The U.S. Soccer Sports Medicine Book

The U.S. Soccer Sports Medicine Book

Editor-in-Chief

William E. Garrett, Jr., MD, PhD
Professor Orthopaedic Surgery
Duke University Medical Center
Medical Director, U.S. Soccer
Federation
Durham, NC

Associate Editors

Donald T. Kirkendall, PhD
Department of Physical and
    Occupational Therapy
Duke University Medical Center
Durham, NC

S. Robert Contiguglia, MD
Clinical Associate Professor
    of Medicine
University of Colorado
Health Science Center
Denver, CO

Williams & Wilkins
A WAVERLY COMPANY

BALTIMORE • PHILADELPHIA • LONDON • PARIS • BANGKOK
BUENOS AIRES • HONG KONG • MUNICH • SYDNEY • TOKYO • WROCLAW

Binder: Port City Press

Copyright © 1996 Williams & Wilkins

351 West Camden Street
Baltimore, Maryland 21201-2436 USA

Rose Tree Corporate Center
1400 North Providence Road
Building II, Suite 5025
Media, Pennsylvania 19063-2043 USA

Accurate indications, adverse reactions and dosage schedules for drugs are provided in this book, but it is possible that they may change. The reader is urged to review the package information data of the manufacturers of the medications mentioned.

Printed in the United States of America

First Edition,

Library of Congress Cataloging-in-Publication Data

The U.S. soccer sports medicine book / editor-in-chief, William E. Garrett, Jr. ; associate
   editors, S. Robert Contiguglia, Donald T. Kirkendall.
      p.   cm.
   Includes bibliographical references and index.
   ISBN 0-683-18249-8
   1. Soccer—Physiological aspects.   2. Soccer injuries.   I. Garrett, William E.
II. Contiguglia, S. Robert.   III. Kirkendall, Donald T.   IV. United States Soccer Federation.
      [DNLM: 1. Soccer—injuries—congresses.   2. Sports Medicine—congresses.
QT 260.5.S7   U87   1996]
RC1220.S57U88   1996
617.1'027—dc20
DNLM/DLC
for Library of Congress   96-1088
                                                                                          CIP

The publishers have made every effort to trace the copyright holders for borrowed material. If they have inadvertently overlooked any, they will be pleased to make the necessary arrangements at the first opportunity.

96 97 98 99

1 2 3 4 5 6 7 8 9 10

To purchase additional copies of this book, call our customer service department at **(800) 638-0672** or fax orders to **(800) 447-8438.** For other book services, including chapter reprints and large quantity sales, ask for the Special Sales department.

Canadian customers should call **(800) 268-4178,** or fax **(905) 470-6780.** For all other calls originating outside of the United States, please call **(410) 528-4223** or fax us at **(410) 528-8550.**

Visit Williams & Wilkins on the Internet: **http://www.wwilkins.com** or contact our customer service department at **custserv@wwilkins.com.** Williams & Wilkins customer service representatives are available from 8:30 am to 6:00 pm, EST, Monday through Friday, for telephone access.

To soccer players and their families
and
To those who teach and care for them.

Preface

The FIFA World Cup was held for the first time in the United States during the summer of 1994. The United States Soccer Federation took this opportunity to assemble a number of the world's authorities on the sports medicine and science of soccer. An international conference was held June 11–15 at the Dolphin Resort in Orlando, Florida prior to the opening of the World Cup. The presentations at this multidisciplinary conference formed the nucleus for this book.

Our purpose in writing this book was to make complex scientific material accessible to all readers; from the volunteer coach without scientific or medical training to the practicing physician. We attempted to cover the basic physiology and biomechanics of soccer performance, applied aspects of nutrition, comprehensive treatment of injuries focusing on mechanism of injury and treatment, and selected topics, such as the female soccer player, youth, and psychological aspects of the sport.

The United States Soccer Federation, through its Sports Medicine Committee, is responsible for the conference and this book. It is important to acknowledge the sponsors who made the conference and this book possible: Snickers, Gatorade, and Aircast. Special thanks to Patty Butterfield and Patty Marchak (US Soccer), Gerry Newton and John Lohnes (Duke University Medical Center), and Darlene Cooke, Sharon Zinner, and Paula Mueller (Williams & Wilkins). Without their help, neither the conference nor this book would have been possible.

William E. Garrett, Jr.
Donald T. Kirkendall
S. Robert Contiguglia

Contributors

Paolo Aglietti, MD
Clinical Orthopaedics
University of Firenze
Firenze, Italy

Michelle Akers-Stahl, MD
USSF National Board of
    Directors
Oveido, Florida

Elizabeth A. Arendt, MD
Associate Professor Orthopedic
    Surgery
Medical Director, Men's &
    Women's Varsity Athletics
Director, Sports Medicine
    Institute
Minneapolis, Minnesota

William R. Barfield, Ph.D
Physical Education & Health
    College of Charleston
Charleston, South Carolina

Jeffrey A. Bauer, Ph.D
Assistant Professor of Exercise
    and Sport Sciences
Director of the Biomechanics
    Laboratory
University of Florida
Member: American Society of
    Biomechanics
Gainesville, Florida

Barry P. Boden, MD
Fellow in Sports Medicine
Duke University Medical Center

Department of Orthopaedic
    Surgery
Durham, North Carolina

Douglas W. Brown, MD
Private Practice - Orthopaedic
    Surgery and Sports Medicine
Orthopaedic Associates of
    Portland, P.A.,
    Portland, ME
U.S. Soccer Medical Advisory
    Committee
Team Physician, U.S. Women's
    National Soccer Team
Portland, Maine

William G. Clancy, Jr., MD
Clinical Professor of
    Orthopaedic Surgery
University of Virginia
Charlottesville, Virginia
Clinical Professor of Surgery
UAB School of Medicine,
    Department of Surgery
Division of Orthopaedic
    Surgery
Staff Orthopaedic Surgeon
Alabama Sports Medicine and
    Orthopaedic Center
Birmingham, Alabama

Kristine Clark, Ph.D, RD
Director of Sports Nutrition
Fellow of the American
    College of Sports Medicine
Past Chair of the American
    Dietetics Assoc. Practice

Group for Sports and
    Cardiovascular Nutritionists
University Park, Pennsylvania

Prof. Eduardo Henrique De
    Rose, M.D., Ph.D., FACSM
Professor of Sports Medicine
Rio Grande do Sul State
    University
President
International Federation of
    Sports Medicine
Porto Alegre, Brazil

Pietro Debiase
Clinical Orthopaedics
Univeristy of Firenze
Firenze, Italy

Randall Dick, MS
Fellow, American College of
    Sports Medicine (FACSM)
Assistant Director of Sports
    Sciences
The National Collegiate Athletic
    Association
Overland Park, Kansas

Professor Bjorn Ekblom, MD
Professor of Physiology,
    Karolinska Institute
Stockholm, Sweden

Ejnar Eriksson, MD
Professor of Sports Medicine at
    the Karolinska Institute
Head, Department of Sports
    Orthopaedic Surgery,

Karolinska Hospital
Stockhom, Sweden

Gregory M. Fox, MD
American Sports Medicine
    Institute
Birmingham, AL 35205

William E. Garrett, MD, Ph.D.
Professor of Orthopaedic
    Surgery
Duke University Medical Center
Medical Director, U.S. Soccer
    Federation
Durham, North Carolina

James Gilbert, MD
Resident, Division of
    Orthopaedics
Duke University Medical Center
Durham, North Carolina

Gil Gleim, Ph.D
Director of Research, Nicholas
    Institute of Sports Medicine
    and Athletic Trauma, Lenox
    Hill Hospital
Adjunct Associate Professor of
    Physiology, New York
    Medical College
New York, New York

Gary A. Green, MD
Clinical Assistant Professor,
    UCLA Division of Family
    Medicine
Los Angeles, California

Emily M. Haymes, Ph.D
Professor of Nutrition, Food,
    and Movement Sciences,
Florida State University
Fellow, American College of
    Sports Medicine
Tallahassee, Florida

William M. Heinz, MD
Portland, Maine

Rey Jaffet, MS, PT, ATC
Director Clinical Services
Health South Rehabilitation
Coral Gables, Florida

W. Benjamin Kibler, MD,
    FACSM
Medical Director, Lexington
    Clinic Sports Medicine
    Center
Member U.S. Soccer Federation
    Sports Medicine Committee
Lexington, Kentucky

Donald T. Kirkendall, Ph.D.
Clinical Associate, Department
    of Physical and
    Occupational Therapy
Duke University Medical Center
Durham, North Carolina

Thomas P. Knapp, MD
Clinical Instructor of
    Orthopedic Surgery, USC
    School of Medicine
Santa Monica, California

Peter Krumins, MD
Private Practice
Team Physician
Pacific Lutheran University
Tacoma, Washington

Beven Pace Livingston, PT, AT, C
Clinical Specialist
Sports Medicine Center
Lexington, Kentucky

John Lohnes, P.A.-C., MHS
Div. of Orthopaedic Surgery
Duke University Medical Center
Durham, North Carolina

Richard Lopez, Ed.D.
Associate Professor
Florida International University
Miami, Florida

James M. Lynch, MD
Team Physician
Associate Member, Graduate
    Faculty, Exercise and Sports
    Science
Penn State Center for Sports
    Medicine
University Park, Pennsylvania

Bert R. Mandelbaum, MD
Chief of Orthopedics
St John's Hospital & Health
    Center
Santa Monica, California
National Team Physician, U.S.
    Soccer Federation
Team Physician, Pepperdine
    University
Malibu, California
Medical Director
Women's Professional
Volleyball Association
Santa Monica, California

John R. McCarroll, MD
Orthopaedic Consultant Indiana
    University Athletic
    Department
Bloomington, Indiana
Clinical Assistant Professor,
    Dept. Of Orthopaedics,
    Indiana University School of
    Medicine
Indianapolis, Indiana
Orthopaedic Surgeon, Methodist
    Sports Medicine Center
Carmel, Indiana

Charlotte C. McIntosh, MS, RD,
    LDN
Clinical Nutritionist
Department of Nutritional
    Services
The Moses H. Cone Group of
    Health Care Services
Greensboro, North Carolina

Michael K. McIntosh, Ph.D.,
RD, LDN
Associate Professor of Nutrition
Department of Food, Nutrition
& Food Service
ManagementThe University of
North Carolina - Greensboro
Greensboro, North Carolina

Robert McKelvain, Ph.D.
Professor and Chair,
    Department of Psychology
Abilene Christian University
Psychology Consultant, USA
World Cup Team, 1994
Abilene, Texas

John McMullen, MS, ATC
Lexington Clinic Sports
    Medicine Center
Lexington, Kentucky

Raymond Rocco Monto, MD
Martha's Vinyard Hospital
Oak Bluffs, Massachusetts

Werner Muller, Prof. MD
Professor extraorinarius for
    Orthopaedic Surgery
    Medical Faculty University
    of Basel
Head Department of
    Orthopaedic Surgery
Bruderholz, Switzerland

G. Naessens, MD
University Hospital Antwerp

Department of Physical
    Medicine and Rehabilitation
Edegem, Belgium

Lars Peterson, MD, Ph.D.
Associate Professor,
    Department of Orthopaedics
University of Goteburg
Clinical Director Gothenburg
    Medical Center
Member Medical Committee of
    FIFA

Bruce Reider, MD
Director of Sports Medicine,
    University of Chicago
Associate Professor of Surgery
    (Orthopaedics), University
    of Chicago
Chicago, Illinois

Thomas Reilly
B.A., Dip. P.E., M.Sc., M.I.
Biology, Ph.D, F.Erg.S.
School of Human Sciences,
Liverpool John Moores
    University
Liverpool, England

Per A.F.H. Renstrom MD, Ph.D.
Professor of Sports Medicine
the University of Vermont
Department of Orthopaedics &
    Rehabilitation
McClure Musculoskeletal
    Research Center
Burlington, Vermont

Tonu Saartok, MD, Ph.D.
Assoc. Professor, Section of
    Orthopaedics, Dept. of
    Surgery, Visby Hospital
Visby, Sweden

Bruce Snell, MS, PT, ATC,
    SCS
Certified Athletic Trainer
Sports Clinical Specialist
Northwest Center for Sports
    Medicine and Physical
    Therapy
Tacoma, Washington

Scott E. Strasburger, MD
American Sports Medicine
    Institute
Birmingham, Alabama

Lars-Ingle Svenson
Folksam Insurance Company
Stockholm, Sweden

Robert A. Swoap, Ph.D
Conroe, Texas

Anders Valentin, MD
Department of Arthroscopy &
    Sports Surgery
Karolinska Hospital
Stockholm, Sweden

Giovanni Zaccherotti, MD
Prima Clinica Ortopedica
Universita de Firenze
Firenze, Italy

Contents

VIII. Sociological and Psychological Aspects

I

• Sports Medicine

1   **Physiological Profile**

Thomas Reilly

Soccer places physiological demands on its participants. These are determined both by the trends in play as the match progresses and by the motivational and fitness levels of the players for high-intensity exercise. Without the necessary combination of physiological attributes, players are unlikely to cope with the demands placed on them by intensely competitive soccer. The physiological effort associated with playing soccer has consequences for both fitness testing and training regimens.

The profile of effort can be determined by motion analysis of players during matches. The exercise intensity can be gauged by indices of work-rate, such as distance covered during the game or exercise-to-rest ratios. A variety of factors influence the work-rate, including styles of play, nutritional status, and fitness status. There are energetic consequences associated with execution of games skills, which are superimposed on work-rate patterns. The link with soccer skills is most obvious in the engagement of players in training. A further consideration in this review is the assessment of game-related performance and factors that affect the scoring of goals.

Work-Rate Profiles
Effort profiles can be classified in terms of type of activity, intensity (or quality), duration (or distance), and frequency. These efforts are produced in the context of contributing to play directly or indirectly. Changes in work-rate profiles may be due to fatigue or failures of fitness. These changes may have been influenced by training programs and have consequences for energy provision and prevention of injury. For example, ill-timed mistakes in tackling or contesting possession are more likely when a player is fatigued.

The pioneering research on motion analysis of soccer was completed by Reilly and Thomas. Observations focused on a single player during a game, and data were collected for more than 50 games. A tape-recorded commentary was made from an elevated vantage point overlooking the pitch and using a map of the playing area in conjunction with cues on the pitch and along its boundaries. Estimation of exercise intensities (walking, jogging, cruising, and sprinting) was validated by concomitant filming of the player observed.

3

The profile incorporated game-related events (headers, tackling, moving in possession of the ball) and unorthodox directions of locomotion, backwards, and sideways.

Activity classes (Fig. 1-1) illustrate that the majority of the overall distance covered is at low intensity, either walking or jogging. Cruising refers to submaximal effort with manifest immediate purpose and is at a higher intensity. Sprinting is all-out effort, but occurs on average once every 90 sec over a mean distance of 14 m. Rest pauses amount to 3 sec every 2 min, but obviously may be longer in pauses for injury. Running in possession of the ball accounts for less than 2% of the total distance covered. The movement is mainly off-the-ball, to seek space for oneself or create space for others, complete decoy runs, support teammates, or counter movements of opponents. This low percentage of distance covered with the ball is characteristic of the other football codes also including Rugby League, Australian Rules, and Gaelic Football.

Each game entails approximately 1000 discrete activities. This means a change in activity about every 6 sec. The activity is acyclical, and the succession of events is temporally unique. Nevertheless, there is remarkable reproducibility of work-rate profiles from game to game, particularly with regard to the high-intensity efforts.

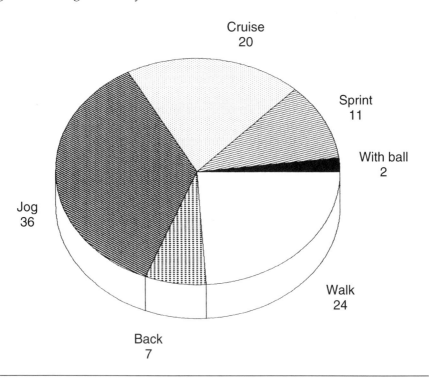

Figure 1-1. Percent of total distance covered according to categories of activity during soccer match-play.

Factors That Affect Work Rate

Playing Position

Although the overall distance covered in a game is approximately 9–11 km, this can be influenced by various factors. One such variable is the positional role of the player (Fig. 1-2).

In teams using a 4-4-2 or 4-3-3 configuration, the greatest distances are covered by the mid-field players. This is due to their linking role between defense and attack. A striker (forward) operating alone in a 4-5-1 formation will have a work rate similar to midfielders.

Sprints are particularly important in gaining possession. The timing and velocity of the sprints will be particularly evident in situations of goal-scoring potential. The midfield players are distinguished from the others in terms of the greater distances covered at low exercise intensities. They use active recovery in reassuming allocated positions following the more intensive bouts of play. Defenders, especially those used in central positions, cover a disproportionate distance moving backwards. This may be retreating strategically to maneuver an attacking player into a less favorable position or going backwards to meet a lofted ball or a 'centered' delivery from the wing.

Fitness and Fatigue

The intense activities around the ball may be anaerobic, and high-intensity efforts can determine crucial events during the match. Nevertheless, aerobic

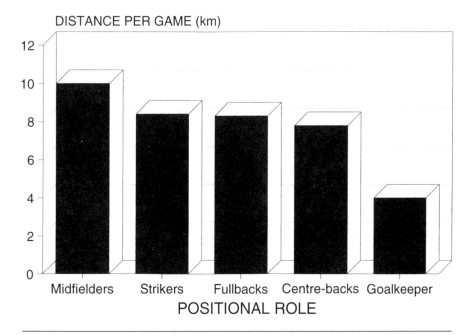

Figure 1-2. Distance covered per game according to playing position. (Data from: Reilly T, Thomas V. An analysis of work-rate in different positional roles in professional football match-play. J Hum Movement Sci 1976;2:87–98).

fitness influences players' abilities to keep up with play. The distance covered in a game is correlated with the maximal oxygen uptake. Possession of high aerobic power also is linked with maintenance of work rate toward the end of a game. As the game progresses, a fall-off is evident in both distance covered and the number of sprints attempted. This fatigue effect has been linked with depletion of muscle glycogen levels and can to a lesser degree be counteracted by pre-game nutrition.

Goals scored tend to increase toward the end of the game, although goals may be scored at any time. The increase in scoring may be due to physiological fatigue, lapses in mental concentration, or a willingness of players in the losing team to take risks to regain the initiative.

Despite a fall in work rate, the heart rate may remain elevated at a high level. This occurs in university players and in some top-level players. The match referee is at a disadvantage because he is obliged to keep up with play as it increases in urgency near the end. Heart rates remain at approximately 170 beats · min-1 in referees throughout the game.

Style of Play

Highly skilled teams may dictate the pace of play and so work rate will be influenced by the style of play. Highly trained players may use their fitness levels to pressurize opponents in possession of the ball and force them into mistakes. The 'direct' method of play, which eschews a slow build-up from defensive positions imposes high work-rate demands on the players; defenders intermingle with midfield players in supporting the target-man or the players in attack.

An example of this style is used by the Republic of Ireland team in the European Championships of 1988 and World Cups of 1990 and 1994. Analysis of behavioral events in Ireland versus England matches showed that the Irish players were rarely caught in possession in their half of the field. This contrasted with the ball-carrying traits of England players who were more frequently dispossessed in their defensive half of the field. Although the Irish style of play has been criticized for its directness, it has evolved to accommodate players with exceptionally high work rates and skilled players with lower work intensities. Norway and Sweden, both qualifiers for the 1994 World Cup tournament, use a form of 'direct method.'

The intricate moves associated with patterns of play and leading to goals can be analyzed from broadcasted recordings and analyzed using computerized methods. This provides comprehensive information, besides the pathways to goals, on individual and team performance. The position, the player involved, the action, and its outcome can be processed to provide an overall picture of patterns of play. This method can be matched with a work-rate analysis if film recordings are obtained on an individual player. The movement intensities, accelerations, and decelerations can be calculated by identifying the coordinates of serial positions on the playing pitch. In this way, the overall work rate of a striker can be outlined (Fig. 1-3). The tactical outcome of movements can be established by the computer-aided program.

Activity Profile of a World Cup Striker

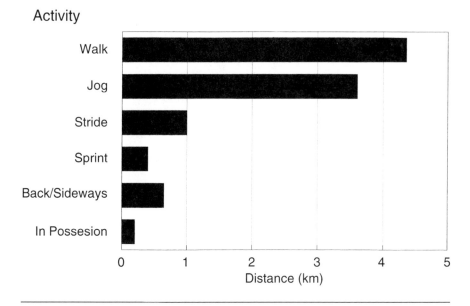

Figure 1-3. Work-rate of a World-Cup striker while playing in English First Division match.

Players are also engaged in tussles for possession, including headers and tackles. They are also engaged in running with the ball. Analysis of the energetic consequences of dribbling the ball has been performed in laboratory conditions. Irrespective of the speed of locomotion, dribbling entails a constant elevation in energy cost. The deflection in lactate with increasing exercise intensity occurs at a lower speed than when running normally. This means that training runs with the ball will provide a higher training stimulus than running normally at the same speed. The running stride is shortened when moving with the ball and is irregular. This works both to control the ball and deceive opponents.

Moving backwards and sideways also elevates the oxygen consumption compared with orthodox running. In these cases, the elevations are disproportionate when the speed of motion is increased.

Effort in Training

Training for competitive soccer incorporates a range of components following warm-up, flexibility, and fitness elements. Players practice skills, games drills, and full-scale or small-sided matches. The relative intensities as indicated by mean heart rate (Table 1-1) demonstrate that the exercise intensity is highest when playing a match. Our comparison of training matches with competitive games indicate that match-play taxes aerobic mechanisms to approximately 75% VO2max on average.

Table 1-1

Relative Intensities of Training Components as Indicated by Mean ($\pm$ SD) Heart Rate (beats min^{-1})	
Warm-up	120 ± 2
Flexibility/calisthenics	112 ± 3
Running	144 ± 4
Circuit and weight training	125 ± 4
Skills practice	128 ± 5
Drills	137 ± 4
Games	157 ± 7
Recovery periods	102 ± 3

Players are reluctant to exercise at high intensities in training drills without the ball. Timed performance tasks have poor reliability when conducted by the coaching staff. Consequently, field tasks that incorporate zig-zag runs, fast turns, and sections with the ball are more likely to motivate players towards maximal effort.

The training load has to be distributed in a cyclic manner throughout the week in preparation for week-end matches. The energy expended peaks in mid-week before a tapering for the game. This avoids reduction of glycogen stores before competition. Training intensity must also be curtailed when matches are scheduled twice in 1 week. Safety and prevention of injury must be emphasized at times of strenuous competitive engagements.

Special attention is required in pre-season training to avoid injury due to an abrupt increase in training load. Players may take a complete break during the off-season and return overweight and detrained. Over-emphasis on endurance or aerobic exercise pre-season may lead to a reduction in muscular strength as the competitive season starts. Fitness elements in the training program should be balanced, especially in the pre-season period.

Aerobic fitness must be maintained throughout the competitive season. This depends on how well the players can be kept together and remain free from injury. Apor showed how average aerobic fitness levels of teams in the top Hungarian League were correlated with finishing position in the league. Success leads to improved fitness and improved group morale, whereas defeats and injuries trigger a downward spiral in fitness and morale.

The predominately aerobic make-up of soccer players is reflected in muscle biopsy samples taken from elite performers. These tend to have oxidative enzymes characteristic of endurance-trained athletes. They nevertheless should pay attention to strength training, in view of the contact components of the game and its anaerobic elements.

Muscle strength at high velocities seems to be the most relevant for soccer play. The balance between hamstrings and quadriceps, particularly the eccentric action of the latter in controlling kicking motions, should be considered.

Training muscle strength can enhance kicking performance, provided it is functionally relevant and added to rather than offered as replacement for normal strength training. Top Belgian players improved their kicking abilities when they used a specially tailored training program. Similar relationships between kicking performance and peak torque at high angular velocities have been noted for female soccer players.

Any asymmetries in limb strength, especially during rehabilitation, should be corrected.

Isokinetic dynamometry can be used both as a training tool and an assessment device. The training must eventually incorporate game-related actions before the player can be deemed ready for match practice.

SUGGESTED READING

Apor, P. Successful formula for fitness training. In. Science & Football (T Reilly, A. Lees, K. Davids (eds) London: E & FN Spon, 1988; 95-107.

Catterall C, Reilly T, Atkinson G, et al. Analysis of the work-rates and heart-rates of association football referees. Br J Sports Med 1993;27:193–196.

Coghlan A. How to score goals and influence people. New Scientist 1990;1719:54–59.

Reilly T. What research tells the coach about soccer. Washington: AAHPERD, 1979.

Reilly T. Physiological aspects of soccer. Biol Sport 1994;11:3–20.

Reilly T. Analysis of work-rate in soccer. In: S.A. Robertson (ed). Contemporary Ergonomics. London: Taylor and Francis, 1994:377–381.

Reilly T, Ball D. The physiological cost of dribbling a soccer ball. Res Q Exerc Sport 1984;55:267–271.

Reilly T, Bowen T. Exertional costs of changes in directional modes of running. Perceptual Motor Skills 1984;58:49–50.

Reilly T, Thomas V. An analysis of work-rate in different positional roles in professional football match-play. J Hum Movement Sci 1976;2:87–98.

Reilly T, Thomas V. Estimated energy expenditures of professional association footballers. Ergonomics 1979;22: 541–548.

Reilly T, Clarys J, Stibbe A (eds). Science and Football II. London: E & FN Spon, 1993.

Reilly T, Lees A, Davids K (eds.), et al. Science and Football. London: E & FN Spon, 1988.

Saltin B. Metabolic fundamentals in exercise. Med Sci Sports 1973;5:137–146.

2  Energy Metabolism

Björn Ekblom

In soccer, periods of short term high-intensity sprinting and running are interspersed with periods of slower running, jogging, walking, and standing still. The average distance covered by an elite outfield male player is in the range of 10–11 km, with little difference in the same player between different games. Approximately 10% of the total distance covered during a game is sprinting or high-speed running. Midfielders cover more, and defenders cover less than the average of the team. In addition, all players perform several different energy-demanding activities such as tackling, jumping, and acceleration. Thus, both aerobic and anaerobic energy systems must be involved in covering the energy demands of match play in soccer. In this overview, current knowledge of the total energy demand and the contribution of the different energy systems are discussed.

Aerobic Energy Yield

Heart Rate

Because direct measurements of the aerobic energy yield during match play in soccer is currently not possible, several methods for estimation of the oxygen consumption must be used. The most obvious physiological factor to be used is heart rate.

Figure 2-1 shows the heart rate for a midfield player in a regular game using a small portable heart rate transmitter. As seen in the figure, the player has a heart rate above 90% of his peak heart rate in many parts of the game. Even if during intermittent exercise, psychological and other factors may superficially increase heart rate, these data indicate that there is a substantial stress on the oxygen transport system chain during soccer match play. Corresponding unpublished measurements from our laboratory on female players during match play showed that the mean heart rate in five outfield players with an average peak heart rate of 195 (±9) during three matches was 177 (±11), 174 (±11), and 173 (±10). These data show that there are no differences in the heart rate response, and consequently aerobic demand, between women's and men's soccer match play.

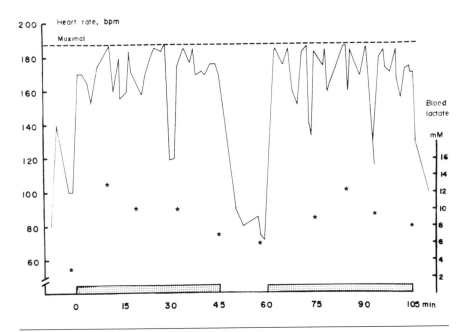

Figure 2-1. Heart rate in a midfield player during match play.

Body Temperature

Measurements of rectal temperature after the game can be used for evaluating the average oxygen demand during exercise. The average rectal temperature during continuous exercise when oxygen uptake is 50 and 75% of maximal aerobic power, is 38.0 and 38.8°C, respectively. In studies on Swedish soccer players, the average body temperature in four teams in four different divisions were between 39.0 and 39.5°C. In 9 of the 125 players, the rectal temperature after the game was >40°C. Measurements of rectal temperature during women's match play showed lower values; mean values were between 38.0 and 38.8°C. However, body temperature is increased above the "normal" relationship between average oxygen turnover and body temperature during both intermittent exercise and after dehydration. This has to be taken into account when evaluating the energy demands. However, these conditions cannot contradict that the average energy demand during match play as evaluated from measurements of body temperature is very high.

Blood Lactates

For evaluating the total energy demand during soccer match play, blood lactates may also be used. In data from Swedish soccer match play, blood lactates in the range of 7–11 mmol/L after the game have been reported. However, in Danish reports, and in reports from other countries, lower values are reported, which among other things may be due to different style of play and climate conditions. In women's match play, blood lactate concentration values in the range of 4–7 mmol/L are found (Fig. 2-2).

BLOOD LACTATES

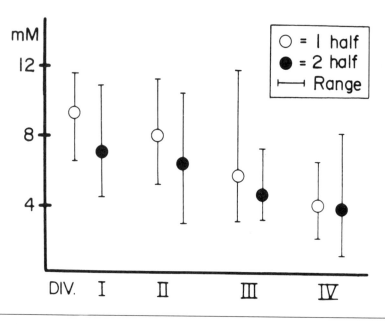

Figure 2-2. *Blood lactate concentration (mean and range) at halftime and after the game in teams for four from different divisions.*

Summary

From measurements of heart rate and body temperature, it can be concluded that in national and international elite match play the average energy turn-over rate is in the range of 75–80% of maximal aerobic power both in men and women. Different styles of play, positions in the squad and other factors, such as climate, may modify average energy turn-over rate. Male players of 70–75 kg body mass and an average maximal aerobic power of approximately 4.5 L/in have a total energy turn-over during a regular elite game in the range of 1600–1800 Kcal. In women's soccer, corresponding values are 1400–1500 Kcal. As a result, the heat production is high. Sweat rate is high with a body mass loss in the range of 2 liters in normal climate conditions. Consequently, in games in hot climates, the stress on the temperature regulation systems is severe. During games in the World Cup in USA 1994, the Swedish National team lost approximately 3 kg body mass, even though the players drank approximately 2 liters before and during the game. This loss in body water causes modifications in different body functions, which will cause considerable reduction in players physical performance. Therefore, games during extreme hot climate conditions are not acceptable.

Anaerobic Considerations

One important observation during soccer match play is the high lactate concentrations. This is evidently a sign that soccer match play puts huge demands on different anaerobic energy systems. Anaerobic metabolism is one of the most important physiological performance-related factors in soccer. There is currently no accepted method to evaluate the contribution of anaerobic metabolism during soccer. In fact, evaluating the capacity of anaerobic metabolism can only be made from indirect testing procedures that are accompanied by many theoretic problems.

Oxygen Deficit

By definition, anaerobic metabolism is used mainly when the supply to, and the availability of oxygen in, the mitochondria is insufficient. Thus, the oxygen deficit during exercise, the part of the total metabolism that is not covered by aerobic metabolism, has several components that are discussed. There is an oxygen deficit both at the beginning of an exercise bout, before the oxygen supply system has accelerated to a steady state level, and in situations when the energy demand exceeds the maximal aerobic power. The oxygen deficit must be repaid after the exercise by increased metabolism over the basal metabolic rate. The "extra" oxygen after exercise is called the "oxygen debt." The oxygen deficit has two main components: the alactacid and the lactacid energy turn-over. In addition, oxygen bound to hemoglobin and myoglobin is available for immediate use for the oxidation of fat and carbohydrates.

Biochemical Background

Anaerobic metabolism includes the alactacid breakdown of energy-rich substrates of adenosine triphosphate (ATP) and creatine phosphate (CP) in the muscle as well as the lactacid breakdown (glycolysis) of glucose units (glucose or glycogen) to pyruvate and lactate.

The rate of energy liberation by the breakdown of ATP to ADP and AMP as well as CP to C (creatine) and P (phosphate) is fast, but the total capacity of these energy-rich compounds is low. Therefore, the build up of ATP and CP must be accomplished by either anaerobic lactacid or aerobic metabolism. The rate of the energy liberation for lactacid metabolism is lower than the rate for the alactacid metabolism, whereas the lactacid capacity is higher.

The ATP and CP stores in the muscle are approximately 30 mmoles/kg muscle. These stores do not change with physical training. Also, the rate of utilization of energy from ATP and CP is probably not significantly affected by physical training. However, supplementation of creatine may enhance total creatine pool in the muscle, which in turn improves the capacity to perform repeated sprints, as in soccer. However, supplementation of creatine has not been beneficial to soccer performance. The oxygen stored in hemoglobin and myoglobin amounts to approximately 5–6 ml O_2 per kg muscle mass. Although physical training may increase the myoglobin content of the muscle, this part of the oxygen deficit is not subject to large variation with physical training.

Contrary to the alactacid anaerobic metabolism and the "stored" oxygen in the muscle, glycolysis may be subjected to changes with physical training. The total anaerobic lactacid capacity is enhanced by high-intensity, short-term exercise, but whether the rate of the glycolysis can be enhanced, by physical training is currently a subject of discussion. A sedentary individual may have a total lactacid capacity, equivalent to 25–30 ml O_2 per kg muscle. This may increase two- to threefold with physical training. This means that the total oxygen deficit in a well-trained athlete from an anaerobic event may reach from 75 even up to 100 ml O_2 per kg muscle. The improvement with physical training is probably due to enhanced lactacid anaerobic metabolism.

Although the "stored" oxygen easily can be repaid after exercise and the alactacid breakdown of ATP and CP restored during and after exercise, the metabolite of the anaerobic glycolysis (lactate) must either be oxidized during and after exercise to C02 and H20 or used in as a substrate in the development of glycogen.

Limitations

As stated earlier, the anaerobic lactacid metabolism seems to be the most important factor for a training-induced improvement of the oxygen deficit. There are many different points of interest concerning lactacid metabolism especially with regard to the limitation in the performance.

- Rate of glycolysis and lactate production. This is limited by the availability of glycogen in the muscle, the concentration of the key enzyme (LDH4-5) and eventually inhibitory factors.
- Accumulation of lactate in the muscle cell. This is limited by the buffer capacity and the pH tolerance.
- Clearance rate. This is limited by both the oxidation of pyruvate in the working and adjacent muscle fiber and the transport of lactate to the interstitial space and the blood. The former is enhanced by increased levels of oxidative mitochondrial enzymes and the latter by increased capillarization, peripheral perfusion, and uptake in other tissues.

Measurement of Anaerobic Metabolism

The best evaluation of total anaerobic metabolism can be made from the measurement of the oxygen deficit. In some cases, oxygen debt can also be used. However, in many situations like soccer, which is characterized as noncontinuous, intermittent, high-intensity exercise, oxygen deficit and debt can not be measured and therefore other indirect measures have to be used.

For the moment, a measure of lactate concentration in the muscle tissue and/or blood is used. However, a concentration is always a balance between production, clearance, and dilution space. Therefore, the obtained values must be interpreted with caution.

In soccer, the most important factor may not be the total oxygen deficit, or the rate of anaerobic energy liberation (except for sprinting), but the integration of anaerobic and aerobic metabolism. Thus, the local muscle adjustment to improved anaerobic metabolism for soccer performance may lie in the integration of the known effects of aerobic physiological factors and the anaerobic factors discussed.

During high-intensity, intermittent exercise, as in soccer match play, lactate is produced in many of the short and long sprints. The performance of the sprints would appear to have an acute component related to alactacid metabolism, and an endurance component (the capacity to perform several sprints during short periods) related to the different limiting factors listed. One of the most important of these factors should be the capacity to clear lactate during the game. The level of muscle glycogen also seems to be important.

Measurement of Anaerobic Metabolism During Soccer

As previously mentioned, lactate has been measured during and after regular games of soccer. In top Swedish teams post-game lactate levels as high as 12 mM have been found, with an average around 7 mM, whereas players from the lower divisions have had lower values. The lowest values were from players playing in the lowest division. In youth soccer, lactate values measured during and after the game were below those of the lower senior players. Although there are limitations that accompany these values, the role of the anaerobic metabolism in soccer is great.

The main question that needs to be addressed from this discussion is "How can anaerobic performance (e.g., during a game of soccer) be improved? Considerations must include different types and effects of training methods and other factors such as the importance of muscle glycogen stores.

Anaerobic Capacity of Soccer Players

Laboratory studies of the anaerobic capacity of soccer players have shown that soccer players have higher values than sedentary individuals, but the differences are small. This may be explained by the fact that the tests used in the laboratory (e.g., using bicycle ergometers) include muscle activity that is not "football specific" and therefore not representative of the movements that are most commonly made by soccer players.

However, the most important factor with regard to anaerobic metabolism in soccer is the ability to sustain repeated bouts of severe fast exercise using anaerobic glycolysis with lactate as metabolite, as well as alactacid energy liberation. There is a high negative correlation ($r = -0.91$) between anaerobic capacity and performance decrement observed during a type of soccer-specific intermittent exercise. This indicates that players with a higher anaerobic capacity showed less performance decrement during repeated bouts of short periods of high-intensity exercise (sprinting) interspersed with longer periods of active recovery. The contribution of alactacid and lactacid anaerobic metabolism during physical activity such as soccer needs further evaluation.

SUGGESTED READING

Balsom P, Soderlund K, Ekblom B. Creatine and creatine supplementation. Sport Med 1994;18:268–280.

Balsom PD, Seger JY, Sjodin B, et al. Maximal-intensity intermittent exercise: effect of recovery duration. Int J Sports Med 1992;13:528–533.

Balsom PD, Seger JY, Sjodin B, et al. Physiological responses to maximal-intensity in-
    termittent exercise. Eur J Appl Physiol 1992;65: 144–149.
Ekblom B (ed). Handbook of Sport Medicine and Science: Football (Soccer). England:
    Blackwell, 1994.
Ekblom B. Applied physiology of soccer. Sports Med 1986;3:50–60.
Ekblom B, Greenleaf CJ, Greenleaf JE, et al. Temperature regulation during exercise
    dehydration in man. Acta Physiol Scand 1970;79:475–483.
Ekblom B, Greenleaf CJ, Greenleaf JE, et al. Temperature regulation during continu-
    ous and intermittent exercise in man. Acta Physiol Scand 1971;81:1–10.
Saltin B, Hermansen L. Esophagheal, rectal and muscle temperature during exercise.
    J Appl Physiol 1966;21:1757–1762.
Tumilty D. Physiological characteristics of elite soccer players. Sports Med 1993;
    16:80–96.

3  Strength, Speed, Flexibility

Gilbert W. Gleim

Most emphasis is placed on the tactical and technical aspects of soccer, so physiological aspects of soccer performance are often unmeasured by coaches. Nevertheless, physiologic performance factors are as important in this game as in any other. The realization of this fact is not lost on the championship teams of the world as evidenced by the routine testing performed on elite teams throughout Brazil, the 1994 World Cup Champions. Dramatic changes in tactical and technical ability have not been proven by such interventions, yet a physically fit body has never been a liability.

In the words of James A. Nicholas, M.D., "we are limited in our knowledge by our ability to measure." This statement underscores many difficulties as they apply to biometrics in sports. Disagreements about definitions, precision and reproducibility of measurements, motivation of the athlete to perform the tests, and time of the training season when testing is performed are all likely to impact measurements.

Strength, flexibility, speed, and agility are all important aspects of soccer performance. The following definitions of these terms will be used: strength, the maximum amount of force exerted by a body segment by means of muscular tension; flexibility, the range of motion available across one or more articulations; speed, the distance covered divided by the time it takes to cover that distance; agility, speed plus the ability to make a sudden change in the direction of movement.

Strength

Strength is perhaps the most studied of all human performance factors. Factors that influence strength are the cross-sectional area of the muscle (proportion of the contractile protein mass), recruitment of motor units (related to the speed of the movement), length of the lever arms involved, motivation of the subject, pain inhibition, and fatigue. Given these determinants, it is a wonder that strength can be measured reliably.

Isometric (same length) strength is the ability to generate force through a nonmoving limb segment (discounting joint compressive forces). This form of strength measurement is the most reproducible because it lends itself to the stabilization of body segments. For recruitment of motor units, an isometric contraction is typically measured over 3–5 seconds. Joint compression may be a limiting factor for force production in subjects with chondral pain, and should not be ignored in the interpretation of isometric strength measurement. This form of strength testing is nonspecific for most activity patterns, including soccer.

Isotonic (same tension) strength measurement is traditionally measured by the ability to perform one maximal repetition (1 RM, the maximum amount of weight a person can lift once). When applied to human movement, the mechanical advantage exerted by the muscle on the bony lever arm is constantly changing during the range of motion. Therefore, this form of strength testing assesses the weakest portion of the range of motion unless some form of cam is used to aid the biological lever arm in its weak areas.

Isokinetic (same speed) strength testing is the most modern technique. The muscle is not shortening at a constant velocity, rather, the angular velocity of the limb segment is constant. Devices for the measurement of isokinetic strength allow for torque documentation of speeds up to 450°/sec. These speeds approach angular velocities of some human movements in sports, but their reproducibility is poor. These devices also allow for measurement of torque produced by concentric contractions (in which active muscle tendons come closer to each other) and eccentric contractions (in which external forces on the limb exceed the shortening capacity so that the muscle lengthens).

Representative knee extension/flexion torque in elite soccer players is demonstrated in Table 3-1. The average soccer player weighs approximately 70 to 75 kg (155–165 pounds). For comparison, our observations of knee extension strength in professional American football players represents 1.2 times the body weight in ft/lb. In the cross-section of soccer players shown in Table 3-1, knee extension torque, when measured at 60°/sec, is approximately 1.5 times body weight.

Strength correlates with kicking performance in soccer players. Poulmedis demonstrated a correlation between ball velocity and peak isokinetic knee extension torque. DeProft, et al. also demonstrated a correlation between the distance of kicks and peak knee extension strength. Both studies showed the correlation to be higher for eccentric torque production than for concentric torque production. Finally, in a modified knee extension, hip flexion isokinetic test, Narcici, et al. found a correlation between kicking velocity and ball

Table 3-1

Mean Knee Strength in Three Groups of Elite Soccer Players, in ft · lb.		
Group	Knee Extension	Knee Flexion
New York Cosmos (NASL)	266	173
Swedish, Oberg et al	246	154
Canadian, Rhodes et al	250	118

velocity. Aging seems to selectively affect the strength of soccer players. In a cross-sectional study by McHugh, et al., older soccer players lost strength in knee extensors and flexors but did not experience strength loss in hip abductors, adductors, or flexors.

Strength testing and training in the elite soccer player can be beneficial. To begin with, a strength measurement made before an injury serves as a benchmark for rehabilitation following the injury. Parity with the opposite limb, a common clinical goal, may not be appropriate for a therapeutic endpoint. Increased strength has never been associated with injury whereas decreased strength has been associated with injury. In the elite soccer player, knee extension torque at 60°/sec should exceed 120% of body weight in pounds.

Strength training can and should be done year round. Changes in sprinting speed should be monitored and strength training stopped if speed decrements result. Strengthening exercises should never be done before hard running, drills, or games in which agility is important. Although it is not the most effective way to strength train, if exercising on a practice day be sure to use weights after practice. Strength will decline faster than aerobic power in the active, aging player.

Flexibility

Because the foot is the primary way of affecting ball movement in soccer, extreme demands are placed on the lower extremity joints to allow for maximal range of motion. The need for dynamic flexibility is imperative, yet we have no known ways to safely measure dynamic flexibility in humans. Joint disruption or muscle tears are possible results of the demands placed on the joints. Therefore, most of our information about flexibility in humans is a result of static measurements in which injuries are unlikely to occur. This leads to possible misinterpretations of findings as they apply to any sport.

Flexibility is a function of physiological and mechanical factors (Fig. 3-1). Skeletal muscle possesses material properties that exhibit viscous and elastic behavior, and is therefore referred to as visco-elastic. If muscle is stretched, it gradually lengthens; an example of its viscous behavior. A rapidly stretched muscle will recoil to a certain extent; an example of its elastic behavior. The degree of underlying muscle tone also may impact flexibility. The degree of myofilament overlap and gamma motor neuron activity are both contributors to this phenomenon. Finally, the conformation of the bony surfaces of the joint, and perhaps capsular structures, can limit flexibility at the extremes of the range of motion.

Resistance to skeletal muscle stretch is both active and passive. The muscle spindle reflex, which is evoked by tendon stretch, is an example of active resistance. Theories of contract-relax stretching techniques are based to some extent on desensitizing this reflex activity so that the muscle can be stretched further before evoking a reflex contraction. Conclusive proof for this contention is lacking.

Passive resistance to stretch is a property of the connective tissue of the muscle. Collagen comprising the various sheaths (endomysium, perimysium,

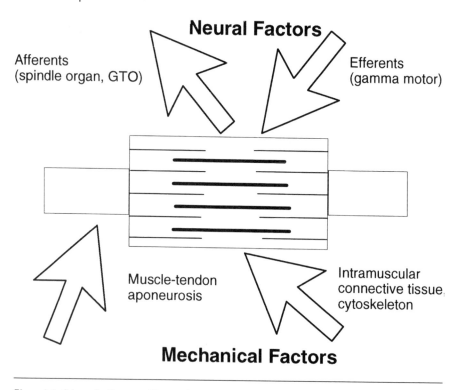

Figure 3-1. Schematic diagram of factors that can influence flexibility.

and epimysium) within whole muscles, and perhaps proteins of the cytoskeleton, may all play a roll in dictating passive resistance to stretch. Resistance to passive stretch is less dependent on the active components and more reliant on the passive components in humans.

Goniometric measurement of joint range of motion is the traditional, clinical method of documenting flexibility. Because of the difficulties in keeping a goniometer precisely over the joint axis of rotation and along the shaft of the bone, it takes a fastidious investigator to reproduce these measurements to within 5°. Also, goniometers only allow for range of motion measures across one joint, while limb position is frequently a function of range of motion across many joints at once.

The sit-and-reach test of posterior (i.e., back, gluteal, hamstrings, and triceps surae) body flexibility is frequently used as a measure. The major disadvantage of this test is that it is related to body segment lengths. Persons having long arms and shorter torsos are at an advantage. Additionally, this form of flexibility testing is unidimensional and does not address the principal planes of human movement; sagittal, coronal, and frontal.

We (see Gleim, 1990) have traditionally used tests that are graded into broad categories of loose (−1), normal (0), and tight (+1) (Fig. 3-2). Such a categorization allows for mass screening and avoids a false sense of precision that

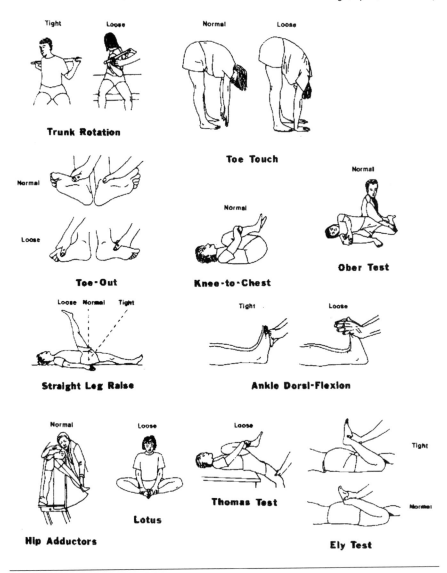

Figure 3-2. Static flexibility tests which are rated into the gross categories of loose, normal or tight.

might be obtained by a goniometer. The tests are designed to address all planes of motion in the body and to span a number of body segments. The summation of these tests yields a range of -2 to $+2$ for the average individual. Areas of individual tightness can be targeted for specific stretching.

There is no consensus about the average flexibility of soccer players. With the exception of goalkeepers, most soccer players tend to be tighter than nonathletes. Data to the contrary have been reported in the United States and England. Virtually any sport that does not use sustained stretch in a principal motion results in tightness. If tightness can result in muscle injury, the only way this can be prevented is by diligent stretching.

Musculoskeletal injuries resulting from sports are multifactorial, and chance undoubtedly plays a major role. Muscle tears, a common injury in soccer, fall into this realm. Muscle tightness has always been blamed as the cause. Muscle strains seem to be unrelated to flexibility, but tend to be more frequent during the second half of the game (see Arnason, 1994). Muscular tightness has been associated with increased walking and jogging economy. Elastic recoil after ballistic stretching of skeletal muscle during normal movement is likely to be greater in tight versus loose muscles. Consequently, there may be advantages (with respect to economy of motion) and disadvantages (with respect to injury) to muscular tightness in the soccer player. More research is necessary in this fundamental area of human movement.

The goal of stretching programs is to produce a plastic deformation of connective tissue within the muscle. The duration of the effect of both acute stretching and chronic stretching exercises is not well known. By examining the decline in tension of the hamstrings during a straight leg raise, a nonlinear relaxation is apparent over 45 seconds. The first 20 seconds of a stretch produce the greatest decline in tension. Repetitive acute stretching is associated with reduced declines as well. Because visco-elastic relaxation is temperature dependent, the greatest plastic deformation occurs after the activity that has heated the muscle. Although unproven, stretching programs after activity are likely to result in the greatest short-term improvement in flexibility.

In addition to static stretching, so called contract-relax and contract-relax-agonist-contract stretching techniques are also used (referred to as proprioceptive neuromuscular facilitation techniques, or PNF). The rationale for these protocols is to inhibit reflex contractile activity of the muscle being stretched. Electromyogram (EMG) studies do not corroborate this belief, but subjects may subjectively experience less pain while stretching. It is probable that the greater the lengthening force applied to the visco-elastic element, the greater the subsequent decrease in tension. Pain within the muscle being stretched often limits the amount of force that can be applied.

Speed

Speed is of primary importance in the soccer player. A mistake in positioning, recovery from a stolen ball, breaking for a header, or outrunning a defender all require explosive speed. Speed can make the talented player exceptional, and the less than average player useful. Speed is one of the characteristics that consistently distinguishes the elite soccer player as unique among players of other sports.

Speed, as a performance factor, relies on the integration of a number of factors that may be real or may give the illusion of speed. Examples of the latter are reaction time (although in track and field, sprinters must have superior reaction time at the blocks to be fast) and the ability to anticipate to get a head start. These factors aside, speed is a function of many physiologic characteristics.

In the physical sense, speed is the ability to generate power or work per unit of time. The more work that can be generated in a period of time, the farther one will move. In a physiological sense, the short-term ability to generate work is a function of anaerobic power. During speed events, which last from a few seconds to perhaps 10 seconds, the principal metabolic pathway for ATP generation is from creatine phosphate. Speed declines following periods longer than approximately 10 seconds because ATP generation becomes a function of the rate of anaerobic glycolysis. Peak rates of ATP production from creatine phosphate are about 2.5 times greater than from glycolysis.

Maximum power outputs are attained at approximately 50% of maximum force production. Maximum force production is ultimately a function of strength. Therefore, speed is in part a function of strength. Consequently, the factors that determine strength also must determine speed. Yet, strength is not the sole determinant of speed, as can be seen in Olympic weight lifters who are not the fastest of athletes.

One of the distinguishing characteristics between strength and speed is that speed relies heavily on the stretch-shortening cycle. The force that is produced by muscles during running also is a function of the stretch of the muscle from the previous portion of the stride. Therefore, speed is dependent on the ability of the muscle to store elastic energy, which is perhaps a function of flexibility, and on the ability of the nervous system to activate the muscle at precisely the right time. This is likely to be dictated by both voluntary and involuntary (i.e., reflex) activation of the muscle.

Anaerobic power is related to speed in the 60-yard dash. In addition, strength training 3 times/week can increase speed. Endurance training added to the strength training tends to decrease strength without effect on speed. Endurance training alone has no effect on speed.

Table 3-2 demonstrates 40-yard sprint times from athletes participating in different types of football. Although the measures made on the soccer players were from a 5-yard running start, those times represent averages for the entire team. The fastest times for the American football players are recorded in wide receivers. Rugby players have the slowest times. The degree of contact in American football and rugby is considerably greater than that in soccer (at least according to the rules), so those other forms of football are seeking some balance between body mass and speed. Soccer, it would seem, selects specifically for speed.

Table 3-2

Representative 40-Yard Sprint Times in Various Types of Football		
Group	*Start Type*	*Time (Seconds)*
US Nat'l Soccer	Running	4.33
US Pro Football	Stance	4.58–5.08
UK First Class Rugby	Stand	5.37–5.9

Training methods for speed and endurance are different. The type of speed necessary in soccer will not benefit from 12 minute runs or other forms of aerobic conditioning. Therefore, in the few weeks preceding and during the season, speed training should be emphasized. The goal of this training is to build power for the stretch-shortening cycle. Plyometric (rebound) training is the most effective way to train the stretch-shortening cycle because it is the most specific. Although it has not been systematically studied, plyometric training has an increased injury risk because the forces involved are larger. This would apply for ligamentous disruptions and muscle tears. Care should be taken not to train the tired player plyometrically.

Strength training also is likely to produce increases in speed to some extent, but one must monitor changes in speed when embarking on strengthening programs. Increased muscle mass is advantageous in virtually any sport as long as speed is not decreased. Soccer players in the early 21st century probably will be considerably bigger and stronger than those playing the game today.

Agility

Shifting directions at high speeds in reaction to a stimulus, which occurs constantly during a match, is the essence of agility. By definition, agility is dependent on speed. In addition, it is dependent on neuromuscular coordination and proprioceptive feedback from joint receptors. Perhaps more than any performance factor, agility is compromised by joint instability, which is likely to affect proprioception.

As a performance factor, agility differs from the other factors discussed because it is also dependent on an environmental factor, namely the shoe-surface interface. When the body shifts direction, firm contact with the ground is necessary. For this to occur, high coefficients of friction must be established at the shoe-surface interface. When this occurs, increased shear forces are transmitted to the knee. As a result of the effort to improve performance through footwear, there is an increased likelihood of ligamentous disruption because of failure of the foot to release.

Although many agility tests exist, we have only been able to find one with direct application to soccer. It consists of a zigzag run in a figure eight pattern around small pylons arranged in a 3 by 5 meter area (Fig. 3-3). Athletes complete three circuits without the ball. The United States Soccer PanAm team of the late 1980s completed the test in an average of 20.95 seconds. Additionally, we found that during a battery of tests which we correlated to the subjective ratings of coaches of various soccer performance indices, this test correlated better than any of the tests of anaerobic capacity used. Coaches were asked to rate the player's ability to move without the ball, track and defend the opponent, and to attain a defensive posture once the ball had been lost (see Gleim, 1988). Further tests are needed that are specific to the agility characteristics of soccer players and to how these abilities change with increasing levels of play.

The issue of developing specific training for agility in soccer may be disputed, since it is an integral part of every match or practice whenever play-

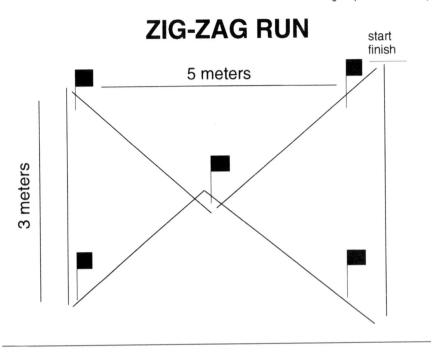

Figure 3-3. Players are timed for 3 consecutive laps in a figure 8 pattern. Dimensions shown.

ers come into contact with the ball, either on offense or defense. Although there is no proof, drills that emphasize agility with the ball may increase the likelihood of injury. It is accepted that agility tends to decrease with age because of decreases in strength, flexibility, and reaction time. Yet, definitive proof of this assertion is lacking. Certainly, before returning a player to competition following an injury, agility drills should be used by the trainer to condition the athlete and to verify the ability to compete.

Summary

The impact of training protocols addressing the performance factors in soccer players is scientifically unknown. Few coaches are willing to train half of their team with the other half acting as controls. Consequently, we are unlikely to know which interventions actually help in the performance of the game. Table 3-3 is a speculation on how the performance factors discussed relate to the game of soccer.

The designation of (+) or (−) in the table is a qualitative assessment of how a particular factor rates under a given category. Improvements in strength are likely to have a large effect on performance and an even greater effect on injury prevention. Strength measurement is generally good, but reproducibility of high speed strength, at the rates of movement in soccer, is poor. Flexibility training may improve performance but may also decrease it by causing the use of more energy. Flexibility training is likely to have a beneficial effect on injury prevention but we can only measure it statically, not dy-

Table 3-3

Selected Performance Factors in Soccer			
Factor	Performance	Injury Prevention	Measurement
Strength	(++)	(+++)	(++/−)
Flexibility	(+/−)	(++)	(+/−)
Speed	(+++)	(++/−)	(+++)
Agility	(+++)	(+++)	(+/−)

This table depicts qualitatively how well a given factor effects performance and prevents injury as well as the state-of-the-art of its measurment. (+) and (−) refer to the positive or negative attributes of the factor.

namically. Speed enhancement can only serve to improve performance and is likely to help prevent injury, although speed is deleterious when impacts occur. Speed is perhaps the easiest performance factor to measure. Finally, improvements in agility will certainly improve performance and help players avoid injury. Measurement of agility is still in its initial stages as it applies to soccer.

SUGGESTED READING

Arnason A, Johannsson E, Dahl HA. Strains, sprains and contusions in icelandic elite soccer players. Med Sci Sports Exec 1994;26(5S),S14.

Bosco C, Komi PV, Tihanyi J, et al. Mechanical power test and fiber composition of human leg extensor muscles. Eur J Appl Physiol 1983;51:129–135.

Cavagna GA, Saibene FP, Margaria R. Mechanical work in running. J Appl Physiol 1964;19:249–256.

DeProft E, Clarys JP, Bollens E, et al. Muscle activity in the soccer kick. In: Reilly T, Lees A, Davids K, (eds.) et al. Science and Football. London: E. & F.N. Spon, 1988.

Ekstrand J, Gillquist J. The frequency of muscle tightness and injuries in soccer players. Am J Sports Med 1982;10:75–78.

Fenn WO. Frictional and kinetic factors in the work of sprint running. Am J Physiol 1929;92:583–611.

Gleim GW, Trachtenberg A, Noyes FR, et al. Tests of anaerobic power in elite soccer players. Med Sci Sports Exerc 1988;20(5S),S81.

Gleim GW, Stachenfeld NA, Nicholas JA. The influence of flexibility on the economy of walking and jogging. J Orthop Res 1990;8:814–823.

Hennessy LC, Watson AWS. The interference effects of training for strength and endurance simultaneously. J Strength and Conditioning Research 1994;8:12–19.

Komi PV. Stretch-shortening cycle. In: Komi PV, ed. Strength and power in sport. Boston: Blackwell Scientific Publications, 1992.

Leatt P, Shepard RJ, Plyley MJ. Specific muscular development in under-18 soccer players. J Sports Sci 1987;5:165–175.

Magnusson SP, Gleim GW, Geismer R, et al. Tension decline from passive stretch. Med Sci Sports Exerc 1993;25(5S),S140.

Margaria RP, Cerretelli F, Mangili F. Balance and kinetics of energy release during strenuous exercise in man. J Appl Physiol 1964;19:623–628.

McHugh MP, Magnusson SP, Gleim GW, et al. Viscoelastic stress relaxation in human skeletal muscle. Med Sci Spots Exerc 1992;24: 1375–1382.

McHugh MP, Gleim GW, Magnusson SP, et al. A Cross-sectional study of age-related musculoskeletal and physiological changes in soccer players. Med Exerc Nutr Health 1993;2:261–268.

Narcici MV, Sirtori MD, Mognoni P. Maximal ball velocity and peak torques of hip flexor and knee extensor muscles. In: Reilly T, Lees A, Davids K, (eds.) et al. Science and Football. London: E. & F.N. Spon, 1988.

Oberg B, Moller M, Gillquist J, et al. Isokinetic torque levels for knee extensors and knee flexors in soccer players. Int J Sports Med 1986;7:50–53.

Osternig L, Robertson RN, Troxel RK, et al. Differential responses to proprioceptive neuromuscular facilitation (PNF) stretch techniques. Med Sci Sports Exerc 1990; 22:106–111.

Poulmedis P. Isokinetic maximal torque power of Greek elite soccer players. J Ortho Sports Med Physical Ther 1985;6:293–295.

Raven PB, Gettman LR, Pollock ML, et al. A physiologic evaluation of professional soccer players. Brit J Sports Med 1976;10:209–216.

Rhodes E, Mosher R, McKenzie D, et al. Physiological profiles of the Canadian Olympic Soccer team. Can J Appl Sport Sci 1986;11:31–36.

Vandewalle H, Peres G, Monod H. Standard anaerobic exercise tests. Sports Med 1987;4:268–289.

Acknowledgments

I would like to thank James A. Nicholas, M.D. for instilling the perspectives which are thematic in this work. Also, special thanks to Arnold Trachtenberg, A.T.C. who has been instrumental in my education about the sport of soccer and the nature of soccer injuries.

4  Dietary Applications

Charlotte C. McIntosh
Michael K. McIntosh

The Need for Nutrients

Food is more than a substance to satisfy taste buds or hunger pains. Food, especially the appropriate amount and variety, is essential for survival. No one could live on sugar water alone because it would provide plenty of calories and fluid, but little nutrition. Without consuming essential nutrients from food and drinking proper amounts of fluids, death would result. Food provides nourishing substances called nutrients that are necessary for growth and development, promoting health, preventing disease, and enhancing mental and physical performance. A well-nourished body is strong, resilient, efficient, and able to adapt quickly to changes in physiological status. When trying to improve eating habits, it helps to think of food as more than just fuel. Hidden in each bite of meat, piece of fruit, plate of pasta, or serving of vegetables are the nutrients that give life.

Why should athletes care about being well-nourished? Can't they function well enough on doughnuts, hamburgers, and pizza? Athletes could certainly get enough calories from eating these foods, however, they wouldn't be able to obtain enough of the vital nutrients needed for optimal performance. People need vitamins and minerals such as those found in a variety of grains, fruits, vegetables, dairy products, and meats to be at their healthiest. The human body is resilient and can tolerate severe nutrient deficiencies before any obvious symptoms of malnutrition become apparent. However, suboptimal nutritional status limits daily performance in both athletes and nonathletes. A car cannot be expected to run well if water was put in the gas tank instead of gasoline or if it was lubricated with vegetable oil instead of motor oil. Chemical reactions in the car's engine need the proper fuels and lubricants. Every breath, heartbeat, contraction of the muscle pulling on the skeleton, and every other function of the human body is a result of a chemical reaction involving nutrients. Food provides nutrients that are transformed into the chemical compounds that provide energy or are used for growth, development, and/or maintenance of the human body. Good nutrition is especially vital for optimal athletic performance.

Types, Functions, and Sources of Nutrients

The six categories of essential nutrients are carbohydrates, lipids, protein, vitamins, minerals, and water. Of these six nutrients, only carbohydrates, lipids, and protein provide energy. Many of the vitamins and minerals serve as cofactors for enzymes involved in metabolism (synthesis and breakdown) of carbohydrates, lipids, and protein. They are also involved in the delivery and use of oxygen by working muscles.

Carbohydrates

Carbohydrates are glucose-rich nutrients found in plant foods that provide immediate sources of energy for all cells. The two major forms of carbohydrates found in foods are simple (i.e., single or double molecules of glucose, fructose, or galactose) and complex (i.e., straight or branched chains of glucose molecules). Simple sugars commonly found in foods include monosaccharides (i.e., single sugars such as glucose, dextrose, fructose, and galactose) and disaccharides (i.e., two monosaccharides joined together such as sucrose, lactose, and maltose). Glucose, sometimes called "blood sugar," is the most abundant carbohydrate in the body. After digestion and absorption, 95% of all carbohydrates in food end up as glucose in the bloodstream. Fructose is the simple sugar that makes fruit sweet. Sucrose, a disaccharide containing glucose and fructose, is found in table sugar, sugar cane, honey, and sugar beets. Lactose, a disaccharide containing glucose and galactose, is abundant in milk products. Maltose, a disaccharide containing two glucose molecules, is found in fermented grain products. Monosaccharides do not require enzymatic digestion in the gut. When ingested alone, they are rapidly absorbed (within minutes following ingestion) into the bloodstream. Therefore, simple sugars are very effective in raising blood glucose levels during activities, such as exhaustive exercise, that result in a decrease in blood glucose levels.

Complex carbohydrates or starches commonly found in plant foods include dextrins (short, straight chains of glucose molecules), polysaccharides (long, straight, and branched chains of glucose molecules), and fiber (indigestible polysaccharides, cellulose, and lignin). Foods rich in complex carbohydrates include whole grains (e.g., wheat, oats, barley, and rice) and their products (e.g., breads, cereals, and pasta), legumes (e.g., dried beans, peas, and lentils), fruits, and vegetables. In contrast to simple sugars, complex carbohydrates require considerable time (approximately 30–90 min.) before they reach the bloodstream. They take more time to be absorbed because each glucose molecule must be digested away from its parent chain of glucose molecules before it can be absorbed into the blood. For this reason, complex carbohydrates help curb the appetite and serve as a sustained energy source during physical activity. The slower rate of absorption of glucose provides a steady supply of glucose to the bloodstream over time. Based on these properties of complex carbohydrates, current dietary guidelines recommend that Americans with average activity levels consume approximately 55% of their daily calories from carbohydrates, with at least 2/3 of these calories from complex carbohydrates. For those individuals engaged in strenuous physical activity or exercise, the American Dietetic Association (ADA) recommends that approximately 60–65% of their daily calories be from carbohydrates with at least 5/6 of those calories from complex carbohydrates. The important role of carbohydrates during soccer training and matches is discussed in detail in Chapter 6.

Lipids

Lipids (or fats) constitute a class of water-insoluble compounds that include triglycerides, fatty acids (saturated, monounsaturated, and polyunsaturated), cholesterol, steroids (e.g., vitamin D and cortisol), phospholipids, and waxes. Dietary fats enhance the flavor and texture of food (Table 4-1).

Most of the lipids found in food and the body are in the form of triglycerides. Whether in french fries or around the waistline, triglycerides are made up of three fatty acids connected to a glycerol backbone. Triglycerides differ from one another based on the types of fatty acids that are attached to their glycerol backbones. Consequently, triglycerides have different physical properties and health implications. Saturated fatty acids (contain no carbon-carbon double bonds) are extremely rigid. When saturated fatty acids are incorporated into cell membranes, the fluidity (flexibility) and functional properties may be adversely altered. Loss of membrane function can lead to numerous metabolic disturbances and contribute to life-threatening diseases such as atherosclerosis, stroke, and hypertension. Animal fats, oils from coconut and palm trees, and vegetable oils that have been hydrogenated (removal of the carbon-carbon double bonds from fatty acids) are high in saturated fatty acids. Saturated fat is solid at room temperature and resembles the hard, white fat around a typical steak or in a can of shortening.

Monounsaturated fatty acids (one carbon-carbon double bond) or polyunsaturated (more than one carbon-carbon double bond) are very fluid. When unsaturated fatty acids are incorporated into cell membranes, they increase the functional capacity of the membrane. Natural oils from soybean, corn, sunflower, and safflower are rich in polyunsaturated fatty acids whereas oils from canola, peanut, and olives are rich in monounsaturated fatty acids. Canola oil is also low in saturated fatty acids (approximately 7%). Polyunsaturated and monounsaturated fats are liquid at room temperature, similar to a bottle of vegetable oil. Consuming too much fat, even oils rich in polyun-

Table 4-1

Uses of Lipids by the Body
Provide essential fatty acids the body cannot make
Provide a concentrated source of energy (9 cal/gm)
Are vital constituents of all cell membranes
Transport the fat-soluble vitamins (A, D, E, and K)
Are building blocks for certain hormone-like substances
Insulate against external temperature fluctuations
Cushion vital organs against injury due to sudden shock or rapid movement

saturated or monounsaturated fatty acids, can lead to obesity and is associated with an increased risk of cancer. Moreover, manufacturers can turn good polyunsaturated oils into hard, saturated fats by the chemical process of hydrogenation. This process converts a liquid oil into a hard, saturated fat. Vegetable oil shortening is a good example of the result of hydrogenation. Excess consumption of vegetable oils that have been hydrogenated (which include all types of stick margarine) contribute to many of the same health problems as saturated fatty acids.

Reducing dietary fat is important for heart health. Most school age children, adolescents, and adults could benefit from eating less fat. Table 4-2 provides some general guidelines for reducing dietary fat consumption. In terms of calories, fat is fat whether it is saturated or unsaturated. Gram per gram,

Table 4-2

Guidelines for Reducing Dietary Fat		
	Use these more often	*Use these less often:*
Meats	lean red meat, skinless chicken & turkey, pork tenderloin or loin chops, seafood (baked, broiled, grilled), 95% fat free lunch meats, 95% fat free hot dogs	choice cuts of red meat, rib eye, T-bone, ribs, fried seafood, bacon, sausage, bologna, regular hot dogs, fast food burgers
Starches	pasta with tomato sauce, rice, dried beans, loaf breads, rolls, potatoes, pretzels, pancakes, low fat or fat free waffles, cereals, low fat or baked crackers, low fat granola bars, bagels, english muffins	doughnut, sweet breads, biscuits, potato chips french fries, fried crackers, taco chips and other fried snacks, regular granola bars, deli muffins
Vegetables	any fresh, plain frozen or canned	vegetables with cream sauces, fried vegetables
Fruit	any kind	avocados
Dairy	reduced fat cheeses, ice milk, frozen yogurt, fat free sour cream, yogurt, sherbert	regular block or sliced cheeses, ice cream, sour cream, cream, cream cheese, dips
Desserts	jello, fruited yogurt, vanilla wafers, angel food cake, ginger snaps, low fat cookies, graham crackers, non-fat or reduced fat frozen desserts, puddings made with skim or 1% milk	fudge, most cookies, candy bars cream filled or frosted desserts, ice cream
Miscellaneous	reduced fat mayonnaise and margarine, reduced fat salad dressings, pickles, mustard, ketchup, relishes, tomato sauces	mayonnaise, margarine, tarter sauce, cream sauces, regular salad dressings

ounce per ounce, saturated and polyunsaturated fats have the same number of calories. Current dietary guidelines from the American Heart Association recommend consuming 30% or less of daily calories from fat with 1/3 or less from saturated fatty acids, 1/3 from monounsaturated fatty acids, and 1/3 from polyunsaturated fatty acids. At least 5% of calories should be from the essential fatty acids linoleic acid (Cl8:2, omega 6) and linolenic acid (Cl8:3, omega 3) found in oils rich in polyunsaturated fatty acids. Cold water fish are an excellent source of omega 3 fatty acids. Athletes consuming 60–65% of their calories from carbohydrates and 15% of their calories from protein would have fat intakes at a level of 20–25% of total calories. On the other hand, ultra-endurance athletes such as triathletes and marathon runners may need to increase their fat intake slightly since it may be difficult for them to consume enough calories from carbohydrates to meet their energy demands.

Protein

Proteins are made up of building blocks called amino acids. These amino acids are linked together in specific sequences that determine the specific structure and subsequent function of the protein. Of the 20 or so amino acids known, 9 are considered to be essential and, therefore, must be present in the diet. These essential amino acids can be obtained by consuming good quality sources of protein such as animal products (meat, eggs, and dairy) and also by including a variety of legumes (e.g., dried beans, peas, lentils, and tofu), grains (e.g., bread, rice, and cereals), nuts, and seeds (e.g., peanuts, cashews, and sunflower seeds) in the daily diet. Protein from vegetables is also a good source of complex carbohydrates, including fiber. Vegetables are low in fat unless margarine, cream spreads, sauces, or salad dressings are added to them.

The Recommended Dietary Allowances (RDAs) for protein are determined based on body weight and age. Most healthy persons between the ages of 4–6, 7–14, 15–18, and those over 18 years of age need, 1.2, 1.0, 0.9, and 0.8 grains of protein per kg body weight daily, respectively. The protein requirement for people engaged in vigorous training and athletic events is not much different from the average healthy individual and can usually be met by consuming extra portions of good quality protein. Unless an amino acid supplement contains all of the nine essential amino acids, these expensive supplements will most likely be used for energy or stored as fat, depending on the person's energy balance. In addition, this conversion of excess amino acids to energy or fat contributes to dehydration and can lead to kidney problems due to the increased workload involved in excreting the excess ammonia. To ensure that dietary protein is used for protein synthesis rather than broken down for energy needs, sufficient calories, especially in the form of complex carbohydrates, must be consumed daily (Table 4-3).

Vitamins

Vitamins are carbon-containing compounds which are required in small amounts by the body. For example, most water soluble vitamins (niacin, thiamin, riboflavin, pantothenic acid, biotin, folate, and vitamins B_6 and B_{12}) serve as cofactors or coenzymes for pathways of carbohydrate, lipid, protein,

Table 4-3

Uses of Protein by the Body
Make up vital body constituents such as muscle, connective tissue, and transporters
Help maintain fluid and acid-base balance
Compromise hormones and enzymes
Are key components of the immune system such as antibodies
Can be used to make glucose
Provide energy

and energy metabolism. Vitamin C, another water soluble vitamin, serves not only as an antioxidant in body fluids, but is also necessary for the synthesis of collagen, hormones, and neurotransmitters. Fat soluble vitamins (vitamins A, E, D, and K), on the other hand, are necessary for the optimal growth, development, and maintenance of tissues and organs. In addition, vitamin E and carotenoids (vitamin A precursors) serve as antioxidants within lipid rich compartments in the body.

The RDAs for the water and fat soluble vitamins are based on a person's age and gender. A diet balanced in carbohydrate, lipid, and protein, selected from a variety of foods from all the food groups, supplies ample vitamins and minerals for most individuals and athletes. Taking vitamin supplements in excess of daily requirements does not improve performance or health. In fact, some may hinder performance if taken in excessive amounts.

Minerals

Minerals are noncarbon containing compounds found in both plant and animal products. Minerals serve a variety of functions within the body. Some minerals such as magnesium, copper, and selenium serve as cofactors for enzymes of metabolism. The two categories of minerals, major and minor, are based on their daily requirements. The major minerals (calcium, phosphorus, sodium, potassium, chloride, magnesium, and sulfur) are required in amounts greater than 100 mg/day. The minor or trace minerals (iron, zinc, copper, selenium, iodide, fluoride, chromium, manganese, and molybdenum) are required in amounts less than 100 mg/day (Table 4-4).

Table 4-4

Uses of Minerals by the Body
Providing skeleton support (calcium and phosphorus)
Transporting oxygen (iron)
Transmitting nerve impulses (calcium, sodium, potassium, and magnesium)
Fluid balance (sodium, chloride, potassium, and phosphorus).

Although plant sources may be rich in minerals, especially trace minerals, their bioavailability (amount available for absorption into the bloodstream) may be low (approximately 5–10%). The best dietary sources of minerals are animal products. For this reason, including a variety of animal products in the daily diet helps to ensure adequacy. Female athletes, especially elite runners and gymnasts, may need to consume extra portions of dietary sources of iron from lean red meats or legumes and calcium from low fat dairy products to decrease the risks of developing anemia and/or osteoporosis. Vegetarian female athletes may need iron and calcium supplements. However, minerals in excess of 150% of the RDA should be taken only under the guidance of a physician since nutrient interactions and toxicity may occur at these increased levels of intake.

Water

Man cannot live without water. The body contains 50–70% water on a weight basis, depending on age, gender, and muscle mass. In addition to the vital role of water in energy metabolism, osmotic balance, nutrient transport, and waste elimination, it also keeps the body from overheating. In fact, water replacement is the most important nutritional factor during prolonged exercise, especially in the heat. Sweating is the body's cooling mechanism to dissipate body core heat produced during exercise and high environmental temperatures. Excess sweat loss between 4–10% of body weight during vigorous exercise in hot, humid weather can lead to elevated body core temperatures, dehydration, and electrolyte losses. These factors cause dizziness, fainting, cramping, fatigue, and, if untreated, heat stroke. A 20% loss of body weight in water results in coma and death. To compensate for water losses consume water before, during, and after physical exercise and avoid diuretics (e.g., caffeinated beverages, pills such as Excedrin, Dexatrim, and No-Doz, and alcoholic beverages). As a rule of thumb, drink two cups of fluid for every pound of weight lost (1 pint/pound) from sweating. Remember, thirst is not an adequate indicator of hydration status. Sport drinks containing simple sugars should be diluted to at least 2.5–5% sugar content and should not be consumed immediately prior to or within the first 30 min. of an endurance activity. They can cause cramping and hypoglycemia if not properly used during physical exercise, especially if they have a high sugar or electrolyte content.

Meeting Nutrient and Energy Needs.

The Recommended Dietary Allowances (RDAs)

The RDAs, established by The National Research Council, enable individuals of all ages to determine the amounts of nutrients they must consume on a regular basis in order to assure proper nourishment. RDAs for 19 nutrients have been established whereas RDAs for the other 26 known nutrients have yet to be set. The RDAs are expressed as average daily intakes over time for groups of individuals and are intended for most average individuals living in the U.S. For some nutrients without RDAs (e.g., biotin, copper, and chromium), estimated safe and adequate daily dietary intakes (ESADDI) have been established. For other nutrients without RDAs (e.g., sodium, chlorine, and potassium), estimated minimum requirements have been established.

To help consumers use the RDAs when making food choices, the U.S. Food and Drug Administration established the U.S. Recommended Daily Allowances (U.S. RDAs) in 1974. The U.S. RDAs, which appear on most packaged foods and supplements, express the content of specific nutrients in each serving as a percentage of the 1968 RDAs for children over the age of four or adults (whichever is highest). Depending on the product, consuming one serving size provides a certain percentage of the 1968 RDAs for those nutrients. For example, if one serving size of the product provides 30 mg of vitamin C, and the highest RDA for vitamin C in 1968 was 60 mg (for adults), each serving provides 50% of the U.S. RDA for vitamin C. The U.S. RDAs are currently being changed to the Reference Daily Intakes (RDI) to reflect more recent research on the requirements of new and previously discovered nutrients, and to reduce the confusion between the RDAs and the U.S. RDAs. Moreover, a new labeling law will require labels on packaged foods to display a new category called the Daily Reference Values (DRVs). The DRVs are standards considered to be the upper intake limit of specific nutrients, many of which do not currently have RDAs, such as fat, saturated fat, cholesterol, sodium, and carbohydrate (sugar and fiber). The current DRVs are based on a 2000 cal/day diet. Therefore, individuals with energy requirements greater than 2000 cal/day will have higher DRVs, with the exceptions of cholesterol and saturated fat.

What are the different types of foods needed and how much of them should be consumed to meet the RDAS, ESADDI and the estimated minimum requirements of the essential nutrients? In general, a healthy diet should contain 12–15% of calories from protein, 55–60% of calories from carbohydrate, and 25–30% of calories from fat. To illustrate these guidelines, the following chart provides examples of approximately how many grams of protein, carbohydrate, and fat should be consumed daily based on different levels of calorie needs.

Examples of Total Daily Grams of Protein, Carbohydrate and Fat Based on Calorie Needs of 15% of Calories from Protein, 55% from Carbohydrate and 30% from Fat

Total Calories Needed	Protein (grams)	Carbohydrate (grams)	Fat (grams)
1600	60	220	53
1800	68	248	60
2000	75	275	67
2200	83	303	73
2400	90	330	80
2600	98	358	87
2800	105	385	93
3000	113	413	100

For example, an individual needing 2400 cal/day should consume approximately 90 gm of protein, 330 gm of carbohydrate, and 80 gm of fat. Table 4-5 provides an example of a 24 hour food plan that would achieve this recommended intake level of protein, carbohydrate, and fat from a variety of common food sources.

The Food Guide Pyramid

The Four Basic Food Groups have recently been replaced by The Food Guide Pyramid which is presented in Figure 4-1. The Food Guide Pyramid, a na-

Table 4-5

Example of a 2400 Calorie Meal Plan that Provides Approximately 15% of the Calories from Protein, 55% of the Calories from Carbohydrate and 30% of the Calories from Fat			
Breakfast	Protein *(grams)*	Carbohydrate *(grams)*	Fat *(grams)*	Calories Content

Food	Protein (grams)	Carbohydrate (grams)	Fat (grams)	Calories Content
1 cup Toasted Oatmeal	4	33	1	160
1 cup 1% milk	8	12	3	100
1 banana	1	27	—	105
1 cup orange juice	—	27	—	112
Mid-morning Snack				
3 graham crackers	3	15	1	60
1 Tbsp. peanut butter	4	4	8	100
1 cup apple juice	—	28	—	112
Lunch				
McDonald's Quarter Pounder	23	34	21	410
small fries	3	26	12	220
large apple	—	30	—	115
1 cup 1% milk	8	12	3	100
Mid-afternoon Snack				
2 Nature Valley granola bars	4	32	8	210
1 can soda	—	38	—	150
Dinner				
3 ounces grilled fish	23	—	6	157
large baked potato (7 oz.)	5	51	—	220
1 cup broccoli	5	8	1	43
1 Tbsp. margarine	—	—	10	100
Totals	91 grams	377 grams	74 grams	2474 calories
% of total calories	14%	60%	26%	

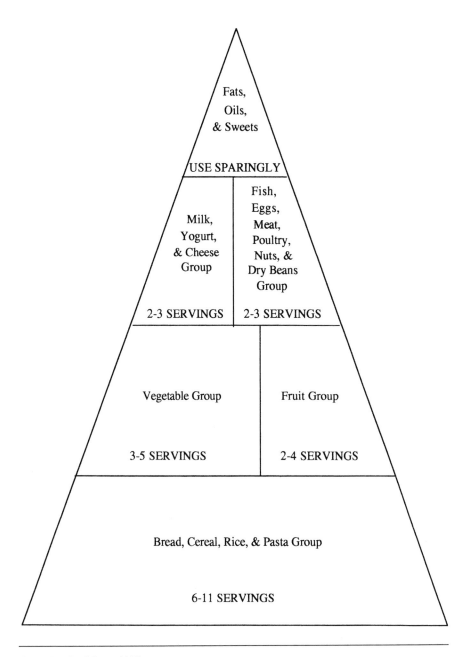

Figure 4-1. Food Pyramid Diagram.

tionally accepted guide to healthy eating developed by the U.S. Department of Agriculture, categorizes foods into six groups and advises Americans how many minimum servings/day from each group they should eat.

One question that may come to mind after looking over The Food Guide Pyramid is, "What is a serving size?" Table 4-6 is a listing of general portion sizes. It is assumed that, within a reasonable range, each portion of that particular type of food has similar nutrients and calories.

By following the previously mentioned guidelines average, healthy people, including athletes, will be well nourished and have no need for vitamin, mineral, or protein supplements. Self-proclaimed magic powders and pills that (falsely) claim to add vigor and health are not necessary and may even be harmful. The Food Guide Pyramid encourages Americans to focus more on starches (breads, cereals, rice, and pasta), fruits, and vegetables while still including protein-rich foods (meats, poultry, fish, legumes, eggs, and nuts) and dairy products in their diets. Currently, Americans tend to consume a lot of high fatty meats, a few basic starches such as potatoes with a lot of butter and sour cream or french fries, "squashy" white breads, one or two servings of fruits and vegetables, and plenty of nutrient-poor, high calorie foods such as

Table 4-6

The Five Food Groups, Calorie Content and Representative Portion Sizes		
Food Group	*Calories/serving*	*Portion Sizes*
Bread, Cereal, Rice, & Pasta	80–100	1 slice of bread 1/2 cup cooked pasta, rice or hot cereal, (e.g., oatmeal)
Fruit	60–80	1 small piece of fresh fruit (apple, orange) 1/2 banana 1/2–3/4 cup of fruit juice
Vegetables	25	1/2 cup cooked vegetables 1 cup raw vegetables
Meat, Poultry, Fish, Eggs, Nuts, & Dry Beans	100	3 oz lean meat, poultry, or fish (about the size of a deck of cards) 1/2 cup cooked beans 2 eggs (<3–4/week if you have high cholesterol or heart disease) small palmful of nuts
Milk, Yogurt, & Cheese	100	8 oz cup of skim milk or plain yogurt 1 oz (1 square inch cube) of cheese

potato chips, pastries, cookies, sugary sodas, and high fat dairy desserts (yes, they do provide a little calcium). It is no wonder that so many people have trouble learning new eating patterns which can allow for the maintenance of a more healthy diet. The Food Guide Pyramid de-emphasizes fats, oils, and sweets while emphasizing carbohydrate-rich foods and balance.

Nutritious Eating Habits

Back when most work was done manually, hard working farmers ate throughout the day. Breakfast was generally the biggest meal of the day, lunch the next largest, and the evening meal the smallest because most of the farmer's energy was spent during the day. The late evening was a time to be more sedentary and, therefore, did not require much energy. Although most people are not farmers, they can still benefit from this example. People are usually more active during the day, especially when participating in athletic events, than during the evenings when activity is more likely to include studying, watching television, or sleeping. Many people skip breakfast, have a small lunch when they find a spare moment, and then sit down to a large dinner in the evening. Surveys indicate that nearly half the calories consumed in a day are taken in between dinner and bedtime. Some of these people do not understand why they are so tired during the day. How well would a car run if the gas tank was empty during the day and then filled to the brim after it was returned to the garage? The point is that people, especially athletes, should consume most of their calories during the times when they are most active rather than when they are not burning much energy. In fact, people who don't eat more than a bite or two during the day are literally starving themselves. Athletes cannot expect to perform well without sufficient fuel.

Ideally, athletes should strive for more of a grazing pattern of eating. This term became popular in the 1980s among health conscious people. It means eating small amounts of food frequently throughout the day. By eating smaller amounts throughout the day, the body is provided with the right amount of fuel when needed. Planning for small, healthy snacks such as fruit or other moderate fat foods throughout the day is a good idea. A snack does not always have to be nutrient rich, but so-called "junk food" should be used as an occasional treat, not a routine snack food. There is no daily requirement for candy or potato chips. Healthy snack foods such as dried or fresh fruit, granola bars, yogurt, or peanut butter crackers should be kept readily available. It is critical to plan nourishing snacks at times when they are needed the most. By following the guidelines presented in The Food Guide Pyramid, it is possible to have a wide variety of food choices at meals and snack time. Spread eating out throughout the day. A 10:00 a.m. and 3:00 p.m. snack break during the day can be very refreshing. Everyone is familiar with the pleasant, calming effect of a good meal. What happens when an athlete is hungry? He's usually weak, irritable and impatient. It may be difficult to think clearly and quickly. It doesn't take much to feel better—a small sandwich and some fruit, a muffin, some crackers, or a bowl of cereal.

Hunger should not be ignored and fought against. It is a genuine signal from the body that energy is needed. When the body is supplied with the right types of fuel, a variety of wholesome, moderate fat choices, innate control mechanisms can help regulate how much is eaten. It is important to listen to the body's signals; eating when hungry and drinking when thirsty (or before, if exercising or working in the heat). One reason hunger is felt is because blood sugar is lower than normal. When food is eaten, it is digested and the energy and nutrients from the food are absorbed into the bloodstream. Blood sugar (glucose) increases and the desire to eat disappears. Stomach fullness also causes a feeling of satisfaction. Although there are many theories on hunger and appetite regulation, suffice it to say that there are many factors that naturally control the amounts eaten. Because of this, an athlete who maintains a relatively healthy diet and eats routine meals and snacks should not have to count calories to maintain a satisfactory weight. It takes a lot of retraining to get to the point where the mind, taste buds, and body signals all work together. It can be done, however, if an athlete learns how to eat the right foods at the right times, taking into consideration the minimum number of servings of each of the five food groups from The Food Guide Pyramid.

An active person does not need to eat a high fat diet to obtain adequate calories and energy. On the other hand, there is no need to be overly strict and eliminate all high fat foods such as fried chicken and pepperoni pizza. Because caloric needs of athletes tend to be higher than sedentary persons, it may be difficult to maintain weight on a strict diet. Moderation and variety are important. Increasing consumption of high carbohydrate foods, eating more frequently, and consuming a well balanced diet help to assure adequate caloric intake. To help Americans maintain health and fight disease, the U.S. Department of Agriculture (USDA) and the U.S. Department of Health and Humans Services (USDHHS) established the Dietary Guidelines for Americans. These seven guidelines are as follows:

1. Eat a variety of foods
2. Maintain a desirable weight
3. Choose a diet low in fat, saturated fat, and cholesterol
4. Choose a diet with plenty of vegetables, fruits, and grain products
5. Use sugars in moderation
6. Use salt and sodium in moderation
7. If you drink alcoholic beverages, do so in moderation

Long term success in learning to eat healthier can't be accomplished unless an individual is willing to expand beyond a "meat and potatoes" diet. All eating habits are learned. People are born with the instinct to eat and to eat a variety of foods. Peculiarities and unhealthy habits are learned behaviors. Some people can be stubborn about changing those habits, but it can be done if desired.

Determining Ideal Body Weight and Energy Needs
Determining Ideal Body Weight (IBW)
Athletes should eat enough to maintain a healthy weight or, in the case of growing adolescents and those who are increasing their muscle mass through exercise, allow for weight gain . Chapter 5, "Nutritional Needs," dis-

cusses the growth needs of adolescents. Energy needs are determined according to a person's age, gender, and current body weight (usually for youth and adolescents) or ideal body weight (IBW) (for adults). IBW for youth and adolescents can be obtained from standardized growth charts from pediatricians or from various health related texts.

Males:

106 lb for the first five feet of height.
Add 6 additional lb for each inch over 5 feet.

For example:
Joe is 5'8". He should weigh:
106 lb + (6 lb × 8) = 154 lb ± 10%

The ± 10% of IBW is used to adjust ideal weight for persons with very small (−10%) or very large (+10%) bone structure. Some people have slender bones and, therefore, should weigh proportionately less than persons of the same height with average bone thickness. Conversely, others may have thicker, heavier bones and should weigh more than the average person for their height. Because of this, an IBW weight range is allowed. Therefore, Joe's IBW range is 154 lb. ±10%. Relative to his frame size, Joe's IBW is:

small bone   = 138 lb {154 − (0.1 × 154)}
medium bone   = 154 lb
large bone   = 169 lb {154 + (0.1 × 154)}

Females:

100 lb for the first five feet of height.
Add 5 additional lb for each inch over five feet.

For example:
Josephine is 5'3". She should weigh:
100 lb + (5 lb x 3) = 115 lb ± 10%

Therefore, Josephine's IBW range is 115 lb ±10%. Relative to her frame size, Josephine's IBW is:

small bone   = 104 lb {115 − (0.1 × 115)}
medium bone   = 115 lb
large bone   = 126 lb {115 + (0.1 × 115)}

An athlete with ample muscle mass, such as a body builder, may weigh more than the IBW range indicates. Muscle weighs more than fat and the IBW calculations are based on the average, nonathletic individual. Being fit and healthy are wonderful goals, but as far as weight is concerned, if an athlete is within a healthy weight range but seems to carry a little more fat than his teammates, he shouldn't be obsessed with weight loss and control.

Determining Daily Energy Needs

How are caloric needs calculated? First, figure out the appropriate IBW range based on height and, unless it is absolutely certain that an individual is small or large boned, use the IBW for a medium-boned person. The desirable weight range of youths and adolescents can be obtained from standardized growth charts available from pediatricians. If they are not readily available, use current body weight since youths and adolescents are still growing and should never be put on an energy-restricting diet. Athletes such as body builders or football players should use the upper range of their IBW, even if they are medium boned, because of increased muscle mass. Calculating caloric needs is not an exact science, but it is possible to get a good idea of energy requirements. One commonly used method to determine energy requirements is according to the Recommended Energy Intake-10th Edition RDA. According to this procedure, energy needs for the average, moderately active person can be calculated by multiplying the person's current weight or IBW in kg by the number of cal/kg IBW in the appropriate age and gender categories. The following is an example of this method:

Determining Daily Energy Requirements Based on Age, Gender, and Weight (in kg)

Category	Ages	Calories/kg
Children	1–3	102
	4–6	90
	7–10	70
Males	11–14	55
	15-18	45
	19-24	40
	25-50	37
Females	11–14	47
	15–18	40
	19–24	38
	25–50	36

Therefore, if Joe (IBW = 154 lb or 70 kg) is a moderately active 18-year-old high school senior, he would need approximately 3150 cal/day. If Josephine (IBW = 115 lb or 52.3 kg) is a moderately active 19-year-old college freshman, she would need approximately 1988 cal/day. Extremely active persons training and playing strenuous sports or doing manual labor full time, may need as much as 25% more cal/kg IBW depending on the intensity and duration of the exercise or physical activity.

The amount of exercise or physical activity level makes a difference in how many calories are needed. Because a calculation such as this cannot take into account each individual person's rate of metabolism, the calculated caloric needs can only give a rough idea of how much should be eaten each day. The most important thing is to eat well balanced, moderate fat, regular meals and snacks throughout the day. If an athlete currently weighs more than his ideal weight, the level of calories needed to maintain ideal weight should promote a very gradual weight loss until he comes within the normal range for his height.

Summary

This chapter has provided information on maintaining a well-balanced diet. This can be achieved by consuming adequate portions from each of the five food groups, outlined in The Food Guide Pyramid, on a regular basis. Unfortunately, there is no magic food, diet, or supplement that will enhance athletic performance above and beyond that of a properly balanced diet. However, poor nutritional habits can have a negative effect on training and performance levels. The athlete's diet should be relatively similar in composition to that of the nonathlete. The primary differences are in caloric and fluid requirements which, for some athletes, can be nearly double depending on the type and duration of their activity levels. These increased demands of physical activity can usually be met by consuming extra portions of carbohydrate-rich foods and fluids. Therefore, eating meals rich in complex carbohydrates (whole grain breads, cereals and pasta, rice, potatoes, legumes, fruits, and vegetables) and low in fat (low fat dairy products and lean meats) and drinking plenty of fluids will help an individual achieve maximal performance, fitness, and health. The following chapters will provide special considerations involving soccer players. Good eating habits can be worked into an individual's daily routine. It may take some extra effort at first, since any type of change takes extra thought and planning. Coaches who work to develop good eating habits in their athletes not only improve their performance and health, but also help to establish the foundation for a lifetime of optimal health. The ultimate goal is to make healthy eating habits an instinctual behavior. With healthy eating habits, athletes will reap many rewards in the form of a stronger and healthier body, better endurance, and enhanced performance overall.

SUGGESTED READING

American Dietetic Association. Position stand on nutrition for physical fitness and athletic performance for adults. J Am Dietetic Assoc 1987;87:933–939.

Berning J. Wise food choices for athletes on the road. Sports Science Exchange. Gatorade Sports Science Institute. Vol. l(l): April, 1988.

National Dairy Council. FOOD POWER: A coach's guide to improving performance-3rd Edition (#0140N). c/o Dairy & Food Nutrition Council, 2300 West Meadowview Road, #106, Greensboro, NC 27407 (1/800-768-6455).

National Dairy Council. YOU: Your Guide to Food, Fitness and Fun. Young Men (#0110N) and Young Women (#0130N). c/o Dairy & Food Nutrition Council, 2300 West Meadowview Road, #106, Greensboro, NC 27407 (1/800-768-6455).

Recommended Dietary Allowance (RDA)-10th Edition. Food and Nutrition Board, National Research Council. National Academy Press. Washington, DC, 1989.

Wardlaw G, Insel P. Perspective in nutrition-2nd edition. St Louis: Mosby-Year Book, Inc., 1993.

5 Nutritional Needs

Kristine Larson Clark

Today, more than ever before, people are concerned about what they eat. The one exception to this rule is adolescents. The teenage attitude of invincibility prevails and spills over into food behavior. For adolescent athletes, food selection is more frequently dictated by peer pressure and socialization than by the nutritional facts. Scientifically, nutrition and sport performance have made great strides. But translating the science of good nutrition to adolescent athletes in an impressionable way continues to be a goal.

Because few adolescent soccer players have the opportunity to individually meet with a sport nutritionist, their parents, coaches, and trainers must have an understanding of what foods promote optimal performance. In addition, "nutrition advisers" need adequate nutrition knowledge to dispel the myths surrounding the notion of "good" and "bad" foods.

What foods adolescent soccer players eat and what time of day they eat relative to playing soccer lay the foundation for promoting appropriate growth patterns and providing calories and micronutrients to support exercise. In this chapter, the nutrition issues that effect exercise performance and nutrition education strategies to promote appropriate eating behaviors for the adolescent soccer player are described.

Energy Needs

Soccer is considered a high-intensity, intermittent sport. Children under the age of 10 participate in games that have four 12 minute quarters. A 5 minute break occurs between the quarters, with a 10 minute break after the first two quarters. Children over the age of 10 participate in games in which there are two halves that range in length from 25 min/half (10 year olds) to 45 min/half (19 year olds). Soccer training and competition results in an increased energy demand that must be accompanied by an increased energy intake to sustain the activity. In addition to the calories the young athletes need to play soccer without undue fatigue, they need an adequate level of calories to promote growth. Because there is no data available on the actual caloric cost during youth soccer match-play or during a practice, it makes sense to be aware of a child's body weight and manage calorie needs based on whether weight appears to be lost or appropriate weight gain achieved. Children should not intentionally lose weight unless a physician has been consulted.

Despite the fact that little research exists to identify specific calorie requirements for adolescents, we do know that energy requirements peak during this period of life. Adolescence is a time of rapid growth and changes in body composition. The adolescent growth spurt begins at approximately 10 years of age in girls and 12 years of age in boys. Energy requirements increase to support this growth. In boys, estimated energy intake is 2500 to 3200 cal/day between the ages of 10–20 years. For girls, the estimated calories range between 1800 to 2000 per day (Diet and Health, National Academy of Sciences, 1989).

Parents and coaches often want information regarding calorie intake for their active children and athletes. The best advice, because data on calorie needs is unavailable, is to make a wide variety of foods available to children at home and on the soccer field. Nutrient-rich snacks should be available while traveling to or from a soccer game. Finally, parents should pay attention to the type and amount of food consumed at school. Find out whether a school food program is offered, what types of foods are served, or mutually plan a bagged lunch with the child. Input from the adolescent will increase the likelihood that the food will be eaten.

Carbohydrate Needs

Carbohydrate is the most important macronutrient in the soccer players diet. As the primary fuel source for skeletal muscle, carbohydrate-rich foods should be selected for meals and snacks more often than high protein or fat containing foods.

Carbohydrates come in several forms including complex carbohydrates that are starchy and fiber-rich and simple carbohydrates, typically made up of sucrose, fructose, lactose, glucose, or a combination of several of these. All carbohydrate sources provide necessary energy for performance, with the exception of fiber. The main difference between the types of carbohydrates is the rate or speed at which the body can digest, absorb, and metabolize them or, in other words, use them for energy. Complex carbohydrates require more digestive time whereas the simple carbohydrates are digested and absorbed at faster rates.

Because of this difference, the type of carbohydrate found in foods is important. Foods containing complex carbohydrates provide an excellent source of energy, but should be eaten two or more hours before vigorous exercise. Simple carbohydrates found in sport drinks, sport bars, candy, fruits, and juices also provide excellent energy, but are more useful immediately before vigorous exercise or during activity.

The misconception that carbohydrates are only found in pasta, bread, rice, and cereal continues in the athletic population. Most athletes, parents, and coaches are unaware of the high carbohydrate content found in all fruits, vegetables, and dairy products, as well as sweetened foods such as cookies, cakes, candies, and other snacks. Table 5-1 outlines a variety of both solid and

Table 5-1

Food Sources of Carbohydrates, Protein, Fat, and Calories				
	Calories	*Protein g*	*Carbohydrate g*	*Fat g*
Milk Group				
Buttermilk, 1 cup	99	8	12	2
Cheese, American, 1 slice	106	6	—	9
Cheese, Cheddar, 1 slice	114	7	—	9
Cheese, Cottage, 1/2 cup	109	13	3	5
Cheese, Swiss, 1 slice	107	8	1	8
Cocoa, 3/4 cup	164	7	19	7
Ice Cream, Vanilla, 1/2 cup	135	2	16	7
Milk, 1 cup	150	8	11	8
Milk, Chocolate, 1 cup	208	8	26	8
Milk, Lowfat (2%), 1 cup	121	8	12	5
Milk, Skim, 1 cup	86	8	12	—
Milkshake, Chocolate, 10.6 oz.	356	9	63	8
Pudding, Chocolate, 1/2 cup	161	4	30	4
Yogurt, Strawberry, 1 cup	225	9	42	3
Meat Group				
Bacon, 2 slices	92	5	1	8
Beans, Refried, 1/2 cup	142	9	26	1
Beef, Roast, 3 oz.	182	26	0	8
Beef Liver, 3 oz.	195	23	5	9
Bologna, 1 slice	86	3	—	8
Chicken, Fried, 3 oz.	201	26	2	9
Egg, Fried, large	83	5	1	6
Egg, Hard-Cooked, large	79	6	1	6
Egg, Scrambled, large	95	6	1	7
Frankfurter, 2 oz.	172	7	1	15
Ham, Baked, 3 oz.	179	26	0	8
Meat Loaf, 3 oz.	230	15	13	12
Meat Patty, 3 oz.	186	23	0	10
Peanut Butter, 2 Tbsp.	186	9	6	16
Peanuts, Salted, 1/4 cup	211	9	7	18
Peas, Blackeye, Immature, 1/2 cup	134	10	22	1
Peas, Blackeye, Mature, 1/2 cup	94	6	17	—
Perch, Fried, Breaded, 3 oz.	193	16	6	11
Pork Chop, 3 oz.	308	21	0	24
Sausage, 2 links	135	5	—	13
T-Bone Steak, 3 1/3 oz.	212	29	0	10
Tuna, 3 oz.	168	25	0	7

Table 5-1 (continued)

	Calories	Protein g	Carbohydrate g	Fat g
Fruit-Vegetable Group				
Apple, medium	80	—	20	1
Applesauce, 1/2 cup	116	—	30	—
Apricots, Dried, 4 halves	39	1	10	—
Asparagus, 4 spears, 1/2 cup	12	1	2	—
Banana, medium	101	1	26	—
Beans, Green, 1/2 cup	16	1	3	—
Beans, Lima, 1/2 cup	94	7	17	—
Broccoli, stalk, 1/2 cup	20	2	4	—
Cabbage, 1/6 head, 1/2 cup	13	1	3	—
Cantaloupe, 1/4 medium	29	1	7	—
Carrots, 1/2 cup	22	1	5	—
Carrot Sticks, 5" carrot	21	1	5	—
Cauliflower, 1/2 cup	13	1	3	—
Celery Sticks, 8" stalk	10	1	2	—
Coleslaw, 1/2 cup	82	1	3	8
Corn, 1/2 cup	70	2	16	1
Corn, 5" ear	114	4	26	1
Fruit Salad, 1/2 cup	99	2	25	1
Grapefruit, Pink, 1/2 medium	48	1	13	—
Grapes, 1/2 cup	48	—	12	—
Greens, 1/2 cup	17	2	3	—
Lettuce, 1/6 head, 1/2 cup	10	1	2	—
Onions, 1/2 cup	30	1	7	—
Orange, medium	65	1	16	—
Orange Juice, 1/2 cup	56	1	13	—
Peaches, 1/2 cup	100	1	26	—
Pear, medium	101	1	25	1
Peas, Green, 1/2 cup	54	4	9	—
Pineapple, large slice	90	—	24	—
Potato, Baked, large	132	4	30	—
Potatoes, Broiled, 2 small	79	2	18	—
Potatoes, French-fried, 20	233	4	31	11
Potatoes, Mashed, 1/2 cup	63	2	13	1
Potato, Sweet, 1/2 medium	78	1	18	—
Raisins, 4 1/2 Tbsp.	123	1	33	—
Strawberries, 1/2 cup	28	1	6	—
Tomato, 1/2 medium	22	1	5	—
Tomato Juice, 1/2 cup	26	1	5	—
Tossed Salad, 3/4 cup	13	1	3	—
Watermelon, 1 cup	52	1	13	—

Table 5-1 (continued)

	Calories	Protein g	Carbohydrate g	Fat g
Grain Group				
Bagel	165	6	28	2
Biscuit, Baking Powder	103	2	13	5
Bread, White, slice	61	2	12	1
Bread, Whole Wheat, slice	55	2	11	1
Cornbread, 2 1/2" × 3"	191	6	30	5
Cornflakes, 3/4 cup	72	2	16	—
Crackers, Graham, 2	54	1	10	1
Crackers, Saltines, 5	60	1	10	2
Hominy Grits, 1/2 cup	62	2	14	—
Noodles, Egg, 1/2 cup	100	3	19	1
Oatmeal, 1/2 cup	66	2	12	1
Pancake, 4" diameter	61	2	9	2
Rice, 1/2 cup	112	2	25	—
Roll, Frankfurter	119	3	21	2
Roll, Hamburger	119	3	21	2
Roll, Hard	156	5	30	2
Toast, White, slice	61	2	12	1
Tortilla, Corn, 6" diameter	63	2	14	1
Combination Foods (foods made with ingredients from more than one food group)				
Beans, Bakes, Pork & Tomato Sauce, 1/2 cup	156	8	24	3
Beef & Vegetable Stew, 1 cup	209	15	15	10
Chili Con Carne, 1 cup	333	19	31	15
Custard, Baked, 1/2 cup	152	7	15	7
Macaroni & Cheese, 1/2 cup	215	8	20	11
Pizza, Cheese, 1/4 of 14" pie	354	18	43	13
Soup, Chicken Noodle, 1 cup	59	3	8	2
Soup, Cream of Tomato, 1 cup	173	7	23	7
Spaghetti & Meat Balls, 1 cup	332	19	39	12
Taco, Beef	216	17	15	10
"Others" Category (fats, sweets, and alcohol)				
Bar, Milk Chocolate, 1 oz.	147	2	16	9
Beer, 1 1/2 cups	151	1	14	0
Butter, 1 tsp.	36	—	—	4
Cake, Devil's Food, 1/16 of 9" cake	234	3	40	9

Table 5-1 (continued)

	Calories	Protein g	Carbohydrate g	Fat g
"Others" Category (fats, sweets, and alcohol)				
Cake, Sponge, 1/12 of 10" cake	196	5	36	4
Chocolate Syrup, 2 Tbsp.	93	1	24	1
Coffee, Black, 3/4 cup	2	—	—	—
Cookie, Sugar, 3" diameter	89	1	14	3
Doughnut, Cake Type	125	2	17	6
French Dressing, 1 Tbsp.	66	—	3	6
Gelatin Dessert, 1/2 cup	71	2	17	0
Highball, 1 1/2 oz.	97	0	—	0
Jelly, Currant, 1 Tbsp.	49	0	13	0
Mayonnaise, 1 Tbsp.	101	—	—	11
Pie, Apple, 1/6 of 9" pie	403	4	60	18
Popcorn, Plain, 1 cup	23	1	5	—
Potato Chips, 10 chips	114	1	10	8
Roll, Danish Pastry	274	5	30	15
Sherbert, Orange, 1/2 cup	135	1	29	2
Soft Drink, Cola, 1 cup	96	0	25	0
Sugar, 1 tsp.	14	0	4	0
Wine, Rose, 3 1/2 oz.	87	—	4	0

liquid carbohydrate-rich foods that should be consumed throughout the day. Notice that eggs, beef, pork, fish, and poultry do not contain carbohydrate.

Protein Needs

Protein needs are greater during adolescence than in adulthood. For soccer players between the ages of 7–10, protein requirements are approximately 1.2 gm/kg of body weight (2.2 pounds = 1 kg). As players become older, protein needs decline to 1.0 gm/kg of body weight for 11–14-year-olds and 0.8 gm for 15–18-year-olds. The Recommended Daily Allowance (RDA) for protein for adults is 0.8 gm/kg of body weight.

Soccer players should have their protein needs assessed by asking them about their food intake. Similar to carbohydrates, few soccer players, parents, or coaches are familiar with the variety of protein sources. Meat, fish, poultry, dairy products, and eggs are obvious sources. Less obvious are beans, tofu, and all foods originating from grains or vegetables. Table 5-2 lists examples of foods adolescents report as "favorites." Serving sizes and protein quantity are also included.

Vegetarians can obtain adequate protein from plant sources, but they typically need to eat substantial quantities of grain-based foods and vegetables to meet their needs. The vegetarian athlete can obtain approximately 2 gm of

Table 5-2.

Favorite Foods of Adolescents and the Amount of Protein Found in Average Servings Sizes		
Food Item	Serving Size	Grams of Protein
Meat, fish, poultry	3 oz. cooked (the size of a deck of cards)	21
Custard-type yogurt	1 cup	9
Egg white	large egg	7
Corn or peas	1/2 cup	2
Soda, sports drink	12 oz.	0
Milk	8 oz.	8
Snickers candy bar	1 bar	6
Pasta	1 cup cooked	4
Beans, garbonzo	1 cup cooked	23.6
Captain Crunch cereal	1 cup	2
Cheerios	1 cup	4
Froot Loops cereal	1 cup	1.7
Lucky Charms	1 cup	2.6
Graham crackers	1 whole cracker	1
Pancakes	3 medium	19.8
French toast	2 slices	11.4
Peanut butter	2 tablespoons of creamy or chunky	9
Cheese pizza	1 slice	8
Hot dog plus bun	1 sandwich	8.5
Peanut butter and jelly on white bread	1 sandwich	12.3

protein per half cup serving of most vegetables and 2 gm of protein per half cup of a cooked grain such as pasta, rice, oatmeal, barley, or corn.

Nonvegetarians can obtain adequate protein by eating protein-rich foods and using the Food Guide Pyramid (Fig. 5-1) to understand how many servings from the meat, dairy, grains, and vegetable groups are needed.

Female athletes may be at risk for low protein intakes because their "fat-consciousness" keeps them from eating meats and dairy products. Fat in the diet is important in moderation and nutritious sources of fat such as meat, fish, poultry, and dairy products provide additional nutrients such as protein, calcium, and iron.

Protein or amino acid supplements are not recommended unless medical or dietary problems limit the use of protein-rich foods. When protein is con-

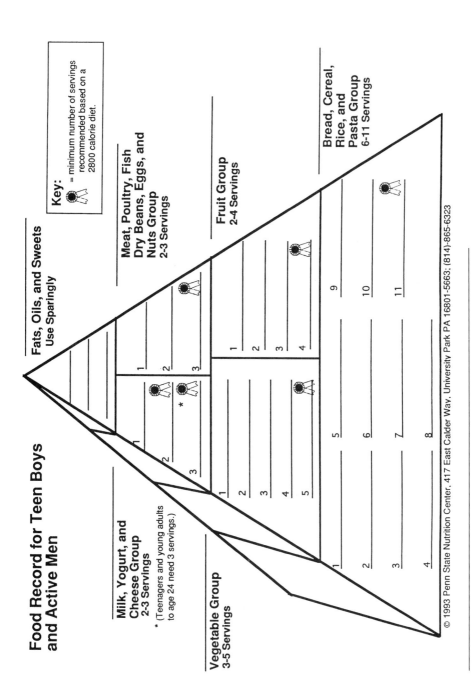

Food Record for Teen Boys and Active Men

Fats, Oils, and Sweets
Use Sparingly

Key:
= minimum number of servings recommended based on a 2800 calorie diet.

Milk, Yogurt, and Cheese Group
2-3 Servings
* (Teenagers and young adults to age 24 need 3 servings.)

Meat, Poultry, Fish Dry Beans, Eggs, and Nuts Group
2-3 Servings

Vegetable Group
3-5 Servings

Fruit Group
2-4 Servings

Bread, Cereal, Rice, and Pasta Group
6-11 Servings

© 1993 Penn State Nutrition Center, 417 East Calder Way, University Park PA 16801-5663; (814)-865-6323

Figure 5-1. The United States Department of Agriculture Food Guide Pyramid.

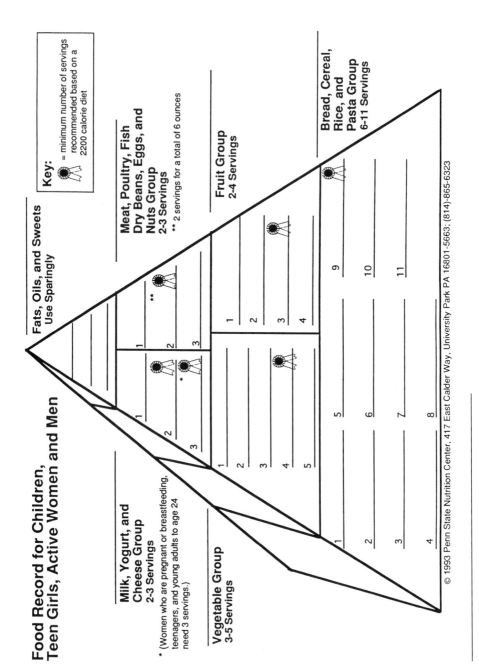

**Food Record for Children,
Teen Girls, Active Women and Men**

Fats, Oils, and Sweets
Use Sparingly

Key:
 = minimum number of servings
recommended based on a
2200 calorie diet

**Meat, Poultry, Fish
Dry Beans, Eggs, and
Nuts Group**
2-3 Servings
** 2 servings for a total of 6 ounces

**Milk, Yogurt, and
Cheese Group**
2-3 Servings
* (Women who are pregnant or breastfeeding,
teenagers, and young adults to age 24
need 3 servings.)

Fruit Group
2-4 Servings

Vegetable Group
3-5 Servings

**Bread, Cereal,
Rice, and
Pasta Group**
6-11 Servings

© 1993 Penn State Nutrition Center, 417 East Calder Way, University Park PA 16801-5663; (814)-865-6323

Figure 5-1. (continued)

sumed in excess of physiological needs, the body converts the extra protein calories into body fat.

Fat: An Essential Nutrient

Fat is an essential component in a healthy diet. All of us need to eat some fat on a daily basis to maintain good health. Although fat is used as an energy source during exercise, the fat content of young soccer players diets should not exceed 30% of their total daily calories. No studies support the idea that children need more fat in their diets than adults. In fact, obesity among children continues to be a problem in the U.S. and may be partially attributed to excessive fat in the diet. Although children and adolescents may be regular participants of soccer, poor food choices and excess intake of total calories often result in weight problems. Fat intake alone is not the cause of an overweight condition in a child.

In 1991, the American Academy of Pediatrics recommended that children consume 10% or less of their fat intake in the form of saturated fat. These fats have been associated with heart disease and are mostly found in foods of animal origin such as beef, pork, poultry, dairy products that are not fat-free, butter, lard, bacon, or sausage products. In addition, many baked products contain saturated fats in the form of partially hydrogenated oils, coconut, or palm oils.

The remaining fat allowed in the diet should come from polyunsaturated (10%) and monounsaturated (10%) fats. Both of these fats are liquid at room temperature. Margarine, however, is typically made from liquid polyunsaturated fats that have been chemically altered to make them hard at room temperature (similar to butter). The chemical alteration increases the level of saturated fat in the margarine, giving it the name "partially hydrogenated" or partially saturated fat. Dietitians and research scientists are recommending that margarines be used sparingly.

Polyunsaturated fats are found in corn, sunflower seed, safflower seed, and cottonseed oils. Monounsaturated fats are predominantly found in olive, peanut, and canola oils. These fats are considered the "heart healthiest" due to their ability to lower total cholesterol levels without lowering the "good" portion of cholesterol, referred to as high density lipoprotein (HDL)-Cholesterol. Research demonstrating the effects of monounsaturated fats on lowering cholesterol levels in children has not been conducted because high cholesterol levels in children and adolescents are not a concern. However, helping adolescent athletes to make wise choices in the selection of oils or fats is an important lesson for future dietary habits.

Eating Meals for Training

With the fundamentals of good nutrition as a framework, sport nutritionists encourage young athletes to spread their daily calories throughout the day for consistent energy. Athletes are reminded to eat three meals a day and not skip breakfast. Although this is good advice, young athletes will not always listen or adhere to it in their daily routines. Instead, the complex lifestyle of adolescents involves snacking and a possible meal once a day.

The eating patterns of adolescents in general, do not seem to be different from adolescent soccer players or other athletes. Sleeping late may influence breakfast habits. The timing of soccer practice may determine how much and what foods are eaten at a given time. Consequently, recommending the "three-meals-a-day" pattern may not apply to young athletes on a daily basis. In addition, many adolescents are responsible for their own food decisions at home and school. The lack of prepared meals at home could predispose young athletes to snacking. Despite these situations, good food choices can be encouraged even if food consumption is not in the form of a traditional meal.

Snacking as a style of eating throughout the day is appropriate as long as the selection of food is varied and provides a mixture of carbohydrates, protein, fat, vitamins, and minerals.

Traditional "snacks," such as sweet, salty, crunchy, high-fat goodies, can be added to a nutritious diet for additional calories to meet the growth demands of young soccer players. Sugar is a misunderstood ingredient found in many foods and beverages. It is a carbohydrate that contributes energy to active adolescents as opposed to an ingredient that leads to obesity, diabetes, or hyperactivity. Sugar can contribute to dental disease and cavities without proper brushing and flossing. Yet, popular foods containing sugar, such as cookies, candy bars, soda, ice cream, and peanut butter can be important sources of energy for soccer players who eat vitamin and mineral-rich foods throughout the day but are unable to maintain their weight or gain desired weight.

Adolescent soccer players who need between 2000–2800 calories daily, should distribute these calories between three separate time periods: morning, afternoon, and evening. For example, from the time they wake up until noon, 1/3 of their calories needed for the day should be consumed. Between noon and late afternoon, another 1/3 should be eaten. The last 1/3 should be consumed before bed. In other words, it does not matter if balanced meals are eaten. It is important that adequate calories from a variety of foods offering a mixture of carbohydrate, protein, and fat are eaten throughout the day. An example of this plan, based on a daily caloric intake of 2500 calories and the recommended number of servings from the food guide pyramid, can be seen in Table 5-3.

Although eating good food throughout the day is a sensible recommendation, teenagers frequently skip breakfast and, when they do decide to eat, select foods with low levels of vitamins and minerals.

In a 1995 survey of teenage male and female swimmers at a Penn State University Sports Camp, the majority said they knew how to eat appropriate meals but did not due to lack of time. In fact, the majority said they did not eat properly because they liked "junk food" too much. These trends are not surprising. Collegiate athletes in all sports report poor eating behaviors due to a perceived lack of time and the convenience of and preference for fast foods and "junk foods."

Table 5-3

Eating Throughout the Day for Consistent Energy and Good Nutrition			
Food	*Amount*	*Main Nutrient*	*Calories*
7 a.m.			
Banana	1 medium	carbohydrate	100
Lucky Charms	1 cup	carb, protein	110
Skim milk	1 cup	protein, carb	80
10 a.m.			
Bread	2 slices	carb, protein	140
Peanut butter	2 Tablespoons	fat, protein, carb	185
Jelly	1 Tablespoon	carbohydrate	48
Orange juice	8 oz. box/can	carbohydrate	112
Total Calories Before Noon= 776			
12 noon			
Noodles	2 cups cooked	carb, protein	280
Spaghetti sauce with ground beef	1 cup	protein, carb, fat	160
Sports drink	8 oz.	carbohydrate	70
1 p.m.			
Frozen yogurt (low-fat)	1 cup	protein, carb, fat	200
Cone	1 plain cone	carb, protein	45
3 p.m.			
Granola bar	1 bar	carb, protein, fat	140
Total Calories in Afternoon = 895			
6 p.m.			
Hamburger	4 oz.	protein, fat	280
Bun	1	carb, protein	140
Am. cheese	1 slice	protein, fat, carb	90
Potato chips	1 sm. bag	fat, carb, protein	110
Carrot sticks	5–6 sticks	carb, protein	25
Celery sticks	5–6 sticks	carb, protein	25
Skim milk	8 oz.	protein, carb	80
9 p.m.			
Apple	1 medium	carbohydrate	80
Total Calories in Evening = 830			

Calories are based on Bowes and Church's Food Values of Portions Commonly Used, 14th edition, 1985.

Eating Before Competition

Food selection before a soccer game should be aimed at eliminating hunger before and during the event. The "Rules of 10" (Table 5-4) are precompetition recommendations that consider four primary points: foods adolescent athletes enjoy, adequate carbohydrate for energy, the need for fluids, and the physiology of digestion. Table 5-5 shows examples of meals that could be eaten before a game.

What to Eat Mid-Game

Orange slices appear at every soccer game and provide two important nutrients players may need mid-game or between games. The first nutrient is carbohydrate in the form of fruit sugar or fructose. The second is water, found in the juice of the fruit. Depending on the food selection and quantity of calories the soccer player had prior to a game determines whether carbohydrate is needed. But young soccer players do need fluids, and the good taste and acceptability of orange juice will provide some. However, orange slices are not the only food selection that will provide carbohydrates and fluid.

Mid-game or between games the nutrient young soccer players need is water. Sport drinks are popular with athletes because they taste good. However, they cost money and are not necessary, especially for young soccer players who are not on the playing field for long periods. Sport drinks, as opposed to water, contain calories in the form of carbohydrates. If a player is feeling fatigued or hungry due to low calorie intake prior to the game, a sport drink or sport bar may be useful. The carbohydrates used in these products are specially formulated to leave the intestines quickly, providing a source of energy faster than more complex foods.

In addition to orange slices, foods young soccer players find appealing mid-game or between games include graham crackers, vanilla wafers, saltine crackers, bananas, or sport bars. If possible, bring both water and sport drinks and encourage drinking fluids in general.

Post-Game Foods

Athletes are encouraged to eat or drink carbohydrate containing foods or fluids as soon after exercise as possible for recovery from the game and to replace glycogen, the body's storage form of carbohydrate. Again, sport drinks and bars are popular, transportable, and excellent sources of carbohydrate. Table 5-6 lists additional foods to select from that are relatively inexpensive and convenient.

Fluids

One of the major causes of fatigue during high-intensity, intermittent exercise is dehydration. Water, diluted fruit juice, or sport drinks are recommended for achieving hydration before a game and maintaining hydration levels during and after a game.

Coaches or parents may want to weigh athletes before and after games and practices to determine how much weight is lost due to sweat. Soccer players

Table 5-4

"Rules of 10" for Optimal Pre-Competition Performance

1. Eat between 500–600 calories.
2. Eat these calories approximately 2–3 hours before the game.
3. Make the calories primarily carbohydrates, such as:
    breakfast cereals
    bread, toast, rolls, english muffins, bagels
    pancakes
    waffles
    french toast
    suitable toppings include syrup, jelly, jam, honey (use butter or
        margarine sparingly)
    fruits, juices
    vegetables
    pasta, rice, potatoes
    low-fat milk, yogurt
    graham crackers, vanilla wafers
    granola bars
    sports drinks or sports bars
4. Use low-fat protein sources moderately, such as:
    turkey, chicken, or fish in a sandwich
    cottage cheese
    low-fat milk or yogurt
    poached or scrambled egg
5. Keep the "added" fat low. Try to limit salad dressings, butter, margarine, and fried foods. Pizza, sausage, bacon, french fries, and ice cream are popular foods among adolescents, but do not make ideal pre-competition foods due to their higher fat contents.
6. Have plenty of fluids, especially water, available. The greater the variety of beverages, the greater the likelihood the soccer players will adequately hydrate themselves. Along with water, sports drinks and diluted juices can be made available.
7. Offer foods that you know your particular team likes. Always have a variety of carbohydrate-rich foods available to increase the interest in eating after the game.
8. Avoid spicy and high fiber foods. Spicy foods may cause indigestion and very high—fiber foods delay digestion.
9. Liquid meals, such as sport drinks, sport bars, or carbohydrate supplements such as Gatorlode may help an athlete get necessary carbohydrate into their body even though their stomach is queasy and they may not feel like eating.
10. Try to arrange a pre-competition meal that is relaxed and in a comfortable atmosphere.

Table 5-5

Sample Meals of Between 500-600 Calories	
Early Morning Game	*Afternoon Game*
Orange juice	Vegetable soup
Corn flakes + banana	Chicken sandwich on wheat bread
Skim milk	Sliced canned peaches
1 slice whole wheat toast	Fruit yogurt
Jelly	

should be encouraged to drink enough to replace their lost weight. General recommendations for fluid intake cannot be made due to individual variation in fluid loss. It is important to have adequate fluids and a variety of choices available before, mid-game, and after a game to promote increased drinking.

Vitamin and Mineral Supplements

Sport nutritionists encourage young athletes to select nutritious foods to fuel optimal athletic performance. Foods selected from the five food groups shown in the food guide pyramid (Fig. 5-1) can provide vitamins, minerals, and calories to support growth and meet individual nutrient needs if adequate amounts of foods are eaten. When young athletes eat well, a vitamin or mineral supplement is not recommended because their needs are being met by the foods they are choosing.

Supplements may be necessary when less than the recommended number of servings from certain food groups are eaten or if an entire food group is avoided. Female athletes frequently lack adequate calcium and iron because they cut back or avoid dairy and meat products. Calcium is a mineral that functions in bone growth, nerve transmission, and muscle contraction (Table 5-7). Iron is a mineral that is involved with oxygen transport to working muscles (Table 5-8).

Table 5-6

Post Game Food Choices
Bagels with peanut butter, cream cheese, or jam
Dry breakfast cereals
Granola or candy bars
Any type of cracker
Bananas, apples, raisins
Peanut butter sandwiches
Muffins

Table 5-7

Food Sources of Calcium

Milligrams of Calcium

300–350	White or chocolate milk, 1 cup Yogurt, 8 oz. container Milkshake, 10 oz.	
200–275	Calcium fortified orange juice (Citrus Hill), 6 oz. Canned sardines or salmon (with bones) 3 oz. Tofu, raw, firm, 1/2 cup	Cheddar, Mozzarella, Swiss, 1 ounce Pizza, 1 piece Burrito Egg McMuffin
150–175	Rhubarb, cooked & sweetened, 1/2 cup Instant oatmeal, 1 pkt Cheese spread, 1 oz.	Jello, cheesecake, 1/8 cheesecake Pudding, regular or instant (prepared w/milk), 1/2 cup Macaroni & cheese, 3/4 cup Canned cream of tomato & mushroom soups (prepared with milk), 1 cup
100–125	Broccoli w/cheese sauce, 1/2 cup Broccoli, 1/2 cup cooked Au Gratin potatoes, from mix or homemade, 1/2 cup Wax beans, 1/2 cup Hershey kisses, 9 pieces Maypo, cooked 3/4 cup American cheese, 1 oz. Vanilla ice cream or ice milk, 1/2 cup	Custard pie, 1/8 pie Taco Cheeseburger Pancakes (fast food), 1 serving Cornbread, 1 piece Frozen french toast 2 slices Pancakes & waffles from mix English muffin
50–75	Corn pudding, 1/2 cup Navy beans, 1/2 cup cooked Okra, 1/2 cup Instant mashed potatoes, 1/2 cup Total cereal, 1 cup Wheaties, 1 cup Pumpkin pie, 1/8 pie	Gingerbread cake, 1 piece Pudding pops, 1 pop Orange sherbert, 1/2 cup Baked beans, 1/2 cup Turkey frank Cottage cheese, lowfat, 1/2 cup Devil's food cake, 1/12 cake
Below 50	Soy milk, 1 cup Kidney Beans, 1/2 cup cooked	

Adolescents need 1200 milligrams (mg) of calcium per day.

All Figures are rounded to the nearest 25 mg.

Dark green leafy vegetables (spinach, kale, etc.) have been excluded because the calcium cannot be absorbed.

Source: Food Values of Portions Commonly Used. *J. Pennington, J. B. Lippincott Co., Phila., 1989.*

Table 5-8

Some of the best sources of dietary iron from plant sources are dried beans. Compare the amount of iron found in the plant foods listed below to those of animal foods at the bottom of the list.

1 cup canned pork and beans = 3.63 grams iron
1 cup three bean salad = .90 mg iron
1 cup cooked black eyed peas = 3.40 mg.
1 cup garbonzo beans (chickpeas) = 6.00 mg
1 cup lima beans = 7.20 mg
1 cup cooked peas = 3.6 mg
Compare the above values with the following:
1 slice of whole wheat bread = .64 mg
1 bagel = 1.46 mg
1 medium tangerine = .09 mg
1 cup of grapes = .27 mg
1 medium baked potato = .70 mg
1 cup frozen corn = 1.8 mg
1 oz. sunflower seeds = 1.99 mg

Iron found in beef, pork, and poultry is absorbed more efficiently

3.5 oz. roasted turkey (no skin) = 1.78 mg
3.5 oz. dark meat chicken roasted w/o skin = 1.33 mg
3.5 oz. ham (lean) cooked = 1.70 mg
3.5 oz. breaded veal cutlet = 4.2 mg
3.5 oz pork tenderloin, roasted = 4.7 mg
3.5 oz roasted leg of lamb = 1.90 mg
3.5 oz lean hamburger patty = 3.9 mg
3.5 oz homemade meatloaf = 2.3 mg

Although meats don't necessarily appear to be much higher in iron than sources of plant iron, the absorption of iron from "heme" or meat sources is better.

(From: Bowe's and Church Food Values of Portions Commonly Used, 14th edition.)

If an athlete expresses interest in becoming a vegetarian, iron and calcium rich foods should be reviewed with special attention to nonanimal based food sources (Tables 5-7 and 5-8). The Recommended Daily Allowance (RDA) for calcium and iron for various age groups is listed in Table 5-9.

Excellent sources of iron from both plant and animal sources are found in Table 5-8. Iron is found in many plants, but the human intestine does not absorb plant iron as efficiently as it does iron from animal sources. Beans are considered the best source of plant iron. In addition, many breakfast cereals and other grains are fortified with iron (read the nutrition labels). Vitamin C rich foods, such as citrus fruits, juices, and most vegetables enhance the absorption of iron from plant sources.

Table 5-9

How Much Iron and Calcium Should the Adolescent Soccer Player Get*		
Age	Iron (mg)	Calcium (mg)
4–6	10	800
7–10	10	800
Males		
11–14	12	1200
15–18	12	1200
Females		
11–14	15	1200
15–18	15	1200

*1989 RDA for iron and calcium, National Research Councils Recommended Dietary Allowances.

Weight Loss or Weight Gain

Although most physicians and sport nutritionists caution young, growing athletes against dieting, there are appropriate dietary strategies that promote a gradual weight loss if the soccer player is overweight.

Nutrition strategies to gradually reduce calories:

1. Enlist a registered dietitian (R.D.) to work with the parents and the player. Contact a Sports Medicine facility, hospital, or clinic to locate an R.D.

2. The soccer player should record everything eaten for approximately 3–4 days. The quantity of each food should also be recorded. This creates an awareness of food choices and how much food is eaten.

3. The R.D. can point out food selections that are contributing excess calories and make suggestions for reducing portion sizes of foods without compromising energy or micronutrients.

4. Increased aerobic activity may be beneficial in addition to a 500 calorie reduction in total energy intake. A 30-minute walk or jog, increased bicycle riding, or swimming will help use stored calories and contribute to a gradual weight loss.

5. Decreasing soda, sport drinks, juices, or any other beverages that contribute calories. Increase intake of water as the fluid of choice.

6. Increase intake of fruits and vegetables.

7. Change any dairy products that have fat in them to reduced or fat-free. Select skim milk, fat-free frozen or custard yogurt, and reduced fat cheeses.

8. Decrease use of butter, margarine, mayonnaise, miracle whip, and salad dressings. Use jam, jelly, or honey on bread, bagels, or English muffins. These foods contain carbohydrate, not fat. Use mustard on sandwiches and tomato salsa on salads or baked potatoes.

9. Measure foods that you may be overeating. Pasta, rice, cereal, frozen

yogurt, and snack foods like popcorn are typically overeaten. One cup of pasta and rice is considered two servings. Many athletes eat 2–3 times that amount. Although pasta, rice, and cereal are excellent sources of carbohydrate, vitamins, and minerals, they also contribute excess calories if they are overeaten.

10. Decrease portions of meat. Eat meat at only one meal and trim all fat off beef, pork, fish, or poultry. Remember, skin is fat, so don't eat the skin on chicken or turkey.

An interest in weight gain is more common among males than females and can be frustrating for soccer players who eat more but still can't gain weight. Opposite to weight loss, weight gain implies that more calories need to be consumed than are burned through daily activity or exercise. Approximately 500–1000 additional cal/day should be eaten to maximize weight gain. Anytime activity increases, food intake must also increase.

Any nutritious foods eaten on a regular basis can assist in gaining weight if they are eaten in larger quantities. For example, if one cup of pasta with a half cup of sauce is eaten, simply add an additional cup of pasta and another half cup of sauce. The result is an additional 140 calories from the pasta and approximately 50–80 calories from the sauce (depending on the ingredients). If you drink one cup of milk at breakfast, try drinking two. Carry food whenever possible and snack frequently. In Table 5-10 are some examples of inexpensive, transportable, and popular foods to eat for additional calories to promote weight gain.

The type of weight that a young soccer player wants to gain is lean muscle tissue versus increased body fat. Along with additional calories, the athlete should be lifting weights to promote new tissue growth and hypertrophy of the muscle cell.

Table 5-10

Examples of Foods to Eat for "Additional" Calories	
Food	*Calories*
Peanut butter and jelly sandwich	420
1 slice of apple pie	450
2 cups frosted mini-wheats cereal	400
8 whole graham crackers	480
1 candy bar	280
Chocolate milkshake	380
Quarter pounder with cheese	524
2 pop-tarts	420
2 granola bars	220
2 large oatmeal cookies	305
2 cups of orange juice	224

Summary

The type and quantity of food an adolescent soccer player eats can influence fatigue levels, hydration status, and overall performance during training and competition. Parents and coaches of adolescent athletes should pay attention to food and beverage choices to ensure that appropriate calories for growth and energy are consumed. Although 55% of an athlete's diet should be comprised of carbohydrate-rich foods, both protein and fat are equally important nutrients, but needed in smaller amounts.

The food guide pyramid should be a resource for assisting young athletes in food selection and portion information. Foods from the five food groups provide a balance of carbohydrate, protein, fat, vitamins, and minerals. Any athlete reporting interest in vegetarian or weight reduction diets should be assisted to avoid compromising calories and nutrients. Both calcium and iron should be reviewed, particularly with female athletes.

Finally, snacking is acceptable. Young athletes should be educated to understand that vitamin and mineral-rich foods qualify as snacks along with less nutritious, but perhaps more appealing, snacks. Guide athletes toward a combination of traditional, fast, and "junk" foods and remind them that moderation, balance, and variety of all foods are the keys to good nutrition for optimal sports performance.

SUGGESTED READING

Brownell K, Rodin J, Wilmore J. Eating, body weight, and performance in athletes. Malvern, PA: Lea and Febiger, 1992.

Clark N. Sports Nutrition Guidebook: eating to fuel your active lifestyle. Champaign, IL: Leisure Press, 1990.

Clark N. Balancing the "Bad-Foods" Diet. Physician Sports Med 1991;19:51–52.

Clark N. Breakfast is for Champions. Physician Sports Med 1992;20:29–30.

Clark N. How to gain weight healthfully. Physician Sports Med 1991;19:53–54.

Coleman E. Eating for endurance. California: Bull Publishing, 1992.

Cowart VS. Dietary Supplements: Alternatives to Anabolic Steroids? Physician Sports Med 1992;20:189–198.

Day B. Fast facts on fast food for fast people. West Fargo, MD: An Apple a Day Publisher, 1995.

Ikeda J. Winning weight loss for teens. California: Bull Publishing, 1987.

Parker DF, Bar-Or O. Juvenile Obesity: The Importance of Exercise—and Getting Children to Do It. Physician Sports Med 1991;19:113–125.

Smith NJ, Roberts BW. Food for sport. California: Bull Publishing, 1989.

Williams M. Nutritional Ergogenics: Help or Hype? J Am Dietetic Assoc 1992;20: 1213–1214.

6  Nutrition and Performance

Donald T. Kirkendall

Chapters 4 and 5 make it clear that nutrition has an effect on exercise performance. The effect of fuel on the performance of muscle was first discussed in 1939. Since then, there have been studies that have proven muscle performance can be improved by improving the fuel supply through good nutrition.

The bulk of studies have been directed toward endurance activities like distance running, cycling, and swimming. Although the distance covered in a soccer game, approximately 10 km, is less than the 42.2 km marathon, nutrition can influence performance in soccer as well as in the marathon. The work requirements of the game, outlined in Chapter 1, are helpful in understanding the influence of nutrition on soccer performance. This chapter, based on the nutritional concepts outlined in the prior two chapters (Chapters 4 and 5), is directed toward the serious players and teams who train regularly and compete frequently.

The primary fuel is glycogen, a string of glucose molecules connected together. This is stored in skeletal muscle and the liver. When muscle glycogen levels are elevated, the time to exhaustion is increased. How can muscle glycogen levels be elevated? The earliest methods required that the athlete eat small amounts of carbohydrate for a few days while training. This depleted the supply of glycogen in the muscles. A couple of days prior to competition, the athlete then increased the intake of carbohydrate while reducing the volume and intensity of training. The result was a rebound of muscle glycogen to above normal levels. This method is not practiced frequently because glycogen levels in training athletes are depleted on a regular basis so there is no need for low carbohydrate intake. Currently, athletes continue training until the period prior to competition when the volume and intensity of training decreases, at which point they increase their carbohydrate intake. It takes approximately 24 hours to replenish the muscle glycogen that has been depleted by intermittent exercise, like soccer.

The athlete with supercompensated muscle glycogen has more fuel for high-intensity exercise and can continue exercise longer. To the marathoner, this means they can hold their pace longer resulting in a faster overall time. The runner with less glycogen slows down sooner and is forced to fuel their running with fat. When exercise is fueled with fat, the intensity is approximately 50% of capacity—a slow jog or a walk. The more glycogen in the muscles, the faster an athlete can run for extended periods of time. This concept is critical to the soccer player.

The bulk of research on nutrition and performance has focused on single, isolated periods of exercise. Yet, the daily training of athletes may influence the amount of glycogen available to muscle. The pattern of muscle glycogen during repetitive days of exercise is shown in Figure 6-1. The low carbohydrate line represents training while eating a normal, western diet (40% carbohydrates, 40% fat, 20% protein) and the high carbohydrate diet contains approximately 60% carbohydrates, 30% fat, and 10% protein. While exercising on the normal diet, the muscle glycogen level gradually declines over three days. The normal diet contains insufficient carbohydrate to replace that used during activity. However, when the diet is high in carbohydrates, there is sufficient carbohydrate intake to replace the glycogen used. This is important in soccer when players may compete with less than 24 hours between games. Inadequate carbohydrate intake will slow down the player in the subsequent game. From the strategic standpoint, if your opponent played yesterday and you did not, your team is at an advantage, assuming they did not eat large amounts of carbohydrates in the interim. The other team will tire out faster and not be able to keep up with your team.

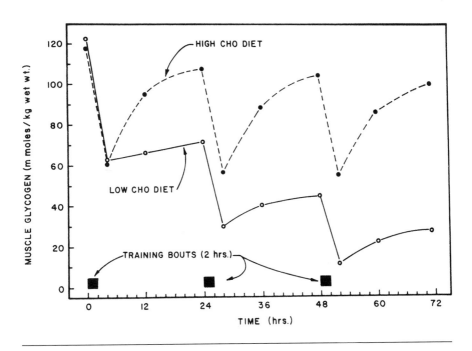

Figure 6-1. The effects of diet on muscle glycogen during multiple days of exercise.

The Fuel Requirements of Soccer

The body can use fat or carbohydrates as fuel for exercise. The mixture of these fuels is based on the intensity of activity. The lower the intensity (walking), the greater the reliance on fat. The greater the intensity (sprinting), the greater the reliance on carbohydrates. No sporting activity requires only fat or only carbohydrates. Low intensity exercises during soccer like walking and jogging (nearly 2/3 of the total game distance) can be mostly fueled by fat. The other 1/3 of the game is played at a higher intensity and is primarily fueled by carbohydrate. This high intensity part of the game depletes the glycogen in the muscles used in running.

In 1970, a series of players had their muscle glycogen levels determined prior to a game, at half-time, and after the game (Fig. 6-2). Figure 6-2 shows three points. First, note the level of glycogen at the start of the game. This value is consistent with the muscle glycogen level of an untrained person. Therefore, these athletes were no different than the spectators because the combination of their training and poor food selection did not allow them to optimize their fuel stores. Second, most of the glycogen depletion occurs in the first half. Dr. Reilly's data, found in Chapter 1, shows that most of the running also occurs in the first half. Therefore, the glycogen data and performance data correlate; the more glycogen, the more running. Third, at the end of the game, the muscle glycogen levels are consistent with the levels seen at volitional exhaustion.

The Nutritional Habits of Soccer Players

Well-trained athletes who make appropriate food selections store approximately 50% or more glycogen than their untrained counterparts. Remember from Figure 6-2 that the players had pregame glycogen levels consistent with those of untrained people. The most likely explanation is related not to their training, but to their food selection. A sigmoid relationship exists between carbohydrate intake and glycogen stored (Fig. 6-3). Notice that the curve tends to plateau at approximately 500 grams of carbohydrate in 24 hours. Therefore, to maximally store carbohydrate in muscles, a total of 500–600 grams of carbohydrate must be eaten over a 24 hour period.

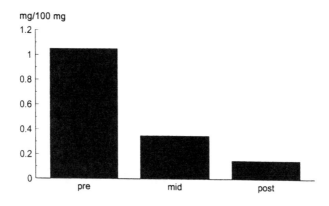

Figure 6-2. Muscle glycogen before, at half-time, and after a soccer game.

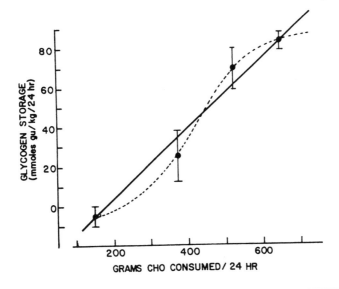

Figure 6-3. The relationship between the amount of carbohydrate ingested and the amount of glycogen stored in skeletal muscle.

A dietary study of professional Swedish soccer players showed that their carbohydrate intake during the 72 hours after a game was insufficient to replenish their muscles with glycogen. After 72 hours, their glycogen levels were still below those of sedentary subjects. Their food selection, approximately 300 grams of carbohydrate a day, would be detrimental to their performance in the next game. A survey of high school (Table 6-1) and college soccer players showed that both groups averaged approximately 250–350 grams of carbohydrate a day; an insufficient amount for their game requirements. Some of these meals were from buffets while traveling. Although a variety of foods high in carbohydrates were available, the players selected meals high in protein and fat.

Soccer is a glycogen depleting game and the volume and intensity of running is inversely related to the amount of glycogen in the muscles. Although it may seem that it is only necessary to worry about diet the day or two prior to a game, the effects of repeated days of exercise on muscle glycogen levels

Table 6-1

5-Day Food Intake of a High School Soccer Team					
	Day 1	*Day 2*	*Day 3*	*Day 4*	*Day 5*
Calories	3326	2718	3101	3027	2807
Carbohydrate	456 gm	327 gm	394 gm	429 gm	333 gm
	(54%)	(48%)	(49%)	(56%)	(45%)
Fat	32%	37%	36%	31%	40%
Protein	13%	13%	12%	12%	15%

must also be considered. In the early part of a season there are multiple days of training. The players must understand the concept of proper food selection so they go to the field the next day with as high a level of glycogen as possible. It may not be a coincidence that more injuries occur later in the week when glycogen levels are decreasing and poor diet is not replenishing the depleted glycogen.

Soccer Performance and Nutrition

A study examined the question, how does the amount of muscle glycogen influence running habits during a game of soccer? Two teams played a game that was filmed. The distance and intensities of individual players were estimated from the film record. The players with low muscle glycogen had levels that were approximately half that of the other players. The players with high muscle glycogen had levels consistent with sedentary people. The players with low levels of glycogen ran out of fuel by the end of the game and covered approximately 25% less distance than the other players during the game. Approximately half of that distance was covered at a walk (Fig. 6-4). Therefore, these players ran less distance at a slower speed. The relationship is clear; the more muscle glycogen, the further and faster the player will run.

Nutritional habits are difficult to change and players will look to supplements that might disguise some of their nutritional inadequacies. The most common supplement is the glucose polymer, a string of approximately six glucose molecules. This supplement can be found in Karo Syrup in addition to numerous commercial products that may be high in calories (e.g., Exceed High Carbohydrate Supplement and Gatorlode). Once ingested, the blood glucose levels start to rise in approximately five minutes and offer an added source of carbohydrates to the working muscle. When given to players prior to a game, their muscle glycogen levels were higher after the game than when they did not have the polymer. Glycogen levels were not depleted and there was more fuel in their muscles. Players ran farther in the second half at higher speeds and were able to sustain their first half intensity longer into the second half. This has also been demonstrated during simulated indoor tournament play.

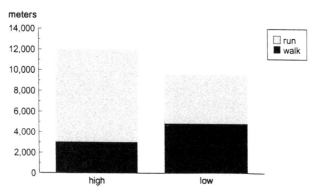

Figure 6-4. The effects of pre-game muscle glycogen levels on exercise volume and intensity.

Table 6-2

Recommendations for Optimal Nutritional Intake and Muscle Glycogen

1. Assess the food selection habits of the players
2. Counsel the players whose food selection habits are less than optimal (see Chapters 4 and 5 for recommended guidelines)
3. Stress eating carbohydrates immediately after the game
4. The acute use of a glucose polymer may be a reasonable nutritional supplement

The Timing of Carbohydrate Intake

In many of the studies mentioned, the carbohydrate intake was spread out over a 24 hour period. The best time for carbohydrate intake would probably be immediately after exercise when the muscle has just been depleted of glycogen. In fact, if even two hours elapse after exercise, the rate of eventual glycogen storage is decreased. The time to start preparing fuel reserves for the next game or practice is immediately after exercise. Carbohydrate should be available immediately after exercise so the players can start preparing for the next training session or game. Suggestions for carbohydrate selection during the day and in the locker room are in Chapter 5.

Summary

Adequate carbohydrate intake is important for successful soccer performance. The game empties the fuel tank and that tank must be filled with a variety of carbohydrates over the course of a 24 hour period, beginning immediately after the workout or game. This better prepares your team for the game. Poor food selection is not the way to prepare for the demands of the game. Follow the recommendations (Table 6-2) and your team will be approaching the game with a full tank of fuel. Remember, the more glycogen and glucose available for the muscle, the farther and faster your players will run.

SUGGESTED READING

Agnevik G. Fotball: Indrottsfysiologi Rapport Nr 7. Stockholm: Trygg-Hansa, 1970.

Costill DL, Bowers RW, Branam G, et al. Muscle glycogen utilization during prolonged exercise on successive days. J Appl Physiol 1971;31:834–838.

Ekblom B. Applied physiology of soccer. Sports Med 1986;3:50–60.

Ivy JL, Katz AL, Cutler CL. Muscle glycogen resynthesis after exercise: effect of time on carbohydrate ingestion. J Appl Physiol 1988;64:1480–1485.

Jacobs I, Wrestlin J, Karlsson J. Muscle glycogen and diet in elite soccer players. Eur J Appl Physiol 1986;48:297–302.

Kirkendall DT. The applied sport science of soccer. Physician and Sportsmed 1985;13:53–59.

Kirkendall DT. Effects of nutrition on performance in soccer. Med Sci Sports Exerc 1993;25:1370–1374.

Saltin B. Metabolic fundamentals of exercise. Med Sci Sports 1973;5:137–146.

Sherman WM, Costill DL. The marathon: dietary manipulation to optimize performance. Am J Sports Med 1984;12:44–51.

7  Fluids and Electrolytes

Donald T. Kirkendall

The first research into the effects of work in the heat was conducted during the construction of Hoover Dam near Boulder City, Nevada. Fluid intake, sweat output, and the consequences of work in temperatures that ranged from 90–120°F were published in the mid 1930s. In the next decade, the military studied work in the heat when they investigated the demands of warfare in the desert. This work was summarized in 1947 in *Physiology of Man in the Desert*. The effects and consequences of physical work in the heat on sweat rate, dehydration, salt loss, and intake have been known for more than half a century.

No exercise physiology text published before 1970 mentioned the potential dangers of exercise in the heat and the consequences of water restriction. Marathoners were ingesting only one or two drinks during a race. Ultramarathoners might withhold water until the 75th mile of a 100 mile run.

Water deprivation during exercise seems absurd and negligent. However, in the world of sports, as long as athletes were winning there was no initiative to encourage fluid intake during exercise.

This chapter discusses the factors of exercise in the heat that affect sports performance, how fluids ingested during exercise affect performance, and the general effects of playing soccer in the heat. The effects of water restriction before exercise (hypohydration) will not be discussed. Rather, the effects of fluid ingestion or restriction that result when a hydrated person exercises in the heat will be reviewed.

Exercise in the Heat

Exercise in the heat places two competitive demands on the circulatory system. The system attempts to balance oxygen delivery to the working muscles with the need to shunt blood to the skin to cool the body. Temperature regulation is an interaction of four methods: conduction (direct contact with cool surfaces; like jumping into a pool), convection (cool molecules flowing over warm molecules; like standing in front of an air conditioner), evaporation (driving water molecules from a liquid to a gaseous state), and radiation (heat exchange with electromagnetic heat waves). During exercise, evaporation is the primary method of losing heat. For every gram of water driven into a gaseous state, .58 kcal of heat are lost. Evaporation, not sweating, cools the body.

Exercise requires energy. The breakdown of adenosine triphosphate (ATP) releases energy, which is used for work and heat. The energy given off as heat warms adjacent tissues, including the blood. The temperature of the core (measured rectally) begins to rise and will continue to rise in the absence of fluid ingestion (rectal temperatures tend to plateau if fluids are given during exercise). The warm blood circulates through the body where it eventually bathes the hypothalamus; the home of our thermostat, which is located in the brain. When the warm blood bathes the hypothalamus, a series of events occur in an attempt to lower the temperature of the blood. The blood is diverted away from the warm core of the body to the cooler shell (in extreme heat stress 15–25% of the cardiac output can be diverted to the skin). This diversion of blood to the skin results in heat loss to the environment through the interaction of the methods defined earlier. Evaporation begins within seconds of the onset of exercise and tends to plateau after approximately 30 minutes of work at a rate that is proportional to the intensity of exercise (because high-intensity exercise demands more energy, the core temperature can go even higher forcing the sweat rate to increase because of the increased heat production). The cooled blood can now return to the warm core where additional heat can be picked up and the process repeated. In addition, hormonal changes occur in an attempt to conserve water (antidiuretic hormone) and prevent sodium loss (aldosterone).

Environmental Factors Influencing Temperature Regulation

Heat

The gradient, or difference, between the core, skin, and air is a critical factor in heat loss. The greater the gradient, the faster the heat loss. Therefore, exercise in the heat results in slower heat loss than exercise in cooler temperatures.

Humidity

The saturation of the air with water also can affect heat loss, especially evaporation, which is determined by a gradient. If the air is dry (low humidity), the water can be easily removed from the saturated skin and changed into a gas. However, if the air is heavily saturated with water (high humidity), the rate at which water is changed into a gas and heat loss are slower. If exercise is maintained, the core temperature builds up faster than the cooling process can lose heat.

Clothing

Clothing limits heat loss because it acts as a barrier and creates a microenvironment between itself and the skin. Water must first pass from the skin to the clothing to get to the larger environment. The rate of heat loss is dependent on the fibers of the clothing. Cotton is a cylindrical fiber that swells when wet and limits heat loss. Newer polyesters with greater surface areas allow for faster rates of evaporation. Rubber clothing creates an environment between itself and the skin that is saturated with water and severely restricts evaporation and cooling.

Consequences of Dehydration

There are many results of fluid loss with exercise. Weight loss of less than 2% of the normally hydrated body weight has little effect on performance. When weight loss exceeds 3% or more, a progressive decline in the ability to exercise results. Core temperature rises and the events that can lead to heat cramps, heat syncope, heat exhaustion (mostly water depletion), and heat stroke are set in place.

Fluid Ingestion

The primary concern is how to minimize the potentially life-threatening consequences of severe dehydration. To keep the body cool sweat must evaporate (mostly water with a little salt and other electrolytes). The sweat (fluid) that is lost should be replaced. This is a simple concept that the military and occupational settings adopted long before the athletic community. The ideal prescription for fluid intake is now the subject of inquiry.

Factors Affecting the Ingested Fluid

A variety of factors can influence the use of ingested fluids by the body during exercise. There are the characteristics of the drink and the process that occurs when the drink leaves the stomach to be absorbed by the intestine and bowel.

THE DRINK

Many factors go into the characteristics of a drink. Some of the variables are the volume ingested, the concentration of electrolytes, the type and amount of carbohydrate, and the temperature of the drink.

Volume

Animals such as the burro, dog, Bedouin goat, and monkey ingest fluids in approximately the exact proportion to the loss of fluid; they lose 5 pounds of fluid and drink the equivalent amount of water. Man's thirst mechanism does not allow for such an exact match of loss and replenishment. Because man's thirst mechanism cannot keep up with sweat loss, a condition known as voluntary dehydration develops. The attempt to match weight loss with fluid ingestion results in a full feeling, which makes exercise uncomfortable.

The amount of fluid emptied from the stomach into the small intestine increases with added volume up to approximately 600 ml (20 oz). The timing and volume suggestions for fluid replacement take this into consideration. The stomach should be able to take in and empty 100–200 ml of fluid every 15 minutes. More volume does not empty any faster. The extra volume stays in the stomach leaving the athlete with an uncomfortable full feeling. If too much fluid is ingested, the volume can exceed the absorptive capacity of the intestine and result in diarrhea.

The small intestine seems to be able to absorb fluid at a rate of approximately 350–450 ml/hr. This is also the limit to the approximate volume that most people will voluntarily drink during exercise. Therefore, there must be a cue that controls fluid intake so that the intestine is not overwhelmed.

The American College of Sports Medicine offers the following guidelines. The volume of fluid ingested should be approximately 400–600 ml (13–20 oz) during the hour prior to exercise. This should be followed by 100–200 ml (3–6 oz) every 10–15 minutes during exercise. Table 7-1 is a modification of the guideline based on the expected amount of weight loss during the period of exercise. Weighing before and after exercise to calculate the amount of weight lost can be used to determine how much fluid should be ingested prior to the next workout. For every pound of weight lost, the athlete should drink 2 cups of water. A simple way to remember the formula is 1 pint per pound.

Electrolyte make-up
The goal is to replace the sweat that has evaporated. Sweat is mostly water with a small concentration of salts and other electrolytes. The drink and sweat should be similar in concentration of salts. In fact, the earliest drinks had an electrolyte and water make-up that was the same as sweat.

The evaporated sweat should be replaced before the next period of exercise. Most research shows that through the diet, people can replace lost electrolytes without the need for salts found in drinks. However, the electrolytes in drinks have advantages in addition to than the replacement of lost salts.

Carbohydrate Type and Content
Scientific research shows that adding carbohydrates to the drink improves athletic performance. The major questions surround the type of carbohydrate and the amount. An added variable to consider is the osmolarity of the drink. In brief, osmolarity is the number of particles in the solution. The fewer number of particles, the lower the osmolarity, and the more particles, the higher the osmolarity. If a drink has fewer particles than what is normally found in body fluids, the drink is called hypotonic. If the drink has more particles, it is termed hypertonic. If it has the same number of particles, the drink is considered isotonic.

Table 7-1

A Recommended Schedule for Fluid Ingestion During a 90 minute Training Session*		
Estimated weight loss (lbs)	Minutes between water breaks	Fluid per break (oz)
1	45	6
2	30	8
3	20	9–10
4	15	8–9
5	15	10–11
6	10	8–9
7	10	8–10

*(Modified from: McArdle WD, Katch FI, Katch VL. Exercise physiology: energy, nutrition, and human performance. 3rd ed. Philadelphia: Lea & Febiger, 1991; 563.)

There are many types of carbohydrates that can be added to a drink. Glucose is the primary form of carbohydrate transport in the blood. Maltodextrins (glucose polymers) are short strings of glucose molecules. Fructose is the sugar found in fruit. Sucrose is table sugar (1 glucose + 1 fructose).

Glucose, polymers, and sucrose all stimulate fluid absorption by the intestine and can improve performance. Many people prefer drinks flavored with a polymer because more carbohydrate is delivered. Remember, osmolarity is the number of particles, not the size of the particles. So one molecule of glucose and one molecule of a polymer both exert the same osmotic pressure. However, the polymer may contain six individual glucose molecules. Therefore, each molecule of the polymer absorbed eventually yields more glucose.

Fructose, on the other hand, slows intestinal absorption of fluids. Drinks that are high in fructose can lead to gastrointestinal distress and osmotic diarrhea. Yet, some fructose is desirable because it improves the taste of the drink.

The amount of carbohydrate in a drink should be between 6–8%. Beverages that contain this amount are absorbed into the system as fast as water with the added benefit of providing an energy fuel. Drinks with less than 6% carbohydrate do not provide enough fuel. Most commercial sodas (Table 7-2) are commonly associated with cramps, diarrhea, and nausea.

Temperature

At constant beverage volumes, cool fluids are emptied from the stomach faster than drinks at body temperature. Cool drinks are preferred by athletes and are most effective.

Table 7-2

		A Comparison of Selected Beverages*			
Beverage	Carbohydrate source	Carbohydrate concentration (%)	Sodium (mg)	Osmolarity	Calories (per 8 oz serving)
Water	—	—	low	10–20	0
Gatorade	sucrose/glucose powder	6	110	280–360	50
Exceed	glucose polymer, fructose	7.2	50	250	70
All Sport	high fructose corn syrup	6.1	55	—	240
Coca-Cola	high fructose corn syrup/sucrose	10.7–11.3	9.2	600–715	105
Orange Juice	fructose sucrose glucose	10–12	5.0	690	100

*Modified from Coleman E. Sports drink update. Sports Science Exchange vol 1, August 1988.

GASTRIC EMPTYING

All the variables discussed interact to influence the ability of the gut to empty fluids from the stomach and the absorption of these fluids by the intestine. For a number of years, the stomach's role as gatekeeper was considered the rate-limiting step in this entire process. Early work showed that the gastric emptying rate during rest slowed when the drink was over 2.5% glucose. Anything more concentrated would impair gastric emptying.

Caloric content also influences gastric emptying. The greater the number of calories, the slower the rate of emptying. The stomach will only allow so many calories/minute to leave for the intestine. Overloading the stomach with calories may slow emptying, but the rate of calories entering the intestine will remain constant.

Osmolarity, defined earlier, is also a factor in gastric emptying. Many people are under the mistaken notion that fluids must be isotonic with the body before they leave the stomach and that osmolarity is the main determinant of gastric emptying. First, most fluids leave the stomach at approximately the same osmolarity that they arrived with. Dilution of gastric contents by water flow across gastric membranes has not been demonstrated. Some minor dilution of gastric contents may be due to other gastric secretions, but not water. Second, studies that tested osmolarity as the factor controlling gastric emptying showed that osmolarity was increased by adding sugar to the drink, effectively increasing the calorie content, a known determinant of gastric emptying.

INTESTINAL ABSORPTION

The more important anatomic site is the intestine where the drink and its contents are absorbed. With respect to fluids, the presence of glucose and sodium enhance the absorption of intestinal fluid. As these two are transported across the intestinal wall, the cells become hypertonic and water is absorbed to balance out the osmolarity. This is the concept behind the use of fluids containing glucose and sodium for combating diarrhea. Water absorption is greatest when the glucose content in the intestine is between 1–3% and sodium is between 90–120 mmol/L. Most drinks are higher in glucose and lower in sodium. The glucose is diluted by the constant secretions (from the salivary glands, stomach, pancreas, and gall bladder) into the gastrointestinal tract and sodium is increased because some of the gastric secretions are high in sodium.

INTENSITY OF EXERCISE

Gastric emptying and intestinal absorption are related to the blood flow through the gut. At low intensities of exercise, there is little competition between the exercising muscle and the gastrointestinal tract for the limited amount of cardiac output. As the intensity of exercise increases to approximately 70% of the person's capacity, the blood flow to the gut is increasingly diverted to the working muscles. The function of the gastrointestinal tract must slow down in consideration of the demands of the working muscles. Thus, the harder the exercise, the less fluid that can be absorbed.

Soccer in the Heat

A discussion of soccer played in the heat will apply the concepts from this chapter to the game and the players. Chapters 1 and 2 outline the demands that soccer places on players. It is also known that the game can be played in extreme weather conditions and the nature of the game limits planned water breaks. Yet, there are only a few reports on the effects of heat on soccer players.

In Africa, a series of games in a variety of climatic conditions were used to study the amount of dehydration in soccer. The range of weight loss was approximately 2–3% of pregame weight. In Illinois during the spring, a soccer team lost an average of only 2% of their body weight. On a larger scale, the US Youth Cup that is held annually in Blaine, Minnesota over the 4th of July holiday had a year in which temperatures for the games were in the high 90s . During the first two days there were numerous cases of heat related illnesses. The doctors requested that the organizers change the tourney format to lessen the possibility of further problems. Games were shortened and half-time was extended so that players had more time to ingest fluids. During the remaining four days of the tourney, less than five heat related illnesses occured.

It might be assumed that extremes of heat and humidity reduce the in-play time of soccer games. The 1994 World Cup in the U.S. was played in some challenging conditions. The average in-play time was nearly five minutes longer than the prior tournament in Italy and, therefore, temperature had little effect on game time. The referees were lenient in allowing water during the times when the ball was out of play, such as injury timeouts.

Summary

One of the most important changes in sports attitudes is in the use of fluids to prevent heat induced illnesses. To prevent heat related illness and improve performance, fluids must be ingested. The ideal fluids will be palatable so that intake is voluntary. To optimize fluid absorption by the intestine, the fluid needs to be a dilute solution of glucose and sodium that is also low in calories. A reasonable schedule of ingestion needs to be followed. This is possible in soccer despite the restricted opportunities during a game. Creative placement of fluid containers around the field, in the goal nets, and available for use during stoppages in the game (injury time-outs) make fluids readily available during a game.

SUGGESTED READING

Coleman E. Sports drink update. In: Sports Science Exchange. vol 1. Barrington, IL: Gatorade Sports Science Institute, 1988.

Coyle EF, Montain SJ. Carbohydrate and fluid ingestion during exercise: are there trade offs? Med Sci Sports Exerc 1992;24:671–678.

Fox EF, Foss ML, Bowers RW. Physiological basis for exercise and sport. 5th ed. Dubuque, IA: Brown & Benchmark, 1993.

Gisolfi CV, Duchman SM. Guidelines for optimal replacement beverages for different athletic events. Med Sci Sports Exerc 1992;24:679–687.

Maughan RJ, Noakes TD. Fluid replenishment and exercise stress: a brief review of studies on fluid replacement and some guidelines for the athlete. Sports Med 1991;12:16–31.

McArdle WD, Katch FI, Katch VL. Exercise physiology: energy, nutrition, and human performance, 3rd ed. Philadelphia: Lea & Febiger, 1991.

Murray R. The effects of consuming carbohydrate-electrolyte beverages on gastric emptying and fluid absorbtion during and following exercise. Sports Med 1987;4:322–351.

Noakes TD. Fluid replacement during exercise. Exerc Sport Sci Rev 1993;21:297–330.

II

● Biomechanics

 # Heading

James M. Lynch
Jeffrey A. Bauer

Heading a soccer ball is a complex series of dynamic events that must be precisely coordinated to ensure accurate placement of the ball. The entire body must be prepared for the act to be successful. The skill becomes more difficult when the player must head a ball while running, jumping, diving, in the presence of opponents, and combinations of a variety of other factors. This chapter will focus on the limited amount of information about the skill of heading.

Biomechanics of Heading

Properly heading a soccer ball is a complex skill that requires a great deal of practice. The ball should be struck by the forehead at the hairline—in the region used to check for the presence of a fever. This is an active motion; that is, the player should strike the ball rather than being hit by the ball in order to accurately direct the play.

When heading a ball, the initial movement of the trunk is backward into extension. The head and body are extended as a unit with the chin tucked in toward the chest. This tilt backward will allow greater velocity forward through the subsequent action of the trunk and hip flexors. The arms are extended forward in front of and away from the body to aid in balance and protect the heading player from oncoming participants. If the act of heading is to be incorporated into a jumping motion, then the legs should be drawn somewhat backward and upward in preparation for striking the ball.

Careful timing is necessary to use the momentum of the body for striking the ball. The head and shoulders are brought forward as a unit during the approach to the ball. This requires activation of the flexors of the hips and trunk. The eyes must remain open and focused on the ball throughout the act of heading. The neck should be rigid at impact and the velocity of the head, relative to the body, should be almost zero. The arms are drawn quickly back and to the sides as the motion is completed. The eyes should be kept on the ball following contact to reduce the velocity of the head and assist in controlling body motion during recovery. It is the ability of the hip and trunk flexors to initiate and sustain the translational motion of the trunk and upper body that ultimately produces an effective momentum transfer between the head and ball. An effective recovery of balance and motion must then be obtained to allow the player to continue in the game. There is much more trunk motion following impact to allow the player to remain tactically involved in the match.

Heading a soccer ball can be divided into three phases: preparation, contact, and recovery.

Preparation

The preparation phase will differ according to the circumstances of play (i.e., standing, running, or jumping). This phase is of crucial importance to ensure accurate timing for proper technique. The trunk dominates the action of heading a ball since it comprises most of the total weight of the body segments. We conducted an investigation using electromyogram (EMG) analysis of the trapezius (upper back) and sternocleidomastoid (neck) muscles during heading. A portable EMG unit was attached to the waist of each subject. Electrodes were attached to the sternocleidomastoid and trapezius bilaterally and a pressure sensor was placed on the forehead under a swimmer's cap. Both the trapezius and sternocleidomastoid muscles are activated during the preparation phase with the sternocleidomastoid initiating first. The activation begins earliest in a jumping header.

Impact

The impact can be characterized as an initial contact with a subsequent ball deformation and resultant recoil off the head. The total contact time has been consistently measured in the range of 10–23 milliseconds (msec) by investigators, using accelerometers or cinematographic analysis. We have obtained similar values from analysis of low-speed videography and measurements taken from a pressure sensor array attached to the forehead.

The impact force sustained during heading has also been measured or estimated by several researchers. Force is a measure that increases as mass and acceleration increase. The relationship is of the form $F = ma$, in which the force, F, is equal to the product of the mass, m, of the object multiplied by its acceleration, a, at any instant of time. It is assumed that the mass of a soccer ball does not change during play. However, the acceleration, or change in velocity over time, of the ball from one moment to the next often varies. When dealing with impact forces, a measure that provides an understanding of the heading event in the human is one that combines force and time. Not only is the magnitude of forces experienced during heading a ball of concern, but also the duration over which the force is applied. The mechanical relationship that combines both force and time is termed the impulse. Impulse is equal to force multipled by the time of force application and is expressed as $I = Ft$, in which I equals the impulse, F equals force, and t represents the time of force application. Most studies dealing with heading have presented peak impact or average impact forces rather than impulse values.

The contact of the ball with the head can be broken into three distinct phases. Phase one consists of contact and deformation of the ball with momentum from the head transferred to the ball to cause a change in the direction of movement of the ball. During phase two, the ball remains deformed and be-gins movement in the same direction as the head of the player. Phase three involves recoil of the ball, in which it regains normal shape and breaks con-tact with the head. All impulse calculations assume that the mass of the ball remains constant and that the change in velocity during this time of impact determines the magnitude of the impulse experienced by the player's head.

Recovery

The trapezius remains active longer than the sternocleidomastoid after im-pact to aid in decelerating the head. When the ball is directed at the ground the sternocleidomastoid turns off faster after impact than in any other situa-tion since the chin must be tucked in prior to impact in order to get the head over the ball to direct it downward.

Filming, accelerometers, a computer simulation, and mathematical model-ing using Newton's Third Law of momentum conservation have been used for analysis of heading . Relatively slow ball velocities used during data col-lection all yielded similar values. Although impact forces have been deter-mined through reverse kinematic analysis and empirical measurement, there has yet to be an investigation that truly reproduces game situations and pro-vides published results.

The physical characteristics of the ball vary depending on its size, weight, and elastic properties. The mass of a soccer ball varies according to the age of the players (Table 8-1).

From a scientific standpoint, the "bounce," or the coefficient of restitution (COR), of a ball is determined by calculating the ratio of how high a ball bounces versus the height from which it is dropped. The COR can be affected by the material of the ball, the inflation pressure, and environmental condi-tions (i.e., wet games). Inflation pressure regulations allow a range of 0.6–1.1 atmospheres (8.5–15.6 pounds per square inch—one pound per square inch equals 6975 Pascals). Molded soccer balls have panels that are bonded to a rubber lining or the entire cover is molded with painted panels.

Stitched soccer balls have hand-sewn panels of leather or some synthetic ma-terial that simulates leather. A slower rise time and more time to dissipate

Table 8-1

Ball Characteristics			
Size	Mass	Circumference	Age Group
#5	396–453 gm 14–16 oz	68–71 cm 27–28 in	14 and over
#4	312–369 gm 11–13 oz	61–64 cm 24–25 in	10–13
#3	312–340 gm 11–12 oz	56–59 cm 23–24 in	6–9

the forces incurred are features of the stitched ball. Stitched balls produce more peak force, but they also weigh more than the molded balls. In a comparison of stitched and molded balls under varying moisture and inflation conditions, wet and over-inflated balls had increased impact forces. Wet balls had more mass while the over-inflated balls had a faster rise time and, therefore, less time to dissipate the force. Dry stitched balls had the slower rise time while the wet stitched balls gained greater mass under wet conditions. It was not clear in this study whether the increased weight gain of the stitched ball was due to absorbency of the stitching or the material of the ball.

Contact time between a ball and a player's head varies from 10–23 msec. Ball velocities during an elite game may reach 25 m/sec. The impact force values determined in the literature have ranged from 200–1200 Newtons. These values have differed in quantity primarily due to the ball velocity used. Extrapolation to conditions of match play produce similar values in the range of 2000–3000 Newtons. The other common measure used in this body of literature is acceleration. The unit of measure is the gravitational unit (G), which is the increase in velocity due to gravity. The range of values obtained have been from 20–55 Gs. A head injury criterion (HIC) value has been calculated in a range of 1.40–10.98 with an average of 5.80 with accelerometer data using ball velocities of 15.5 m/sec. Two percent of the population would be expected to sustain a serious brain injury with a HIC value of 500 or more and 15% would sustain brain injury with a HIC of 1000. A computer simulation of heading calculated HIC values of 0–2362 and angular head accelerations of 138–6986 radians/second. Estimations of human tolerance have ranged from 3000–18,000 radians/second.

Impact values have been described in several other sports. American football has impacts lasting from 200–350 msec with peaks of 150–450 Gs. Heavyweight boxers can deliver a blow of 6000 Newtons and 100 Gs over a duration of 14 msec. In a study of volunteer boxers during matches in which no injuries occurred, impact time ranged up to 18 msec with linear accelerations of 20–159 Gs and angular accelerations up to 16,234 radians/second. The

Table 8-2

Impact in Sport		
Activity	*Duration*	*Force*
Soccer heading	10–23 msec	2000–3000 Newtons 30–55 Gs
American football	200–350 msec	150–450 Gs
Boxing	14–18 msec	6000 Newtons 100 Gs
Karate kick	8–10 msec	90–120 Gs

HIC values calculated in this study were 5–348. Kicks to the head in full-contact karate can generate 90–120 Gs (Table 8-2).

Acknowledgment

The authors would like to acknowledge the efforts of our research group: Nigel Sparks, Susan Mulligan, Sarah Richardson, Richard Park, and Joseph Leluga. We would also like to thank Coach Barry Gorman, the Penn State soccer team, and Paromed for their cooperation.

SUGGESTED READING

Levendusky RA, Armstrong CW, Eck JS, et al. Impact characteristics of two types of soccer balls. In: Science and Football: proceedings of the first world congress of science and football. London: E. & F.N. Spon, 1988;385–393.

Mawdsley HP. A biomechanical analysis of heading (summary of Masters thesis at University of Massachusetts). Edinburgh: Momentum, 1978;3:30–40.

9  Biomechanics of Kicking and Biomechanics of the Ball

William R. Barfield

Biomechanics is used to define the anatomical and mechanical methods for describing movement. The biomechanics of soccer, techniques, equipment, and the ball itself have been vigorously studied over the past several years. This chapter summarizes areas of interest to the soccer community, including those interested in sports medicine, teaching, and coaching. Primary areas of interest include: developmental levels, kicking kinematics and kinetics, approach angle, ground reaction forces while kicking, temporal patterning, ball contact, muscle activity, isokinetically evaluated strength measures, and the ball itself. Finally, a few suggestions for future study are suggested.

In soccer the primary skill used by players is kicking. Because of its fundamental importance in the game this particular technique has been frequently investigated in the literature.

Developmental Levels

Studies on the developmental levels in kicking among players between ages 2–5 show that there is virtually no run-up when kicking a stationary ball. Among 6–12 year old children, there is a greater tendency toward faster, more angled approaches and more optimal segmental timing with respect to velocity of the swing limb. However, the most surprising finding is the wide range of abilities displayed among players within age groups.

Because soccer is a stop-and-go sport, it may be expected that leg strength would be greater among soccer players than other types of athletes. Sixth-grade boys were tested before and after a nine-week season to determine if the stop-and-go nature of soccer would increase leg strength. The results were inconclusive since both controls and subjects increased in strength. Findings may have been confounded by maturation factors and the fact that intensity of training for subjects may have been inadequate to produce significantly different training effects.

Kinematics and Kinetics

Kicking is the biomechanical issue that has received the most scientific attention. Kicking differs from walking and running because the primary force for the kick comes from the swing, not the support limb. In addition, the speed of limb movement is faster than that seen in walking and running.

Most research leads to the conclusion that there are two key components of kicking: (1) development of velocity in the swing limb, particularly the shank and foot at ball impact and (2) occurrences with the foot during contact with the ball. Successful kicking, when evaluated by resultant ball velocity and/or velocity of swing limb movement, is based on optimal coordination of acceleration and deceleration of adjacent body links with one segment dominating at one stage while another dominates at a later stage. Contributing factors to swing velocity during instep kicking include velocity of the kicker, angle of approach, and optimal timing. Foot placement on the ball and rigidity of the foot and ankle at ball contact are crucial variables at impact in predicting success when kicking the ball powerfully.

Approach Angle

Kickers of various ages and ability levels can be observed approaching the ball from a variety of angles. With a one-step approach, peak ball velocity can be achieved at a 45° angle. Peak ankle and toe velocities, but not ball velocities, can be achieved at a 30° approach angle. A significant relationship between swing limb velocity and ball velocity implies that both approach angles should result in equal ball velocities. The most plausible explanation for the difference in approach angles is increased striking mass resulting from greater fixation of the knee and ankle joints at a 45° approach angle. Further work on the approach angle, speed of approach, and desired outcome of the kick (shot, goal kick, pass) is needed.

Ground Reaction Forces

In analysis of ground reaction forces (GRF), the peak vertical component is greater than medio-lateral or anterio-posterior and is not greatly influenced by the angle of approach. However, as approach angle becomes greater, the frictional impact becomes oriented in an increasingly lateral and less anterior direction. This inverse relationship of lateral and frontal forces should be expected.

When comparing differences between dominant and nondominant sides, medio-lateral GRFs are highly correlated with ball velocity for the dominant side. Skilled players also generate greater GRF and ball velocity than unskilled players. The conclusion is greater ball velocity among skilled players is partly due to greater forces generated in the support limb. The assumption can be made that dominant side kicking produces an ideal model and nondominant kicking produces a less desirable result, similar to differences between skilled and unskilled kickers. Figure 9-1 shows typical GRF of the support limb during kicking following a 45–60° approach angle. The peak medio-lateral force (F-y) blocks body momentum prior to peak anterior-posterior force.

Torque at support foot impact is a measure of vertical twist imparted to the body by action of the swing leg. This torque is reduced with increasing approach angle. In a straight approach there is no torque imparted. At an approach angle of 45–60° the active torque, supplied by the asymmetrical

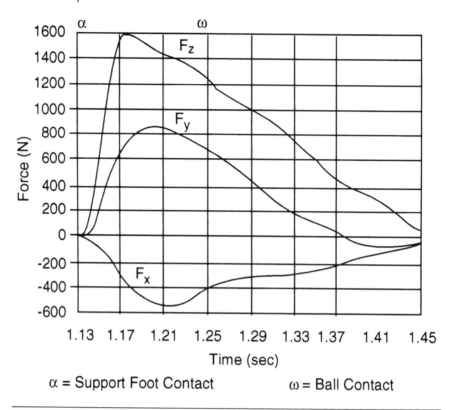

Figure 9-1. Ground reaction forces (GRF) on the plant foot when the dominant limb is kicking (Fz = vertical GRF, Fy = medio/lateral GRF, Fx = anterior/posterior GRF).

movement of the swing limb, balances the resistive torque on the plant foot through ground reaction and may be considered a sound injury prevention technique.

Temporal Patterning

Proper timing of body segments seems to be one of the primary keys to successful kicking. The precise transfer of energy from one body segment to another and the exact mechanism by which this occurs is unclear. Several authors have investigated the sequential movement of the thigh and lower leg (shank) during the toe kick. Findings show that the thigh begins to rotate forward while the leg (defined from knee to ankle) continues to rotate backward. As the leg begins to rotate forward the thigh begins to decelerate, and is almost stationary at impact while the leg and foot reach peak acceleration.

Invariant Patterning

Temporal patterning does not seem to vary greatly among various age groups. This may indicate that the patterning in skilled kicking is similar in type and timing. In addition, the relative timing of the pelvis, thigh, and lower leg vary little. The shank sequentially follows combined pelvic rotation and hip flexion.

One of the differences between a toe kicker and a soccer-style kicker is that soccer-style kickers display more consistent temporal distance parameters than toe kickers. From an injury perspective, 15% of the energy from the kick is transferred to the ball while the rest is dissipated through soft tissues of the leg after ball contact. Optimum performance is dependent on the prevention of energy loss inherent in the lower limb prior to ball contact. This reduces the time needed to dissipate energy and the muscle forces required to slow the limb during follow-through. Immediately after contact, flexion torque at the knee (280 N · m) can exceed extension torque (230 N · m), which guards against hyperextension. If flexion torque is initiated too early, the leg is slowed leading to a less than optimal performance. The muscles are in greatest danger of injury after the kick. Additional anterior or medial loads produced at impact create ideal conditions for a knee injury.

There are measureable differences between the dominant and nondominant leg. Linear velocity of the fifth metatarsal (toe) and lateral malleolus (ankle) at ball contact correlate with resultant ball velocity on the dominant side. Figure 9-2 is an example of velocity of the toe, knee, and hip for the dominant limb. Linear velocity of the toe is close to maximum at ball contact. Maximum angular velocity at the knee occurs almost simultaneously with ball contact on the dominant side, which is a desirable finding. Maximum angular velocity of the knee occurs after ball contact on the nondominant side. Figure 9-3 displays angular position, velocity, and acceleration at the knee.

Ball Contact

Studies show foot rigidity at ball contact to be a critical factor in powerful kicking. A significant relationship between the speed of the kicking foot and ball speed also has been found. Skilled players typically contact the ball closer to the ankle (less "give" at the joint) and position the plant foot closer to the ball rather than behind. The position between the kicking foot and ball seems to distinguish the skilled players from the unskilled players. Displacement at the ankle ("give") during ball contact on the dorsal surface occurs even among skilled players as displayed in Figure 9-4. Note the oscillation after ball contact. Impact plantarflexes the foot until the supporting structures reach extremes in their range of motion. To achieve optimal kicking performance, players should strike the ball as close to the ankle as possible.

Electromyogram (EMG)

During the "cocking phase" of the kick and in the acceleration of the shank during knee extension, the quadriceps play a critical role. Flexion of the knee and rotation of the leg backward seem to provide loading for the knee extensors, which is later used in accelerating the leg forward. EMG data support this contention.

There appears to be a "kicking paradox"; the quadricep muscles seem to be most active during flexion of the knee (when they are antagonistic to the movement) while the hamstrings are most active during knee extension (when they are antagonistic to the movement). Based on EMG studies, the vastus lateralis and medialis (2 of the 4 quadriceps) are most active at the end of knee flexion (loading phase). Compared to recreational players, well-

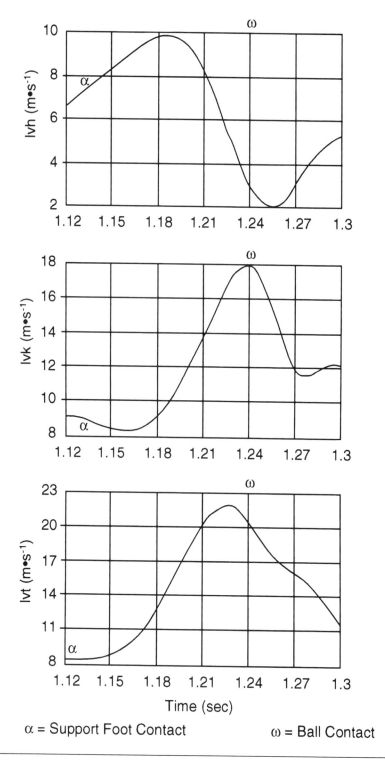

Figure 9-2. Linear velocity of the toe (lvt), knee (lvk), and hip (lvh) for the dominant limb during kicking.

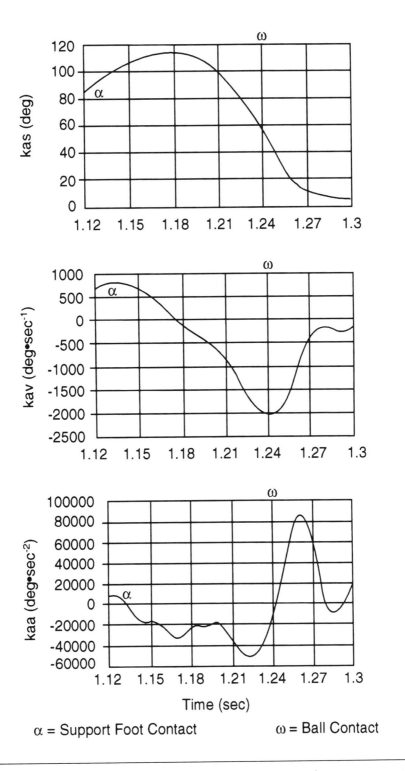

Figure 9-3. Dominant side trial depicting angular position (kap), velocity (kav), and acceleration (kaa) at the knee.

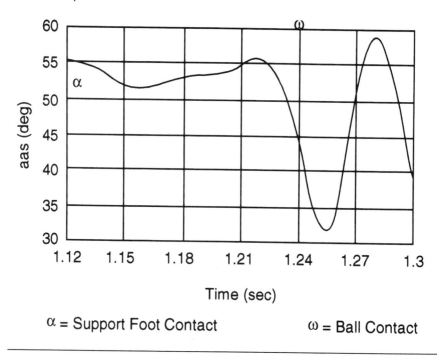

α = Support Foot Contact   ω = Ball Contact

Figure 9-4. Displacement of the ankle during ball contact.

trained soccer players appear to have more efficient use of kicking limb muscles, thereby increasing the importance of technical motor skills.

During soccer coaching clinics, there are discussions concerning where the power for instep kicking occurs. For members of the Canadian Olympic Soccer Team, 90% of the work in instep kicking was supplied by the hip muscles. Hip flexors dominated motion of the thigh during the majority of the swing phase, but just prior to ball contact, the hip extensors (hamstrings) became dominant in slowing the leg, which is contrary to what might be expected. The knee extensors, which were thought to be important in swing-to-ball contact, showed limited activity immediately prior to ball contact. In fact, the flexors were dominant and acted eccentrically to slow extension of the knee. Explanations given for the slowing of knee extension prior to ball contact were that: (1) flexors worked to prevent hyperextension at the knee and (2) due to the speed of knee extension the force-velocity relationship prevented forceful contraction by the knee extensors.

Ball Impact

Investigations concerning ball type, inflation pressure, and increased mass due to wetness have been conducted. In one investigation, molded and stitched balls (9 psi) were dropped from a height to ensure a constant velocity (17–18 m · s^{-1}) at impact. The stitched ball exerted a force of 912 N while the molded ball yielded 851 N of force. Both balls exerted forces clearly within the limits shown to cause concussions and fractures.

The molded ball demonstrated 12.43 N · s^{-1} of impulse (force × time) force at impact and the stitched ball 13.72 N · s^{-1}, which are both below that needed to cause a head injury. Because the head is moving, the change in momentum will be different from that seen in the laboratory with an impulse that is likely to be greater. Since impulse is the product of force and time, the greater the temporal variable the better the chances of reducing injury since the force can be dissipated over a longer period of time.

Mean rise time (time needed to develop the impact forces) was 3.3 seconds for the molded ball and 4.2 seconds for the stitched ball. The shorter the rise time, the greater the possibility of injury. The rise time for the stitched ball was 28% greater than that for the molded ball, which supports the use of stitched balls in terms of injury prevention and giving players the desired "feel" or "touch" of the ball.

When three different sizes of soccer balls were tested, peak impact force was greater for the larger balls. Size 5 impact forces exceeded sizes 4 and 3 by 26% and 35%, respectively. Since less mass decreased the amount of force, there may be a decreased likelihood of injury. As ball size decreased, there was also a decrease in total impulse, thereby reducing the possibility of impact injury. This has particular application to youth players and coaches since younger children generally have less body mass. Therefore, a smaller ball will decrease the possibility of injury.

Ball Wetness

During play on wet ground, a ball may accumulate moisture, which will increase its mass and affect its impact characteristics. In the previously mentioned study, the peak impact force of a wet stitched ball was increased by 8.5% while the molded ball increased by 2.8%. Impulse also increased in the wet condition due to increased mass (7.5% for stitched and 1.3% for molded), since the time variable in the impulse equation was thought to be unaffected by the moisture.

Increased inflation levels produce greater levels of peak force due to a decreased rise time, indicating an increased rate of deceleration. Molded balls had lower rise times (17.96%) than stitched balls, which would suggest that molded balls generate greater peak force. Yet, results found that greater stitched ball mass negated the differences in deceleration.

Although others have found that the type of ball is more important than inflation pressure, the less the pressure and weight of the ball the less the force of impact.

Summary and Conclusions

Despite the number of investigations on the biomechanics of kicking and the ball, further investigation is required. Future areas of interest include the influence of age and gender on kicking mechanics and the total influence of the upper body on kicking. Each of these areas may lead to new avenues of investigation that could impact training style from a teaching and coaching perspective and improve methods of injury prevention.

SUGGESTED READING

Asami T, Nolte V. Analysis of powerful ball kicking. In: Matsui H, Kobayashi K, eds. Biomechanics VIII-B. Champaign, Il: Human Kinetic Publishers, 1983;695–700.

Barfield WR. Effects of selected biomechanical variables on a coordinated human movement: instep kicking with dominant and nondominant feet. Dissertation Abstracts International 1993;54, 08–A. (University Microfilms No. AAD94–02068).

Brady EC, O'Regan M, McCormack B. Isokinetic assessment of uninjured soccer players. In: Reilly T, Clarys J, Stibbe A, eds. Science and football II. London: E. & F.N. Spon, 1993;351–356.

De Proft E, Clarys JP, Bollens E, et al. Muscle activity in the soccer kick. In: Reilly T, Lees A, Davids K, eds. et al. Science and football. New York: E. & F.N. Spon, 1988;434–440.

Hirsh AH. Current problems in head protection. In: Caveness WF, Walker AE, eds. Head injury conference proceedings. Philadelphia: J.B. Lippincott Company, 1966;37–40.

Huang TC, Roberts EM, Youm Y. Biomechanics of kicking. In: Ghista DN, ed. Human body dynamics: impact, occupational, and athletic aspects. Oxford: Clarendon Press, 1982;409–443.

Isokawa M, Lees A. A biomechanical analysis of the instep kick motion in soccer. In: Reilly T, Lees A, Davids K, eds. et al. Science and football. New York: E. & F.N. Spon, 1988;449–455.

Levendusky TA, Armstrong CW, Eck JS, et al. Impact characteristics of two types of soccer balls. In: Reilly T, Lees A, Davids K, eds. et al. Science and football. New York: E. & F.N. Spon, 1988;385–393.

Narici MV, Sirtori MD, Mognoni P. Maximal ball velocity and peak torques of hip flexor and knee extensor muscles. In: Reilly T, Lees A, Davids K, eds. et al. Science and football. New York: E. & F.N. Spon, 1988;429–433.

Rodano R, Tavana R. Three-dimensional analysis of instep kick in professional soccer players. In: Reilly T, Clarys J, Stibbe A, eds. Science and football II. New York: E. & F.N. Spon, 1993;357–361.

10 Soccer Shoes and Playing Surfaces

Raymond Rocco Monto

Although the soccer shoe has gone through an impressive transformation over the past two decades, it has remained largely forgotten. Due to the international growth of the game, athletic shoe manufacturers are now focusing on the development of the soccer shoe and equipment. As a result, new shoe designs are flooding into the soccer market. The purpose of this chapter is to better prepare players, coaches, and trainers for this revolution in soccer equipment.

To understand what drives athletic shoe design it is necessary to appreciate the two most fundamental but conflicting concepts involved. The prevention of injury due to excessive load or trauma and the enhancement of performance. To complicate matters further, the modern soccer player also desires style and affordability.

Epidemiology

In the course of a typical soccer match or practice, dependent on position, a player will run approximately 10 kilometers. Given an average stride length, most players sustain approximately 4200 heelstrikes during a game and more than 75,000 heelstrikes during a typical month of training. Shear forces in the foot while running have been estimated at approximately 50 times those seen during walking and must be absorbed at 5 times the rate. Add to this the usual load absorption of the lower extremities, between 3 and 6 times body weight with each heelstrike, and it is understandable that soccer players are at high risk for overuse injuries.

The standard soccer ball weighs 400–450 grams and can be kicked at speeds in excess of 120 km/hr. Biomechanical studies of the kick have demonstrated significant translational and rotational torque loads to the knee and foot during the kick. The majority of this torque is generated by the hip flexors acting concentrically with the knee extensors as agonists to accelerate the lower leg toward the ball. These torques have been estimated at 2000 Newton-meters, with the lower leg absorbing all but 15% of this kinetic energy. The body absorbs these excessive loads through a chain of violent eccentric muscular co-contractions that begin in the foot and lead to the hamstring and adductor muscles to decelerate the leg after ball contact.

The general injury rate for soccer runs between 4–20 injuries per thousand hours of play. Although this rate is average for most contact sports, the injury rate for indoor soccer is seven times higher. Injuries to the foot and ankle make up a disproportionate percentage of this trauma and account for the majority of lost playing time. A recent radiographic survey of elite young soccer players shows that 98% display bone changes in the foot and ankle. These radiographic changes range from fractures to bone spurs and may be the result of years of cumulative microtrauma to the foot and ankle during soccer (Fig. 10-1).

Evolution

Modern soccer was born in the crucible of the Industrial Revolution. As a game designed to occupy the laboring masses, it was natural that it took its equipment from the workplace. The first modern soccer shoes were stiff, "high-top" leather or canvas mining boots that had been handstudded on their soles with wooden spikes. Although shoe manufacturers eventually industrialized their production, little change was seen in the basic soccer shoe for nearly 100 years.

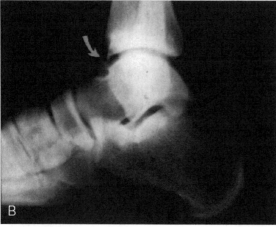

Figure 10-1. A,B; 98% of soccer players may develop radiographic abnormalities by age 23.

In the mid-1950s the growing emphasis on ball-handling and individual skills led to a need for more flexibility in the shoe. The growth of soccer in South America and other warm climates also led to a demand for lighter, less restrictive shoes. Gradually, low-cut soccer shoes appeared, becoming almost universal by the mid-1960s. The 1970s were marked by the dominance of molded plastic cleats and the rise of a new and problematic playing surface—artificial turf (first called "astro-turf" from its introduction in the Houston Astrodome). Still, the general design and stud array changed little and the 1980s offered few modifications despite the revolution underway in running and basketball footwear.

Presently, however, new concepts are reshaping the form and function of the old miner's soccer boot. Energy conservation and load dissipation have been incorporated into design equations and everything from fins to metallic blades have been used to improve performance and sales. To differentiate important new design elements from ineffectual or cosmetic changes, it is necessary to understand the form and function of the human foot and ankle.

Anatomy of the Foot and Ankle

The ankle joint consists of the tibia, fibula, and talus joints forming a mechanically stable "mortise and tenon" construct. The mortise is created by the medial and lateral malleoli of the ankle with the wedge-shaped talus acting as the tenon (Fig. 10-2). As the ankle joint dorsiflexes, the wider anterior portion of the talus fills up the mortise and stabilizes the joint. When the ankle and foot plantarflexes, the tenon releases from the mortise and the ankle becomes primarily dependent on its ligamentous supports for stability. At this point the ankle is most vulnerable to injury. The risk of deltoid ligament medially is decreased by the extra length of the fibula laterally because it helps prevent excessive eversion of the ankle. Conversely, the relative shortness of the medial malleolus allows forceful inversion and potential lateral ligament damage. Normal ankle laxity allows twice as much inversion as eversion (Fig. 10-3). For further information, see Chapter 32.

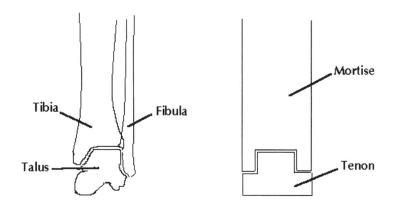

Figure 10-2. The ankle gains mechanical stability from "mortise and tenon" architecture.

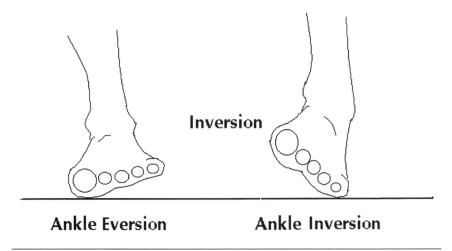

Figure 10-3. Normal ankle inversion is twice that of eversion.

The primary lateral ankle ligaments consist of the anterior talofibular, posterior talofibular, and calcaneofibular ligaments. The anterior talofibular ligament and anterior joint capsule are most commonly injured when the ankle is flexed downward and inverted (Fig. 10-4a). When the ankle is forcefully inverted and flexed upward, as if stepping in a hole, the calcaneofibular ligament is exposed to injury (Fig. 10-4b). Forced external rotation of the ankle, seen in tackling, can also damage the anterior ankle with tearing in the vital tibiofibular syndesmotic ligaments (Fig. 10-4c). These syndesmotic injuries are less common than inversion injuries, but are much slower to heal. New research has implicated impaired proprioception as a factor in recurrent ankle sprains. Other studies show decreased ankle inversion with increased shoe-top height, which may impair flexibility and performance levels.

The kinematics, or dynamic anatomy, of the ankle joint also plays a critical role in gait. The talus is irregularly shaped on its medial border as it articulates with the calcaneus to form the subtalar joint. This creates a functional mismatch between the medial and lateral axes of motion. As a result, the talus wobbles on the calcaneus like a poorly mounted tire (Fig. 10-5). The oblique hinge created in the subtalar joint helps prevent injury of the foot and ankle in several critical ways. Its primary role is to act as an efficient torque convertor to convert vertically direct loads into well-distributed longitudinal forces. Along with the normal internal rotation of the tibia, the oblique hinge of the subtalar joint drives the pronation and supination of the foot during gait.

When the foot makes initial ground contact it is normally supinated (Fig. 10-6). As weight is transferred to the foot, the internally rotated tibia and the obliquely hinged subtalar joint combine to initiate pronation. Forefoot pronation acts as an active force dampener for the foot and ankle. As weight is transferred to the foot and ankle after heelstrike, pronation attenuates the force of impact by extending the amount of time and area over which it can be absorbed. Therefore, elevated pronation velocity may play as important a role in producing overuse

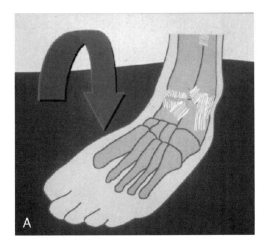

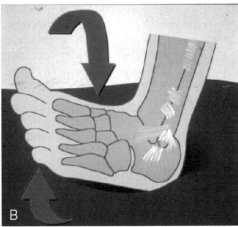

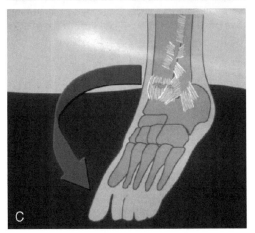

Figure 10-4. A; The anterior talofibular ligament is torn when the ankle is flexed downward, B; The calcaneofibular ligament is torn when the ankle is flexed upward, C; The tibiofibular syndesmotic ligaments are torn when the ankle is rotated.

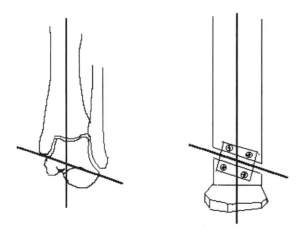

Figure 10-5. The irregular axis of the subtalar joint creates an oblique hinge.

injuries as exposure to excessive shear forces. Abnormal levels of pronation magnitude or velocity may contribute to other running problems such as patellar tendonitis, iliotibial band friction syndrome, and patellofemoral pain. For research purposes, the relative velocity of pronation can be studied by examining the rate of calcaneal eversion (Fig. 10-7). The effects of heel height and orientation on maximal pronation velocity will be reviewed later in this chapter.

The central two metatarsal bones of the forefoot are fixed in position. The border metatarsals are free to move and contour to loading during gait (Fig. 10-8). This may be why the second and third metatarsals are frequently involved in stress reactions and fractures. The anatomy of the forefoot also features the formation of three discrete arches (Fig. 10-9). The talus, cuboid, and central cuneiform bones work as keystones to support these arches while the spring ligament below provides a soft-tissue "tie beam" to improve pressure distribution. For many years it was believed that people with flexible flatfeet were at higher risk for injury. This condition led to the discharge of otherwise healthy U.S. Army recruits during World War II. New research shows that players with flexible flatfeet are actually at lower risk for injury than

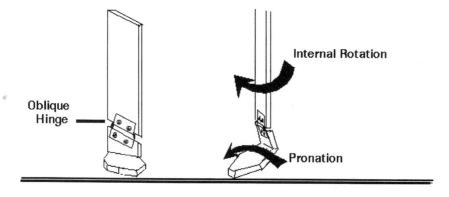

Figure 10-6. The oblique hinge of the subtalar joint drives progressive foot pronation.

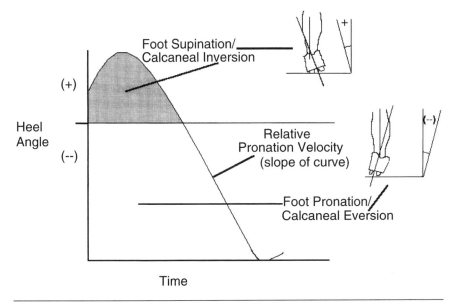

Figure 10-7. Relative pronation velocity can be measured by calcaneal (heel) eversion. Adapted from Nike, Inc. Beaverton, Oregon.

those with stiff, high arches (cavus feet). Recent studies suggest that the extrinsic and intrinsic musculature of the foot and ankle may also participate in dynamic arch support. The fascial plantar aponeurosis also acts as a "windlass" mechanism to shorten and elevate the arch during upward flexion of the toes (Fig. 10-10). It has been suggested that the arch functions as an efficient reservoir of kinetic energy during gait and may provide some energy return as a result. Studies on barefoot runners demonstrate active arch elevation through training. This is believed to be a result of increased activ-

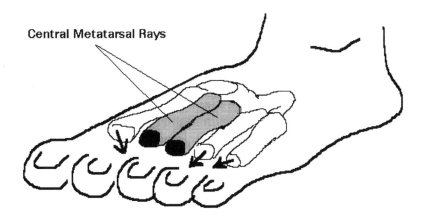

Figure 10-8. The central two metatarsal bones remain fixed during normal gait. This may increase the risk of stress fracture.

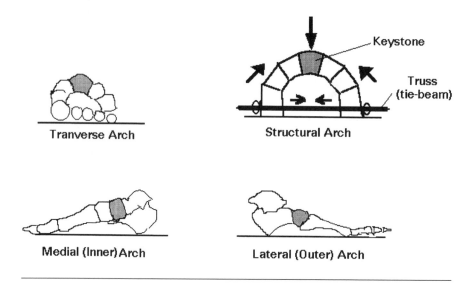

Figure 10-9. The forefoot contains both longitudinal and transverse arches for support.

ity in the muscles of the foot. Some researchers now recommend occasional barefoot training to improve foot muscle function. This is in contrast to traditional beliefs that the foot muscles play a limited role in gait.

The morphology of the human foot has a direct effect on shoe design. Evidence of sexual dimorphism (male and female shape differences) has been recognized in the foot and ankle, resulting in the introduction of differing last and outsole designs. The male foot is proportionally wider and thicker than the female foot at any given length. Another important morphologic feature of the foot stems from its role as a type 1 biomechanical lever with the ful-

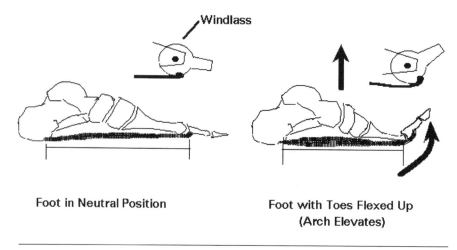

Figure 10-10. The plantar fascia acts as a functional "windlass" to elevate the arch.

crum at the ankle joint. Foot length increases with body size on an isometric, or proportional, scale to maintain a constant mechanical advantage. This is similar to the relationship between body height and weight in that the width and height of the foot increase on an allometric scale with disproportionately slower increases in body size. This may allow the maintenance of relatively static plantar pressures with increases in body mass. To achieve improved comfort and fit, modern soccer shoe design must incorporate sexual dimorphism and combine isometric and allometric scaling.

Anatomy of the Soccer Shoe

Although not as complex as the foot and ankle, the modern soccer shoe has several universal components that have evolved (Fig. 10-11). The shoe begins with a toe-box usually made of soft, supple leather. The upper of the shoe should be ventilated to allow the estimated 250,000 sweat glands of the foot to breathe. Ventilation also speeds heat dissipation and decreases moisture build-up in the shoe. Some companies are using synthetic water impermeable materials to keep the shoe from gaining detrimental water-weight on wet or muddy fields.

The upper extends to a padded tongue that protects the foot from the laces. Various types of tongues are available, including flip-over, conventional, monotongue, and internal sleeve designs. The insole is a removable liner that can provide additional padding and support to the foot. It can be replaced with an off-the-shelf or custom orthotic. The role of orthotics has been limited in soccer shoes because of their low height and snug fit. Some manufacturers now offer relatively expensive, extra-depth shoes that are intended to accommodate the addition of custom orthotics. This solution does not address the many shortcomings of the current mainstream soccer boot.

Anatomy of the Soccer Shoe

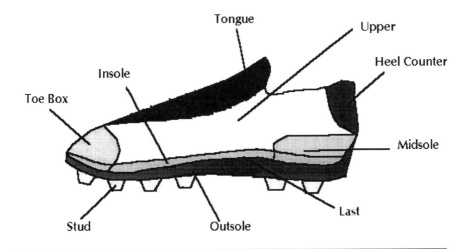

Figure 10-11. Anatomy of the soccer shoe.

The last lies beneath the insole and is an important determinate of shoe flexibility. A board-lasted shoe is a fairly stiff but stable construct. This is because the upper is bonded to a uniform board pattern inside. Board-lasted athletic shoes are uncommon today. A slip-lasted shoe is much more flexible since the upper is stitched around the last in one piece, allowing it to be slipped out. Most modern shoe designs use a hybrid or combination-last to gain the stability and pronation control of the board-last while maintaining the flexibility and comfort of the slip-last. The heel counter of the shoe is padded to protect the rearfoot. It is often contoured in a V-shaped pattern to accommodate the Achilles tendon during hyperflexion of the ankle.

The midsole is the heart of the athletic shoe. Although the midsole has been the focus of over two decades of research in other sports, it has been largely ignored in soccer. Many of the lessons learned from the study of basketball and running are now being applied to soccer with varying degrees of success. The majority of the shockwave at impact is absorbed by the midsole. It also creates a guidance system to control the amount and rate of pronation as the foot proceeds after heelstrike. Both of these features are believed to be key elements in the prevention of injury. Many different types and combinations of materials have been used in midsole construction (Table 10-1). These materials have been chosen for their cushioning characteristics and resistance to fatigue damage and wear. The optimal aspects of midsole design will be further discussed in the sections on cushioning, guidance, and support.

Shoe manufacturers have devoted the majority of their time and resources to the outsole. Myriad styles of stud shapes and patterns have been used. The use of computer-assisted design and manufacture (CAD/CAM) has become an integral part of this effort. Despite these innovations, most outsole designs continue to be derivative and are almost indistinguishable from one another. Most removable studs maintain a central metal post, which may represent a site of high plantar pressure concentration (Fig. 10-12). Recent outsole designs have responded to this problem by using protective plates of composite materials to improve pressure distribution. The actual success of these changes remains to be seen.

Table 10-1

Midsole Material Composition
Polyurethane foam
Ethylene vinyl acetate (EVA)
Air cells
Gel
Hexalite
Foam rubber
Hydroflow
Dual-density (hybrid)

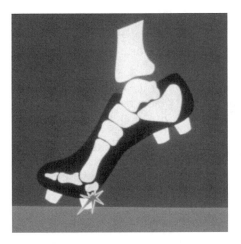

Figure 10-12. The central post of studs may concentrate plantar pressure and cause pain.

The length of the stud also is important. Long studs increase the length of the moment arm of the shoe in relation to the body and can create potential instability if not widely distributed on the outsole. On hard natural surfaces a low-profile molded multistud shoe is recommended. Longer screw-in metal-posted studs should be reserved for use on wet or soft natural turf to maintain traction. In terms of children, one major problem with studded cleats is that they tend to be too long in relation to body height. This creates a potentially dangerous mismatch with an increased relative moment arm. Some youth designs have tried to combine flat rear outsoles with studded forward outsoles to improve stability. These attempts may worsen the situation by creating tractional conflicts within the outsole itself while still allowing the instability of long studs. In general, children under the age of 12 should avoid the use of high-profile studded cleats and wear comfortable flat or corrugated athletic shoes for soccer.

Orthotics

Orthotics function as replacement insoles and are molded to contour and support the foot. They are available in custom, semi-custom, and off-the-shelf versions. Orthotics vary greatly in price, stiffness, and effectiveness. They are most useful in providing additional cushioning and longitudinal arch support to the flexible, overpronating foot. Stiff, high-arched, or cavus feet are more difficult to effectively treat with orthotics. Advanced orthotic designs seem to improve plantar pressure distribution patterns in the foot and can help improve minor gait irregularities. Many relatively inexpensive off-the-shelf orthotics function as well as more costly semicustom or full custom versions. As soccer shoe design continues to evolve, the need for these types of devices should decrease.

Surface Considerations

The game of soccer may seem ideally suited to a sunny, well-manicured, natural grass field. In reality, soccer is played on all types of surfaces and extreme weather conditions. From the sandy, glass-lined fields of the inner city to the most advanced synthetic stadium field, each surface type and condition creates a unique challenge for shoe designers. The indoor game also presents new demands with the widespread use of hardwood and relatively un-forgiving artificial surfaces. To increase performance and decrease injury rates, each of these challenges must be considered as the soccer shoe evolves into more specialized forms.

Artificial turf is a classic example of how the introduction of a new surface type can affect players. The rapid initial spread of synthetic grass fields was due to their greater versatility, durability, and economy compared to natural grass. The potential cost savings are dramatic. The cost of maintaining an ar-tificial grass field is only 15% of that needed to maintain a natural grass field. The multi-use capability of synthetic fields allows far greater usage than nat-ural grass fields could sustain without expensive increases in maintenance.

Despite these obvious advantages, concerns over a rise in injury rates slowed the acceptance of artificial turf. It was believed that increased rotational fric-tion was to blame for this increase in knee and ankle sprains. In fact, the real problem was not the surface type, but the shoes. Both soccer and American football players used their outdoor studded cleats to play on the artificial turf. The long studs gave them high traction and many felt quicker on the new surface. The problem was that a mismatch in frictional profiles between the shoe and the surface was created. This led to excessively high amounts of traction, with the shoe remaining firmly planted in the turf while the rest of the body twisted in a new direction. Torsional injuries of the ankle and knee resulted. Using studs on the hard synthetic surfaces also led to in-creased relative moment arms and platform instability. Injury rates dropped dramatically when players used shoes with flat or low-profile outsoles on the artificial turf.

Aside from a slight increase in abrasion rates, current research indicates no significant difference in injury rates between artificial and natural grass. Many players now routinely coat their exposed legs and arms with petro-leum jelly or wear compression shorts to combat the abrasion problem. An-other difficulty unique to artificial turf is excessive heat build-up during hot weather conditions. On older fields, this can lead to carpet shrinkage and po-tentially dangerous open seams and exposed flaps.

Indoor soccer injury rates are 6–8 times higher than those seen in outdoor soccer. This is almost certainly a result of the hard surfaces and confined spaces of the indoor game. Slide tackling is particularly hazardous indoors and some leagues have moved to ban it altogether. Injury rates have fallen to levels comparable to outdoor soccer when open tackling has been restricted. The use of smaller balls, mandatory shinguards, and padded containment boards should also decrease the injury rates in indoor soccer.

Biomechanics

At the core of modern athletic shoe design is the theory that load reduction leads to injury prevention. Although this equation has yet to be proven, there has been enough supportive research to justify extensive design modifica-tions toward this goal. An increasing number of scientific studies link exces-sive repetitive impact loading with cumulative foot and ankle trauma. Stress fractures, osteoarthritis, shinsplints, and anemia have been reported. One study supports the finding of anemia in runners by demonstrating increased levels of hemolytic blood products in those wearing harder-soled shoes.

The effects of cyclic stress loading are not all detrimental. If kept within safe limits, repetitive loading can strengthen biomaterials like collagen. This is best seen in the successful use of aggressive rehabilitation protocols in the treatment of ankle and knee sprains. The laboratory assessment of force is difficult, partly due to the many forms and orientation that force can take. Its primary forms are compression, tension, and shear. Most bench and field research is based on measuring externally generated compressive force. The magnitude and orientation of tensile and shear forces continue to frustrate researchers. The presence of internally generated forces further clouds the significance of current work.

Bench testing of impact force levels is done in several ways. Impact force can be estimated by measuring the net force acting at the body's center of mass with floor mounted force plates. An alternative method is "drop testing." This method uses a series of weighted metal shafts that simulate the impact of running and jumping on athletic shoes. Load cells attached to the end of the shaft measure impact force. A more sensitive estimation of relative force is obtained by using limb-mounted accelerometers. Another technique is to examine force distribution patterns in the shoe itself. This is accomplished by placing flexible pressure transducer grids within the insole to monitor peak vertical plantar pressure (Fig. 10-13).

Cushioning is aimed at attenuating the violent shock waves created in the foot and ankle by running and jumping. Although the actual magnitude of impact force is only modestly decreased by midsole cushioning, the force is absorbed over a longer period of time. This delay in onset of maximal impact force attenuates the effects of repeated impact loading by improving its absorption and distribution. Impact testing leads to the creation of force-deflection curves, which are equivalent to stress-strain models. Shock attenuation through cushioning is represented by a decrease in the slope of this force deflection curve (Fig. 10-14a). The area beneath this curve is equivalent to the amount of force absorbed by the midsole. This is called the impulse. The pattern of this curve during unloading allows the generation of a hysteresis graph that estimates the amount of energy lost by the shoe during transfer (Fig. 10-14b). Severe irregularities of these curves result when the shoe bottoms out and functional cushioning is lost.

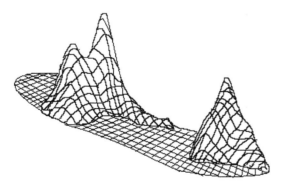

Figure 10-13. Flexible pressure transducer grids are used to monitor plantar pressure.

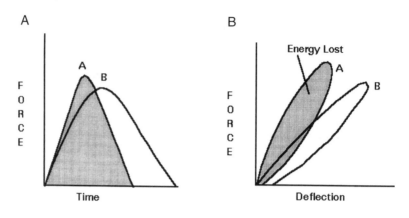

Figure 10-14. A; Cushioning leads to shock attenuation. Curve B represents a better cushioned shoe than Curve A. B; Energy is lost during the gait cycle and is dissipated as heat.

One important feature of cushioning is the effect of the rate of force application. This is due to the viscoelastic nature of most cushioning (and biologic) materials. When load is applied faster, viscoelastic materials become functionally stiffer. Conversely, slow application of force leads to softer, more compliant behavior. Because of the different viscoelastic profiles of various cushioning materials, designers make extensive use of hybrid engineering and composite materials. Another advantage of using composite material is that it limits the effects of vibration due to increased cushioning. The real benefits in dampening vibration in athletic shoes are unclear since there are not sufficient data available on the type and amount of internal force generated by the foot and ankle.

There are additional problems associated with increased shoe cushioning. Regardless of the amount of cushioning present, the ultimate magnitude of

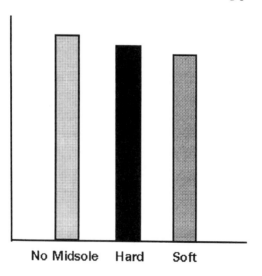

Figure 10-15. Cushioning has little effect on overall impact shock levels.

impact force changes little (Fig. 10-15). There are two reasons for this finding. First, force plate technology is limited in sensitivity. Force plates measure the ground reactive force associated with the acceleration of the body's center of mass and are not able to easily assess local shock impact in the foot and ankle. Leg shock accelerometers and plantar pressure transducers are more effective. The second reason for the consistency of shock impacts at different cushioning levels relates to kinematic adaptation.

Kinematic adaptation refers to the subconscious adjustments the body makes when running or jumping in athletic shoes of differing hardness. Runners with poorly cushioned shoes tend to flex at the knee more at foot strike and more rapidly following heel strike than runners with better cushioned shoes. In this way, the lower extremity becomes a more compliant spring to reduce peak impact forces. This, however, may result in elevated energy demands. This is one of the costs of cushioning.

Another cost of cushioning is the added weight it brings to the shoe. The body is sensitive to increased weight on the foot while running. In fact, running shoes themselves result in a 3–5% increase in energy consumption compared to running barefoot. There is an average increase of 1% in energy consumption at moderate running speeds for every 100 grams added to the weight of the shoe. Additional problems of increased cushioning are increased bulk, decreased flexibility, and decreased rearfoot stability. Despite these factors, bigger athletes need proportionally more cushioning than smaller athletes because body mass scales allometrically. Decreased foot and ankle flexibility results in performance degradation. Rearfoot instability results in excessive medial heel deformation at heelstrike. This will depend on individual variation of pronation or supination

Stability

Rearfoot stability is critical in the efficient control of load transfer and absorption. Midsole height, width, flare, and material composition all contribute to rearfoot stability and the initiation of controlled pronation. The magnitude and rate of pronation must be controlled to allow enough time for effective transfer and distribution of the impact force. Midsoles composed of stiffer or less cushioned materials compress less at contact than softer midsoles. This causes more medio-lateral orientation of the ground reactive force axis at heel strike. This leads to a longer moment arm in relation to the subtalar axis. Increased lateral leverage of the heel results. This cascades and creates increased levels of calcaneal eversion and elevated maximal pronation velocity, which potentially increases the risk of cumulative foot injury. Conversely, soft midsoles decrease calcaneal eversion and slow maximal pronation velocity. Extremely soft or poorly cushioned midsoles bottom out at heelstrike and behave like stiff midsoles. Athletic shoes are now engineered to take full advantage of these findings.

Composite midsoles use softer, more compliant material laterally. Stiffer material is used medially to create a functional varus wedge. With the force of impact shifted medially, the moment arm is decreased and pronation rate slowed. The soccer shoe has yet to take full advantage of this midsole technology. Heel flare is a midsole design element that has not been used in soccer. Lateral heel flare tends to increase pronation while medial heel flare decreases pronation. This is the reason why serious pronators should wear shoes with a straight last. Midsole hardness has a greater effect on pronation velocity than heel flare. Increased midsole width (up to 90 mm) has been shown to reduce pronation velocity and magnitude. Further increases in width, however, increase lateral leverage and pronation velocity.

The height of the heel also influences pronation. When hard materials are used in the midsole, increases in heel height increase lateral leverage and speed pronation (Fig. 10-16). It is believed that the use of softer materials that deform more at impact will lessen the negative effects of increased heel height due to added cushioning.

To summarize, the goal of contemporary midsole design is to create a heel with minimal height, moderate width, minimal flare, and bidensity composition. Soft cushioning material should be used laterally and stiffer material medially to slow pronation and improve shock distribution. These factors should theoretically combine to attenuate force impact and allow its effective absorption.

A unique determinant of stability in the soccer shoe is the stud shape and length. The longer the stud, the greater the instability of the platform. This is due to the increased moment arm the stud introduces to the system. Many times the studs are placed centrally on the outsole, further increasing potential instability. By placing the studs peripherally on the outsole, stability can be improved. Most stud designs use a central metal post, which may lead to possible pressure concentration over the sesamoids and metatarso-phalangeal joint of the great toe (Fig. 10-17). Foot pain is common in soccer players and radiographic studies have disclosed a high percentage of sesamoid bone fragmentation. It is not known whether this fragmentation is pathologic

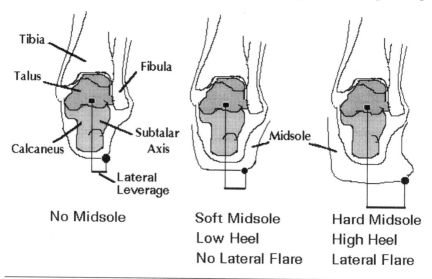

Figure 10-16. A hard midsole serves to create lateral heel leverage and speed pronation. Adapted from Nike, Inc., Beaverton, Oregon

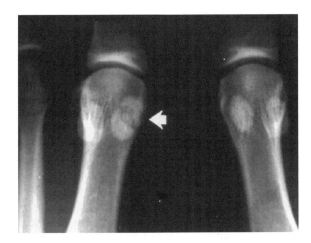

Figure 10-17. Fragmented sesamoid foot bone commonly seen in soccer players.

or adaptive in nature. Newer outsole designs are engineered with polydensity composite materials to improve force distribution and decrease foot pain.

Guidance

The role of guidance in the shoe is to control load and movement after heel-strike. One approach is to create increased torsional or twisting flexibility through the midfoot. This is thought to promote rearfoot stability and dynamic control of pronation. Increased torsion has not been well accepted by soccer players who, in general, prefer greater midfoot platform stability. As research proceeds in this area, new methods of rear and midfoot guidance will be tested and applied to the soccer shoe. Newer designs attempt dynamic foot guidance through platform contouring and strategic cushioning.

Friction

The role of friction (traction) is critical to the balance between injury prevention and performance enhancement. Friction is usually divided into two primary components; translation and rotation. It is thought that translational friction dictates a player's ability to make quick stops, starts, and aggressive cuts. The coefficient of translational friction depends on the interaction between the outsole and the playing field. The coefficient also is influenced by the relative velocity at contact between the shoe and surface.

Rotational friction depends on the moment of rotation, which depends on the pressure distribution in the contact area and its size. This relationship is believed to increase injury rates when rotational friction levels are high. Traditional shoe design has attempted to minimize the presence and effects of rotational friction. This has proved to be difficult, since rotational friction is increased when there are gains in translational friction. When rotational friction is limited, translational friction also decreases and performance degrades.

If friction levels are too high, the loaded leg may remain fixed to the ground too long after ground contact while the body twists to change direction. This places high torsional and shear stresses on the foot, ankle, and knee leading to injury. When friction is limited, slipping leads to poor performance. The optimal level of friction varies considerably depending on the shoe, surface, sport, and playing conditions. For example, the optimal coefficient of friction for a soccer shoe on a dry, artificial turf field should be between 0.8–1.2. In contrast, the optimal coefficient of friction for a tennis player on a hard court is only 0.5. As outsoles evolve, the issue of friction will continue to be a challenge.

Flexibility

The flexibility of the soccer shoe is another major concern. Most players desire a supple, snug-fitting boot that gives them a feel for the ball. Some shoe designers have attempted to make the instep of the soccer shoe stiffer to increase ball velocity during the kick, but did not succeed. The rigidity of the midfoot bones far exceeded that of the materials and dominated velocity production during the kick. Despite this failure, other major companies continue to experiment in this area. One major manufacturer has added fins and ridges to the instep and toe, claiming novel ball aerodynamics and increased shooter power. These claims have yet to be substantiated by monitored scientific study and players have been reluctant to accept their use.

The shoe can also be too flexible. Increases in torsional flexibility were not well received by most players and supple toe-boxes can cause injury. Repetitive microtrauma and macrotrauma of the toes and forefoot are among the most common of soccer injuries, occurring in 40% of players. Classic turf-toe is well described in soccer players. It results from chronic hyperextension of the great toe (Fig. 10-18a). There is also a variation of turf-toe called soccer-toe (Fig. 10-18b). Soccer toe is the result of joint damage from hyperflexion of the great toe metatarso-phalangeal joint. Both injuries are caused by violent foot contact in the normally supple soccer shoe toe-box. Another chronic problem of a lightweight, flexible shoe is that they allow subungual hematomas from blunt trauma or pressure. This is seen in 60% of players and can combine with blistering to severely hamper performance. A wider, stiffer toe-box may alleviate some of these problems.

Energy Conservation

The assumption that performance can be enhanced through shoes that improve energy conservation is suspect. Wearing shoes costs the body a 3–5% oxygen penalty. Each additional 100 g of padding further increases this by 1%. Intelligent shoe design can curtail some of these losses through energy transfer efficiency. The efficiency of athletic performance is the result of energy exchange between body segments containing muscles, tendons, and ligaments. In running, this exchange of potential and kinetic energy is more than 500 Joules per step. The quadriceps cycle through 70 Joules of this while 70 Joules is stored and transferred by the Achilles tendon to initiate the next step. An unknown quantity is absorbed and transferred by the windlass mechanism of the arch (Fig. 10-10). In contrast to this, the athletic shoe absorbs less than 10 Joules during each step and returns only 6 Joules. Approximately 40% of the energy transferred to the shoe is lost, with most of it dissipated as heat. Complicating matters further is the inability of the shoe to easily convert axially directed force into horizontal distribution force. This is a complex task that the human subtalar joint performs gracefully during gait. Eventually, many of the

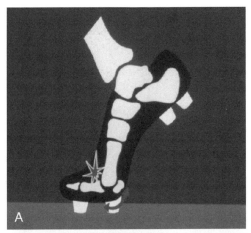

Figure 10-18. A; Turf-toe results from chronic hyperextension of the great toe. B; Soccer-toe results from chronic hyperflexion of the great toe.

lessons of energy conservation learned from radical new prosthetic designs for amputees will find their way into athletic shoe design. For now, the prospects of performance enhancement through energy conservation by the shoe are limited in scope. Energy return is even less likely and will require advanced technologic breakthroughs in material design and engineering.

It is more likely that performance enhancement through energy conservation and return will first come from advancements in artificial surfaces because the spring constants and surface areas of such fields are so much greater. This can already be seen in track and field and will probably influence contact sports such as soccer. These new surfaces will bring a new set of challenges to shoe designers.

Conclusion

As soccer shoes and equipment advance, players and coaches will face the daunting task of finding those products that truly limit injury and improve performance. As we have seen, these goals are often conflicting and require sophisticated design and execution. Future research will result in new midsole and outsole designs. Hopefully, this chapter has provided some insight into the once inaccessible world of athletic shoe performance and design.

SUGGESTED READINGS

Eichner ER. The epidemiology of running injuries. Techniques in Orthopedics 1990;5:1–7.

Ekstrand J, Nigg BM. Surface-related injuries in soccer. Sports Med 1989;8:56–62.

Fu FH, Feldman A. The biomechanics of running: practical considerations. Techniques in Orthopedics 1990;5:8–14.

Lohnes JH, Garreft WE, Jr., Monto RR. Soccer. In: Fu F, Stone DA, eds. Sports injuries—mechanisms, prevention, treatment. Baltimore: Williams & Wilkins, 1994;603–624.

Lufter LD. Shoes and orthoses in the runner. Techniques in Orthopedics 1990;5:57–63.

Nigg BM, Segesser B. Biomechanical and orthopedic concepts in sport shoe construction. Med Sci Sports Exerc 1992;24: 595–602.

Nike Research Review. Lateral Ankle Sprains. July/August, 1989.

Nike Research Review. Rearfoot Stability. November/December, 1989.

Nike Research Review. Physical Tests. January/February, 1990.

Volpe AJ, Amis JA. Evaluation and management of foot disorders in the runner. Techniques in Orthopedics 1990;5:47–56.

III

• Soccer Team Physician

11

The Role of the Team Physician

Douglas W. Brown

Introduction

The role of team physician varies depending on the type of team, the location, team management, and many other factors. This chapter will discuss the role of the team physician from both a general perspective and the specific perspective of a national team physician traveling to international competitions. The author has had 10 years' experience traveling with various U.S. National Teams during international competition and accompanied the Women's National Team to the World Cup in Sweden in June 1995, and the Men's National Team to the World Cup in Italy in 1990.

Personal Qualities of a Team Physician

It is important for the team physician to want to be part of the team. The successful team physician needs to assume a subservient role. In many ways, the team physician is the least essential member of the team. Certainly the players, coaches, and trainer contribute more directly and routinely to the team's mission. When someone is ill or seriously injured the team physician becomes essential. In this context, the customary role of the physician involving leadership and responsibility is required. The most successful team physician is one who has the respect of the players, coaches, and team administrators as a knowledgeable health professional and can comfortably adapt to a supportive team player role.

The team physician should be committed to being useful and helpful to the team. Often, international team travel delegations are small in number, and there are many chores and duties that need to be done. Although most of these chores are not in the usual domain of a physician, he/she should be willing to help whenever possible. Reports from coaches, administrators, and players indicate that the best team physicians are those who are willing to help in a variety of ways when they are not practicing medicine. Chasing balls during training, carrying equipment, and running errands are some of the ways the team physician can be of assistance. The cardinal sin for a team physician is to be unavailable to players or coaches. Shopping and sightseeing need to be limited and carefully scheduled. When traveling with teams, the players are the first priority with the needs of the coaches, administrators, and personnel from other teams addressed only after the needs of the players have been met.

Efforts to maintain optimal communication with the coaches, players, and administrators are also important. It is essential to work closely with the trainer to maintain a professional and unified approach to managing injuries and illness. It is unacceptable to compete with or undermine the role of the trainer, whose credibility with the team is essential to his/her ability to function effectively. In most situations, the trainer has worked with the players for a long time and knows them better than the team physician. Therefore, a team physician should not do anything to diminish the trainer's rapport with all members of the team, including the physician. There is no place for medical rivalry or competition on any team.

The physician needs to maintain a professional demeanor and at the same time strike a balance between being too aloof and too cozy. Being upbeat and optimistic is always appropriate. Traveling long distances for international competition is stressful, and teams can use good humor and positive energy.

Finally, the team physician s role is not to second guess or to make soccer judgments regarding players or coaches. Although it is important to understand some aspects of team politics and interpersonal relationships to perform more effectively and professionally, it is risky to become too involved. It is better for the team physician to be perceived as neutral and above team politics.

Responsibilities

The team physician's first responsibility is the safety and well being of each athlete.

Thoughtful and thorough preparation is the team physician's most effective tool. The following list summarizes the most important issues that lend themselves to thorough preparation:

1. Learn the history of the team. This includes accomplishments, successes, failures and their coaching and player histories.

2. Know the names of all players and as much about their athletic and personal histories as possible.

3. Know where you will be traveling, especially the local public health issues. You can consult with the Center for Disease Control (CDC) in Atlanta for details on issues such as local health conditions and recommendations for immunizations. The U.S. State Department can also supply information about embassies and consulates. These resources can be useful for information about quality local medical personnel and facilities. Research into these issues should be done before travel.

4. Select appropriate medications and equipment for your trip. William Heinz, MD developed a standardized medical kit for U.S. Soccer (see Chapter 12) based on extensive travel and sports medicine experience. Reviewing the contents of this kit, or other similar sources, can be helpful in anticipating your medicine and equipment needs. If you are traveling to a location where traveler's diarrhea is likely, you need to

bring enough medications to treat an outbreak and provide prophylaxis for the entire team or delegation. It will be necessary to know the prescribing information and side effects of all the medications in the kit. In this regard, the *Physicians Desk Reference* (PDR), the *Washington Manual of Medical Therapeutics,* and other medical texts are available in an electronic book format.

5. Talk with people who have been with the team previously or have traveled to the same locale. It is essential to talk to the trainer (and coaches, if appropriate) and any other physicians who have been with the team recently.

6. Find out about any special medical problems, current injuries, and previous significant injuries for any members of the team and delegation. Effectiveness will be greatly enhanced by knowing this information ahead of time. Most teams have records for each player that list all pertinent medical information, past medical histories, medications, allergies, hospitalizations, surgeries, and other information. Be sure that either these records or personally created summaries of them accompany the team for possible reference. Ideally, previous contact with the players, including periodic or pre-participation screening, will familiarize the physician with the players.

7. Finally, find out about drug testing that might be done. Many over-the-counter cold preparations and herbal remedies contain banned substances, so players must be educated and advised to avoid inadvertent positive drug tests. In all drug testing situations, be on constant alert so that medications containing banned substances are not accidentally prescribed. Be thoroughly familiar with all the categories of banned substances and with all of the medications in the kit that contain them. Labeling all such medications with highly visible warning labels (to remind the physician, trainer, and players) and keeping them separate from the rest of the drugs in the medical kit can be helpful. Up-to-date information on drug testing and banned substances can be obtained from the U.S. Olympic Commmittee in Colorado Springs, CO, and through the following Hotline [(800) 233–0393 (M-F 8AM–5PM Mountain Time)].

In Country

After arrival, it is necessary to think about possible escape routes and emergency medical facilities and personnel. If a player sustains a serious head, neck, eye, cardiac, chest, abdominal, or musculo-skeletal injury at training or during a game, it is necessary to know ahead of time where and how to take them for emergency care. Often, in foreign countries, language and communication are issues. Fortunately, most international competitions have local organizing committees that assign liaisons to deal with the team. Be sure to make arrangements with them to be available in the case that local medical care is needed or the player and team physician need to be accompanied to the hospital.

Besides an acute injury to a player, other medical situations could arise that require help. Sometimes an illness in a player or member of the team delegation can become serious. Appendicitis, cholecystitis, cardiac conditions, and serious or prolonged gastroenteritis can all occur during travel to different countries, and hospitalization or consultation with an appropriate specialist may be necessary. Do not forget that there is always the option of calling familiar expert consultants back home for advice.

For serious injuries or illnesses, the team physician must insure proper care, even when other medical personnel are directly involved. Sometimes the best option is to fly the patient home, by international air ambulance if necessary. Often, the best choice is to allow local medical specialists to treat the patient. In this case, the team physician should be prepared to monitor and assist in whatever way is best for the patient. Physicians traveling with U.S. teams have been called upon to oversee abdominal surgery in the Soviet Union, hospitalization for a serious head injury in China, emergency eye surgery in Hong Kong, and transient quadriplegia accompanying a cervical spine injury in Mexico. All of these situations were handled well because the team physician acted appropriately and responsibly to secure and monitor local specialized medical care.

Food and water

Good food and safe drinking water are essential issues for every traveling team. Although rarely necessary, the team may need to bring their own food and water. In every location the team physician and staff need to work together to secure adequate sources and supplies. As a general rule, it is best to rely on bottled water in virtually every location. Gastroenteritis can develop after drinking tap water, even in first class hotels in developed countries.

The problem with unsafe water is often the worst in tropical or sub-tropical climates where adequate hydration is most essential for players. Adequate water supplies (sometimes 2 liters or more per player) need to be available at training and games. Players must be educated about the risks of even washing out their mouths or brushing their teeth with potentially contaminated sources. Ice is also a problem, since it is often made from questionable sources. If necessary, players have to be educated to drink fluids that are warm.

In addition to being responsible for securing safe water and educating the players about avoiding all sources of contamination, the team physician must also be thoroughly familiar with the physiology of exercise and hydration as it applies to athletic performance so he/she (along with the trainer) can advise players and coaches about what they should be drinking and when. Although not within the scope of this chapter, it is also important for the team physician to be well informed about the proper use of carbohydrate sports drinks, the role and proper timing of carbohydrate ingestion to enhance athletic performance, and nutrition in general. Personal experience shows that all athletes are eager for advice regarding nutrition, especially as it applies to enhancing athletic performance. There are many opportunities for education and discussions on these issues during travel situations.

Food can also be a source of contamination and disability from gastroenteritis. In most locations, especially in hot climates and developing countries, raw vegetables should be avoided. Although salads can be tempting, keep in mind that players have been disabled with gastroenteritis from eating raw vegetables in salads in a setting that seemed perfectly safe.

Food can be a problem simply because it is unfamiliar and, therefore, players do not consume it in sufficient quantities to sustain intense athletic performance. Try to work with the hotel to provide American style dishes that the players will readily consume in sufficient quantities and in the proper ratios of carbohydrate, protein, and fat. The U.S. Women's National Team practices good nutrition and recognizes the relationship between proper diet and performance, especially in intense competition. For example, at the World Cup in Sweden in June 1995, they had to play 6 strenuous matches in 11 days. Team personnel worked closely with each hotel staff in Sweden to have familiar, popular, and appropriate dishes served at each meal.

In summary, food and water are important issues for the traveling team and the team physician. Too much attention cannot be given to insuring proper hydration and nutrition during international team travel and competition. The successful team physician should be thoroughly familiar with all the medical and nutritional issues. Long airplane flights and changes in climate can quickly induce dehydration. The physician should be prepared to help players stay free of unnecessary illness (or treat it when it occurs) and provide nutritional counseling, especially as it relates to performance enhancement. The team physician needs to be prepared to make the decision to treat players with prophylactic antibiotics to prevent traveler's diarrhea by weighing the cost and side effects of the prophylaxis against the risk of illness.

Dress and Demeanor

The following thoughts are based on personal experiences and those of colleagues. These issues can be very important to the success of the team physician.

Personal appearance is an important issue for physicians in the hospital, office, and while working as a team physician. When traveling with a team, it is better to avoid looking like a player or a fan. The team physician should dress with some consideration for professional image, especially when not familiar with the team (in which case the players will be more likely to make judgments based on appearance). Informality, in dress and manner, is generally good around athletes. When carried out appropriately, and especially after the physician is known and accepted by the team, informality enhances communication. When informality and familiarity are interpreted by players as the team physician trying too hard to be one of the players or trying to impress, then it works to the physician's disadvantage. It is best to be open and approachable and to recognize the distinction between the players and the physician. The physician's position on the team is unique as neither player, coach, or administrator. The team physician must be friendly and open to enhance effectiveness, but also remember that the ability to be effective requires respect from the players.

At games and at training the physician may often get involved and should dress appropriately. Many national team physicians dress in business suits or a jacket and tie. Although this is appropriate and supports their professional image, dressing in the same game warm-up apparel that the coaching staff wears is not inappropriate.

The team physician will not get along with all players, coaches, administrators, and staff. Yet, it is essential to try. The distraction of interpersonal problems between the physician and players is detrimental to the team and is not tolerated by coaches.

It is useful if the team physician adopts the attitude that he/she is there to serve the medical needs of the team and the coaches. It is not appropriate or effective to try to impress players, coaches, or anyone else associated with the team. This is especially true in medical situations. The most effective team physician is honest. If confronted with an unfamiliar situation admit lack of knowledge and do thorough research to arrive at an answer.

Most elite athletes have had a lot of experience with doctors. Perhaps some of it has been bad, but more often than not, the experiences are good. As team physician, it is necessary to measure up to the level of the players favorite doctors back home. Since the players have not chosen their team physician, but have been assigned, the situation requires humility and honesty on the part of the physician. Being helpful and willing to go the extra mile also improves the physician's chances of acceptance.

Attributes of a Good Team Physician

The role of the team physician was discussed with several elite U.S. National Team players. They were asked what they thought were the key attributes of a good team physician. Their responses coalesced on the following three general categories.

Affability, or general social skills, was recognized as an important quality in a team physician. This includes the ease with which the players can talk to the physician and the ability to communicate well with members of the team and staff.

Availability was also cited as an important factor. The physician should be there when needed by players either medically or just to talk. The physician is not effective or helpful when out every night or shopping during the day. The best way to be available is to spend time in the training room (on the road, a hotel room is designated as the training room). In that setting, the physician can watch players interact with each other and with the trainer, and become part of the interaction. It is useful to arrange specific times when the training room will be open for players who want to see the physician or the trainer. Before training, when the trainer is taping, is an appropriate time. Meals are also an ideal time. While eating, the physician can announce availability or arrange meetings with specific players. It is best for the team physician to attend all team meals, since this is such a reliable time to communicate. Contact with the trainer during meals is also important to insure regular communication.

Ability refers not only to actual skills and ability, but to the confidence that is conveyed nonverbally when examining players. One player explained that she had been examined so many times by so many different doctors that she could get a sense of a physician's competence and confidence simply by the way he examined her and explained things. Just as players are being watched and evaluated when they play, the team physician is being watched and evaluated when providing care.

Qualifications of a Team Physician

Since many injuries in soccer are musculo-skeletal, a team physician needs to have a good understanding of orthopaedic diagnosis and treatment. At the same time, the team physician will encounter many general medical problems including upper respiratory infections, gastroenteritis, asthma, migraine headaches, and acute allergic reactions. The best team physician, therefore, is one with both orthopaedic and general medical skills. It is beneficial to have experience dealing with athletes and teams under travel situations. It is also essential to have an athletic trainer to work with who has similar skills and experience.

Coaches

It is essential for the coaches and the team physician to have an appropriate relationship, governed by mutual respect. Without the respect of the coach, the team physician cannot function effectively. A good coach will communicate directly and openly with the team physician (and vice versa) and will defer to the physician in matters of medical judgment and player safety. In an ideal relationship there is no need for the physician to be assertive. Yet, the physician must be prepared to be assertive to protect players from injury, inappropriate risk, or abuse. If the coach and physician understand and appreciate each others' roles, responsibilities, professionalism, and value to the team they can work together to solve problems effectively.

Helpful Hints

1. Have small paper envelopes for dispensing medications. Names, doses, and times can be written on the envelope to help busy and forgetful players remember to take their medications.
2. Dispense medications only one or two days at a time and keep careful records of who is getting what. This insures frequent communication with the athletes being treated.
3. Keep a log of who is being treated, for what, and with what medications. It is easy to get distracted and forget to finish a course of medication or to skip medication that would be useful. Players can be forgetful under stressful circumstances. Through good organization the physician can prevent oversights.
4. Meals are a good time to dispense medications, especially nonsteroidal antiinflammatory drugs (NSAIDs) since they are best taken with meals. Many players take them and it is easy for them to leave their medications in their rooms.
5. Because so many players are accustomed to taking NSAIDs on their own, and since multiple varieties are now available over-the-counter, it may be necessary to counsel players about taking multiple agents at the same time and overdosing.

SUGGESTED READINGS

Bangsbo J. Fitness training in football: a scientific approach. Denmark: August Krogh Institute, University of Copenhagen, 1994.

Bangsbo J. The physiology of soccer: with special reference to intense Intermittent exercise. Denmark: August Krogh Institute, University of Copenhagen, 1993.

Clark K. Nutritional guidance to soccer players for training and competition. J Sports Sci 1994;12:543–550.

DuPont H, Ericsson CD. Prevention and treament of traveller's diarrhea. N Engl J Med 1993:328:1821–1827.

Foods, Nutrition and Soccer Performance. Proceedings of an International Scientific Consensus held February 10–11, 1994 in Zurich. J Sports Sci 1994;12 (Special Issue).

Maughan RJ, Leipor JB. Fluid replacement requirements in soccer. J Sports Sci 1994;12:529–534.

Reilly T, Lees A, Davids K, et al. Science and football. New York: E. & F. N. Spon, 1988.

Washington Manual of Medical Therapeutics. Franklin Electronic Publishers, 122 Burrs Rd., Mt. Holly, NJ 08060 [(800) 762–5382]

12  Medical Equipment for the Team Physician

William J. Heinz

The decision about which medications and supplies to take to an athletic event can be difficult. Only some of the factors that must be considered are type and location of event, weather conditions, number of players, and their sex. The complexity increases when traveling internationally with a large team. In these situations, the team physician needs to function as a portable emergency room because it may not be possible to rely on the local medical community for care of an illness or injury. Preparing a medical kit of this magnitude can overwhelm even a well-experienced team physician because of the scope and amount of medications required. The initial costs and the costs to maintain and restock the kit can be staggering. Because it is assumed that the physicians traveling with the National Teams have strong backgrounds in orthopaedics, these issues are not addressed. It is also assumed that the physicians are competent in performing basic life support. Because of space limitations and infrequent use, the medications and supplies necessary for advanced cardiac life support (ACLS) are not included.

The physicians with US Soccer were confronted with a multitude of potential problems when they traveled with the National Teams. Therefore, the Sports Medicine committee of US Soccer elected to develop standard medical kits for use when the National Teams travel internationally. These kits are maintained by US Soccer and are transported with the team equipment, minimizing the handling and customs problems. A unique feature of the US Soccer Medical Kit is its design based on a medical guide (see Appendix). This guide describes treatment options for many medical and emergent conditions encountered when traveling with a team. It is arranged in a cookbook fashion, using major body systems as categories. It includes information and warnings about medication dosing, common side effects, and drug interactions. It also identifies any medications in the kit that are subject to drug testing. All of the medications described in the medical guide are included in the medical kit.

The US Soccer Medical Kit is too big to be contained in a simple black bag. It is comprised of one large case and several smaller bags (Fig. 12-1). The case is portable, lockable, waterproof, and virtually indestructible. It allows quick, easy access and protects the contents from damage. The bags contain

Figure 12-1. US Soccer Medical Kits.

large splints and bulky materials, such as casting supplies. The tropical kit contains IV solutions with set-up equipment and extra medications for traveler's diarrhea. A fanny pack, called the break-out kit, allows ready access to frequently-used medications. This is especially useful when the main kit is inaccessible, such as on a plane.

When the main case is first opened the contents appear to be in total chaos (Fig. 12-2). However, there is a logical order to the location of the contents. The plastic bags on top contain medications and supplies grouped together for specific body systems (i.e., eye kit; ear, nose, and throat (ENT) kit; dental trauma kit; suture kit; creams/lotions; and dressing supplies). These are designed to allow access to all supplies and medications necessary to treat a specific problem, such as a laceration or epistaxis.

Under the plastic bags are the vials of medications (Fig. 12-3). Each is labeled on the top and front, providing easy identification both in and out of the case. Also included on the label is the strength and expiration date of the medication. All medications are repackaged into uniformly-sized vials to conserve space. The medications are grouped by category (i.e., anti-inflammatories and antibiotics) starting on the left side of the case. Instruments (i.e., diagnostic kit and blood pressure cuff) and tall bottles of liquids are located on the right side. A copy of the medical guide and lists of all medications and supplies included in the kits are located under the foam in the lid of the case.

Standardizing the medical kits and providing a medical guide insures that all US Soccer National Teams are adequately covered from a medical stand-

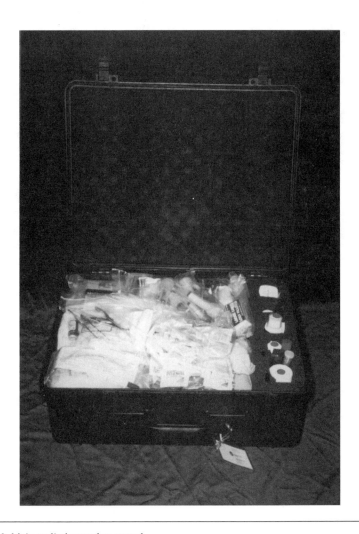

Figure 12-2. Main medical case when opened.

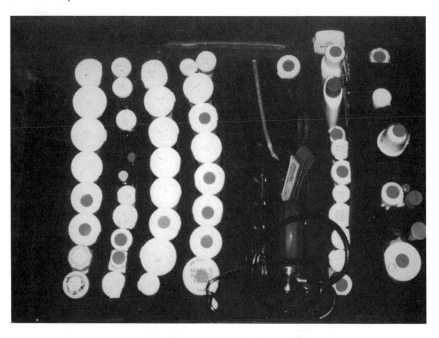

Figure 12-3. Vials of Medications.

point when they travel. However, these kits and guides are not perfect. They cannot contain every medication or supply the physician may need to treat a medical condition. The medical guide deals only with medical and dental conditions.

It is helpful for every physician to customize the kits. Minor modifications in types or brands of medications can make the kits easier to use and the physician more comfortable. For example, if the physician treats traumatic epistaxis with a nasal pack of surgical patties soaked in a cocaine solution, it is necessary to include the cocaine since it is not part of the standard kit. It is also recommended that the physician include surgical gloves that fit and extra nonsteroidal anti-inflammatory medication. All physicians who use the US Soccer Medical Kits and Guide provide feedback so that the kit can be improved.

Table 12-1 is the list of medications and supplies included in the medical kits. These lists are divided into: (a) prescription medications, (b) non-prescription medications, (c) equipment/supplies, (d) tropical kit, and (e) break-out kit. The US Soccer Medical Guide follows the medications and supplies list.

This information about the US Soccer Medical Kits and Guide should help the team physician to devise and develop a personal black bag. With the kit and careful planning, the physician should be able to handle most medical and emergent conditions at sporting events and while traveling.

Table 12-1

List of Medications Included in the U.S. Soccer Medical Kits

Prescription Drugs

Drug	Generic	Quantity
Augmentin	amoxicillin, 500 mg; clavulinic acid, 125 mg	50
Bactrim DS Caplets	trimethoprim, 160 mg; sulfamethoxazole, 800 mg	50
Benadryl injectable 50 mg/ml 1 cc	diphenhydramine	2
Cipro, 500 mg	ciprofloxacin, 500 mg	50
Cleocin T-Gel, foil packs	clindamycin	30
Compazine injectable, 10 mg/2 cc*	prochlorperazine, 10 mg/2 cc	2 vials
Cortisporin otic suspension 10 cc**	polymyxin B-neomycin-hydrocortisone	1 bottle
Decadron tabs 1.5 mg*	dexamethasone, 1.5 mg	100
Depo-Medrol, 40 mg/ml, 1 cc*	methylprednisolone, 40 mg/ml, 1 cc	2 vials
Doxycycline 100 mg tablets	doxycycline, 100 mg	50
Entex-LA*	phenylpropanolamine HCl, 75 mg; guaifenesin, 400 mg	50
Epinephrine ampule 1:1000, 1 cc*	epinephrine	2
Flagyl 250 mg tablets	metronidazole, 250 mg	30
Flexeril 10 mg	cyclobenzaprine, 10 mg	25
Halcion 0.25 mg tablets*	triazolam, 0.25 mg	50
Hismanal 10 mg	astemizole, 10 mg	50
Hydrocortisone cream 1% 1 oz**	hydrocortisone cream	2
Indocin 25 mg	indomethacin, 25 mg	30
Lidex cream 0.05% sample tubes**	fluocinonide, 0.05%	50
Lidocaine 1% without epinephrine, 10 cc vial*	lidocaine, 1%, without epinephrine, 10 cc	2 vials
Lidocaine 2% with epinephrine, 10 cc vial*	lidocaine, 2%, with epinephrine, 10 cc	1 vial
Marcaine 0.5%–10 cc vial**	bupivacaine 0.5%	1
Monistat 3 suppositories	miconazole	3
Morphine ampule, 10 mg/cc, 1 cc*	morphine, 10 mg/cc, 1 cc	2
Motrin 800 mg caplets	ibuprofen, 800 mg	30
Naprosyn 500 mg caplets	naproxen, 500 mg	30
Nasalide nasal spray 25 ml**	flunisolide, 25 ml	2

Table 12-1 (continued)

Prescription Drugs

Drug	Generic	Quantity
Neosporin ophthalmic ointment, 1/8 oz tube	polymyxin B-bacitracin-neosporin	2
Neosporin ophthalmic solution, 10 ml bottle	polymyxin B-bacitracin-neosporin	2
Nizoral cream 2% sample tubes	ketoconazole 2%	50
PCE tabs 500 mg	erythromycin, 500 mg	50
Pen-VEE K, 500 mg	penicillin V, 500 mg	50
Pepcid, 40 mg	famotidine, 40 mg	30
Procardia 10 mg	nifedipine, 10 mg	12
Proventil inhaler–17 gm	albuterol, 17 gm	2
Pyridium 200 mg tabs	phenazopyridine	15
Rocephin, 1000 mg vial	ceftriaxone, 1000 mg vial	1
Silvadene cream 20 gm tube 1%	silver sulfadiazine	2
Silver nitrate sticks	silver nitrate sticks	1 canister
Sulf-10 10% ophthalmic solution, 1 cc	sulfacetamide	4
Tetracaine ophthalmic 0.5%, 1 cc**	tetracaine ophthalmic	4
Tigan suppositories 200 mg*	trimethabenzamide	5
Tylenol #3*	codeine, 30 mg.; acetaminophen, 300 mg	50
Tylox capsules*	oxycodone, 5 mg; acetaminophen, 500 mg	25
Valium injectable vial–5 mg/cc-2 cc*	diazepam, 5 mg/cc–2 cc	2 vials
Valium tabs, 5 mg*	diazepam, 5 mg	20
Zovirax ointment 5%, 3 gm tube	acyclovir 5%	1

* *Substances are banned by USOC/NCAA.*

**Substances that need written notification for testing officials.*

Table 12-1 (continued)

Over-the-Counter Drugs

Item	Generic	Quantity
Advil 2-tablet packs	ibuprofen	30
AlternaGEL, 5 oz	aluminum hydroxide	1 bottle
Anbesol gel 0.25 oz	benzocaine	1 tube
Aspirin, 325 mg, enteric	acetylsalicylic acid, 325 mg, enteric	50
Benadryl 25 mg	diphenhydramine, 25 mg	30
Benadryl cream 0.5 oz	diphenhydramine	1 tube
Betadine ointment 1 oz	povidone-iodine, 10%	1
Chapstick 10 gm	lip balm	1 tube
Ex-Lax tabs	phenolphthalein	18
Gaviscon tabs chewable	alum. hydroxide, 80 mg; mag. trisilicate, 20 mg	42 (1 box)
Hibiclens 4 oz	antimicrobial skin cleanser	1
Imodium caplets, 2 mg	loperamide	24
Kaopectate tabs	attapulgite	40
Mastisol	dressing adhesive	2 amp
Mycitracin ointment	polymyxin B-bacitracin-neomycin	30
Neo-Synephrine Nasal Spray 1%, 15 ml*	phenylephrine	1 bottle
NIX 1% Lotion	permethrin	1 bottle
Pepto-Bismol tabs	bismuth subsalicylate	30
Phillip's Milk of Magnesia tabs	magnesium hydroxide	24
Pre-Sun 39 sunscreen 4 oz	para-aminobenzoic acid	1
Robitussin DM, 8 oz bottle*	guaifenesin, dextromethorpan	1
Saline, sterile, nonpreserved 8 oz	saline, sterile	2
Solarcaine spray 3 oz	benzocaine	1 bottle
Tears Plus, 15 cc	lubricant eye drops	2
Tinactin powder 1.5 oz	tolnaftate	1
Tylenol Extra-Strength, 2-packs, gelcaps	acetaminophen	50

Substances are banned by USOC/NCAA.

Table 12-1 (continued)

Breakout Kit

Item	Generic	Quantity
Advil, sample packets	ibuprofen	20
Band-Aids, coverlet	coverlet bandages	20
Benadryl, 25 mg	diphenhydramine	10
Cipro, 500 mg	ciprofloxacin	10
Dramamine tabs*	dimenhydrinate	36
Epi-pen*	insect sting emergency kit	1
Gaviscon chewable tabs	alum. hydroxide, 80 mg; mag. trisilicate, 20 mg	6
Imodium, 2 mg	loperamide, 2 mg	20
Lidex, 0.05% cream, samples**	fluocinonide	10 tubes
NTG, 1/150 gr	nitroglycerin 1/150 gr	1 bottle
Sudafed tablets	pseudoephedrine	48
Swiss Army knife, multi-purpose		1
Transderm Scop, 1.5 mg	scopolamine patches, 1.5 mg	1 box
Tylenol Extra-Strength packets	acetaminophen	20
Tylenol No. 3*	codeine, 30 mg; acetaminophen, 300 mg	10

* *Substances are banned by USOC/NCAA.*

***Substances that need written notification for testing officials.*

Tropical Kit

Item	Generic	Quantity
Alcohol sponges		10
Angiocath, 18 gauge		2
Angiocath, 20 gauge		2
Copper wire, 12 gauge (to hang IV bag)		2 feet
D5 Ringer's lactate, 1000 cc bags		4 bags
Gauze sponges, 3 × 3		10
IV tubing, extension and spike		2 set-ups
Non-sterile gloves		2
Tape, Dermacel, 1"		1
Tape, Dermacel, 1/2"		1
Tourniquet, rubber		1
Bactrim DS	trimethoprim, sulfamethoxazole double-strength	50

Table 12-1 (continued)

Tropical Kit

Item	Generic	Quantity
Cipro, 500 mg	ciprofloxacin, 500 mg	300
Imodium AD caplets, 2 mg	loperamide hydrochloride, 2 mg	100
Kaopectate tabs	attapulgite	100
Pepto-Bismol tabs	bismuth subsalicylate	60

Equipment

Item	Quantity
Adaptic 3 × 3	5
Adhesive tape remover pads (Clinipad)	5
Alcohol sponges	20
Alumafoam finger splint, 3/4″	1
Band-Aids, coverlet, elasticized	30
Blood pressure cuff	1
Casting tape–Fiberglass-2″	4
Casting tape–Fiberglass-4″	4
Cautery, battery-powered	1
Cervical collar–soft	1
Chux	5
Coban–4″	2
Cotton-tipped applicators–sterile	10
Drape, barrier, sterile	2
Drape, towel, fenestrated, sterile	2
Dressing, Surgipad–5″ × 9″	2
Eye patch sponges	4
Fluor-1 strip (ophthalmic)	5
Forceps, angled, nasal	1
Gauze sponges, 3 × 3	20
Gloves, latex medical, sterile	2 pairs
Gloves, latex non-sterile	10
Inflatable forearm splint	1
Inflatable leg splint	1
Inventory list	
Knee immobilizer	1
Medication envelopes 2″ × 4″	50
Nasal speculum	1
Nasopharyngeal tubes, adult	1
Nasostat hemostatic nasal balloon	1
Needle-18 gauge–1.25″	5
Needle-22 gauge–1.25″	5
Needle-27 gauge–1.25″	5

Table 12-1 (continued)

Equipment

Item	Quantity
Otoscope/ophthalmoscope kit (Welch Allen)	1
Plastic bags, heavy duty	5
Pocket mask with unidirectional flow valve	1
Razors, disposable	2
Reflex hammer	1
Scalpel, disposable, sterile #11	3
Scalpel, disposable, sterile #15	3
Scissors, bandage, all-purpose	1
Shoulder immobilizer, large	1
Steri-strips-1/4" × 4" packs	5
Sterile cottonoid (Codman) patties	1 package
Stethoscope-Littman	1
Stockinette, elastic–3" × 36"	1
Stockinette, elastic–4" × 36"	1
Suture kit, sterile (5 pieces*) reusable	1
Suture, 0 Ethilon	2
Suture, 4-0 Ethilon	3
Suture, 4-0 Silk	3
Suture, 4-0 Vicryl	3
Suture, 6-0 Ethilon	3
Syringe–12 cc	5
Syringe–3 cc w/attached 22-gauge needle	5
Syringe–35 cc	2
Tape measure	1
Tape, Dermacel, 1"	1
Tape, Dermacel, 1/2"	2
Tape, Elasticon, 2"	1
Telfa dressing, 3" × 4"	5
Thermometer, oral	1
Tongue depressors, sterile	10
Vaseline packing strip (nasal) 1/2" × 72"	1
Velcro tourniquet	1
Webril cast padding–2" roll	4
Webril cast padding–3" roll	4
Webril cast padding–4" roll	4

Suture kit contents:

1. *Needle holder-4 3/4"*
2. *Iris scissors-4 1/2"*
3. *Suture forceps*
4. *Suture scissors*
5. *Mosquito clamp*

Appendix: US Soccer Medical Guide

This medical guide and the travel kits were put together in an attempt to make life a little simpler for the physicians traveling with US Soccer. I tried to include everything typically needed while traveling with the soccer teams. However, the kits are not all inclusive, so it is important you look over the lists of drugs and supplies prior to leaving to see if there is anything you want to add or substitute. Also, you should check with the team trainer before leaving to see if any of the players have medical conditions which require medication not included in the kits (such as Theo-Dur for asthma). It is recommended you bring several sheets of your office letterhead and a prescription pad (in case needed.)

This Medical Guide is meant to be just that—a *guide* which provides suggestions for treatment of medical and emergent problems (not orthopaedic problems). There are different ways to treat problems, so don't feel you must use the suggestions provided. Generally, it is recommended you use the primary treatment guidelines unless there is an allergy or contraindication. I would welcome all input (good and bad) about the Guide and the Kits. Good luck, (and enjoy your trip.)

William M. Heinz, M.D.
May 1994

Kits

The Medical Kits are divided into sections: (a) prescription medications; (b) over-the-counter medications; (c) supplies/equipment; (d) Third World Country Kit, and (e) break-out kit (hip pack). The prescription medications, over-the-counter medications, and supplies/equipment (large black case) should go with the physician/team to all practices and games. Cast supplies will be in the trainer's kit. The break-out kit is meant to be used for easy access to medication while traveling and on day trips. The Third World Country Kit includes IV fluids and apparatus, extra anti-diarrheal medications and antibiotics. This Kit will only be included in trips to third world countries. When traveling to third world countries, it is recommended you contact the CDC (*CDC, Health Information for International Travel, Superintendent of Documents, U. S. Government Printing Office, Washington, DC 20402 — Phone: [404] 332–4559*) or State Department beforehand to obtain information about malaria prophylaxis and/or other local medical problems, as well as facilities you might use in case of a significant problem.

Please Note: All banned or "permission only" substances will be notated:
*Substances are banned by USOC/NCAA, and
**Substances which need written notification given to testing officials.

For these substances, usage must be declared by the team physician in writing (in the case of the USOC, via the Chief Medical Officer to the International Olympic Committee). The following information *must* be provided: the compound used, date used, time of administration, route of administration, and amount given. For questions about medications banned by the International Olympic Committee, call the U.S. Olympic Committee's drug hotline at 1–800–233–0393.

Medical Guide

Head

This guide for evaluation and treating head injuries was developed by the Colorado Medical Society and appears to be very useful and appropriate. I have reproduced it here for your convenience. Copies may be obtained by writing the Colorado Medical Society at P.O. Box 17550, Denver, Colorado 80217–0550.

Eye

1. *Corneal Abrasions* typically present with complaints of a lot of pain and photophobia. They are diagnosed with the aid of fluorescein stain and a cobalt blue filtered light. (This is in the ophthalmoscope apertures.) The damaged epithelium stains a brilliant yellow-green color. Install fluorescein stain by first wetting the fluorescein with a drop of saline solution then, pulling the lower lid down, place the tip of the fluorescein strip in the lower cul-de-sac. The fluorescein may sting a little bit, so caution the patient about this. Remember to check for a foreign body. I recommend you do *not* patch the eye, but if you do, patch for *no longer than 8 hours.*

> *Treatment*
>
> *Primary:* Sulf-10 (sulfacetamide), 2 drops, q 2 hours, while awake; Sulf-10 ointment, qhs.
>
> *Alternative:* Neosporin (polymyxin B-bacitracin-neomycin) ophthalmic solution, 2 drops, q 2 hours while wake; Neosporin ophthalmic ointment, qhs.
>
> *Duration:* The primary/alternative treatments are to continue for two days.
>
> *Analgesia:* May need analgesic, as abrasions can be very painful.
>
> *Equipment:* Sunglasses (for photophobia).

2. *Conjunctivitis* presents with redness and sensation of grittiness, rarely with pain. Mucopurulent discharge is present in bacterial conjunctivitis; watery discharge in viral conjunctivitis. Usually 3 to 5 days of treatment is sufficient. Avoid patching; keep fingers out of eyes; isolate patient to prevent spread to roommates.

Table 12-1

Medical Guide: Concussion Guidelines

Grading Concussions in Sports and Guidelines for Return to Play

Severity	Signs/Symptoms	First Concussion	Second Concussion	Third Concussion
Grade I (mild)	Confusion without amnesia No loss of consciousness	May return to play if asymptomatic* for at least 20 minutes	Terminate contest/practice. May return to play one week after asymptomatic*	Terminate season. May return to play in three months if asymptomatic*
Grade II (Moderate)	Confusion with amnesia** No loss of consciousness	Terminate contest or practice. May return to play one week after asymptomatic*	Consider terminating season but may return to play one month after asymptomatic*	Terminate season. May return to play next season if asymptomatic*
Grade III (Severe)	Loss of consciousness	Terminate contest or practice and transport to hospital. May return to play one month after two weeks asymptomatic* Conditioning allowed after one week asymptomatic*	Terminate season. May return to play next season if asymptomatic*	Strongly discourage return to contact/collision sports

(Adapted from Colorado Medical Society. Guidelines for the management of concussion in sports. Sports Medicine Committee, Colorado Medical Society, May 1990)

*No headache, confusion, dizziness, impaired orientation/consciousness or memory dysfunction during rest or with exercise.

**Post-traumatic amnesia: amnesia for the events following the impact.

Treatment

Primary: Neosporin ophthalmic (polymyxin B-bacitracin-neomycin) drops, 2 drops, q 2 hours while awake; Neosporin ophthalmic ointment, qhs.

Alternative: Sulf-10 (sulfacetamide), 2 drops, q. 2 hours while awake; Sulf-10 ointment, q.h.s.

Duration: Both primary and alternative treatments are to continue for 3 days.

3. Foreign bodies present with pain, redness and tearing. Use tetracaine** ophthalmic drops in affected eye for topical anesthetic. These drops sting, so be sure you warn the patient. Evert upper lid to look into the superior cul-de-sac; remove an embedded foreign body with an 18-gauge hypodermic needle placed on the end of a cotton-tipped applicator.

Treatment

Anesthetize cornea and conjunctiva, remove foreign body, instill antibiotic.

Primary: Neosporin (polymyxin B-bacitracin-neomycin) ophthalmic ointment.

Alternative: Sulf-10 (sulfacetamide), 2 drops, q. 2 hours while awake; Sulf-10 ointment, q.h.s.

Duration: Double eye patch for 8 hours, then discontinue eye patch. Continue Neosporin ophthalmic (polymyxin B-bacitracin-neomycin) drops, 2 drops, q. 2 hours, while awake; Neosporin ophthalmic ointment, q.h.s., × 48 hours.

4. Hordeolum (stye): This is an inflammation of the meibomian glands of the upper lid.

Treatment

Primary: Hot soaks, incise with tip of needle and drain, no antibiotic needed unless there is a diffuse cellulitis, then treat for Staph. aureus: Augmentin (amoxicillin, clavulinic acid), 500 mg., p.o., q. 8 hours, × 10 days) (alternative: PCE (erythromycin) 500 mg., q. 12 hours × 10 days).

C. Ear

1. External otitis (swimmer's ear): Signs and symptoms—itching, pain, discharge from ear canal.

Treatment

Cortisporin** (polymyxin B-neosporin-hydrocortisone) otic suspension, 4 drops into ear canal, q.i.d., × 10 days. Use cotton plug to keep drops from dripping out when patient stands up. If auricle is red or lymphadenopathy is present, add Augmentin (amoxicillin, clavulinic acid), 500 mg., q. 8 hours × 10 days (*Alternative:* PCE (erythromycin), 500 mg., q. 12 hours × 10 days).

2. Otitis media: Signs and symptoms—fever, pain, recent upper respiratory infection or sinus congestion, hearing loss. Tympanic membrane usually red and bulging. There may be discharge if the tympanic membrane has ruptured.

Treatment

Primary: Augmentin (amoxicillin, clavulinic acid), 500 mg., q. 8 hours × 10 days.

Alternative: Bactrim DS (trimethoprim, sulfamethoxazole), 1, q. 12 hours × 10 days.

Note: Add **Cortisporin**** (polymyxin B-neosporin-hydrocortisone) otic suspension, four drops, q.i.d., × 10 days to ear canal if tympanic membrane has ruptured. Use cotton plug to keep drops from dripping out when patient stands up.

3. *Auricular hematoma:* (bleeding between the cartilage and the perichondrium).

Treatment

Primary: Aseptic aspiration and compressive dressing to prevent re-accumulation of the hematoma.

D. Nose

1. *Nosebleed*

Treatment

Primary: Manual pinching of the nares for 4 to 5 minutes. Use silver nitrate cautery if you can localize the area of bleeding. If unable to control bleeding, use surgical patties soaked in **epinephrine*** 1:1,000 or **Neo-Synephrine*** (phenylephrine) nasal spray 1% and pack anterior nasal chamber until full. Keep pack in place for 30 minutes or more. If still unable to control bleeding, use Nasostat hemostatic nasal balloon. Inflate with 15–20 cc. of air or saline. If a posterior nasal bleed is present, admission to hospital is required for a posterior pack (Do not try this on your own— ENT consult is needed for control of airway.)

2. *Sinusitis:* Usually tender to percussion over affected sinus.

Treatment

Primary: Septra DS (trimethoprim, sulfamethoxazole), 1, q. 12 hours, × 10 days.

Alternative: Augmentin (amoxicillin, clavulinic acid), 500 mg., q. 8 hours, × 10 days.

Note: Also, use Neo-Synephrine* (phenylephrine) nasal spray to help decrease swelling, p.r.n. Avoid decongestants as these can dry the sinuses too much and interfere with the treatment of the infection.

3. *Allergic rhinitis:* Felt to be IgE-mediated degranulation of mast cells and basophils. Symptoms include congestion, itching, rhinorrhea and swelling of nasal membranes.

Treatment

Hismanal (astemizole), 10 mg., daily (H-1 antihistamine) [*NOTE: Use of Hismanal with erythromycin or ketoconazole is contraindicated because of possible cardiac reactions: prolonged QT, torsades de pointes, cardiac arrest.*]; **Nasalide**** (flunisolide), 2 sprays each nostril, b.i.d. (This is a steroid spray and must be used prophylactically; therapeutic benefit requires several days to weeks of use before evident. Warn patient that the spray stings for several minutes when administered.) Use Entex LA* (phenylpropanolamine hydrochloride, 75 mg. and guaifenesin, 400 mg.), b.i.d., for congestion.

E. Mouth/Throat

1. *Tooth Trauma*

(a) *Fracture involving only enamel:* This is primarily a cosmetic problem. Use emery board to smooth edges.

(b) *Fracture of enamel and dentin or caries that are sensitive to cold/heat or pressure:* IMR (intermediate restorative material) is a compound that contains cloves and is useful as an analgesic when there is exposed sensitive pulp or nerve. It is mixed 1 drop liquid to 1 scoop of powder until a paste is made, this is then packed into the cavity or the fracture. This will set up over several hours and is a temporary filling material until definitive treatment can be obtained. If the injury or carie is not sensitive and you just want to fill a cavity, you can use Cavit-G which is already premixed as a paste. This, however, has no analgesic effect.

(c) *Avulsed tooth:* If a player entirely avulses a tooth, the tooth should be carefully recovered with care not to touch any of the roots. It should be rinsed in tap water or in saline, and should be placed back into the socket with attention paid to the orientation of the tooth. The tooth then needs to be stabilized. That can be accomplished by mixing equal portions of Dycal (base ivory plus base dentin) and applying this to the teeth in front and behind the avulsed tooth forming a bridge to help stabilize it. This is a temporary stabilizing method and permanent stabilization will need to be accomplished within several days.

(d) *Loose crowns/bridges:* These can be stabilized by mixing equal proportions of Dycal (base ivory and base dentin) and using this around the sides of the crown or bridge to help hold it in place. This is a temporary repair and a permanent repair needs to be done within several days.

(e) *Abscessed tooth:* The definitive treatment is to remove the tooth. The patient should also be treated with an antibiotic. *Primary:* Pen Vee K (penicillin V, 500 mg., q. 6 hours on an empty stomach, × 7 days. *Alternative:* Cipro (ciprofloxacin) 500 mg., b.i.d., × 7 days.

2. *Oral Soft Tissue Injury*

Treatment

Close mucosal lacerations with silk suture (to avoid irritation). Through-and-through lacerations should receive antibiotic coverage of Augmentin (amoxicillin, clavulinic acid), 500 mg., q. 8 hours, × 7 days (alternative: Cipro (ciprofloxacin), 500 mg., b.i.d., × 7 days).

3. *Sore Throat (exudative pharyngitis):* Group A/Group C Strep, "viral," infectious mononucleosis are the most common etiologies.

Treatment

Primary: Pen-Vee K (penicillin V), 500 mg., q. 6 hours on empty stomach × 10 days.

Alternative: PCE (erythromycin), 500 mg., q. 12 hours, × 10 days.

Note: Avoid ampicillin/amoxicillin (Augmentin [amoxicillin×clavulinic acid]) if suspicious of mononucleosis, as this will cause a rash. Do not use Bactrim DS (trimethoprim-sulfamethoxazole).

F. Respiratory

1. *Asthma:* Remember that not all that wheezes is asthma. Upper airway obstruction, chemical irritants and allergic reactions can also cause wheezing. Also, asthma may present as a cough and not as wheezing.

Treatment

Proventil* (albuterol) inhaler, 2 puffs, q. 5 minutes, until wheezing has broken. Proventil is a beta-2 sympathomimetic medication that is frequently used for exercise-induced asthma (EIA). Some of the players may be on other asthmatic medications, including different beta-2 sympathomimetic agents such as Ventolin (albuterol), Brethaire (terbutaline), Maxair (pirbuterol) or Alupent (metaproterenol). These all work to relax the smooth muscles in the bronchials. There is some cross-over to beta-1 receptors, which can cause tachycardia. Other medications used for exercise-induced asthma include Intal (cromolyn sodium), which is believed to inhibit release of mediators of hypersensitivity in the lung by preventing degranulation of mast cells (must be used prophylactically). Inhaled corticosteroids are frequently used prophylactically for EIA, including Beclovent* (beclomethasone) and Azmacort* (triamcinolone). Oral theophylline preparations (Theo-Dur, Slo-bid) are also used in the treatment of asthma. *None of these other medications are included in the kit* as they do not work as rapidly as the beta-2 agonists. If the wheezing does not break with Proventil, consider the possibility that it is due to an allergic reaction.

If wheezing is due to an allergic reaction, use: (see also Allergic Reactions)
- (a) *EpiPen** (epinephrine), 0.3 cc., 1:1000, subcutaneously or IM (thigh);
- (b) Benadryl (diphenhydramine), 50 mg., IV or deep IM; (H-1 antihistamine)
- (c) Pepcid (famotidine), 40 mg., p.o., (H-2 antihistamine);
- (d) *Systemic steroids*.*
- (e) Control airway.

2. Acute bronchitis: Etiology is usually viral, but also caused by Mycoplasma, Chlamydia and Pertussis.

Treatment

Primary: PCE (erythromycin), 500 mg., q. 12 hours, × 14 days.

Alternative: Doxycycline, 100 mg., q. 12 hours, × 14 days.

For cough, treat with Robitussin DM*, 10 cc., q.4–6 h. *Codeine** is also a very effective cough suppressant (Tylenol No. 3*).

3. *Pneumonia:* The most common etiologies are viral, Mycoplasma and Strep. pneumoniae.

Treatment

Primary: PCE (erythromycin), 500 mg., q. 12 hours, × 14 days.

Alternative: Doxycycline, 100 mg., q. 12 hours, × 14 days.

Note: If very sick, add Rocephin (ceftriaxone, 500 mg., IM/IV, q. 12 hours, or Augmentin (amoxicillin, clavulinic acid), 500 mg., p.o., q. 8 hours, × 14 days.

G. Cardiac

1. *Chest pain:* Myocardial infarction frequently presents with left-sided chest pain/pressure radiating to the neck, jaw, left arm or shoulder, shortness of breath, nausea, diaphoresis or anxiety. Try to relieve pain. Get help.

Treatment

Step #1

Primary: Nitroglycerin 1/150, sublingual, q. 3 minutes, up to 3.

Alternative: Procardia (nifedipine), 10 mg., sublingual (use needle to pierce capsule and squirt contents sublingually).

Step #2

Morphine sulfate*, 2 mg., IV for pain and anxiety control

Step #3

Start IV fluid and oxygen when available.

H. Gastrointestinal

1. *Travelers' diarrhea*

Prophylaxis

Primary: Bactrim DS (trimethoprim-sulfamethaxazole), 1 daily.

Alternative: Cipro (ciprofloxacin), 500 mg., 1, daily.

On trips to third world countries, I usually start prophylactic antibiotics on all players and coaches/staff on the first day of the trip, and continue to the end of the trip. ***Bactrim DS must be immediately discontinued at <u>first</u> signs of skin rash or adverse reaction.*** If diarrhea develops, stop the prophylactic antibiotic and start treatment (see below). Do not allow the players to drink *any water which is not bottled,* including ice. Also, do not allow them to eat food from street vendors or from marketplaces, and no salads or uncooked vegetables. It is acceptable, however, to drink soft drinks, beer/wine and drinks prepared from boiled water.

Treatment

Primary: (A) Cipro (ciprofloxacin), 500 mg., b.i.d., plus (B) Imodium (loperamide), 4 mg. initially, followed by 2 mg. after each unformed stool (up to 16 mg. per 24 hours [replacement for Lomotil]), plus (C) Kaopectate (attapulgite), 2 caplets per day.

Alternative: (A) Septra DS (trimethoprim, sulfamethaxazole), 1, b.i.d., plus (B) Imodium (loperamide), 4 mg. initially, followed by 2 mg. after each unformed stool (up to 16 mg. per 24 hours), plus (C) Kaopectate (attapulgite), 2 caplets per day.

Note: Be sure to maintain hydration and don't be afraid to use IV fluids. When diarrhea stops, you can stop the higher doses of antibiotics and resume the prophylactic treatment.

2. *Nausea/Vomiting*

Treatment: Add more medications, as needed, to control nausea/vomiting

(a) Pepto-Bismol (bismuth subsalicylate) is a good, all-around choice. This also helps treat diarrhea, if that develops.

(b) Tigan* (trimethobenzamide) suppositories, 1 per rectum, t.i.d. to q.i.d.

(c) Compazine* (prochlorpenazine) injectable, 5–10 mg., deep IM injection (upper outer quadrant of buttocks), q. 3–4 hours. Compazine* can be given very slowly IV (not to exceed 5 mg./minute as this can cause hypotension). Total dose Compazine*: IM and/or IV - not to exceed 40 mg. per 24 hours.

3. *Motion Sickness:*

(a) Transderm Scop patches (scopolamine patches). This is for prevention of motion sickness. It can cause dizziness and some people cannot tolerate it. Apply four hours prior to start of travel. The patch lasts for three days. Be sure to wash your hands after application, as the scopolamine will dilate your pupils.

(b) Also available are Dramamine* (dimenhydrinate) tablets for 1–2 tabs, q. 4–6 hours, as needed.

4. *Gastritis/Heartburn:*

Antacids are very effective and they work quickly. Options in kit are Gaviscon (aluminum hydroxide, magnesium trisilicate) and AlternaGel (Aluminum hydroxide). Pepcid (famotidine) is also very effective at 40 mg., t.i.d., as needed (H-2 antihistamine works to block HCl production in stomach).

I. Genitourinary

1. *Sexually-transmitted diseases:*

(a) Gonorrhea: Symptoms are spontaneous urethral discharge and dysuria.

Treatment

Primary: Rocephine (ceftriaxone), 250 mg., IM (single dose), plus Doxycycline, 100 mg., p.o., b.i.d., × 7 days (to treat for Chlamydia).

Alternative: Cipro (ciprofloxacin), 500 mg., p.o., × 1 dose, plus Doxycycline, 100 mg., p.o., b.i.d., × 7 days (to treat for Chlamydia).

(b) Nongonococcal urethritis: Etiologies are Chlamydia, ureaplasma, Trichomonas; only gonorrhea has spontaneous urethral discharge.

Treatment

Primary: Doxycycline, 100 mg., p.o., b.i.d., × 7 days.

Alternative: PCE (erythromycin), 500 mg., p.o., b.i.d., × 7 days.

2. *Prostatitis:*

Treatment

Primary: Cipro (ciprofloxacin), 500 mg., p.o., b.i.d., × 14 days.

Alternative: Septra DS (trimethoprim, sulfamethoxazole) or Doxycycline, 100 mg., p.o., b.i.d, × 14 days.

3. *Urinary tract infection (cystitis/urethritis):*

Treatment

Primary: Septra DS (trimethroprim, sulfamethoxazole), 1, p.o., b.i.d. × 3 days.

Alternative: Doxycycline, 100 mg., p.o., b.i.d., × 3 days.

Note: If the patient fails to improve on a three-day regimen, culture the urine and treat for two weeks. Also, for local treatment of dysuria, use Pyridium (phenazopyridine), 200 mg., p.o., t.i.d., p.c., until symptoms resolve. This has a topical analgesic effect on the mucosa of the urinary tract. It turns the urine orange and can stain soft contacts and clothes.

4. *Vaginal yeast infections:* Symptoms: pruritis; thick, cheesy discharge.

Treatment

Primary: Monistat 3 (miconazole), one suppository, intravaginally × 3 days.

5. *Pubic lice (crabs/scabies):*

Treatment

Primary: NIX (permethrin) 1% lotion applied to affected areas for 10 minutes, then rinse off. Use fine-tooth comb to pubic hair to help remove the nits.

J. Skin/Soft Tissue

1. *Minor Abrasions/Minor Lacerations/Burns:*

Treatment

If minor, treat topically with Silvadene (silver sulfadiazine) cream and Adaptic dressing changes daily. If a cellulitis develops, add Pen-Vee K (penicillin V), 500 mg., q. 6 hours on empty stomach, × 10 days (alternative: PCE [erythromycin], 500 mg., q. 12 hours, × 10 days.

Note: All of the players should have their tetanus status updated prior to leaving on the trip and the trainer should be aware of their tetanus status. Therefore, tetanus vaccine is not included in the kits.

2. *Deep wounds/Lacerations/Human bites:* Cleaning, irrigation and debridement are the most important treatment. If at all possible, don't close these wounds, (except on the face for cosmetic reasons). *Treat them all prophylactically with antibiotics.*

Treatment

Primary: Augmentin (amoxicillin, clavulinic acid), 500 mg., q. 8 hours, × 10 days.

Alternative: PCE (erythromycin), 500 mg., q. 12 hours × 10 days.

3. *Contact dermatitis:* Symptoms: pruritus, erythema, serous-filled bullae.

Local Treatment

Primary: **Lidex**** (fluocinonide), 0.5% cream, t.i.d. to affected areas. **This is much too strong for use on the face.** For the face, use **Hydrocortisone**** cream 1% t.i.d.

Note: In addition, an antihistamine can be used to help with the itching.

Primary: Hismanal (astemizole), 10 mg., p.o., daily. [**NOTE:** *Use of Hismanal with erythromycin or ketoconazole is contraindicated because of possible cardiac*

reactions: elevated QT, torsades de pointes, cardiac arrest.]
Alternative: Benadryl (diphenhydramine), 25 mg., p.o., q.i.d.

For widespread contact dermatitis, treat with systemic steroids, using a *dexamethasone** taper dose, utilizing *Medical Guide Charts 2 and 3,* provided below.

Table 12-2

Relative Steroid Potencies (The following oral steroids and dosages are equally potent)	
Steroid	Dosage
Hydrocortisone*	20 mg
Cortisone*	25 mg
Prednisone*	5 mg
Methylprednisone*	4 mg
Dexamethasone*	0.75 mg
Betamethasone*	0.6 mg

Table 12-3

Medical Guide Chart: Dexamethasone Taper Dosages (Decadron* (dexamethasone), 1.5 mg. tabs, should be taken in the following amounts, and can be taken all at once, q.A.M. The total number of tablets taken will be 63.)		
Day	Number of Tablets	Running Total
1	6	6
2	6	12
3	6	18
4	6	24
5	6	30
6	6	36
7	5	41
8	5	46
9	4	50
10	4	54
11	3	57
12	3	60
13	2	62
14	1	63

4. *Fungal infections (athlete's foot/jock itch/tinea versicolor):*
Treatment
Primary: Nizoral (ketoconazole) cream 2%, apply daily to affected areas for 14 days. *Alternative:* Tinactin (tolnaftate) power to feet and groin.

K. General

1. *Allergic reactions:* Treat according to level of severity.
Treatment
(a) *Mild reaction,* including a mild rash, itching, no wheezing or airway compromise: Hismanal (astemizole [H-1 antihistamine]), 10 mg., p.o., daily.

[*NOTE: Use of Hismanal with erythromycin or ketoconazole is contraindicated because of possible cardiac reactions: elevated QT, torsades de pointes, cardiac arrest.*]

(b) *Moderate reaction* with diffuse rash, more itching but still not wheezing or airway compromise, add Pepcid, 40 mg., t.i.d. (famotidine [H-2 antihistamine]). Consider oral steroids (Decadron* [dexamethasone] taper dose) and see *Contact Dermatitis,* under SKIN/SOFT TISSUE, for dosage and schedule. (page 10)

(c) *Severe allergic reaction* with rash, itching and wheezing/airway compromise will require:

(1) *EpiPen** (Epinephrine), 0.3 cc IM (thigh), q. 5 minutes until wheezing is resolved.
(2) Control airway.
(3) IV fluids.
(4) Systemic steroids (*Decadron** [dexamethasone], taper dose).

13 Preparticipation Physical Examination

W. Benjamin Kibler
G. Naessens

Preparticipation physical exams (PPFE) may be discussed in terms of their usefulness, who needs to perform them (a medical doctor, physical therapist, athletic trainer, primary care physician, or the team physician), what aspects of fitness should be screened, and what are the financial and legal implications of the examinations. This chapter will deal with these points and try to create a framework for preparticipation physical examinationss in soccer players that will benefit coaches, players, and team physicians.

Purposes

The purposes of the PPFE are to do an evaluation that is specific to soccer demands, prepare the athletes to play soccer, and minimize the risk of injury. To fully achieve these purposes, a framework must be created to collect the appropriate data.

Framework

This framework should be based on the "critical point" model of the athlete interaction in sport. In this model, the "critical point" in athletic activity that determines maximum performance and injury occurs when the specific demands of the activity interact with the individual's musculoskeletal base for response to those demands (Fig. 13-1). For soccer this would involve knowledge of the anatomic (running, jumping, start/stop, kicking), biomechanical (kinetic chains of kicking and jumping), and physiologic (metabolic and motor unit recruitment) demands inherent in the sport at various age and skill levels. It would also include a plan for evaluation of the medical and musculoskeletal base of the athlete that focuses on the areas that will experience the most demand during play.

Goals

One of the primary goals of the PPFE is to identify athletes "at risk." The "at risk" athlete may be susceptible to medical conditions, incompletely rehabilitated from an old injury, or predisposed by biomechanical or physiological maladaptations to a new injury. Since soccer acts as a stressor on many organ systems throughout the body, the entire body needs to be able to respond in a normal physiological manner through functional and structural

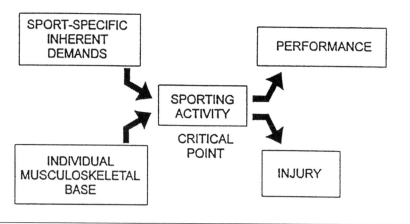

Figure 13-1. Critical Point for interaction between the sport and the athlete.

adaptation to the demands. Therefore, all systems should be checked for medical conditions that could be worsened by the high demands of sports or that have a higher exposure injury risk in a contact, endurance sport like soccer. Some of these conditions include cardiovascular abnormalities and risk factors, mononucleosis-induced fatigue, splenomegaly, exercise-induced bronchospasm, or diabetes. Emphasis should be placed on the musculoskeletal system, since it is the most injured or dysfunctional system in soccer. In addition to evaluation of incompletely healed injuries, it is necessary to look for other musculoskeletal conditions that could predispose a player to injury such as flexibility, strength, and alignment. A small percentage of athletes will have conditions that will disqualify them from soccer. A larger number will have biomechanical or physiological maladaptations that need to be corrected for maximum play. For the majority of the athletes, however, the goal of the PPFE is to provide a starting point for soccer specific conditioning programs. The PPFE, by defining the capabilities of the athletes in strength, flexibility, and aerobic base, can serve as a starting point to improve or refine these capabilities.

Methods

History

All participants in the PPFE should complete questionnaires concerning their past medical, musculoskeletal, and family histories. This outlines areas to focus on during the physical examination. However, this information must be checked by medical personnel because the athletes can be incomplete or unsure. Several examples of medical, family, and orthopedic history forms are referred to in the suggested readings. The questions should be in a simple "yes-no" format. Tables 13-1–13-5 are examples of some of these forms.

The personal history should contain questions about all medical problems that the athlete may experience and questions about health-related symp-

Table 13-1

Personal Medical History Questionnaire			

Name _____

Have you personally had any of the following medical problems?

	Yes	No	Physician's comments
Allergies	___	___	_____
Asthma	___	___	_____
Chronic cough	___	___	_____
Pneumonia	___	___	_____
Tuberculosis	___	___	_____
Heart disease	___	___	_____
Chest pains	___	___	_____
Shortness of breath	___	___	_____
Heart murmur	___	___	_____
High blood pressure	___	___	_____
Epilepsy	___	___	_____
Fainting spells	___	___	_____
Diabetes	___	___	_____
Cancer	___	___	_____
Hernia	___	___	_____
Missing kidney or other paired organ	___	___	_____
Emotional illness	___	___	_____
Excessive weight loss	___	___	_____
Mononucleosis	___	___	_____
Contusions	___	___	_____
Vision problems	___	___	_____
Hearing problems	___	___	_____
Operations	___	___	_____
Irregular menstrual periods	___	___	_____
Heat intolerance	___	___	_____
Frequent headaches	___	___	_____

Table 13-2

Orthopedic History Questionnaire

Name _____

Have you personally had any of the following orthopedic problems?

	Yes	No	Physician's comments
Neck injury	___	___	_____
Back injury	___	___	_____
Shoulder injury	___	___	_____
Elbow injury	___	___	_____
Wrist injury	___	___	_____
Hand injury	___	___	_____
Other arm injury	___	___	_____
Rib injury	___	___	_____
Hip or pelvis injury	___	___	_____
Knee injury	___	___	_____
Ankle injury	___	___	_____
Foot injury	___	___	_____
Other leg injury	___	___	_____

Table 13-3

Family Medical History Questionnaire

Name _____

Has anyone in your immediate family (father, mother, grandparents, brothers, or sisters) had any of the following?

	Yes	No	Physician's comments
Death under age 40 from heart disease	___	___	_____
Heart disease	___	___	_____
Diabetes	___	___	_____
High blood pressure	___	___	_____
Tuberculosis	___	___	_____
Alcohol or drug abuse	___	___	_____
Fainting spells	___	___	_____
Asthma	___	___	_____

Table 13-4

Annual Health Status Review

Name _____ School _____

Age _____ Date of Birth _____ Sex _____

Date of initial medical evaluation _____

Date of current medical reconsideration _____

Please answer the following questions.

1. Have you ever been hospitalized or had surgery or a major   Yes   No
   illness since your aforementioned initial medical evaluation?

2. Are you currently ill in any way?   Yes   No

3. Have you had a major injury (including brain concussion)   Yes   No
   since your aforementioned initial medical evaluation?

4. Do you currently have any incompletely healed injury?   Yes   No

5. Are you taking any medication on a regular or   Yes   No
   continuous basis?

6. Are you currently taking any short-course medication   Yes   No
   for a specific current illness or another reason?

7. Do you know of or do you believe there is any health   Yes   No
   reason why you should not participate in the
   _____ (school)
   _____ (sport) athletic program at this time?

Table 13-5

Exercise-Induced Bronchospasm (EIB) Questionnaire

Name _____

Instructions: For "yes" answers, indicate whether you have experienced the symptoms recently, whether you experience it with a cold or infection, and whether it occurs related to exercise.

	Yes	No	Recent (within past 2 months)	With (colds infection)	Exercise (before, during, after)
1. Eyes					
A. Itchy	___	___	_____	_____	_____
B. Watery	___	___	_____	_____	_____
C. Puffy	___	___	_____	_____	_____
2. Nose					
A. Itchy	___	___	_____	_____	_____
B. Stuffy	___	___	_____	_____	_____
C. Sneezing	___	___	_____	_____	_____
D. Runny	___	___	_____	_____	_____
E. Hay fever	___	___	_____	_____	_____
F. Postnasal drip	___	___	_____	_____	_____
3. Sinus infection					
A. Yellow/green nasal discharge	___	___	_____	_____	_____
B. Tender sinuses/ headache	___	___	_____	_____	_____
4. Ears					
A. Popping sensation	___	___	_____	_____	_____
B. Ears feel full/congested					
C. Sensation of being in rising elevator	___	___	_____	_____	_____
5. Chest (after exercise)					
A. Cough	___	___	_____	_____	_____
B. Wheezing	___	___	_____	_____	_____
C. Noisy breathing	___	___	_____	_____	_____
D. Chest congestion	___	___	_____	_____	_____
E. Chest tightness	___	___	_____	_____	_____
F. Unable to get deep breath					
G. Asthma	___	___	_____	_____	_____

Table 13-5 (continued)

	Yes	No	Recent (within past 2 months)	With (colds infection)	Exercise (before, during, after)
6. *Skin Reactions*					
A. Hives	___	___	_____	_____	_____
B. Itchy skin	___	___	_____	_____	_____
C. Dry skin	___	___	_____	_____	_____
D. Swelling of skin	___	___	_____	_____	_____
E. Eczema	___	___	_____	_____	_____
F. Atopic dermatitis	___	___	_____	_____	_____
7. *Contact Dermatitis* (skin reacts to things that touch the skin)					
A. Underwrap	___	___	_____	_____	_____
B. Tape	___	___	_____	_____	_____
C. Sweat bands	___	___	_____	_____	_____
D. Deodorants	___	___	_____	_____	_____
E. After-shave lotion	___	___	_____	_____	_____
F. Elastic	___	___	_____	_____	_____
G. Other	___	___	_____	_____	_____
8. *Food and Medication*					
A. Aspirin	___	___	_____	_____	_____
B. Penicillin	___	___	_____	_____	_____
C. Sulfa drug	___	___	_____	_____	_____
D. Other medication	___	___	_____	_____	_____
E. Food allergy	___	___	_____	_____	_____
9. *Allergy or sensitivity to the following:*					
A. Dust	___	___	_____		
B. Animals/pets	___	___	_____		
C. Mold/mildew	___	___	_____	_____	_____
D. Pollen/grass	___	___	_____	_____	_____
E. Air pollution	___	___	_____	_____	_____
10. *Life-Threatening (systemic) reactions requiring hospital treatment*					
A. Shock from bee sting	___	___	_____		
B. Difficulty breathing	___	___	_____	_____	_____

Table 13-5 (continued)

	Yes	No	Recent (within past 2 months)	With (colds infection)	Exercise (before, during, after)
11. If you ran 1 mile and rested 15 minutes					
A. Would your chest feel tighter?	___	___	_____		
B. Would you experience coughing?	___	___	_____		
If yes to A or B above, are you more likely to have these sensations in					
A. Cold weather?	___	___	_____		
B. Certain seasons of the year?	___	___	_____		
C. Periods of air pollution?	___	___	_____		
12. Have you had skin test for allergies in the past	___	___	_____		
13. Have you had allergy shots? (immunotherapy)	___	___	_____		
14. Recent colds/chest colds	___	___			
15. Headache after exercise	___	___	_____		
16. Stomachache after exercise	___	___	_____	_____	_____
17. Have you taken any of the following medications?					
A. Antihistamine	___	___	_____	_____	_____
B. Decongestant/ cold medicine	___	___	_____	_____	_____
C. Antibiotics	___	___	_____	_____	_____
D. Bronchodilators (to open breathing passages)	___	___	_____	_____	_____
E. Other	___	___	_____	_____	_____
F. Are you taking any of these medications now?	___	___	_____	_____	_____
18. Have you ever been hospitalized for the following?					
A. Pneumonia	___	___	_____		
B. Asthma	___	___	_____		
C. Bronchitis/bronchiolitis	___	___	_____		
D. Other lung problem	___	___	_____		

(Note: The EIB Questionnaire was developed, printed, and distributed by the United States Olympic Committee, Colorado Springs, CO. Copyright 1990 by the USOC. Reprinted by permission.)

toms that may not be considered an illness, such as weight loss, fainting, or dizziness. Attention should be given to exercise-related symptoms such as abnormal tiredness or dizziness and risk factors such as mononucleosis (organ enlargement), viral symptoms (myocarditis), and smoking (reduced endurance capacity, heart and lung disease). The orthopedic history questionnaire is best organized by anatomical area and is useful for focusing the clinical exam on injury-prone anatomic areas. The value of the family medical history lies in identification of potential problems, which can be exacerbated by exercise. Examples would include family history of coronary arteriosclerosis, diabetes, hypertension, sudden death in exercise, and exercise-induced bronchospasm. Family histories of alcohol and drug abuse indicate risk factors for physiological health and socio-economical and cultural interaction of the athlete. This is especially true for children, because it can influence their attitudes toward sports. A specific questionnaire is used for exercise induced bronchospasm (EIB) (Table 13-5) because it is common (8–10% in adolescents), underdiagnosed, and often a cause of decreased performance in endurance activities. In soccer, which has a major endurance component and is mostly played on grass fields, this may be significant.

Testing Battery

The testing battery for the PPFE should consist of a screening medical examination, a musculoskeletal and posture examination, and an examination for performance parameters of flexibility, strength, and endurance. This medical examination should not be considered a replacement for the annual physical examination. Unfortunately, this is sometimes the only extensive examination an athlete gets during the year. Therefore, it should cover all major organ systems and be of sufficient depth to identify major problems. Once again, forms should be used (Tables 13-1–13-5). In the head, eye, ear, nose, and throat (HEENT) area, it is necessary to look for a normal eye function, healthy teeth, adenopathy, masses, and restriction of head motion. The chest examination focuses on cardiac murmurs and extra sounds, blood pressure (especially in the older athlete), wheezing and bronchospasms, chest deformities, gynaecomastia, and breast development in young girls, which can give an estimation of skeletal maturity. All diastolic murmurs and systolic murmurs that increase with Valsalva maneuver or that do not diminish when changing from a lying to a standing position should be investigated more intensively. The emphasis in the abdominal examination should be on intra-abdominal masses and hernias. Examination of the testicles, pubic hair pattern, and penis can determine maturational age and check for undescended testicles. Skin inspection for contagious diseases, arterial pulsations of the groin and legs, and a routine neurological screening should complete the general medical examination.

The musculoskeletal examination is a screening examination for conditions that may predispose to injury or incompletely rehabilitated conditions that may be reinjured. Information to guide the examination can be obtained from the musculoskeletal history questionnaire. Some examples of incompletely rehabilitated or healed problems are recurrent ankle sprains, knee instability secondary to anterior cruciate ligament (ACL) deficiency, or chronic hamstring muscle strain. Predisposing conditions to injury may be related to anthropometric characteristics like body composition (height, weight, fat distribution, somatotype), joint malalignment, ligamentous laxity, muscle inflexibility due to sport specific maladaptations, or bony problems such as tibial torsion or cavus feet.

First inspect the spine looking for scoliosis or hyperlordosis and then check general posture in the standing position. In this position, alignment of the lower extremities are observed. Specific attention is paid to leg length differences, genu recurvatum, knee varus or valgus and pes planus, and cavus or excessive pronation. All major joints must be checked for range of motion, alignment, and general muscle strength. The extent of this examination will be determined by the questionnaire and the amount and type of demands that will be placed on the athlete. Laboratory examinations are not recommended for routine PPFEs. Urinalysis as a screening test for kidney or blood analysis is difficult to justify on routine examination and needs to be reserved for specific indications such as suspected or actual diabetes, prolonged decreased performance, anemia, or chronic sore throat.

Performance parameter testing should be included in the PPFE. This may be as simple as field tests for toe touch, push-ups, and a mile run. However, more information can be obtained about an athlete's ability to withstand the demands of soccer through a more extensive and sport-specific screening, which is related to injury risk and conditioning. The first parameter to screen for is flexibility. Inflexibility may be a sports-related muscular maladaptation or it may be related to injury or treatment. There are several anatomic areas that may be inflexible as a result of playing soccer. The most common inflexibilities are the hamstrings, psoas, and hip adductors. The quadriceps, hip rotators, iliotibial band, and gastrocnemius are involved to a lesser extent. Although it appears that inflexibility places the athlete at some biomechanical disadvantage, there is a lack of consensus about the role inflexibility plays in injury risk. The combination of inflexibility and increased ligamentous laxity makes soccer players and other running athletes more prone to muscle strains and other overuse injuries.

Specific tests for flexibility are the sit and reach test (lower back and hamstrings), calf dorsiflexion with extended knee (gastrocnemius), spread sit (long hip adductors), cross sit (short hip adductors), maximal hip adduction in side lying (iliotibial band), maximum knee flexion in the prone position with pelvic stabilization (quadriceps), maximum hip extension under the same condition with knee flexed (psoas), maximum hip flexion with knee extended (hamstrings), and maximum internal and external hip rotation in 90° flexed hip position (hip rotators). Ligamentous laxity is screened by the amount of knee, finger, and elbow hyperextension, patellar mobility, thumb hyperabduction, and ankle inversion. Lower body joints, such as the knee and ankle, should be checked for posttraumatic instability. Flexibility evaluation is important in soccer players because flexibility is easily improved, soccer players are generally inflexible, and many young soccer players will be inflexible due to rapid bone growth during adolescence.

The second parameter to screen for is strength. Strength is composed of different factors (e.g., static force, dynamic force, explosive force, force endurance, maximal force) and depends on muscle mass and neuromuscular coordination. Soccer players need force for kicking the ball, sprinting activities, and body contact charges. Evaluation of force is specific to muscle and movement and is related to performance and injury risk prevention. The muscles primarily tested for soccer screening are the quadriceps, hamstrings, and gluteals. They may be tested by manual muscle testing, the amount of maximum weight for 1 repetition or 10 repetitions (1 rep or 10 rep max), and isokinetic devices (peak torque, total work, endurance ratio, quadriceps/hamstring [Q:H] ratio). Although there is no consensus on isokinetic testing values, the numbers (especially Q:H ratio) are objective and do have some relationship to force production and joint stabilization. In addition, soccer players frequently demonstrate hamstring, abdominal, and back muscle weakness. Therefore, leg raises and sit-ups should also be part of the strength screening evaluation program.

The third parameter to evaluate is power (force per time unit and explosive force). Soccer is a game of explosive, high intensity, short duration power bursts. More differences exist between high-level and low-level soccer players in anaerobic alactic (anaerobic power) characteristics than in aerobic power or endurance. Power can be measured by the standing vertical jump test (best suited for routine soccer screening), depth jumps, standing broad jump, or medicine ball throw. Other tests include maximum power development during a 10-second bicycle ergometer test, the Margaria stair climbing test, or calculations of time to peak torque from isoknetic measurements.

The fourth parameter to evaluate is anaerobic endurance, especially the alactic component. Movement analysis shows that soccer players usually cover short distances at high speed, although they cover up to 6 miles per match. The tests used to screen for this parameter are timing in the 20-yard dash, 3 by 5 point shuttle run with or without a ball, or the 5-dot drill (Figs. 13-2 and 13-3). Although the shuttle run is more soccer specific, the 5-dot drill will also

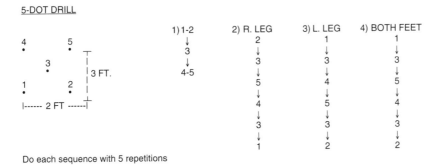

Figure 13-2. 5-Dot drill. The dots are laid out as shown. Each sequence should be done in the order as listed and should be completed five times.

3 X 5 DRILL

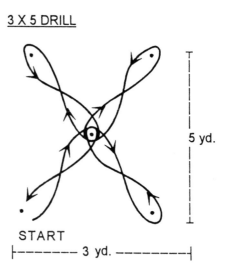

5 yd.

START

|——————— 3 yd. ————————|

Figure 13-3. 3 × 5 Drill. Start on one corner and go around the center as shown by the arrows. May run or may dribble the ball.

evaluate agility. Other tests that use onset of lactate production for measuring alactic characteristics are more sophisticated, but give no additional information than the above mentioned tests. The total work in the 30 second all-out Wingate test relies more on the lactic system, which is less important in soccer.

The last parameter to check for is aerobic endurance. Taking into account the average distance covered during a game (6–7 miles), the mean heart rate during a match (approximately 170), and laboratory values for average maximal oxygen consumption (VO$_2$max) of soccer players (55–65 ml/kg/min), this parameter certainly plays a role in performance and injury. This parameter may be more important in recovery episodes after anaerobic activity during the match. Therefore, a minimal endurance capacity is necessary and should be evaluated and conditioned since it is easily improved. Evaluation can be done by tests on the field and in laboratory conditions. Distance covered during the Cooper test, timing on a mile run, or a more specific soccer field run (Fig. 13-4) are useful for a general screening, although they may also rely on a contribution from the lactate system. Practice heart rate recovery measurements, indirect measurements of VO$_2$max by submaximal tests (step tests, physical working capacity at a heart rate of 170 [PWC170], Astrand-Rhyming nomogram), or estimations by maximal tests (Wmax) in endurance testing have some value and are appropriate for physiologic screening. Laboratory measurements of VO$_2$max and lactate threshold or lactate measurements on the field with determination of maximal running time can better characterize the metabolic systems involved, and may be beneficial at the highest levels of competition. Skilled interpretation is needed for proper evaluation of these tests.

SOCCER FIELD RUN

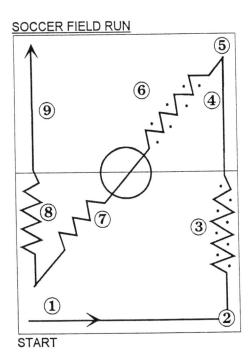

1. Sprint
2. Jump and head a ball
3. Run around cones
4. Run backwards
5. Pick up soccer ball
6. Dribble around cones
7. 3 running jumps
8. Plyometric jumps over lines
9. Sprint

START

Figure 13-4. Soccer field run. Follow the running requirements to test soccer skill and endurance.

Station Format

The organization of the PPFE depends on many medical and nonmedical factors. One of the major factors is the medical structure of the local community. While some communities offer highly organized programs and protocols, others are loosely organized, and some have no organization. The organization of the PPFE should be carried out as a "mass screening" in a station format, especially for the younger athlete involved in organized sports activities such as soccer. The station format can also be used on a smaller scale for smaller numbers of highly skilled athletes. This format allows for the smoothest traffic flow and best use of time, equipment, space, and personnel. Large areas such as a sports medicine center, a local school, or the local training facilities should be used. Clear lines of authority are necessary. Since a medical doctor is responsible for the medical part of the screening, he or she can be in charge. The station program can be oriented in a space available method or straight line method (Fig. 13-5). This requires the involvement of a diverse group of people including medical doctors, physical therapists, athletic trainers, nurses, interested parents, or other students. Tests need to be performed in a correct and reproducible manner. Therefore, the examiners and the person being examined need to be well instructed.

Proceeding to the next station should be allowed only after completion of the previous stations. This is best accomplished when each examiner signs the data collection paper the athlete carries. Finally, all data are collected at the

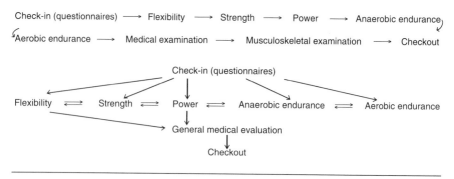

Figure 13-5. Organization of the stations: straight line (upper) or space available (lower).

final checkout. Here, they are analyzed and discussed by the physician and the people directly involved in the athlete's care.

Individual PPFEs can be done in individual doctor's offices. Although the privacy and increased individual attention may result in better medical examinations, this situation will not provide information about performance parameters, which are key to maximum effectiveness of the PPFE.

Selection of Specific Tests for Age and Skill Level

The previous discussion outlined the framework and methods of the PPFE. Age, maturation, skill level, and gender necessitate the use of an evaluation specific for the needs and demands associated with each category. Estimation of skeletal maturity (clinically or radiologically), which is a major determinant of the physiological profile of the growing child, needs to be done to adjust for age specific norms and needs. Prepubescent children have a reasonably well developed endurance capacity system, lower glycolytic system, and less efficient movement pattern. Therefore, puberty is important in influencing the physiological profile.

Problems with flexibility and certain overuse injuries, such as Sever's apophysitis and Sinding-Larsen apophysitis, are common in prepubescent athletes, especially those participating at a high level. A basic PPFE should be done on these athletes. It should start with emphasis on the axial skeletal posture. Flexibility should be checked in the lower back (sit and reach), hamstrings, quadriceps, and calf. Abdominal muscle strength can be checked by sit-ups. Shoulder girdle muscle strength, a measurement of the general strength of axial muscles, can be checked by push-ups. A general aerobic endurance test for this age group, such as a mile run, is helpful in the soccer screening and for education toward a general positive physical fitness attitude. Obese children in poor condition should especially be counseled in this context. During puberty, decreased flexibility is due to different rates in growth of bone and muscles. Since soccer players in general have decreased flexibility of the leg muscles, special attention should be paid to these characteristics in this age group.

Although strength gains during and after puberty may be impressive due to the effect of testosterone, muscle imbalances are common and should be evaluated carefully. Agility may remain decreased until coordination of the strength gains is achieved. Aerobic endurance measurements are important because they may be decreased during puberty. For college or high level athletes, the complete testing battery needs to be used. This is a time of maximum demands and maximum musculoskeletal base.

At a certain age, a decrease in physical profile characteristics is apparent. This directs the PPFE toward focusing more on the medical examination, such as screening for cardiovascular diseases, metabolic diseases, and musculo-osteoarticular degenerative pathology. Emphasis should be placed on prevention of potential problems by proper stretching, strengthening, and establishment of a good aerobic base.

Female athletes also need specific attention. Before puberty they can compete with their male peers. After puberty, size and power differences dictate sex specific play. Three areas for evaluation in females are increased joint laxity (e.g., patello-femoral problems, ACL injuries), the female athlete triad (amenorrhea, osteoporosis, eating disorders), and a higher risk for developing anemia. It is important to screen for these factors in the PPFE, since early detection of these abnormalities and corrective measures may prevent further problems. Laxity measurements, specific questionnaires for the female athlete triad, and a blood analysis (when necessary) are useful for screening. Similar to males, females develop muscle inflexibility and should be evaluated for the same types of inflexibilities.

Proposed guidelines for age-related soccer testing batteries are illustrated in Table 13-6.

Recording and Storage of Data

The data resulting from the PPFE should be stored in an easy, accessible manner. Specific examination forms filled out by hand can be organized by name, sports activity, school, or team. Storing data in a computer program is more desirable. A good storage system makes it possible to analyze the data uniformly and makes a longitudinal follow-up of the soccer player easier. Examiners can use all data for research purposes, setting up norms for performance, and detecting injury risk factors. In this manner, specific programs for performance enhancement or injury risk reduction can be easily constructed.

Feedback and Storage of Data

At the final checkout, test results need to be discussed in an appropriate way. The physician needs to make a judgment about the athlete's ability to participate in soccer based on the highest standard of medical care available. The ultimate decision can range from approval with or without restrictions, deferred approval, or disqualification. Approval with restrictions would require some modification to allow the athlete to withstand the demands. Examples would include ankle or knee bracing, high impact lenses for athletes with one eye, or kidney protection for athletes with one kidney. Deferred approval would involve further evaluation or treatment, such as work-up of high blood pressure, unexplained heart murmur, or the completion of rehabilitation after injury.

Table 13-6

Recommended Test Battery		

Youth Teams under 15

Flexibility	*Strength*	*Power*
Sit and Reach	Sit-Ups	Vertical Jump
Quadriceps	Push-Ups	
Hamstrings		

Anaerobic Endurance		*Aerobic Endurance*
40-Yard Dash		Soccer Field Run
3 × 5 Test		Mile Run

Youth Teams 15–19

Flexibility	*Strength*	*Power*
All Tests	Cybex for Quads,	All Tests
	Hams	

Anaerobic Endurance		*Aerobic Endurance*
40-Yard Dash		Mile Run
3 × 5 Test		Soccer Field Run
5-Dot Drill		

College or Elite

Flexibility	*Strength*	*Power*
All Tests	All Tests	All Tests
		Other Lab Tests

Anaerobic Endurance		*Aerobic Endurance*
All Tests		Mile Run
		Soccer Field Run
		Other Lab Tests

Adult

Flexibiltiy	*Strength*	*Power*
Sit and Reach	5 Rep Max Squat	Vertical Jump
Quadriceps		
Hamstrings		
Gastrocnemius		*Medical Evaluation*
Hip flexors		Exam Appropriate for Age

Anaerobic Endurance		*Aerobic Endurance*
40-Yard Dash		Soccer Field Run

Although rare, disqualification might be necessary for cardiomyopathies, bleeding disorders, uncontrolled diabetes, or hypertension. This decision will be primarily based on the accumulation of "negative" information from the PPFE. Other athletic and fitness options should be stressed to those athletes who are disqualified because of musculoskeletal base.

Much of the data collected is "positive" information and is not used to restrict sports participation. Rather, by using norms and standards for soccer players, weak points in the athlete's capabilities can be addressed in order to provide a basis for injury prevention and enhance performance. The findings should be explained and stressed to the athletes and their coaches, especially when correction of the deficiencies is easy. Inflexibility, lack of endurance, muscle weakness or imbalances, and incompletely healed injuries are examples of deficiencies. Special exercise programs (e.g., stretching exercises) written down in an illustrative layout help the athlete accomplish these goals.

Cost Considerations and Legal Implications

The PPFE should be relatively inexpensive and cost effective. For this reason, the detailed examination should not be done every year for every athlete. Each athlete should have the general medical examination when entering the athletic program. The competitive level, age, and medical history of the player, which can be screened for by an annual health status review questionnaire, will determine the need for the detailed examination. The performance examination should be done every year to help the athlete maintain maximum fitness and conditioning. Most preparticipation examinations in the young athlete are done under the sponsorship of a school or other organization (e.g., youth soccer association). Although the PPFE is required in all states for organized interscholastic sports activities, it is not uniform in content. Informed consent should be obtained for the possible (low) risk of accidents during the PPFE and the athlete should be informed that the PPFE is not a replacement for the annual physical examination. Good data storage and adequate procedure documentation are necessary to decrease the chances of litigation. Descriptions of the legal implications of sports medicine liability in the PPFE are in literature.

Conclusions

The PPFE plays a role in the evaluation and preparticipation of athletes for soccer participation. To play soccer the athlete needs to be in adequate physical and psychological health. The PPFE should address these goals to allow or restrict soccer activities and to evaluate the critical interaction point of the soccer-specific demands and individual musculoskeletal base leading toward performance enhancement and injury prevention. To achieve these goals the soccer PPFE should be specific for age, gender, and skill level. Feedback of the collected data to the athlete and coaches is essential.

SUGGESTED READINGS

Ekstrand J, Gillquist J. The avoidability of soccer injuries. Int J Sports Med 1983;4: 124–128.

Herbert W. Legal considerations in sports medicine. In: Kibler WB, ed. Handbook for the team physician. Baltimore: Williams & Wilkins, 1996 (in press).

Jackson DL, Nyland J. Club lacrosse: A physiological and injury profile. Ann Sports Med 1990;5:114–117.

Kibler WB, Chandler TJ, Uhl T, et al. A musculoskeletal approach to the preparticipation physical examination: preventing injury and improving performance. Am J Sport Med 1989;17:525–531.

Kibler WB. Advances in conditioning. In: Griffin LY, ed. Orthopaedic knowledge update sports medicine. Illinois: American Academy of Orthopaedic Surgeons, 1994:65–72.

Kibler WB. The sport preparticipation fitness examination. Champaign, Illinois: Human Kinetic Books, 1990.

Knapik JJ, Bauman CL, Jones BH, et al. Preseason strength and flexibility imbalances associated with athletic injuries in female collegiate athletes. Am J Sport Med 1991;19:76–81.

Lombardo J. Preparticipation examination. In: Cantu RC, Micheli LJ, eds. ACSM guidelines for the team physician. Philadelphia: Lea and Febiger, 1991:127–132.

Smith B. Preparticipation physical examination. Sp Med Arthro Rev 1995;3:84–94.

14   Tournament Coverage

W. Ben Kibler
Beven Pace Livingston
John McMullen

Youth soccer tournaments are an important part of the U.S. Soccer Federation Program. These tournaments, which usually last 3–4 days, bring together 200–2000 children who play as many as 25 games per tournament. Based on statistical probability, a significant number of injuries should be expected. These could range from musculoskeletal injuries to medical problems and heat-related illnesses that may affect players, referees, and fans. Because of these risks, onsite medical coverage should be given high priority by tournament organizers. Undertaking such detailed medical coverage is complex. It requires organization, planning, personnel, and resources to allow safe participation by the athletes. This chapter discusses the basic principles of planning and implementation for medical coverage of youth soccer tournaments.

Planning

Organizations

Planning of medical coverage should involve the sponsoring soccer organization and the responsible medical organization. Each organization should have clearly defined, specific duties and responsibilities. They should agree to cooperate and should start meeting early in the planning process for each tournament. Implementation of the medical coverage is more efficient if the planning process creates agreement between the organizations on goals, objectives, and methods.

The sponsoring soccer organization has control over all aspects of the tournament. To insure maximum safety for participants, the organizers must recognize the importance of medical coverage. In some tournaments, medical coverage is an afterthought, resulting in little coverage or cooperation. The sponsoring organization should emphasize the importance and availability of on-site medical coverage to staff, players, and coaches. The organizers should be prepared to use resources to provide proper medical coverage and personnel to assist the medical coverage. The soccer organization should designate a medical services coordinator to act as a formal liaison with the medical organization.

The responsible medical organization should have coherence and direction. It should not be a loose collection of individuals who do volunteer work because their children play soccer. There should be a director of medical services, a formally designated liaison, and a list of available and willing resources including doctors, therapists, trainers, host hospitals, and emergency treatment services. This organization should be responsible for assembling and implementing delivery of medical services.

Agreement

A written agreement listing the responsibilities of each organization should be considered to make sure responsibilities are divided properly and the individual organizations understand their roles. The agreement should specify which organization is responsible for providing what equipment or resources, including publicity, tents, banners, carts, phones, emergency supplies, treatment supplies, and transportation. It should establish lines of communication between the two organizations and a hierarchy of authority for difficult decisions about play such as stoppage, alteration, and return to play criteria for extreme conditions such as lightning, rain, heat, or cold. Each organization can then assemble and use resources based on their specific responsibilities. An example of such an agreement is found in Table 14-1.

Specific Responsibilities

The sponsoring soccer organization is responsible for providing equipment and services to support the medical services (Table 14-2). The primary equipment needed are tents or rooms designated for medical care. These will not be shared with referees, coaches, or vendors. The organizers need to supply portable phones or walkie-talkies to facilitate communication between the field and the medical tent or emergency personnel. Golf carts or other means of transportation on the fields will need to be supplied. Finally, there must be secure storage to lock up medical supplies during the night.

In addition to the designated medical services coordinator, the soccer organization will need to provide an adequate number of field marshals to cover all the fields at a site. These marshals are usually assigned to two fields to monitor for problems. The marshals are often the first tournament official contacted in the event of a medical problem. The field marshals should be able to communicate with the medical tent to give an estimate of the injury and need for personnel.

Finally, the soccer organization should publicize the availability and extent of the medical coverage and recognize the involvement of the medical organization. This can be done in pretournament brochures and on banners and signs at the tournament.

The responsible medical organization should provide most basic and some advanced capabilities to handle medical problems at soccer tournaments. Immediate evaluation and early management of acute injuries should be available. Definitive treatment for mild injuries and stabilization and referral for more serious injuries should also be available. Follow-ups for possible return to play after mild injuries should be scheduled. The medical organization should supply all medical equipment and supplies to achieve

Table 14-1

Outline of Agreement Between the Sponsoring Soccer Organization and the Responsible Medical Organization

Duties

A. Medical Director—
- Review all policies and procedures
- Establish liaison with hospitals
- Render on-site or referral care

B. Physicians—
- Render on-site or referral care
- Determine playing status
- Consult on environmental conditions

C. Medical coverage coordinator—
- Coordinate all medical coverage activities
- Plan equipment and personnel at field sites

D. Trainers, EMT, Therapists—
- Assist in care of athletes, coaches, and players
- Compile data regarding injuries
- Assure basic and advanced life-support care
- Render definitive care for mild injuries

E. Medical Services Coordinator—
- Liaison from sponsoring organization
- Provide materials for medical coverage

LIAISON CHECKLIST

This list should be reviewed during the planning process. It will be signed by liaison representatives from each organization before the tournament.

FIELD SITES _____   DATE _____

	Completed	*Not Completed*	*Problems*
1. Emergency Phone List			
2. Communication Setup (Type _____)			
3. Medical Backup Secured and informed			
4. First Aid Supplies Ordered and Secured			
5. Trainer			
6. Trainer's Kit			
7. Tent or Room with Exam Table			
8. Coolers with Ice and Water			
9. Water Access Identified			

Table 14-1 (continued)

	Completed	Not Completed	Problems
10. Injury Forms			
11. Protocol for Emergency Care and EMS Activation Reviewed			
12. Consent to Treat Forms			
13. Medical Coverage Information Given to Coaches			
14. Medical Coverage			
15. Stabilization Equipment			
16. Transportation Equipment			

these goals. This includes emergency resuscitation equipment, stretchers, crutches, examination tables, tape, wraps, and medications ranging from aspirin and other nonsteroidal antiinflammatory drugs (NSAIDS) to bee sting kits. A complete list of stocks for each field site is listed in Table 14-3.

Medical personnel with a wide range of expertise should be available. Certified athletic trainers are a prerequisite at each site. Physical therapists, nurses, emergency medical technicians (EMTs), and aides may be involved depending on the location availability and past experience. Medical doctors should be assigned to field sites on a rotation basis. They should have backgrounds in on-the-field assessment and emergency resuscitative activities and be able to work with the other medical personnel.

Medical backup should be arranged in advance. Hospitals that have trauma capability should be notified that the soccer tournament is being held and may generate a variety of medical problems. Coverage for musculoskeletal trauma, head injuries, and medical problems should be arranged with physicians who have agreed to be on call. Finally, emergency transportation by ambulance should be arranged with the ambulance either on-site or within five minutes away. Detailed directions to the field sites are given to the ambulance dispatchers.

Coordination

Regular planning sessions should start 3–4 months before the event. With each tournament the sessions usually become easier and more efficient. Early planning should involve information about the number of teams, fields, and field sites, the starting times for the games, and the physical resources (e.g., tents, carts, phones, and medical supplies needed at each site). Any physical peculiarities about the field sites, such as distance from other sites, limited vehicular access, or distance from water, should be known. Proper medical resources can then be developed and assigned for each of the sites.

Table 14-2

Specific Responsibilities for Each Organization

Sponsoring Soccer Organization

Equipment
>   Designated—use tents or rooms
>   Portable phones
>   Walkie-talkies
>   Golf carts
>   Secure storage space

Personnel
>   Designated liaison
>   Field marshals

Publicity
>   Availability and extent of coverage
>   Recognize involvement

Responsible Medical Organization

Equipment and Supplies
>   Emergency resuscitative equipment
>   Stretchers
>   Crutches
>   Exam tables
>   Tape
>   Wraps
>   Medications
>   First aid supplies

Personnel
>   Certified athletic trainers
>   Physical therapists
>   EMT
>   MD

Medical Coverage
>   Immediate evaluation and early management
>   Definitive treatment
>   Stabilization
>   Referral
>   Evaluation for return to play

Medical Backup
>   Hospitals
>   Other specialists
>   Ambulance

Table 14-3

Medical Supplies and Equipment for Each Field Site
Tables for evaluation and taping
Ice chest, ice, and bags
Cold water
Defibrillator and cardiac medications
Splints for arms and legs (immoblizers, air casts, slings)
Crutches
Litters
Taping supplies
Blood pressure cuff and stethoscope
Thermometers
Elastic bandages
First aid supplies
Gauze
Disinfectant
Wound cleanser
Antibiotic ointment
Adhesive bandages
Blister care supplies
Wound closure strips
Gloves
Biohazard disposal bags
Padding supplies

Implementation

Pretournament

Medical personnel must be present at the pretournament coaches meeting. The scope of services and the location of treatment areas are described. How injuries will be evaluated and treated at the field site must be discussed. Coaches are required to inform the medical director of current medical problems such as incompletely healed muscle strains, fractures still in casts, or insulin-dependent diabetics. This is necessary for adequate preparation. The coaches must be made aware of potential weather problems. The opening presentation by the medical director must also stress the importance of preventive measures such as stretching, nutrition, and hydration. Finally, it is important to confirm that all permission to treat forms, allowing acute emergency evaluation and stabilization, are current and in the possession of the coaches.

The backbone of medical coverage during youth soccer tournaments is the certified athletic trainer. This is the first person contacted at the time of an injury. The number of trainers must be adequate for the number of fields and the number, age, and skill levels of the players. An adequate ratio is 1–2 athletic trainers for every 6–10 fields and at least one per field site. Higher staff coverage is necessary at areas with a higher risk of injury. Based on injury data from past tournaments, the highest risks are on fields where females 13-years-old and 18-years-old or males 16–19-years-old are playing.

Nurses or EMTs can be used where they may be most valuable. They are usually in the tent area to provide emergency services, resuscitation, or monitoring for mild cases of concussion, heat illness, dizziness, or diabetic reactions.

Physical therapists are used to help in diagnosis. However, they mainly provide definitive care of mild musculoskeletal problems such as first degree ligament sprains and muscle strains. They also provide modality treatment for appropriate conditions, strengthening or flexibility education for injury rehabilitation, or an exercise prescription for the athlete to take home to their personal therapist.

Medical doctors should be assigned to oversee medical coverage at the field sites. They should be on-site most of the time. The medical doctors should have team physician or on-the-field experience and be knowledgeable about the musculoskeletal, medical, and environmental problems that may occur at a soccer tournament. The physicians usually serve as backups to the athletic trainer in acute mild musculoskeletal injury evaluation and management. However, in more serious cases, the physicians must be ready to assume full control. The physicians also staff a "drop-in" clinic every morning during the tournament for injury evaluation and to allow return to play for old injuries.

Injury Evaluation

The athletic trainer is usually at the medical tent and responds to direct visualization of the injury or a call from the field marshal. The trainer has full authority to see the injured individual and assist or provide medical care at the site of injury. The trainer also has the authority to suspend play, if it is necessary to keep the player on the field for safety reasons, and to decide when and how the player may be safely moved. After initial evaluation and stabilization transport to the side of the field, tent, or hospital may be done. The trainer may transport by foot, crutches, or golf cart.

Many times traveling soccer teams bring physicians either as part of the team structure or because their children play on the team. Cooperative and coordinated efforts should be established so that proper care may be given.

Medical consultation is obtained for all injuries with a questionable diagnosis or any injury that will require doctor approval for return to play. Consultation is also sought for injuries sent to the hospital.

The trainer may activate the emergency medical services (EMS) system if the injury is severe enough to warrant monitored or supervised transportation to the hospital. Guidelines have been established for this process. Transportation by EMS or by private car is mandatory for any fractures with obvious deformity or possible neurovascular compromise, suspect fractures with enough clinical signs and symptoms to warrant a radiograph, concussions with retrograde amnesia, loss of consciousness, persistent headaches, and lacerations that require deep closure.

The trainer, therapist, or physician may be able to render definitive treatment for mild musculoskeletal conditions or concussions at the site or during the tournament. This ability will be enhanced by the availability of splints, braces, tape, or modalities at the field site.

Before any treatment other than emergency evaluation and stabilization is started, legal permission should be obtained since the majority of athletes will be under the age of consent. Permission can be obtained directly from the parents or legal guardians on-site, another adult who has a permission to treat form (such as the coach), or by contacting the parents. Good Samaritan laws usually apply in the acute situation, but not necessarily in the nonacute situation.

Every injury seen by a member of the medical coverage staff, either on the field or in the tent, is logged on to a standardized injury report form (Table 14-4). The format of this form is compatible with the ALFIE Computerized Injury Reporting System. This form allows input on multiple injury variables including position, type of injury, mechanism of injury, severity of injury, treatment, results of treatment, and playing status. After each tournament, the injury data is reviewed and compared to reports from previous years. This type of follow-up shows what types of injuries and injury mechanisms are most prevalent to determine any trends or changes in injuries or injury patterns. The effect of any rule or coaching technique changes implemented in the past are immediately visible. Suggestions for future tournaments in terms of equipment, fields, or refereeing can be discussed. For example, fewer injuries caused by tripping from behind are seen because of more severe penalties and closer refereeing. More lower leg contusion injuries, due to being deliberately kicked or stepped on, have prompted the tournament refereeing committee to watch this mechanism of injury closely.

Summary

Medical coverage of youth soccer tournaments is an important part of the success of the program. It involves attention to detail and organization and a commitment to cooperation. It is accomplished through a planning process that starts far in advance of the tournament. Although the logistics of organizing the resources for such an undertaking may be difficult at first, allowing each organization to do what it does best overcomes most difficulties. Financial considerations play a role in the coverage and should also be solved in advance. Possible arrangements include each organization paying for its own contribution, the soccer organization paying for medical coverage, or the medical organization acting as a paying sponsor of the tournament.

Both organizations benefit from this type of cooperation. The soccer organization receives on-site full-time service for the inevitable medical problems that occur during a large tournament. The provision of efficient medical coverage by the tournament organizing committee is often seen by participating

Table 14-4

Injury Report Form

NAME: _____   AGE: _____   DATE: _____

ADDRESS: _____

         (street)   (city)   (state)   (zip)

INJURY DATE: _____SPORT: _____SCHOOL: _____

BODY AREA: HEAD/NECK/UPPER EXT./LOWER EXT./TORSO/GENERAL MEDICAL/GENITALS

SPECIAL STRUCTURE: _____   SIDE: RIGHT/LEFT/BILATERAL/MIDDLE/NA

INJURY: CONTUSION / CONCUSSION / FRACTURE / SPRAIN / OTHER

MECHANISM: PLANTAR FLEXION   VARUS   HYPERFLEXION   DIRECT CONTACT

                 DORSI FLEXION   VALGUS   HYPEREXTENSION   CONGENITAL

                 INTERNAL ROT.   INVERSION   SUPINATION   ENVIRONMENTAL

                 EXTERNAL ROT.   EVERSION   PRONATION   REPETITIVE STRESS

                 LATERAL FLEXION   TORSION   IMPINGEMENT   N/A

                 OTHER _____

ONSET: ACUTE / ACUTE REINJURY / GRADUAL / CHRONIC REINJURY

CAUSE: ENVIRONMENTAL: HEAT/COLD   CONGENITAL DEFECT   CONTACT WITH PERSON

           CONTACT W/ A SPORTS TOOL   DYNAMIC OVERLOAD   OVERUSE

           TURF: ARTIFICIAL/NATURAL   MUSCLE IMBALANCE   OTHER _____

SEVERITY:

    1:    INJURED BUT ABLE TO RETURN WITHIN PRACTICE/GAME. MINIMAL TO NO DAMAGE.

    1+: BORDERLINE TOWARDS 2. MAY OR MAY NOT BE ABLE TO RETURN TO ACTIVITY. MINIMAL DAMAGE WITH SOME SLIGHT SWELLING.

    2:    UNABLE TO RETURN TO ACTIVITY FOR AT LEAST ONE DAY. MODERATE DAMAGE WITH MODERATE SWELLING.

    2+: BORDERLINE TO TOTAL TISSUE RUPTURE. REQUIRES MEDICAL EVALUATION. SEVERE SWELLING.

    3:    TOTAL DISRUPTION WITH GROSS SWELLING. MAY REQUIRE E.R. ASSISTANCE.

POSITION OF ATHLETE: _____

ACTIVITY: OFF SEASON   GAME   INDIVIDUAL DRILL   INTRAMURALS

           NON ATHLETIC   SCRIMMAGE   NON CONTACT DRILL   CONDITIONING

           GENERAL MEDICAL RUNNING   DEFENSIVE DRILL   WGT TRAINING

           N/A   OTHER _____

TIME: PRACTICE / GAME / NON ATHLETIC / CHRONIC / OTHER

PLATOON: DEFENSIVE / OFFENSIVE / INDIVIDUAL / NON ATHLETIC / OTHER _____

DISPOSITION: HOSPITAL _____   WHICH ONE _____

               DOCTOR _____   SPECIALTY _____

               RETURNED _____   SAT OUT   OTHER _____

STATUS: FULL   – NORMAL ACTIVITY

          GO AS CAN   – PARTICIPATES FULLY EXCEPT WHEN HAVING PAIN, THEN BACKS OFF

          ALTERED PRACTICE   – LIMITED TO SPECIFIED PARTICIPATION BY DOCTOR OR PHYSICAL LIMITATIONS

          NO PRACTICE   – OUT DUE TO ILLNESS OR INJURY

FLEXIBILITY: ROM NORMAL

                ROM LIMITED / WHICH WAY _____

STRENGTH: _____

MISSED ACTIVITY: NUMBER OF DAYS: _____   NUMBER OF GAMES: _____

HISTORY: _____

Table 14-4 (continued)

INSPECTION: _____

_____

_____

PALPATION: _____

_____

FUNCTIONAL TESTS: _____

_____

SPECIAL TESTS: _____

_____

PLAN: _____

_____

FOLLOW UP: _____

COMPLETED BY: _____   DATE: _____

---

teams as a benefit and is a significant factor in their decision to return to the tournament from year to year. The medical organization does community service, may receive some financial compensation, and gains access to a large amount of clinically significant data which can be analyzed and reported.

The most important benefit for each organization, however, is the achievement of their primary goal of a competitive but safe soccer tournament.

Acknowledgment

We would like to thank the staff of the Lexington Clinic Sports Medicine Center, past and present, who participated in tournament coverage and contributed to the collective knowledge that is presented in this chapter.

SUGGESTED READINGS

Kibler, WB. Injuries in Youth Soccer. Med Sci Sports Exerc 1993;25:1330–1332.

IV

• Injuries

15   Acute Injuries

Werner Muller

This chapter offers the reader the benefit of 25 years' experience in the orthopaedic care of professional soccer players. The data have been collected from 1967–1991 during the author's activity as an orthopaedic surgeon of the FC Basel 1893 Soccer Team; a team that was in the first division for 20 of the 25 years. All the data presented concern the 22 players of the premier team. From 1967–1991, of over 3000 injuries reported to the club's insurance, primary operative treatment was necessary in 83 specific injuries.

The data indicate the part of the body where the lesions mainly occur and the percentage of total injuries according to the location of the injury (e.g., upper or lower extremity). Certain questions are of interest. Where do we find these injuries? Which are benign injuries with good prognosis to return to the field? Which are so severe that there is no possibility of return?

Material and Methods

There were a large number of minor injuries, which were not registered for insurance claims, that were treated by the club's physician and physiotherapists in the stadium. These minor injuries were not reported. If the injured player needed radiographs, had to see the club's physician, or needed more specific treatment and was unable to play (nonworkman's compensation), then the injury was reported to the insurance company and registered in their documentation. All injuries reported and documented between 1987–1991 were analyzed. Estimates of the total number of injuries over a 25 year career were based on this 4 year period.

Interpolation, Interpretation, and Estimation

There were 485 injuries within 4 years. It was extrapolated that there were over 3000 insurance registered major accidents (IRMA) over the 25 years. These injuries lead to 83 operations in the same period. The percentage of the operatively treated injuries was 2.7%. The injuries that needed operative treatment were cases in which the lesion was so serious that without operative treatment no full restitution could be expected or the healing time would have been significantly longer. Table 15-1 lists the nonoperative injuries according to the type of injury. Table 15-2 lists the number and percentage of the total nonoperative injuries by the region of the body.

Table 15-1

Global Distribution of all the Injuries, 1987–1991 (N = 485)		
Injury	*Number*	*Percentage*
Contusions	188	38.8
Ligament sprains	127	26.2
Muscle lesions	87	17.9
Wounds	40	8.2
Spine	18	3.7
Tendon sprains	11	2.3
Teeth	4	0.8
Nose	2	0.4
Others	8	1.7

All injury cases within the nonoperative treatment group were able to go back to the same high level of competitive soccer in first division. The healing time lasted anywhere from a few days to a few weeks or even several months. Operative treatment was chosen in seriously injured cases immediately or when nonoperative treatment was unsuccessful (less than 10% of the 83 interventions).

There were eight injuries treated nonoperatively that deserve special attention. These included four clavicle fractures, one elbow dislocation (goalkeeper), and three fractures of the radius (loco classico). There were no forearm fractures within all these years. The elbow dislocation was treated with

Table 15-2

Regional Distribution of the Involved Parts of the Body		
Locations	*Number*	*Percentage*
Head	55	11.3
Neck	6	1.2
Trunk	28	5.8
Upper extremity		
shoulder/arm	13	2.7
hand	51	10.5
Groin	22	4.5
Lower extremity		
thigh	79	16.4
knee	64	13.3
Leg	38	7.8
Foot	129	26.6
Total	485	100

a removable splint. The splint was removed only to allow daily controlled motion and early muscle training. The three radius fractures were reduced and fixed in a plaster, which was replaced 7–10 days later with a special anatomically adapted leather brace for the games. This was necessary due to the soccer rules, which do not allow plaster or any other hard fixation-like braces during the game for safety reasons. The players had to show this up-holstered brace to the referee together with a medical declaration for approval before the game. Because of the rules of the game, all treatments had to exclude the possibility of using braces. This was especially challenging in the treatment of knee injuries, which had to be treated operatively in many cases.

Table 15-3 details the 83 injuries that were treated by surgery. These cases are tabulated according to their location and the specific type of injury. The percent of total IRMA and the percentage of total surgeries are listed.

The Leg

The healing time for a transverse tibial fracture can be very long and the risk of a re-fracture is high in soccer players. Even tibial nails can bend and break. Soccer players often do not wait long enough before they go back to play. For this reason, after 6–8 weeks a carefully adapted open Judet-decortication to the primary internal fixation was added to stimulate an early strong callus formation, which allows the player to go back to competition months earlier than if they had not had this treatment.

The Foot

Foot lesions account for more than 26% of the IRMA, but only 20% of the operations. Many of the lesions can be treated successfully without operation. Among those are fractures of the toes, avulsion of toe nails, some metatarsal fractures, and many fibulo-tarsal ligament lesions.

In three cases a rupture of the aponeurosis plantaris (plantar fascia) occurred. These cases needed 8–12 weeks of recovery time. High-level soccer players need mobile and stable feet to play with good technique. Ankle ligament instabilities can create additional problems in the Achilles tendon or in the peroneal tendons with secondary degenerative processes and chronic ruptures.

In some cases of severe complex fibulo-tarsal ligament lesions, the recovery time was shorter when an anatomic suture repair was performed with full functional postoperative treatment. Since 1976 a circular rigid fixation has not been used by the authors in the postoperative treatment of ankle ligament surgery. Therefore, the players were allowed to move and run very early so that they were back in the field playing full games after 8 weeks. This experience has proven beneficial for all patients.

The Deltoid Ligament

The stabilizing function of the deltoid ligament is important for soccer players and ballet dancers. If there was a clinically evident rupture of this ligament, a primary open anatomic repair was done. In many other cases, it was necessary to operate to restore insufficient deltoid ligaments and bring the

Table 15-3

Surgical Summary of the Surgically Treated IRMA		
Shoulder / arm / hand	13.2% of total IRMA	11 of 83 = 13.3%
Recurrent shoulder dislocation	3	
A-C dislocation	2	
Lateral clavicle fracture	1	
Humerus fracture	1	
Perilunar wrist dislocation	1	
Metacarpal fracture	1	
Finger dislocation	2	
Spine	3.7% of total IRMA	1 of 83 = 1.2%
Herniated disc	1	

Nonoperative treatment was applied in a player with temporarily painful spondylolisthesis. He remained on the premier team for over a decade and played 28 times on the Swiss national team.

Pelvis	4.5% of total IRMA	8 of 83 = 10.3%
Adductor gracilis tenoplasty	5	
Nesevic rectus tenoplasty	3	
Lower extremity	64.1% of total IRMA	65 of 83 = 78.3%
Quadricep muscle rupture	1	
Semimembranosus tendon rupture	1	
Knee	41	
Leg	5	
Foot	17	
Knee lesions	13.5% of total IRMA	41 of 83 = 49.4%
Meniscus, arthroscopic or open	18	
15 partial meniscectomies		
3 repair		
Anterior cruciate ligament (ACL) primary reconstruction	7	
Chondral lesions	6	
Medial collateral ligament (MCL)	4	
MCL + meniscus fixation	3	
Posterior cruciate ligament (PCL)	1	
Patella recurrent dislocation	1	
Plica	1	

Of the knee lesions that were reported (IRMA contusions, sprains, etc.), there was a 1 MCL, 1 PCL and 1 ACL (a goalkeeper) ligament ruptures that were treated nonoperatively

Leg lesions	7.8% of total IRMA	5 of 83 = 6.0%
Transverse fracture tibia + fibula	1	
Direct isolated fibula fracture	1	
Malleolar fracture Weber type C	3	

Table 15-3 (continued)

Foot lesions	26.6% of total IRMA	17 of 83 = 20.5%
Ruptured fibulo-tarsal ligaments	10	
Rupture deltoid ligament	2	
Recurrent primary dislocation of peroneal tendons	2	
Rupture anterior syndesmosis	1	
Fracture/dislocation of cuneiform	1	

tendon of tibialis posterior back into a correct tendon sleeve for pain relief. This sleeve is mainly formed by the superficial and the deep layer of the deltoid ligament.

Often, small avulsion fragments are torn away from the tip of the medial tibial malleolus by the most important, strongest, shortest, and isometric fiber bundle of the deltoid ligament. This can create chronic inflammation with pain and further ligament deterioration. In this case, it may be necessary to excise the tiny fragments later, together with debridement of the ligament with precise refixation of the main ligament bundle.

Therefore, Watson Jone's statement, "it is worse to sprain an ankle than to break it," is still valid. Ankle lesions, especially in soccer players, need good examination, precise diagnosis, and correct treatment.

The Success Rate and Failures of Operative Treatment

All but three of the 83 operative patients came back into the premier team of the FC Basel. The following three players could not come back to the previous level of first division.

The first player was a goalkeeper with a grade IV disruption of his right acromioclavicular joint. There was a dePalma type III anatomic variation with a slope in the joint contact area. Even after a second operation, residual pain at reactions with high elevated arm was limiting the capacity to box out the ball from the upper right goal corner.

The second operative patient unable to return to play was 28-years-old, with a residual anterior knee pain after a straight-leg trauma to the knee in hyperextension. The transverse ligament and the lateral meniscus were torn away (sulcus terminalis in hyperextension) at the hiatus popliteus. The cruciate ligaments were not distorted or ruptured. There never was more than 3 mm anterior-posterior play compared to the noninjured knee. Yet, the anterior knee was painful and at various magnetic resonance imaging (MRI) examinations the meniscus had healed, but black scars in the front were impressive and were probably the reason for increasing pain after playing a halftime.

The third player, also 28-years-old, was a highest class player with well-known anterior cruciate ligament (ACL)-insufficiency prior to playing with

FC Basel. This player sustained a new trauma with complete meniscus desinsertion. After meticulous resuture, the meniscus healed and he was able to play again at the same level for another 4 years. But at the age of 33, the meniscus was torn again and trapped by a new serious trauma. There was no possibility to repair the meniscus so it was removed. In this osteoarthritic knee with visible severe cartilage lesions, the deterioration of the knee did not allow further playing in high-class soccer.

When injuries occur in players above the age of 28, it is harder to bring them back to professional soccer. This may be an ideal time for them to end their careers, especially when the insurance contract offers a good compensation.

Percentage of Severely Injured Players Needing Operations

From 1967–1992 the transfer of players between teams was not as intensive as it is currently. Approximately 200 players were involved in the premier team during this time. Of the 200 premier players, 83 injuries required surgery for an average of approximately 0.4 operations per player. But these 83 operations were done in only 58 players. Therefore, these players had an average of 1.4 primary operations. This shows that some of the players were especially at risk for severe injuries due to their personalities and physical conditions. A total of six players had 20 severe lesions that required surgery, comprising almost 25% of the total operations (Table 15-4)

Conclusion

For the best level of restoration in a short time, there must be a wide range of experience in broad diagnostic fields. Good knowledge of functional anatomy is mandatory for precise diagnosis and a good treatment plan.

Foot lesions, accounting for more than 26% of the injuries, play an important role. The career of a famous soccer player may end due to a Weber type C malleolar dislocation fracture or a deltoid ligament rupture with very small cartilage fragments. Arthroscopy often does not show the problem because the cause of the pain and dysfunction is outside of the joint. Goalkeepers need stable tarsal joints with an excellent proprioceptive feeling for jumping and landing. They may sustain severe ankle injuries when they land on one foot and are simultaneously hit by another player.

The knee injuries represent the most serious group of injuries in the soccer team (49.4% of the 83 operations). Beside severe cartilage injuries, the cruciate ligament lesions are among the most serious in terms of healing time and outcome. The authors first performed a full ACL reconstruction with an autologous patellar tendon graft in 1976 on the center forward of the team. The player returned to the game after 4 months. He played at the same level for another couple of years until the end of his playing career, at the age of 32. Even now, 19 years later, he is still a very active international referee with a perfectly stable knee.

Later, when the scientific data concerning graft remodeling were published, ACL reconstruction patients were not permitted to go back to sports before

Table 15-4

The Players with the Most Surgeries

Player A: 4 surgeries
   meniscus rupture
   fracture/dislocation upper talar joint type C
   acromioclavicular dislocation, grade IV
   big chondral fragment, locking the knee
Player B: 4 surgeries
   medial collateral ligament (MCL) + meniscus refixation left knee
   anterior cruciate ligament (ACL) + MCL right knee
   chronic adductor tendon injury
   cartilage defect left knee
Player C: 3 surgeries
   ACL and meniscus rupture
   fibulo-tarsal ligament ruptures
   quadriceps rupture, chronic painful cyst
Player D: 3 surgeries
   fracture/dislocation of the 1st cuneiform
   humeral shaft fracture
   transverse fracture of the tibia and fibula
Player E (goalkeeper):   3 surgeries
   MCL + meniscus, refix grade III
   fibulo-tarsal ligament ruptures
   acromio-clavicular dislocation, grade IV de Palma type III
Player F: 3 surgeries
   MCL + meniscus refixation
   chronic fibulotarsal instability
   adductor + rectus tendonitis
Player G: 2 surgeries
   meniscus bucket
   fibulotarsal ligament ruptures
Player H: 2 surgeries
   recurrent shoulder dislocation
   chronic dislocation of peroneal tendons
Player I: 2 surgeries
   chronic dislocation of peroneal tendons
   meniscus rupture
Player K: 2 surgeries
   recurrent shoulder dislocation
   fibulo-tarsal ligament ruptures
Player L: 2 surgeries
   open finger dislocation
   perilunar dislocation wrist right and left

Table 15-4 (continued)

Player M: 2 surgeries
   meniscus refixation, medial
   meniscectomy, medial
Player N: 2 surgeries
   meniscectomy
   finger dislocation
Summary:

4 operations	2 players
3 operations	4 players
2 operations	7 players
1 operation	45 players

6–9 months. Sometimes they needed 1 year until a complete comeback. The current wisdom is to allow athletes to return to play and high-level sports activity much earlier, usually after 5–6 months. This reflects how clinical experience and scientific laboratory data may differ and sometimes delay progress for years. Controlled follow-up is mandatory for all treatments in soccer and sports medicine.

16 Acute Head and Neck Injuries

James M. Lynch
Jeffrey A. Bauer

One of the many unique aspects of soccer is the purposeful use of the head to direct the ball. Heading is a thrilling component of the game. The head can be used to pass a ball, settle it to the ground for control, or score a goal. An analysis of first division matches indicated an average of 100 headers per game. If added to the unknown number of headers during training, the result could be several thousand headers throughout a successful soccer career. Numerous reports have raised the question of both chronic and acute injury associated with heading a soccer ball.

Epidemiology

Head and neck injuries account for approximately 10% of injuries in soccer. This is consistent with the fact that the head and neck comprise approximately 10% of the total body surface area. Literature reports a range of 4%–22% of injuries in soccer involving the head and neck. It has been postulated that the mechanism of head injury in soccer has changed over the years. Prior to 1960, most reports seemed to be of head-to-ball contact injuries. A plastic coating was added to the ball to decrease water saturation and subsequent weight gain. Reports after 1980 seem to identify head-to-head contact as the primary mechanism of injury.

In an emergency room study done in Norway, head and neck injuries accounted for 8.2% of soccer injuries over a 1 year period; 8.5% in males and 5.5% in females. Head injuries occurred more frequently in games than practices. Total soccer injuries accounted for 28.4% of all sports injuries during this year long project. A Finnish study using insurance records documented head and neck injuries as comprising 14% of male and 9% of female soccer injuries. Fractures of the facial bones or the skull accounted for 9% of the total fractures in this review. A Nigerian prospective study of an intensive 8 week training camp reported a 20% incidence of head and neck injuries. The reported concussion rate in this study was 15%, which is high when compared to other reports. In a study of a North American professional soccer team involving 15 players during a 4 month season of 24 games, a nasal fracture was the only injury involving the head or neck.

During a Danish youth soccer tournament with 6600 participants, 5.2% of the players were injured with an incidence of 19.1 per 1000 playing hours. Of these injuries, 4.9% involved the head and face with 1.2% being concussions. The Dana Cup involved 12,907 players during a five day tournament and reported a 9% incidence of head and face injuries. A large youth tournament in the United States recorded an incidence of 2.38 injuries per 1000 playing hours with head injuries comprising 8% of the total. The Norway Cup recorded an injury incidence of 14 per 1000 playing hours in boys and 32 per 1000 playing hours in girls. Ten percent of these injuries involved the head and face.

A Danish male youth (12–18-years-old) soccer club system reported an injury incidence of 3.7 per 1000 playing hours over a year. Injuries to the head totaled 4.3% with 1.2% being concussions and 1.9% involving the eye region. A youth league in the United States involving 80 teams and 1272 players was surveyed weekly to assess injuries. The injury rate was 0.51 per 1000 playing hours for the boys and 1.10 for the girls. There was a total of 34 injuries, five (14.7%) of which involved the head or neck. One of these was a conjunctivitis from contact with the lime used to mark the field. Another study in the United States conducted a weekly survey of 253 teams with 4018 participants. One hundred and seventy-six injuries occurred during the 4 month spring season. Five (2.8%) were concussions, one was a neck injury, and five involved the face. A retrospective survey mailing, which compared outdoor and indoor youth leagues in the midwestern United States, yielded a response rate of 63% of the players (455/723). Head and face injuries comprised 22% of the outdoor and 8% of the indoor injuries. An insurance claim review for high school soccer injuries in the northwestern United States showed 436 claims among 10,634 players over 2 years. Head and neck injuries accounted for 9.2% of the injuries and attributed to 12.4% of the costs.

A review of soccer head and neck injuries submitted to an Italian otolaryngology service over an 8 year period indicated that the majority (130/135) were caused by contact with another player. Active elite male soccer players in the United States were surveyed to assess the cumulative incidence of head injuries. Eighty-nine percent had sustained head trauma during their soccer careers. Of the 60 injuries in which mechanisms were reported, 14 (23%) were due to contact with the ball. Thirty-six were secondary to contact with another player, seven with the ground, and three with the goalpost.

Mechanics of Head Injuries

The head consists of a skull, covered by the scalp, which contains the brain, dura mater, pia-arachnoid complex, blood vessels, and cerebrospinal fluid. The skull can be considered a rigid container under the conditions involved in heading a soccer ball. The brain is a gelatinous structure containing nerve cells (grey matter) and their axons (white matter), which are supported by glia cells. In mechanical terms, the central nervous system (CNS) can be considered a viscoelastic mass hydraulically shock-mounted in a stiff container with external shock-attenuating layers.

Head injuries encompass three broad categories. Focal injuries cause local damage and consist of subdural, epidural or intracerebral hematoma, and cortical contusions. Epidural hematomas occur between the dura mater and inner table of the skull and are often caused by a laceration of the middle meningeal artery. Subdural hematomas occur between the dura and the thin pia-arachnoid complex and are usually of venous origin. Diffuse injuries are associated with widespread disruption of the structure or function of the brain. A skull fracture can occur with or without damage to the brain. Physical input to the head can be slow (static loading) or, more commonly, rapid (dynamic loading). Static loading of the head implies that force is applied gradually over a period of 200—500 milliseconds or longer. Dynamic loading occurs more commonly in sports, with force application lasting less than 200 milliseconds.

Head injury can result through two major mechanisms. The first is contact phenomena and the second is inertial or acceleration effects. Contact phenomena are a group of mechanical events that may occur both locally and distant from the site of impact. These cause skull deformation and shock wave propagation through the brain. Shock wave propagation is most likely to result in impacts less than 5 milliseconds in duration. Inertial loading of the head accelerates or decelerates the head. From a mechanical point of view, the physical input of both acceleration and deceleration are considered to differ only in direction. The inertial loading may result from impact or impulsive loading. Impulsive loading occurs when the head is not directly hit but is set into motion through other means, such as impact to the body. Acceleration of the head may be translational (in one plane of motion) or angular (rotational). The physiological effects of these two types of accelerations are different. Focal injuries are more likely to result from translational acceleration while angular accelerations will cause more diffuse injuries.

Although head injuries technically encompass any structural damage to the head, the term has become synonymous with the more limited concept of brain injury. The low-risk group includes those who are asymptomatic, have minimal symptoms, or have scalp injuries but no neurologic abnormalities. The moderate-risk group are those with a change in the level of consciousness, under the influence of drugs or alcohol, with multiple trauma, or with skull fractures. The high-risk group includes patients with a depressed or decreasing level of consciousness, focal neurologic signs, or depressed skull fractures. Documenting the player's level of consciousness is the most important initial step following a head injury. The Glasgow Coma Scale is almost universally accepted and requires grading of eye opening, verbal, and motor responses. The duration of altered consciousness and post-traumatic amnesia and the presence of focal neurologic signs are also important considerations.

Of the head and neck injuries in soccer registered through insurance records in Finland, 40% involved dental injuries, 7% were concussions, and 6% were ocular injuries.

Neck injuries have been reported in soccer players. A hyperextension of the cervical spine can cause a vascular injury which could result in a central cervical cord syndrome. A cervical disc herniation has also been reported in a soccer player. Neither report discusses previous injury history in these players, however.

Facial injuries should be evaluated in a step-by-step manner. The player should be asked how the teeth fit together when the jaws are tightly closed. If the teeth feel out of line, a jaw fracture should be suspected. The player can be asked to bite down on a tongue blade. If a jaw fracture exists, there may be pain at the site. It is also necessary to do a systematic palpation and inspection of the facial features to compare the two sides. Particular attention should be paid to the orbit. Visual acuity and the presence of double or blurred vision must also be evaluated. Dental injuries can be managed on a temporary basis until definitive care can be obtained. A tooth fracture that involves only the enamel is primarily a cosmetic problem that requires an emery board to smooth sharp edges. A fracture of enamel and dentin will require a temporary filling material to cover any exposed and sensitive edges. A completely avulsed tooth should be recovered without touching any of the roots. The tooth should be rinsed in saline or tap water and placed back in the socket with careful attention to the orientation of the tooth. The tooth then needs to be bridged to the surrounding teeth until permanent stabilization can be accomplished.

Eye injuries have been reported in a five year study of 24 contusion eye injuries from soccer ball impact. Hyphema (50%), vitreous hemorrhage (29%), corneal abrasion (21%), angle recession (8%), and retinal tears (4%) were seen. All the injuries were unilateral. Fourteen patients (58%) were initially seen with more than one identifiable injury on examination. Ten (42%) had both anterior and posterior chamber injuries. Seventy percent of the patients initially had at least one-line visual loss. All but two achieved final visual acuity of 20/20. Only the patients with hyphema were hospitalized, but did not experience rebleeding. When compared to the literature on other sports, the injuries in this study were much less severe. This is probably due to the large diameter of a soccer ball. Impacting objects with a diameter larger than 10 centimeters (4 inches) deliver most of their energy to the orbital rims. The globe and orbit are adult size by age seven while rim growth matches that of the paranasal sinuses, which expand slowly until puberty and then rapidly reach adult size. Therefore, younger players will have less protection from the normal bony anatomy. Several eye injuries seen during this study were secondary to head-to-head contact but only the injuries directly due to the soccer ball were reported.

A retrospective survey of elite male players in the United States was done at a national tournament. Sixty-four of the 72 respondents (89%) had sustained head injuries during their soccer careers. There were 65 concussions in 36 players, 15 fractures in 10 players, 27 lacerations in 18 players, 30 nose bleeds in 25 players, 6 eye injuries in 5 players, and 20 mouth injuries in 16 players.

Management of Head and Neck Injuries

A concussion is a traumatically induced alteration of consciousness, which does not necessarily include a loss of consciousness. A concussion can be considered a disorder of information processing. This diffuse brain injury most often results from a rotational acceleration with a shearing force applied to the brain. Confusion and amnesia can result if the shearing forces involve the cortical, subcortical, or deeper diencephalic structures. Loss of consciousness will occur if the reticular activating system is involved. Several grading systems have been proposed that allow classification of the concussion and provide guidelines for return to play. The classification of a concussion depends on the development of symptoms over time. Symptoms do not have to occur at the time of impact. The fact that amnesia or postconcussion symptoms may occur several minutes after the injury suggests that the pathological process occurs gradually. Therefore, serial neurologic examinations are important in the decision to return to practice or competition. The neuropsychologic examination should focus on three major areas: postconcussion symptoms, information-processing efficiency, and memory functions. Anterograde or posttraumatic amnesia occurs when there is no recollection of the period immediately following the injury. Retrograde amnesia involves loss of memory of the events prior to the injury. An athlete with continued symptoms should not be allowed to return to activity. An athlete who has lost consciousness should be closely evaluated and free of symptoms for a period of time before returning to activity.

A postconcussive syndrome can occur. It is associated with headache, exertional headache, dizziness, fatigue, irritability, and impaired concentration and memory. The various symptoms can be grouped into physical, cognitive, integrative, and affective categories. Second-impact syndrome is a consideration in athletes who still have symptoms. This syndrome involves rapid brain swelling after apparently minor head trauma and can be fatal. It is conjectured that vascular autoregulation in the brain is disrupted with the initial insult and that the second injury results in vascular engorgement. Migraine headaches have been reported in soccer players as a result of heading a ball. Although the pathophysiology of severe head injury is well understood, minor traumatic brain injury remains unclear. Concussive injury appears to be cumulative. The threshold at which cumulative subconcussive trauma may become clinically significant remains unclear. The long term effects of head injuries in soccer players is discussed in Chapter 17.

Summary

Acute head and neck injuries occur in soccer as in any other contact sport. Approximately 10% of soccer injuries involve the head and neck. This region does not seem to be at particular risk since the head and neck comprise only 10% of the surface area of the body. A large number of head and neck injuries in soccer occur by mechanisms other than heading a ball. Although significant forces are produced when heading a soccer ball, these are of a lesser magnitude than forces involved in other sports. The mass of the ball and the duration of impact are important in determining the magnitude of these forces. Some protective equipment (i.e., a helmet) does not appear to be an effective strategy, although addition of mouth guards and other rule changes may be useful.

Acknowledgments

The authors would like to acknowledge the efforts of our research group: Nigel Sparks, Susan Mulligan, Sarah Richardson, Richard Park, and Joseph Leluga. We would also like to thank Coach Barry Gorman, the Penn State soccer team, and Paromed for their cooperation.

SUGGESTED READINGS

Fields KB. Head injuries in soccer. Physician and Sportsmedicine 1989;17:69–73.

Hugenholz H, Richard MT. The on-site management of athletes with head injuries. Physican and Sportsmedicine 1983;11:71–78.

LeBlanc KE. Concussions in sports: guidelines for return to competition. Am Fam Physician 1994;50:801–806.

Nelson WE, Jane JA, Gieck JH. Minor head injury in sports: a new system of classification and management. Physician and Sportsmedicine 1984;12:103–107.

Schmidt-Olsen S, Jorgensen U, Kaalund S, et al. Injuries among young soccer players. Am J Sports Med 1991;19:273–275.

Tysvaer AT. Head and neck injuries in soccer: impact of minor trauma. Sports Med 1992;14:200–213.

White RJ, Likavec MJ. The diagnosis and initial management of head injury. N Engl J Med 1992;327:1507–1511.

17  Chronic Head and Neck Injuries

Gary A. Green
Sheldon E. Jordan

Introduction

Although the average soccer player heads the ball up to 10 times per game, few studies have examined the effects on the head and neck. It is as if the head is not subject to the same type of injury risk as other body parts, such as the lower extremities, that have been more extensively studied. However, the head and neck are at risk for acute and chronic injuries. This chapter outlines the types of injuries that occur and the management, treatment, and prevention of such occurrences. Compared to sports such as boxing and football, soccer is considered to be relatively safe for the head and neck, despite being classified as a contact/collision sport by the American Academy of Pediatrics. The ways that the head and neck can be injured during a soccer match will be discussed in this chapter. The first way results in an acute traumatic event and occurs when there is significant impact with another player, the ground, or a fixed object such as a goalpost. The next type of injury is a result of the acute head or neck injuries experienced by soccer players throughout their careers and leads to the development of chronic head and neck symptoms. Finally, repetitive minor head impacts with the ball can possibly cause a cumulative encephalopathy.

Epidemiology

A review of worldwide medical literature yields numerous anecdotal descriptions of acute head and neck injuries. Table 17-1 summarizes several types of catastrophic injuries described in the medical literature that have occurred during soccer matches. These injuries are serious, but they do not seem common considering the large number of matches and practices (potential exposures) that take place each year in soccer.

Despite the fact that soccer is popular worldwide, few studies have accurately examined the actual incidence of injury to the head and neck. The frequency of acute head injuries has commonly been quoted as 9%–12%, although one study measured the frequency as high as 24%. A study of soccer players in Nigeria revealed that concussions accounted for approximately 15% of all soccer injuries. A Norwegian study determined that 60% of 43 former soccer players with neck injuries had decreased cervical range of motion

Table 17-1

Acute Head and Neck Injury Case Reports in Soccer

Two cases dissection of internal carotid artery
Epileptic seizure after acute occipital injury
Bilateral conductive hearing loss after head injury with ball
Fatal penetrating head injury on collision with fence
Extended coma, temporal fracture after knee to head injury
Central cervical cord syndrome after heading
Acute cervical disc herniation
Temporal skull fracture and brain edema

and 5 of these players had healed cervical fractures. A 1981 study of 128 active Norwegian players determined that 5% complained of protracted neck symptoms.

The above studies provide some information regarding the epidemiology of head injuries, but they are of limited value in establishing an incidence. The numbers quoted in the above studies are typically expressed as a percentage of reported injuries. To ascertain the actual incidence of acute head and neck injuries in soccer it is necessary to determine a denominator, such as athlete exposures. The National Collegiate Athletic Association (NCAA) developed an injury surveillance system for all sports that reports injuries in terms of athlete exposures. Athlete exposure refers to any situation in which an athlete is at risk of injury (i.e., a single practice or game). Injury rates are then expressed in terms of number of injuries per 1000 athlete exposures.

During the collegiate 1993–1994 soccer season, the rate of concussions for men and women was 0.14 and 0.15 concussions per 1000 athlete exposures. Although this rate is approximately half of that seen in American intercollegiate football, it may be significant in a professional soccer player who is exposed to over 200 practices and games per year over a 20 year career (equivalent to 4000 athlete exposures). The NCAA also calculated the rate for significant neck injuries and found that these occur at a lower rate than acute head injuries. The rate for neck injuries in men's and women's soccer between 1993–1994 was 0.07 and 0.08 per 1000 athlete exposures.

Mechanism of Head Injuries

Acute head injuries are not uncommon among soccer players and usually are the result of a violent collision, rather than routine heading of the ball. An Italian study examined consecutive admissions to an ear, nose, and throat service for facial trauma resulting from athletic activity. It was found that 7% of the injuries occurred in soccer. The cause of the injuries was determined to be contact with another player (97%), contact with fixed equipment (2%), or contact with the ground (1%). Although this study looked at facial trauma, the mechanisms of injury are similar to observations of head and neck injuries. Many of the acute head injuries in soccer occur as a result of dangerous play and could be prevented through enforcement of the rules. Renstrom and Peterson found that head injuries are common in goalkeepers as a result of contact with other players or collision with the goalpost. Janda, et al. addressed the latter point in a study of padded goal posts and found a significant reduction in acute traumatic events secondary to collision with the posts.

Case report: In the course of a World Cup match, two players became entangled. An injury occurred when the opposing player used his elbow to strike the other player in the temple. Following the blow to the head, the player was briefly unconscious and suffered a seizure. He was immediately transported to the hospital where magnetic resonance imaging (MRI) and a computerized axial tomography (CAT) scan were performed. These are shown in Figures 17-1–17-3. He was hospitalized for observation and neurosurgical consultation. After conservative management he was released. This demonstrates the damage that can be done in a situation that is outside the bounds of legal play. As a consequence of this event, the player who committed the flagrant act received a red card and was dismissed from the tournament. The injured player suffered a temporal skull fracture, grade III concussion, brain edema, and was unable to play soccer for 6 months. He eventually returned to play without any sequelae.

It is not unusual for players to experience several acute head traumas throughout their careers. The long-term effects of such injuries have been debated among the sports medicine community, especially in sports with high concussion rates, such as boxing and American football. Extensive neuropsychiatric testing is pobably necessary to detect the subtle signs of chronic encephalopathy that may result from cumulative acute head injury. Alves' study of American intercollegiate football players who experienced concussions found that there did not seem to be any lasting impairment after a first concussion, as measured by a battery of neuropsychiatric tests. The study sounded a warning, however, in that a second head injury occurring in close proximity to the first resulted in longer lasting impairments than injuries occurring further apart. Clearly, further longitudinal research is required in this area.

The effects of repetitive heading of the ball on the head and neck is also of interest. It has been postulated that the cumulative impact of heading a ball could lead to a chronic encephalopathy, similar to that observed in boxing. This frequently seen syndrome in boxing has been classified as dementia pugilistica or chronic progressive traumatic encephalopathy of boxers, and was first noted in professional boxing in 1928. Because the frequency of this syndrome correlates with the length of a fighter's career, it is felt that it occurs secondary to repetitive blows to the head. It is a progressive syndrome that begins 7–35 years after the start of a boxer's career and the incidence may be as high as 25% in professional fighters. It is characterized by early findings such as mild affective disturbances and incoordination. It progresses to decreased cognitive functioning and increasing psychiatric symptoms, such as dementia and parkinsonism. Neuroradiologic findings in dementia pugilistica include central and cortical atrophy, ventricular enlargement, and possibly an increased incidence of cavum septum pellucidum. Despite the

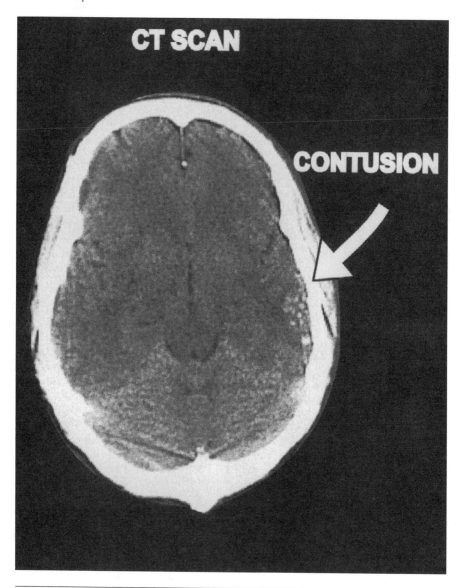

Figure 17-1. CT scan of elbowing injury to temporal area with contusion.

frequency of this syndrome, it is unclear whether it results from recurrent acute head injuries (knockouts), repetitive microtrauma from punches that do not cause concussions, or a combination of both. Multiple studies of amateur boxers from several countries have failed to demonstrate clinical or neuroradiologic findings of dementia pugilistica. This suggests that because amateur boxing is tightly regulated in terms of return to competition after knockouts, there is a decreased incidence of dementia pugilistica. Studies of

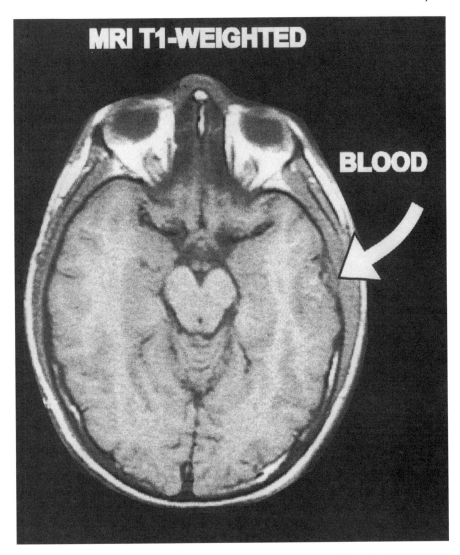

Figure 17-2. "T-1 weighted MRI image" of temporal lobe contusion.

boxers and chronic encephalopathy are significant in the discussion of potential repetitive head trauma in soccer players.

Several soccer researchers have proposed that a similar syndrome may occur in soccer players because of the repetitive microtrauma that the brain receives through contact with the ball. Tysvaer performed several studies on active and former soccer players and found extensive electroencephalogram (EEG) abnormalities, including cerebral atrophy in one-third of the players and 81% with mild to severe neuropsychological impairment. These results have not been reproduced by other authors and their conclusion, that a

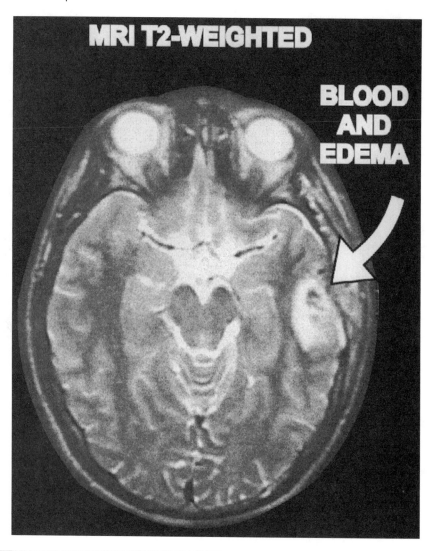

Figure 17-3. "T-2 weighted MRI image" of temporal lobe contusion.

chronic encephalopathy results from repetitive heading, has been ques-tioned. Among the limitations cited in Tysvaer's studies are lack of a suitable control group, failure to control for acute head injuries, lack of adequate screening for alcohol, and failure to appropriately blind the researchers. A recent presentation by Witol and Webbe found that soccer players with the highest reported frequency of heading had the largest percentage of deficits on an IQ test and various neuro-psychiatric tests. However, the study was limited by small numbers, the lack of a control group, inappropriate control for acute head trauma, and possible selection bias.

In addition, the neuropsychiatric and neuroradiologic findings in these studies do not conform to the pattern of chronic traumatic encephalopathy seen in dementia pugilistica. Finally, if repetitive heading of the ball does lead to chronic brain damage, it would be expected that those with the greatest absolute number of career headers would have the greatest neurologic changes. Previous studies have failed to adequately examine this important variable.

There are several distinctions between soccer and boxing with regard to chronic brain injury. First, the forces involved in a boxing punch are much greater than those associated with heading a soccer ball. Studies have demonstrated that a soccer ball can travel 26.82–53.64 m/sec, although the speed typically diminishes by the time it reaches a player's head. Studies from the University of Delaware using ball speeds of 15.5 m/sec (35 miles per hour), demonstrated head acceleration forces of 20 gs with peak forces reaching 1200 newtons. This is several orders of magnitude less than the forces seen in boxing, in which a punch can produce enough force to accelerate the head at 100 gs. An English study by Townend in 1987 confirms these findings. More significantly, a boxing punch may generate a rotational force to the head and brain. These rotational forces (Fig. 17-4) can be very destructive to the bridging veins of the brain. In contrast, soccer players encounter a more linear force when heading a soccer ball. Figure 17-5 illustrates a straight linear force, which is better absorbed and produces less brain damage.

The forces generated on the cervical spine are not clearly understood. Heading a soccer ball is a complex task that involves positioning the muscles of the lower extremities, trunk, and neck to meet the ball. Biomechanical studies from Penn State University measured impact times and electromyographic (EMG) analysis of muscles during heading. The studies found that the flexors of the hip and trunk combined with the flexors of the neck to properly head a ball. Tysvaer also found that the flexors of the neck are active in preventing the head from snapping forward after heading the ball. All of

ROTATIONAL FORCE

Figure 17-4. Punching impact in boxing often produces rotational force.

Figure 17-5. Soccer heading typically produces linear force to head.

these forces can be responsible for cervical flexion strain and compression of the cervical vertebrae. The neck is an area where incorrect heading technique can contribute to injury through the improper dissipation of forces.

The final type of injury is a traumatic fracture/dislocation of the cervical spine. In the United States, American football is responsible for the majority of these injuries related to sports. This is not true in other countries where soccer contributes to a greater extent. A study from Scotland revealed that 6% of all para and quadraplegics occurred as a result of playing soccer. Although hyperflexion and hyperextension injuries to the neck occur, the current research of Torg and others has implicated forced axial loading as the main mechanism in the development of cervical spine fracture/dislocation. As with acute head injuries, many of these occur outside the bounds of legal play.

Management of Head and Neck Trauma

Acute Head Injuries

In the management of sports related injury there are several important issues. First of all, it is necessary to assess the acuity of injury so that emergency transport to the hospital and the need for emergency imaging of the brain and neck can be considered. Furthermore, it is important to decide whether or not the player needs stabilization of possible acute neck injury. In less severe instances of head injury, returning to competition is an important issue.

The taking of a history by the trainer or on-field physician is of critical importance. Through direct observation or history, it is important to establish whether the player lost consciousness and if there is amnesia for events subsequent to the impact. A seizure at the time of the impact has some relevance in terms of understanding why a player may be confused or be in an amnestic state immediately after the impact. Typical complaints with a concussion include headache, ringing in the ears, dizziness, nausea, and vomiting. The presence of double vision, hearing loss, or extreme vertigo signifies the presence of injury to the cranial nerves and/or the possibility of a basal skull fracture. The patient should be asked about neck pain, if the pain radiates down the arms, and any numbness or weakness in the arms or legs. If there is any question of neck injury, the neck should immediately be stabilized with an immobilization device and the patient transported appropriately.

An examination should include testing for orientation to time, place, and person. The player should be questioned about recent events and tested for immediate recall and short-term memory. The level of alertness and the presence or absence of an amnestic state should be reevaluated every 5 minutes for an observation period of at least 20 minutes.

The discharge of spinal fluid from the nose or ears signifies a cerebrospinal fluid (CSF) fistula and indicates severe injury to the skull base. Typically, blood behind the tympanic membrane or along the mastoid process around the periorbital tissues is not seen for several hours after a basilar skull fracture. Marked asymmetry in deep tendon reflexes, strength, and sensation or the presence of Babinski responses, disconjugate eye movements, or abnormal pupillary responses also signify the presence of a neurosurgical emergency and indicate the need for emergency transportation, imaging, and neurosurgical consultation.

There are several different systems that outline the criteria for returning a player to competition. The recommendations of the Colorado Medical Society is one of the most widely used systems. According to these guidelines, a grade I concussion does not involve a loss of consciousness but does include confusion without amnesia. A player suffering from a grade I concussion should be removed from the contest and reexamined every 5 minutes for amnesia or postconcussive symptoms at rest and with exertion. If none of these develop after 20 minutes of observation, the player may return to the contest.

A grade II injury is defined as no loss of consciousness with confusion and amnesia. In this case, the player should be removed from the contest and not allowed to return. The player should be reexamined frequently and the next day for neurological deficits. Participation in practice should be considered only after 1 week without symptoms, either at rest or with exertion.

A grade III concussion is associated with loss of consciousness. The player should be transported by ambulance to the hospital with the use of spinal immobilization. Imaging and neurology or neurosurgical consultation should be obtained in the hospital. The player should only be allowed to return after 2 weeks without symptoms. Generally speaking, a CT scan with the use of bone windows should be obtained in any patient with loss of consciousness. The Colorado Medical Society guidelines are summarized in Table 17-2.

Table 17-2

Colorado Medical Society Guidelines for the Management of Concussion in Sports

Grade 1: Confusion without amnesia, no loss of consciousness

    Remove from contest

    Examine immediately and every 5 minutes for the development of amnesia or postconcussive symptoms at rest and with exertion

    Permit return to contest if amnesia does not appear and no symptoms appear for at least 20 minutes

Grade 2: Confusion with amnesia, no loss of consciousness

    Remove from contest and disallow return

    Examine frequently for signs of evolving intracranial pathology

    Reexamine the next day

    Permit return to practice after 1 week without symptoms

Grade 3: Loss of consciousness

    Transport from field to nearest hospital by ambulance (with cervical spine immobilization if indicated)

    Perform thorough neurological evaluation immediately

    Admit to hospital if signs of pathology are detected

    If findings are normal, instruct family for overnight observation

    Permit return to practice only after 2 weeks without symptoms

Adapted from: Kelly JP, Nichols JS, et al. Concussion in sports: guidelines for prevention of catastrophic outcome. JAMA 1991; 266:2867–2869.

The above criteria have been established to avoid the results of a second impact before a player has had a chance to recover from the loss of vascular or regulatory capacities after an initial concussion. There have been several cases reported of severe brain swelling, in which the player was returned to competition before fully recovered from the initial concussion. There is a need for concern in the case of a player who suffers a concussion and does not appear to be recovering as expected. On physical examination, it is often difficult to discern a postconcussive syndrome or traumatic migraine from a subdural hematoma. In these cases, it is prudent to obtain a CT or MRI scan to eliminate the possibility of intracranial pathology.

Chronic Head Injuries

There is a possibility that repeated concussions can lead to cumulative brain injury. However, the ability to reliably predict the probabilities and extent of such a syndrome is not within our present capabilities. As a result, a player who returns to competition after a concussion is taking an undefined risk in terms of the potential for a delayed cumulative brain syndrome. In our own studies, we have not been able to establish the presence of a cumulative brain syndrome due specifically to repeated heading. However, head to head or head to ground collisions can be a possible source of cumulative brain injury.

There are general guidelines for the return of an athlete to play following multiple concussions. The most widely followed are Cantu's guidelines for football players, which mandate termination of a season after a player experiences either three grade I or II concussions or two grade III concussions. A soccer player who suffers multiple concussions in a season requires a complete neurologic evaluation prior to return to play. The mechanism of injury and the forces involved in each incident need to be examined. It is an ominous sign when a minor blow results in a concussion. In addition, the individual style of play should be evaluated in light of multiple head injuries. Based on our work, it is suggested that a soccer player who suffers a concussion should not participate in heading until all symptoms have disappeared.

Published guidelines should be used only as suggestions. Each player with a head injury should be individually evaluated by the team physician and appropriate consultants before a decision on return to play is made. Periodic examinations are necessary in the periconcussive period and need to be repeated as the athlete is gradually returned to full play. Return to play after a concussion should be viewed as a conditional status guided by the presence of symptoms. Although there are many published guidelines regarding return to play after acute head trauma, there is not enough data to make recommendations regarding the prevention of brain injury from repetitive heading of the ball.

Neck Injuries

Cervical spine injury is probably the most feared consequence of athletic participation. Although cervical spine injuries are infrequent, it is important to always be prepared. Adequate preparation in terms of equipment and staff is the key to managing this injury. The protocols for transport should be reviewed at the start of each season so that all personnel are aware of procedures. The next step is recognition of the injury. A cervical spine injury should be assumed in any event involving loss of consciousness. Due to the possibility of cervical spine injury in the unconscious player, ammonia capsules should never be used in this situation. An immediate evaluation of the airway, breathing, and circulation should be performed. In any situation in which a cervical spine or neck injury is suspected, the neck should be stabilized and the athlete transported on a spine board to a trauma center for more extensive evaluation.

Long-Term Sequalae

To determine whether a chronic encephalopathy exists in soccer players, a study was done by Jordan, Green, Galanty, Mandelbaum, and Jabour. The study examined the hypothesis that if repetitive heading leads to brain injury, there should be a dose response effect whereby those players with the greatest cumulative exposure would have the greatest neurologic changes. The study also attempted to correct factors that have limited past research, such as previous acute head trauma, alcohol use, and properly blinded investigators. The study group consisted of 25 soccer players invited to attend the U.S. Men's National Team Training Camp. They were compared to 20 male elite track athletes with no history of playing soccer.

Both subject groups were questioned about demographics, past medical history, sports participation, and acute head injuries. They also completed a questionnaire on the use of alcohol. The groups then answered a 10 symptom questionnaire regarding head and neck complaints, which addressed both current and past symptoms. These questions were developed from common complaints reported among soccer players in other studies.

To assess the cumulative effect of heading a soccer ball, a scale of heading exposure was developed. A grading system was created in conjunction with the coaches and trainers of the U.S. National Team. This system was weighted with regard to the length of a particular season and the potential for heading exposure. For example, a European outdoor professional league season was given the standard of 1.0 because it tends to have the most games and practices and a style of play that encourages heading. An indoor soccer player participating in a full season was assessed at 0.25 because there is relatively little heading during the average indoor game. High school and college seasons were scaled down because of fewer games. The grading system is shown in Table 17-3. Multiplying the number of years at each level of play by the grading score and summing the respective scores at each level results in a total participation score for each player, called the heading exposure index. The coaches found these scores to be reasonable estimates of soccer participation and heading experience.

The final part of the study involved a brain MRI scan for both groups that was independently read by two certified neuro-imagers blinded to the subject's group and identity. Following a review of neuro-radiographic studies of boxers and soccer players, a scoring system was developed to account for any positive neuro-radiologic findings reported as being associated with brain trauma.

The results of the study demonstrated no statistical differences between the track athletes and soccer players with regard to symptom scores or MRI scans. Alcohol use was similar for both groups. Among the soccer players, the symptom questionnaire and the MRI scans did not correlate with age, years of play, reported number of headers, or heading exposure index. The study found that a history of acute head trauma had a high correlation with

Table 17-3

Grading of Soccer Participation	
League	Score/Season
High School	0.5
College	0.75
European League	1.0
US Outdoor League	0.8
US Indoor League	0.25
US National Team (Full Time)	1.0
National Team Games	5 games = 0.1

current reported head symptoms, especially in the soccer players (r = 0.63). Although the same trend was seen in the track athletes, it was not statistically significant. These results seem to indicate that any findings of encephalopathy among soccer players is likely to occur secondary to acute head injury rather than from the repetitive effects of heading. It also suggests that future studies examining the effects of heading should consider the past history of acute head injury.

Summary

Although acute head injuries in soccer result from random collisions, they occur at a predictable rate in organized games. It is imperative that medical personnel are present at soccer practices and matches and are trained in the recognition of acute head and neck injuries. The proper emergency equipment, such as spine boards, should be readily available along with appropriate transportation to a trauma center.

Some things can be done to decrease the possibility of head injury associated with soccer. The uniform application of strict refereeing principles would reduce the possibility of dangerous play. High kicking, jumping at a player, and heading in the presence of another player should all be penalized according to the principles of dangerous play. Fighting should result in expulsion to discourage such outbursts. Although some youth soccer fields use padding around goal posts, there has been no action taken to apply this safety measure at other levels of play.

In terms of chronic head and neck injuries in soccer, there are more questions than definitive answers. This has the dual effect of providing an area for potential research, while at the same time making it difficult to make concrete recommendations. Further research needs to examine the influence of proper heading technique from a biomechanical viewpoint with respect to various ages and levels of play. The use of a dry, light ball should also reduce the apparently small chances of cumulative injury associated with heading. Studies done in Scandinavia suggest that wet, heavy soccer balls may be the cause for the possible development of a cumulative brain syndrome associated with heading. The new plastic coated balls reduce this occurrence, even under wet conditions.

Future studies could focus on a longitudinal examination of soccer players throughout their careers and into retirement. Jordan and Green developed a heading exposure index that can be applied to various populations of soccer players to determine if there is any evidence that repetitive heading does have an adverse effect on the brain. It may also be useful to incorporate neuropsychiatric testing and functional imaging, such as position emission tomography (PET) scanning, into future studies. Studying large numbers of soccer players may reveal important distinctions that contribute to head injury, such as heading style. The study by Jordan and Green revealed the importance of controlling for acute head trauma when examining the effect of heading a ball. By teaming multiple specialists together, such as epidemiologists, neurologists, neuro-imagers, neuro-psychologists, biomechanists, and team physicians, the identification, management, and prevention of head and neck injuries in soccer can be definitively established.

SUGGESTED READINGS

Cantu RC. Guidelines for return to contact sports after a cerebral concussion. Physician and Sports Med 1986;14:75–83.

Haglund Y, Eriksson E. Does amateur boxing lead to chronic brain damage? American J of Sports Med 1993;21:97–109.

Janda DH, Bir C, Wild B, et. al. Goal post injuries in soccer. American J of Sports Med 1995;23:340–344.

Jordan SE, Green GA, Galanty HL, Mandelbaum BR, Jabour BA. Acute and chronic brain injury in United States national team soccer players. Am J Sports Med 1996;24:205–209.

Kelly JP, Nichols JS, Filley CM, et al. Concussion in sports: guidelines for the prevention of catastrophic outcome. JAMA 1991;266:2867–2869.

Scoppetta C, Vaccario ML. Central cervical cord syndrome after heading a football. Lancet 1978;1:1269.

Smodlaka VN. Medical aspects of heading the ball in soccer. Physician and Sports Med 1984;12:127–131.

Sortland O, Tysvaer AT, Storli OV. Changes in the cervical spine in association football players. Brit J of Sports Med 1982;16:80–84.

Townend MS. Is heading the ball a dangerous activity? In: Reilly T, ed. Proceeding of the First World Congress of Science and Football. New York: E. & F.N. Spon, 1987.

Tysvaer AT, Storli O. Soccer injuries to the brain: a neurologic and EEG study of active football players. American J of Sports Med 1989;17:573–578.

Tysvaer AT, Lochen EA. Soccer injuries to the brain: a neuropsychologic study of former soccer players. American J of Sports Med 1991;19:56–60.

18

Upper Extremity Injuries

James Gilbert

Introduction

In soccer, injuries to the upper extremities are not as common as injuries to the lower extremities. They have been estimated to comprise 10%–15% of all injuries. Upper extremity injuries commonly occur in collisions between players or when a player strikes the ground with the edge of the shoulder or outstretched hand (Fig. 18-1). While hand injuries are more commonly seen in goalkeepers, other upper extremity injuries are evenly distributed among players.

Some injuries, especially to the shoulder region, can be severe due to high impact energy. Other injuries associated with high impact energy must not be overlooked because they can be serious. Head and neck trauma must be assumed until proven otherwise, and because neurovascular structures are also commonly at risk, a high index of suspicion must be maintained. The joint above and below the injury must be examined. Because of the energy involved, these injuries may be open or develop compartment syndromes, which are orthopaedic emergencies requiring prompt surgical management.

After a thorough physical examination, most injuries can be immobilized with a sling or splint. Injuries with vascular compromise or gross deformity should first be reduced with gentle longitudinal traction. This is usually followed by radiographs and referral to an orthopaedist when indicated. Finally, return to play should be allowed only after neurovascular injury has been ruled out and the player demonstrates a functional range of motion with near normal strength.

This chapter is a comprehensive review and will discuss some of the more common injuries seen in the upper extremities of soccer players. For more in-depth information, see the suggested readings provided at the end of the chapter.

Shoulder Girdle Fractures

Clavicle Fractures

MECHANISM OF INJURY

Clavicle fractures are very common. They are usually the result of direct trauma, but can occur from a fall on the shoulder or outstretched hand. The

Figure 18-1. Common mechanism of a shoulder injury.

middle one third of the clavicle is typically involved (Fig. 18-2). The deformity is usually obvious with the shoulder on the affected side appearing lower. Palpation will cause tenderness and crepitus. The athlete can splint the shoulder by holding it up at the elbow with the opposite hand.

MANAGEMENT OF THE INJURY

Immediate management should involve a search for possible associated injuries. Although these are rare, they can be life threatening, such as when the lungs or subclavian vessels are injured. The shoulder should be placed into a sling or some form of immobilization for comfort and radiographs obtained to confirm diagnosis. Surgical intervention is rarely needed. Although some physicians recommend a figure-of-eight splint, a simple sling is sufficient in most athletes until there is radiographic evidence of union. In young athletes, this can be approximately 3–6 weeks, while in older patients it can be 6–8

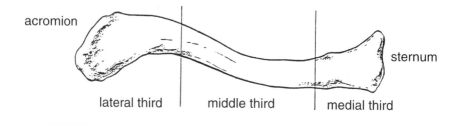

acromion

sternum

lateral third   middle third   medial third

Figure 18-2. The middle third of the clavicle is the most commonly injured.

weeks. The athlete should not return to vigorous play until a painless range of shoulder motion can be demonstrated and there is near normal strength. This often takes 3–4 months.

Although fracture callus may be prominent, there are rarely long term functional limitations. Failure of the clavicle to heal in 4–6 months may require open reduction and internal fixation (ORIF) with bone grafting.

Acromioclavicular Injuries

MECHANISM OF INJURY

Acromioclavicular (AC) separation is a common injury seen mostly in adults. It results from a direct fall on the tip of the shoulder. There are six types of AC joint injuries (Fig. 18-3). The critical distinction is between the more common incomplete AC strains or subluxations (Types 1 and 2) and those injuries that are completely displaced (Types 3, 4, 5, and 6).

MANAGEMENT OF THE INJURY

Surgery is not required for incomplete injuries, and only rarely needed for complete injuries. Athletes with complete AC separations will have tenderness to palpation over the AC joint, drooping of the involved shoulder, and a prominent distal clavicle (Fig. 18-4). A distinction should be made between a clavicle fracture and a dislocated shoulder. Radiographs can be helpful in this regard. It may be necessary to perform stress radiographs by hanging weights from the arms to accentuate a complete separation. In incomplete strains or subluxations, only a sling is needed and can be discarded when the athlete is comfortable. There is rarely any long-term disability from this type of injury and the athlete may return to full activity when the criteria are met. Only rarely will late onset posttraumatic arthritis need to be addressed. Most complete AC separations can also be treated nonoperatively. The natural history of a conservatively treated complete AC separation is usually as good as the operatively treated injury, without the risk of complication. If the athlete remains symptomatic, there are stabilization procedures that can be effectively performed at a later time.

However, there are some injuries that may require surgery. Certain widely displaced complete separations or separations in which the distal clavicle is trapped posteriorly within the trapezium muscle or underneath the coracoid process of the scapula may need surgery. For this reason, all complete AC separations should be referred to an orthopaedist.

Shoulder Dislocations

MECHANISM OF INJURY

Shoulder dislocations are common injuries in adolescents and young adults involved in contact sports. The glenohumeral joint can dislocate anteriorly, posteriorly, inferiorly, or superiorly. Anterior dislocations account for approximately 95%–98% of all glenohumeral dislocations. Posterior glenohumeral dislocations account for approximately 2%–4% of dislocations. The inferior and superior dislocations are rare. Anterior shoulder dislocations typically occur when there is trauma to the arm in a position of abduction (outstretched) and external (outward) rotation. Goalkeepers have a disproportionately high incidence of shoulder dislocation, although field players are also at risk.

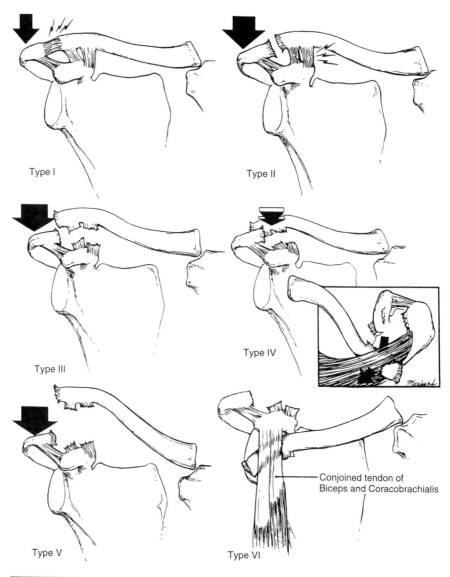

Figure 18-3. Grading of acromioclavicular injuries.

MANAGEMENT OF THE INJURY

The acutely dislocated shoulder is painful because the muscles are in spasm to stabilize the joint. The athlete can splint the affected shoulder through slight abduction and external rotation with the opposite arm. The shoulder is squared off and the humeral head can be palpated anteriorly and inferior to the coracoid process. The axillary nerve function should be checked because of its frequent association with the injury (Fig. 18-5). Sensation to the skin over the lateral aspect of the shoulder and active firing of the deltoid

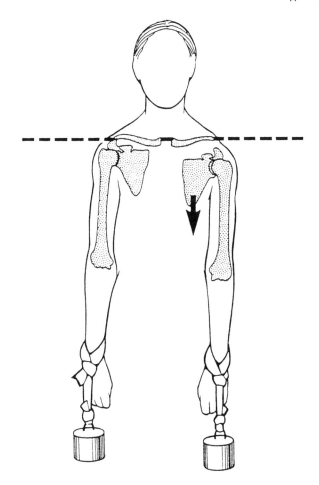

Figure 18-4. The effect of stress on a grade III acromioclavicular dislocation.

muscle are indications that the axillary nerve is intact. Patients who have re-current dislocations or anterior subluxation might experience the dead arm syndrome, in which pain and numbness occur when the arm is abducted and externally rotated. Although the pain usually subsides when the shoulder is in a neutral position, the shoulder may remain sore and weak for several days.

The management of anterior shoulder dislocations and recurrent shoulder instability is controversial. The acute management involves reduction by some form of traction-counteraction method followed by a brief period of immobilization (Fig 18-6). Although the period of immobilization is debat-able, 4–6 weeks is preferred by many orthopedists. Recurrent shoulder dis-locations are a consequence of initial injury, with some studies reporting a redislocation rate of 55%–90% in athletes less than 20-years-old. In older ath-

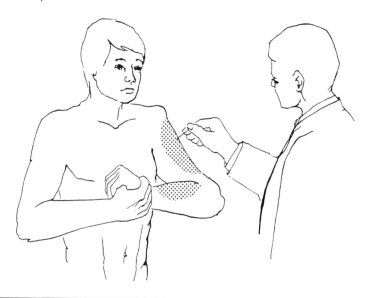

Figure 18-5. Damage to the axillary and musculocutaneous nerves should be determined prior to reduction of an anterior dislocation. Nerve function is tested by testing for skin sensitivity.

letes, the redislocation rate is much less. For young athletes with their first dislocation, most orthopedists still recommend immobilization followed by an aggressive rehabilitation program to strengthen the shoulder muscles and rotator cuff. Some studies support the use of rehabilitation in the prevention of recurrent dislocation. If rehabilitation fails, open repair is usually indicated. For some athletes, recurrent instability results in a prolonged period away from sports. Players with recurrent episodes of instability may dislocate easily while playing soccer, although there is little ball contact with the hands in field players. Treatment of recurrent instability should be individualized. Early arthroscopic techniques or open surgical repair may provide the best opportunity to return to play the following season.

Humerus Fractures

Proximal Humeral Fractures

MECHANISM OF INJURY

Although these fractures commonly occur in elderly, osteoporotic individuals, they may be seen in athletes. They are rarely seen in children before the growth plates are closed. They occur as the result of a fall on the shoulder or outstretched arm. The deformity is usually obvious with crepitus on palpation and severe pain with attempted motion.

MANAGEMENT OF THE INJURY

Neurovascular injury is not uncommon. The function of the axillary nerve must be carefully checked. On-field immobilization in a sling and swath is necessary before transport to an emergency facility where the necessary radiographs can be obtained. The Neer Classification is useful for the treatment of these injuries. Proximal humeral fractures can be classified as nondis-

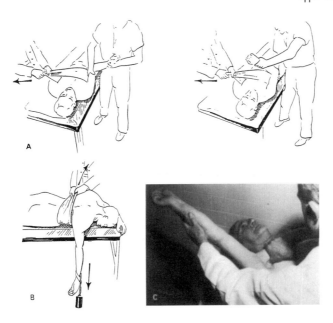

Figure 18-6. Three methods of reducing an anterior shoulder dislocation. A; Kocher method, B; Stimson method, C; Elevation method.

placed, two-part, three-part, or four-part fractures. The parts used to classify these fractures are the greater and lesser tuberosities, humeral shaft, and humeral head. In this system, displacement of 1 cm or angulation of > 45° results in classification as a part (Fig. 18-7). Nondisplaced and two-part fractures can be treated in a shoulder immobilizer, with reduction prior to immobilization if necessary. Motion should be started as soon as it is tolerable. In young patients with good bones the humeral head should be saved, although avascular necrosis or loss of blood flow to the humeral head can occur. Therefore, in young athletes, all three and four-part fractures should undergo open reduction and internal fixation. In the elderly population with poor bones, most three and four-part fractures indicate placement of a hemiarthroplasty. In young patients, it is also important to stabilize two-part fractures involving the greater tuberosity to preserve rotator cuff function and avoid subacromial impingement. Two-part lesser tuberosity fractures, which are rare and often associated with posterior dislocation and seizures, can result in an injured subscapularis tendon.

Humeral Shaft Fractures

MECHANISM OF INJURY

Humeral shaft fractures can occur as the result of a direct blow to the humerus or a fall on the outstretched hand.

MANAGEMENT OF THE INJURY

Humeral shaft fractures can almost always be treated without surgery. The main complication is damage to the radial nerve, which runs in the spiral groove in close association with the shaft of the humerus. Injury to the radial

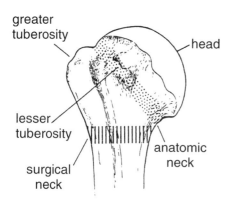

greater
tuberosity

head

lesser
tuberosity

anatomic
neck

surgical
neck

Figure 18-7. Pertinent
structures of the proximal
humerus.

nerve resolves itself in a large percentage of cases and, therefore, surgical explorations are delayed for 3–4 months. If the nerve does not recover, it should then be explored. On the other hand, if the radial nerve is functioning prior to reduction and then is found to be dysfunctional, most would recommend surgical exploration. Humeral shaft fractures can be reduced by longitudinal traction and then immobilized in a coaptation splint, which is a plaster splint placed like a sugar tong from the tip of the shoulder, around the elbow, and brought up underneath the axilla. An angulation of up to 30° is acceptable and allows for excellent function. Once the fracture has become sticky, it can be placed into a fracture brace. This uses the soft tissues to maintain reduction while allowing for elbow motion.

Adult Distal Humerus Fractures

MECHANISM OF INJURY

Distal humerus fractures are uncommon in adults. They usually occur in elderly, osteoporotic individuals. However, they can occur in athletes as the result of high energy trauma, such as falling on an outstretched arm. They are often highly comminuted with intra-articular T or Y type fracture patterns (Fig. 18-8). As expected, neurovascular injuries are common.

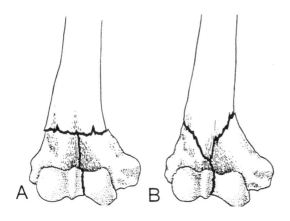

A   B

Figure 18-8. Intraarticular
fractures of the distal humerus.
A; T-shaped fracture, B; Y-
shaped fracture.

MANAGEMENT OF THE INJURY

Nondisplaced fractures can be treated with immobilization followed by early motion. In individuals who are good operative candidates, open reduction and internal fixation is required for displaced fractures.

Elbow Injuries

Elbow injuries in soccer are rare. However, because of the high degree of bony joint congruity, they are often difficult to manage. In addition to bone injuries, articular, muscle, tendon, and ligament injuries may be seen. The injuries and treatment differ between children and adults. Acute management should consist of a thorough neurovascular examination and immobilization. Associated injuries should not be overlooked. The wrist and shoulder must also be evaluated. Although treatment varies according to the injury, early motion of the elbow to prevent contracture is usually indicated. Finally, these injuries should be referred to an orthopaedist. Improper diagnosis and management can lead to disastrous consequences.

Radial Head Fractures

MECHANISM OF INJURY

The most common bony injury to the elbow is probably the radial head fracture. It occurs from a fall on an outstretched hand. It is characterized by swelling and painful motion.

MANAGEMENT OF INJURY

Radiographically, a radial head fracture is suspected when there is displacement of the fat pads of the elbow with intra-articular fluid. A positive fat pad sign without evidence of a fracture should initially be treated as a nondisplaced fracture. Radial head fractures are classified into three types (Fig. 18-9). Type I are nondisplaced fractures and can be treated by a short period of immobilization. Type II fractures are displaced. For these fractures, open reduction and internal fixation is recommended when the fracture is depressed more than 3mm, if the fracture involves more than 30% of the articular surface, or if the fracture is angulated more than 30°. Type III fractures should be fixed with open reduction and internal fixation. If this is not possible, then excision is required. However, excision of the radial head is contraindicated with a concurrent ligamentous injury to the elbow or injury to the wrist. A controversial option is placement of a radial head prosthesis after excision.

Supracondylar Pediatric Elbow Fractures

MECHANISM OF INJURY

Supracondylar elbow fractures are extra-articular fractures that occur in the distal humerus. They are rare after the growth plates have closed. However, these fractures are considered the second most common fracture seen in children, especially ages 5–10. The fracture occurs in the metaphyseal bone of the coronoid and olecranon fossas of the humerus after a fall on an outstretched hand and is usually an extension-type injury (Fig. 18-10). There is usually an obvious deformity.

MANAGEMENT OF THE INJURY

Supracondylar fractures are associated with neurovascular injuries to structures around the elbow, including the brachial artery medial, ulnar, and radial nerves. Ischemic contractures of the arm and hand can result if this in-

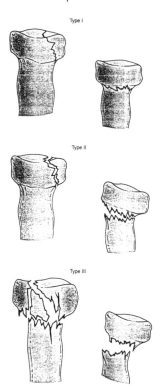

Figure 18-9. Fracture grades of the radial head.

jury is misdiagnosed or mismanaged. Supracondylar elbow fractures are classified into three types. Type I is nondisplaced. Type II is displaced with an intact posterior cortex. Type III is displacement with no cortical contact. Treatment for Type I injuries involves immobilization in flexion in a long arm cast or splint. Increasing elbow flexion stabilizes the fracture but also increases the risk of vascular compromise. Therefore, most orthopedists recommend elbow flexion of approximately 90° for nondisplaced fractures. For displaced Type II fractures, reduction can be attempted by traction, correction of medial and lateral displacement, and then flexion to lock the distal fragment into place on the end of the distal humerus. After reduction, the neurovascular examination and radiographs must be checked. If there is neurovascular compromise after reduction and flexion of the elbow, the elbow must be flexed less until documented function returns to normal. Failure to attain normal function or a stable reduction is an indication for surgical treatment. All Type III or unstable Type II fractures require either percutaneous pinning or open reduction and internal fixation performed with fluoroscopy. Any athlete treated for a displaced supracondylar fracture should be admitted for 24–48 hours to monitor the neurovascular examination.

Elbow Dislocations

MECHANISM OF INJURY

The elbow is the most commonly dislocated joint in athletes less than 10-years-old. In adults, dislocation of the shoulder is more common. Elbow dislocations occur by hyperextension from a fall on an outstretched hand.

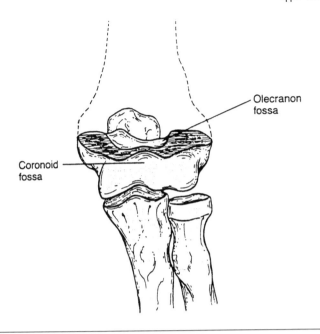

Figure 18-10. A supracondylar fracture typically occurs through the weakest part of the bone. This cross section of the distal humerus shows where a fracture is likely to occur.

MANAGEMENT OF THE INJURY

Elbow dislocations are classified according to the direction of the dislocated olecranon process of the ulna. Posterior dislocations are more common than the rare anterior dislocation. Associated fractures of the radial head, capitellum, coronoid process, and epicondyles are common. Ulnar nerve injury and elevated compartment pressures can also occur. Always examine the wrist and shoulder and perform a detailed neurovascular examination. Treatment involves reduction followed by a period of immobilization determined by stability testing. The reduction maneuver is done by longitudinal traction, manipulation of the olecranon posterior to anterior over the distal humerus, and then flexion to lock-in the reduction (Fig. 18-11). For uncomplicated dislocations that are stable when brought into extension, immobilization for 7–10 days in a sling is recommended. However, if instability occurs in extension, the anterior band of the medial ulnar collateral ligamentous has been disrupted and an extension block splint is needed. It takes approximately 3 weeks for the collateral ligament to heal. The extension block can then gradually be decreased. A full range of motion is usually attained in 6–8 weeks. Even in uncomplicated cases, some loss of full extension should be expected. The outcome is poorer in complicated cases. Some injuries can require 6–18 months to recover. Functional range of motion and stability are rarely lost.

Olecranon Fractures

MECHANISM OF INJURY

Olecranon fractures occur as the result of a fall on the elbow, usually in flexion. The pull of the triceps causes displacement of the fracture fragments (Fig. 18-12).

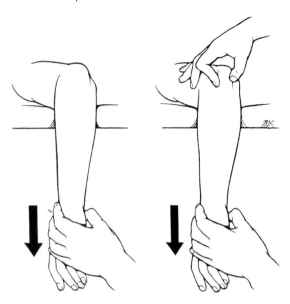

Figure 18-11. The Meyn and Quigley method for reducing an elbow dislocation. The forearm hangs and gentle traction is applied at the wrist. The physician guides the olecranon with the opposite hand.

MANAGEMENT OF THE INJURY

Nondisplaced fractures have less than 2 mm of separation and are stable with flexion to 90°. These fractures can occasionally be treated nonoperatively in a long-arm cast with the elbow in extension. For displaced fractures, the recommended treatment is open reduction and internal fixation. Comminuted fractures are best treated with plate fixation. For highly comminuted fractures in low-demand individuals, excision of up to two thirds of the olecranon followed by reattachment of the triceps can be performed without loss of stability.

Other Elbow Injuries

Isolated fractures of the capitellum, trochlea, and coronoid process are rare. They are usually associated with other elbow injuries. Displaced fractures and those fractures blocking elbow motion are usually treated operatively. Nondisplaced fractures can be immobilized with early range of motion. Me-

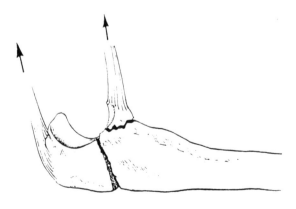

Figure 18-12. Fractured olecranon and coronoid processes of the ulna. Notice that muscle contraction can distract the fragments.

dial epicondyle fractures are more common in young throwing athletes who subject their elbows to repetitive high valgus stresses (little leaguer's elbow). Lateral condyle fractures are rare and can occur from a direct blow to the elbow or a varus stress. They can be seen in association with a radial head injury.

Fractures Of The Forearm

Fractures of the Radius and Ulna

MECHANISM OF THE INJURY

These are fairly uncommon injuries in soccer. When they occur, they are frequently the result of direct contact with an opposing player or a goalpost. In addition, they can be caused by a direct fall onto an outstretched hand, through which sufficient forces are transmitted to fracture the radius and ulna.

MANAGEMENT OF THE INJURY

Fractures of the radius and ulna are known as both bones forearm fractures. In adults, fractures of the radial and ulnar shafts should be treated with open reduction and internal fixation. In children, these injuries can be managed with cast immobilization. For children less than 10-years-old, up to 10° of angulation can be accepted because remodeling with growth will improve angulation. There is controversy over the need to remove plates in adults. Recent studies suggest that plates should not be removed for at least 2 years. When they are removed, the forearm needs protection for 6 weeks because the screw holes act as stress risers. An isolated fracture of the shaft of the ulna is known as a night stick fracture. With minimal displacement, these can be treated with a functional brace.

Injuries Of The Wrist And Hand

Although injuries to the wrist and hand are more common in other contact sports, they are seen in soccer. The goalkeeper is the most likely to sustain such an injury. Yet, falls onto an outstretched hand can occur to any outfield player. Soft tissue injuries, such as sprains and strains, are most common. Distal radius, scaphoid, and phalangeal fractures are also commonly seen in soccer.

A detailed history and physical examination followed by appropriate radiographs will usually lead to diagnosis and treatment. Acute management can be accomplished with a plaster splint. Immobilization is rarely required for more than 3 weeks. Most injuries should be referred to an orthopaedist for definitive management.

Distal Radius Fractures

MECHANISM OF INJURY

Fractures of the distal radius are common. They can occur as the result of a variety of traumatic events, including falls and other types of collisions.

MANAGEMENT OF THE INJURY

The treatment of the classic Colles fracture, with its dorsally angulated distal fragment, in an elderly osteoporotic female is different from treatment in young athletes. In the young athlete, the goal is to restore the anatomy to normal. Closed reduction and cast immobilization in a long-arm cast for 3–4 weeks with conversion to a short-arm cast for another 3–4 weeks has been the traditional method of treatment. This may be appropriate for some nondisplaced fractures. However, for displaced fractures, it is important to restore radial length, radial inclination, and the palmar tilt of the distal radius. Failure to restore these parameters to normal results in decreased wrist motion, advanced degenerative changes, and impingement of the wrist with the distal radius. In addition, an articular step-off of more than 2 mm has been shown to result in the progression of degenerative changes. Current treatment options now include external fixation, open reduction, and internal fixation with plates and screws. Recent studies have supported the use of the external fixator over traditional methods. Through ligamentotaxis, external fixation maintains radial length and inclination and restores palmar tilt and joint congruity with a low complication rate.

Scaphoid Fractures

MECHANISM OF INJURY

Scaphoid fractures are the most common fractures involving the bones of the wrist (Fig. 18-13). They occur from a fall on an outstretched hand and are manifested by tenderness in the anatomic snuff box at the base of the thumb.

MANAGEMENT OF THE INJURY

Scaphoid fractures should be immobilized in a thumb spica, excluding the thumb interphalangeal joint. Most orthopaedists agree that for a documented fracture, or when there is a high suspicion, the cast should come above the elbow to provide for more rigid rotational control. The reason for such concern over scaphoid fractures is the chance of developing avascular necrosis or nonunion. This is related to the peculiar vascular supply that en-

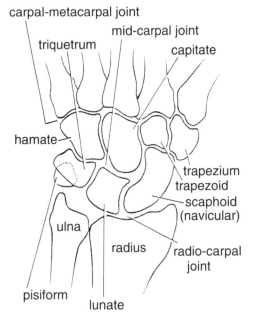

Figure 18-13. Bones of the wrist.

ters the scaphoid distally. Therefore, fractures through the middle and proximal one third of the scaphoid have a high rate of avascular necrosis and nonunion. In addition to anterior-posterior (AP) and lateral radiographs, a scaphoid view with the wrist in ulnar deviation is often helpful to see the fracture. Some orthopaedists recommend a computerized tomography (CT) scan for all documented fractures to accurately determine displacement. Nondisplaced fractures can be managed with closed treatment. A scaphoid fracture should initially be immobilized in a long arm thumb spica cast with the wrist in slight palmar flexion and radial deviation for 6 weeks. This can then be changed to a short arm thumb spica cast until there is clinical and radiographic evidence of union. Union usually takes 15–18 weeks. There are special synthetic and padded casts that allow participation in soccer. For the elite athlete, ORIF should be considered to allow for quicker return to play. A separation of 2 mm or more is considered a displaced fracture. Displaced fractures require anatomic reduction to avoid the complications of avascular necrosis, nonunion, and malunion, which can lead to debilitating wrist arthritis. The most reliable method for anatomic reduction is through ORIF, using various threaded bone screws. Bone grafting and internal fixation is usually required if there is no evidence of union by 6 months. There are some revascularization techniques that are also effective.

Fractures of the Metacarpals and Phalanges

MECHANISM OF INJURY

Falls and collisions can result in fractures of the metacarpals and phalanges. In sports, crushing trauma (having the hand or fingers stepped on) is common.

MANAGEMENT OF THE INJURY

Fractures of the long bones in the hand can usually be treated with closed reduction and immobilization, provided that the fracture remains stable and there is no malrotation or angulation. Failure to correct malrotation or angulation can result in fingers that under or overlap. The fingernails should all lie in essentially the same plane and the fingers, when flexed, should point to the scaphoid bone (Fig. 18-14). In general, when intra-articular fractures are less than 30% of the total surface, they can be managed with closed treatment. ORIF should be considered when there is volar subluxation of the more distal phalanx. Severely broken intra-articular fractures are usually best treated closed with early range of motion. For closed treatment, the hand is immobilized in the position of safety (Fig. 18-15). The metacarpal-phalangeal (MP) joints are immobilized in 70°–90° of flexion and the joints of the fingers are immobilized in 10°–20° of flexion. This is approximately the position required to hold a drink in a can. Failure to immobilize the hand in a functional position can result in contractures of the collateral ligaments. Rarely should the fingers be immobilized for more than 3 weeks. Buddy taping followed by early motion is encouraged for all stable fractures. For unstable fractures, such as long spiral metacarpal fractures, or for large intra-articular fractures that involve the condyles, closed reduction and percutaneous pinning is often used. Intramedullary fixation of unstable transverse fractures and fixation of adjacent metacarpals with external fixation devices are other options.

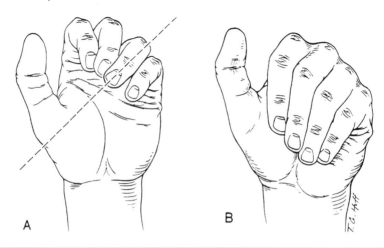

Figure 18-14. A; For proper alignment of the bones, the nails should be parallel with the digits. B; In flexion, the fingers should all point toward the scaphoid.

Bennett and Rolando's Fractures

MECHANISM OF INJURY

The mechanism of injury is essentially the same as that for other hand and finger fractures.

MANAGEMENT OF THE INJURY.

The Bennett fracture is a fracture of the thumb metacarpal base. A small ulnar fragment remains associated with the trapezium and the thumb metacarpal is usually dislocated proximal and radial by the pull of the abductor pollicis muscle. A comminuted intra-articular fracture involving the thumb metacarpal base is referred to as a Rolando's fracture (Fig. 18-16). These fractures typically require reduction and stabilization with percutaneous pinning to the adjacent metacarpal.

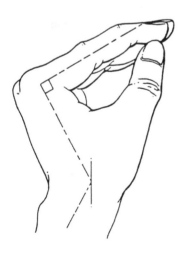

Figure 18-15. The "safe" position for splinting the hand.

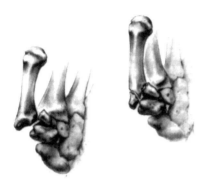

Figure 18-16. Intraarticular fractures of the thumb. Type I is a fracture-dislocation (Bennett's) and Type II is a fracture (Rolando's).

Ligamentous Injuries and Dislocations of the Finger Joints

MECHANISM OF INJURY

Dorsal proximal interphalangeal (PIP) joint dislocations are commonly caused by excessive hyperextension. Volar PIP dislocations are rare.

MANAGEMENT OF THE INJURY

The deformity is obvious and often the injury is self-reduced by the time the athlete comes to the sidelines. If there is any doubt that a fracture might be present, a radiograph should be obtained. For the majority of injuries, the dislocation can be reduced by recreating the mechanism of injury. This involves exaggeration of the hyperextension deformity to unhinge the middle phalanx and flexion of the middle phalanx over the proximal phalanx. Occasionally, reduction is blocked by interposition of the volar plate (Fig. 18-17). A follow-up radiograph should be taken to rule out a complicating fracture. The joint is then immobilized with a padded aluminum splint in extension for 4–5 days followed by buddy taping until the athlete is comfortable. Long-term complications are rare and are not usually of clinical significance. Sprains and ruptures of the collateral ligaments are also common.

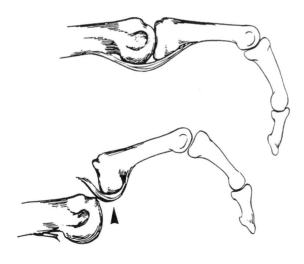

Figure 18-17. (Top) Normal position of the volar plate. (Bottom) Interposition of volar plate between the finger and the metacarpal.

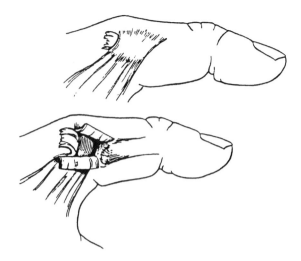

Figure 18-18. The Stenar lesion is an interposition of an adductor tendon between the ends of the ulnar collateral ligament.

They are caused by radial or ulnar forces. The radial collateral ligament is commonly injured in the fingers and the ulnar collateral ligament is commonly injured in the thumb. These injuries can be treated with buddy taping until the athlete is comfortable, usually 10–14 days.

Gamekeeper's Thumb

MECHANISM OF INJURY

This common skiing injury is usually seen in the goalkeeper and is the result of a valgus stress to the metacarpal-phalangeal joint of the thumb, producing an injury to the ulnar collateral ligament.

MANAGEMENT OF THE INJURY

On physical examination, there is tenderness over the ulnar collateral ligament with increased laxity to valgus stress. Stress radiographs are sometimes used to distinguish partial from complete rupture of the ulnar collateral ligament. An opening of greater than 35°–45° is suggestive of a complete injury. Interposition of the adductor tendon between the ends of the ulnar collateral ligaments is known as a Stener lesion. Partial injuries can be treated with immobilization. The current recommendation for complete injuries and Stener lesions (Fig. 18-18) is surgical repair.

SUGGESTED READINGS

Browner BD, Jupiter JB, Levine AM, et al, eds. Skeletal trauma. Philadelphia: WB Saunders, 1992.

Charnley JS. The closed treatment of common fractures. Edinburgh: E. and S. Livingston, 1968.

Green DP, ed. Operative hand surgery. 3rd ed. New York: Churchill Livingstone, 1991.

Greenspan A, ed. Orthopedic radiology. 2nd ed. New York: Raven Press, 1992.

Orthopaedic Knowledge Update 4. Home Study Syllabus. Chicago: American Academy of Orthopaedic Surgeons, 1993.

Orthopaedic Knowledge Update. Sports Medicine. Chicago: American Academy of Orthopaedic Surgeons, 1994.

Rockwood CA, Green DP, Bucholz RW, eds. Fractures in adults. 3rd ed. Philadelphia: J.B. Lippincott, 1991.

Rockwood CA, Wilkins KE, King RE, eds. Fractures in children. Philadelphia: Lippincott, 1991.

19   Back and Trunk Injuries

John R. McCarroll

Epidemiology

Injuries above the waist are uncommon in soccer. Combined injuries to the thorax, back, abdomen, pelvis, and groin account for less than 10% of injuries that result in loss of playing time. In review of the literature on soccer injuries, the incidence of injuries to the trunk range from 0%–13% (Table 19-1). In the National Collegiate Athletic Association (NCAA) database of injuries, the incidence of back and thoracic injuries is .41 per 1,000 athletic exposures (AE) in men and .43 per 1,000 AE in women.

All injuries to the trunk in soccer players at Indiana University since 1975 (Table 19-2) were recently reviewed. The most common injury was to the lumbar spine followed by injuries to the hip, thoracic spine, and abdomen. Most of these injuries were contusions and mild sprains or strains. Few needed to be seen by a physician. There was little playing time lost and only one case involving a lumbar disc required surgery.

Abdominal Injuries

Internal Organs

Although abdominal injuries to the soccer athlete are not frequent, they are a potential serious injury that can have fatal consequences if not recognized immediately.

MECHANISM OF INJURY

The abdomen can withstand the majority of blows received in normal contact because of the protection afforded by the bony pelvis, ribs, and the muscles attached to them. The degree to which the muscles and bones protect the internal abdominal structures depends on the force of the blow, the angle it strikes, how well developed the muscles are, and whether penetration through the muscles occurs.

Most injuries are caused by two players colliding, a player struck by a moving object, or a player colliding with the goal (Fig. 19-1). The most commonly injured viscera in this type of trauma are the solid organs such as the kidneys, spleen, liver, and pancreas.

Table 19-1

Percentage of Total Injuries by Region of the Body	
Site	Percentage*
Head	10
Upper Extremity	13
Trunk and Pelvis	22
Lower Extremity	66
Thigh	16
Knee	17
Leg	16
Ankle	24
Foot	12

*Average of percentages from multiple studies. The column will not add up to 100%

(Adapted from: Lohnes J, et al. Soccer injuries. In: Fu FH, Stone DA, eds. Sports injuries. Media: Williams & Wilkins, 1991; 607.)

Table 19-2

Trunk Injuries in Indiana University Soccer			
Part injured	# Players injured	# Players that missed days of play	# Seen by M.D.
Lumbar spine	81	19/51 days	14
Hip contusion	42	4/22 days	3
Hip pointer	10	1/1 days	0
Thoracic spine	26	8/21 days	6
Abdominal muscle	16	4/8 days	3
Ribs	15	5/11 days	3
Coccyx	2	1/2 days	1
Rhomboids	3	1/5 days	1
Kidney	1	1/6 days	1
Latissimus dorsi	3	0/0 days	0
Pectorals	2	0/0 days	0

Figure 19-1. Contact in area of spleen and kidneys.

MANAGEMENT OF THE INJURY

Blunt injuries are more difficult to diagnose and may escape initial detection. If there is any question regarding the possibility of internal injury, the athlete must be taken immediately to a medical facility for further examination and testing. Failure to do so could result in a serious situation or even death.

The suggestion of intraabdominal hemorrhage can be confirmed by peritoneal lavage or laparoscopy. In most major trauma centers, computed tomography (CT scan) is helpful in detecting injuries to the abdominal organs. Routine radiographs are usually not helpful. When a kidney injury is suspected, an intravenous pyelogram (IVP) will provide valuable information. Although magnetic resonance imaging (MRI) can provide good soft tissue views, it is not a practical tool for emergencies.

The spleen is usually the most commonly injured organ because of its location. If the organ is enlarged as a result of mononucleosis the athlete is particularly vulnerable to splenic rupture. There has been some dispute about the length of time the athlete recovering from mononucleosis needs to avoid contact sports. Because no definite study exists, a 6 month span seems to be the safest for the amateur athlete (and for the legal protection of the sports medicine physician). However, this recommendation is not always followed.

Splenic injury can range from a small subscapular tear to a total disruption, which can have fatal results. Immediate diagnosis with peroneal lavage and/or CT scan is important. Presently, the spleen is no longer removed as it was in the past. The spleen is important to the immune system of a young person. It can be salvaged by the use of blood clotting agents combined with hemostatic suturing. The spleen may even be wrapped in mesh.

It is not uncommon for the spleen to undergo a delayed rupture. If there is any question of a serious injury in an athlete who sustains a blow to the left upper abdomen or left rib cage, it is best to transport the player to a medical facility.

In soccer, the kidney is injured almost as frequently as the spleen. Symptomatically, these patients usually exhibit mild tenderness in the upper abdomen or flank. In addition, there can be gross or microscopic hematuria, progression to flank swelling, hypotension, and increasing pain. In less obvious cases, CT scan is a choice for diagnosis. In runners, transient hematuria can occur. Approximately 1 in 5 marathon runners has hematuria after a race. Therefore, care must be taken to avoid a false diagnosis.

Renal injuries might be suspected from a blow to the kidney area followed by flank pain. A simple on-site test is to have the athlete void, then examine the urine for blood visually and with dip stick testing. If the first test is negative, wait 10 minutes and repeat. If a positive test is found, hospitalization is indicated. At the hospital, a definitive examination is done. When splenic injury is suspected, emphasis should be placed on the possibility that the athlete may have had mononucleosis in the past. Studies have found that as many as 44% of splenic injuries in sports are related to this disease.

In many cases renal injuries can be managed with conservative treatment, which includes bed rest, IV fluids, antibiotics, and careful observation. However, if symptoms are severe, surgical exploration of the kidney is undertaken.

If no surgical procedure was involved, all evidence of injury must be absent and proven by follow-up studies before allowing the athlete to return to play. Return is determined by the physician. If surgery of the abdomen is involved, healing may take up to 8 weeks for noncontact and 12 weeks for contact sports.

Abdominal Muscle Injury
MECHANISM OF INJURY
Abdominal wall contusions and muscle tears are frequent injuries in soccer. An abrupt twist can cause a tear in the rectus abdominis muscle. A hematoma then forms and the pain may restrict athletic activities.

MANAGEMENT OF THE INJURY
Early treatment should begin with ice, compression, and rest. When the pain decreases, physical therapy is begun to restore strength to the abdominal muscles. Pain or soreness acts as a guide to when the athlete can return to more strenuous exercise.

Chest Injuries
Rib Injuries
MECHANISM OF INJURY
Rib fractures or contusions are the most common chest injuries. The most commonly fractured or contused ribs are in the middle level or the 4–7 ribs. This usually is the result of a direct blow.

MANAGEMENT OF THE INJURY

When rib injury is suspected, a chest radiograph should be obtained to rule out life threatening interthoracic injuries such as pneumothorax, hemathorax, and pulmonary contusion. Further studies may be needed to detect additional rib fractures.

The treatment for isolated rib fractures is symptomatic. The most common recommendations include rest, a compression dressing such as a rib belt, and protection when coughing or sneezing such as splinting the side of the injury with a pillow or holding the humerus to the side and using it as a splint. When the pain improves, a protective rib device may be used for return to sports. The athlete must also be cautioned that a repeat blow could cause thoracic or abdominal injury if an organ is penetrated by a fractured rib. If a fracture is present, some time may be needed for healing before allowing the patient to return to contact sports. In the case of rib contusion, pain can be the most useful guide.

Other injuries to the chest and thoracic areas such as scapula fractures, sternal fractures, costal chondral injuries, clavicle fractures, and serious injuries to the lungs and cardiac region must be considered, although they are not common soccer injuries.

Spine Injuries

Thoracic Spine

MECHANISM OF INJURY

Thoracic spine injuries must also be considered in soccer, especially if the athlete has had a violent collision with another player or the goalpost. However, these are rare and have not been reported in current medical literature.

Lumbar Spine Injuries

MECHANISM OF INJURY

Most of the problems we have seen (Table 19-2) are related to the lumbar spine. Predisposing factors to lumbar spine pain in athletes are increased trunk length and stiff lower extremities. Spina bifida occulta is found in a high percentage of patients who develop lower lumbar spondylitic defects. The relationship of exercise and back pain in athletes compared to the average population does not demonstrate an increased incidence of back pain in athletes. In fact, one report suggests that back pain is more common in students who avoid sports.

The Indiana data shows that 80% of back injuries occur during practice, 6% during competition, and 14% during preseason conditioning. A total of 80% of male players and 6% of the female players have injuries. The nature of the injuries is acute for 59% of the cases, overuse in 12%, and aggravation of pre-existing conditions in 29%.

MANAGEMENT OF THE INJURY

Again, a proper diagnosis precedes an aggressive treatment program. In diagnosing the exact etiology of lumbar spine pain, age is an important factor. Young athletes are more likely to have stress fractures and diseases that effect growing cartilage (e.g., Scheuermann's Disease). In the mature athlete, the pain may be related to disc problems. One of the most important diag-

Table 19-3

Locations of Soccer Injuries (Percent of Total)

Head	Upper Extremity	Trunk	Pelvis	Lower Extremity	Thigh	Knee	Leg	Ankle	Foot
7	8	—	20	—	—	18	29	—	—
7	5	3	3	71	8	13	16	19	10
12	13	1	1	61	—	—	—	—	—
—	2	7	—	—	—	59	—	9	—
—	—	—	13	—	14	20	29	26	12
22	6	—	6	63	15	23	9	—	9
8	20	—	8	58	—	—	—	—	—
2	27	—	15	57	—	—	—	33	—
17	14	1	1	61	—	—	—	—	—
—	—	7.5	—	—	—	—	—	—	—
9	7	5	6	—	17	18	7	21	9.5
7	7	6	4	—	18	17	9	22	10
—	—	—	—	84	22 (includes groin)	18	—	—	—
10	15	7	—	68	12	14	13	16	13
9	26	—	4	58	—	12	—	—	—
—	—	—	—	59	—	—	—	—	—
14	12	9	—	64	—	—	—	—	—
9	16	7	—	68	—	—	—	—	—
5	—	1	1	81	—	—	—	44	1
15	17	—	—	65	—	12	—	41	—
4	—	—	—	—	24	19	—	27	19

Reprinted with permission from: Lohnes J, Garrett WE. Soccer injuries. In: Fu FH, Stone DA, eds. Sports injuries. Media: Williams & Wilkins, 1991.

noses to make in an athlete with back and leg pain is that of peripheral nerve injury and peripheral nerve entrapment, such as piriformis syndrome. These diagnoses must be ruled out before disc disease is seriously considered.

A variety of pathologic conditions can be diagnosed on radiographs. The bone scan and single photon emission computed tomography (SPECT scan) are vital tools for the diagnostic imaging needs of the physician in caring for lumbar problems, especially in the younger athlete. The MRI and CAT scan are helpful in diagnosing certain spine conditions, such as herniated nucleus pulposus. After a thorough history and physical examination, most athletic injuries to the lumbar spine can be categorized as mechanical, actual, back, or leg pain. Lumbar spine injuries can fall into four major categories or syndromes.

Annular Tear of the Intravertebral Disc

This is usually caused by a compressive rotating injury producing severe back spasm and pain. The pain is increased by coughing, sneezing, sitting, and the upright posture. There is usually a positive straight leg raising sign and possible neurologic defects. MRIs are helpful in diagnosing these problems.

Facet Syndrome

Injuries that occur with extension and rotation can affect the facet joints of the lumbar spine. Symptoms can be reproduced by extension on physical examination and point tenderness over the paraspinous area and may have referred leg pain. Straight leg raising may be negative and there are usually no neurologic findings. These injuries can usually be treated well with conservative treatment.

Lumbar Muscle Strains and Contusions

Strains and contusions of the lumbar muscles are probably the most common injuries and respond well to nonoperative and conservative treatment.

Sacroiliac Joint Pain

Localized sacroiliac joint pain can be common in sports such as soccer due to the rotation and hyperextension movements of the game. This condition responds well to nonoperative care. After proper diagnosis, nonoperative care in lumbar spine injuries should be aimed at minimizing inflammation with the use of rest, ice, antiinflammatory agents, and soft tissue mobilization techniques to relieve the spasm caused by the injury.

Physical therapy is then started to restore strength and flexibility. After therapeutic execises can be performed easily and without pain, aerobic conditioning can be started with careful attention to the spine. Weight lifting and other exercise programs should not affect or re-injure the lumbar area. The player can return to full function if symptoms have resolved and the movements involved in soccer can be performed without significant back trauma.

If nonoperative care does not work and the proper diagnosis has been made, then surgical treatment is needed. In the review of spine injuries at Indiana University, only one soccer player with lumbar pain eventually required surgery.

Stress Fractures

Spondylolysis in Soccer Athletes

Spondylolysis is a defect usually caused by stress in the pars intra-articularis (Fig. 19-2). European literature describes the defect as congenital spondylol-

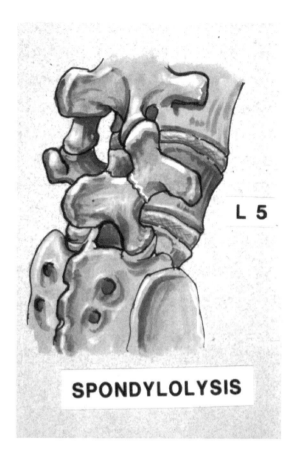

Figure 19-2. Picture of spondylolysis.

L 5

SPONDYLOLYSIS

ysis, which means it is present at an early age and not related to athletic activity. Little mention is made of stress fractures to the pars intra-articularis in this literature.

MECHANISM OF INJURY

Spondylolysis, or stress fracture of the pars intra-articularis, may occur in goalkeepers because of the repetitive lumbar hyperextension required during diving saves. Many believe that the mechanism causing stress fractures of the pars intra-articularis is due to increased axial loading during hyperextension and tarsal movements and repeated cycles of flexion to extension. Over one-third of young athletes with significant lumbar pain have positive bone scans that indicate a stress fracture of the pars intra-articularis. In the Indiana review, 30 stress fractures of the pars intra-articularis in soccer athletes were treated.

Using high speed video filming, pressure plates, and electromyographic (EMG) studies, the biomechanical forces on the lumbar spine have been performed on football lineman, golfers, and soccer players. The stress across the pars intra-articularis in soccer athletes was similar to that in American football lineman. Numerous studies show an increased incidence of pars intra-articularis stress fractures with compression across the pars intra-articularis being 7.4 times the body weight with increased shear forces.

In soccer, the kicking action (Fig. 19-3) can be divided into approach, contact, and follow through. During the follow through, the muscles rotate the trunk resulting in rotation and hyperextension stress on the lumbar spine.

MANAGEMENT OF THE INJURY

Most patients with spondylolysis have a history of aching low back pain lasting from a few weeks to several months. The pain can be unilateral or bilateral. There is usually no leg pain. The back pain limits sports activity.

On physical examination there are usually no neurologic findings or limitations on range of motion testing. The hallmark sign is pain on hyperextension. These patients may have a positive single leg hyperextension test (Fig. 19-4). Standing on the leg on the same side as the back pain and leaning backward recreates the pain. They may also have increased hamstring tightness.

These patients must have routine radiograph examinations including anteriorposterior (AP), lateral, and oblique views of the lumbar spine. If these radiographs are negative, the patient should undergo a bone scan. If the bone scan is negative, a SPECT scan should be done because it picks up the 10%–15% of findings not seen with a normal bone scan.

From 1989–1995, we have seen 30 stress fractures of pars intra-articularis in soccer athletes with a positive bone or SPECT scan at the Methodist Sports Medicine Center. There were 28 males and 2 females with an age range of 12–20 years and an average of 16 years. Twenty-nine were field players and

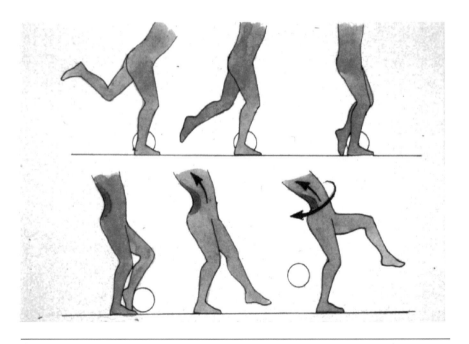

Figure 19-3. The 3 phases of kicking. Top: approach and impact. Bottom: follow through with stress on spine.

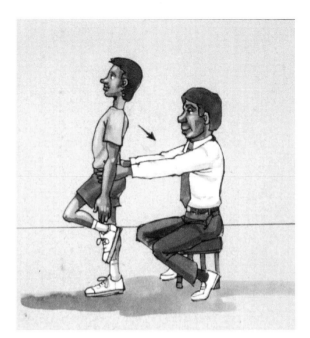

Figure 19-4. One leg hyperextension test.

one was a goalie. These patients were treated with an antilordotic Boston overlap brace for 12 weeks. For the first 10 weeks, the patients wore the brace 23 out of 24 hours per day. For the next 2 weeks, the patients wore the brace 12 out of 24 hours per day. If the pain disappeared after 3 weeks, the patients were allowed to return to soccer wearing the brace. If the pain returned, they rested another 3 weeks before attempting another return. After 6 weeks they were started on physical therapy, which included antilordotic exercises.

If the pain continued after more than 3 months, the patients wore the brace for another 3 months. If they still continued to have pain, we considered further diagnostic studies, such as CAT scan.

In our work, follow-up radiographs were taken at 3 months, 6 months, and 1 year. Twenty-nine of the 30 athletes returned to soccer in the same season. Twenty-eight of the 30 defects were at L5 level and 2 of the 30 at L4 level, the levels of the fifth and fourth lumbar vertebra. In 19 of the 30 athletes the lesion was on the same side as their dominant kicking leg. In 10 of the 30 athletes the lesions were bilateral. In one athlete the lesion was on the opposite side from their dominant kicking leg. There was one reoccurrence with a new lesion on the opposite side pars intra-articularis, resulting in a bilateral injury.

Summary

Injuries to the trunk in soccer are not common and usually not serious. However, in the young soccer player with lumbar pain, stress fracture of the pars intra-articularis must be suspected and treated.

20 Groin Injuries

Lars Peterson

Introduction

Soccer is one of the most popular and widely played sports in the world. More than 400 million males are active in soccer, approximately 200 million players are licensed, and an additional 200 million are recreational players. Female soccer is one of the fastest growing sports with approximately 30 million players estimated to be playing in organized games. World championships in soccer attract large crowds and a worldwide television audience. Soccer is a body contact sport and traumatic injuries and overuse are common. The most frequent injuries in the groin region affect the adductor longus, rectus abdominis, rectus femoris, and iliopsoas muscle-tendon units. The most important symptom is pain. But pain in the groin can also be referred from other sources. When the pain is caused by injuries to the muscle-tendon units, the injury is not a diagnostic or therapeutic problem when treated in the early stages (Fig. 20-1). With chronic groin pain, the symptoms may be vague and uncharacteristic. This requires a careful analysis of the history, mechanism of injury, and thorough examination.

Epidemiology

Injuries in soccer may be caused by overuse or trauma. The injury rate is between 15–20 injuries per 1000 play-hours. The injury rate is 3 to 4 times higher during matches than during training. The injury rate seems to be higher among female players than among male players. Males have 7.6 injuries per 1000 play-hours contrasted with a rate of 29.9 injuries per 1000 play-hours among females. In a prospective study of soccer injuries in Sweden, groin injuries constituted 5% of the total number of injuries. Groin injuries caused by overuse seem to be more common on artificial turf than on grass.

The mechanism of injury, treatment, and prevention strategies will be presented in the sections that discuss each injury.

Adductor Longus

The adductor longus muscle (Fig. 20-1) is the most common location of groin injuries. The mechanism of injury could be overuse, which causes microle-

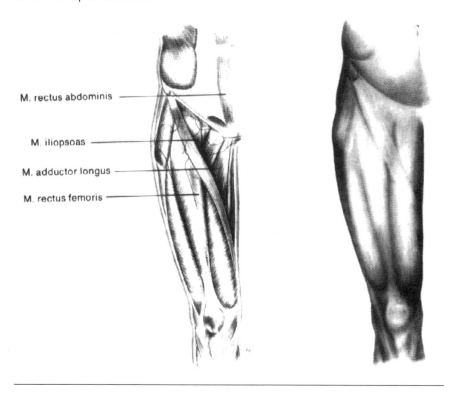

M. rectus abdominis

M. iliopsoas

M. adductor longus

M. rectus femoris

Figure 20-1. The groin region, including the adductors, rectus abdominis, rectus femoris, and iliopsoas muscles.

sions, inflammation, and repair. The muscle could also be injured from sudden or repeated overload (or trauma) with forceful adduction against an opposite force (e.g., an opponent), which results in a partial or total rupture.

Strain

The injury is usually located in the tendinous insertion at the tendon or muscle-tendon junction. In acute cases, there is a stabbing pain in the groin area. The pain is recurring when the injured player tries to continue playing. Locally, there is pain on palpation, hemorrhage, and swelling. These symptoms can usually be seen during the couple of days after the injury. The diagnosis is determined by the history of injury, localized tenderness, and pain on active adduction against resistance.

IMMEDIATE CARE OF THE INJURY

The player is immediately removed from the field. Ice is applied to the injured area with a compression bandage. The limb is elevated while the player rests. When the diagnosis is confirmed, partial weight bearing with crutches can begin. Range of motion exercises can start early. Isometric contraction without resistance is followed by gradually increasing resistance, with pain being the primary source of limitation. When the player is free of pain and dynamic contraction against resistance is achieved, dynamic training with increasing resistance can be started. The return to swimming, bicycling, running, and soccer training must be gradual. It is important not to return to training and matches too soon because the most common complication is recurring symptoms. In chronic conditions, remaining or recurring symptoms are from an acute injury. Otherwise, the symptoms start insidiously and the pain is more diffuse, radiating up and down from the origin of the adductor longus. Coughing and sneezing are often painful. Swelling is rarely seen. Pain and stiffness before and after exercise and in the morning are common. Often, there is localized tenderness over the origin of the adductor longus or its tendon. Tenderness may also be present at the insertion of the rectus abdominis muscle on the same side. If the diagnosis is not clear, a rectal examination should be performed.

Examination of the scrotum, lymphatic and neural structures of the lower leg, and for the location of a hernia should be carried out. Routine radiographs should be performed (Figs. 20-2a and 20-2b). If necessary, ultrasonography, bonescan, magnetic resonance imaging (MRI), and other tests should be done. Herniography could be of value if there is a suspicion of incipient hernia. Laboratory tests and arthroscopy should be done if there is a suspicion of hip joint changes such as chondral injuries, osteochondritis dissecans, or labral tears. Nerve entrapment should be ruled out. Treatment with antiinflammatory medication or local steroid injection in the tender region could be tried once or twice in combination with rest for 2 weeks. Isometric training to the limits of pain, gradual increase of dynamic training with resistance, and stretching exercises should be done.

SURGICAL TREATMENT

If 6 months of conservative treatment is unsuccessful, surgery may be necessary. Several surgical procedures are used, such as tenotomy. The policy in our practice has been to excise the pathologic lesion. Preoperative ultrasonography, a valuable procedure before surgery, may reveal the location and extent of the lesion. Surgery is done with general anesthesia and the leg dressed so that it may be freely moved. The leg is placed in 45°–60° of hip flexion and the knee in 90° of flexion, a position that exposes the adductor longus tendon for inspection and palpation. A transverse or a longitudinal incision is made over the tendon. The fascia and paratenon are incised to explore the tendon from the insertion to the muscle-tendon junction. The area is palpated and inspected. Over the discolored and swollen area, a longitudinal incision over the tendon is made and opened like the pages of a book. Sometimes a discolored area of scar tissue is found. The scar tissue is excised along the direction of the fibers until normal resection surfaces. Sometimes scar tissue without fiber structures is seen, which should be excised longitudinally until normal fibers are reached. If the exploration is negative or there is extensive inflammatory scar tissue, a tenotomy is made at the origin of the adductor longus. Should there be an inflammatory reaction, the inflamed area is excised radically. Postoperatively, the patient can walk using crutches with weight bearing that is limited by pain. Rehabilitation includes range of motion training and isometric exercises with progressive resistance. When free of pain, isometric contractions, dynamic progressive weight training, and functional training can progress. Return to training and matches usually takes 16–24 weeks.

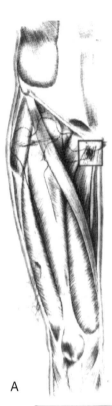

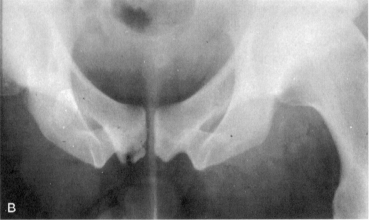

Figure 20-2. A; The adductor longus muscle with partial rupture in the tendon close to the pubic bone. B; Avulsion fracture of the adductor longus origin.

Complete Rupture

Complete rupture of the adductor longus may occur in the origin on the pubic bone or in the insertion on the femur. The mechanism of injury is an explosive overloading of the groin on contact (forceful adduction met with sudden resistance by an opponent). There is sudden pain and loss of power. The adductor longus muscle is inactive on adduction against resistance. If the injury is located proximally in the origin of the tendon, there is often a palpable and tender defect close to the insertion. Treatment requires surgery with reinsertion or suturing of the tendon. If the rupture is distal, a large hematoma may increase muscular pressure. Surgery can evacuate the hematoma and reinsert the muscle to the insertion of the femur with bone sutures. The postoperative treatment is the same as the surgical treatment of chronic cases. If the distal rupture is overlooked or not treated, it may later simulate a tumor (Fig. 20-3).

INJURY PREVENTION

Special attention should be paid to general conditioning of the player, and specifically the strength, endurance, and flexibility of the thigh muscles. Isometric and dynamic muscle strength and endurance training should be included in the training program along with warming up before and cooling down after every training and match. Heat, which increases the elasticity of the collagen, should be applied with the use of neoprene pants during warm up or matches in cold weather conditions.

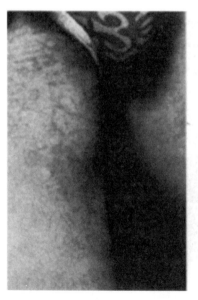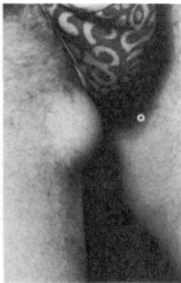

Figure 20-3. Complete distal avulsion of the adductor longus muscle and the late result with a tumor-like hypertrophy. Left; during muscle relaxation. Right; during muscle contraction.

The Rectus Abdominis Muscle

Strains

Microlesions and partial ruptures are seen at the muscle-tendon insertion on the pubic bone. They can occur from overuse during sit-ups, strength, and shooting training. They can also occur in heading or as a result of throw-ins. The pain is insidious when caused by explosive overloading. There is localized tenderness and pain on active lifting of the head and both legs at the same time. In an acute case, there can be discoloration. Most of the time there is no notable bleeding or discoloration. The treatment is conservative and similar to that for the adductor longus. In chronic cases, surgical treatment may be necessary following the same guidelines described for the adductor longus.

Complete Rupture

Total rupture or avulsion of the tendon insertion is uncommon. There is always a history of sudden pain. On palpation, there is a defect at the insertion of the rectus abdominis tendon and no activation of the distal part of the muscle during active muscle contraction. The total rupture can be verified by ultrasonography and a bone avulsion can be verified by radiographs. Surgical treatment is required and involves suturing the rupture or reinserting the avulsed tendon or bone fragment (Fig. 20-4).

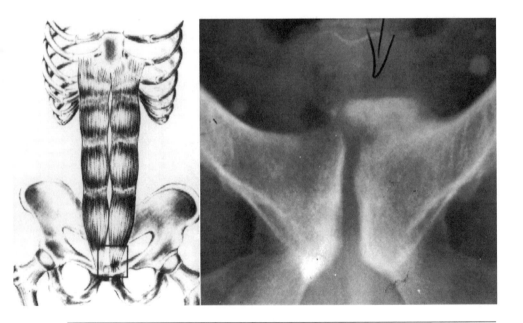

Figure 20-4. Avulsion of the bone insertion of the rectus abdominis insertion in the pubic bone. One year after initial injury.

The Rectus Femoris

Strains

The rectus femoris is commonly injured in its tendon origin above the acetabulum. There is a distinct tenderness over the tendon at the acetabular origin. Pain is elicited on flexion of the hip and extension of the knee. Microlesions can result from overuse during intensive shooting training. A partial rupture can be due to sudden overloading during explosive training movements or forceful shooting events. Partial ruptures can also occur as a result of a collision with an opponent during a forceful contraction of the rectus femoris muscle. The treatment is usually conservative and, in principle, the same as for the adductor longus. Ultrasonography may reveal the location and extent of the lesion. In chronic cases, when conservative treatment fails, surgery may be necessary. A longitudinal incision at the tendon's origin is performed. The scar tissue or granulated tissue is excised according to the guidelines given for the surgical treatment of the adductor longus.

Complete Rupture

Total rupture or avulsion of the tendon insertion is uncommon. Complete rupture or avulsion of the bony attachment at the origin of the rectus femoris tendon may be a result of forceful shooting, explosive sprint training, or a collision with an opponent against forceful contraction of the rectus femoris. Sudden, localized pain is felt deep in the groin. Discoloration or swelling can occur, but usually only after a few days. The player is unable to activate the rectus femoris muscle and may have a palpable defect in the proximal part of the tendon close to origin. Radiographs or ultrasonography may be helpful in verifying the diagnosis.

On palpation, there is a defect at the insertion of the rectus abdominis tendon and no activation of the distal part of the muscle during active muscle contraction. Surgical treatment involves suturing the rupture or reinserting the avulsed tendon or bone fragment (Fig. 20-5). In late cases, calcification or bony healing of avulsed fragments may cause chronic pain and limited range of motion. This bone formation can be removed surgically in a late stage when necessary.

The Iliopsoas

Strains

Injuries to the iliopsoas usually occur in the muscle-tendon junction, the tendon itself, or its insertion on the lesser trochanter. Repeated or forceful flexion maneuvers of the hip and jumping, sprinting, and shooting training may cause microlesions or partial ruptures of the iliopsoas. Strength training with weight lifting and sit-ups can lead to overuse injuries. The iliopectineal bursa, which lies behind the iliopsoas tendon and extends and encloses the tendon in front, is usually involved in the condition. There is local tenderness in the region of the lesser trochanter, which may be hard to reach on palpation. Bimanual palpation from the front and back on the medial aspect of the upper femur can identify the lesser trochanter and elicit pain. Pain is also experienced when flexing the hip against resistance, with passive extension of the hip, and with passive internal rotation of the hip in 90° of flexion. In principle, the treatment is the same as outlined for the adductor longus.

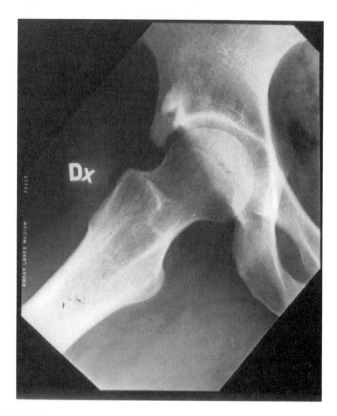

Figure 20-5. Bone formation limiting the range of hip motion after avulsion of the tendinous origin of the rectus femoris.

Complete Rupture

A complete rupture of the iliopsoas tendon can occur from a forceful flexion of the hip against resistance. It is felt as a sudden pain or click in the groin. There is a pronounced weakness in flexion at the hip, but there is usually no visible swelling or discoloration. Radiographs may reveal avulsion of a bony fragment. If the fragment is dislocated more than 10 mm, it should be reinserted. Ultrasonograpny may verify a total rupture, which should be sutured.

With chronic pain conditions in the iliopsoas tendon region, there is usually a secondary bursitis. This may give rise to snapping in the front of the groin, which can be elicited with flexion against resistance. Usually, there is a hypertrophic thickening of the synovial bursa, which gives rise to the snapping phenomena. Bursography or MRI may be used for diagnosis. In the case of painful snapping, extirpation of the bursa may be indicated (Fig. 20-6).

Surgical Treatment of Groin Pain

The following information represents experience from the clinic. Forty-six patients, 36 males and 8 females with an average age of 26 years, were oper-

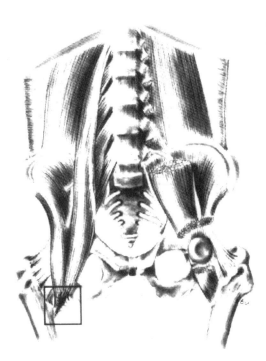

Figure 20-6. The iliopsoas tendon and the illopectineal bursa.

ated on for long-standing chronic pain conditions in the groin. In 22 patients the lesion was located in the adductor longus, the rectus femoris in 14, the rectus abdominis in 6, the iliopsoas in 3, the pectineus in 1, and the adductor brevis in 1. In 44 cases, local excisions and adaptation sutures were performed. Two patients underwent tenotomy and excision of the scar tissue.

All but 6 patients could return to their preinjury level of activity. Forty patients were completely free of symptoms, 4 were improved, and 2 were unchanged.

Groin Pain in the Adolescent Player

Young, growing players with open epiphyses have a high risk of avulsion fractures of the muscle-tendon origin or insertion and should always have radiographs done in the evaluation of acute groin pain. The pain could occur in the groin in the region of the anterior superior and inferior iliac spines, on the greater and lesser trochanter, or on the tuberosity. An avulsion should be looked for when there is boney tenderness at the muscular attachement. Surgery should be considered if the avulsed fragment is dislocated by more than 10 mm (Fig. 20-7).

Injuries to Other Muscle-Tendon Units in the Groin

Other adductors (e.g., the adductor magnus, adductor brevis, peroneus, or gracilis) could also be injured in the groin area. It is important to elicit and localize the pain with functional muscle testing. In principle, the treatment is the same as outlined for the adductor longus.

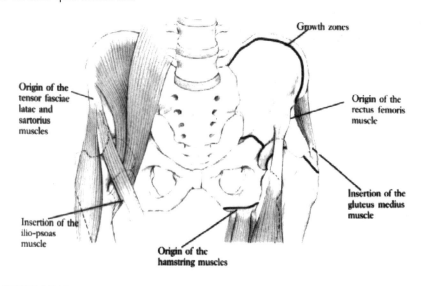

Origin of the
tensor fasciae
latae and
sartorius
muscles

Growth zones

Origin of the
rectus femoris
muscle

Insertion of the
gluteus medius
muscle

Insertion of the
ilio-psoas
muscle

Origin of the
hamstring muscles

Figure 20-7. Apophyses where avulsion fracture should be suspected in the adolescent players.

Differential Diagnosis for Groin Pain

Fractures

Table 20-1 lists the possible diagnoses associated with groin pain. Fractures of the pubic bone and femoral neck are rare, but may occur after trauma. If there is adequate trauma, tender bones, and pain with motion of the hip joint, fractures should be expected and ruled out with radiographs. The treatment of femoral neck fractures usually requires surgery.

Stress Fractures

Fatigue, or stress, fractures may occur in the upper femur, femoral neck, and pubic bones. A history of pain during exercise and high intensity or high mileage training is usually reported. It is not common among soccer players, but must be considered. If the bone is accessible for palpation, pain and light swelling is often found. Otherwise, radiographs and bone scans should be taken as soon as possible to rule out stress fractures of the neck, femur, or upper femoral shaft. Stress fractures of the femoral neck have a high incidence of caput necrosis and should be treated surgically.

Injuries or Diseases in the Hip Joint

Pain in the groin is often experienced from the hip joint as a result of inflammatory conditions, such as early osteoarthritis and osteochondritis dissecans. Traumatic injuries causing labral tears and chondral injuries can also cause pain in the groin. There is usually pain with movement of the hip. Radiographs, including MRI, may be necessary for the diagnosis. Arthroscopy or arthrography could be helpful for diagnosis of intraarticular conditions. Slipped femoral epiphyses should be considered in adolescents.

Osteitis Pubis

Many soccer players have pain in the groin area close to the symphysis. Mechanical strains from abnormal motion or trauma may cause inflammation

Table 20-1

Differential Diagnosis of Groin Pain
Fractures
Stress fractures
Injury or disease of the hip
Osteitis pubis
Nerve entrapment
Hernias

and pain. Sometimes it is combined with an instability in the symphysis. Radiographs and bonescans can support the diagnosis. The treatment is conservative.

Nerve Entrapment

Any nerve running across the groin region may cause pain due to entrapment. This could be caused by direct trauma to the nerve, resulting in scar tissue and entrapment of the nerve. It could also be caused by an inflammatory response to local anatomic conditions such as narrow passages, restrictive ligaments, or muscles. The nerves that could be symptomatic are the lateral cutaneous femoral nerve, anterior cutaneous branches of the femoral nerve, ilioinguinal nerve, genitofemoral nerve, iliohypogastric nerve, and obturator nerve. In addition to pain, the player often experiences numbness in the skin. The diagnosis may be confirmed with local anesthetics along the nerve. If pain continues after conservative treatment, surgical lysis of the nerve may be necessary. In persistent cases, nerve resection may be needed (Fig. 20-8).

Hernias

Inguinal and femoral hernias are common causes of groin pain. All players with groin pain should be examined for hernias. Incipient hernias may be diagnosed by herniography. Treatment requires surgery.

Groin Pain Arising from Tissue Outside the Groin

Referred pain from tissues outside the groin should be looked for when the diagnosis is unclear. Conditions that affect the spinal nerves to the leg, such as L4-L5 syndrome of the sciatic, should be looked for as well as other diseases of the spine, such as spondylolysis or spondylolisthesis.

Intraabdominal diseases or urogenital diseases should also be included in the differential diagnosis of groin pain. Tumors such as osteosarcomas, chondrosarcomas, malignant schwannomas, or metastatic tumors should always be considered.

Summary

Groin injuries usually affect the adductor, rectus abdominis, rectus femoris, and iliopsoas muscle-tendon units in the groin area. Diagnosis and therapy is straightforward in early stages. In chronic cases, diagnosis may be difficult and should include a broad differential diagnostic background. A history

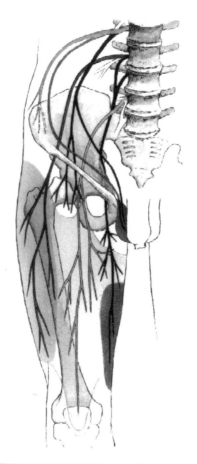

Figure 20-8. Entrapment of nerves in the groin region. The areas of loss of sensation are marked. From medial to lateral; genitofemoral, ilioinguinal obturator, anterior femoral cutaneous, lateral femoral cutaneous, and iliohypogastric nerves.

and analysis of the injury mechanism should be followed by a clinical examination and functional tests. Further examinations may be needed, such as routine radiographs, ultrasonography, MRI, bonescan, and laboratory examinations. For effective and successful treatment of groin pain, a correct diagnosis is a necessity.

SUGGESTED READINGS

Abrahamson PA, Westlin N. Symphysitis and prostatitis in athletes. Scand J Urol Nephrol 1985;19 (suppl 93):42.

Akermark C, Johansson C. Tenotomy of the adductor longus tendon in the treament of chronic groin pain in athletes. Am J Sports Med 1992;20:640–643.

Ekberg 0, Persson NA, Abrahamson PA, et al. Longstanding groin pain in athletes—a multidisciplinary approach. Sports Med 1988;6:56–61.

Ekstrand J. Soccer injuries and their prevention. Dissertation. Sweden: University of Linkoping, 1982.

Estwanik JJ, Sloane B, Rosenberg MA. Groin strain and other possible causes of groin pain. Physician Sportsmed 1990;18:59–65.

Jacobson T, Allen WT. Surgical correction of the snapping iliopsoas tendon. Am J Sports Med 1990;18:470–474.

Kalebo P, Karlsson J, Sward L, et al. Ultrasonography of chronic tendon injuries in the groin. Am J Sports Med 1992;20:634–639.

Martens MA, Hansen L, Mulier JC. Adductor tendinitis and musculus rectus abdominis tendopathy. Am J Sports Med 1987;15:353–356.

Peterson L, Renstrom P. Injuries in sports. London: Dunitz, 1985.

Peterson L, Stener B. Old total rupture of the adductor longus muscle. Acta Orthop Scand 1976;47:653–657.

Renstrom P, Peterson L. Groin injuries in athletes. Br J Sports Med 1980;14:30–36.

Smedberg SG, Broome AE, Gullmo A, et al. Herniography in athletes with groin pain. Am J Surg 1985;140:378–382.

Smodlaka VN. Groin pain in soccer players. Physician Sportsmed 1980;8:57–61.

Westman M. Ilioinguinalis—och genitofemoralis-neuralgi. Lakartidn 1970;67:47.

21   Athletic Pubalgia and Chronic Groin Pain

John Lohnes

The diagnosis and treatment of persistent groin pain in athletes can be difficult. The symptoms are often vague and nonspecific and the physical examination is not always definitive. The differential diagnosis includes tendinitis, strain of abdominal, hip, or thigh muscles, hip joint pathology, hernias, pelvic floor muscle defects, lumbar neuropathy, genito-urinary tract disorders, and osteitis pubis.

Epidemiology

Specific statistics regarding the incidence of these injuries is lacking. Most studies group injuries by region and not by specific injury. Also, it is difficult to estimate the number of exposures to a specific sport to give meaningful results.

The repetitive stresses of dribbling, kicking, and passing the soccer ball can result in a condition known as pubalgia. The condition is well described in Europe where it has been called pubalgie in France and Gilmore's groin in Great Britain. It has also been observed in sprinters, American football players, and other high performance athletes.

Mechanism of Injury

The condition is characterized by chronic, persistent groin pain that is the result of a weakness or defect near the pubic insertion of the rectus abdominus and internal oblique aponeurosis. The repetitive stresses of sprinting and kicking on the pelvic floor musculature are thought to cause micro-tearing or stretching near the already lax inguinal ring. The condition has many of the symptoms characteristic of a direct inguinal hernia, but without a palpable mass. The cause of the pain is obscure in these cases, but may be due to irritation or entrapment of the iliohypogastric, ilioinguinal, or genital branch of the genitofemoral nerves. The condition is seen mostly in males and rarely in females. This is probably due to an inherent weakness of the inguinal canal musculature in males. Athletes with this condition have been treated successfully by a Bassini-type herniorraphy to reinforce the pelvic floor musculature.

Athletic pubalgia typically occurs in elite or professional level players who are involved in daily training and competition. The condition is also seen in older players who have a long playing history and continue to play competitively. In some cases there is a history of acute injury involving a strain or pull of the hip flexors or adductors. More commonly, the player describes an insidious onset. Table 21-1 outlines the symptoms of pubalgia.

Initially, pain is more localized in the inguinal area. With strenuous exercise the pain may radiate both proximally into the lower abdomen and distally to the testicles and/or inner thigh. The pain may be felt unilaterally or bilaterally, although one side is typically more painful. The dominant kicking leg is more often the affected side in the soccer player.

Pain symptoms are frequently vague and difficult for the player to describe. The player may experience sharp or burning pain with activity, aching pain lasting several hours after exercise, and a tight sensation in the groin, lower abdomen, or inner thighs. Hard kicking, shooting, and sprinting are most painful. In the majority of cases, symptoms resolve completely after several days of rest. Invariably, the pain returns when the player attempts to run or play again, even after weeks or months of rest.

Numbness or other dysaesthesias, severe or persistent pain at rest, back pain, and urinary, bowel, or sexual dysfunction symptoms are unusual in athletic pubalgia. These symptoms suggest other sources of the groin pain.

The hallmarks of athletic pubalgia are tenderness at the pubic tubercle and pain with resisted hip flexion, internal rotation, and abdominal muscle contraction. Resisted hip adduction with the hips in neutral position also elicits pain in the groin. However, the adductor muscles and tendons are generally nontender. Some individuals may have tenderness and weakness palpable in the inguinal ring, but seldom is a true hernia present. Hip and back flexibility should be full and painless. The neurologic examination of the lower extremities should be normal.

Palpation of the inguinal canal, spermatic cord, and testicle should be performed to detect hernias, masses, or tenderness. Rectal and prostate examinations may also be indicated, especially in the older athlete.

The diagnosis of athletic pubalgia is primarily a diagnosis of exclusion. For this reason, several diagnostic studies should he considered to rule out

Table 21-1

Symptoms of Publagia
Inguinal pain
uni- or bilateral
radiate to lower abdomen or inner thigh
Pain with:
kicking
shooting
sprinting

other causes of groin pain. Plain radiographs of the pelvis, lower back, and hips will identify osteoarthritis, bony neoplasms, or osteitis pubis. A bone scan will occasionally be indicated if stress fractures or stress reaction is suspected. Magnetic resonance imaging (MRI) will identify most lumbar or abdominal soft tissue lesions or inflammation. In athletic pubalgia, most radiographic imaging studies are normal. In some cases, increased marrow signal in the pubic tubercle or pubic symphysis may be observed on MRI.

Although laboratory tests are not generally needed, a urinalysis should be done to rule out urinary tract infection.

Differential Diagnoses

Muscle Strains and Ruptures

A strain or rupture of the adductor longus, rectus abdominus, iliopsoas, or rectus femoris is usually the result of an acute overload injury, particularly forceful kicking or shooting. The player recalls a sudden event characterized by a painful tearing or pulling sensation. Physical examination often demonstrates bleeding and edema at the site of injury and, in the case of rupture, a defect with retracted mass of muscle belly may be palpable. In children and adolescents, avulsion fractures should be suspected and ruled out with plain radiographs.

Hip Joint Pathology

Osteoarthrosis, avascular necrosis of the femoral head, and stress fractures of the femoral neck can occur in soccer players and are often insidious. Some epidemiologic studies indicate a slightly higher incidence of degenerative hip disease in older soccer players. In the adolescent athlete, slipped capital femoral epiphysis should also be considered. Osteitis pubis, or degenerative disease of the pubic symphysis, is not common but should also be considered. All of these conditions should be apparent on plain radiographs or bone scans (Table 21-2).

Hernias

Direct and indirect inguinal hernias and femoral hernias are common in athletes and usually cause groin pain with exertion. Hydroceles and varicoceles are related hernia formations, which may also cause groin pain. Although careful physical examination usually reveals a hernia, sometimes the weakness and associated bulge or mass is difficult to detect manually. Herniography can help to diagnose incipient hernias.

Intra-Abdominal or Genito-Urinary Inflammation

Prostatitis, epididymitis, or testicular tumors should be suspected in a male with chronic groin pain. In females, gynecologic disorders should be considered and a pelvic examination performed. In both sexes, urinary tract infections should be ruled out by history, physical examination, and urinalysis.

Nerve Entrapment

After direct trauma to the groin, peripheral nerves may become contused or entrapped. The ilio-inguinal, genito-femoral, and ilio-hypogastric nerves are particularly associated with this problem. Lumbar nerve root or obturator

Table 21-2

Differential Diagnosis of Pubalgia
Muscle strains
Adductor longus
Rectus abdominis
Iliopsoas
Rectus femoris
Avulsion fracture (children)
Hip joint pathology
Osteoarthritis
Avascular necrosis
Stress fractures of the femoral neck
Slipped capital femoral epiphysis
Hernias
Inguinal
Femoral
Hydroceles
Varioceles
Inflammation
Prostatitis
Epididymitis
Testicular tumors
Urinary tract infections
Nerve entrapment
Ilio-inguinal
Genito-femoral
Ilio-hypogastic
Lumbar nerve root
Obturator nerve

nerve impingement from the lower back can cause referred pain to the groin and should be ruled out by physical examination, plain radiographs, and MRI.

Management of Athletic Pubalgia

Some authors have found that specific strengthening exercises relieve pain symptoms. Abdominal and hip adductor/flexor strengthening with light to moderate resistance done daily for several weeks has been indicated as a successful form of treatment. Complete rest and antiinflammatory medications also relieve pain symptoms, but the effect is usually temporary.

In cases that fail to respond to conservative measures after several months, surgery should be considered after all other possible causes of groin pain have been ruled out. Although surgery for athletic pubalgia is still considered controversial in the United States, surgeons in Europe have had good results treating the condition with a Bassini-type herniorraphy. The procedure involves plicating the transversalis fascia and suturing the lateral edge of the rectus abdominus to the shelving edge of the inguinal ligament. Some surgeons have also recommended tenotomy of the adductor longus tendon, but only if pain is clearly localized in the tendinous origin. Most players undergoing surgery may return to athletic activity after 4 months. Recommended recovery and rehabilitation includes 4–6 weeks of rest immediately following surgery, only normal daily activities, and no heavy lifting or exertion. Pool walking, gentle stretching, and stationary biking are the next step of recovery, followed by progressive strengthening exercises. Particular attention should be paid to strengthening abdominal and adductor muscles. Most players are ready to run 3 months after surgery and may then resume sport-specific training as tolerated. The majority of athletes will be able to return to full competitive sports 4–6 months postoperative.

SUGGESTED READINGS

Abbeele K, Verhelst M, Martens C, et al. Bassini's hernial repair and tenotomy of the adductor longus in the treatment of chronic groin pain in athletes. Unpublished manuscript.

Gilmore OJ. Gilmore's Groin. Sportsmedicine and Soft Tissue Trauma 1992;3:2–4.

Hackney RG. The sports hernia: a cause of chronic groin pain. Br J Sports Med 1993;27:58–62.

Hasselman CT, Best TM, Garrett WE. When groin pain signals an adductor strain. The Physician and Sportsmedicine 1995;23:53–60.

Renstrom P, Peterson L. Groin injuries in athletes. Brit J Sports Med 1980;14:30–36.

Taylor DC, Myers WC, Moylan JA, et al. Abdominal musculature abnormalities as a cause of groin pain in athletes: inguinal hernias and pubalgia. Amer J Sports Med 1991;19:239–242.

22  Treatment Options in Anterior Cruciate Ligament (ACL) Injuries

Paolo Aglietti
Giovanni Zaccherotti
Pietro DeBiase

Epidemiology

Soccer injuries to the leg are frequent due to the high number of participants (approximately 22 million worldwide) and the specific mechanisms involved in kicking, cutting, and tackling. The epidemiology of soccer injuries has been studied by several authors (Table 22-1). The incidence of injury ranges from 4.0–7.6 for every player per 1000 hours of play. Lower extremities are most at risk, accounting for 64%–93% of the lesions. Knee injuries represent 18%–26% of all soccer injuries and mostly involve ligaments or meniscal lesions. The anterior cruciate ligament (ACL) is frequently involved and is the most disabling injury for a soccer player. Injuries to the ACL account for approximately half of all knee ligament injuries.

Disability

The disability of an athlete after an ACL tear has been considered and documented in the literature. Only a few soccer players returned to full soccer participation without surgery on the torn ACL. This kind of injury often sidelines an athlete for a long time and, in some cases, permanently. For example, 36 competitive soccer players with ACL insufficient knees were observed for an average of 3.5 years after arthroscopic partial meniscectomy. Eleven (31%) of the 36 were able to return to the same competitive level, 7 (19%) dropped to a recreational level, 9 (25%) had to change to a less demanding sport, and 9 (25%) were unable to participate in any sport. The long-term outcome of rim-preserving meniscectomy depends primarily on the condition of the ACL . Five years after meniscectomy, players with a ruptured ACL were less involved in soccer than the players with an intact ACL. The players with a ruptured ACL also had further meniscectomies, more radiologic signs of articular degeneration, and more operations for osteoarthritis.

From these data there is strong evidence that after an acute ACL injury only a minority of the patients will be able to resume full participation in a sport requiring jumping, cutting, and pivoting. A rehabilitation course may de-

Table 22-1

Incidence of Injuries in Soccer			
Author	*Year*	*Injuries/1000hr (Games)*	*Remarks*
Ekstrand	1983	16.9	180 Senior Players
Jorgesen	1984	4.1	Players over 18 years
Nielsen	1989	14.3	3 Competition Levels
Engstrom	1990	13	64 Elite Players
Schmidt-Olsen	1991	3.7	496 Boys 12–18 years
Aglietti	1994	4.0	1018 Players (11 seasons) 3 Competition Levels

crease the symptoms, but counseling and reduction of the activity level is mandatory. Athletic patients willing to return to high level soccer activity risk reinjury of the menisci and cartilage.

Reconstruction

Graft Choice

Presently, intraarticular ACL reconstruction is accepted as the surgical treatment of choice for ACL lesions. Primary repair results in a failure rate of 17%–30% of cases, which can be reduced with an augmentation technique. The operation is being performed more frequently with a variety of autogenous tissues and satisfactory results. In acute cases, the timing of surgery is important. Patients operated on acutely can have significantly more arthrofibrosis compared with those undergoing delayed surgery. We prefer to operate when the patient has regained almost complete range of motion and muscular control, and pain and swelling is reduced.

Advances in instrumentation and technique during the last decade have allowed surgeons to perform ACL reconstructions with greater precision and safety, less rehabilitation time, and more predictable results. Basic parameters have been discussed with agreement on the use of strong autologous grafts, correct positioning, secure graft fixation, and early mobilization with an accelerated rehabilitation.

The selection of a high-strength graft and an appropriate surgical technique are the most important factors in the result of an ACL reconstruction. The patellar tendon (PT) graft is considered the golden standard for its structural properties (stiffness and ultimate load to failure). The semitendinosus and gracilis tendons (STG) show good mechanical properties, although lower than the PT. To improve the cross-sectional area of the STG tendons, surgeons began to use them in a three or four stranded fashion.

A comparison of arthroscopically assisted ACL reconstruction with PT versus doubled STG tendons revealed no differences, although the same rehabilitation regimen was used. In another project, 72 patients were evaluated after the two types of surgery. No significant differences were noted between the groups with respect to subjective complaints, functional level, or objective laxity evaluation including KT-1000 measurements. Seventeen of 72 patients (24%) experienced anterior knee pain after ACL reconstruction. Overall, 46 of 72 patients (64%) returned to their preinjury level of activity. Mean KT-1000 scores were 1.6 ± 1.4 mm for the PT group and 1.9 ± 1.3 mm for the STG group. Significant weakness in the harmstrings resulted when reconstruction was performed with the double STG tendons.

In all categories (acute versus chronic and meniscectomy versus no meniscectomy) the PT patients had consistently greater knee stability compared with the doubled STG group. Over 3 years, the doubled STG group had 94%, 83%, and 81% yearly success rate compared with 98%, 96%, and 96% in the PT group. These results indicate that although both grafts are good choices in ACL reconstruction, the PT graft provides more knee stability.

In a recent study, the results of intraarticular ACL reconstruction with the PT or the STG were compared in a consecutive series of 60 chronic ACL injuries (Table 22-2). A single surgeon performed arthroscopic assisted reconstruction in an alternating sequence (30 PT and 30 STG grafts). The STG tendons were detached distally and doubled (four strands). The patients were reviewed with an average follow-up of 28 months (range 22–39). Analysis of the preoperative and operative data revealed no significant differences between the two groups. There were no significant differences in symptoms and recurrent subjective instability was present in only one STG knee. Return to participation in sports involving agility, cutting, and jumping was more frequent in the PT group (80%) than in the STG group (43%). KT-2000 testing showed anterior tibial displacement >5 mm at the 30 pounds test in 13% of the PT group and 2% of the STG group. A grade II pivot-shift was found in only one STG knee. A $1°–3°$ extension loss was more frequent in the PT group (47%) than in the STG group (3%). A patello-femoral crepitation developed in 17% of the PT and 3% of the STG knees. A decreased height of the patella was found in 13% of the PT and 3% of the STG group. Cybex II evaluation at $60°$, $120°$, and $180°/sec$ revealed that there was no selective deficit in the peak extensor or flexor torques after a PT or an STG graft. In conclusion, this study identified only two significant differences between the STG and PT groups. Activity level was higher in the PT group and there was a higher incidence of minor extension loss. The PT graft seemed to offer a slightly better objective stability, but resulted in more patello femoral problems. However, these differences did not have statistical significance.

It is probably wise to use the PT graft in the younger, motivated individuals with high demands and the STG graft in the less motivated, older patients. We also use the doubled (four strands) STG graft in cases of reoperation for failed reconstruction with PT. Fixation of STG grafts with soft tissue washers is successful and comparable to the fixation obtained with PT and interference screws. Both grafts approximated the intact ACL in strength, but only the PT grafts secured with interference screws were comparable in stiffness.

Table 22-2

Patellar Tendon versus Double Semitendinosus and Gracilis Tendon in ACL Reconstruction		
CLINICAL RESULTS	PT	STG
Symptoms		
pain	13%	10%
swelling	3%	3%
giving-way	0%	3%
Range of Motion		
extension loss (<3°)	47%	3%
flexion loss (<6°)	20%	20%
Stability		
KT 2000 (30 lbs) ssd difference		
average	3.2 mm	3.8 mm
> 5 mm	13%	20%
pivot shift		
absent	79%	70%
glide	21%	27%
clunk	0%	3%
Patellofemoral Problems		
absent	50%	60%
minor	33%	37%
moderate	17%	3%
severe	—	—
Cybex II (operated vs. normal knee)		
peak extension torque		
60°/sec	91.1%	89.3%
180°/sec	94.1%	94.7%
peak flexion torque		
60°/sec	97.8%	94.0%
180°/sec	98.6%	91.6%

Techniques

Several surgical techniques have been developed. Arthroscopically assisted ACL reconstruction has become the technique of choice for many surgeons. There are different techniques for producing the femoral tunnel. It can be performed with two incisions from outside-in using specific guides, or with one incision from inside-out (through the tibial tunnel) using an atraumatic reamer.

The differences between the double and single incision technique have been evaluated with KT-2000 and radiologic results. The center of the femoral tunnel exit in the joint was 6 mm anterior to the "over the top" position at the junction of the roof and the lateral wall of the notch.

Fifty patients with chronic ACL deficient knees were randomly allotted to a double or single incision technique and evaluated for an average of 12 months (range 8–16 months) (Table 22-3). The following radiographic parameters were measured: 1) the direction of the femoral and tibial tunnels in the anteroposterior (AP) and lateral (LL) views; 2) the location of the intraarticular exit hole of the femoral tunnel (expressed as the percentage of the sagittal width of the condyles, with 100% being the most posterior point); 3) femoral interference screw divergence with the bone block (considered significant if 2:200). At follow-up, the International Knee Documentation Committee (IKDC) form and the KT-2000 were used to evaluate the results.

With the double incision technique, the femoral and tibial tunnels were divergent and crossed the joint at an angle of 37° and 72°. With the single incision technique, the bone tunnels in the AP view were almost parallel and crossed the joint with an average angle of 68°. The location of the intraarticular exit of the femoral tunnel was posterior with the double and single incision technique (63% and 66%). Screw divergence ($\geq$20°) on the femoral side was absent in the double incision group and present in 12% of the single incision group. An extension loss of less than 3° was detected in 20% of the double incision and 16% of the single incision patients (Table 22-4). An extension loss of 3°–5° was present in 20% of the double and single incision groups. No patients lost more than 5° of extension. A flexion loss of less than 10° was present in 8% of the double incision group and 16% of the single incision group. There were no differences in pivot-shift between the two groups. One patient from the double incision group showed a jerk. KT-2000 evaluation gave com-

Table 22-3

Comparison of Radiographic Parameters with Three Arthroscopic Techniques for ACL Reconstruction			
	Double Incision	*Single Incision*	*Modified Single Incision*
Anteroposterior Angulation (average)			
Femoral Tunnel	37°	68°	49°
Tibial Tunnel	72°	69°	67°
Intrarticular Tunnel Exit (average)			
Femoral	63%	66%	68%
Tibial	28%	27%	30%
Femoral Screw Divergence (>20°)	—	12%	—
Impingment			
Absent	50%	71%	77%
Moderate	50%	29%	23%
Severe	—	—	—

Table 22-4

Comparison of Clinical Results using Two Arthroscopic Techniques for ACL Reconstruction		
	Single Incision	Double Incision
Range of Motion		
Extension Loss (<5°)	36%	40%
Flexion Loss (<6°)	16%	8%
Pivot-Shift		
Absent	84%	80%
Glide	16%	16%
Clunk	0%	4%
KT 2000 (30 lbs) ssd difference		
average	2.64 mm	1.98 mm
> 5 mm	0%	4%

parable results in the two groups. The average side to side differences revealed by the manual maximum test were 1.98 mm in the double incision group and 2.64 mm in the single incision group. Even without straight line tunnels, satisfactory stability was achieved.

The single incision technique may be preferable because of less postoperative pain and swelling. To avoid screw divergence, consistently obtain precise femoral tunnel positioning with a good posterior wall, and make drilling of the femoral tunnel independent from tibial tunnel, we recently started to use a modified single incision technique. The femoral tunnel is prepared through the low antero-medial arthroscopic portal with the knee fully flexed. The femoral interference screw is introduced from the same portal, which makes parallel alignment with the bone plug easier. The fully flexed position and use of the central portal (through the defect in the PT) allow an improved visualization of the notch with a limited notchplasty.

Summary

In conclusion, the recent improvements in surgical techniques and accelerated rehabilitation programs have decreased the incidence of complication (i.e., patello-femoral problems and loss of range of motion) while maintaining satisfactory results in terms of objective stability (Tables 22-5 and 22-6). Although ACL injury is a major soccer lesion, it can be successfully treated leading to full recovery and a return to sports in approximately 6 months.

Table 22-5

Complications in ACL Reconstructions: Acute Lesions		
Suture + STG Augmentation (Cast)	ST + G Reconstruction (Early Mobilization)	ST + G Reconstruction (Accelerated Rehabilitation)
Arthrofibrosis		
Extension Loss (>5°) 2.5%	3%	0%
Flexion Loss (>10°) 21%	14%	0%
Patellofemoral Problems		
Crepitation		
(moderate and severe) 42%	16%	0%
Patella Infera 17%	8%	0%
Graft Failure Rate 7%	11%	12%

Table 22-6

Complications in ACL Reconstructions: Chronic Lesions		
PT Open (Cast)	PT Closed (Early Mobilization)	PT Closed (Accelerated Rehabilitation)
Arthrofibrosis		
Extension Loss (>5°) 8%	7%	0%
Flexion Loss (>10°) 24%	10%	0%
Patellofemoral Problems		
Crepitation		
(moderate and severe) 29%	21%	17%
Patella Infera 32%	14%	13%
Graft Failure Rate 17%	12%	13%

SUGGESTED READINGS

Aglietti P, Buzzi R, Zaccherotti G, et al. Patellar tendon verus doubled (four strands) semitendinosus and gracilis in ACL reconstruction. Am J Sports Med 1994;22:211.

Aglietti P, Zaccherotti G, DeBiase P, et al. Injury in soccer: mechanism and epidemiology. In: Renstrom PAFH, ed. The encyclopaedia of sports medicine: clinical pratice of sports injury prevention and care. Oxford, England: Blackwell Scientific Publications, 1994;277.

Andersson C, Odensten N, Good L, et al. Surgical or non-surgical treatment of acute rupture of the anterior cruciate ligament: a randomized study with long-term follow-up. J Bone Joint Surg 1989;71A:965.

Bonamo JJ, Fay C, Firestone T. The conservative treatment of the anterior cruciate deficient knee. Am J Sports Med 1990;18:618.

Engstrom B, Forssblad M, Johansson C, et al. .Does a major knee injury definitely sideline an elite player? Am J Sports Med 1990;18:101.

Friden T, Zatterstrom R, Lindstrand A, et al. Anterior cruciate insufficient knees treated with physiotherapy: a three year follow-up study of patients with late diagnosis. Clin Orthop 1991;263:190.

Marder RA, Raskind JR, Carrol M. Prospective evaluation of arthroscopically assisted anterior cruciate ligament reconstruction. Patellar tendon versus semitendinosus and gracilis tendon. Am J Sports Med 1991;19:478.

Neyret P, Donell ST, Dejour D, et al. Partial meniscectomy and anterior cruciate ligament rupture in soccer players. Am J Sports Med 1993;21:455.

Otero AL, Hutchenson L. A comparison of the doubled semitendinosus/gracilis and central third of the patellar tendon autografts in arthroscopic anterior cruciate ligament reconstruction. Arthroscopy 1993;9:143.

Sgaglione NE, Warren RF, Wickiewicz TL, et al. Primary repair with semitendinosus tendon augmentation of anterior cruciate ligament injuries. Am J Sports Med 1990;18:64.

Shelbourne KD, Wilckens JH. Arthrofibrosis in anterior cruciate ligament reconstruction: the effect of timing of reconstruction and rehabilitation protocol. Am J Sports Med 1990;18:292.

Zaccherotti G, Aglietti P, Menchetti PPM, et al. ACL reconstruction: a randomized study of tunnels position using two techniques. Presented at the 6th Congress of the European Society of Sports Traumatology, Knee surgery, and Arthroscopy. Berlin, 1994.

23  Posterior Cruciate and Collateral Ligament Injuries

William G. Clancy, Jr.
Scott E. Strasburger

The Posterior Cruciate Ligament

The posterior cruciate ligament (PCL) is the strongest ligament of the knee and is twice as strong as the anterior cruciate ligament (ACL). The bulk of the PCL arises from the posterolateral portion of the medial femoral condyle and inserts into the central posterior sulcus of the tibia. There are two functional bands: the large, taut in flexion anterior band and the small, taut in extension posterior band.

The length of both the PCL and ACL is approximately 38 mm. The PCL is approximately 2 mm wider than the 11 mm wide ACL. Approximately 95% of the strength used to resist posterior displacement is provided by the PCL. The PCL is also responsible for drawing the femur posteriorly during flexion. PCL insufficiency produces increased tibial translation in the posterior direction, resulting in abnormal knee biomechanics and increased shear across the articular surface.

Mechanism of Injury

Although the PCL is injured frequently, it is injured approximately one-tenth as often as the ACL. Isolated PCL injuries usually occur by one of three mechanisms. The most common mechanism is the dashboard injury, in which the knee is propelled into the dashboard, driving the tibia posteriorly and rupturing the PCL. The second most common mechanism is a fall on the flexed knee. If the foot is in dorsiflexion, the blow is usually delivered to the patellofemoral joint. If the foot is in plantar flexion, the blow is delivered to the tibial tubercle, driving the tibia posteriorly (Fig. 23-1). The third mechanism is a fall on the proximal tibia, which results in hyperflexion of the knee. The latter two mechanisms often fail to produce a posterior capsular injury. This limits the total amount of tibial translation so that the PCL undergoes deformation without gross disruption. PCL injuries can be associated and combined with other ligament injuries in the knee area. Hyperextension injuries of the knee can result in PCL injury, but usually after the rupture of the ACL. Less common are PCL injuries associated with medial collateral ligament (MCL) injuries and posterolateral injuries.

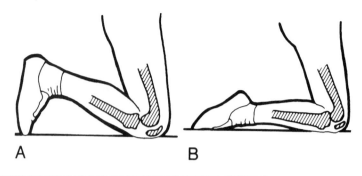

A   B

Figure 23-1. During a fall on the knee, the load is sustained on the patelofemoral joint (A) if the foot is in dorsiflexion. If the foot is in plantar flexion (B), the tibial tubercle may sustain most of the load, driving the tibia backward and producing a PCL injury. (Reprinted with permission from: Clancy WG. Repair and reconstruction of the posterior cruciate ligament. In: Chapman MW, ed. Operative orthopaedics, Vol 3. Philadelphia: J.B. Lippincott Co., 1993;2094).

Isolated PCL injuries usually result in mild bloody effusions, as opposed to the gross bloody effusions seen in acute isolated ACL injuries. The patient usually has minimal pain with full extension. Although the patient can flex to at least 90°, pain increases with greater flexion. When the knee is flexed to 90° there is usually a mild posterior sag due to gravity. With quadricep spasm, the tibial sag may not be present. An anterior drawer performed with the knee at 90° may be misinterpreted as positive due to the gravity-induced posterior sag being reduced by the examiner (Fig. 23-2). Therefore, it is important to determine if the knee is in neutral position when testing for an anterior or posterior drawer. This can be determined by flexing both knees to 90° and palpating the normal anteromedial and anterolateral tibial plateau stepoff in the normal knee. The anterior tibial plateau in the normal knee has an anterior stepoff of approximately 10 mm. If no stepoff is present in the injured knee and the anterior tibial crest is flush with the medial and lateral femoral condyles, there is at least 2+ posterior drawer, indicating complete PCL inadequacy. If the anterior tibial crest is posterior to the medial and lateral femoral condyles, there is a 3+ posterior drawer. If the stepoff is less than the normal knee, but still palpable, it is considered a 1+ posterior drawer (Fig. 23-3). This test should be performed with the tibia in the neutral position and internal tibial rotation to limit any posterolateral rotation, which may be present in patients with a combined PCL and posterolateral injury.

COMBINED PCL INJURIES WITH MEDIAL OR LATERAL COLLATERAL LIGAMENT INJURIES

In the acutely injured knee, if marked valgus or varus laxity is present with the knee at full extension, one or both cruciate ligaments are disrupted. Disruption of the ACL is more common. However, injury to the PCL must be suspected. Flexion to 90° and palpation of the anterior tibial stepoff should confirm the presence or absence of an intact PCL.

PCL AND POSTEROLATERAL INSTABILITY

When evaluating cruciate ligament injuries, posterolateral instability must be addressed. If it is ignored, a severe functional instability will ensue despite treatment of the cruciate injury. In the presence of posterolateral instability,

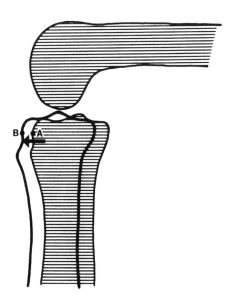

Figure 23-2. If there is an insufficient PCL and the knee is flexed to 90°, the tibia displaces posteriorly due to gravity and sits in a posterior subluxed position (A). With an anterior drawer the tibia translates forward to its normal neutral position (B). This forward translation is often misinterpreted as a positive anterior drawer. In fact, it is only a reduction of the posterior subluxation. (Reprinted with permission from: Clancy WG. Repair and reconstruction of the posterior cruciate ligament. In: Chapman MW, ed. Operative orthopaedics, Vol 3. Philadelphia: J.B. Lippincott Co., 1993;2094).

the tibia will rotate posterolaterally if the PCL or ACL insufficiency is addressed. Consequently, the tibial insertion of the PCL will rotate medially, resulting in a shortened distance between its origin on the medial femoral condyle and its tibial insertion. This will produce a functionally lax PCL and ACL. Isolated sectioning of the PCL does not produce excessive external tibial rotation. Therefore, significant increase in posterolateral rotation must result from injury to the posterolateral structures. Injury to the popliteus muscle tendon complex is the most important cause of posterolateral instability.

Treatment

The method for treating acute and chronic PCL injuries is controversial. Numerous reports emphasize the success of PCL deficient patients treated without surgery. This implies that functional instability seldom accompanies acute PCL injury if there is no other major ligamentous instability. Other authors believe that a chronic PCL deficiency will lead to degenerative arthritis and, therefore, conclude that early repair is the treatment of choice.

Due to insufficient follow-up, most studies of current surgical techniques do not demonstrate whether surgery can prevent long-term articular changes associated with PCL injury. Successful restoration of the biomechanics of the PCL should produce a more beneficial result. Surgical intervention must produce an objectively stable knee. Since nonoperative treatment can produce a functionally stable knee, which can still lead to significant articular destruction, surgery should only be done if it can produce an objectively stable knee.

Magnetic resonance imaging (MRI) should be done on all acute isolated PCL injuries to determine whether there is a complete interstitial failure or an interstitial failure in continuity. In the latter case, the treatment should generally be nonoperative. The ligament will often tighten, reducing a 2+ posterior drawer to a 1+ or trace posterior drawer.

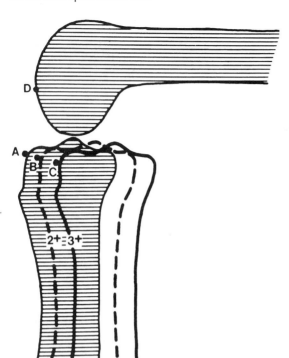

Figure 23-3. With the knee flexed to 90°, the anterior tibial plateaus should have an 8–10 mm anterior stepoff (A). If the posterior cruciate ligament is insufficient, there should be a complete loss of this stepoff and the anterior aspect of the tibial plateaus (B) should be flush with the medial and lateral femoral condyles (D). This would be considered a 2+ posterior drawer. If the anterior tibial plateau (C) is displaced posterior to the anterior femoral condyles (d), this would be considered a 3+ posterior drawer. (Reprinted with permission from: Clancy WG. Repair and reconstruction of the posterior cruciate ligament. In: Chapman MW, ed. Operative orthopaedics, Vol 3. Philadelphia: J.B. Lippincott Co., 1993:2095).

TREATMENT OF ACUTE PCL INJURIES

Not all patients with an acute rupture of the PCL will require major ligamentous surgery because few will develop functional instability. Although some will develop significant disability and accelerated articular injury, it is impossible to predict. Surgical reconstruction may provide higher static stability, but only long-term follow-up will determine whether it can produce enough static stability to protect the knee from early traumatic arthritis. If surgery is recommended, the surgeon must be confident that the surgical technique will consistently produce a posterior drawer of 0 or a trace. A 1+ posterior drawer should be considered less than acceptable in providing excellent biomechanical static stability. A patient with a posterior drawer greater than 2+ has more than an isolated PCL injury and should be considered for surgical repair and reconstruction.

Conservative Treatment

A nonsurgical approach involves early functional rehabilitation programs. Cast immobilization is unwarranted and could be detrimental. A vigorous quadricep strengthening program should be initiated within the first two weeks. Hamstring musculature strengthening should start 4–6 weeks after injury. Return to a vigorous life-style is allowed 6–8 weeks after injury if there is full range of motion and equal strength, power, and endurance when compared to the uninjured knee. Quadricep exercises should be continued three times a week. Currently, a yearly bone scan is performed for those treated without surgery. The goal of this study is early detection of patients who are beginning to develop medial compartment or patellar articular surface degeneration.

Surgical Treatment

Injury to the PCL includes bony avulsion and interstitial injuries. If PCL stability is important, repair can consistently lead to successful objective stability. For PCL bony avulsion injuries, surgical fixation is almost universally recommended and produces excellent objective results at long-term follow-up. The follow-up should include a complete ligamentous evaluation under anesthesia and diagnostic arthroscopy to evaluate the menisci and all compartments. An isolated PCL bony avulsion from the tibia can be approached in two different ways. The direct posterior approach gives the best view of the avulsion and allows for easier internal fixation of the fragment with a screw. The second approach combines anteromedial arthrotomy and, when necessary, posteromedial arthrotomy.

Tensile testing of knee ligament preparations in which bony avulsions have occurred suggest that plastic deformation may occur in the ligament, resulting in a permanent increase in length. Therefore, any bony avulsion should be countersunk at the time of fixation so that proper functional length will result.

The reported results of primary repair of interstitial mid-substance tears reveal a failure to provide objective stability. Reconstruction of the PCL using patellar tendon graft has a success rate of approximately 90% in terms of static results. Further improvements of this technique have been developed. Use of a strain gauge to find the most physiometric area on the medial femoral condyle and the posterior tibia has probably been the most important contribution to improving static stability. Correct tibial and femoral tunnel placement is the most important technical factor for a successful result. A 10 mm patellar tendon graft (PTG) is strong enough to reconstruct the anterior lateral band of the PCL. To reconstruct the posterior medial band, a second small tunnel is made through the medial femoral condyle using a 6 mm strip of the quadricep tendon or a semitendinosis graft for reconstruction.

Physical Therapy

The patient is placed in a knee mobilizer in full extension. Range of motion exercises (0°–90°) and full weight bearing on crutches are started the second day. At 6 weeks the knee mobilizer is removed, additional motion is encouraged, and the patient begins to use an exercise bike. Quadricep strengthening through a progressive range of motion is also begun at 6 weeks. Hamstring strengthening starts at 4 months. Running is permitted at 4 months on an every third day basis. Noncontact participation is allowed at 6 months, and contact participation at 9 months.

The Lateral Ligaments of the Knee

The lateral ligament complex of the knee has three layers. The superficial layer consists of the iliotibial band and tendon of the biceps femoris. The patellar retinaculum makes up the middle layer, and the deep layer consists of the fibular collateral, arcuate, fabello-fibular ligament, and joint capsule.

The lateral aspect of the knee has an intimate association with the posterolateral structures, which include the popliteus tendon and the arcuate-posterolateral capsular complex. The lateral ligament complex resists only varus rotation of the knee. The posterolateral structures stabilize the knee against varus rotation, external rotation and, to a limited degree, posterior translation. Isolated injury to the lateral collateral ligament produces maximal varus instability at 30° of knee flexion. Varus instability can be significantly increased with injuries to the posterolateral structures. Varus laxity in extension indicates posterolateral structure insufficiency. Injury to the posterolateral structures results in a significant increase in external rotation of the tibia with maximal rotation occurring at 30° of flexion. The lateral structures are also important as secondary restraints to anterior tibial translation when associated with anterior cruciate ligament insufficiency.

Mechanism of Injury

Isolated injuries to the lateral ligaments of the knee are uncommon. The varus producing stress needed to produce isolated injury is often caused by a direct blow to the medial aspect of the knee. Protection from this mechanism of injury is usually provided by the contralateral knee, preventing isolated trauma to the medial aspect of the knee. This type of injury may occur when the opponent tries to tackle the ball and impacts the inside of the leg. Injury to the lateral aspect of the knee is often associated with rupture of one or both of the crucial ligaments. Injuries to the lateral ligaments must be addressed during cruciate ligament reconstruction to avoid unsatisfactory results. This is especially significant when patients have a concomitant injury to the PCL and posterolateral structures.

Injury to the lateral collateral ligament complex is often accompanied by extensive disruption of the posterolateral complex and posterior cruciate ligament. These injuries are all detectable clinically. Due to the significant force required to produce these injuries, occult knee dislocation must be considered and a complete neurovascular examination performed. A significant number of these patients have signs of common peroneal nerve injury.

Varus instability at 30° knee flexion indicates injury to the lateral collateral ligament complex. Varus instability at 0° of knee flexion indicates more extensive injury, including the posterolateral structures and cruciate ligaments. The posterior cruciate ligament is often associated with this injury pattern. A marked increase in external rotation of the tibia compared to the uninjured extremity at 30° of flexion is associated with injury to the posterolateral structures. At 90° of knee flexion, a marked increase in external rotation is also associated with injury to the PCL.

An isolated partial injury to the lateral collateral ligament is usually not associated with an effusion, whereas an isolated complete tear produces a small effusion. Diagnosis is confirmed by tenderness along the lateral collateral ligament. The inability to palpate the structure in varus laxity at 30° of flexion confirms this injury.

Treatment

CONSERVATIVE CARE

Isolated injury to the lateral collateral ligament is uncommon. Injuries not associated with an avulsion of the lateral collateral ligament from the fibular styloid may be treated conservatively. Patients can be started on a rehabilitation program as pain allows and athletes can return to sports participation when strength and endurance equal the uninjured leg.

SURGICAL TREATMENT

Lateral collateral ligament injuries associated with a displaced avulsion fracture of the fibular styloid indicate surgical repair. If the fracture fragment is large enough, the avulsed fragment of bone can be repaired to the fracture site using a 4.5 mm cancellous screw and smooth washer. If the fracture fragment is small, a suture weaved through the torn end of the ligament and bone can be secured through drill holes in the proximal fibula.

PHYSICAL THERAPY

Postoperatively, the patient is treated with a hinged knee brace and full weight bearing for 3–6 weeks. Limited passive range of motion is initiated and rehabilitation is progressed after 6 weeks.

Lateral collateral ligament injuries associated with posterolateral instability and injury to the PCL are usually an indication for surgical repair. Along with repair of the lateral collateral ligament, primary repair of the posterolateral structures and reconstruction of the PCL are indicated.

Postoperatively, full weight bearing and passive range of motion from 0°–60° is initiated and continued for 6 weeks, at which point full range of motion is allowed. Hamstring resistance exercises are usually delayed until 3 months postoperatively, but quadricep exercises are started at 6 weeks. Return to sports requires at least 6 months of aggressive rehabilitation.

The Medial Ligaments of the Knee

Injury to the medial side of the knee is one of the more common knee injuries in athletics. Improvements in evaluation and a more exact diagnosis have led to improved treatment protocols. Nonoperative results are no different than surgical treatment of the acute isolated medial knee injury. The emphasis on nonsurgical treatment of medial knee injuries should not de-emphasize the importance of this injury. Appropriate rehabilitation and protection of the injury is required before the patient can return to a satisfactory competitive level.

Mechanism of Injury

The medial collateral ligament of the knee can be injured from a blow to the outer side of the knee, twisting injuries away from the weight bearing foot, or falls in which the body weight provides a valgus force to the knee in external rotation. The medial collateral ligament is the primary restraint, preventing excessive valgus rotation.

Abnormal laxity of the medial structures can result in occasional functional instability. This will produce a sensation of instability during direction change, particularly while running. This must be differentiated from a pivot shift, which produces a similar feeling of instability. The latter instance is consistent with deficiency of the ACL allowing anterior tibial subluxation.

Recent studies show that up to 80% of knee injuries occurring in contact sports, especially soccer and football, involve isolated injury to the MCL (Fig. 23-4).

Figure 23-4. Soccer play.

Medial instability, demonstrated by joint opening with valgus stress when the knee is in full extension, indicates a lesion of the MCL, medial capsule, posterior capsule, and the ACL or PCL. Any significant opening of the medial joint space when valgus stress is applied at 0° extension signifies a tear of the PCL. However, this is seldom the case. The ACL is more frequently torn. Marked laxity in full extension signifies that one or both cruciate ligaments are torn.

Thirty degrees of flexion eliminates the posterior capsule as a stabilizing structure, allowing isolated evaluation of the medial collateral ligament. Grading of medial collateral ligament injuries depends on the amount of opening to valgus stress and the firmness of the end point (Table 23-1). Grading of medial collateral ligament repair is detailed in Table 23-2.

Medical literature is not consistent concerning the grading of injury to the medial collateral ligament due to the lack of consistency in describing the complex make up of the MCL. The MCL consists of two parts. The anterior half of the medial collateral ligament consists of parallel fibers that insert on the medial femoral epicondyle and, seen distally and anteriorly, insert on the anterior medial tibial plateau approximately three finger breadths below the

Table 23-1

Grading of MCL Injuries

Grade 1:   0–5 mm opening with end point
Grade 2:   6–10 mm opening with end point
Grade 3:   more than 10 mm opening with no end point

joint line. The posterior half of the MCL, referred to as the posterior oblique ligament, consists of fibers that run in the opposite diagonal direction; anterior to posterior inserting on the posteromedial portion of the tibia. This is not a separate ligament, but the posterior part of the MCL.

Surgical findings indicate that isolated tears of the posterior oblique portion rarely occur and that the anterior fibers must be torn before the posterior fibers. When a knee opens 6–10 mm with valgus stress at 30° of knee flexion and minimal flexion at 0°, then at least part of the oblique fibers are intact. When there is significant laxity present at 30° of flexion, both parts of the MCL are torn and a true Grade III sprain exists.

The athlete usually associates a valgus mechanism of injury to the knee with a loud pop and a feeling of instability. In the acute stage, there is effusion or localized swelling and tenderness to the medial aspect of the knee. Tenderness is usually present over the substance of the MCL, localized by palpating from the medial epicondyle of the femur down to the insertion. Immediate swelling of the knee indicates a possible ACL tear. A block of extension or flexion suggests a meniscal tear, although this can be difficult to assess due to muscle spasm in the acute stage.

Within a day, an isolated partial tear will display a loss of 15°–30° of flexion because the MCL is most lax at 20°–30° of flexion, the least painful position. Recent studies reveal that an interbody tear of the medial meniscus seldom

Table 23-2

Grading of MCL Reconstruction

Grade 1:
Failure of only a few fibers with minimal loss of strength, minimal lengthening, and no significant abnormal laxity.
Grade 2:
Partial tearing of the fibers, with some compromise of strength of the tissue and lengthening of the ligament. There is abnormal opening of the medial side, but a definite end point is recognized.
Grade 3:
Greater than 10 mm opening with no detectable end point consistent with the complete tear of the ligament.

accompanies an isolated MCL strain. This is consistent with the mechanism of injury in that the force distracts rather than compresses the medial joint. A meniscofemoral or meniscal tibial capsular tear always accompanies a grade II or III sprain. Although lateral meniscus tears and lateral tibial plateau fractures are possible, these injuries are uncommon. Chronic medial laxity produces a sensation of instability as the patient turns away from the weight bearing leg. This is accentuated by twisting and pivoting while running. Patients often complain of the knee "giving way." This is different from the pivot shift phenomena, in which the event is more dramatic and elicits the response of the knee "going out." Physical examination of a medial collateral ligament knee injury is suggested by the abduction or valgus stress test with the knee in flexion. The MCL then becomes the primary restraint being tested. An opening of more than 10–15 mm suggests that a secondary restraint, such as the ACL, is involved. Injuries are graded as I–III.

The abduction stress test with the knee in 0° of flexion evaluates the MCL, capsule, and posteromedial capsule constraints. Usually, an abduction stress in this position does not produce any medial joint opening. A slight opening of up to 5 mm indicates a tear of the MCL and possibly the posteromedial capsule. An opening of 5–10 mm indicates that the posterior capsule is no longer maintaining its secondary restraint. An opening of more than 10 mm suggests involvement of the cruciate ligaments.

Treatment

An acute isolated injury to the MCL is a nonsurgical problem. Grade I and II injuries are initially treated with restriction of activities, active range of motion (ROM), and weight bearing as tolerated until the acute inflammatory reaction subsides. At this time, a functional rehabilitation program is initiated. Full activity, including return to contact sports, is allowed after completion of the rehabilitation program and an examination revealing no significant abnormal laxity. Isolated Grade III injuries are rare and it is necessary to rule out associated ACL, PCL, or meniscal injuries. If there is a Grade III MCL injury, treatment remains nonsurgical. Immobilization of the knee in full extension and weight bearing as tolerated is started, as well as early ROM until the acute inflammatory reaction subsides. At this time, passive and active range of motion is encouraged as tolerated and strength training is incorporated. The functional running rehabilitation program is again incorporated when painless full ROM is achieved. When the knee is clinically stable and rehabilitation is complete, the athlete may return to contact sports usually 6–8 weeks after injury.

Surgical treatment is indicated if chronic instability is present, which is rare if both cruciate ligaments are normal. Patients with a chronic functional problem often have not completed a full rehabilitation program. The original injury and decreased use of the leg results in uncorrected muscle weakness. A rehabilitation program may restore enough support to allow the desired activity level without instability. These patients occasionally require functional bracing as an alternative to surgical reconstruction. If functional instability is not resolved by these measures, surgical reconstruction allows an improved activity level.

Surgical treatment can include a direct repair of the MCL, while chronic injuries usually require a reconstructive technique. Most indications for surgical treatment of chronic medial instability are associated with cruciate deficiencies, usually of the ACL. Therefore, surgical treatment must include a reconstructive procedure for the ACL and medial stability.

SUGGESTED READINGS

Allen WC, Marder RA. Injuries of the lateral ligaments of the knee. In: Chapman NW, ed. Operative orthopaedics. Philadelphia: J.B. Lippincott Co., 1993.

Clancy WG, Shelbourne KD, Zoellner GB, et al. Treatment of knee joint instability secondary to rupture of the posterior cruciate ligament: report of a new procedure. J Bone Joint Surg 1983;65A:310–322.

Clancy WG. Repair and reconstruction of the posterior cruciate ligament. In: Chapman MW, ed. Operative orthopaedics. J. B. Lippincott Co., 1993.

Fowler PJ, Messich SS. Isolated posterior cruciate ligament injuries in athletes. Am J Sports Med 1987;15:553.

Hughston JC. The importance of the posterior oblique ligament in repairs of acute tears of the medial ligaments in knees with and without an associated rupture of the anterior cruciate ligament. J Bone Joint Surg 1994;76A:1328–1344.

Indelicato PA. Nonoperative treatment of complete tears of the medial collateral ligament of the knee. J Bone Joint Surg 1983;65A:323.

Gollahon DL, Torzill PA, Warren RF. The role of the posterolateral and cruciate ligaments. J Bone Joint Surg 1987;69A:233.

Jokl P, Kaplan N, Stovall P, et al. Nonoperative treatment of severe injuries to the medial and anterior cruciate ligaments of the knee. J Bone Joint Surg 1984;66A:741–744.

Linton RC, Indelicato PA. Medial ligament injuries. In: DeLee JC, Drez D, eds. Orthopaedic sports medicine. Philadelphia: W.B. Saunders, Co., 1994.

Noyes FR, Grood ES, Tarzill PA. The definitions of terms for motion and position of the knee and injuries of the ligament. J Bone Joint Surg 1989;71A:465–472.

24   Menisci

Barry Boden

The menisci serve several purposes, the most important being the transmission of force from the femur to the tibia. While the leg and knee are prone to injuries in soccer, the twisting, cutting, and pivoting inherent in the game often result in injury to the menisci. Studies localize the injury to a particular joint and not according to specific injury. As a result, useful statistics on the incidence of meniscal injuries are limited.

Unstable meniscal injuries often lead to mechanical symptoms blocking a smooth, full range of knee motion. Removal of the menisci excessively loads the articular cartilage of the femur and tibia, thereby accelerating the development of arthritis. Depending on the size and location of a meniscal tear, management can vary from nonoperative therapy to arthroscopic partial meniscectomy or meniscal repair. Future treatment modalities may involve injection of substances that promote meniscal healing or meniscal transplantation.

Anatomy

The medial and lateral menisci are semilunar fibrocartilage structures interposed between the femur and tibia (Fig. 24-1). The menisci have a blood supply, which decreases with age, that is limited to the peripheral 20%–30%. Therefore, only certain tears in this peripheral location have the potential to heal. Although the menisci contain no nerve fibers, unstable meniscal tears may be painful because the meniscus can pull on the richly innervated capsule.

There are several differences between the medial and lateral menisci. The C-shaped medial meniscus covers approximately half of the medial tibial plateau while the O-shaped lateral meniscus constitutes more than three-fourths of the lateral tibial plateau. Therefore, results of a total removal (total meniscectomy) of the lateral meniscus tend to be worse than total medial meniscectomy. The medial meniscus is more firmly attached to the surrounding capsule of the knee than the lateral meniscus. The lack of mobility of the medial meniscus results in a higher incidence of medial meniscal tears.

Function

The menisci act as shock absorbers to dampen the forces transmitted from the femur to the tibia. Forces across the knee joint vary from 2–4 times body weight

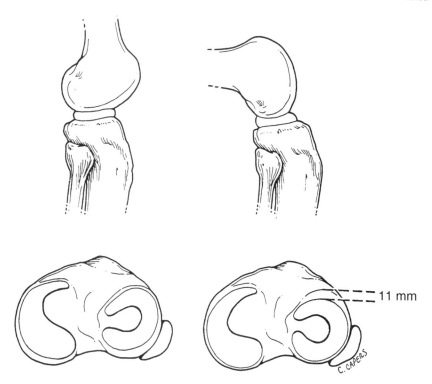

Figure 24-1. Normal meniscal anatomy.

depending on the position of the knee and the activity being performed. Between 50% and 100% of the load is transmitted to the meniscus. Meniscectomy can result in a 40%–60% increase in contact stresses between the femur and tibia. Even partial meniscectomy can result in a significant increase in articular contact forces. These increases in contact area forces have been shown experimentally and clinically to lead to degenerative joint conditions.

Mechanism of Injury

Meniscal injuries are common in sports such as soccer, which involve cutting, twisting, and pivoting. A combination of compression and rotational forces are the most common causes of meniscal injuries. These forces can shear the meniscus between the femoral and tibial condyles, resulting in a tear. As the knee is flexed, a progressively larger percentage of weight is borne by the meniscus due to the decreased contact area between the femur and tibia. Therefore, most meniscal tears occur with the knee in flexion. Few studies address methods to reduce the incidence of meniscal injuries. This is probably due in part to the unavoidable stresses placed on the knee during soccer.

The mechanism of injury in traumatic injuries can be recalled 80%–90% of the time. The athlete experiences a sudden onset of knee pain after a twisting injury. Often the player complains of mechanical symptoms, such as locking or catching, when the torn meniscus interferes with the normally smooth range of knee motion. Although the pain may abate after several days and allow a return to the activities of daily living, few patients are able to resume their previous level of sports activity.

Classification

Although there is no universal classification system for meniscal tears, most can be classified as traumatic or degenerative and further subdivided according to the geometry of the tear. Traumatic tears generally occur in young, active soccer players and may be isolated or associated with other ligamentous or articular injuries. Degenerative tears occur in older individuals and reflect cumulative stresses on the menisci, age-related changes, or both. The four basic patterns of meniscal tears (Fig. 24-2) include longitudinal, horizontal, oblique, and radial configurations. Bucket handle tears are extensive longitudinal tears in which the central half of the tear may flip 180° into the center of the knee, often resulting in a locked knee.

Treatment

The soccer player with a meniscal tear often has a small knee effusion in the acute setting, tenderness along the medial and lateral joint line, and pain when squatting. Locking or loss of full knee extension indicates a meniscal lesion. Commonly performed tests that are nonspecific for a meniscal tear attempt to reproduce the symptoms by maneuvering the knee through certain positions. Normal radiographs rarely reveal changes due to an acute, isolated meniscal tear, but may rule out a bony defect. Magnetic resonance imaging (MRI) is a noninvasive study with excellent soft tissue detail. The disadvantages of MRI include the cost, inability to classify the tear, and high incidence of overinterpretation.

In addition to the meniscus, soccer players also can injure the articular cartilage. Articular cartilage injury may appear similar to a meniscal injury. Often, the player does not remember the exact time of injury. Examination often demonstrates a generalized pain with less specific joint line tenderness. Effusions are more common in chronic injury to the articular cartilage.

Management of the Injury

Acute treatment of meniscal tears consists of ice, compression, and elevation. Crutches may be used for comfort. Immobilization is not necessary and will result in a stiff knee. Definitive treatment options for a meniscal tear include nonoperative or operative care (Table 24-1). Unless the knee is in a locked position or full range of motion is unobtainable, most isolated meniscal tears should be treated with rest and protected weightbearing.

SURGICAL TREATMENT

The majority of meniscal tears require operative treatment. Diagnostic arthroscopy is widely used to determine the location, stability, and configuration of the tear. Partial thickness tears and stable vertical longitudinal tears in the peripheral vascular portion of the menisci have excellent healing potential without any intervention. These tears are often incidental findings during arthroscopy performed for other reasons.

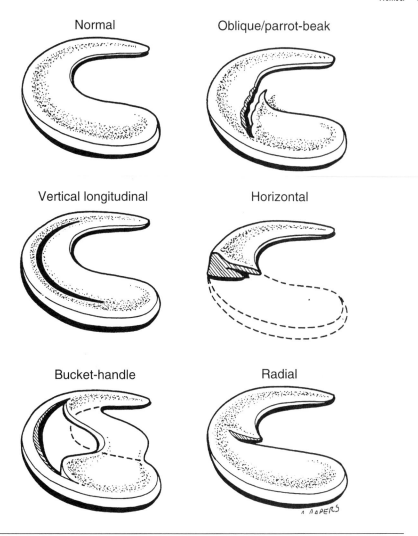

Figure 24-2. Classification of meniscal tears.

To preserve as much meniscal tissue as possible, the treatment for symptomatic, unstable tears is partial meniscectomy or meniscal repair. Partial meniscectomy is indicated for symptomatic, unstable meniscal tears with no potential to heal in the inner, central, or avascular portion and for complex peripheral tears. The goal of partial meniscectomy is to resect only the unstable or catching portion of the meniscus. The technique involves maintaining as much of the normal meniscus as possible, especially the peripheral, capsular portion. The meniscal edge is smoothed and contoured to prevent further meniscal injury.

Table 24-1

Treatment of Meniscal Tears

Conservative Treatment
  Asymptomatic, stable tears in peripheral 1/3
Partial Meniscectomy
  Unstable tears in central 2/3
  Complex tears
Meniscal Repairs
  Unstable tears in peripheral 1/3

The advantage of meniscal repair is that the entire meniscus is preserved. However, only tears in the peripheral vascular third have the potential to heal after suture repair. Longitudinal or bucket-handle tears in young individuals are usually responsive to repair. Concomitant anterior cruciate ligament reconstruction increases the chance of meniscal healing due to the postoperative hemarthrosis. The bloody effusion bathes the menisci with nutrients that promote healing.

REHABILITATION

Due to advances in arthroscopic techniques and anesthetic protocols, most isolated meniscal tears can be treated as outpatient procedures. Immediately after diagnostic arthroscopy or partial meniscectomies, patients are allowed to weight bear as tolerated. A full range of motion should be regained within 2 weeks, at which time activities such as swimming and cycling are begun. By 6–8 weeks, most athletes are asymptomatic, have regained full strength, and may return to playing soccer.

Rehabilitation after a meniscal repair is more prolonged. Range of motion exercises are started immediately. Most surgeons allow weight bearing only in full extension for the first 6 weeks to avoid the high contact pressures with knee flexion. Full weight bearing and a strengthening program may begin at 6 weeks postoperatively. By 3 months swimming, cycling, and jogging are started. The athlete is usually ready to return to soccer 6 months after surgery. More aggressive rehabilitation protocols are advocated by some surgeons.

Future Treatment Possibilities

Several experimental modalities are promising for athletes with meniscal pathology. As scientists gain a better understanding of the biological factors responsible for meniscal healing, repair of the avascular portion of the meniscus may become possible. One study using a fibrin clot shows promising results. For patients with unsalvageable meniscal pathology, meniscus transplantation may be an alternative, although initial results using this procedure have had limited success. Results of meniscal transplantation in degenerative knees have also been poor. Prospective studies on methods to reduce the incidence of meniscal injuries are lacking.

Summary

The menisci are dynamic structures with important load transmission functions. Due to the demands of soccer, the menisci are frequently injured. Although a limited number of meniscal tears can be treated nonoperatively, most require surgical therapy. The goal of surgery is to preserve the maximum amount of meniscal tissue to prevent degenerative knee conditions. Improvements in arthroscopic techniques have enhanced the ability to achieve this goal.

SUGGESTED READINGS

Arnoczky SP, Warren RF, Spivak JM. Meniscal repair using an exogenous fibrin clot: an experimental study in dogs. J Bone and Joint Surg 1988;7OA:1209–1217.

Belzer JP, Cannon D, Jr. Meniscus tears-treatment in the stable and unstable knee. J Amer Acad Ortho Surg 1993;l:4147.

DeLee JC, Drez D, Jr. Orthopedic sports medicine principles and practice. Philadelphia: WB Saunders, 1994.

Fu FH, Stone DA. Sports injuries: mechanisms, prevention, and treatment. Baltimore: Williams & Wilkins, 1994.

Hardin GT, Farr J, Bach BR, Jr. Meniscal tears: diagnosis, evaluation, and treatment. Ortho Review 1992;21:1311–1317.

Hede A, Hempel-Poulsen S, Jensen JS. Symptoms and level of sports activity in patients awaiting arthroscopy for meniscal lesions of the knee. J Bone and Joint Surg 1990;72A:550–552.

Omeara PM. The basic science of meniscus repair. Ortho Review 1993;22:681–686.

Weiss CB, Lundberg M, Hamberg P, et al. Non-operative treatment of meniscal tears. J Bone and Joint Surg 1989;71A:811–822.

25 Patellofemoral Problems

Bruce Reider

Patellofemoral problems are common in all sports, including soccer. However, these problems tend to be rare at the elite levels of soccer. This may be due to well developed quadriceps muscles, which protect elite players from many common causes of patellofemoral pain. Also, patellofemoral problems are so disabling that soccer players predisposed to them may not reach the elite level.

The nature of patellofemoral disorders changes according to the age of the athlete. For example, patellar problems in youth soccer players may be influenced by developmental variations in parameters such as limb alignment, patellar morphology, patellar stability, and dysplastic variations of quadriceps development. Older athletes may be affected by attritional changes, such as breakdown and erosion of patellar articular cartilage and degeneration of the patellar tendon.

At any age, patellofemoral symptoms may be caused by trauma. Acute trauma, such as a direct fall on the knee, may produce a frank patellar fracture or, more commonly, traumatic chondrosis of the hyaline cartilage of the patella or femoral trochlea. Chronic overuse may also produce progressive chondrosis of the patella or tendinosis of the patellar or quadriceps tendons. Overuse may be related to kicking, running, or strength and endurance training.

Mechanism of Injury

Although patients describe patellofemoral pain in different ways, they are usually trying to indicate a deep anterior pain. They will often grab the front of the knee and state that the pain is "in the knee," "deep in the knee," or "under the kneecap." (Fig. 25-1) Activities that increase patellar compression, such as quadriceps contraction, typically incite pain. In soccer, pain inducing activities include running, kicking, landing from a jump, or falling on the knee. Off of the soccer field, pain is typically experienced when kneeling, squatting, climbing stairs, or sitting with the knee flexed. Athletes may have episodes of functional instability, described as collapsing or giving out of the knee. This occurs when the patient is running forward, in contrast to the

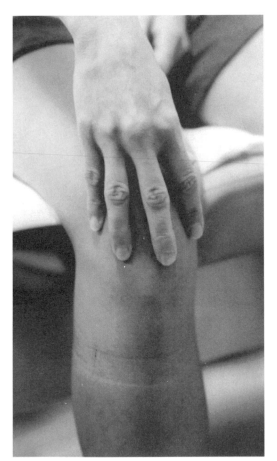

Figure 25-1. Whatever words they may use to describe their symptoms, athletes with patellofemoral pain will often grab their knee like this to indicate a deep anterior knee pain.

functional instability associated with anterior cruciate ligament insufficiency, which occurs when the athlete is cutting or pivoting.

In more advanced cases, when frank chondrosis is present, the athlete will complain of crunching or crepitus. Recurrent effusions also suggest the presence of advanced chondral damage. Players with patellar dislocation will have an acute (or recurrent) episode accompanied by considerable pain, swelling, and disability. When the extensor mechanism development is normal, there will usually be a history of direct trauma to the knee.

Physical Examination

The physical examination of the athlete with patellofemoral symptoms begins with an assessment of limb and extensor mechanism alignment. The athlete stands with the feet together and facing forward (Fig. 25-2). The patellas should also face directly forward. In some patients with patellofemoral pain, the patellas will squint or face inward toward each other. The Q angle, a traditional assessment of limb and extensor mechanism alignment, is used

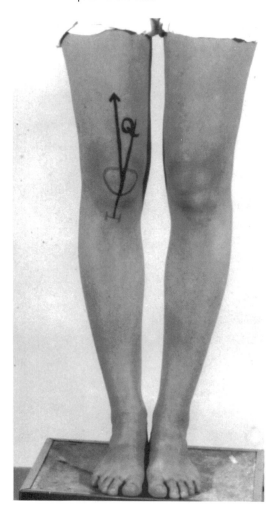

Figure 25-2. The Q angle is formed by a line from the anterior superior iliac spine to the center of the patella and a line from the center of the tibial tubercle to the center of the patella.

when the patient is in this position. The angle is formed by a line from the anterior superior iliac spine to the center of the patellar, and another line from the center of the tibial tubercle to the center of the patella. While the athlete is standing, the clinician should examine the feet for evidence of relative overpronation or loss of the medial longitudinal arch. This foot deformity produces internal rotation of the entire limb, which may aggravate any preexisting malalignment.

The alignment of the extensor mechanism may also be assessed in the seated position by evaluation of the tubercle-sulcus angle (Fig. 25-3). A line down the middle of the patellar tendon and a line perpendicular to the floor and horizontal line created by the femoral condyles creates the tubercle-sulcus angle. The normal range of this angle is approximately 80° in females and 50° in males.

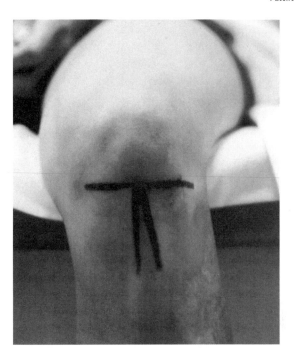

Figure 25-3. To measure the tubercle sulcus angle, the clinician draws a line down the middle of the patellar tendon and another line perpendicular to the floor and the horizontal line created by the femoral condyles on the seated patient.

During the initial inspection of the limb, the prominence formed by the vastus medialis obliquus should be examined carefully. Normally, this muscle is well developed in soccer players. A lack of this prominence bilaterally suggests an underlying dysplasia of the quadriceps mechanism, while an asymmetrical decrease in the vastus medialis obliquus (VMO) development suggests disuse atrophy. Next, dynamic patellar alignment in tracking is assessed. The athlete, sitting on the side of the table, extends the knee from 90° to full extension. The path of the patella as the knee extends is observed. Normally, the patella moves proximally with a slight lateral deviation or tilt at terminal extension. The greater the lateral shift or tilt at terminal extension, the greater the potential of patellar instability.

The potential for patellar instability is also assessed by measuring the patellar glides. The amount of excursion is assessed as the patella is pushed passively medially and laterally (Fig. 25-4). The normal excursion is approximately 1 cm in either direction. Hypermobility puts the patient at risk for clinical patellar instability, although many athletes with hypermobile patellas do not have clinical instability problems. Clinical instability is unlikely with tight patellar glides.

Next, passive patellar tilt is tested. The lateral facet of the patella is lifted from the lateral femoral condyle. Tightness with this maneuver suggests excessive

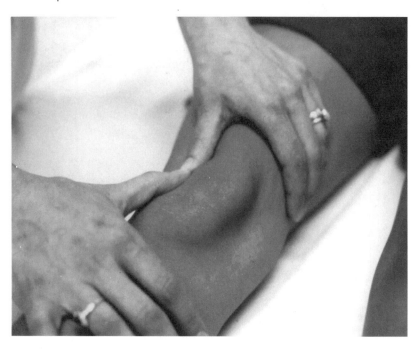

Figure 25-4. Passive patellar mobility (patellar glides) is assessed by pushing the patella medially and laterally while the quadriceps are relaxed.

lateral pressure syndrome, especially when the pain is localized in the lateral patellar facet. In these cases, the examiner should palpate carefully for the lateral patellofemoral ligament, which may be tender.

The dynamic test for patellar instability is known as the apprehension test (Fig. 25-5). The patient is supine and relaxed with the knee in full extension as the patella is pushed passively lateral and the knee is flexed over the side of the table. This maneuver mimics the instability episode and will usually cause apprehension and guarding in the patient with patellar subluxation or dislocation.

If breakdown of the normal articular surface of the patella or femoral trochlea is present, crepitus will often be detectable. One of the most sensitive ways to elicit this sign is to palpate the patella while the patient climbs on a small stool (Fig. 25-6). Crepitus will often be palpable and sometimes audible.

The final portion of the examination involves looking for specific areas of tenderness. With the knee in full extension, the patella is passively subluxed medially and the medial facet is palpated. The patella is then pushed laterally and the lateral facet is similarly examined. The patellar compression test, which involves gently pressing on the patella while passively flexing the knee, can be painful for the patient and should be done carefully. Pushing the patella laterally will tense the lateral patellofemoral ligament, which can often be distinctly palpated. Tenderness of this ligament, in conjunction with

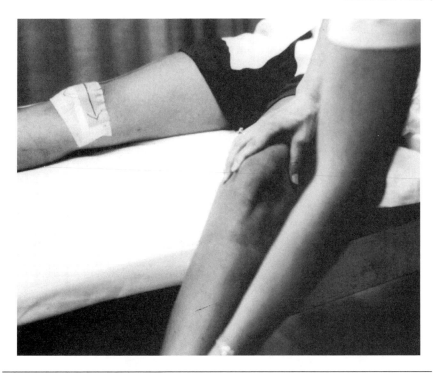

Figure 25-5. During the apprehension test, the examiner attempts to simulate an instability episode by pushing the patella laterally while passively flexing the knee.

pain localized to the lateral aspect of the patella and tight patellar glides, suggests a lateral patellar compression syndrome.

Localized swelling can suggest a specific disorder of the extensor mechanism. Swelling and tenderness of the tibial tubercle are the hallmarks of Osgood-Schlatter's disease, commonly seen in early adolescence. Sinding-Larsen-Johanssen disease is rare and is marked by tenderness and prominence at the inferior pole of the patella. In older athletes, swelling and tenderness at the inferior pole of the patella are indicative of patellar tendonitis.

Radiographic Examination

In mild cases of patellofemoral pain, treatment may be initiated on clinical grounds without obtaining radiographs. In cases of long-standing or severe pain, particularly in the older athlete or when effusion or crepitus are present, radiographs are usually obtained. The purposes of these radiographs are to detect bony changes such as degenerative arthritis or osteochondritis dissecans of the patellofemoral joint, look for loose bodies or other fracture fragments following an episode of patellar instability, rule out other bony pathology, and supplement the clinical assessment of patellar alignment (Fig. 25-7).

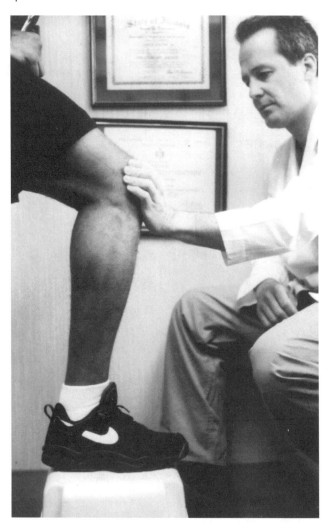

Figure 25-6. One of the most sensitive ways to elicit patellofemoral crepitus is to palpate the patella while the patient climbs onto a small step stool.

A standing anterior-posterior (AP) radiograph is useful as a screening tool for the assessment of knee alignment and tibiofemoral degenerative changes, although it is probably the least useful view for abnormalities specific to the patellofemoral joint. The AP view is also useful in the assessment of bipartite patella, which is usually characterized by an unfused supralateral bone fragment. Although this may be an incidental finding, pathologic motion at the fibrous union of the accessory fragment to the main patella may produce localized pain.

The lateral radiographic projection has several uses. It is the best projection for detecting the ossicles that may form within the patellar tendon near the

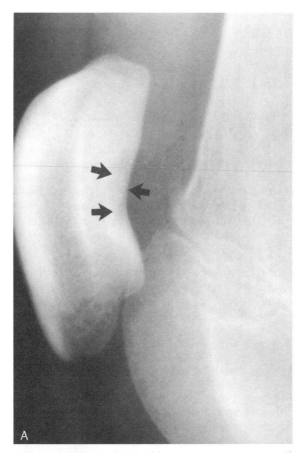

Figure 25-7. Osteochondritis dissecans of the patella in a high school soccer player seen on the lateral (A) and skyline (B) radiographs (arrows).

tibial tubercle in Osgood-Schlatter's disease or near the inferior pole of the patellar in Sinding-Larsen-Johanssen disease. Because these ossicles may be easily missed, a bright light should be used to examine these areas when suspicion is aroused by localized swelling in the adolescent patient.

Degenerative patellar osteophytes are most easily seen on the lateral view. Subtle sharpening of the posterior-superior or posterior-inferior corners of the patella on the lateral view may be the first sign of osteophyte formation. Patellar height, the relationship of the length of the patellar tendon to the other dimensions of the patella and the rest of the knee, is also assessed on the lateral projection. Patella alta, or high riding patella, has been associated with patellar instability. The ratio of the longest length measurement of the patella to the length of the patellar tendon is measured, with a ratio of less than 0.8 considered diagnostic of patella alta. This method may be difficult to use if the patellar shape is unusual or the location of the tibial tubercle is difficult to determine on the radiograph.

The tangential projection, often called an axial, sunrise, or skyline view, is important in the radiographic assessment of the patellofemoral joint. It is often the most useful view for detecting osteochondritis dissecans of the patella or femoral trochlea. Osteophytes, loose bodies, or avulsion fractures, which typically arise from the medial aspect of the patella during episodes of patellar dislocation, can be seen on this projection. Narrowing of the patellofemoral joint space in the presence of advanced patellofemoral arthritis is also visible.

If it is obtained in a standardized fashion, the tangential view is useful in classifying patellar morphology and detecting elements of malalignment. The Merchant view is the most popular standardized method and is obtained with the patient's knees flexed 45° over the edge of the examination table while the radiograph beam is directed at both patellofemoral joints at an angle of 30° to the axis of the femur. The angle of the femoral trochlear sulcus is outlined and bisected. The angle between this bisector and a line drawn from the apex of the patella to the deepest point of the trochlear sulcus is called the congruence angle (Fig. 25-8). As the patella shifts laterally, the congruence angle increases. According to Merchant's studies, a lateral or positive congruence angle of 16° or greater is considered diagnostic of lateral patellar subluxation. Although subject to error due to rotational positioning of the femur, patellar tilt or rotation in the transverse plane can also be estimated using this projection. Ideally, the lateral patella facet should parallel the lateral facet of the femoral trochlea. The more these two facets converge laterally, the more likely that abnormal lateral patellar tilt is present.

Computed tomography (CT) has been advocated as a more reliable method of assessing patellar malalignment. Patellar tilt may be more accurately assessed by comparing the orientation of the lateral facet to the orientation of a line formed by the posterior aspects of the femoral condyles. Because it is expensive and inconvenient to obtain, CT is usually reserved for surgical decision making when routine clinical and radiograph assessment of patellar alignment is insufficient.

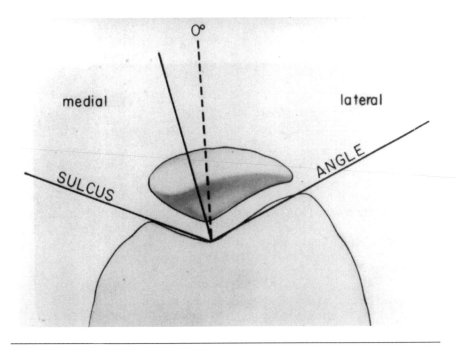

Figure 25-8. Merchant's congruence angle is formed by a line bisecting the trochlear sulcus and a line from the apex of the patella to the deepest point of the trochlear sulcus on a standardized radiograph.

Management of the Injury

Conservative

Conservative treatment options should be sufficient for the majority of soccer players with patellofemoral problems. Although surgery is the final treatment option for patellofemoral pain, players with pain severe enough to require surgery may not be able to return to soccer even after successful surgical treatment. Similarly, patients with patellar instability due to significant dyplasia of the quadriceps mechanism are probably not candidates for highly competitive soccer participation. On the other hand, patients with normal extensor mechanisms who experience patellar dislocation following specific acute trauma might be able to return to play after surgical repair.

Most aspects of conservative treatment fall into the general category of physical therapy techniques, including patellar taping and/or bracing, strengthening exercises, flexibility exercises, physical therapy modalities, and foot orthoses.

Analgesics and antiinflammatory agents play a limited role in the treatment of these disorders. The routine prescription of nonsteroidal antiinflammatory drugs does not seem to significantly improve the condition of patients just suffering from pain. Therefore, these medications are reserved for cases with identifiable synovial thickening or effusion. Athletes are encouraged to limit the use of drugs, such as ibuprofen, to a p.r.n. (as needed) basis for specific episodes of pain. Cryotherapy techniques are also helpful for analgesia.

Diana Gray, head orthopaedic physical therapist at the University of Chicago, outlined four guiding principles for the treatment of patellofemoral pain:

1. Evaluate and rehabilitate the entire lower extremity
2. Train in the most functional way possible
3. Understand that control, endurance, and balance are more important than strength
4. Never have the patient work through pain during exercise

Not every player will require an elaborate treatment program. Athletes with mild, intermittent pain may be appropriately treated with a simple home program, which might consist of a modified quadriceps exercise and the use of a functional patellar knee sleeve. The purpose of the quadriceps program is to further strengthen the quadriceps using a range of motion that is not painful or crepitant. For most patients, this means avoiding the last 30°–40° of extension during progressive resistive knee extension exercises. A wedge can be placed under the thigh to increase knee flexion, so knee extension exercises can be performed in a range from approximately 110°–40°. If there is a specific arc of motion during which the patient experiences patellofemoral pain or crepitus, the patient is instructed to avoid that arc of motion during knee extension exercises. If there is no painful or crepitant arc, the patient is told to exercise in the range from 110°–40° of flexion. Patients are told to perform two or three sets of 15–20 repetitions at each session using light weights and to slowly progress their resistance in amounts of 1 kilogram or 2.5 pounds. Each leg is exercised independently to prevent the healthy limb from shielding the symptomatic limb from the load.

If symptoms are mild, no modification in sports activities is necessary. If it is necessary, practices can be shortened or lightened without being discontinued completely. The athlete is fitted with a patellar knee sleeve and instructed to wear it for all activities that would incite symptoms. The elastic sleeve with an oval cutout for the kneecap and a horseshoe or circular pad surrounding the kneecap is the most effective. The knit elastic sleeves are generally tolerated more easily than the neoprene versions. The athlete is checked for progress 6 and 12 weeks after the start of treatment.

Athletes with more severe symptoms or who fail this simple home program are treated with a more elaborate program supervised by a physical therapist or athletic trainer. In the supervised program, the patellar knee sleeve is often replaced with McConnell taping. The McConnell taping may be thought of as a customized patellar knee sleeve tailored to the biomechanics of the knees of the patient. The supervised treatment program also includes weight bearing exercises for the knee, hip, and foot; flexibility exercises for the iliotibial band, hamstrings, and calf; biofeedback; electric muscle stimulation; and foot orthoses.

When designing the treatment program, the therapist thoroughly evaluates the patient using many of the same tests described under "Physical Examination." The therapist looks for a tight lateral retinaculum and iliotibial band, a weak vastus medialis obliquus, poor quadriceps control or endurance, abnormal hip rotation (version), excessive foot pronation, and limited flexibility of quadriceps, hamstrings, or gastrocsoleus.

McConnell taping is a new and controversial treatment modality. The technique was originated by the Australian physical therapist, Jenny McConnell, and has grown in popularity worldwide. Currently, there is little controlled research in the orthopedic literature concerning the efficacy of McConnell taping. Empirically, it is a useful adjunct in the treatment of patellofemoral pain. McConnell taping is only intended for use as a facilitative component of a complete treatment program. Although McConnell taping may temporarily relieve symptoms, they will generally recur after the tape is removed. The goal of the taping program is to temporarily place the patient in a pain-free state, permitting the performance of strengthening exercises and other rehabilitation techniques.

Not all patients are suitable subjects for McConnell taping. To be a candidate, an athlete should have pain that can be reproduced by a standardized provocative test. Stepping down from a standard stool is often used clinically, although a standardized running or ballhandling drill may be more appropriate for some athletes. When it has been established that the provocative test reliably evokes the pain, the McConnell taping is systematically applied. After each component of the taping is applied, the provocative test is repeated to see if the pain is relieved. When the pain is eliminated, the taping is considered complete. If the pain can not be largely or completely relieved by taping, the patient is not a candidate for this treatment technique.

McConnell describes the application of tape to try to modify four components of patellar alignment:

1. Glide, or medial-lateral translation in the coronal plane
2. Tilt, or rotation in the transverse plane
3. Rotation, or rotation in the coronal plane
4. AP tilt (flexion-extension), or rotation in the sagittal plane

When treating a patient, the therapist first assesses the four components of patellar tracking just mentioned. The provocative test is performed to verify that it reliably reproduces the pain. To protect the skin from the shear stresses exerted by the tape, the anterior knee is covered with an adhesive cloth-like cover roll (Fig. 25-9). The glide correction, the most important and useful portion of the taping process, is done first. Usually, this involves applying the tape to the anterior knee and pulling it medially (Fig. 25-10). The provocative test is then repeated to see whether relief has been obtained. This initial component of taping often provides sufficient relief so that no additional taping is required.

The second correction attempted is patellar tilt. Since abnormal tilt is usually lateral, the tape is applied at the center of the patella and pulled medially and posteriorly in an attempt to reduce pathologic lateral tilt (Fig. 25-11). It has not been verified that measurable changes in patellar tilt result from this taping, although it is possible that changes in patellar position sufficient to alter

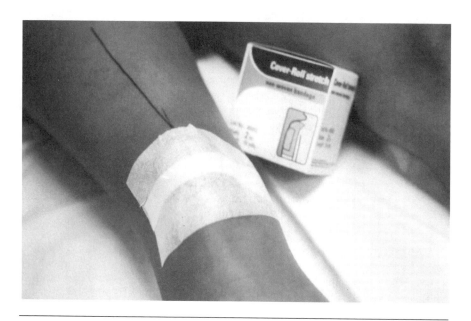

Figure 25-9. To protect the skin from the shear stresses of taping, an adhesive cover roll is first applied to the knee.

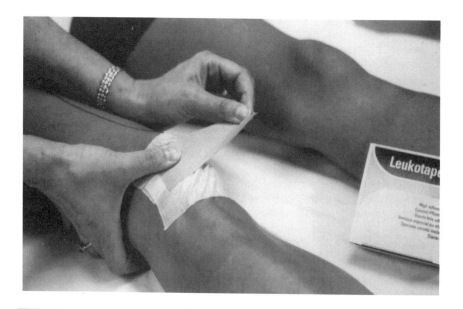

Figure 25-10. The most common correction of patellar glide involves pulling the patella medially.

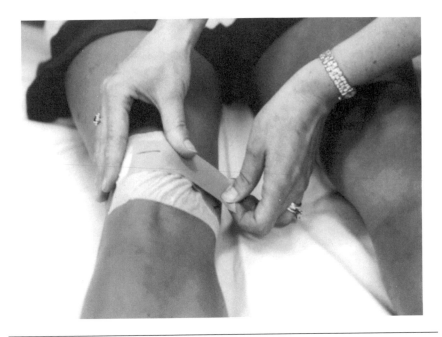

Figure 25-11. Patellar tilt is addressed by starting at the midpatella and pulling the tape medially and posteriorly.

symptoms may be too small to measure with currently available techniques. After the tilt component of taping has been applied, the provocative test is repeated. Again, if the pain is relieved, further taping is not required.

The final two components of taping are rotation and AP tilt (Fig. 25-12). This last component of taping is usually directed at depressing the superior pole of the patella and pushing the inferior pole anteriorly. If the pain does not improve with patella taping or if the skin does not tolerate the tape, a patellar knee sleeve may be used. If neither of these techniques is successful, the following rehabilitation program is carried out.

One objective of the rehabilitation program is to strengthen the VMO in relation to the rest of the quadriceps. The VMO is an important dynamic patellar stabilizer. It may be inhibited by patellar pain, potentially resulting in a vicious circle in which pain produces VMO inhibition, which produces functional patellar malalignment, which produces more pain. Methods of biasing the VMO during quadriceps rehabilitation include the use of weight bearing quadriceps exercises, in which knee extension is combined with hip adduction, and the use of biofeedback (Fig. 25-13). An example of such an exercise is shown in Figure 25-14. The athlete performs partial squats while simultaneously squeezing a heavy rubber ball between the knees.

In many patients, pathologic lateral tilt of the patella is associated with a tight iliotibial band. This is usually addressed by a combination of indirect stretch-

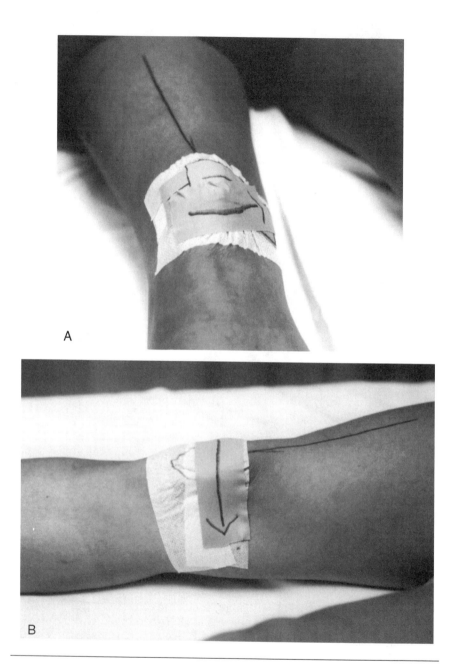

Figure 25-12. The final two components of taping are rotation (A) and AP tilt (B). The goal of this last component of taping is to depress the superior pole of the patella and push the inferior pole anteriorly.

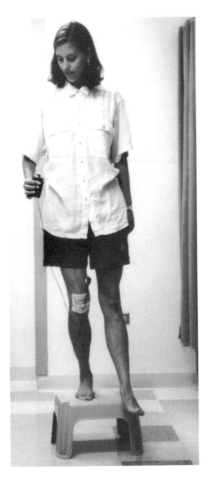

Figure 25-13. A biofeedback device placed over the VMO may be used to train an athlete to fire the VMO during rehabilitation exercises such as the step-down shown here.

ing techniques, which the patient performs several times daily, and manual stretching performed by the therapist.

Other factors that affect functional limb alignment may need to be addressed in some patients. For example, weakness or lack of endurance of the gluteus medius may lead to sagging of the pelvis and malalignment of the limb. For these patients, gluteus medius strengthening is important. In other patients, hyperpronation of the foot produces increased internal rotation of the entire lower limb. The prescription of a neutral functional orthotic may help these patients.

As symptoms improve, players temporarily suspended from soccer participation are reintroduced to controlled running and ball-handling drills. When the players are ready to return to full soccer participation, exercises are continued on a maintenance basis as necessary.

Summary

When patellofemoral pain occurs in soccer players, conservative treatment can usually improve the symptoms and permit continued participation. Mild

Figure 25-14. An exercise that tries to bias VMO activity by asking the athlete to perform a partial squat while squeezing a ball between the knees.

instability problems may also respond to conservative management. In all cases, treatment should be tailored to each patient according to the anatomic and functional etiologic factors present.

SUGGESTED READINGS

Fulkerson JP, Kalenak A, Rosenberg TD, et al. Patellofemoral pain. Instructional Course Lectures. American Academy of Orthopaedic Surgeons 1992;XLI:577–591.

Fulkerson JP, Shea KP. Disorders of patellofemoral alignment. J Bone Joint Surg 1990;72-A:1424–1429.

Fulkerson JP. Hungerford DS-disorders of the patellofemoral joint, 2nd ed. Baltimore: Williams & Wilkins, 1990.

Fulkerson JP. The etiology of patellofemoral pain in young, active patients. Clin Orthop 1983;179:129–133.

Malek MM, Mangine RE. Patellofemoral pain syndromes: a comprehensive and conservative approach. J Orthop Sports Phys Ther 1981;2:108–116.

McConnell J. The management of chondromalacia patellae: a long-term solution. Austral J Physiother 1986;332:215–223.

Radin EL. A rational approach to the treatment of patellofemoral pain. Clin Orthop 1979;144:107–109.

Reider B, ed. Patellofemoral joint surgery. Operative Techniques in Sports Medicine, Vol 2 #4. 1994;237–342.

Shea KP, Fulkerson JP. Rehabilitation of the patellofemoral joint. In: Griffin LY, ed. Rehabilitation of the injured knee. St Louis: Mosby Year Book, in press.

26  Chondral Injuries of the Knee

William E. Garrett, Jr.
Donald T. Kirkendall

Injuries to the articular cartilage of the knee are receiving increasing attention from sports medicine personnel involved with soccer. In recent years there has been interest in the basic and clinical aspects of the anterior cruciate ligament in soccer, resulting in general agreement on the concepts of diagnosis and management. In contrast, little has been written about articular cartilage injuries and there is no consensus regarding the clinical management of this condition. Although most of these injuries can be managed in a way that allows a return to sports, some of these injuries end careers.

There are two types of cartilage in the knee. All freely moving synovial joints have a thin layer of articular cartilage that surrounds the ends of the bones. This hyaline cartilage has impressive stiffness, compression, resilience, and ability to distribute loads. The cells are widely spaced. These functions and the low density of cells minimize the stress on the subchondral bone that lies under the cartilage. The cartilage is relatively void of neural input, has no lymphatic drainage, and is largely devoid of blood vessels. Damage to articular cartilage results in little inflammation because of this lack of vascularity. The cells of articular cartilage receive their nutrients from the synovial fluid that bathes all surfaces of the joint. Normal joint function can last over a lifetime in many people.

The other type of cartilage in the knee, the two crescent moon shaped menisci, are made up of fibrocartilage and are well suited for absorption of loads. These pads sit on the flat surface of the tibia. When an athlete has arthroscopic surgery for a cartilage injury and returns to competition only weeks later, it can be assumed that the menisci were treated by partial excision. The menisci are discussed more in Chapter 24.

Epidemiology
The only data on incidence suggests that chondral defects can be found in approximately 4% of arthroscopies, indicating that this injury is not common. However, as will be described later, this injury can be easily missed. Although there are no reliable data on the incidence of chondral injuries in sports, there seems to be a high incidence in soccer. A recent description of the clinical experience in soccer players reported 21 articular cartilage in-

juries in 13 soccer players over 5–7 years. Other references do not give a reasonable estimate of the incidence of the injury. However, sports-related injury to the cartilage seems to be more frequent in team field sports like soccer, lacrosse, field hockey, rugby, and related sports.

Mechanism of Injury

Several factors are thought to be related to chondral injuries. Running long distances may be a predisposing factor. Soccer requires approximately 10 km per game for adult professionals. Soccer also requires considerable pivoting and cutting, which may lead to high shear forces in the knee. Soccer shoes or boots are designed for traction to allow quick direction change or acceleration and have very little padding. Although basketball players also cut, they do not accumulate the same distances and their shoes have more padding. The impact is also reduced in ice hockey players because they skate rather than run. Football players do not cover the long distances run by soccer players. There are few data on selected sports to prove or disprove these ideas.

Chondral injuries have been classified according to their appearance at arthroscopy or on gross inspection (Fig. 26-1). The cartilage is often fibrillated or otherwise abnormal at its surface, giving the appearance that injury occurs from the surface toward the base. Another injury type involves a chondral fracture running from the articular surface to the calcified cartilage with fur-

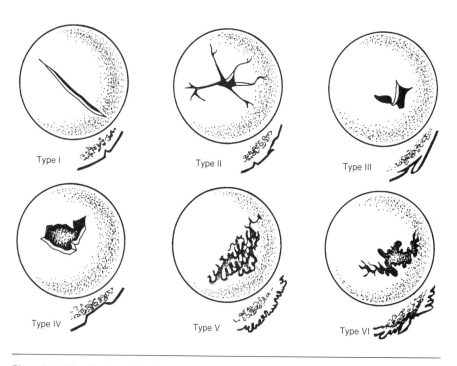

Figure 26-1. Classification of chondral lesions. (Reprinted with permission from: Harris JR. Chondral lesions. In: Baker C, ed. The Hughston Sports Medicine Book. Media: Williams & Wilkins, 1995.)

ther disruption of the cartilage at the junction between soft cartilage and calcified cartilage. This junction is called the tidemark. The delaminating flap of cartilage may appear normal at its surface. However, probing the cartilage demonstrates the instability of the chondral fragment.

The chondral injuries may involve any of the articular surfaces of the knee. The femoral condyles, the trochlea, and the patella are the most common locations.

Cartilage has a limited ability to repair itself. This is partly due to its lack of blood supply and the need for undifferentiated cells (cells that can differentiate into various types with appropriate signals) for repair. The available cells are well encased in a matrix, limiting their mobility and potential to migrate to damaged areas of the cartilage. The minimal blood supply also limits cells from migrating to damaged areas. The low density of cells and the limited ability of cells to migrate to damaged areas means that repair of cartilage can be compromised by lack of raw materials. The tear can extend into the well-vascularized subchondral bone giving access of the blood supply to the defect.

The fractures have been classified according to their arthroscopic appearance (Fig. 26-1). Table 26-1 outlines the descriptive appearance of the defects. Figure 26-2 shows an arthroscopic view of one type of chondral defect. Some of these defects can be difficult to see arthroscopically. To illustrate, imagine a cut in the carpet. If the tear has been tamped down, it may be impossible to see unless there is suspicion of a tear. This is also the case with chondral lesions. The surgery must be approached with a high degree of suspicion or the defect may be missed. Because of this difficulty, the 4% figure quoted previously may be too low.

Diagnosis of chondral defects is difficult because there are no definitive diagnostic signs. Vague symptoms suggestive of mensical problems like locking, catching, and giving way may be described. Often, there is an aching sensation during and after play. Although a traumatic episode may have occurred months earlier, a single injury is rarely recalled. The knee may be stiff in the morning with some impairment of movement. Going up stairs will probably be more difficult than going down stairs. There may be pain with turning or rotation and there may or may not be an effusion about the knee. During flexion and extension the knee may pop or catch.

Table 26-1

Classification of Chondral Defects
Type I - linear crack
Type II - stellate crack
Type III - chondral flap
Type IV - condral crater
Type V - fibrillar appearance
Type VI - degraded

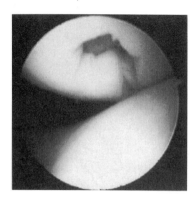

Figure 26-2. Arthroscopic photograph of a chondral lesion. (Reprinted with permission from: Harris JR. Chondral lesions. In: Baker C, ed. The Hughston Sports Medicine Book. Media: Williams & Wilkins, 1995.)

Further physical findings may suggest meniscal involvement. There may be some quadriceps atrophy depending on the length of time the player has had the injury. Effusion may or may not be present. An effusion is more common on chronic injuries than mensical injuries. There may be joint line tenderness around the area of the defect. Extremes of flexion and extension are often painful. Direct patellofemoral pressure may elicit some tenderness. The joint is rarely unstable in the absence of ligamentous injury. Standard radiographs are usually not diagnostic. Magnetic resonance imaging (MRI) is not accurate in the diagnosis of chondral injury, although MRI is accurate for meniscal injuries. The only way to obtain a definitive diagnosis is arthroscopically. Thus, the diagnosis of a chondral injury is a clinical diagnosis confirmed arthroscopically.

Management of the Injury

The best initial care is conservative. If there is no reason to suspect meniscal problems, the athlete may return to play. Pain will be the main guide in determining sports participation. Some players with chondral defects improve spontaneously. Although symptoms may persist for months, they may not be severe enough to prevent play. Persistent effusions are often the sign of a chondral lesion. Suspected chondral lesions may improve with time. It is uncertain whether physical therapy or other conservative measures contribute to the speed of recovery. Repetitive low intensity motion exercises may be the best choice for therapy with emphasis on nonimpact exercises, such as cycling or swimming.

Surgical treatment of the defect is sometimes necessary. The loose pieces of cartilage are removed to the point of a stable rim of hyaline cartilage. The base of the lesion (although the floor of the lesion looks like bone, there is still a layer of fibrocartilage) is drilled or abraded so that growth of the fibrocartilage is stimulated. If the defect is isolated to the cartilage, surgical disruption will result in proliferation of cartilage cells in the area surrounding the injury.

If the defect extends through the cartilage to the vascular, subchondral bone, repair follows inflammation. The bone defect and a portion of the cartilage defect fill with new cells and matrix. Within 6 months, the subchondral bone defect fills with bone cells and blood vessels. The chondral portion rarely fills completely and the tissue that is there is a hybrid of hyaline and fibrocartilage tissue.

The prognosis is largely based on the size of the injury. If the lesion is small and does not alter normal joint function, then the injury can heal more predictably than larger defects. In studies on animals, lesions of 2–3 mm were created. Approximately 12 weeks later tissue remodeling began. In humans, the lesions are 5–20 mm and require a longer time to recover. Although age has not been systematically investigated, young, immature bone and growing synovial joints remodel more effectively than those of skeletally mature adults.

Little is known about the appropriate course of therapy to follow. After surgery, a gradual progression back to athletic activity is begun. Table 26-2 summarizes the steps. There is controversy about each level of rehabilitation. Some advocate protection of the knee while others encourage weight bearing and range of motion as tolerated. Continuous passive motion is advocated for the first week after surgery. Cyclical motion (cycling, swimming) is encouraged for range of motion because these activities are nonweight bearing. This cyclical motion enhances nutrition of the cartilage and further stimulates the cells to differentiate, which should accelerate healing. Strengthening should be confined to the pain-free arcs of motion. If the injury is old, atrophy may need to be addressed. However, low strength may be due to pain inhibition, which would suggest that strengthening exercises may not be necessary. Regardless, strength is important. Although it increases patellofemoral forces, strength also increases the activity of the quadriceps muscle, which can reduce joint impact. Another source of controversy regarding strength training is the issue of closed versus open chain activities. Open chain activities increase shear forces in the 0°–30° range while closed chain stress the 60°–90° range. Because the defects can occur anywhere on the condyles of the femur or patella, the effectiveness of these methods cannot be predicted. Knowing the location of the defect helps determine which method to use.

The return to impact activities needs to be gradual to allow for adequate healing, increase in strength, and impact absorption. It may take 3–6 months before the knee can be fully functional. If the lesion is less than 1 cm, the player can usually return to full activity with only mild residual symptoms. If the lesion is larger, especially those over 2 cm, only partial relief can be expected

Table 26-2

Steps in Post-Surgical Rehabilitation of Chondral Defects
Weight bearing as tolerated
Range of motion as tolerated
Cyclical motion
Strengthening (at arcs that do not add compressive/ shear forces to the defect)
No impact for 1–3 months
Gradual progression to impact activities

and the lesion may progress. Patellar lesions may not recover as well as lesions to the femoral condyles or trochlea. It is not known whether return to soccer accelerates progression of the lesion.

At the present time, surgery is indicated for pain relief and preservation of function. Even with subchondral abrasion, it is not known whether long-term results of surgery are superior to those of conservative treatment. The regenerated cartilage is not normal hyaline cartilage and experimental studies do not support the ability of surgery to lead to regeneration of normal cartilage. Therefore, conservative treatment seems appropriate if symptoms are not limiting performance. Although surgical treatment often affords symptomatic improvement and an ability to retun to play, it may not provide complete relief.

Summary

Condral injuries of the knee are frequent in soccer players. Activity related pain and aching are characteristic symptoms. On examination, there is often an effusion without the characteristic joint line tenderness of a meniscal injury. Diagnosis is based on the clinical presentation since MRI and radiographs may not be diagnostic. Conservative treatment is often adequate. When conservative treatment does not allow return to sport, surgical treatment may be beneficial. Symptomatic relief can be achieved and return to play is usually possible. However, the pain relief may not be complete and progression of the lesion is possible.

SUGGESTED READINGS

Buckwalter JA. Mechanical injuries of articular cartilage. In: Finerman GAM, Noyes FR, eds. Biology and biomechanics of the traumatized synovial joint: the knee as a model. Rosemont, IL: American Academy of Orthopedic Surgeons, 1992.

Harris JR. Chondral lesion. In: Baker C, ed. The Hughston Sports Medicine Book. Media: Williams & Wilkins, 1995.

Levy A, Garrett WE. Chondral delamination of the knee in soccer players. Presented at the 3rd World Congress of Science and Football. Cardiff, Wales. 1995.

27   Muscle Strains

William E. Garrett, Jr.

Muscle injuries are well known to soccer players and sports medicine professionals involved with their care. Indirect injury to muscle does not result from direct trauma but, rather, from too much stretch or tension in the muscle. These indirect injuries are often called strains or pulls. In engineering terminology, strain is a precise measure for stretch. Strain injury is usually cited as the most frequent injury in sports and comprises approximately 30% of the injuries seen in a sports medicine practice.

Epidemiology

There are numerous studies on injury epidemiology. The leg is the most injured limb with the ankle being the primary area effected. These epidemiology studies estimate that strain injuries account for 10%–30% of all soccer injuries. Although time may be lost from play, many players participate with these injuries even though their performance is significantly hampered.

Mechanism of Muscle Strain Injury

Every sport has characteristic muscle strain injuries. The physiological demands of soccer include sprinting, endurance running, rapid acceleration and deceleration, rapid direction changes, jumping, heading, and many other activities putting muscle groups at risk. The thigh muscles are at most risk. Strains are more prevalant in soccer than in any other sport. Hamstring injuries are the most common, followed by quadriceps strains.

Hamstring strains occur during sprinting, stretching the leg to strike or trap a ball, or during high kicks. They are characterized by pain in the posterior thigh anywhere from the buttock to the knee. There is frequent bruising (ecchymosis) in the posterior thigh and knee. Knee extension, hip flexion, sprinting, and kicking are painful. Any of the hamstring muscles can be injured proximally near the buttock or distally toward the knee. Imaging studies show that the biceps femoris long head and semimembranosus muscles are especially at risk.

The second most commonly strained muscle group is the quadriceps. The knee extensor group is especially at risk during powerful kicks and when the foot catches on the ground and the quadriceps are activated. The rectus femoris muscle is the sole component of the quadriceps group that crosses two joints and is the most frequently injured muscle. It can be injured distally and retracted proximally. This leaves a prominent muscle mass in the proximal thigh. The muscle can also be injured within its substance from a position of the proximal attachment. This leaves a prominent proximal muscle bulge.

The adductor muscles are also frequently injured. The adductor longus is most at risk. It is often injured when the hip is abducted to play a ball or forced into abduction (e.g., during a slip on a wet field). Tenderness is usually in the medial thigh near the pelvis. The injury is along the proximal muscle-tendon junction, although the injury can also be distally near its attachment to the femur. The muscle injury is usually incomplete and does not create much asymmetry. The injuries prevent hip abduction and strong instep kicks due to pain.

Other muscles are injured to a lesser extent than the thigh muscles. The triceps surae and the medial head of the gastrocnemius can suffer strains from soccer. The injury is usually in the mid calf and medially. Injury to the back muscles is also common. The injuries cause pain with powerful trunk motion when hard kicking or heading.

These specific muscle injuries are all common in soccer. Imaging studies have defined the specific muscles at risk. Currently, the diagnosis can be made based on the specific history and physical examination.

Noncontact or indirect injuries to skeletal muscle include delayed onset muscle soreness (DOMS), partial strain injury, and complete muscle rupture. These three conditions are more prone to occur with eccentric exercise. DOMS is characterized by generalized muscle soreness and weakness, which is maximal 1–2 days after eccentric exercise and is usually not associated with long-term morbidity. In contrast, partial strain injury and complete muscle rupture involve more focal pain and weakness during exercise with significant morbidity resulting. This is the common muscle pull or strain that is experienced as an acute painful injury during exercise. This chapter focuses on acute muscle strain injuries including partial injury and total muscle rupture. Clinical observations and data from animal experiments are reviewed in an effort to develop some consensus on the pathophysiology, mechanism of injury, and methods of treatment and prevention.

Management of the Injury
Conservative Care

Treatment strategies for muscle strain injuries vary and are often based more on success in clinical practice than basic scientific data. Immediate treatment usually involves rest, ice, and compression of the affected soft tissue and extremity. Additional treatment modalities typically include physical therapy to promote range of motion, functional strengthening exercises, and medications. Medications include anesthetics, analgesics, muscle relaxants, and antiinflammatory medicines (steroidal and nonsteroidal agents). Nonsteroidal antiinflammatory drugs (NSAIDs) are usually started as soon as possible and are used for a short period (5–7 days) since they may interfere with subsequent tissue repair and remodeling. In the case of severe injury a period of enforced rest (e.g., brace or cast) is sometimes recommended.

The repair process for strain injuries involves two competitive events; regeneration of muscle fibers from the remaining viable muscle fibers and satellite cells and the simultaneous production of connective scar tissue. NSAIDs, which inhibit prostaglandin production, are typically prescribed to inhibit the inflammatory response. Despite their known effects on prostaglandin inhibition, studies have failed to demonstrate that administration of NSAIDs decreases muscle edema or swelling after acute injury. It may be that the inhibitory effects on prostaglandin production are of little consequence since other inflammatory mediators such as histamine, serotonin, and oxygen free radicals are not inhibited by NSAIDs. Many questions remain regarding the effects and role of NSAIDs in the treatment of acute muscle strain injuries. The optimal time course for therapy and dosage schedules are not well known. It may be that the analgesic properties of NSAIDs promote earlier and more effective rehabilitation after injury due to pain reduction rather than effects on inflammation.

Traditionally, clinicians have advised a period of immobilization of the muscle and affected extremity. When muscle fibers are immobilized for a long period under stretch, the immediate effect is that the fibers are larger and the constituent myofibrils longer. Sarcomere lengths are initially increased, but return to normal length after several weeks. Additional sarcomeres are added at the muscle-tendon junction (MTJ) and the length-tension relationship shifts to the right so that less passive force is generated in response to the same stretch. Prolonged immobilization can lead to detrimental effects, including muscle atrophy, loss of muscle extensibility and strength, and an increased propensity for re-injury. Consequently, a short course of immobilization followed by early mobilization has become a popular form of treatment. The basis for this treatment strategy is experimental data that shows early mobilization after a contusion muscle injury (3–5 days after the injury in rats) improves the mechanical properties of the muscle and less necrotic muscle tissue. The appropriate length of immobilization and start of mobilization following acute muscle strain injury has not been studied in humans. Also, no experimental studies have been performed to evaluate different rehabilitation techniques.

Physical Therapy

Our preference for rehabilitation of most strains involves rest of the muscle without immobilization, range of motion exercises, and stretch. If the injured athlete administers the stretch, it is unlikely to increase the area of injury and is stretching the scar tissue at the site of injury. As motion is restored, gentle strengthening is begun. Isometric, concentric, and isokinetic exercises at low intensity are most helpful. As comfort allows, intensity is increased, jogging, and light exercise are begun. Sprinting, cutting, and ball drills can be added when tolerable. These injuries have a high rate of recurrence when competition is resumed. Near full recovery of strength, functional ability, and full motion are desired before returning to competition.

Surgical Care

Occasional surgical intervention has been advocated in cases of complete dissociation of the muscle-tendon unit. Injury at the muscle-tendon junction is difficult to repair. Complete disruption of the origin or insertion of all or one head of a muscle-tendon unit may be required for adequate function or pain. Although complete disruption of the adductor longus may produce a clear mass, it often causes little functional deficit. However, complete hamstring disruption from the ischium is possible and may require reattachment for athletic function. Similarly, a strain of the rectus femoris involving the indirect head may be disabling to a soccer player, especially during forceful kicking.

Injury Prevention

A number of factors predispose muscle to strain injury. Most athletes routinely stretch because it is thought to prevent muscle injury. Adequate warm-up is also cited as a method of prevention. Training programs employing adequate stretching and warm-up may decrease the incidence of muscle injuries. However, these programs involve a number of variables and the effects of single factors has not been determined.

Muscles are most often injured during eccentric action while resisting stretch. The muscles may be protected by being able to stretch further before injury or resist being stretched. Studies in animals show several other factors to be important. Muscles contracting eccentrically are decelerating joint motion to control and absorb energy. Fatigue results in less energy absorbed before failure. Strength allows muscle to absorb more energy before failing. This has been shown by differential stimulation of muscle demonstrating that more force production results in more energy absorbed before failure.

A minor injury predisposes to a more serious injury. Therefore, supervised care and careful return to activity may prevent extension of the injury. Swedish studies show that careful supervision can be effective in the prevention of soccer injuries.

In addition to these preventive measures of stretching and warm-up, there are some additional risk factors that may be avoided. Fatigue is thought to predispose muscle to injury. Previous injury is thought to predispose an affected muscle to a subsequent injury. Although such factors are widely felt to be important risk factors for muscle injury, there have been few solid clinical or laboratory studies to support these beliefs.

Clinical Studies of Muscle Strain Injury

Mechanism of Injury in the Lab

Despite a large amount of clinical data on injury to skeletal muscle, the exact mechanism of muscle strain injuries remains unknown. It is clinically accepted that muscle strain injuries occur in response to forcible stretching of a muscle either passively (without muscle activation) or, more often, when the muscle is activated (eccentric contraction). With eccentric contractions muscle may be more prone to injury due to the forces produced by the contractile element and the extrinsic forces stretching the muscle.

The muscles that are most susceptible to injury are the two-joint or biarticular muscles. These muscles cross two or more joints and are subject to stretch at more than one joint. Another characteristic of commonly injured muscles is their ability to limit the range of motion of a joint due to the intrinsic tightness in the muscle. For example, hamstring muscles can limit knee extension when the hip is flexed. Similarly, the gastrocnemius can limit ankle dorsiflexion when the knee is extended. Muscles at risk for injury often function in an eccentric manner to control and regulate motion. Much of the muscle action involved with running or sprinting is eccentric. For instance, the hamstrings act not so much to flex the knee as to decelerate the lower extremity during knee extension. Similarly, the quadriceps act as much to prevent knee flexion as to power knee extension in running.

Muscle strain injuries occur most often in sprinters or speed athletes. They are most common in sports and positions requiring rapid changes in velocity or acceleration/deceleration, such as American football, basketball, rugby, soccer, and sprinting.

Structural Changes with Muscle Strain Injury

Clinical data are relatively sparse regarding the nature of changes within the muscle following a strain injury. The injury can be partial or complete depending on whether the muscle-tendon unit is grossly disrupted. Complete tears are characterized by muscle asymmetry at rest compared to the contour of the opposite limb. With contraction, the injured muscle will demonstrate a bulge towards the affected side, which is still attached to bone.

Direct injury or contusion causes injury to muscle at the place of contact. However, the location of pathological changes in a muscle following strain injury was not well defined until recently. The vulnerable site in indirect strain injury appears to be near the MTJ or the tendon-bone junction. The extent of the MTJ in certain muscles is often surprising. For example, the hamstring muscles have an extended MTJ in the posterior thigh. The proximal tendon and muscle-tendon junctions of the biceps femoris and semimembranosus extend well over half the total length of these muscles. Although surgical exploration of muscle strain injuries is not commonly performed, there are a number of references in the literature regarding surgical findings. These studies confirm tears near the MTJ in the gastrocnemius medial head (incorrectly called plantaris rupture), rectus femoris muscle, triceps brachii muscle, adductor longus muscle, pectoralis major muscle, and semimembranosus muscle. More recently, high resolution imaging studies have localized hamstring injuries to the region of the MTJ. Computerized tomography (CT) scans reveal areas of low density consistent with edema at the site of injury in all patients. In another study, 50 athletes with acute muscle strain injuries were imaged by CT or MRI within 96 hours of injury. On MRI, T_2-weighted images were most effective in identifying free fluid shifts and differentiating these areas from injured tissue. In contrast, T_1-weighted images were most appropriate as an adjunct for specifically identifying hemorrhage. Within a given synergistic muscle group, certain muscles were more prone to injury than others. For example, the adductor longus was the most often injured of the adductors and the rectus femoris was the most commonly injured quadriceps muscle. Reasons for this are unknown. In all cases, injury occurred at the MTJ with fluid collections at the injury site extending along the epimysium. Muscle tissue remote from the MTJ showed extensive injury and changes consistent with edema and inflammation.

Although bleeding often occurs after a muscle injury, it usually takes one or more days to detect subcutaneous ecchymosis. Subcutaneous blood collections demonstrate that the bleeding is not confined to the muscle proper, but escapes through the perimysium and fascia to the subcutaneous space. In other instances it appears that bleeding can occur and a hematoma or seroma can collect between the muscle tissue and the surrounding fascial compartment, as shown by ultrasonography. This is in contrast to findings seen with direct muscular contusion in which bleeding often occurs within the muscle substance.

Experimental Data on Acute Muscle Strain Injury

Skeletal muscle is subjected to a range of loading conditions in vivo and it is difficult to experimentally reproduce the kinematics and kinetics of these conditions. One of the first studies of muscle strain injury demonstrated that normal tendon did not rupture when the muscle-tendon unit was strained to failure. Rather, failure occurred at the tendon-bone junction, the myotendinous junction, or within the muscle. Our laboratory previously studied recovery in rabbit hind limb muscles following muscle laceration and repair. This model has been adapted to the study of acute muscle strain injuries.

Initial experiments demonstrated that activation of normal muscle by nerve stimulation alone did not cause complete or incomplete disruption. Force diminished and failure of excitation occurred, but no disruption resulted. To achieve gross or microscopic muscle injury, stretch of the muscle was required. The forces produced at the time of failure without muscle activation were several times the maximum isometric force produced by the muscle itself. This data suggests that the passive component of the total muscle force may be as important as the active component in strain injuries. Since these initial experiments, a number of studies have been conducted to investigate various aspects of muscle strain injuries.

Site of Injury

Clinical studies have shown that the MTJ is the most common site of damage in acute muscle strain injuries. Laboratory studies using a variety of test preparations have produced injury at or near the MTJ. The reason why the MTJ is susceptible to injury is not well understood. This finding would not be predicted from a maximum stress theory of failure because the MTJ has a larger cross section and the same loads as the distal tendon. Recent data suggests that the MTJ may be predisposed to injury due to large strains locally at the site of injury.

Active Stretch

Conditions were devised to evaluate the powerful eccentric contractions during which muscle injuries are believed to occur. Muscles were stretched to failure under three conditions of motor nerve activation: 1) tetanic stimulation, 2) submaximal stimulation, and 3) unstimulated. Muscle stimulation did not change the site of failure—the MTJ. Total deformation to failure was not different between the three groups. Force at failure was 15% higher in stimulated muscles. However, the energy absorbed was approximately 100% higher in activated muscles stretched to failure. These data confirm the importance of muscles as energy absorbers. Although the passive components of stretched muscle have the ability to absorb energy, the potential is greatly increased with active muscle contraction.

The above concept may explain how muscle can prevent injury to itself and associated joint structures. There are two components of the muscle's ability to absorb energy. The passive component is not dependent on muscle activation and is a property of the connective tissue elements within the muscle. It includes the muscle fibers and the connective tissue associated with the cell surface and existing between fibers. There is an additional ability to absorb energy within the contractile element of the muscle. Based on the above experiments, the contractile element can double the ability of the muscle to absorb energy (Fig. 27–1). At small muscle displacements the majority of energy absorption is due to the active component. Therefore, conditions that diminish the contractile ability of muscle may diminish its ability to absorb energy. Muscle fatigue and weakness are often considered predisposing factors to muscle injury.

Nondisruptive (partial injury)

The previously cited studies evaluated the biomechanics of muscle stretched to failure to complete muscle disruption. Most strain injuries to muscle did not result in total rupture and dissociation of the MTJ unit, but in partial or incomplete injury. Experiments have been performed in an attempt to better understand partial strain injuries. Nonrupture injuries were created by stretching passive muscle to 80% of the force necessary to fail the contralateral muscle. Histological studies show that injuries nondisruptive to whole muscles cause disruption of a small number of muscle fibers near the MTJ (Fig. 27–2). The fibers do not tear at the junction of the muscle fiber and the tendon, but within the fiber a short distance from the tendon. Initially,

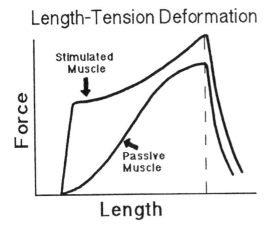

Figure 27-1. The differences in relative energy absorbed to failure in stimulated vs. passive muscle are shown as the area under each length-tension curve.

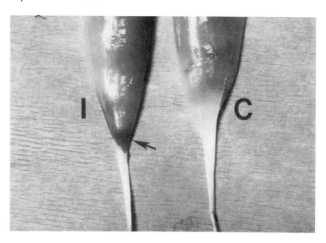

Figure 27-2. Site of strain injury (arrow) in and injured (I) tibialis anterior muscle of a rabbit. An uninjured muscle (C) is shown for comparison.

nondisruptive injuries are marked by disruption and some hemorrhage within the muscle. By 1–2 days, an inflammatory reaction becomes pronounced. Invading inflammatory cells and edema are present. By 7 days, the inflammatory reaction is being replaced by an increase in fibrous tissue near the region of the injury. Although some regenerating muscle fibers are present, normal histology is not restored and scar tissue is persistent.

The functional recovery of the muscle can be determined by physiological testing of maximal force production in response to nerve stimulation. Immediately after injury, the muscle can produce 70% of the force production of the noninjured controls. After 24 hours, only 50% of normal force production is typical. After 7 days, recovery is 90% complete, demonstrating that recovery of the contractile apparatus is relatively rapid. These results have been confirmed in later work that evaluated the effect of nonsteroidal antiinflammatory drugs (NSAIDs) on healing muscle injuries. The tensile strength of muscle following a nondisruptive strain injury was also evaluated. Seven days postinjury, tensile strength was 77% of noninjured controls. In contrast, active force generating ability approached 90% of the control side. Based on these studies, tensile strength may be an indicator of the susceptibility of muscle to injury. Therefore, a previous injury may predispose muscle to a second injury.

Subsequent studies used electron microscopy to evaluate the immediate structural response at the MTJ to acute injury. Sixty minutes postinjury, sarcomeres closest to the site of fiber rupture were hypercontracted. There was a progressive increase in sarcomere length, which became normal by 300–500 μm away from the site of rupture. Six hours after injury, necrosis was noted in the transition region between hypercontracted and normal sarcomeres. These findings suggest that after acute injury, an intracellular barrier effectively restricts the injury response to less than 50 μm from the initial site of rupture.

The fact that muscle contractile ability can recover prior to tensile strength after injury suggests that a threshold or continuum for injury may exist. We have tested this hypothesis and shown that at the smallest forces necessary to produce injury, the contractile ability of the muscle was impaired, electromyographic (EMG) voltage was diminished, and variable injury occurred near the MTJ. At higher levels of applied force, contractile ability and EMG amplitude continued to decline while the MTJ and distal muscle belly were injured. Forces that stretched the muscle beyond 80% of the control's failure force resulted in changes in the passive tensile properties and diminished contractile ability and EMG voltage. Histology confirmed disruption at the MTJ, distal muscle belly injury, and connective tissue damage. Therefore, it appears that a continuum for acute muscle strain injury exists. Indices other than biomechanical data may also be useful measures of muscle-tendon unit injury.

Summary

Muscle strain injuries are common in soccer. The lower extremity muscles, including the flexors, extensors, and adductors of the hip, are most commonly injured. Strains occur in muscles that are being stretched while undergoing strong activation to decelerate or control the limb. This situation is common in soccer when sprinting, shooting, and stretching the leg to trap or tackle. Clinical and basic studies emphasize that strains occur within the muscle near the junction with the tendon. The bleeding usually escapes the muscle epimysium. There is an inflammatory reaction in muscle followed by regeneration of muscle fibers and connective tissue.

Imaging of muscle strains is useful for determining pathologic changes and the exact location of injury.

Injury prevention should concentrate on improving the ability of muscle to absorb energy without excessive stretch and allowing the muscle to stretch without injury. Conditioning to avoid fatigue and improving muscular strength contribute to the ability of muscle to absorb energy. Stretching and flexibility are discussed in Chapter 36.

SUGGESTED READINGS

Garrett WE Jr, Best TM. Ortho basic science. In: Simon S, ed. Anatomy, physiology and mechanics of skeletal muscle. American Academy of Orthopaedic Surgeons, 1994;89–126.

Garrett WE Jr, Rich FR, Nikolaou PK, et al. Computed tomography of hamstring muscle strains. Med Sci Sports and Exer 1989;21:506–514.

Garrett WE Jr. Muscle strain injuries. Med Sci Sports and Exer 1990;22:436–443.

Hasselman CT, Best TM, Mastey R, et al. An explanation for various rectus femoris strain injuries using previously undescribed muscle architecture. Amer J Sports Med 1995;23:493–499.

Sallay PI, Friedman RL, Coogan PG, et al. Hamstring injuries in water skiing: functional outcome and prevention. Submitted to Amer J Sports Med, 1994.

Speer KP, Spritzer CE, Goldner JL, et al. Magnetic resonance imaging of traumatic knee articular cartilage injuries. Am J Sports Med 1991;19:396–402.

28 Acute and Chronic Tendon Injuries

William G. Clancy, Jr.
Gregory M. Fox

Introduction

Soccer players are particularly vulnerable to acute and chronic tendon injuries due to the cutting, twisting, kicking, rapid acceleration and deceleration, and repetitive, nonstop action of the game. With most chronic tendon injuries, the onset of symptoms is usually not related to a particular traumatic event. Symptoms usually begin insidiously and worsen with an attempt to maintain the previous level of performance. Acute tendon disruptions occur when the stress point of a normal or pathologic tendon is exceeded by the load applied to the tendon. In this chapter tendon anatomy, pathologic conditions, and the issues related to nonoperative and operative treatment of acute and chronic tendon injuries of the knee are addressed.

Tendon Anatomy

Tendon consists of regularly arranged collagen connecting muscle to bone. The collagen fibers run the entire length of the tendon in a matrix structure composed of complex carbohydrate called polyglycans. Collagen fibers group together to form primary bundles. These primary bundles are gathered in a hexagonal shape with a cross-sectional area of 0.125–0.375 mm to form secondary bundles or fascicles. The secondary bundles then form tertiary bundles. A packing of loose connective tissue containing the vascular supply, lymphatics, and nerves separates the bundles. The connective tissue layer directly surrounding each fascicle is the endotenon. The next layer engulfing the grouping of fascicles is the epitenon. It is of similar construct and is continuous on its inner surface with the endotenon. The epitenon is surrounded by a third layer, the paratenon, which allows the tendon to glide through the surrounding tissue with as little friction as possible. A double layered paratenon containing a synovial cell layer is called tenosynovium. The flexor tendon sheaths of the hand and forearm are tenosynovia. In the absence of a synovial lining, as seen in the Achilles tendon sheath, the layer is referred to as tenovagium. Perpendicular layers in the paratenon are called mesotendon and allow the passage of vascular supply from the paratenon into the epitenon (Fig. 28–1).

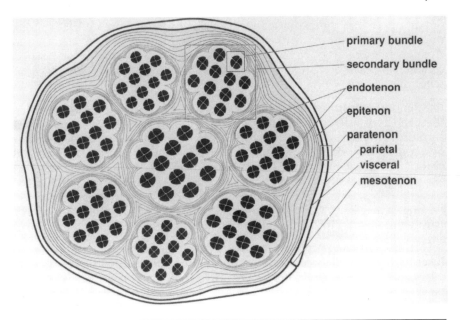

Figure 28-1. A cross section of a typical tendon. A double layer tendon sheath called the paratenon surrounds the tendon. The outer or parietal layer is connected at points to the inner or visceral layer by bridges, the mesotenon. The tendon consists of primary collagen bundles grouped together to form secondary bundles. The secondary bundles are held firmly together by the intertwining connective tissue called the endotenon. All the secondary bundles are further surrounded circumferentially by connective tissue called the epitenon that lies adjacent to the visceral layer of the paratenon.

Pathologic Conditions

With knowledge of tendon anatomy and universal nomenclature, accurate terminology can be used to describe corresponding pathologic conditions. The terms most descriptive of the conditions are paratenonitis, tendinitis, tendinosis, paratenonitis with tendinosis, partial tendon rupture, complete tendon rupture, and insertional tendinitis. The term paratenonitis describes an inflammation of the outer layer of the tendon (paratenon). The first layer affected by direct mechanical irritation to the tendon is the paratenon, whether it is a single layer of loose (areolar) connective tissue or a more defined double-layer sheath. The term paratenonitis includes the terms peritendinitis, tenosynovitis, and tenovaginitis.

Tendinitis is an inflammatory response in the tendon. Acute tendon injury may lead to a secondary inflammatory response in the paratenon, although this has not been proven. Tendinitis describes a condition in which the tendon, the primary site of injury, undergoes an inflammatory response. An associated reactive paratenonitis is present.

Tendinosis refers to tendon degeneration without an inflammatory response. Degeneration of tendon occurs without clinical manifestation of disease. Histologic examination shows signs of tendon degeneration without an inflammatory response in the tendon or paratenon, which explains the lack of symptoms. In cases of tendon rupture, specifically in the Achilles tendon, areas of tendinosis show hypocellularity, loss of normal collagen architecture, and amorphic zones with mucinoid degeneration of tendon.

Paratenonitis with tendinosis is probably the most appropriate term for the condition referred to as chronic tendinitis. Biopsy specimens reveal significant tendon degeneration and inflammation of the paratenon, but no observable inflammatory cellular response in the tendon. The classic chronic inflammatory cellular response in the tendon has only been observed in patients with grossly observable partial tendon rupture. Gross, partial, and spontaneous complete tendon ruptures have characteristic findings consistent with an inflammatory response in the tendon and paratenon layers. In addition, there are areas of tendinosis at the rupture site.

Insertional tendinitis refers to an entity that can be described as a subcategory of paratenonitis with tendinosis. These patients experience pain at the bone-tendon junction. Although patients with prolonged symptoms frequently have positive bone scans, biopsy of the bone may not show signs of an inflammatory response. The tendon shows evidence of collagen degeneration without any of the classic signs of inflammatory response.

Specific Tendon Injuries

Quadriceps Tendon: Acute Ruptures

MECHANISM OF INJURY

Injury to the quadriceps tendon commonly occurs with rapid quadriceps contraction when the knee is flexed. Less common mechanisms include direct blows or lacerations to the tendon. Quadriceps tendon ruptures occur more commonly in athletes over the age of 40. Extensor mechanism ruptures are often seen in association with long-term steroid use, diabetes mellitus, uremia, rheumatoid arthritis, systemic lupus erythematosus, gout, hyperparathyroidism, or repeated microtrauma. Acute ruptures in athletes are usually the end result of altered extensor mechanism mechanics combined with chronic inflammatory change. One case report discusses a 16-year-old female who sustained a quadriceps contusion from a direct blow and then tore the quadriceps tendon when she fell on a flexed knee. Quadriceps tendon rupture has also been reported after a central third patellar tendon anterior cruciate ligament reconstruction.

A quadriceps tendon rupture is usually associated with a sudden pop followed by pain. With a complete rupture, the athlete will be unable to bear weight on the injured extremity. Physical examination reveals a large hemarthrosis, palpable gap, mobile patella, loss of extensor mechanism function, and tenderness in the distal tendon. A straight leg raise with the knee locked in extension may be possible because of an intact extensor retinaculum. Passive flexion of the knee demonstrates patella baja (a patella that rides low) when compared to the uninjured knee. Although an extensor lag may exist in partial tears, extensor function may be near normal.

MANAGEMENT OF THE INJURY

Patella baja is best seen on lateral radiographs with the knee flexed. A small avulsion off the superior pole of the patella may be noted. Although magnetic resonance imaging (MRI) shows disruption of the tendon, it is only necessary to confirm the diagnosis of a partial tear or acute strain. Surgical repair is required for treatment of complete quadriceps tendon ruptures.

After surgical treatment of acute or chronic quadriceps tendon ruptures, athletes are allowed immediate full weight bearing with the knee immobilized in extension for 6 weeks. Passive and active assisted range of motion is begun within a limited arc determined by the quality of tissue and strength of repair. Active range of motion and isometric strengthening is begun at 6–8 weeks. Athletes may begin running when isokinetic peak torque at $180°/sec$ is 70% of the unaffected side. 85% isokinetic peak torque and successful completion of a running program (Fig. 28–2) is the goal for return to competition. This running program was designed to provide an objective assessment of readiness for return to competition.

Successful completion of the running program requires the athlete to perform each phase in succession without pain. If pain developes at any phase of the program the athlete must stop and start again from the beginning.

Partial quadriceps tendon ruptures may be treated with a short period of immobilization followed by an aggressive rehabilitation program. Criteria for return to competition is the same as for complete tendon rupture.

Patellar Tendon: Acute Ruptures

MECHANISM OF INJURY

In contrast to quadriceps tendon ruptures, patellar tendon ruptures occur in athletes younger than 40. However, the mechanism of injury is also rapid quadriceps contraction against rapid knee flexion.

Patellar tendon ruptures are often associated with underlying systemic diseases or use of steroids. Many athletes without underlying diseases have preexisting inflammation. Athletes who deny any prodromal symptoms may have prerupture tendon disease at a subclinical level.

The association between patellar tendon rupture and previous tendon injections has been well described. While the marked antiinflammatory effects of glucocorticoids are well recognized, it is also accepted that collagen biosynthesis is inhibited by glucocorticoids.

MANAGEMENT OF THE INJURY

Athletes with a patellar tendon rupture complain of severe anterior knee pain and inability to bear weight. A history of preexisting inflammatory symptoms is often present. Lateral radiographs may reveal a small avulsion off the inferior patellar pole and patella alta (a patella that rides high). Examination will reveal hemarthrosis, tenderness inferior to the patella, patella alta accentuated by passive knee flexion, and a loss of active knee extension.

Surgical repair is required for treatment of patellar tendon ruptures. Rehabilitation protocol and criteria for return to competition are identical to those discussed for quadriceps tendon injuries.

The following running program should be used as a measure of an athlete's progress as s/he returns from an injury to the lower extremity. When the athlete has completed the ENTIRE program, they are ready to return to competition.

The athlete may begin the running program when s/he can hop up and down on the toes of the injured extremity 5 times without bearing weight on the other leg.

OUTDOORS

1. Jog one mile. Stop immediately when limping is noticed or when there is mild pain. When the athlete can jog one mile pain free:*
    a. do 6 eighty yard sprints at 1/2 speed. If no pain or limp:
    b. do 6 eighty yard sprints at 3/4 speed. If no pain or limp:
    c. do 6 eighty yard sprints at full speed. If no pain:
    d. do 6 eighty yard runs cutting at 3/4 speed. If no pain:
    e. do 6 eighty yard runs cutting at full speed. Always plant on the outside foot to cut. If no pain:

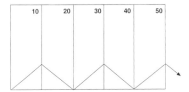

2. Do 10 minutes of running and/or jumping drills related to your sport. When the athlete has completed the entire running program, s/he is ready to return to competition**

INDOORS

1. Jog eighteen laps around the basketball court. Stop immediately when limping is noticed or when there is mild pain. If pain free:*
    a. do 15 lengths of the gym at 1/2 speed. If no pain:
    b. do 15 lengths of the gym at 3/4 speed. If no pain:
    c. do 15 lengths of the gym at full speed. If no pain:
    d. do 15 lengths cutting at 3/4 speed. Be sure to plant on the outside foot with each cut. If no pain:
    e. do 15 lengths cutting at full speed. If no pain:
2. Do 10 minutes of running and/or jumping drills related to your sport. When the athlete has completed the entire running program, s/he is ready to return to competition**

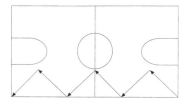

*If the athlete does not complete the entire program on a particular day s/he should start at the beginning the following day.
**Each running workout must be followed by a 15 minute application of ice.

Figure 28-2. Running Program

Quadriceps Tendinitis
MECHANISM OF INJURY
Quadriceps tendinitis occurs less frequently than patellar tendinitis. In adolescents, avulsion injuries of the proximal patellar apophysis are more common than quadriceps tendinitis. In younger athletes, quadriceps tendinitis is usually secondary to repetitive microtrauma from rapid acceleration and deceleration. However, quadriceps tendinitis may be seen in association with the previously mentioned systemic diseases.

MANAGEMENT OF THE INJURY
Athletes with quadriceps tendinitis usually complain of the insidious onset of pain near the proximal pole of the patella. Physical examination reveals tenderness directly over the quadriceps tendon and pain with passive knee hyperflexion and extension against resistance. Radiographs are usually normal. MRI may be helpful if there is a question of partial rupture.

Nonoperative rehabilitation is the primary treatment for quadriceps tendinitis. A short period of rest is followed by a return to nonirritating activities and an extensive stretching program focusing on the quadriceps, hamstrings, and achilles tendon. Therapeutic modalities include ice, heat, ultrasound, phonophoresis, iontophoresis, and a course of antiinflammatory medication. A strengthening program focuses on the balance between the quadriceps and hamstrings. Athletes may return to activity when they are symptom-free and have successfully completed the running program.

Surgical treatment is only indicated for refractory quadriceps tendinitis. Surgery involves excising degenerative tissue with side to side repair of healthy tendon.

Patellar Tendinitis
MECHANISM OF INJURY
Soccer players are particularly vulnerable to patellar tendinitis, or jumper's knee, due to repetitive trauma from running, jumping, and kicking. Strong quadriceps contraction produces forces that exceed the tensile strength of the patellar tendon. This leads to microtears, focal mucoid degeneration, and fibrinoid necrosis. The lesion usually occurs in the deep fibers of the patellar tendon near its insertion on the inferior pole of the patella. Forces on the patellar tendon may reach 9000 N during fast running, 8000 N when landing from a jump, and 500 N during level walking.

Athletes with patellar tendinitis typically complain of pain localized in the lower pole of the patella or in the tendon itself. This pain increases with activities that stress the extensor mechanism such as jumping, running, or kicking. Symptoms are usually insidious in onset without any particular inciting event.

MANAGEMENT OF THE INJURY
Physical examination reveals specific localized tenderness over the patellar tendon, usually near the inferior pole of the patella. Thickening of the tendon may be noticed by the physician. Knee flexion in the prone position may reproduce pain and reveal quadriceps tightness, particularly associated with the rectus femoris. Hamstring and achilles tendon tightness may also be present. Although radiographs are usually normal, they may show bony changes at the inferior pole of the patella.

An extensive rehabilitation program is the first step in the treatment of patellar tendinitis. This program should aim to gradually increase stresses on the patellar tendon and, consequently, increase tensile strength of the tendon. A stretching program focusing on the quadriceps, hamstrings, and achilles tendons is also important. Strengthening of the quadriceps should involve eccentric exercises with a gradual increase in speed, weight, and repetitions. Nonsteroidal antiinflammatory medication and other therapeutic modalities such as ice, heat, ultrasound, phonophoresis, and iontophoresis should be used as necessary. Infrapatellar straps may be useful in the treatment of patellar tendinitis. McConnell's patellofemoral taping technique may also reduce symptoms. Steroid injections should not be used in the treatment of patellar tendinitis.

Athletes with patellar tendinitis need encouragement. Long-term tendinitis may require many weeks before improvement. Surgical treatment is indicated for athletes with persistent symptoms despite a prolonged rehabilitation program. Several procedures have been recommended for treatment of patellar tendinitis. We recommend debridement of all abnormal tendon tissue and excision of a small portion of the inferior patella to stimulate a healing response. Postoperative rehabilitation should include immediate weight bearing, range of motion, and a program used for the treatment of patellar tendinitis.

Hamstring Tendinitis
MECHANISM OF INJURY
Inflammation due to overuse around the knee is not limited to the extensor mechanism. The hamstring tendons of the biceps femoris, semimembranosus, and semitendinosus are subject to overuse and inflammation in soccer, which requires constant stopping, starting, and cutting. Irritation of the semitendinosus tendon also involves the gracilis and sartorius tendons, which are not true hamstring tendons. The insertion of these three collective tendons into the anteromedial aspect of the proximal tibia is known as the pes anserine. A bursa lies between the aponeurosis of these three tendons and the medial collateral ligament. Pes anserine bursitis is usually caused by overuse or direct contusion. Although it is clinically difficult to distinguish between pes tendinitis and bursitis, the treatment for both is the same.

MANAGMENT OF THE INJURY
At the proximal tibia, stress fractures are more common than tendinitis. For proper radiographic evaluation, AP, lateral, and both oblique views are required. If the radiographs are normal and the entity has been present 3 weeks or less, a bone scan is indicated.

Athletes with pes anserine tendinitis or bursitis complain of pain and swelling over the pes bursa. Physical examination reveals localized tenderness at the bursa or along the pes tendons. It is important to rule out other intraarticular knee pathology, which may be the cause of compensatory overuse of the pes anserine muscle-tendon unit.

Treatment begins with activity modification, antiinflammatory medication, therapeutic modalities, and stretching or strengthening of the hamstring, quadriceps, and adductor. Corticosteroid injections are helpful in relieving inflammation in the inflamed pes bursa. Athletes return to play when symptoms allow. Semimembranosus tendinitis usually is suspected when there is persistent aching pain on the posterior medial aspect of the knee. This may occur as a result of repetitive loading of the muscle-tendon unit due to running, acceleration and deceleration, or compensation for other knee problems. The maximal area of pain to palpation is at the posteromedial corner of the knee immediately below the joint line. Direct palpation of the semimembranosus reproduces and exacerbates this pain. As with pes tendinitis, stress fractures of the tibia are not uncommon in this area and need to be ruled out.

Over 90% of patients with semimembranosus tendinitis usually respond to activity modification, nonsteroidal antiinflammatory medication, stretching, therapeutic modalities, and local steroid injection. The remaining 10% are typically treated with exploration of the semimembranosus tendon, excision of pathologic tissue, drilling of the insertion site, and rerouting the semi-membranosus tendon parallel to the posterior edge of the medial collateral ligament. Twelve months after surgery, semimembranosus pain is usually eliminated. In some cases, the rolling of the tendon over a bony ridge on the edge of the posterior aspect of the medial femoral condyle causes pain and results in a pop that can be heard and felt. Knee arthroscopy should be performed to rule out intraarticular pathology. Biceps femoris tendinitis is an uncommon type of hamstring tendinitis. This may occur as a result of secondary compensation due to other intraarticular knee pathology. Treatment is nonoperative.

Popliteus Tendinitis
MECHANISM OF INJURY
Popliteus tendinitis is an uncommon cause of posterolateral or lateral knee pain in athletes. The main functions of the popliteus tendon are to initiate and maintain tibial internal rotation on the femur and to assist the posterior cruciate ligament. Pain usually occurs during running and weight bearing with 15°–30° of knee flexion.

MANAGEMENT OF THE INJURY
The physical examination may be normal or reveal tenderness along the popliteus tendon near its insertion into the lateral femoral condyle. Differential diagnosis includes lateral meniscus tears, iliotibial band syndrome, or biceps tendinitis. Treatment is as described for hamstring tendinitis. Avoiding downhill running may be beneficial. Return to sports is determined by symptoms.

SUGGESTED READINGS

Clancy WG Jr. Tendon trauma and overuse injuries. In: Leadbetter WB, Buckwalter JA, Gordon SL, eds. Sports induced inflammation. Rosemont, IL: American Academy of Orthopaedic Surgeons, 1990.

Kelly DW, Carter VS, Jobe FW, et al. Patellar and quadriceps tendon ruptures: jumper's knee. Am J Sports Med 1984;12:375–380.

Ferretti A, Ippolito E, Mariani P, et al. Jumper's knee. Am J Sports Med 1983;11:58–62.

Curwin S, Stanish WD. Tendinitis: its etiology and treatment. Lexington, MA: Collamare Press, 1984.

Ray JM, Clancy WG Jr, Lemon RA. Semimembranosus tendinitis: an overlooked cause of medial knee pain. Am J Sports Med 1984;16:347–351.

29   **Contusions and Hematomas**

Tonu Saartok

Introduction

Soccer is a contact sport in which the players are at risk for contusion injuries to the body from intentional tackles, illegal tackles, and accidental collisions. The resulting contusions may be regarded as a normal part of the game, the result of a violation, or an accident.

Muscular contusions are nonpenetrating blunt impact trauma to skeletal muscle tissue resulting in the acute crushing of muscle fibers, bleeding, and localized hematomas. Even if contusions to the head, thorax, or abdomen are infrequent, these injuries may be life-threatening. Therefore, prompt diagnosis and management of these injuries is required.

Classification of Muscle Contusions

Intramuscular bleeding that has not spread outside the epimysium, the tight sheath of a muscle belly, can lead to osmotically active intramuscular hematomas. These hematomas can result in increased intramuscular tissue pressure, severe pain, and disability. This condition may require surgery.

Intermuscular hematomas in which the hemorrhage spreads outside the muscle fascia and subcutaneously are often benign. Cutaneous eccymosis or intraarticular effusion below the injury site often appear 2–3 days after injury. Surgery is seldom indicated.

Epidemiology

Muscle contusions are common injuries in soccer. Epidemiologic data do not always indicate this due to the benign nature of most contusions, which are often considered part of the game. Significant skeletal muscle contusions in soccer often occur in the lower extremities.

The incidence of contusions in soccer is reported to be approximately one-third of all injuries. In youth soccer, contusions account for approximately 50% of injuries.

Mechanism of Injury

The severity of a skeletal muscle contusion is defined by the impact (i.e., energy per area), material properties of the contused tissue (i.e., subcutaneous fat or skeletal muscle), and underlying tissue (i.e., a bone).

A small impact area concentrates energy leading to more severe fiber disruption. The same energy applied to a larger area seems to result in more extensive hematoma. The repair of muscle contusions is similar to that of other kinds of posttraumatic muscle regeneration. The crushed muscle fibers and hematoma at the injury site are followed by edema, an inflammatory cleanup phase, and a regenerative phase. Other than the increased diameter of the venules, cold therapy after a contusion does not seem to change the reaction of the muscular microvessels. This leads to increased surface for reabsorption of extracellular fluid, thereby reducing the edema. According to preliminary data from Duke Orthopaedic laboratory, early cold therapy can decrease the inflammatory cell response without undesirable long-term effects.

Early inflammatory response seems to be a prerequisite for the later repair phase, including vascular and connective tissue ingrowth. Therefore, the frequent use of antiinflammatory agents such as nonsteroidal antiinflammatory drugs (NSAIDs) for the benefit of these injuries can be questioned. On the other hand, Bazin et al stated that if the inflammatory process persists beyond the first few days, the regenerative process can result in the formation of increased fibrosis. Lehto et al stated that the muscle regeneration process competes with the connective tissue scar formation after muscle contusions. Short, early immobilization for approximately 5 days (for contused rat gastrocnemius muscle) promotes the formation of beneficial granulation tissue matrix. Longer immobilization leads to increased and contracted scar formation and poor muscle regeneration. Although early mobilization can increase the healing response, excess mobilization can blunt the positive effect. Stretching and other forms of tensioning of the injured muscle tissue can be beneficial because they result in lower tissue pressures and possibly maintain an intact venous and lymphoid drainage. Tensioning of an injured muscle may also lead to increased regenerative capacity of the injured site. In summary, contused muscle should be tensioned and stretched early after injury to acquire the optimal conditions for muscle fiber regeneration and healing.

Clinical Appearance

Two clinical conditions of muscle contusions seem to be most common in soccer.

Quadriceps Contusions

This injury is reported to be one of the most frequent injuries in soccer, rugby, and American football. In soccer, the blunt impact to the thigh usually comes from the knee or foot of an opponent. This can happen frequently and results in subcutaneous hematomas. Only a significant contusion leads to serious muscle injury with increasing pain, progressive weakness, and limping. The injury may result in the immediate inability to play or appear after the game due to continued bleeding. The severity and prognosis of this injury may be classified within 24 hours.

Contusions to the Anterior Compartment of the Lower Leg

According to a retrospective study of soccer, every fifth contusion injury occurs at the shin and half of those shin injuries are the result of inadequate or absent use of shin guards. After the introduction of mandatory shin guards, this injury has been significantly reduced. This injury may develop into a compartment syndrome of the anterior compartment of the lower leg.

Immediate Care of the Injury

Immediate treatment consists of rest (i.e., stopping activity to prevent the injured area from increasing), elevation, cooling and/or compressing the injured area, and RICE therapy (Rest, Immobilization, Cold, Elevation), which is applied on-field. Immobilization of a contused muscle in a tensioned position seems to be favorable. Aronen et al reported that the immediate immobilization of a contused quadriceps muscle in tension with the knee in 120° of flexion for the first 24 hours, in combination with RICE and passive tension, can dramatically reduce the time required for return to athletic activities. These promising preliminary reports, also supported by the data from basic science studies, have to be supported by more extensive and prospective clinical investigations and long-term follow-up.

Management of Injury

Diagnosis

The history of muscle contusion cannot always be separated from the strains and other injuries that may have occurred. However, suspicion of a muscle contusion injury based on witnessing the injury and the history of the player calls for immediate treatment, including RICE.

The clinical diagnosis of a tender muscular mass (e.g., an intramuscular hematoma) can be confirmed by ultrasonography (most cost efficient), computerized tomography (CT) scans, or magnetic resonance imaging (MRI). Random intramuscular calcification can be seen on plain radiographs and eventually lead to myositis ossificans in an unknown percentage of cases. A surgical biopsy and/or removal can be used to differentiate the calcified mass from a malignant osteogenic sarcoma.

Conservative Treatment

It is suggested that acute compression be maintained for at least 48–72 hours. During this time isometric and passive range of motion (ROM) exercise can be started.

The pharmacologic treatment usually includes NSAIDs, which can act as pain relievers and possibly diminish the risk of heterotopic bone formation. This treatment may not be optimal because NSAIDs depress coagulation and formation of IGF-I, one of the apparent primary substances involved in skeletal muscle regeneration. Two recent reports suggest adverse long-term effects of early NSAIDs on skeletal muscle regeneration.

The injection of hyaluronidase to increase the reabsorption of the hematoma and diminish the intracompartmental pressure has been attempted, but not fully scientifically evaluated.

Physical therapy may include therapeutic ultrasound and high-voltage galvanic stimulation, but neither therapy has been clearly evaluated. Although therapeutic ultrasound can increase satellite cell proliferation in a muscle contusion injury, the final time and outcome of muscle regeneration is not influenced. Massage in the early post traumatic period should be avoided because it can increase the incidence of myositis ossificans. Early rehabilitation is designed to regain full ROM by increased stretching of the muscle using continuous passive motion (CPM) devices or physical therapy. Daily workouts for the remaining healthy extremities should also be performed to increase circulation and provide benefits from circulating growth factors with healing properties. Before full ROM is regained, active strengthening exercise should be implemented. Maximal isometric exercise can be started even earlier. Eccentric exercise should be started early, since muscle tension seems to be the most important stimulus for satellite cell activation in muscle regeneration.

A suggestion for the initial treatment of muscle contusions in soccer is presented in Table 29-1.

Surgical Treatment

Aspiration or limited surgical evacuation of the hematoma may be considered to diminish the size and relieve intramuscular pressure. Increased pain and decreased ROM from an intramuscular hematoma indicates surgical evacuation. However, surgery in this early phase includes a high risk for infection and has to be performed under sterile conditions and antibiotic prophylactics.

Resuture of the muscle should only be considered if there has been a total rupture with retraction of both ends. Other indications may be signs of compartment syndrome or nerve palsy. Physical therapy implemented after surgery is similar to that used for conservative treatment.

Return to Activity Criteria

In addition to regained agility, eccentric strength should be recovered 80%–90% before return to preinjury level can be recommended. The risk for a strain injury in the same injury area in a muscle is likely to be increased, although no comparative clinical studies have supported this observation.

Long Term Sequelae

The late diagnosis and treatment of muscle contusions can be challenging (Table 29-2).

Heterotopic Bone Formation

Severe contusions and those close to the periosteum are likely to cause heterotopic bone formation and myositis ossificans. The incidence is calculated as 9%–20% of all quadriceps contusions. While the heterotopic bone seems to be deposited in skeletal muscle, myositis ossificans has contact with the

Table 29-1

Suggested Initial Treatment of Muscle Contusions

On-field:

1. Probable muscle contusion injury.

 —Get the history from the player and witnesses. Mechanism? Energy?

2. Compress the contused area with a cold pack and elastic bandage.

 —Take the player aside to check for the severity of injury and possible associated injuries.

Off-field:

3. Quadriceps contusion: can the player actively move the knee in full ROM?

 —If yes, the player can test the leg by running. If there is no or minimal pain, he/she can try to play again.

 —If no, or pain with running, wrap the elastic bandage so the knee is flexed to 120° or to tolerance. Crutches. Keep the cold pack as tolerated and interchange it with a compressive pad every half hour the first day.

4. Anterior shin contusion: can the player actively dorsiflex the foot with some resistance?

 —If yes, the player can try running. If there is no or minimal pain, he/she can try to play again.

 —If no, or pain with running, wrap the elastic bandage so the foot is plantarflexed. Crutches. Keep the cold pack as tolerated and interchange it with a compressive pad every half hour the first day.

5. Keep the increased tension in the thigh or shin for at least 24 hours. Use regular analgesics (e.g., paracetamol) and avoid NSAIDs.

Office or rehab-center:

6. Day 1–3 (5) after the injury:

 —Start isometric exercises with the knee or ankle in various flexion angles. Smooth eccentric and active ROM exercises.

 —Strength and aerobic exercise for the rest of the body.

7. Between the rehabilitation periods: keep the extremity immobilized, preferably in a tensioned position (as tolerated), and use crutches.

8. After day (3)–5:

 —Increase active ROM exercises and increase the tension of the eccentric exercises.

 —Start closed-chain weight-bearing active and eccentric exercises.

9. Back to training and play after regaining full ROM and a test jog (without more pain and limping).

periosteum and the bone. Intensive massage of a contused muscle and purely intramuscular localization of a contused area are also risk factors for these conditions. Although the mechanism still remains obscure, the differentiation of muscle progenitor cells into osteoblasts due to some growth factors is believed to be a contributing process. The random heterotopic calcification can mature into myositis ossificans. These seem most common in the upper arm and thigh over the length of the long bone. In terms of treatment, there

Table 29-2

Long Term Sequelae of Contusion Injuries
1. Heterotopic bone formation or myositis ossificans
2. Bleeding dyscrasis or disorders
3. Iatrogenic bleeding dyscrasis
4. Soft tissue tomors
5. Compartment syndromes
6. Nerve palsy

should be at least 6–12 months of observation before surgical intervention is considered due to the tendency for recurrence of this condition. In the first half year, some of the benign heterotopically localized calcifications can be gradually resorbed. A contused muscle seems to be prone to reinjury and can result in recurrent muscular hematomas from strains or new contusions.

Bleeding Dyscrasis

Recurrent hematomas may be caused by subclinical bleeding dyscrasis or disorders. Recently, the prevalence of von Willebrand's bleeding disorder was reported to be as high as 1% in apparently healthy children. In the athletic population, the frequent use of NSAIDs can result in iatrogenic bleeding dyscrasis.

Soft Tissue Tumors

The vascularly rich soft tissue tumors (e.g., malignant fibrous histiocytomas) can appear as recurrent muscular hematomas. Myositis ossificans can mimic calcifying soft tissue tumors, such as osteogenic sarcomas. Therefore, repeated hematomas and an unusual history preceding a muscle hematoma or myositis ossificans should lead to the suspicion and investigation of a possible malignant tumor.

Compartment Syndromes

Muscular hematomas are space-occupying and can cause compartment syndromes in exposed areas. Quadriceps contusions can cause impairment of the major nerves of the thigh (femoral or saphenous nerves). Gluteal and hamstring contusions can affect the ischiadic nerve. Although compression is part of the early treatment of muscle contusions, decompression is ideal when the muscle tissue with its nerves (or vessels) is compressed by space-occupying lesions, such as compartment syndromes. The frequent use of NSAIDs in athletes can lead to increased and prolonged bleeding, which increases the risk of compartment syndromes in muscle contusion injuries. However, no scientific investigations have addressed this connection. A long-standing or undiagnosed compartment syndrome can lead to a muscle contracture with loss of joint motion and Volkman's ischemic contracture. The ideal treatment of a compartment syndrome includes prompt diagnosis and surgical fasciotomy, thereby evacuating the hematoma and reducing the edema.

Nerve Palsy

Muscular hematomas can cause nerve palsy by indirect pressure and tensioning of the nerve. Several cases of femoral nerve palsy have been described in athletic youngsters without any defect in clotting mechanisms. The mechanism is a posttraumatic intramuscular hematoma resulting in a space-occupying bulge of the muscle, which affects the local nerve.

Injury Prevention

Although it seems clear that shin guards can protect against contusion injuries to the shin, the role of thigh pads against primary or secondary quadriceps contusions has not been evaluated.

A contusion injury to the leg that causes pain when moving the leg or limping should sideline the player for evaluation due to the higher risk of muscle strain injury associated with a muscle contusion. Minor contusions can turn into more severe muscle injuries, such as a strain injury or new contusion, if the athlete continues to play.

Kicks or tackles intended to interfere with another player and resulting in contusion injuries should result in a short time penalty, such as 10–15 minutes off the field.

Summary

Minor muscle contusions are frequent in soccer. Early short-term (3–5 days) immobilization of the injured muscle in both a compressed and tensioned position seems favorable. The initial treatment on-field aims to diminish the injured area, thereby limiting the risk of developing compartment syndromes or myositis ossificans. When these conditions develop, the differential diagnoses of soft tissue tumors, osteogenic sarcoma, and bleeding dyscrasis as well as treatment can be challenging. Early ROM and some eccentric exercises seem to be the fastest and safest way to rehabilitate contused muscle. However, there is little data to support various rehabilitation modalities and models.

SUGGESTED READINGS

Almekinders LC. Anti-inflammatory treatment of muscular injuries in sports. Sports Med 1993;15:139–145.

Aronen JA, Chronister R, Ove P, et al.Thigh contusions: minimizing the length of time before return to full athletic activities with early immobilization in 120 degrees of knee flexion. Abstract, 16th Annual Meeting of the American Orthopaedic Society of Sports Medicine, Sun Valley, Idaho, July 16–19, 1990.

Aronen JG, Chronister RD. Quadriceps contusions: hastening the return to play. Phys Sportsmed 1992;20:130–136.

Ekstrand J, Gillquist J. The frequency of muscle tightness and injuries in soccer players. Am J Sports Med 1982;10:75–78.

Jackson DW, Feagin JA. Quadriceps contusions in young athletes: relation to severity. J Bone Joint Surg 1973;55-A:95–105.

Järvinen MJ, Lehto MUK. The effects of early mobilisation and immobilisation on the healing process following muscle injuries. Sports Med 1993;15:78–89.

Kaeding CC, Sanko WA, Fischer RA. Quadriceps strains and contusions: decisions that promote rapid recovery. Phys Sportsmed 1995;23:59–64.

Leach RE, Corbett M. Anterior tibial compartment syndrome in soccer players. Am J Sports Med 1979;7:258–259.

Lehto M, Järvinen M, Nelimarkka O. Scar formation after skeletal muscle injury. Arch Orthop Traum Surg 1986;104:366–370.

Ove PN, McDevitt ER, Chronister RD, et al. Quadriceps contusions in collegiate athletes: decreased myositis ossificans following treatment by immediate flexion-bracing. Abstract, 17th Annual Meeting of the American Orthopaedic Society of Sports Medicine, Orlando, Florida, July 8–11, 1991.

Rothwell AG. Quadriceps hematoma: a prospective clinical study. Clin Orthop 1982;171:97–103.

Ryan J, Wheeler J, Hopkinson W, et al. Quadriceps contusions. West Point Update. Am J Sports Med 1991;19:299–304.

Saartok T, Garrett WE Jr. The potential role of human growth hormone (hGH) and insulin-like growth factor-I (IGF-I) in skeletal muscle development and injury in sports. A brief review. Scand J Med Sci Sports (in review).

30   Stress Fractures

Thomas P. Knapp
Bert R. Mandelbaum

Introduction

In 200 B.C., Aristotle correctly characterized "Olympic Victors" by stating that they are " . . . those who do not squander their powers by early and over-training." Overuse injuries have received various names when diagnosed in the tibia, including exertional posterior compartment syndrome, fatigue fractures, shin splints, anterior tibial periostitis, and medial tibial stress syndrome.

Pentecost describes an insufficiency fracture as that produced by normal or physiological stress applied to bone with deficient elastic resistance. In contrast, a fatigue (stress) fracture occurs when abnormal stress is applied to a bone with normal elastic resistance.

Stress fractures in amateur and professional soccer players are becoming common. For example, 9 of the 24 players on the 1994 US National World Cup Soccer team were diagnosed with stress fractures.

In the United States today there are over 18 million soccer players competing and training including elite, recreational, youth, and female athletes. Each of these groups should be considered separately. If not properly diagnosed early, stress fractures can cause significant lost time from participation or even early retirement. Due to more participants, longer playing time, and the increased intensity of soccer, sports medicine professionals must understand the proper diagnosis, treatment, and prevention of these problems.

The purpose of this chapter is to review the history, epidemiology, and etiology of stress fractures. The proper diagnosis, confirmatory studies, and treatment regimens will be discussed. Finally, the timing of the athlete's return to soccer and stress fracture prevention will be reviewed.

History

The description of stress fractures was introduced by Briethaupt, a Prussian military physician, in 1855. He described the clinical signs, symptoms, and time course in the development of a stress fracture of the metatarsal. This was commonly known as a march fracture or Deutschlander's fracture. It took 40 years before the advent of radiographs allowed visual confirmation of his theory.

Devas, in 1958, was the first to describe this injury in athletes. Since then there have been numerous reports of stress fractures in athletes.

Epidemiology

Stress fractures have been described in relation to age, race, sex, specific sport, and bone location patterns. In terms of age, the earliest report of a stress fracture was in an 18-month-old child. More typical is a nonexperienced, nonconditioned runner who tends to jog rather than participate in competitive or competitive- recreational running. These indviduals usually run less than 20 miles a week and develop discomfort with the sudden initiation of an intensive training program.

The common belief, confirmed by few reports in literature, is that stress injuries are rare in populations with dark skin. However, Markey found that in a racially mixed population undergoing the same military training the incidence of stress fractures was similar for all races.

There appears to be a lower incidence of stress fractures in men, for whom lean body mass is greater and overall bone structure is larger; the converse is true for women. According to Markey, the higher incidence of female-related stress injuries in running sports may reflect the fact that the shorter women, in comparison to the men, are being overstressed.

Several authors have shown that women develop up to 10 times as many stress fractures as men on the same training course. In over 300 army trainees during 8 weeks of basic training, women had a significantly higher incidence of time-loss injuries (44.6%) than men (29.0%). A study by Markey in 1987 showed that in children under 16 years, the number of stress fractures was equal between the sexes. This is important since fewer girls participate in running and jumping activities.

Literature review of sports-related stress fractures reveals an approximately 2% soccer-related incidence. The most common location of soccer-related stress fractures is in the metatarsals (the fifth and second are the most common), tibia, fibula, femur, anterior iliac crest, and pars interarticularis. Studies of sports in general reveal the tibia as the most frequent site of stress fractures. The most common bones involved in specific sporting activities are listed in Table 30-1.

Matheson's work on 320 cases of bone scan-positive stress fractures showed that the tibia was the most frequent site of injury (49.1%) and the tarsals were the second most common (25.3%). The remaining stress fractures were to the metatarsals (8.8%), femur (7.2%), fibula (6.6%), pelvis (1.6%), sesamoids (0.9%), and back (0.6%). Of all the cases, 16.6% were bilateral. Femoral and tarsal stress fractures were more common in older athletes while fibular and tibial stress fractures were more common in young athletes. Others report that the metatarsals are the most common (35.2%) followed by the calcaneus (28.0%), tibia (24.0%), ribs (5.6%), femur (3.2%), fibula (3.2%), spine (0.4%), and pubic ramus (0.4%).

Table 30-1

Table of Sporting Activities and the Bones(s) most Vulnerable to Stress Fractures	
Sport/Athletic Activity	*Bone Commonly Involved*
Running	
sprint (rare)	
middle distance	Fibula-tibia
long distance	
Hiking	Metatarsal (rare)
	Pelvis
Jumping	Pelvis, femur
Tennis	Ulna, metacarpal
Baseball	
pitching	Humerus, scapula
batting	Rib
catching	Patella
Basketball	Patella, tibia, os calcis
Javelin	Ulna
Soccer	Tibia
Swimming	Tibia, metatarsal
Skating	Fibula
Curling	Ulna
Aerobics	Tibia, fibula
Ballet	Tibia
Cricket	Humerus
Fencing	Pubis
Handball	Metacarpal

Mechanism of Injury

Soccer-related stress fractures may be common because of hard playing fields, inadequate shoe design, training errors, and overtraining. To fully comprehend how these extrinsic factors impact on the soccer athlete, it is necessary to understand basic connective tissue physiology.

It is hypothesized that connective tissue adapts to stress. Wolf's Law of Transformation states that connective tissue responds to external forces. Consequently, every change in form and function of bone results in a change in internal architecture. Figure 30-1 is the dose-response curve in relation to bone adaptation to stress. The y-axis represents the dose of a given activity (including duration, intensity, and frequency). The x-axis is the response to adaptation. A stress fracture is a maladaptation response to abnormal doses of stress. By modulating the application of stress in a judicial manner, the injury is preventable. Adequate adaptive response requires that stress be ap-

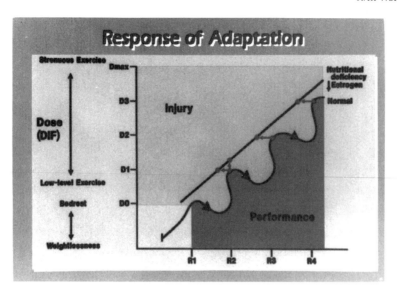

Figure 30-1. Dose-response curve for bone adaptation to stress.

plied in a cyclic fashion, alternating with periods of rest. The amount of rest and stress allowable is determined by the biologic status of the host. This modulation is affected by intrinsic factors, including nutrition and endocrine variables. Given the points on the curve between weightlessness and bed rest, performance adapts negatively and results in decreased bone mineral density, decreased tensile strength, and decreased new periosteal bone formation. This is because both of these activities lack ground reactive forces.

The exercise portion of the curve demonstrates that it is essential that bone adapt in a cyclically progressive fashion. All points below the cyclical curve allow a positive adaptation, minimizing the probability of injury. Increasing the activity dose in a manner inconsistent with the athlete's pattern and quality of response to adaptation, such as in a progressive training program, results in a maladaptive response and injury. In the moderate and high doses of exercises (as in any specific training program) dose response is the key to understanding and integrating details of the adaptive response. This includes quality, quantity, and temporal relationships of the progress. Negative influences such as hormonal deficiency, nutritional deficiency, or increase in the duration, intensity, and frequency outside of the typical response will also cause negative response to adaptation. When the maximal dose (D max) is exceeded, a negative response will result in maladaptation and stress fracture. This hypothesis provides the sports medicine professional with a conceptual and practical mechanism for interpreting stress maladaptation.

There are varied theories that try to explain stress fracture etiology. The most widely held concept is that repetitive stress causes a periosteal resorption that outstrips the rate of bone remodeling, weakens the cortex, and results in a stress fracture. The previous concept of stress fractures stated that fatigue failure in the bone was preceded by fatigue in the surrounding muscles, which then allowed excessive forces to be transmitted to the underlying bone. However, Stanitski believed that the reverse of this mechanism was true. He proposed that highly concentrated muscle forces acting across a specific bone from particular, repetitive tasks enhanced loading. The rhythmic, repetitive muscle action causes subthreshold, mechanical insults that sum up beyond the stress-bearing capacity of the bone and result in a stress fracture. This persistent overuse of bone unaccustomed to stress causes a rapid, focal, circumferential, periosteal resorption of bone formation of a small, cortical cavity. At a lower rate, more dense, stronger lamellar bone is laid down along the lines of stress to the tibia. As the periosteal resorption outstrips the stronger lamellar bone formation there is transient weakening of the cortex, which may rupture with continued stress and overuse. Although multiple biologic and mechanical factors are involved in creating a stress injury to bone, the fracture process appears to be similar in trabecular bone and cortical bone. This process is altered by various factors. An example of these factors are disorders of collagen formation or nutrition that may prolong fracture healing or produce nonunion in a stress fracture of bone.

Simple mechanical evaluation of bone does not explain the biologic process involved in the development of a stress response and ultimate fracture. There are predilections for certain bones and sites on bones depending on the type of stress, age of the patient, and biologic fitness. For instance, in runners the tibia is the most frequent site of stress fractures because it bears 5–6 times the body weight (running magnifies the ground reactive forces by three times as compared to walking). Additional examples are seen in athletes with tarsal navicular fractures who typically sustain repetitive high doses of stress. Intrinsic variables include foot abnormalities, including a short first metatarsal and metatarsus adductus, limited dorsiflexion of the ankle, and limited subtalar motion. Microangiographic studies of the blood supply to the tarsal navicular by Torg demonstrate relative avascularity of the middle third of the bone. All of these findings suggest that repetitive cyclic loading, associated with some unidentified intrinsic variations in foot structure, may result in fatigue failure through the relatively avascular central portion of the tarsal navicular.

Therefore, stress fractures must be considered as an injury spectrum (from stress response to stress fracture) because they do not all progress to the point of disruption of bony cortices and intramedullary changes that are detectable on radiographs. For example, simple cortical hypertrophy along the posterior medial cortex of the tibia may be the only radiographic sign. A colleague averaged 20 young athletes over 5 years who had pain associated with this process; benign cortical hypertrophy secondary to continued stress and overuse.

Training errors are the most frequently encountered cause of stress fractures. In fact, training errors may be the cause of over 20% of stress fractures. Most athletes develop stress fractures during a period of sequential stair-step increase/increase dose progression. Pronated feet were most commonly found in tibial stress fractures and tarsal bone fractures and were least common in metatarsal fractures. Cavus feet were mostly found in metatarsal and femoral stress fractures.

In 1987, Jones found in his study of lower extremity injuries that 2.4% of the men had stress fractures versus 12.3% of the women. In 1985, Marcus found that menstrual irregularities are a predisposing cause of stress fractures. Particularly running-related fractures are more frequent in amenorrheic women. Although it appears that extreme weight-bearing exercise partially overcomes the adverse skeletal effects of estrogen deprivation, amenorrheic runners remain at high risk for exercise-related fractures. Prepubescent girls who initiate serious training and competition before menarche may have delayed menarche and be at increased risk for secondary amenorrhea and stress fractures. Amenorrheic female athletes may have a decrease in mineral density of the lumbar vertebrae (primarily trabecular bone), but not in the radius (primarily cortical bone).

The amount of physical activity reported by amenorrheic athletes does not protect them from loss of vertebral bone. The mineral density of the lumbar spine in amenorrheic runners is typically lower than that in cyclic women and age-matched controls, but higher than that in runners with secondary amenorrhea who are less physically active. Mineral density of the radius is normal in both groups. Those with stress fractures are more likely to have lower bone density, lower dietary calcium intake, current menstrual irregularity, and lower oral contraceptive use. Bone mineral density measured by dual-energy radiograph absorptiometry is significantly lower in the spine, femoral neck, Ward's triangle, and greater trochanter. Therefore, the etiology of stress fractures is based in maladaptive responses to periods of stair-step increase/increase activity doses rather than the proper adaptive cyclic progression. The adaptive/maladaptive responses are modified by various intrinsic and extrinsic factors.

Management of the Injury

It is imperative that the stress fracture is diagnosed early since delay may increase morbidity. Femoral neck stress fractures diagnosed up to 14 weeks after the onset of symptoms forced athletes to end their competitive careers because of the delay in diagnosis. Therefore, prevention and early diagnosis are ultimate objectives of the sports medicine professional.

Soccer players with stress fractures have a predictable, stereotypic, historic course. In almost every instance, there is a change in the dose of activity. This change may occur over time or it may be a single event. Symptoms are gradual in onset over 2–3 weeks, and in some cases up to 5 weeks. According to Markey, a prodrome of less than 24 hours generally indicates cancellous bone involvement.

Devas, in 1958, described the crescendo process. "The symptoms start insidiously: at first the athlete feels a dull gnawing pain in one or other shin, which occurs toward the end of a run. The intensity of the pain, at first mild, gradually increases over the days, and will ultimately become so severe that running or sprinting cannot be continued. At first the pain passes off with rest, but recurs with further running. Over the days shorter and shorter distances produce the pain, which persists for some hours after athletic activity has ceased. Finally the pain continues during the night, but does not prevent sleep, and any attempt at running causes severe pain at once and training has to be discontinued. With a few days rest from sport the athlete feels better and tries to run again, only to find that the pain recurs; in this way a whole season of training is [spoiled]."

In addition to the athlete's history, physical examination is important in correctly diagnosing the injury. The examiner must determine the point of maximum tenderness. Additionally, intrinsic anatomic variations (e.g., cavus or pronated feet, pes planus, bony nodules, hyperkeratosis) and other problems mimicking stress fractures must be evaluated. The differential diagnosis must include tumor (e.g., osteoid osteoma), chronic compartment syndrome, medial tibial stress syndrome, and infection.

Each stress fracture type has specific history and physical issues that aid in proper diagnosis. In the tibia, it is important to differentiate shin splints from stress fractures. Shin splints, according to the AMA Subcommittee Report on Classification of Sports Injuries, are characterized by " . . . pain and discomfort in the leg from repetitive running on hard surfaces, or forcible, excessive use of the foot dorsiflexors; diagnosis should be limited to the musculotendinous inflammations, excluding fracture and ischemic disorders." Shin splint pain is present at the beginning of workout and for several hours after. It is usually a dull, aching discomfort with a broad spectrum of intensity. There is usually a 3–6 cm area of tenderness over the posteromedial distal third of the tibia. Stress fractures show greater induration, erythema, warmth, and a more localized pisiform-shaped area of tenderness. Shin splint pain occasionally is aggravated by active plantar flexion and inversion of the foot against manual resistance. In addition to local tenderness and edema, percussion at distance to the fracture causes transmission pain to the fracture site. Metatarsal stress fractures generally involve vague mid/forefoot pain. It is often difficult to localize a point of maximum tenderness. Toe-walking will often aggravate the pain. Occasionally, mild soft tissue swelling will be present.

Tarsal navicular stress fractures are an underdiagnosed source of prolonged disabling foot pain in young athletes. Symptoms of the tarsal navicular stress fracture include the insidious onset of vague pain over the dorsum of the medial midfoot or the medial aspect of the longitudinal arch. The pain is an ill-defined soreness or there is a localized tenderness over the tarsal navicular or along the medial longitudinal arch. There is little, if any, swelling and no discoloration or lumps. There may be an associated decrease in dorsiflexion or subtalar motion. The interval between the onset of symptoms and the diagnosis can range from less than 1 month to 38 months because a fracture may not be evident or can be overlooked on routine foot radiographs.

Confirmatory Studies

Although the majority of stress fractures are diagnosed from the history and physical examination, it is important to corroborate the diagnosis with confirmatory studies. The clinical and radiographic criteria for the diagnosis of a stress fracture include premorbid normal bone, no direct trauma, a definite inciting activity, and pain and tenderness before radiographic evidence of fracture. Follow-up films must show resolution or remodeling at the fracture site.

The multifaceted variables in the development of the stress response account for the variation in radiographic appearance. Since this is an injury continuum, the exact time in the course of a developing stress fracture when the radiograph is taken determines the radiographic appearance. Stress fracture radiographic signs may show nothing (Fig. 30-2), periosteal new bone formation, and sometimes a lucency (Fig. 30-3). Periosteal new bone is at a maximum by 6 weeks. In actual practice, only 50% of stress fractures will be seen on plain films (Fig. 30-4).

The diagnostic gold standard is the technetium-99 diphosphonate three-phase or single-phase bone scan (Figs. 30-5 and 30-6) or SPECT scan. Table 30-2 compares the bone scan appearance of stress fractures with shin splints.

Because this isotope is incorporated by the osteoblast in new bone formation, the area of a fracture will be easily detected. This may be 48–72 hours following clinical signs of injury.

Bone scans offer a highly sensitive technique for the early diagnosis of stress fractures. Abnormalities on scans can be identified before radiographic

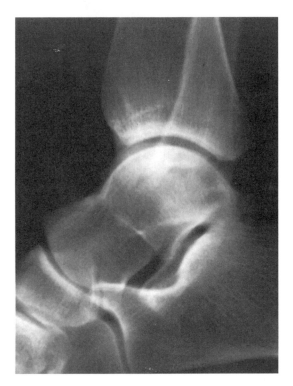

Figure 30-2. Soccer athlete with complaint of ankle pain. Plain radiographs appear normal.

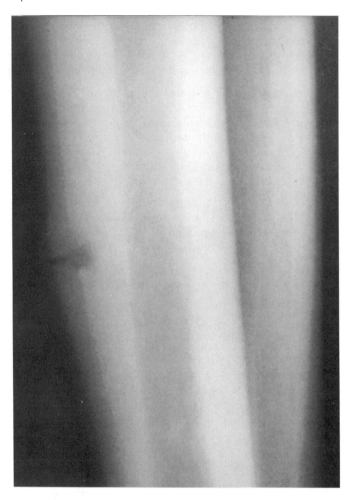

Figure 30-3. Stress fracture of tibia.

changes are observed. Although the bone scan is highly sensitive in detecting stress fracture, it lacks specificity. Prather reported the plain radiographic false negative rate for stress fractures as 71% and the false positive rate for scintigraphy as 24%. The sensitivity and accuracy of the bone scan can be enhanced with high-resolution views of the suspected areas and comparison scans of the uninvolved limb. A negative bone scan virtually excludes the diagnosis of stress fracture. Table 30-3 compares the sequential pattern of stress fractures in regard to symptoms, bone scan, and plain film results.

Although computerized tomography (CT) may be useful to confirm a fracture, it is not a routinely accepted test. It may be of value in determining fracture location, morphology, and state of healing.

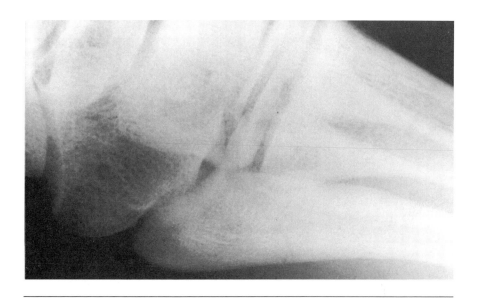

Figure 30-4. Plain radiographs show early stress fracture of fifth metatarsal (missed initially).

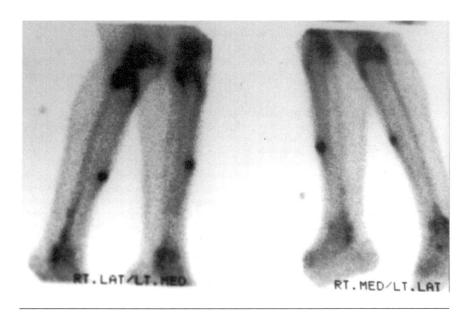

Figure 30-5. Bone scan of the same tibia stress fracture.

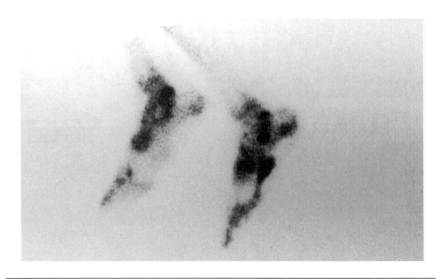

Figure 30-6. Bone scan shows increase uptake indicative of a stress fracture.

Early reports show that magnetic resonance imaging (MRI) is not superior to bone scanning in the assessment of stress fractures. The relative sensitivity of MRI compared to scintigraphy for detection of stress fracture has not been the subject of critical study. MRI, by virtue of its enhanced soft tissue contrast resolution, may permit early (preradiographic) detection of stress injuries of bone. Prefracture stress responses are most readily demonstrated on MRI in areas in which bone marrow is overwhelmingly fatty. This is an advantage when imaging the foot and lower extremity, which are overwhelmingly composed of fatty marrow.

On MRI, stress responses appear as globular foci of decreased signal on T1-weighted sequences that are graphically demonstrated against a background of fatty (bright) marrow. The signal variably increases in intensity on T2-weighted sequences. Stress responses are well demonstrated on Short Tau [Tl] Inversion Recovery (STIR) sequences, in which they are depicted as areas of high signal intensity against the suppressed background of fatty marrow (Fig. 30-7). Although the detection of stress responses in fatty marrow is straightforward, demonstrating the abnormalities in hematopoietic marrow can be difficult. STIR sequences can be of considerable value in this setting. Therefore, MRI may be more specific than the bone scan.

Treatment

Treatment must be multifaceted and multidisciplinary. Categorically, treatment is divided into general, psychological, medical, physical (duration, intensity, frequency), and surgical issues.

In general, soccer players must maintain adequate nutritional integrity to avoid injury, especially the young female athlete. Proper nutrition includes

Table 30-2

Bone Scan Appearance: Stress Fracture versus Shin Splints		
Characteristic	Stress Fracture	Shin Splints
Bone Scan	any phase can be positive	only positive on delays
Intensity	can be 1+ to 4+	usually 1+ or 2+
Shape	round/fusiform	linear/vertical
Location	anywhere in lower leg	mid-posterior tibia

a low fat, high carbohydrate diet with avoidance of phosphate containing sodas (studies suggest that excess phosphate intake may be an important variable in stress maladaptation). Calcium balance must be achieved at all times since negative balance will result in maladaptation. Supplementation should be encouraged because most female athletes require 1000–1500 mg of calcium per day. Vitamins and trace elements are used to prevent deficiency (the use of high dose vitamins or trace elements has not been shown to be of benefit).

Eating disorders must always be considered. This is especially true in the female athlete with multiple, recurrent stress fractures. When this problem is identified the physician must involve the coach, trainer, parent, athlete, and a psychiatrist/psychologist in the treatment program.

Medically, the athlete must be evaluated to ascertain that no concurrent medical condition exists that may affect bone integrity. Abnormal menstrual patterns in the female athlete must be identified. If present, the primary care physician should evaluate for possible estrogen supplementation.

After these factors have been evaluated, the athlete is treated using the bone specific treatment algorithm. The most common factor found to modulate this injury in the healthy individual has been the application of cyclic stress.

Table 30-3

Sequential Pattern of Stress Fractures			
Stage	Symptoms	Scan	Radiographs
Normal bone remodeling (uneventful)			
Accelerated bone remodeling (stress remodeling)		+	
Bone fatigue (stress fracture)	+	+	
Bone exhaustion (cortical break)	+	+	

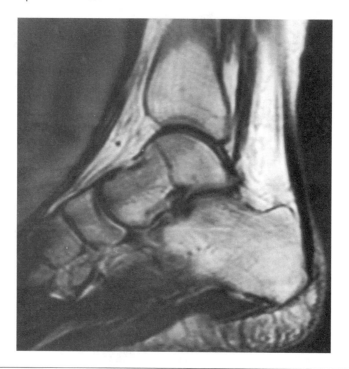

Figure 30-7. MRI reveals stress fracture of talar body.

The cessation of stress (i.e., rest) allows repair to dominate over resorption and usually requires 6–8 weeks for most fractures. Pubic rami fractures heal in 2–5 months. In a study of midshipmen, 97 men with shin splints were divided into five treatment regimens. All were effective to varying degrees. Prohibition of running was common to all the treatments.

Although bracing may be important in limiting motion that aggravates the injury, it can also transfer stress to other areas which may become symptomatic. A group of competitive athletes with tibial stress fractures were fitted with pneumatic leg braces. All were able to ambulate without pain and allowed to resume light training in an average of 1 week. They resumed intensive training at an average of 3.7 weeks post injury. They returned to competition at the preinjury level in an average of 5.3 weeks after application of the brace. The effect may have been the result of accelerated healing due to a venous tourniquet.

Surgery should only be considered for bones in which a complete fracture would have serious complications. Examples of this are the tibia (Fig. 30-8), tarsal navicular, 5th metatarsal, and femoral neck.

Figure 30-9 represents our treatment algorithm for athletes with suspected tibial stress fractures. After the history is taken and the athlete is examined, a plain film radiograph should be obtained. This is done for the occasional

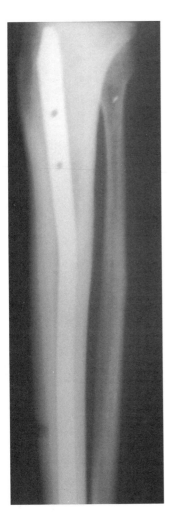

Figure 30-8. Stress fracture required tibial nailing after failure to heal by nonoperative measures.

positive study and documentation for future radiographs. If these films are negative, proceed with a bone scan or MRI. After the diagnosis is confirmed, the athlete begins 6 weeks of rest from the aggravating activity. Crutches are used if a limp or significant pain is present. During this time, the athlete should be allowed to maintain cardiovascular tone by cross training including swimming or bicycling. The athlete is reevaluated after 6 weeks. If pain free, the athlete is allowed to return to sporting activities via cyclical progression. If pain persists and plain films are negative for fracture propagation, cyclical progression is instituted. If plain films are positive for propagation of the fracture, step 1 is repeated for an additional 6 weeks. Upon reexamination after an additional 6 weeks, pain will determine whether return to soccer is allowed. When pain remains we proceed with a CT scan (if radiographs are equivocal). If a large lucency is present or the CT scan is positive, reamed intramedullary rodding of the tibia is undertaken. The athlete is then able to return to soccer by way of cyclical progression.

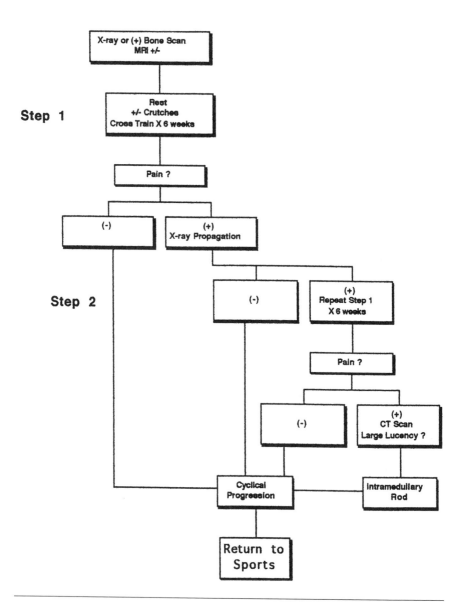

Figure 30-9. Tibial stress fracture treatment algorithm.

Figure 30-10 represents our treatment algorithm for the management of metatarsal stress fractures. The concepts are the same as for the tibia with the exception that surgical intervention involves cancellous screw fixation ± bone graft.

Figure 30-11 is the treatment algorithm for tarsal navicular fractures developed by Torg. Uncomplicated, partial fractures and nondisplaced, complete fractures of the tarsal navicular should be treated by immobilization in a plaster cast with nonweight bearing for 6–8 weeks. Return to weight bearing and activity should be guided by the patient's clinical condition and roentgenographic evidence of the union. Complete, displaced fractures can be treated with immobilization in a plaster cast with nonweight bearing for 6–8 weeks or with open reduction and internal fixation followed by immobilization and nonweight bearing for 6 weeks. Fractures complicated by delayed union or nonunion should be treated with medullary curretage and inlaid bone grafting. In these situations, a fibrous union may exist and no attempt should be made to reduce the fragments. If the fragments are mobile, internal fixation should be effected using a malleolar screw. Following medullary currettage and inlaid bone grafting with or without internal fixation, the patient should be placed in a nonweight-bearing short-leg cast for 6–8 weeks. Again, mobilization and return to activity should depend on clinical and roentgenographic evidence of healing.

In fractures treated by bone grafting, the healing course may be protracted with firm bony union not occurring for 3–6 months. Partial fractures complicated by a small dorsal transverse fracture may require excision of the dorsal fragment. Complete fractures complicated by a large dorsal transverse fracture will go on to union with immobilization and do not require excision of the fragment. Associated dorsal talar beaks and small dorsal transverse fragments should be excised. Sclerotic fragments associated with delayed union and nonunion should not be excised. These should be treated with medullary currettage and inlaid bone graft as indicated. The nonweight-bearing cast immobilization is the treatment of choice for tarsal navicular stress fractures. The treatment compared favorably with surgical treatment for patients who failed weight-bearing treatments. CT scan appearance of healing fractures did not mirror clinical union. It is suggested that postimmobilization management should be managed clinically because 28 of 35 patients (80%) healed with nonweight-bearing cast immobilization versus 12 of 40 patients (30%) healed with limitation of physical activity. Only 1 of 5 patients healed with continued sporting activity.

Although the only required medications are analgesics, hormonal replacement in amenorrheic thin female athletes is often necessary. Rare metabolic abnormalities should be considered in the otherwise healthy athlete. Altered magnesium and copper metabolism can result in a poor crystalline structure of bone. Osteomalacia rickets, whether primary or secondary, requires vitamin D supplementation and calcium to prevent insufficiency fractures.

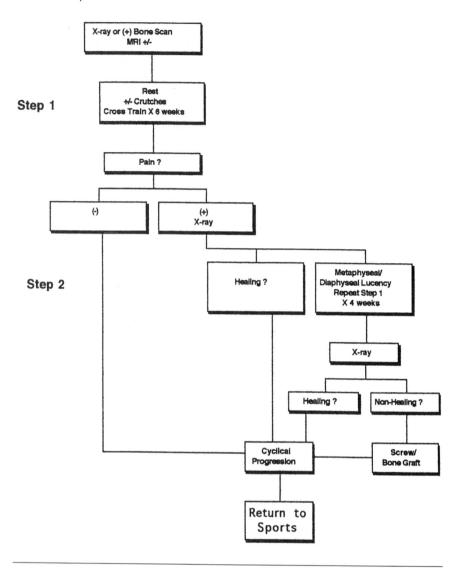

Figure 30-10. Metatarsal stress fracture treatment algorithm.

Ultrasound is contraindicated because it aggravates pain in the area of the fracture, although some studies suggest it may be of some diagnostic value. Application of ice and massage with gentle exercise relieve pain and increase blood supply to the subcutaneous area by reflex vasodilatation.

Return to Play Criteria

Most athletes will be able to return to soccer activities in 3–8 weeks (Fig. 30-12). The athlete must be pain free and remain so during physical activity to begin rehabilitation.

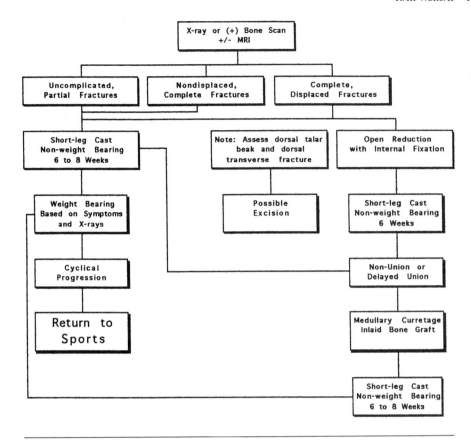

Figure 30-11. Tarsal navicular stress fracture treatment algorithm.

Injury Prevention

A study of approximately 3000 first year midshipmen used four prophylactic programs for prevention of shin splints including heel pads, tennis shoes, stretching exercises, and a graduated running program. None was effective.

We have developed the following treatment guidelines for the prevention of stress fractures in soccer players:

1. Educate athletes, coaches, parents, trainers, and doctors.
2. Use different shoes for training and games.
3. Train in a cyclical progression and in a dose responsive adaptation progression.
4. Cross-train with e.g. bicycle, pool, or Stairmaster.
5. Make quality a priority over quantity.
6. Monitor physical activity periods and rest periods carefully.
7. Individualize training programs.
8. Be especially careful with year-round programs. The highest

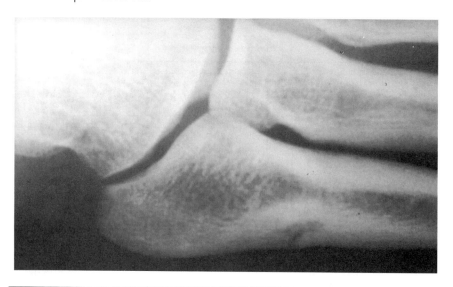

Figure 30-12. Same stress fracture as seen in Figure 30-6 showing progression. Healed after treatment algorithm applied.

concentration of stress fractures are found in areas such as California and Florida.

9. Consider changing the field if stress fractures seem to be inordinately high.

10. Heed Aristotle's warning, "The child is not a small adult." Individualize programs by puberty stage and not by age.

11. Be observant for eating disorders. Watch for multiple stress fractures.

Summary

Detailed studies must be done on the prevalence and incidence of soccer injuries. Biomechanical studies should be designed to look at shoe design and force concentration. Several trainers have raised the possibility of peroneal fatigue and its implications for soccer injuries. Finally, nutritional concerns need to be addressed (e.g., vitamins, trace elements, and antioxidants).

SUGGESTED READINGS

Andrish JT, Bergfeld JA, Walheim J. A prospective study on the management of shin splints, J Bone Joint Surg 1974;56A:1697–1700.

Deutsch AL, Mink JH, Kerr R. MRI of the foot and ankle. New York: Raven Press, 1992.

Devas MB. Stress fractures of the tibia in athletes or "shin soreness." J Bone Joint Surg 1958;4OB:227–239.

Jones BH, Bovee MW, Harris JM, et al. Intrinsic risk factors for exercise-related injuries among male and female army trainees. Am J Sports Med 1993;21:705–710.

Marcus R, Cann C, Madvig P, et al. Menstrual function and bone mass in elite women distance runners. Ann Intern Med 1985;102:158–163.

Markey KL. Stress fractures. Clin Sports Med 1987;6:405–425.

Matheson GO, Clement DB, McKenzie DC, et al. Stress fracture in athletes. Am J Sports Med 1987;15:46–58.

McBryde AM. Stress fractures in athletes. J Sports Med 1975;3: 212–217.

Pentecost RL, et al. Fatigue, insufficiency and pathologic fractures. JAMA 1964;187: 1001–1004.

Prather JL, Nusynowitz ML, Snowdy HA, et al. Scintigraphic findings in stress fractures. J Bone Joint Surg 1977;59A:869–873.

Torg JS, Pavlov H, Cooley LH, et al. Stress fractures of the tarsal navicular. J Bone Joint Surg 1982;63A:700–712.

Viitasalo JT, Kvist M. Some biomechanical aspects of the foot and ankle in athletes, with and without shin splints. Am J Sports Med 1983;11:125–130.

31 Acute Foot and Ankle Injuries

Per A.F.H. Renstrom

Ankle and foot injuries are common in sports. In fact, there is approximately one inversion ankle ligament injury per 10,000 people in the United States. These injuries tend to occur primarily in young people, probably because so many youths participate in sports and physical activities. Ankle injuries are the most common injuries in sports and recreational activities. Twenty-nine percent of all injuries to the lower extremities are to the ankle and of these, 75% involve the lateral ligaments. In high school students, ankle injuries are the most frequent injury in all sports except tennis and swimming. The sport with the highest percentage of ankle injuries is basketball, in which a little over half of all injuries involve the ankle.

Epidemiology

Ankle sprains constitute 17%–20% of all soccer injuries. This incidence of ankle sprains varies between 1.7 to 2.0 per thousand hours of exposure to playing soccer. Despite the high frequency of ankle injuries, there is a great variation in clinical diagnostic techniques and methods of treatment. Although injuries of the foot are also common in soccer, the incidence is not well known. This chapter will discuss factors of importance in the mechanism of ankle and foot injuries in soccer and common foot injuries.

Mechanism of Ankle Injuries

A 2 year prospective study of 17 soccer teams was carried out. The teams registered injuries that occurred during training and competition on different playing surfaces during the 2 year period. Injuries were defined functionally; an injury was one which prevented the player from training or competing. In total, 184 injuries were reported that resulted in time away from soccer for more than 1 week. Table 31-1 outlines the frequency and location of injuries during the project. Table 31-2 lists the activities that caused the injuries. Body contact was the cause for more than 60% of the injuries. Poor warming up was considered to be an important factor for injury in 4%.

Table 31-1

Injury Type and Location in 17 Teams over a 2 Year Period	
Type of Injury	*Incidence*
Muscle tendon strains	30%
Ligament sprains	30%
Fractures	9%
Location	
Knee	24%
Ankle	19%

Seventy-nine percent of the injuries occurred during games. The players trained 2.5 times as often as the played games, which means that the risk for injury was much higher during games. There was a tendency for most injuries to occur at the beginning of the first period or toward the end of the second period. The type of injury did not differ significantly between the different playing positions. Ankle injuries were most common in wing forward players, which might be explained by the fact that these players often shoot long shots from the side to the center and are often tackled from the side in tight positions. Injuries in general were most common in wing defense players, caused by heading or sliding tackles. Groin injuries were experienced most in middle field players and forwards.

The design of the shoe and its relation to the playing surface are important for ankle and foot injuries. Seventy-three percent of the players that were injured on artificial turf used cleated shoes, compared to only 43% of the players whose shoes did not have cleats. These results show that cleats are an im-

Table 31-2

Actions that Cause Injuries in Soccer	
Action	*Incidence*
Tackling with the body	16%
Kicking	12%
Nodding with body contact	10%
Sliding tackle	9%
Tripping	8%
Chasing the ball	8%
Overuse	9%

portant factor in the injury mechanism on artificial turf. Players using 6–10 cleats were wounded less often on grass. In conclusion, it seems that players should not use cleated shoes when playing on artificial turf and that 6–10 cleats are preferrable when playing on grass. It is important to have the shoes that are adapted to the turf.

Based on this set of data, it can be said that ankle injuries are more common on grass, lower leg and groin injuries are more common on artificial turf, and thigh injuries are more common on gravel. Knee injuries are equally common on the different playing surfaces.

Ankle injuries

The anterior talofibular ligament (ATFL), the calcaneofibular ligament (CFL), and the posterior talofibular ligament (PTFL) of the lateral ankle function as a unit. Although one may resist a specific motion, the primary stabilizing ligament is dependent on foot position. As the foot plantarflexes the strain in the ATFL increases, while the strain in the CFL decreases. Although ATFL is the weakest ligament, it is clinically the most significant. Clinical ligamentous damage is primarily a function of tensile loading and is only secondarily affected by twisting and shear forces. The most common injury mechanism is a combination of plantarflexion, inversion, and some internal rotation.

Ankle Ligament Injuries

As a result of sprain, complete rupture of one or more of the lateral ankle ligaments will occur. When injured ankles were surgically explored, an isolated ATFL tear was present in approximately two-thirds of the cases. The second most common injury was a combined rupture of the ATFL and CFL, which occurs in approximately 20%–25% of the cases. The PTFL is rarely injured, except in severe ankle trauma.

A medial ankle sprain can occur when the foot is everted and externally rotated. Isolated ruptures of the medial deltoid ligament are rare and usually occur in combination with fractures of the lateral malleolus.

The anterior and posterior tibial fibular ligaments, the syndesmosis, can occasionally be ruptured. It is usually ruptured in combination with fractures and deltoid ligament tears. In approximately 3% of the cases it can be ruptured as isolated lesions. The risk for future arthrosis development and ankle instability is great if this injury is not recognized and treated correctly. Therefore, it is important that the doctor is aware of the risk for this injury and that it is diagnosed adequately through the use of history, location of tenderness, and the external rotation squeeze and cotton tests.

GRADES OF INJURY

Damage after an ankle ligament injury can be classified in a number of ways. There is no universally accepted, standardized system for grading ankle sprain severity. Table 31-3 summarizes Hamilton's guidelines. Another method classifies lateral ligament injuries as single or double ligament tears rather than first, second, or third degree sprains. A single degree would involve only the ATFL while a double degree would involve the ATFL and the CFL.

Table 31-3

Grades of Ankle Sprains

Grade I (mild sprain): a partial tear of the lateral ligament complex
Grade II (moderate sprain): a torn ATFL with an intact CFL
Grade III (severe sprain): a tear of the entire lateral ligament complex

STABILITY TESTING

Clinical stability tests are often included in the physical examination of an acutely sprained ankle. Two popular tests are the anterior drawer test and the talar tilt test.

The Anterior Drawer Test

This test evaluates ATFL integrity by the amount of anterior talar displacement that can be produced in the sagittal plane. The stability of the ankle depends primarily on the integrity of the ATFL and can be measured by the amount of anterior displacement that occurs during the anterior drawer test. Rupture of the ATFL is indicated by a positive result of the test.

Biomechanically, the greatest amount of anterior drawer is at 10° of plantar flexion when the ATFL is intact. The greatest change in displacement on ATFL sectioning and the ankle position of highest ATFL elongation is also at 10° of plantar flexion. The anterior drawer test should be tested with the ankle held in 10° of plantar flexion. In addition, the foot internally rotates with increasing anterior drawer test in the plantar flexed foot with relaxed or ruptured ATFL. Both laxity and stiffness should be evaluated to quantify load displacement behavior during the anterior drawer test.

The Talar Tilt Test

This test evaluates CFL and ATFL integrity by the size of the angle formed between the articular surface of the talus and the tibia in response to a supination force applied to the hindfoot.

MANAGEMENT OF THE INJURY

The goal of initial treatment for acute ankle sprains is to protect the damaged ligaments from further injury and control the amount of edema that may develop in the joint. Treatment of severe ankle sprains, when there is complete rupture of the lateral ligaments, is conservative or operative. Many studies in literature compare results of both treatment methods to determine the best management for stabilizing the ankle. Functional treatment should be the first method of choice for complete lateral ankle ligament rupture. This type of treatment includes a short period of ankle protection with tape, bandage, or brace and allows early mobility and weight bearing. Rehabilitation exercises are the most important step in the treatment process. The goal of rehabilitation is to stabilize the injured ankle to preinjury condition by reestablishing ankle range of motion, muscle strength, and neuromuscular control.

Some authors recommend operative repair of acute severe ankle sprains in young athletes. Table 31-4 lists the indications for acute repair. Most techniques described for repair of acute ligament injuries are similar.

Table 31-4

Indications for Surgical Repair of Ankle Injuries

1. A history of momentary talocrural dislocation with complete ligamentous disruption
2. A clinical by increased anterior drawer sign
3. 100° more tilt on the affected side with stress inversion testing
4. Clinical or radiographic suspicion of tears in both the AITL and CFL
5. Osteochondral fracture

In 10%–20% of cases there are residual problems. If a patient has continuous pain and swelling 3–4 months after ankle ligament sprain, attention should be focused on intraarticular lesions or other differential diagnoses. It is important to be aware of the many differential diagnostic possibilities.

Ankle Fractures and Tears of Tibiofibular Syndesmosis

Ankle fractures are common and occur in the lateral, medial, and posterior malleolus. Lateral and posterior processes of the talus may also fracture.

Isolated complete syndesmosis injuries without fractures are rare and little information exists about ankle instability in the absence of fracture. In a series of more than 400 ankle ligament ruptures, only 12 cases of syndesmosis rupture in soccer and winter sports were noted. Partial tears of the anterior inferior tibiofibular ligament are not uncommon in soccer. The injury mechanism is often a violent external rotation with the ankle in plantarflexion.

These are ruptures often associated with ruptured deltoid ligaments, fibular fractures, or fractures involving the medial and posterior malleolus. Ankle fractures with syndesmosis injury and major displacement should be treated operatively.

Chondral Injuries and Osteochondral Fractures

Chondral lesions occur in 60% of all ankle sprains and osteochondritis disscans in 6.4%. The etiology is traumatic as a single event or multiple microtraumatic insults. Table 31-5 lists the stages of osteochondral lesions.

Table 31-5

Stages of Osteochonral Lesions

Stage I: Compression injury, causing microscopic damage to an area of subchondral bone. Plain radiographs are negative.

Stage II: Partially detached osteochondral fragment, detectable on careful examination of adequate series of plain radiographs.

Stage III: Osteochondral fragment is completely detached, but remains in anatomic position.

Stage IV: Detached fragment displaced elsewhere in the joint.

The patient usually has a history of a sprained ankle. Sometimes a pop is heard. With a recent injury, there is moderate to severe swelling of the joint. Tenderness is typically located just distal to the anterior tibiofibular syndesmosis or behind the medial malleolus, depending on the location of the lesion. After an inversion injury, the symptoms from a concomitant anterolateral osteochondral lesion may be obscured in the signs of the ligament tear.

When an osteochondral lesion is suspected, a plain radiographic examination is needed including anterior-posterior (AP), lateral, and oblique views of the ankle. Mortise views in plantar flexion should disclose a posteromedial lesion. A corresponding view in dorsiflexion reveals an anterolateral lesion. If the patient is treated for the ligament injury alone (usually immediate functional rehabilitation), symptoms persist (i.e., pain just distal to the anterior syndesmosis, recurrent swelling, and catching or locking), and a renewed plain radiograph is negative, further imaging of the ankle is necessary. Although a bone scan is sensitive, it is nonspecific. If the bone scan is positive for bone damage over the talus, further evaluation is sometimes needed using plain tomography, CT scans, or MRI to accurately determine the exact location and extent of the lesion.

MANAGEMENT OF THE INJURY

Appropriate staging and early treatment of osteochondral lesions of the talus provide the best results. Healing depends on capillary overgrowth from the body of the talus. Immobilization of the area seems to be necessary to prevent frictional effects of an uneven joint surface, which can cause the lesion to progress into more advanced stages and nonunion. Lesions in stages I, II, and III without established nonunion signs (marked sclerosis, grossly uneven joint surfaces, or osteoarthrosis) are treated with a nonweight-bearing lower leg boot for 4–6 weeks, followed by a weight-bearing boot until there is radiographic evidence of healing. An interarticular injection of 10 cc lidocaine can be effective in stage I lesions. Delayed nonoperative treatment of stage III lesions often fails. Stage III and IV lesions are often treated surgically to prevent further deterioration of the joint. Although many of these lesions can be reached arthroscopically (removal of detached lesion and or debridement of the lesion bed), open approaches are occasionally needed. Reattachment of the osteochondral lesions might be considered in the acute phase. Postoperative weight bearing is delayed for 2–6 weeks (a full 6 weeks if osteotomy of the medial malleolus was performed). The prognosis following early nonoperative treatment in stages I, II, and III is good in 75% of the patients and surgery in late stage III and IV lesions render good results in 40%–80% of patients. Advanced lesions, in which treatment is delayed more than one year, generally have a poor outcome.

Ankle Impingement Syndrome

Ankles that show boney osteophytes over the anterior rim of the tibia are called soccer player's ankle. These injuries are usually secondary to traction injury of the joint capsule of the anterior rim of the ankle, which occur when the foot is repeatedly forced into extreme plantar flexion.

Anterior tibiotalar impingement is a condition in which soft tissues are entrapped between the anterior lateral part of the tibia and the talus during dorsiflexion of the ankle. Meniscoid lesions are caused by increased scar tissue or folded ligaments that fill the anterior lateral aspect of the joint. This injury is usually chronic, but can be reactivated by an acute trauma and cause swelling and discomfort. These problems are successfully treated with arthroscopy.

Acute Tendon Injuries Surrounding the Ankle
MANAGEMENT OF THE INJURY
Subluxation or dislocation of the peroneal tendons may occur in soccer. The peroneus longus and brevis tendons run downward on the lateral aspect of the ankle and midfoot to their insertions on the plantar side of the first metatarsal, medial cuneiform, navicular, and the proximal end of the fifth metatarsal. The tendons pass behind the lateral malleolus beneath the superior and inferior retinacula, which holds the tendons in position.

Subluxation or dislocation of the peroneal tendons requires a major trauma with internal rotation and inversion. This injury is painful and feels like the tendon is subluxing or dislocating over the lateral aspect of the lateral malleolus. Twisting activities are painful for the patient. Although treatment of these injuries is often surgical, some doctors prefer a short period of immobilization in a walking boot.

If subluxing or dislocating tendons become chronic, surgery is indicated. A patient with this injury cannot play soccer without pain and fear of dislocating or subluxing the tendon. Surgery includes deepening of the peroneal groove and imbrication of the retinacula. If there is a chronic pathologic condition in the tendon itself, a surgical incision and removal of the pathological tissue can be valuable, although this kind of surgery is not common.

Peroneal tendinitis or tendinosis of the peroneal tendons is typically elicited via stenosis under the overlying retinacula. A longitudinal tear can occur with trauma or overuse. A common predisposing factor to peroneal tendon disease is distortion of the local anatomy caused by a fracture of the lateral malleolus, calcaneus, or by an ankle sprain. Pain, swelling, and point tenderness are located posterior and inferior to the lateral malleolus. Although there may be increased pain with weight bearing, forced plantar flexion, inversion, and resisted eversion of the ankle are more painful. Physical examination must include evaluation of tendon stability. Subtalar motion is usually decreased. Treatment is primarily conservative with rest, ice, NSAIDs, and crutches as acute measures. Short-term immobilization can be helpful in some patients. Surgery with correction of the cause is sometimes necessary.

Ruptures of the tibialis posterior and flexor hallucis brevis tendons may occasionally occur. They are managed similar to acute tendon injuries.

Achilles tendon rupture can be complete or partial and is associated with degenerative changes in the tendon. Complete tears can occur with different traumas and are most common in soccer players over the age of 30. Treatment is usually operative with early functional rehabilitation and motion. Management of a partial tear is difficult. Functional treatment in a walking boot for up to 4 weeks is recommended.

Foot Injuries

Midtarsal Injuries

MIDTARSAL SPRAINS

These sprains are not common. The midtarsal joint or transverse tarsal joint, often called Chopart's joint (i.e., the talonavicular and calcaneocuboid joints), hold a key position in the medial and lateral longitudinal arches. The midtarsal joint acts together with the subtalar joints in inversion and eversion. Midtarsal sprains are potentially disabling injuries with healing times often longer than anticipated. In general, substantial forces are required to cause significant injury to these joints. The soccer shoes give some protection.

Management of the Injury

In addition to plain radiographs, CT scans are helpful in delineating the extent of severe injury in this region. Undisplaced injuries are usually treated nonoperatively. Due to potential instability, 4–6 weeks in a nonweight-bearing walking boot followed by 2 weeks with increasing weight bearing is sometimes recommended. During rehabilitation, a shoe with a firm sole and a longitudinal arch support should be worn. Displaced fractures, subluxations, and dislocations need to be reduced. Although closed reduction is occasionally successful, open means are usually required. Internal fixation is performed, followed by restricted weight-bearing casting for 3–6 weeks.

The prognosis after midtarsal injuries is highly dependent on whether reduction is achieved. Nonreduced injuries and extensively displaced fractures often do poorly. An arthrodesis should be considered in these cases.

Tarsometatarsal Injuries (Lisfranc's Joint)

The second metatarsal base is the primary bony stabilizer of the tarsometatarsal articulation. It sits in a tight mortise between the distal parts of the first and third cuneiforms. The cuneiforms and the metatarsal bases are wedge-shaped and their dorsal width contributes to the transverse arch of the metatarsals. Motion in the joints is restricted. Together, the tarsal and metatarsal bones allow some pro- and supination of the forefoot. Severe trauma to Lisfranc's joint caused by direct or indirect forces on the midfoot can result in a varying pattern of fractures and dislocations. Indirect forces along the metatarsals may result in dislocation of the joint with or without fractures through the plantar aspect of the metatarsal base. Soft tissue injuries are often extensive following fracture dislocations of the Lisfranc joint complex.

MANAGEMENT OF THE INJURY

Injuries to the Lisfranc joint are notorious for missed initial diagnosis and inadequate treatment. The most constant, reliable radiographic sign is a slight widening between the bases of the first and second metatarsals, second and third metatarsals, or between either of the cuneiforms. It is necessary to look for fractured fragments between the first and second metatarsal bases and between the medial and middle cuneiforms. Oblique views are necessary for adequate descriptions of radiographic findings.

The goal of treatment is a stable, anatomic reduction. Due to interposing soft tissues or fractured fragments, reduction is rarely successful by closed means. Therefore, open reduction-internal fixation (ORIF) is recommended. Postoperatively, partial weight bearing for 6 weeks followed by 4–6 weeks in a walking boot is recommended.

Combinations with lower leg, calcaneal, or ankle fractures can occur with substantial risk for compartment syndrome development. Intracompartmental pressure measurements are mandatory and, when indicated, fasciotomy is performed without delay. The prognosis is good provided the injury is closed and reduction/fixation is adequate. Although degenerative arthritis may occur, it is benign if good primary reduction is achieved. However, open injuries and inadequate reduction lead to unsatisfactory results.

Metatarsophalangeal (MTP) Sprains and Dislocation

Repetitive hyperextension loads on the first metatarsophalangeal joint predisposes the plantar aspect of the capsule around the joint to injury. Alternately, the dorsal aspect of the joint is sprained following a hyperflexion event. There is local pain, tenderness, and swelling.

MANAGEMENT OF THE INJURY

Treatment of MTP sprains is nonoperative using ice, compression, and elevation. Initial immobilization is required with weight bearing as tolerated. NSAIDs are beneficial. Recovery time can be as long as 10 weeks. Injections of local anesthetics or steroids can aggravate the injury and should be avoided. An orthosis (steel or orthoplast) limiting dorsiflexion of the first MTP joint can be placed in the shoe during rehabilitation. Surgical capsule repair and removal of loose bodies is occasionally indicated. Strenuous activities, such as running and jumping, are resumed when the patient is asymptomatic.

Forced hyperextension of the MTP joints beyond physiologic limits may lead to rupture of the plantar plate either through the sesamoids as fractures or proximally. Surgery is often indicated. Dislocations with sesamoid fractures are usually readily reducible by closed means.

MTP dislocations of the lesser toes typically can be reduced by closed means. Once reduced, the joint is usually stable and cross-over taping is sufficient.

Metatarsal Fractures

Soft tissue coverage of the dorsum of the foot is thin and vulnerable with a suboptimal blood supply. There are strong ligamentous connections between the metatarsal necks distally and strong bands between the bases, except between the first and second where the soft tissue connection is between the second base and medial cuneiform. Injury mechanism is often a direct blow to the dorsum when an opposing player lands on the foot (e.g., after heading). Direct forces on the metatarsals usually result in transverse neck fractures of the second, third, and fourth metatarsals while indirect forces lead to spiral shaft fractures. The common plantar flexion-inversion trauma results in a fifth metatarsal base fracture. Following severe injuries to this region, compartment pressures in the foot should be monitored and fasciotomy performed when indicated.

MANAGEMENT OF THE INJURY

Treatment of nondisplaced fractures affecting the lesser metatarsals include the use of a firm metatarsal pad, circumferential taping, and a firm boot with a crepe sole. Weight bearing is allowed as soon as it is tolerable. Undisplaced fractures through the first metatarsal require a carefully molded nonweight-bearing short-leg cast for 2 weeks followed by progressive weight bearing.

With only one displaced metatarsal fracture, closed reduction is attempted. If successful, 6 weeks of nonweight-bearing casting follows. With multiple fractures, surgery using screws and plates or intramedullary retrograde pinning is recommended. Casting is unnecessary following stable internal fixation. With fractures through the metatarsal neck, closed reduction is virtually impossible. Fixation with K-wire is commonly used.

Stress fractures

Stress Fractures of the Foot and Ankle

Stress fractures are the most common fractures of the foot and ankle in athletes and workers. They are often chronic and can cause acute pain. Typical stress fracture locations are the distal fibula, tibia, calcaneus and navicular bone, and metatarsals. Bone is continuously adapting to new loading patterns. A stress or fatigue fracture is the failure point in a normal adaptive process. The periosteum gives early warning signs (pain) of overloading. If fatigue microdamage occurs too rapidly, new bone cannot develop fast enough and the bone weakens. Gradually, a stress fracture develops.

The muscles play a major role in shock absorption. Muscle fatigue impairs shock absorption leading to altered stress distribution and increased compressive loads on the bone with a greater risk for stress fracture. Another contributing factor in the development of a stress fracture is biomechanical imbalance, such as skeletal asymmetry and leg length discrepancy. The short leg is more susceptible to stress reaction and fracture. Some anatomical abnormalities predispose to stress reactions on an unpredictable basis. For example, a rigid foot puts increased stress on the metatarsals. The second metatarsal is at risk when playing on a hard surface with a tight heel cord, with a long second metatarsal, or a flexible, nonsupportive great toe. Other factors include improperly supportive shoes and injury to the opposite extremity. The patient protects the injured limb by placing more weight on the opposite limb.

MANAGEMENT OF THE INJURY

A common clinical course is insidious onset of vague pain. With continued stress, pain increases and becomes more localized with possible soft tissue swelling. On clinical examination, there is distinct tenderness over the lesion. The diagnosis is verified by bone scan. Plain radiographs typically become positive at 3–8 weeks. Treatment consists of activity modification and nongravity exercises. Immobilization is recommended with multiple fractures, intolerable pain, or fragmentation. Although healing of a properly treated stress fracture usually occurs in 4–15 weeks, it could take 6 months. A useful clinical healing test has the patient hop on the affected limb without pain. Screening for hormonal imbalance or endocrine dysfunction is indicated in multiple or recurrent stress fractures. Site specific treatment options are detailed.

Hindfoot Stress Fracture

Calcaneal stress fractures are relatively uncommon. They have been reported in military recruits doing over 16 hours of vigorous physical training per day. There is diffuse pain about the heel, which is aggravated by compression of the heel from medial to lateral. Pain is not localized only to the plantar aspect of the heel. Weight bearing as tolerated with crutches, a shock absorbing heel insert, NSAIDs, and at least 6–8 weeks are required for healing.

Metatarsal Stress Fracture

Up to 20% of stress fractures in the lower extremity are located in the metatarsals. The second ray is the most common site in a metatarsal stress fracture. Hypermobility of a metatarsal can predispose to adjacent metatarsal stress fracture. Typical locations are the medial base of the first metatarsal, the distal shaft of the second and third, the middle or distal shaft of the fourth, or proximally on the fifth. Symptoms progress slowly in a crescendo effect. It can take 1–2 months or more before stress fractures become visible on plain radiographs. A bone scan is the key to early radiographic confirmation of stress fractures.

Metatarsal stress fractures are generally treated nonoperatively. In early nondisplaced fractures, activities are limited for 4 weeks. Running in water is beneficial because it protects the forefoot from heavy repetitive loading.

Stress fractures through the fifth metatarsal need special attention. Nonoperative treatment requires 6–8 weeks of nonweight-bearing casting. Less restricted nonoperative treatments have high failure rates. Several investigators advocate internal fixation early because it decreases the time required for healing and return to strenuous activities. Signs of chronicity of the fracture (cortical thickening or intramedullary sclerosis) strongly indicate that only open treatment will be successful. Return to strenuous activities requires clinical and radiographic healing in 8–12 weeks.

Hallux Sesamoid Stress Fractures

Hallux sesamoid stress fractures are much rarer than sesamoiditis, a difficult differential diagnosis. Bipartition of the sesamoid is not uncommon, making radiographic diagnosis difficult. Furthermore, a bone scan is positive in both stress fractures and sesamoiditis. The stress fractures, however, do not heal with immobilization or prolonged inactivity. If other causes of pain can be excluded, a sesamoid stress fracture is treated with excision, which results in a good prognosis. Surgical access to the lateral sesamoid is difficult. Safe removal of the lateral sesamoid requires significant surgical experience in this area.

Tarsal Navicular Stress Fracture

Navicular stress fractures are uncommon in the nonathlete. The condition is characterized by insidious onset of vague pain in the arch, increased pain in the midfoot with motion, and limited dorsiflexion of the ankle. Activity increases the discomfort. Typically, there is localized tenderness over the navicular bone. Plain radiographs are usually normal and a bone scan is required for diagnosis. Plain or computerized tomography delineates the extent of the fracture. The fracture is sagittally oriented in the central 1/3 of the bone. This might be due to a relative avascularity of the central part of the navicular.

Treatment of acutely displaced fractures require ORIF with screws. Nondisplaced fractures should be treated in a nonweight-bearing cast for 6–8 weeks.

Metatarsalgia

Metatarsalgia, pain in the metatarsophalangeal region, is a condition with many possible etiologies. Hallux rigidus, sesamoiditis, and Morton's neuralgia are some chronic conditions. A common predisposing factor to metatarsalgia is altered forefoot biomechanics. These can be extrinsic or intrinsic, such as those listed in Table 31-6.

In the static standing position, all metatarsal heads bear loads with the first metatarsal head bearing double the load of the others. In the dynamic take-off phase of walking and running, this relative first ray overload is even more evident. A disturbance of this load distribution between the metatarsals may be caused by an abnormally short or hypermobile first ray or by a long second metatarsal. With a hypermobile first metatarsal, a significant part of the load is transferred to the second and third rays.

Management of the Injury

Treatment is conservative in the majority of cases. Supporting orthotics that relieve the overload on the metatarsal heads are often beneficial. With a hypermobile first ray and a pad just proximal to the second and third metatarsal heads and/or underneath the first ray may be useful. Stretching of a tight heel cord is essential. If significant discomfort persists for 6 months, in spite of adequate orthotics and flexibility treatment, surgery has to be considered. Soft tissue and skeletal corrections may be indicated.

Capsulitis of the second metatarsophalangeal joint is related to hallux valgus, in which the hallux forces the second toe to sublux dorsally. Tenderness over the dorsal capsule and pain on the passive dorsiflexion of the second MTP joint is diagnostic. Typically, there is no interdigital pain or

Table 31-6

Predisposing Factors for Metatarsalgia

High heeled shoes—alters load from hindfoot to forefoot region

Equinus foot—caused by a tight heel cord, and/or anterior impingement of the ankle, preventing ankle dorsiflexion

Cavus foot—support is by the metatarsal heads and the heel resulting in overload of the forefoot

Irregular distribution of load between the metatarsal heads

tenderness. Strapping of the second toe in a reduced, plantar flexed position is usually helpful. Rarely is an extensor tenotomy, with or without capsulotomy, required.

Nails

Ingrown Toenails

Ingrown toenails are common and potentially disabling. Posttraumatic nail deformation due to injury of the nail matrix may elicit the problem. Toenail shape is congenitally different. Some are flat and others are folded. Frequently, there is a conflict between the lateral and medial edges of a folded toenail and the adjacent nail. The problem grows when there is increased external pressure from a tight sock or a soccer shoe with a narrow toe-box. If the edge of the nail penetrates the skin, bacterial infection and voluminous granulation tissue result. Although this painful condition typically engages the lateral side of the great toe, any toe could be affected.

MANAGEMENT OF THE INJURY

Good foot hygiene, properly fitting footwear, and appropriate nail trimming habits are essential to prevention. Once a week the nails should be cut transversely because they may grow down into the nail fold when cut to a rounded outline. Once established, acute phase infections should be drained and the area soaked in an antiseptic solution followed by a dry cover. Avoid surgery in the acute phase due to high risk for postoperative infection, including potential osteomyelitis. In chronic cases, the ingrown part of the nail, including the nail matrix, should be surgically removed. Allow 3 weeks for healing postoperatively.

Subungual Hematoma

Black nail, or soccer toe, is a bleeding of the nail bed from a direct blow to the nail. This condition can be the result of being stepped on or a toe-box that is too narrow. The hematoma shines through the nail making it appear black or dark blue. The condition may be painful in the acute stage.

MANAGEMENT OF THE INJURY

The hematoma is evacuated via a small hole through the nail made with a hot, straightened paper clip. The procedure is often painless and gives immediate relief. This procedure also preserves the nail, which would otherwise fall off after 2–3 weeks due to disruption of the blood supply.

Subungual Exostosis

As a result of repetitive direct blows a reactive exostosis formation may develop on the dorsal aspect of the outer phalanx of the toe underlying the nail. Intense tenderness prompts treatment, nail removal, and, occasionally, removal of the exostosis. Good shoes often provide foot protection.

Fissures

Fissures of the weight-bearing area of the sole can be painful and disabling. Fissures are related to hyperkeratosis but are also seen in conjunction with psoriasis and fungal infection. Obesity and shoes without counters also contribute to the development of fissures. Hyperkeratosis related fissures are treated with topically applied salicylic acid. Steroid ointments or creams might be added for a limited time. A concomitant fungal infection may require oral antifungal medication.

Summary

The foot and ankle joints are complex mechanisms. In soccer, the focus of injuries should be directed at the feet and ankles. These can be small, nagging injuries or major problems requiring surgery, extensive rehabilitation, or severe limitation of playing. Too often, the player views such injuries as minor consequences of playing soccer and does not seek adequate medical advice, which could minimize time out of the game and significantly improve the long-term outlook.

SUGGESTED READINGS

Brostrom L. Sprained ankles: treatment and prognosis in recent ligament ruptures. Acta Chir Scand 1966;132:537–550.

Cox JS. Surgical and nonsurgical treatment of acute ankle sprains. Clin Orthop 1985;198:118–126.

Ekstrand J, Nigg B. Surface related injuries in soccer. Sports Med 1985;1:56–62.

Ekstrand J, Tropp H. Incidence of ankle sprains in soccer. Foot and Ankle 1990;1: 41–43.

Fritschy D. An unusual ankle injury in top skiers. Am J Sports Med 1989;17:282–286.

Garrick JM. The frequency of injury, mechanism of injury, and epidemiology of ankle sprains. Am J Sports Med 1977;5:241–242.

Grana WA. Chronic pain persisting after ankle sprain. J Musculoskel Med 1990;7: 35–49.

Hamilton WG. Foot and ankle injuries in dancers. Clin Sports Med 1988;7:143–173.

Kannus P, Renstrom P. Treatment for acute tears of the lateral ligaments of the ankle: operation, cast, or early controlled mobilization. J Bone Joint Surg Am 1991;73: 305–312.

Leach RE, Schepsis AA. Acute injury to ligaments of the ankle. In: Evarts CM, ed. Surgery of the musculoskeletal system, vol 4. New York: Churchill Livingstone, 1990;3887–3913.

McCulloch PG, Holden P, Robson DJ, et al. The value of mobilization and nonsteroidal anti-inflammatory analgesia in the management of inversion injuries of the ankle. Br J Clin Pract 1985;2:69–72.

Renstrom P, Wertz M, Incavo S, et al. Strain in the lateral ligaments of the ankle. Foot Ankle 1988;9:59–63.

Renstrom P, Theis M. Biomechanics and function of ankle ligaments: experimental results and clinical application. Sportverletz Sportschaden 1993;7:29–36.

Sandehn J. Acute sports injuries. A clinical and epidemiological study. Thesis, University of Helsinki. Helsinki, Yliopistopaino, 1988, pp. 1–66.

Torg J, Quedenfeld T. Effect of shoe type and cleat length on incidence and severity of knee injuries among high school football players. Research Quarterly 1971;42: 203–224.

32

Ankle Sprains and Impingement Syndromes

Thomas P. Knapp
Bert R. Mandelbaum

Acute ankle sprains and chronic pain/instability syndromes are common and disabling in soccer athletes. The most common injury in soccer, the most popular sport in the world, is ankle sprains. Minor ankle sprains are common and the athlete can return to competition and training with minimal time away from the game. Moderate and severe sprains can cause significant morbidity leading to long down time, chronic and recalcitrant pain, functional instability, weakness, loss of proprioception, and athletic disability. Management goals for ankle sprains should include prevention, minimization of morbidity, and performance facilitation.

This chapter defines the pathomechanics, pathogenesis, and spectrum of acute ankle sprains and chronic ankle pain syndrome (impingement). In addition, a systematic algorithm allowing efficient diagnosis, effective treatment, and rehabilitation with restoration to preinjury athletic activity will be discussed.

Epidemiology of Ankle Sprains

Lateral ligamentous sprains represent the most frequent injuries sustained by athletes. In fact, 85% of all ankle injuries are sprains. Approximately one-third of soccer, one-half of basketball, and one-quarter of volleyball injuries are acute ankle sprains. Therefore, ankle sprains are a common athletic injury.

Anatomy

The cornerstone for understanding the pathoanatomic spectrum is the definition of normal anatomy. This requires understanding all types of anatomic information including gross, planar, topographic, and arthroscopic anatomy. Gross anatomy includes bone-cartilage in the tibia, fibula, and talus; the peroneal, anterior tibialis, and posterior tibialis tendons; and ligaments including the anterior talofibular (ATFL), calcaneofibular (CFL), posterior talofibular (PTFL), deltoid, and distal tibiofibular syndesmosis (ligamentous tissue that joins the tibia to the fibula). Planar anatomy is important when interpreting computerized tomography (CT) scans and magnetic resonance imaging (MRI) in coronal, sagittal, and axial planes. Topographic anatomy identifies points of maximum tenderness, discontinuities, and deformities to correlate with the physical examination. It is essential to accurately define arthroscopic portals. Finally, arthroscopic anatomy refers to complex soft tissue transitions of surfaces, spaces, and additional masses. Therefore, the clinician must think logically and systematically and have access to multiple types of anatomic information.

Ankle Sprains

Mechanism of Injury

Plantar flexion/inversion is the most common mechanism of ankle sprain injury. The ATFL tears are the most common, followed by injuries to the CFL and PTFL. There are more lateral ligament injuries than medial ligament injuries for a number of reasons. First, the longer lateral malleolus obstructs eversion of the ankle whereas the shorter medial malleolus offers little obstruction to inversion. Second, there is a natural tendency for inversion. Third, the ATFL sustains the least maximal load to failure of all the components of the lateral complex and is injured most frequently. Finally, the deltoid ligament (superficial and deep) is stronger than the lateral complex ligaments and more difficult to tear. Eversion, or syndesmotic sprains, are less frequent but may have greater morbidity.

Management of the Injury

The diagnosis of an acute ankle sprain is relatively straightforward. All athletes have painful range of motion, swelling, and an inability to perform. It is necessary to obtain a complete history from the athlete. Details of the incident, including the injury activity and position/rotation of the foot and ankle during the acute event, must be obtained. It is also important to know about previous ankle sprains.

The physical examination is done after a thorough history is obtained. The examination must include the knee and foot because combination injuries are often encountered. Physical examination should document the point of maximum tenderness. Comparison with the opposite ankle should be made. Although anterior drawer testing can be attempted, it often must be delayed for several days until pain diminishes. Changing the position of the foot relative to the tibia changes the contribution of the anterior talofibular and calcaneofibular ligaments to ankle stiffness because of their alignment. Therefore, testing with the ankle perpendicular (90°) to the tibia primarily stresses the calcaneofibular component while plantar flexion increases the contribution of the anterior talofibular ligament.

Injuries to the distal tibiofibular syndesmosis must be carefully evaluated because they are often missed. This is done with the squeeze test (medial compression of the fibula against the stabilized tibia will elicit pain anterolaterally) and the external rotation stress test (external rotation of the foot causes anterolateral pain).

Radiographic evaluation follows and includes anterior-posterior (AP), lateral, and mortise views of the ankle and AP, lateral views of the tibia and fibula (watch out for proximal fibular fractures indicative of a Maisonneuve ankle fracture). If clinically indicated, obtain AP, lateral, and oblique views of the foot. Secondary diagnostic tests, including bone scan and MRI, are rarely indicated in the acute setting unless an occult stress fracture is suspected.

Stress views are generally too painful for the athlete in the immediate, post injury setting. These stress views are frequently inaccurate because of ankle swelling and muscle guarding. Therefore, reserve stress views for the fully rehabilitated athlete with continued instability symptoms.

It is important not to over-read radiographs. Many have been fooled into believing they have discovered the source of the acute symptoms when it is simply the acute discovery of chronic disease. There is a high prevalence of radiographic changes in asymptomatic ankles of professional soccer players. Approximately 50%–60% of ankles show radiographic images that seem to indicate the existence of an osseous remodeling phenomena in response to overuse and overstress of the ankle. The phrase, "radiographic arthrosis of sportsman," has been used to describe these radiographic findings in the asymptomatic athlete. Described were changes in the neck of the talus (squatting facet) and the anterior articular border of the distal epiphysis of the tibia (talotibial exostosis).

After the examination is completed, it is important to grade the injury because the grade will determine when the athlete may return to soccer. O'-Donoghue is credited with developing the most widely accepted grading scale (Table 32-1).

Conservative Treatment

Operative versus nonoperative treatment of acute ankle sprains has been a controversial issue. Kannus, in 1991, reviewed 12 prospective, randomized studies comparing surgical with functional treatment of acute ankle sprains and concluded that early, controlled movement was the treatment of choice. Additionally, he found that secondary reconstruction compares favorably with acute repair and should only be performed if the patient remains symptomatic after complete rehabilitation.

Immobilization and early range of motion are also controversial. Konradsen reported on 80 patients with grade III lateral ligament sprains treated with immobilization in a walking cast or early mobilization in a stabilizing orthosis. Although functionally treated patients resumed work and sports earlier than immobilized patients, there were no differences in ankle stability or symptoms after 1 year. Ninety-five percent of the ankles in both groups were

Table 32-1

Grades of Ankle Sprains
Grade I: Involves stretching or microtearing of ligament fibers. There can be some minimal swelling, but no joint instability is present.
Grade II: Some pain, edema, ecchymosis, and point tenderness will be found over the involved structures. There will be partial loss of joint motion. Some ligament fibers may be completely torn, but overall stability of the joint remains intact.
Grade III: The ankle will exhibit gross instability with complete tearing of all ligament fibers. Examination will reveal marked swelling and severe pain.

radiographically stable after treatment. Residual symptoms were present in 13% of the functionally treated and 9% of the cast-mobilized ankles. Therefore, acute ankle sprains are optimally treated with functional rehabilitation.

Rehabilitation conditioning and restoration are essential on all levels of play in soccer. It is important for the sports medicine professional to think algorithmically. There are four phases in rehabilitation of the acute ankle sprain (Table 32-2).

Initial treatment includes measures that limit soft-tissue swelling. The popular acronym is PRICE (protection, rest, ice, compression, elevation). The early application of ice reduces posttrauma edema. Ice may also act as a local anesthetic. It should be used 3–4 times daily for 15–20 minutes each time. Compression can be added with an ace wrap and/or air-cast. Progression to phase III and IV is as tolerated. Cross training is essential at all phases to maintain cardiovascular conditioning.

Taping and ankle braces facilitate athletic performance and prevent ankle injuries. Laced up stabilizers, with or without hightop shoes, are more affordable and effective when compared to taping or no preventive measures.

It is important not to overlook injuries to the syndesmosis. Acute rupture of the distal tibiofibular syndesmosis is treated with a syndesmotic screw. Chronic tears should be treated with a syndesmotic screw or arthrodesis.

If this protocol is followed, the athlete with an acute ankle sprain should be able to return to soccer by 6 weeks (Table 32-3). This information should be discussed with the athlete, coach, and parents when the diagnosis is made.

Ankle Impingement Syndromes

Epidemiology

Despite the best rehabilitation programs, there is a subgroup of athletes with residual symptoms. These symptoms include pain, weakness, functional instability, gross instability, and inability to play soccer. As many as 40%–50% of basketball players have residual symptoms from ankle sprains. In up to 15%, symptoms compromise performance.

Table 32-2

Acute Ankle Sprain Rehabilitation	
Goals	*Rehabilitation Elements*
Phase I: Decrease pain and swelling	PRICE
Phase II: Mobilization	Ice, compression, early ROM, WBAT
Phase III: Rehabilitation	Ice, ROM, strengthening, proprioceptive exercises
Phase IV: Functional	Sport-specific functional progression, strengthening, flexibility, proprioceptive exercises

Table 32-3

Guidelines for Return to Soccer After Ankle Sprains	
Acute Ankle Sprains	Return to Activity
Grade I	10–14 days
Grade II	2–6 weeks
Grade III	More than 6 weeks
Residual impingement syndromes	6 weeks–1 year

The descriptive terms for these residual symptoms include chronic ankle sprains, meniscoid lesions, and unstable ankles. This syndrome spectrum should be viewed as an overlapping of pain, instability, and impingement. The definition, classification, diagnosis, and treatment of this subgroup of disorders is the focus of the remainder of this chapter.

History of Ankle Impingement Syndromes

In 1950, Wolin was the first to define the term "chronic ankle sprains" when nine patients experienced intractable anterolateral pain, no instability, and a palpable mass in the anterolateral ankle joint after ankle sprains. He theorized that the mass was hyalinized connective tissue from the talofibular joint capsule. Wolin believed that repeated pinching of the tissue lead to pain and swelling. These patients underwent arthrotomy and exploration. Surgical findings included a meniscoid mass between the fibula and talus in the lateral gutter. Histologic sections revealed a combination of ligamentous, fibrous, fibrocartilaginous, and inflammatory tissue and hypertrophic synovium. The mass of tissue involved with dynamic impingement is more extensive and not localized in the lateral gutter. A dense mass of hypertrophic tissue is found in the anterolateral tibiotalar joint space extending from the anterior capsule posteriorly into the lateral gutter.

Histologically, these studies have corroborated the findings of Wolin and improved our understanding of the pathoanatomic changes leading to anterior capsular impingement.

Identical lesions have been seen in soccer players. A repetitive inversion injury that lead to chronic pain anterolaterally was termed an anterolateral corner compression syndrome. In 1990, Bassett reported impingement from a separate distal fasciae of anterior tibiofibular ligament. He theorized that a tear of the ATFL caused increased laxity, allowing the talar dome to extrude anteriorly in dorsiflexion, causing impingement. Bassett's ligament is present in most human ankles and may be a cause of talar impingement, abrasion of the articular cartilage, and pain in the anterior aspect of the ankle. Resection of this ligament will usually alleviate the pain caused by the impingement.

What is the cause of anterolateral pain seen with chronic ankle sprains? Healing of ligament sprains is accompanied by scarring. Recurrent sprains lead to an abundant scar mass in the area of the ATFL and in the anterolateral capsule. This mass may be a combination of scarified capsule and ligamentous tissue. A stem-like mass of scar tissue and hypertrophic synovium may protrude into the joint. The hypertrophic tissue impedes normal healing and complete symptomatic resolution. With significant impingement, patients fail to improve with conservative means. Sprains may cause ankle ligament laxity and attenuation and, therefore, fail to limit undesirable motions. As a consequence, the ankle becomes relatively unstable. The combination of this occult instability with the pathologic scar mass results in clinical and subjective complaints of pain, functional instability, and loss of function. It is this spectrum from impingement to instability that is our algorithmic focus.

Management of the Injury

Diagnosis is made by employing a systematic approach and maintaining a high level of suspicion. Past ankle injuries and treatments must be considered. Ankle impingement syndrome characteristically involves repetitive sprains and intractable anterolateral ankle pain despite an intensive program of physical therapy, pharmacologic intervention, and rehabilitation. Subjective symptoms include pain with exertional activities, such as pivoting and pushing off. Pain is only present with activities and exercise. Symptoms are often absent before or after exertion. Physical examination reveals anterolateral tenderness, bagginess, and occasionally erythema and diffuse swelling. Plain radiographs and stress views are obtained to corroborate the absence of pathologic ligamentous laxity. Subjective functional instability may be present secondary to pain, but laxity is not a component of the syndrome. Ankle injuries may be divided into unstable (with or without impingement) and stable (with or without impingement). Diagnostic techniques (e.g., bone scan, CT scan, MRI) can facilitate interpretation and aid in diagnosis.

There are many entities that cause anterolateral ankle pain. The astute sports medicine professional includes the possibilities listed in Table 32-4 in the differential diagnosis. Table 32-5 is a proposed classification system for stable ankles with soft tissue impingement symptoms.

Conservative Treatment

There is not much literature on the treatment of this important pathologic entity. Fortunately, arthroscopic intervention has expanded the spectrum of therapeutic alternatives. Anterior capsular impingement requiring arthroscopic surgical intervention represents a small percentage of ankle injuries.

Table 32-4

Differential Diagnosis of Ankle Impingement Pain
1. Osteochondral lesions of the talus
2. Calcific densities beneath the medial or lateral malleoli
3. Peroneal subluxation or dislocation
4. Tarsal coalition
5. Subtalar joint dysfunction
6. Degenerative joint disease

Table 32-5

Ankle Impingement Syndrome Classification

Grade I: Normal radiographs, anterolateral capsular thickening seen on MRI and verified arthroscopically

Grade II: Extraarticular or intraarticular osteophytes with articular surfaces entirely normal

Grade III: Bony abnormalities involving articular surface (i.e., osteochondritis dissecans)

Grade IV: Previous intraarticular fracture

During arthroscopic debridement, the anterior talofibular ligament must not be excised in the attempt to debride the pathologic mass.

The success rate for a properly diagnosed, arthroscopically treated ankle is excellent. Approximately 75%–85% of patients usually have excellent or good results after arthroscopic debridement and return to sports in approximately 6 weeks.

Chronic Ankle Instability

Lofvenberg recently detailed the outcome of nonoperated patients with chronic lateral instability of the ankle in a 20-year follow-up study of patients with chronic lateral ankle instability who were treated conservatively. They were studied 18–23 years after their initial visits. Of the 49 ankles, 32 were still instable. Degenerative changes were observed in 6 of 46 radiographically examined ankles. The key finding of this study was the lack of correlation to age or persistent instability. Although instability may persist, it appears that there is no increased incidence of degenerative changes.

Management of the Injury

Diagnosis of instability requires demonstration of abnormal radiographic stress views. However, stress views can result in contradictory information. Stress testing can be performed in a device that controls the position of the foot and amount of force applied during the examination of inversion testing in the anteroposterior plane and anterior drawer testing in the lateral plane. There is usually no difference in the inversion test between ankles tested in neutral and plantar flexion. In functionally normal ankles, the range of inversion talar tilt is 0°–8° while the maximum of anterior displacement on drawer testing is 3 mm. Anterior drawer testing appears to evaluate lateral ligamentous integrity of the ankle more critically than the talar tilt test. Although stress views have a place in the evaluation of chronic instability, comparison views should also be obtained. Moreover, we have found lateral radiographs with an anterior drawer test to be more helpful than talar tilt comparison. Despite this, an anterior drawer of greater than 3 mm or a talar tilt greater than 5° is considered diagnostic of instability.

The first step in the management of an ankle with chronic instability is to differentiate the entity from the incompletely rehabilitated ankle, which can also be present with chronic anterolateral pain and functional instability. An exhaustive systematic therapy program incorporating strengthening and mobilization, modalities, nonsteroidal antiinflammatory agents, and occasional steroid injections is pursued.

The first step in this therapy program involves a rehabilitation program that uses an initial baseline assessment of range of motion and baseline isokinetic testing. The physical therapy protocol incorporates modalities (ice, phonophoresis, electrical and muscle stimulation), exercise and strengthening (isometrics, isokinetics, and isotonics), range of motion activities (stretching, joint mobilization), and functional progression as indicated with multidirectional exercises, proprioceptive training, and sport simulation.

If the first step is unsuccessful, it is necessary to proceed to the second step, which involves diagnostic arthroscopy and modified Brostrom lateral ligament reconstruction. The success rate of this protocol is 85%–90%.

Summary

In summary, acute ankle sprains must be recognized and rehabilitated aggressively. Nonoperative management with functional bracing is as effective as surgical intervention and results in an earlier return to soccer. One cause of chronic lateral ankle pain is the anterior capsular impingement syndrome. This is an entity that develops in a subgroup of ankles after recurrent sprains. It is characterized by the formation of hypertrophic scar tissue, synovium, and fibrocartilage in the anterolateral aspect of the ankle joint. A constellation of symptoms refractory to conservative management, including pain, weakness, functional instability, and diminution in performance, is the result. Surgical management through arthroscopic debridement has yielded good and excellent results, especially in grade I and grade II injuries.

SUGGESTED READINGS

Attarian DE, McCracken HJ, DeVito DP, et al. Biomechanical study of human lateral ankle ligaments and autogenous reconstructive grafts. Am J Sports Med 1985;13: 377–381.

Baiduini FC, Tetzlaff J. Historical perspectives on injuries of the ligaments of the ankle. Clin Sports Med 1982;1:3–12.

Bassett FH, Gates HS, Billys JB, et al. Talar impingement by the anteroinferior tibiofibular ligament. J Bone Joint Surg 1990;72A:55–59.

Boruta PM, Bishop JO, Braley WG, et al. Ankle acute lateral ligament injuries: a literature review. Foot Ankle 1990;11:107–113.

Cox JS. Surgical and nonsurgical treatment of acute ankle sprains. Clin Orthop 1985;198:118–126.

Ekstrand J, Tropp H. The incidence of ankle sprains in soccer. Foot Ankle 1990;11: 41–44.

Ferkel RD, Karzel RP, Del Pizzo W, et al. Arthroscopic treatment of anterolateral impingement of the ankle. Am J Sports Med 1991;19:440–446.

Kannus P, Renstrom P. Current concepts review: treatment of acute tears of the lateral ligaments of the ankle. J Bone Joint Surg 1991;73A:305–312.

Katznelson EL, Militiano J. Ruptures of the ligaments about the tibio-fibular syndesmosis. Injury 1983;15:170–172.

Konradsen L, Holmer P, Sondergaard L. Early mobilizing treatment for grade III ankle ligament injuries. Foot Ankle 1991;12:69–73.

Lofvenberg R, Karrholm J, Lund B. The outcome of nonoperated patients with
chronic lateral instability of the ankle: a 20-year follow-up study. Foot Ankle
1994;15:165–169.

Wolin L, Glassman F, Sideman S, et al. Internal derangement of the talofibular component of the ankle. Surg Gyn Obstet 1950;91:193–200.

33  Rules and Referees

Per A.F.H. Renstrom

Rules form the framework within which a sport must be conducted. The rules must be established early. The first official rules for soccer were published in 1848 at Trinity College in Cambridge, England. The 17 rules of soccer have been the same for the last 100 years. The current rules in soccer are compiled in a rule book that has been in the same form, with a few exceptions, since 1938. The rules in soccer can only be changed by the International Football Association Board, which was founded in London in 1886. This board consists of four delegates from the Great Britain (English, Scottish, Irish, and Wales) Associations with one representative each and four representatives for the International (Soccer) Football Federation (FIFA). Changes in the rules can only be made at the annual meeting of the board in June and must have at least 75% of the votes of the members present. Regardless of how sensible or appropriate changes may be, the national associations of FIFA are not allowed to make any changes without the prior decision of the board.

Rules and Risk for Injury

Rules are specific for the demands of certain sports. One main objective of rules is to make the sport as safe as possible. This is especially important in a contact sport such as soccer. In top-level international soccer, the rules are often interpreted and applied differently compared to national or local-level soccer. This results in greater risk of injury for the international players.

The danger of attacking from behind has been discussed for many years. There are not rules specific enough to control this potentially traumatic event. Although most players tackle from behind with the intent to reach the ball, it is not uncommon that the intent is to stop a player. This kind of tackling from behind constitutes a major risk for injury.

Tackling from behind may also be a serious distraction since it can often stop the player from scoring a goal. The penalty for such a tackle is usually a free kick and, occasionally, a penalty kick. There is a need for further discussion concerning tackling from behind because of the great potential for injury. Also, the form of punishment should be determined in relation to the magnitude of the distraction.

There either needs to be a rule modification concerning tackling from behind or the existing rules should be enforced. When these rules are changed or enforced, they should be applied strictly and in the same way at all levels of soccer. FIFA finally showed that they recognized the seriousness of these problems by enforcing the rules during the World Cup of 1994. Soccer fans all around the world were grateful for this change of mind by FIFA.

Substitution and Injuries

There are other rule changes that can be discussed. Free substitution of players is possible in most sports. Allowing substitution in soccer decreases the risk of injury. Free substitution is defined as the possibility to substitute players at any time during a match. A recent study looked at an intervention group consisting of 30 randomly chosen test teams. The control group consisted of 15 randomly chosen teams. Both groups were observed for 2 years. The results showed no significant differences between the groups in injury incidence or injury pattern per 1000 match hours. However, in the intervention group, the duration of minor injuries was significantly lower than in the control group. The positive compliance of players, the coach, and referees with the free substitution was remarkable. Although it was concluded that a free substitution rule should be introduced in international soccer, this study needs to be confirmed. If the results are valid, FIFA should allow free substitution. The lack of negative consequences implies that at least modified free substitution should be allowed.

Other Problems

Many international soccer players play in extreme heat or high altitude conditions. It took many years before FIFA changed the rules so that players could drink during the game. Soccer players must be allowed to drink at any time during a game.

There is discussion about whether functional knee braces should be allowed in soccer. Although functional knee braces are not allowed in international soccer, they are allowed in college and high school soccer in the US. Functional knee braces are considered to be a risk for injury. Scientific studies are needed to support this theory.

The Referees

The referees are the key people in the medical supervision of a game. They have several important functions. When a player is injured, the referee must make a quick decision. The referee should be aware of the causes and symptoms of soccer injuries, such as head injuries with or without unconsciousness, chest and stomach/abdominal injuries, injuries to the joints, and fractures. The referee must also observe and make an immediate decision concerning the cause of the trauma, such as foul play, attack by an opponent, ball contact, or falling. Perhaps the referee should be given the right to consult an instant replay video in difficult situations, similar to what is used in ice hockey.

The referee has the power to determine whether injuries should be treated on the field. According to the new rules, the referee is the only one who can allow the doctor or trainer to enter the field. It is stated that the referee should do this when convinced that the player is seriously injured. This puts tremendous responsibility on the referee. After a sign from the referee, two medical assistants can enter the field and make an evaluation of the injured player. This should be done as quickly as possible. All major treatment must be done outside of the playing area. On-field treatment is limited to serious injuries, especially in the case of unconsciousness, shock, and bleeding. The new rules state that the player should be carried off of the field as soon as possible. If the player has a serious injury, which can sometimes be difficult even for an experienced sports medicine doctor to diagnose, it can become worse if not recognized early. Therefore, the demands put on the referee are enormous. The referee must be well educated and use common sense. Unfortunately, there is a lack of sports medicine education for referees.

There are some players that intentionally appear to be the victims of trauma. The closer to the penalty box that the fall occurs, the worse it appears. These players sometimes lay on the field and complain as if they had a serious injury, whether they do or not. This kind of behavior is unacceptable. Players who intentionally imitate a traumatic injury should be given warnings. One way to solve this problem is to have a referee committee look at the TV film from the match and if there is clear simulation of trauma by a player, that player should be given a red card. Faking trauma or injury is not fair play and makes the work of the referees more difficult.

A correct diagnosis must be made before the injury is treated. The ice treatment that is given on the field for almost any injury is an effective painkiller and can mask the extent and severity of an injury. If a severe muscle hematoma is iced, there will be a decrease in pain and the injury may become worse when the player returns to the game. The medical responsibility must always rest with the doctor. However, the referees can be instrumental if they have an education in sports medicine. Therefore, courses in sports medicine should be organized for referees.

Role of the Team Doctor

The demands on the doctor can be high because they have a double loyalty. There is potential conflict in the employer mandate versus the player. Pressures from the coach, athletes, and the employer should be evaluated against medical indications. Sports medicine doctors often have no specific written contract. Cooperation with the team is often based on a gentleman's agreement. There is no established minimum salary and the majority of the work is done voluntarily without financial reward.

The doctor often faces a dilemma when treating athletes. He must consider the interest of the patient and medical ethics (Table 33-1). The medical ethics should be compared to the sports medicine ethics, which can differ.

Responsibility of Others

Coaches have a great responsibility and are always under pressure. They are placed in a difficult position because they carry the blame for the success or failure of the team. Coaches have been known to send players on the field with instructions to stop opponents by any means possible. Coaches should

Table 33-1

Issues that Doctors Must Consider
<ul><li>The main goal is the health of the athlete</li><li>Sports medicine activities must never cause an injury, make an injury arise, or make an injury worse</li><li>The individual has the right to decide over his/her life and body</li></ul>

participate in campaigns to eliminate all unfair tactics, unsportsman-like conduct, and maneuvers deliberately inflicting injury.

Rule Changes

The rules should continuously be adjusted and changed as the sport itself changes. Soccer rules may need adjustments based on opinions from different points of view. See Table 33-2 for some considerations.

When soccer rules change, it is important that orthopaedic sports medicine specialists and other team doctors are given the chance to analyze possible injury risks that may result from the new rules. Although a rule can be changed with good intent, there can be an increased risk of injury because of the new rule. Therefore, every new rule must be analyzed by sports medicine experts. Rules are often changed to control unreasonable danger. To understand the risks and danger in soccer, it is important to collect soccer injury data. There are several studies available in the literature that study soccer injury incidence. Studies should be supported by the soccer community and FIFA. Without an awareness of what injuries occur in soccer and how they occur, injures cannot be prevented. Soccer players that are at a high risk for injury must also be identified.

It is also necessary to understand the complex interaction of possible risk factors in soccer. It is necessary to have increased knowledge about the etiology of soccer injuries. Intrinsic risk factors include increased joint flexibility and muscle tightness, functional instability, previous injuries, and inadequate rehabili-

Table 33-2

Possible Rule Changes in Soccer
<ul><li>Increasing interest of the public results in the demand for more scoring</li><li>Moving offside line to the middle of the attacking field</li><li>Kicking the ball from the side instead of throwing it</li><li>Playing with fewer players or increased substitutions</li><li>Increasing the size of the goal</li><li>Changing how to decide a game that ends in a draw</li><li>Changing rules due to economic and administrative considerations</li><li>Changing rules according to injury prevention and sports medicine research</li></ul>

Table 33-3

Guidelines Followed by the NCAA
1. Safety for the athletes
2. Applicable for all institutions
3. A coachable rule
4. Administrable to all officials
5. Balance of offense and defense
6. Interest in spectators
7. Economic impact not probibited

tation. The menstrual cycle and use of oral contraceptives, maximal aerobic capacity, and certain soccer skills are associated with soccer injuries. These findings need further confirmation. Extrinsic risk factors associated with soccer injuries include inadequate equipment such as shin guards and shoes, playing field conditions, and foul play. In our investigation from Goteborg, Sweden, we found a relationship between injury risk and play on different turfs. These results showed that injury trauma and the type of injury differ between different turfs. Therefore, rules need to be clear and specific. Rule adjustments can be made according to the techniques used by the NCAA (Table 33-3).

It is not possible to have a completely injury-free sport. Athletes will continue to ignore the rules and injuries will occur. The skill levels between players will vary and, thereby, increase the risk for injury.

Summary

Soccer cannot be adequately played and controlled without rules. If the rules are not followed or increase the risk for injury, they should be changed. If effectively enforced, well thought out rules can decrease the frequency and severity of injuries in soccer. Rule changes should be analyzed by sports medicine experts to ensure that they do not increase the risk for injury. With the new rules, referees are given great authority to decide the seriousness of injuries. This puts added stress and responsibility on referees. To manage this new role, referees need sports medicine education. It is also important to try to minimize and prevent soccer injuries. This can best be done by increasing knowledge of existing traumas and injuries, which requires sports medicine research. This research should be supported by FIFA and the soccer world as a whole.

SUGGESTED READINGS

Eissmann HJ. The referees in football. Ekblom B, ed. An IOC Medical Commission Publication. Oxford, England: Blackwell Scientific Publication, 1994;1OO–101.

Inklaar H. Soccer injuries II: etiology and prevention. Sports Med, 1994;18:81–93.

Jorgensen U, Sorensen J. Free substitution in soccer: a prospective study. In: Togt van der CR, Kenper ABA, Koornneef M. Proceedings of the 3rd meeting Council of Europe. Sports injuries and their prevention. Oosterbeek: National Institute for Sports Health Care, 1988.

Peterson L, Renstrom P. Soccer injuries: frequency and type. Lakartidningen 1980;77: 3621–3626.

34  Late Results and Sequelae After Soccer

Ejnar Eriksson
Lars-Ingle Svensson,
Tho Kam San,
Anders Valentin

Soccer is popular worldwide. It is estimated that at least 40 million people play soccer. Therefore, soccer is the source of a large number of injuries. Many studies have determined the incidence of different types of injuries in soccer. Few, however, have studied the long-term effects of soccer injuries. One example is the work of Roos and colleagues who reported the prevalence of radiographic signs of knee osteoarthrosis and the relation to past knee injuries. They compared 286 former soccer players with 572 age-matched controls. The subjects averaged 55 years of age. The prevalence of knee osteoarthrosis among the controls was 1.6%, in the nonathlete soccer players it was 4.2%, and in the top players it was 15.5%. Of the 71 elite players studied, 7 had an anterior cruciate ligament (ACL) injury and 40 had undergone meniscectomies.

Neyret reported on a minimum 20-year follow-up of 77 soccer players who had meniscus resection for an isolated meniscus injury or a combination of meniscus and ACL tear. The group with isolated meniscus injury showed radiologic evidence of osteoarthritis in 24% while the ACL tear group showed evidence of osteoarthritis in 77%. In the isolated group, 49% were involved in sports, while no more than 22% of the ACL insufficient players were active in sports.

Most long-term studies deal with relatively limited groups of soccer players. Sweden offers a unique opportunity to study large groups of athletes. Soccer is the most popular sport in Sweden with 165,000 registered soccer players in 1990. Sweden does not have the high school or university sports organizations found in the US. All soccer players in Sweden play for a soccer club. When the players join the club and pay the membership fee, they are automatically insured with Folksam, an insurance company. This insurance company maintains a unique database of injuries. Mainly the severe injuries are reported to the Folksam insurance company. Minor injuries that only result in a short time away from sports are probably not fully reported. Permanent disabilities are frequently reported since athletes can receive substantial economic benefits from such reports.

The Folksam insurance company has regularly published reports of the injury frequency in soccer and most other sports. The aim of this chapter is to review the incidence of soccer injuries in a large group of Swedish soccer players and to study the incidence and nature of permanent disabilities in this group.

The Findings of Folksam

From 1976–1983, Folksam registered 10,659 injuries in soccer. These data were reported and analyzed in a report by Folksam in 1985. From 1986–1990, 26,015 injuries were collected in the same way. To compare the changes in the patterns of injuries, the data from 1986, 1988, and 1990 were analyzed and published by Folksam in 1994. The injuries from 1986–1990 that resulted in permanent disability were analyzed. The injury data were classified by age distribution, level of play (elite to juniors), and sex. A large number of soccer clubs in the elite division, first to seventh divisions, junior clubs, and boys clubs were contacted to develop an average exposure time for players at different levels and for male and female players. This data was used to relate the injury frequency with the time of exposure.

The total number of injuries and the number of injuries analyzed from 1986–1990 are shown in Table 34-1. Notice that less than half of all injuries that occurred were examined, while approximately 90% of injuries that resulted in permanent disability were examined. The distribution of injuries according to levels of play is shown in Table 34-2. Although injuries to players in the elite and first division make up 6% (men) and 9% (women) of all injuries, these players only represent 1%–2% of all the insured players. The exposure time for sustaining an injury in the different divisions for men and women can be seen in Table 34-3. From these data it can be concluded that the higher the divison, the higher the incidence of injuries. The causes of the soccer injuries that occurred in 1990 are given in Table 34-4. For men, over 40% of the injuries were due to a collision or from a kick or blow. For women, approximately 50% of the injuries were due to the same factors as the men, in addition to getting their feet stuck on the ground. The anatomic distribution of the different injuries is shown in Table 34-5. In men, 49% of the total injuries

Table 34-1

					Relative Injury Frequency by Sex and Year			
Year	Number of injuries	Number examined	%	Number of insured	Injury frequency/ 1000 insurance	Male	Female
1986	4605	1980	43	188,152	24	25	24
1987	4859			187,042	26		
1988	5128	2353	46	184,821	28	28	27
1989	5720			179,618	32		
1990	5703	2535	44	165,396	34	35	33
Total	26,015	6868					

Year	Number of permanent disabilities	Number examined	%
1986–90	1500	1312	87

Table 34-2

Distribution of Injuries in Different Series of Soccer in Sweden			
Males	Number of injuries	%	% of all insured
Elite & 1st division	126	6	1
2nd–3rd division	237	12	3
4th division & lower	1175	59	62
Juniors	259	13	14
Boys	157	8	20
Missing	50	2	0
Total	**2004**		
Females	Number of injuries	%	% of all insured
Elite & 1st division	41	9	2
2nd div & lower	304	64	39
Juniors	41	9	22
Girls	77	16	36
Missing	9	2	0
Total	**472**		

Table 34-3

Injury Frequency per 1000 Hours Match and Training for Injuries During 1990		
Males	Injury/1000 hours	Injury/1000 insured
Elite & 1st division	0.71	346
2nd–3rd division	0.36	121
4th division & lower	0.14	33
Juniors	0.13	31
Boys	0.06	14
Total	**0.14**	**35**
Females	Injury/1000 hours	Injury/1000 insured
Elite & 1st division	0.37	126
2nd div & lower	0.21	54
Juniors	0.06	13
Girls	0.07	15
Total	**0.14**	**33**

Table 34-4

	Cause of Injuries that occurred in 1990			
	Males		Females	
Cause	Number of injuries	%	Number of injuries	%
Collision	405	20	96	20
Kick or blow	433	21	77	16
Fall	116	6	28	6
Foot stuck on ground	187	9	59	12
Tackling	155	8	32	7
Hit by ball	70	3	35	7
Traffic injury	7	0	4	0
Twist	134	7	45	9
Wear	65	3	14	3
Overuse	88	4	14	3
Hitting the ball simultaneously	60	3	15	3
Heading-duel	87	4	8	2
Other causes	137	7	33	7
No information	106	5	25	5
Total	**2050**		**485**	

Table 34-5

	Males		Females	
Injured part	Number of injuries	%	Number of injuries	%
Head	127	6	35	7
Teeth	211	10	21	4
Shoulder	88	4	9	2
Breast	13	1	4	1
Neck and back	94	5	20	4
Arm	38	2	10	2
Hand	142	6	31	6
Hip and abdomen	88	4	13	3
Knee	609	30	210	43
Leg	183	9	24	5
Foot	386	19	91	19
Multiple injuries	34	2	8	2
No information	37	2	9	2
Total	**2050**		**485**	

were to the knee and foot. In women, the knee and foot accounted for 62% of all injuries. The percentage of permanent disability for different parts of the body in all the male injuries that occurred in 1986–1990 is shown in Table 34-6. These data show that the knee was the main site of injury that resulted in some degree of disability. The data from knee injuries in males was classified by specific type of knee injury (Table 34-7). These results show that isolated or combined injuries to the anterior cruciate ligament are the major source of disability. The same data for women are shown in Tables 34-8 and 34-9. Soccer does not result in the highest degree of permanent disability when compared to other sports insured by Folksam (Table 34-10).

What the Findings Mean

The Folksam report of 1976–1983 showed an over representation of knee injuries. The same is even more true for the study of 1986–1990. Although the number of insured soccer players has diminished, the total number of injuries has increased from 10,659 to 26,015. This could be due to the bad economics of Sweden, which probably caused more players to report minor injuries. The increase of permanent disabilities from 427 to 1500 is more disturbing. It cannot be ruled out that soccer has become a more physical game.

It is often thought that the incidence of soccer injuries is highest in the lower divisions, in which the players are fairly unskilled. These data do not support that theory. The risk of sustaining an injury is approximately six times higher in the elite players than players in the lower divisions.

When the different permanent disabilities are analyzed, it is evident that knee injuries, especially the anterior cruciate ligament injury in combination with other injuries to the knee, lead to the largest number of permanent disabilities. The degree of permanent disability for these injuries is mostly 5%–10%. This usually means that the players have given up their sport careers or have selected to play in lower divisions. However, the players are still able to work. The primary mechanism of these ACL injuries seems to have occurred when the player's foot became stuck in the ground and the body rotated around the lower leg. To reduce this high incidence of ACL injuries and diminish their permanent disability, it is necessary to first try to prevent ACL injuries. Studies on the length of cleats and friction between different types of cleats and different types of surfaces are important. It may be that different methods of cutting the grass or different types of artificial turf influence the rate of ACL injuries. Studies on the possibility of preventing ACL injuries with different types of muscular training should also be undertaken. The diagnosis and treatment of ACL injuries should also be improved. It has been pointed out by Roos that there is no difference in the outcome of ACL injuries in operatively and nonoperatively treated patients. Technical procedures (e.g., the unit-tunnel drill guide) may influence such findings. Recent work has shown that such a drill guide sometimes leads to a less advantageous positioning of the reconstructed ACL. The absence of a difference between treated and untreated ACL injuries could be due to improper placement of the ACL graft in the operated cases. In a long-term follow-up of patients with ACL injuries whose ligament was repaired with an

Table 34-6

Males				Degree of Permanent Disability per Different Parts of the Body									
	1–4%	5%	6%	7%	8%	9%	10%	12%	15%	20%	25%	70%	Total
Eye		1			1		3			1			6
Head & face	3	7		3			3					1	17
Shoulder	6	11			1		2						20
Neck & back	1	4					1		2				8
Arm & elbow	4	8		1	1		2		1				17
Wrist	2	12		3	2						1		20
Hand	4	6		3	2		2		1				18
Finger	14	4		1									19
Hip, abdomen	1	4					1						6
Knee	45	435	1	22	67	1	149	6	20				746
Leg	14	35			4		3	1	1	1			59
Thigh		2											2
Ankle	9	37		5	4		7	1	3				66
Foot & heel	7	9			2								18
Multiple injuries	1	6					1				1		9
Missing		4											4
Total	111	585	1	38	84	1	174	8	28	2	2	1	1035

Table 34-7

Distribution of Permanent Disability in Different Types of Knee Injuries									
Males	1–4%	5%	6%	7%	8%	9%	10%	12%	15%	Total
Meniscus injury	5	19		3	3		2		1	33
Collateral ligament	4	13					4			21
ACL	21	195	1	6	30		55	3	6	317
PCL		13		1	2		6			22
Joint line		5					1		1	7
Knee cap	3	6					4			13
Meniscus & ACL	6	96		8	17	1	37		2	167
ACL + other injuries	5	77		4	13		35	2	8	144
Other injuries without ACL	1	11			1		5	1	2	21
Missing					1					1
Total	45	435	1	22	67	1	149	6	20	746

Table 34-8

Degree of Permanent Disability per Different Parts of the Body									
Females	1–4%	5%	6%	7%	8%	10%	12%	15%	20%	Total
Eye	1					1				2
Head & face					1					1
Neck, back	1									1
Hand	5						1			6
Finger	2			1						3
Hip, abdomen	2	3								5
Knee	16	143	2	8	18	45	1	4	1	238
Leg	4	4								8
Thigh		1								1
Ankle	2	4				1				7
Foot & heel	3	1								4
Missing		1								1
Total	35	158	2	9	19	47	2	4	1	277

Table 34-9

Distribution of Permanent Disability on Different Types of Knee Injuries

Females	1–4%	5%	6%	7%	8%	10%	12%	15%	20%	Total
Meniscus injury	3	4								7
Collateral ligament					1					1
ACL	7	84	2	4	6	24	1	2	1	131
Joint line		2								2
Knee cap	1	3			1	1				6
Meniscus & ACL	2	26		1	8	10		1		48
ACL + other injuries	2	20		2	1	9				34
Other injuries without ACL	1	3		1				1		6
Missing		1			1	1				3
Total	16	143	2	8	18	45	1	4	1	238

Table 34-10

Average Degree of Permanent Disabilities in Different Sports; 1986–1990

Sports	Degree of permanent disability	Permanent disability per 1000 insurances
Rugby	6.9	3.05
Team handball	6.3	2.00
Soccer	6.3	1.66
Basketball	7.0	1.10
Bandy	8.1	0.77
Floor Ball	6.0	0.45
Freestyle skiing	6.0	10.33
Alpine skiing	8.0	1.40
Wrestling	12.9	0.97
Gymnastics	11.2	0.35
Martial arts	9.2	0.19
Cross country skiing	9.9	0.13

isometric technique at the Karolinska Hospital, it was found that 5–10 years after ACL reconstruction approximately 70% of the players were still active in sports and did not diminish their degree of activity.

Rule changes or reinforcing existing rules should be considered as a way to diminish injuries from collisions, kicks, blows, or rough tackling.

The costs to the Swedish society for these permanent disabilities in Sweden is estimated to be approximately $4,000,000 based on an annual incidence of 500 permanent disabilities. For the US, that figure corresponds with $120,000,000. It is disturbing to see that popular sports lead to so many injuries with such a disturbingly high frequency of permanent disabilities. Therefore, it is essential that all who engage in soccer do everything possible to reduce the frequency of injury.

SUGGESTED READINGS

Feller JA, Glisson RR, Seaber AV, et al. Graft isometry in a unitunnel anterior cruciate ligament reconstruction: analysis of influential factors using a radiogaphic model. Knee Surg Sports Traumatol Arthroscopy 1993;1:136–142.

Folksam. Idrottsskador (Sports Injuries) 1986-1990. A report from Folksam. Stockholm, Sweden: Folksam, 1994.

Folksam. Sports Injuries 1976-1983. A report from Folksam. Stockholm, Sweden: Folksam, 1985.

Johnson RJ, Eriksson E, Haggmark T, et al. Five to ten year follow-up evaluation after reconstruction of the anterior cruciate ligament. Clin Orthop 1984;183:122–140.

Lindberg H, Roos H, Gardsell P. Prevalence of coxarthrosis in former soccer players. Acta Orthop Scand 1993;64:165–167.

Neyret P, Simon TD, Dejour D, et al. Partial meniscectomy and anterior cruciate ligament rupture in soccer players: a study with a minimum 20 year follow-up. Am J Sports Med 1993;21:455–460.

Odensten M, Gillquist J. A modified technique for anterior cruciate ligament (ACL) surgery using a new drill guide for isometric positioning of the ACL. Clin Orthop 1986;213:154–158.

Roos H. Exercise, knee injury and osteoarthrosis. Academic Thesis. Lund, Sweden: Lund University, 1994.

Roos H, Lindberg H, Gardsell P, et al. The prevalence of gonarthrosis in former soccer players and its relation to meniscectomy. Am J Sports Med 1994;22:219–222.

V

• Injury Prevention & Rehabilitation

35 ⚽ **Warmup and Stretching**

William E. Garrett, Jr.

Introduction

Stretching and warmup are advocated by most athletes and sports medicine personnel as a way to improve and maintain flexibility, improve performance, and prevent injury. Although this is a widely held belief, the scientific basis for stretching is not well developed. The scientific rationale is different than that available for strength training, endurance training, and anaerobic training for which there is a highly developed body of physiological literature to quantify the advantages and proper techniques of gaining improvements in those areas. For warmup and flexibility, the basic principles remain in an early stage of development and the clinical application lags even further behind.

We can define flexibility as a total range of motion available to a joint or a body segment containing several contiguous joints. That range of motion will be limited by the inherent range of motion available to the joint and to limitations on that motion by muscles that cross the joint. For instance, the knee can be fully extended when the hip is in a neutral position. The amount of extension is limited by intrinsic structures of the knee. However, when the hip is maximally flexed, knee extension is significantly limited for most people. Limitations under the latter conditions include tightness in the posterior thigh muscles and the hamstrings, whose inherent extensibility will not allow the knee to be extended. Generally, flexibility and warmup are done to improve or increase the range of motion allowed by the muscles rather than the joints themselves. This chapter will concentrate on the muscular contributions to flexibility and warmup.

Basic Science of Muscle Stretching

Warmup and stretching can be considered from two standpoints. First, the acute effects of warmup and stretching must be evaluated. Secondly, the chronic effects of repeated stretch must be evaluated. The effects of warmup and stretching should also be evaluated in two ways. The changes in muscle that effect its performance must be examined. Also, the changes in muscle that might effect its propensity to injury must be considered.

A number of texts and manuals emphasize that the response seen by muscle to acute stretching is probably due to reflex activity within the muscle. Sensory receptors within the muscle are related to the spinal cord and the active resistance of muscle to stretching is inhibited. Although there is probably some component of active resistance to muscle stretching, it is much more likely that most of the resistance is due to the inherent viscoelasticity of the muscle unaffected by any activation of muscular contraction by the nervous system. Electromyography studies of muscle stretching show near complete silence. It is incorrect to assume that muscle near its limit of flexibility is being limited because of active resistance. Connective tissue in the form of ligaments, tendons, or bones all have inherent viscoelastic characteristics. Among the viscoelastic properties of connective tissue are stress relaxation, creep, and strain-rate dependence. The property of stress relaxation defines the response of connective tissue that is stretched to a certain length and held at that length. Although shortening is not allowed, the force or stress measured within that muscle declines or relaxes with time. A purely elastic material would maintain the same resistance following stretch. Therefore, this is a property that is both elastic and viscous. The property of creep describes the condition of muscle when a given load is applied to it. The muscle initially stretches to a certain length. After attaining this length there is a slow, time dependent increase in length over time (Fig. 35-1). Finally, the response of muscle to applications of forces or stretches is dependent on the rate at which the strains or stretches are applied. A muscle loaded faster will have a higher load than a muscle loaded slowly (Fig. 35-2).

Stretching is often done as a series. Laboratory studies on animals have shown that a muscle repeatedly stretched until a given force was reached, and then relaxed and stretched again, showed progressive increase in the length of the muscle. The change seems to plateau after 3–5 stretches held for no more than 30 seconds. Finally, a muscle repeatedly cycled between stretches to a given length will show a continuous decrement in force with subsequent stretches. These properties make it clear that the viscoelasticity existing in muscle is similar to that seen in other connective tissue, such as ligaments and tendons. It was also apparent in these early studies that cutting the nerves supplying the muscle made no difference in the response of

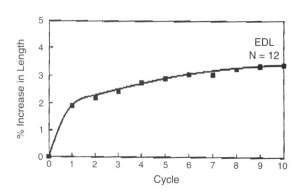

Figure 35-1. Increase in muscle length with repeated stretching to the same tension. The major portion of the increase in length occurs during the first four stretches.

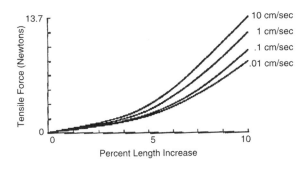

Figure 35-2. The effect of loading rate on the force-length relationship.

the muscle. In addition, no electrical activity was recorded within the muscles showing lack of reflex activation.

These acute changes seen in response to stretching mean that muscle is less stiff after stretching. It can attain the same length with less tension developed within the muscle. This may certainly effect the flexibility.

Stretching and Injury Prevention

Although it is believed that acute stretching makes muscle less susceptible to acute injury, these beliefs do not have a firm scientific basis. Recent studies have shown, however, that muscles subjected to a routine of cyclic stretching and active activation followed by a biomechanical test to failure seem to be protected from injury. Muscles not stretched and warmed up showed micro-failure at a much shorter length than the preconditioned muscle and reached macro-failure at a longer length. These laboratory studies lend support to the common belief that stretching can prevent acute muscle injury.

The chronic effects of stretching have also been evaluated by basic science models. These studies have generally not taken the form of routine stretching exercises. Rather, they have looked at the response of muscle to chronic stretch, such as that due to immobilization, in either a lengthened or shortened position. Immobilization in a lengthened or stretched position causes a longitudinal growth of muscle. In immature animals, both the muscle fibers and tendons lengthen. In mature animals, the muscle fibers grow in length as the muscle fibers lengthen at the region of the muscle-tendon junction. Skeletal muscle does not have a growth plate like the skeleton. The primary factor causing length increase in muscle may be the stretch imposed by the growing skeleton. The lengthened muscle also develops more tension prior to failure.

Flexibility Training

In clinical and athletic practice, flexibility is defined as the range of motion possible in a joint. There is a range of motion inherent to a joint itself. In addition, under certain conditions the muscles can limit joint motion. As stated earlier, with maximal hip flexion the knee usually cannot be fully extended due to tightness in the hamstrings. In general, flexibility training is designed to lengthen the muscles that limit the motion.

Flexibility can be increased with specific training. Stretching exercises can be successful if done regularly and properly. Several techniques are often advocated.

Stretching Techniques

BALLISTIC

Ballistic stretching involves bouncing motions and fast stretching of muscle. This is not widely used due to a potential for injury to muscle.

STATIC

Static stretching involves a slow and steady stretch of muscle. Sustained stretches of 5–30 seconds allow for the previously discussed viscoelastic changes to occur in the stretched muscle groups. Several slow stretches seem to be beneficial, although most of the length increase occurs with the first stretches.

PROPRIOCEPTIVE NEUROMUSCULAR FACILITATION (PNF)

There are several different techniques of PNF. These are thought to help inhibit reflex contractility in the stretched muscle. Although muscle contractility infrequently limits muscle stretch, the routine practice of PNF has produced increased flexibility.

All three stretching techniques have been successful in producing increases in the muscle flexibility immediately after the stretch. To improve the inherent muscle flexibility on a day-to-day basis requires regular and diligent practice. Muscle flexibility is also increased with heat. Therefore, passive warming of muscle or an active warmup to increase the intramuscular temperature is helpful. For the most effective stretching regimen, the muscle should be warm, which cannot be accomplished by stretching itself. A program to increase flexibility should be done approximately three times a week. Maintaining flexibility increases requires stretching on a regular basis.

For participation in sport, it is probably best to warmup with relatively gentle exercise followed by stretch of the necessary muscle groups. It is also helpful to warmup and stretch after cooling or long periods of inactivity in competition. A final stretch after exercise is also helpful.

Flexibility and Soccer

There have also been investigations specific to soccer. Ekstrand and others have shown that soccer players are less flexible than normal individuals in hip abduction, hip extension, knee flexion, and ankle dorsiflexion. Soccer players were more flexible only in hip flexion. Two-thirds of soccer players had one or more less flexible muscle groups.

It has also been shown that a supervised injury prevention program, including flexibility training, was successful in reducing the injury rate. After heavy exercise there is a decrease in muscle flexibility for several days. A post exercise stretching program was shown to be successful in eliminating this loss of flexibility.

In summary, it is apparent that stretching and flexibility exercises can produce changes in muscle that increase the immediate flexibility of a muscle. Longer periods of stretch or regular stretching routines can increase the flexibility of muscle. There is good theoretical reason to consider that flexibility can decrease the potential for muscle injury. In addition, a regular flexibility program seems to be beneficial in the reduction of injury rate in soccer and sports in general.

SUGGESTED READINGS

Ekstrand J, Gillquist J. Soccer injuries and their mechanisms: a prospective study. Med and Science in Sports and Exer 1983;15:267–270.

Ekstrand J, Gillquist J. The frequency of muscle tightness and injuries in soccer players. Amer J Sports Med 1982;10:75–78.

Ekstrand J, Gillquist J, Möller M, et al. Incidence of soccer injuries and their relation to training and team success. Amer J Sports Med 1983;11:63–67.

Hughes GC IV, Hasselman CT, Best TM, et al. The effect of a combined regimen of stretching and muscle activation on prevention of experimental muscle strain injury, In press.

Kime RC III, Seaber AV, Garrett WE Jr. Effect of passive tension during immobilization on muscle biomechanical properties. Surg Forum 1989;4:518.

Taylor DC, Dalton JD Jr, Seaber AV, et al. Viscoelastic properties of muscle-tendon units: the biomechanical effects of stretching. Amer J Sports Med 1990;18:300–309.

Taylor DC, Seaber AV, Garrett WE Jr. Cyclic repetitive stretching on muscle-tendon units. Surg Forum 1985;36:539.

Wiktorsson-Möller M, Öberg B, Ekstrand J, et al. Effects of warming up, massage, and stretching on range of motion and muscle strength in the lower extremity. Amer J Sports Med 1983;11:249–252.

Zachazewski JE. Flexibility in sports. In: Sanous B, ed. Physical therapy. Stanford, CT: Appleton Lange Publishers, 1991;201–238.

Zachazewski JE. Improving flexibility. In: Barnes ML, Scully RM, eds. Physical therapy. Philadelphia, PA: J.B. Lippincott, 1989;698–738.

36  Taping, Bracing, and Protective Equipment

Ray Jaffet
Richard Lopez

Ankle

Soccer, like any contact sport, has an inherent risk of injury. The incidence of soccer injuries during a season ranges from 70%–90%. Most of these injuries (64%–88%) involve the lower limb, with the ankle being the most frequently injured joint. Consequently, athletic trainers and other sports medicine personnel have attempted to reduce the incidence of initial and recurrent injuries. Through the years, a variety of prevention strategies have been employed. Efforts to enhance the dynamic stability of the ankle have included muscle strengthening, heel cord stretching, adequate warm up, specially designed footwear, and taping. Despite these efforts, an extremely high incidence of ankle sprains has persisted. Recently, new prophylactic measures have been taken. These include the development of lace-up and semirigid ankle braces.

Taping

Traditionally, nonelastic adhesive taping has been the preferred method used to reduce the number and severity of ankle injuries. Recently, its effectiveness as a prophylactic measure has been questioned. Although the prophylactic value of taping is supported by anecdotal evidence and some clinical data, there is some question regarding its ability to provide support over time. Several studies have shown that tape loosens within 10 minutes of exercise, providing only 50%–60% of its original support. One study showed that after 1 hour of exercise taping may offer no support. On the other hand, some studies suggest significant support retention. Explanations for the different findings include variations in taping procedures, the type of exercise employed, and the conditions under which the exercise occurred. Some possible variations in the taping procedures include the type of tape used, the orientation of the taping strips relative to the axis of ankle motion, the amount of tension applied to the strips, the experience of the trainer applying the strips, the use or absence of prewrap, the use of benzion, and the degree of adherence to the skin. Variations in the intensity of exercise and the types of movement employed could also affect the laxity of the tape. Finally, because perspiration reduces the adherence of the tape to the skin, environmental factors, such as heat and humidity, can affect support retention.

Although taping loses some of its support with time, there is epidemiological evidence to show that taping is effective in reducing the incidence of ankle sprains. One study concluded that ankle taping may lose some of its support, however, it is still effective in limiting the extremes of motion associated with ankle inversion sprains. Another explanation for the effectiveness of taping is that it can alter the proprioceptive function of the ankle joint by stimulating the contraction of the peroneus brevis muscle.

A criticism of ankle taping is the expense of materials and labor. Table 36–1 shows the possible savings if a 12 person basketball team was braced instead of taped. This assumes that the cost of taping a basketball player over a 25 week basketball season would average $435 and the braces would cost (based on two pairs per season) approximately $160.

Braces

Ankle braces are an alternative to taping. The increasing popularity of ankle bracing is in part due to the superiority of ankle braces over taping in reducing ankle injuries. Unlike taping, the semirigid ankle braces restrict ankle inversion before and after exercise. Braces are also considerably less expensive over the course of a season and can be applied without the assistance of a trainer. This increases the amount of playing time available, which is important when athletes arrive at a site and the amount of time available for practice is limited.

A common design objective of braces is to restrict eversion and inversion movements while permitting maximal plantar flexion and dorsiflexion. There are a variety of designs for ankle braces (Table 36–2). The lace-up and sleeve-like braces are similar in appearance to spats. They are often constructed of canvas material and cover the midfoot and ankles. They are worn over socks and laced similar to a shoe. The semirigid bimalleolar orthosis is made of thermoplastic material and generally contains preinflated air cells. The air cells are positioned on the inner walls of the supports to protect the ankle from pressure injuries and improve ankle stability. It is worn over a sock and held in place by velcro straps. The strut-like orthosis consists of a hard plastic posterior strut, which is positioned directly along the posterior axis of the tibia. The strut is connected to a heel cup and secured to the heel counter of the shoe with velcro tab fasteners. A velcro calf strap affixes the brace proximally.

Table 36-1

Estimated Cost Savings Using Braces Instead of Taping for a Basketball Team		
	Taping	Bracing
$ per player	$435	$160
× 12 players	$5220	$1920
Savings		$3300

Table 36-2

Types of Ankle Braces
• Lace-up braces
• Sleeve-like braces made of fabric
• Semi-rigid bimalleolar orthoses
• Posterior strut orthoses with rigid heel cups

BRACES VERSUS TAPING

Research suggests that the lace-up ankle braces are superior to taping in preventing ankle injuries. Taping is relatively ineffective in preventing injuries and reinjuries in six seasons of collegiate football practice and games. The ineffectiveness of taping may be due to the fact that athletes can get taped 6 hours before the game or practice, which results in loose tape before the game or practice even begins. On the other hand, lace-up stabilizers are self-applied and can easily be retightened to their level of maximal support.

Semirigid ankle braces are effective in reducing the incidence of ankle sprains among soccer players with previously injured ankles. The braces also reduce the incidence of more severe ankle sprains in players with a history of previous ankle injuries. The braces may not alter the incidence of ankle sprains in previously uninjured ankles. Other data suggest that athletes without braces have three times the risk of ankle injuries than athletes with braces.

Some of the literature comparing the effectiveness of bracing (laced and semirigid bimalleolar) to taping has demonstrated their effects in restricting joint motion. Braces and tape both restrict eversion and inversion before exercise. After exercise, however, braces and taping permit considerable eversion. Following exercise, the semirigid bimalleolar brace is the most successful in restricting inversion. Other data support the use of braces over taping in limiting inversion after exercise (walking and running on a laterally tilted treadmill).

Until recently, the benefits of bracing and taping were attributed to the stability they provided in restricting eversion and inversion. Taping and lace-up braces lose a significant amount of their restricting ability while still providing some protection against injury, suggesting that other mechanisms may contribute to their protective effect. Taping may alter proprioceptive function of the ankle joint by stimulating the contraction of the peroneus brevis muscle during the swing phase of running. Although this has been studied for taping and not bracing, this effect probably applies to any external support that is attached firmly enough to stimulate the mechanoreceptors of the skin. It is possible that external support of the ankle joint may reduce the incidence of injury, particularly in the previously injured ankle, by improving the functional stability of the ankle.

A COMPARISON OF BRACES IN RESTRICTING MOTION

Much of the recent research related to ankle prophylaxis emphasizes comparisons of the different available braces. The support provided before and after exercise by a lace-up brace, bimalleolar brace, and strut-type brace was compared. The lace-up brace lost significantly more support with exercise, while the strut-type brace lost no support and the bimalleolar brace lost some support.

The bimalleolar brace and the strut-like brace restrict inversion and eversion before exercise. Both braces permit significantly greater eversion after exercise and provide more eversion support than the unbraced condition. More importantly, both braces significantly restrict inversion following exercise. The strut-like brace, however, provides greater support against inversion than the semirigid bimalleolar brace.

The four most common commercial braces, including the lace-up brace, semirigid bimalleolar brace, strut-like brace, and neoprene velcro strap brace, were compared in their ability to limit eversion and inversion before and after exercise. All braces restricted eversion and inversion before exercise. The strut-like brace and the semirigid bimalleolar brace were more effective in restricting motion than the lace-up brace or the neoprene velcro strap brace.

It appears that taping provides good initial support, even greater than bracing, but loses much of its restraining ability over time. The lace-up brace and the neoprene velcro strap brace also lose much of their restraining ability with exercise. The strut-like brace and the semirigid bimalleolar brace are the most effective in restricting inversion movements following exercise.

Another consideration in the selection of braces is the athlete's receptivity to the braces. Most athletes report that the strut-like braces and the semirigid bimalleolar braces provide more support, while the neoprene velcro strap brace and the lace-up brace are more comfortable. It could be that comfort and stability are inversely related. During a season, athletes change their opinions from negative to mostly positive about the effectiveness and benefits of braces. This change in attitude is important because of its implications for compliance. The findings also suggest that the more an athlete uses a brace, the more likely the athlete is to accept its value. Nonetheless, comfort and compliance must be considered.

THE EFFECT OF TAPING AND BRACING ON PERFORMANCE

The effects of taping and bracing on the muscle of the ankle should be considered. The effects of unsupported, taped, and four commercially available braces on the isometric strength of selected foot muscles was compared. No differences were observed in the isometric forces recorded during rear foot inversion and eversion, indicating that neither taping or bracing constricted the lower leg musculature.

Taping does not appear to reduce speed, balance, agility, or jumping ability. On the other hand, several studies showed that taping can significantly decrease performance in the vertical jump, standing long jump, agility runs, and sprinting. The effects of several different braces (lace-up brace and a neoprene velcro strap brace) and taping on performance in the long jump, vertical leap, 10-yard shuttle run, and 40-yard sprint have been compared. Compared to the no support condition, ankle taping resulted in significantly decreased performance in the vertical jump, 10-yard shuttle run, and 40-yard sprint. The lace-up brace decreased performance in the vertical jump, long jump, and the sprint. The neoprene velcro strap brace only decreased performance in the vertical jump. The brace that reduced performance the least, which was the neoprene velcro strap brace, was rated as the most comfortable. It is likely that the most comfortable brace reduced performance the least because it provided the least support. The use of a semirigid bimalleolar brace appears to decrease base running speed.

Elite soccer players were tested for speed, balance, agility, and vertical jumping under unsupported, taped, and braced conditions. Only vertical jump performance was significantly diminished as a result of wearing a brace. Due to the small decrease in performance when wearing a brace or being taped, these methods can be justified as a means for achieving ankle protection.

Knee

Bracing

The knee is the second most commonly injured joint in athletics. Damage to the knee ligaments represents the most frequent serious injury sustained by soccer players. Injuries to the knee ligaments often result in prolonged disability or complete inability to return to the game. In an attempt to prevent initial injury and reinjury to the knee, a variety of knee orthotic devices (e.g., braces) have been developed. The effectiveness of these braces is of interest not only because of their potential benefits, but also because of concerns regarding legal liability if they are not used.

In 1984, the Sports Medicine Committee of the American Academy of Orthopedic Surgeons (AAOS) conducted a symposium on knee bracing to review the related research and make recommendations for future research. One important outcome of the symposium was the categorization of the commercially available knee braces into three categories; prophylactic, rehabilitative, and functional (Table 36–3).

PROPHYLACTIC BRACES

These braces are constructed primarily to protect against medial collateral ligament injuries resulting from laterally applied impact forces near the joint line. Although each brace offers different design features, they are all constructed to provide knee stability while permitting functional movement. They are supposed to prevent excess lateral movement and limit hyperextension and rotation. Although these braces vary, most consist of single sided

Table 36-3

Types of Knee Braces	
1. Prophylactic	To prevent or reduce initial knee injuries
2. Rehabilitative	To support surgically reconstructed ligaments
3. Functional	To provide stability to the knee that is unstable due to disruption, repair, or reconstructive surgery to one or more soft tissue stabilizing structures

strut composed of metal or heavy plastic. Some braces have two struts. The strut generally has a single hinge, but some double hinged struts are available. The strut can be attached externally to an elastic sleeve or encased in an elastic sleeve. Prophylactic braces are popular among high school and college players of American football. They are used mostly by the players at greatest risk and who can afford to sacrifice a slight loss in speed and maneuverability. Consequently, they are most often used by offensive and defensive linemen and tight ends. They are used less frequently by linebackers and are rarely used by offensive or defensive backs.

The available information regarding the ability of these braces to prevent or reduce the severity of knee injuries is controversial. Although some studies have reported a decrease in the number and severity of knee injuries, other studies have reported that the braces may not reduce injuries but may actually increase injuries.

The safety of prophylactic knee braces can be challenged because there are data that show the use of knee braces may increase knee injuries and have adverse effects on adjacent structures. An increased incidence of injuries to the lower leg, including ankle sprains, stress fractures of the fibula, ruptured achilles tendon, and fractures to the talus and metatarsals, has been reported. The braces may alter the way biomechanical stresses are applied to the knee and shift traumatic forces to nearby supporting structures.

In 1987, the AAOS developed a statement regarding the effectiveness of prophylactic knee braces. They noted that the routine use of prophylactic knee braces has not been proven to be effective in reducing the number and severity of knee injuries. The American Academy of Pediatrics (AAP) issued a recommendation that the lateral unidirectional knee braces not be used by young football players. However, despite their questionable efficacy in the minds of many clinicians, the use of prophylactic knee braces is still popular among high school and collegiate football players.

REHABILITATIVE KNEE BRACES

These braces are longer and designed with features that provide selective control over the range of motion. Their use is widespread in orthopedics and their effectiveness is widely accepted during the early recovery stage. The AAOS has endorsed their use for this application.

FUNCTIONAL KNEE BRACES

Originally, these braces were designed to provide stability in situations involving a repaired, not reconstructed, ligament. There is little question regarding their effectiveness when used for this application. Along with advances in surgical technology, the use of functional braces has expanded. Today, these braces are used in ligament deficit cases and with reconstructed knees. Functional knee braces are often used as prophylactic devices providing protection to repaired, reconstructed, or healing ligaments and grafts.

The use of functional knee braces is a relatively recent phenomenon. The Lenox Hill Derotation Brace, which appeared in the late 1960s, was the first commercially available functional brace. This was followed by the appearance of other commercially available functional braces in the early 1970s. The advent of numerous braces on the market lead the AAOS to call for research assessing their efficacy.

The effectiveness of a functional knee brace as a rehabilitative device has received little challenge. In this regard, the AAOS has endorsed their use. Today, these braces are being used earlier in the rehabilitative protocol as devices to control the range of motion.

Controversy arises when the functional brace is used as a prophylactic device to help injured athletes return to competition. In an attempt to reduce the probability of reinjury, more athletes are using functional knee braces while residual knee laxity exists. Coaches, administrators, and athletic trainers are under subtle pressure to use the braces to reduce reinjury and return the athlete to play sooner.

Functional Knee Brace Effectiveness
Most of the research related to the efficacy of functional knee braces has dealt with biomechanical considerations. The majority of functional knee braces studied appear to reduce anterior tibial translation under low clinical loading conditions. Their effectiveness in controlling internal-external rotational displacements of the tibia on the femur is more variable. In general, most of the biomechanical studies demonstrate that functional knee braces provide increased mechanical stability to the knee under low loads. It appears that functional braces eliminate the compensatory muscular activity in the ACL deficient knee, thereby restoring normal knee kinematics. Functional braces also seem to provide strain shielding effects to the ACL graft under low loads.

Although there is ample evidence that functional braces provide increased stability under low loads, there is concern as to whether the braces provide mechanical stability under the increased loads found in sports. Unfortunately, there are no studies that have measured the effectiveness of these braces under high physiological loads.

In addition to studying the effects of functional knee bracing on tibial translation and rotation, several studies have attempted to investigate its effect on functional movement patterns. The use of force platforms and high-speed photography can be used to evaluate the effects of functional knee bracing on running and cutting maneuvers. Subjects with a braced ACL deficient knee may be able to generate shear and torque forces similar to those generated by nonACL deficient subjects. This is particularly important during cutting maneuvers. The braced knee experienced significantly increased shear forces compared to the unbraced knee. In most cases, running velocity was improved when the brace was worn. The brace may be beneficial in subjects with strength deficits in the quadriceps.

There are also kinematic changes in the unbraced ACL deficient knee when compared to the braced ACL deficient knee. In an ACL disrupted knee, there is a series of compensatory mechanisms evidenced by significantly different muscle firing patterns. These changes in muscle firing patterns most likely represent intuitive compensatory adjustments using muscular contractions to stabilize the knee. Braces can eliminate the need for some of these compensatory contractions by increasing mechanical stability or creating a greater sense of stability.

Functional knee braces increase the energy cost of a task and slightly decrease endurance performance. Runners who wore a Lenox Hill Derotation Brace during horizontal treadmill running showed approximately a 5% increase in oxygen consumption when running with a brace as opposed to without a brace. Another study examined the effects of running with a brace at four different speeds. The braces caused increases of 3%–8% in oxygen consumption, heart rate, and ventilation when compared to running without the brace. Peripheral ratings of perceived exertion were also elevated. The increase in metabolic costs were related to the weight of the braces. Although braces may decrease performance and increase the metabolic load, most users adapt or compensate for the loss because they continue to use the braces after rehabilitation.

In soccer, there is sustained activity, periods that require short bursts of speed, and periods of little or no activity. In this regard, the functional knee braces appear to have little effect on strength and motor performance, but may decrease forward running speed. The braces do not seem to reduce backward speed or agility when the patient becomes accustomed to their use.

Another area of investigation related to bracing is the effect of braces on proprioception. Proprioception is a neurosensory feedback mechanism rather than a neuromuscular control system. There is significant proprioceptive deficiency associated with ligament and capsular injuries. The research related to the effects of functional knee braces on proprioception initially appears contradictory. Little difference in muscle firing patterns between braced and unbraced patients should be expected because ligament receptors bring about very little reflex action, which indicates that they are primarily sensory and are weak controllers of movement. As a result, braces do not have a significant proprioceptive effect on the knee. However, functional knee bracing may enhance both static and dynamic balance abilities in the ACL deficient knee. A properly applied device, such as a knee brace, may enhance kinesthetic awareness through cutaneous stimulation in place of the normal, disrupted internal sensory pathways. Functional knee bracing serves to protect the injured, repaired, or reconstructed ligament from overload during that portion of the recovery period when proprioceptive ability is compromised.

In addition to objective data regarding functional knee bracing, subjective patient responses must be considered in the evaluation of effectiveness. However, the subjective responses should correlate with the objective data. Approximately 90% of patients report significant functional improvement when using the braces, significantly fewer incidents of giving way, and a greater sense of stability and confidence. This greater sense of confidence may play a positive role in compliance with the rehabilitative protocol.

Undesirable psychological effects may also result from the use of braces. The use of a brace may result in an exaggerated dependence on the brace. Some may depend on the brace for all activity and others may continue to use the brace after stability has returned. Also, if an athlete uses the brace at all times there is a possibility that their proprioceptive ability may never return to preinjury level. Another disadvantage is the possibility that the patient may feel a sense of invulnerability and engage in high-risk behaviors.

Still another concern with the use of knee braces is that providing increased rigidity to the knee might place the ankle and foot at risk in noncontact sports, such as soccer. Players who use knee braces should receive additional support of the ankle, such as taping or another protective ankle device. Finally, another consideration is that the brace may become a target for the unscrupulous player. In this case, instead of accelerating recovery, the probability for reinjury is increased.

SUGGESTED READINGS

Alves JW, Alday RV, Ketcham DL, et al. A comparison of the passive support provided by various ankle braces. J Sport Phys Ther 1992;15:10–18.

Baker BE, Van Hanswyk E, Bogosian S, et al. A biomechanical study of the static stabilizing effect of knee braces on medial stability. Am J Sports Med 1987;15:566–570.

Cawley PW, France EP, Paulos LE. The current state of functional knee bracing research: a review of the literature. Am J Sports Med 1991;19:226–233.

France EP, Paulos LE, Layaraman G, et al. The biomechanics of lateral knee bracing. Part II: Impact response of the braced knee. Am J Sports Med 1987;15:430–438.

Garrick JG, Requa RK. Prophylactic knee bracing. Am J Sports Med 1987;15: S118–S123.

Grace TG, Skipper BJ, Newberry JC, et al. Prophylactic knee braces and injury to the lower extremity. J Bone Joint Surg 1988;70:422–427.

Gross MT, Ballard CL, Mears HG, et al. Comparison of Don Joy Ankle Ligament Protector and Aircast Sport-Stirrup orthoses in restricting foot and ankle motion before and after exercise. J Ortho Sports Phys Ther 1992;16:60–67.

Gross MT, Lapp AK, Davis JM. Universal ankle support and Aircast Sport Stirrup orthoses and ankle tape in restricting eversion-inversion before and after exercise. J Ortho Sports Phys Ther 1991;13: 11–19.

Paris D. The effects of Swede-0, New Cross, and McDavid ankle braces and adhesive ankle taping on speed, balance, agility and vertical jump. J Athletic Training 1992;27:253–256.

Rovere GD, Clarke TJ, Yates CS, et al. Retrospective comparison of taping and ankle stabilizers in preventing ankle injuries. Am J Sports Med 1988;16:228–233.

Sitler M, Ryan J, Topkinson N, et al. The efficacy of a prophylactic knee brace to reduce knee injuries to football: a prospective, randomized study at West Point. Am J Sports Med 1990;18:311–315.

Sitler M, Ryan J, Wheeler B, et al. The efficacy of a semirigid ankle stabilizer to reduce acute ankle injuries in basketball: a randomized clinical study at West Point. Am J Sports Med 1994;22:454–461.

Surve I, Schwellnus MP, Noakes T, et al. A fivefold reduction in the incidence of recurrent ankle sprains in soccer players using the Sport Stirrup Arthrosis. Am J Sports Med 1994;22:601–605.

Wojty EM, Loubert BP, Samson SY, et al. Use of a knee-brace for control of tibial translation and rotation: a comparison, in cadavera, of available models. J Bone Joint Surg 1990;72:1323–1329.

Rehabilitation and Return to Play Criterion

Bruce J. Snell

Many times, the most difficult decisions for the medical team to make are those determining when an injured athlete can return to athletic participation. The decision making process must involve all members of the medical team including the doctor, trainer, coach, and player. The many factors involved in this decision will be outlined later. However, a systematic approach must be taken so that the determination is as objective as possible. Functional progression is the tool used to make the process objective.

Historically, treatment of an injured athlete has been divided into the rehabilitation of the injury followed by an assessment of the athlete's ability to return to competition. Rehabilitation is actually a continuum that culminates in a return to play decision. Therefore, rehabilitation must be integrated into the process of determining when an athlete may return to competition. This is accomplished through the functional progression.

Determining When an Athlete Should Return to Sports

Clinically based success alone may not guarantee safe athletic performance. The goal of rehabilitation, and the susequent decision making process, should be safe participation and effective performance. If rehabilitation is limited to the clinical setting, the result may be incomplete recovery of athletic function. There are three aspects to successful rehabilitation.

Clinical Parameters

These are the traditional measures of range of motion, strength, endurance, pain, and swelling.

Functional Stability

Laxity tests alone are not a reliable predictor of functional stability. Functional stability is a term coined by Frank Noyes, M.D. There are four factors relating to the stability of a joint (Table 37–1).

Functional Progression

This concept is designed to improve not only clinical parameters and functional stability but, more importantly, neuromuscular coordination and agility. A functional progression is defined as a planned sequence of progressively more

Table 37-1

Factors Relating to the Stability of a Joint
1. Passive restraints of the ligaments
2. Joint geometry
3. Active restraints of the muscles
4. Joint compressive forces that occur with activity and approximate the joint

difficult activities specific to the demands of the sport. The sport is divided into parts and the athlete works from the simple to the more difficult activities. Thus, the athlete begins to adapt to the specific demands encountered during a game. The three benefits of functional progression are psychological, the determination of a rehabilitation stage, and an objective participation decision.

Psychologically, athletes react to injuries in different ways. Some may experience the wounded animal syndrome, which results in withdraw from teammates and coaches and feelings of being left out. Partial participation during practice, either in noncontact exercises or with the trainer on the side, keeps the athlete involved. This involvement encourages resumption of social relationships. In addition, athletes may be apprehensive as to whether the injury will withstand the demands of training sessions and games. If athletes methodically work through the stages of the progression, they will prove to themselves that they are ready to resume training and competition. Anxiety regarding potential loss of performance skills during a prolonged layoff is a common concern, especially in high-caliber athletes. In this case, a functional progression may be helpful in two ways. First, resumption of some activities early in rehabilitation will minimize loss of skills. Second, during the progression, players have a chance to reacquire skills prior to full participation with the rest of the team or opponents.

The functional progression is also beneficial because it determines the stage of rehabilitation. As the player progresses to more difficult activities, a point of failure is reached. At that point, rehabilitation commences with the last tolerated task and continued work on previous activities. The failure point is then retested periodically to assess progress.

Finally, the most important benefit may be an objective return to play decision. When the player successfully completes the progression, the trainer, doctor, coach, and athlete are all aware that it is time to resume normal participation. This relieves the pressure that a trainer or physician may feel from the coach or player regarding the player's return.

Specific Adaptation to Imposed Demands

When creating a functional progression, the SAID principal (Specific Adaptation to Imposed Demands) is used as a guideline. The body adapts or accommodates to varying stresses. An example would be when the collagen fibers of a healing ligament align themselves along the lines of stress. Therefore, it is necessary to introduce specific demands that will occur during match situations. The first step is to perform an analysis of the demands.

Sport

Within each sport there are different demands. In soccer, physical demands can differ based on the player's position. For example, midfielders and forwards have different physical demands. See Chapter 1 for a more detailed explanation of the demands of the game.

Physical Contact

This analysis includes the player's position and personality. The aggressiveness of the player should be considered. Does the player go in on every tackle or shy away from contact?

Strength vs. Endurance

In this analysis, the individual strengths of the player are examined. The areas in which the player excells should be determined. These areas include endurance, strength, speed, and skill.

Skill Level

The skill level refers to the level at which the player participates in soccer. The player may be a U-14 recreational player or a premier league professional.

Additional Considerations

There are other important factors to consider when developing a functional progression. For example, soft tissue healing is an issue that encompasses surgical protocols (or time-tables) and conservative management of sprains and strains. General muscle strength should also be considered. Many clinicians require a 70% strength return prior to initiating a functional progression. Neuromuscular coordination can be evaluated by determining whether balance and proprioception have adequately returned. Psychosocial considerations are also important. Many times there are secondary motivations (positive or negative) that affect the player. The player may be a starter trying to return to the position too early or one who has been playing poorly and is looking for an excuse not to return. Another important consideration may be the intuition of the clinician. These feelings, gained through experience in successes and failures, are a valuable instrument.

As a player moves through the progression, there must be continual evaluation. The clinician must assess the carriage, control, and confidence of the player. Are movements symmetrical (carriage)? Can the athlete start and stop smoothly and cut without undo stress (control)? Does the athlete look comfortable and eager (confident)?

During the functional rehabilitation process, progression should be stopped prior to failure, even though the clinician and athlete may not feel it is necessary. This leaves the athlete feeling good about the progress and eager to return the next day. The method of progression should stop somewhere between taking the athlete to failure (i.e., poor carriage, control or confidence) and leaving them eager to return.

Soccer Specific Functional Progressions

Running Sequence

Running is required of all positions. Therefore, it is a good starting point for all players. Other position-specific progressions may commence along with the running program.

FULL WEIGHT BEARING

This functional progression involves work on a normal gait pattern. This process may induce pain.

WALK-JOG SEQUENCE

For this functional progression, distances must be tightly controlled. Initially, it begins with 200 meters at a walk and 200 meters at a jog for a total of 1600 meters. Then, the total distance jogging is increased while the total distance walking is decreased until the entire distance is covered at a jog.

FIGURE-8 RUNNING

The athlete begins with a large circle (center circle) as 1/2 of the 8 and works to smaller 8s. The speed begins at a jog and increases to 3/4 pace.

CUTTING SEQUENCE

This progression begins with 45° cuts and works up to 90° cuts while increasing speed to a 3/4 pace. Cuts must be side step (i.e., plant right foot to cut to the left) and cross over (i.e., plant left foot to cut left). It should also begin at a predetermined spot and progress to an on-demand basis determined by the trainer.

CARIOCA RUNNING

This involves side to side running with alternating cross-over (Fig. 37–1).

Kicking Sequence

In these sequences (Tables 37–2 through 37–4), a moving ball is generally easier to kick when played directly to the player. The moving ball has energy and the player only changes its direction.

Figure 37–1. Carioca running sequence.

Figure 37–2. Kicking a dead ball with the side of the foot.

Figure 37–3. Driving a dead ball.

Figure 37–4. Shadow defense—passively defend an attacker who is moving side to side.

Figure 37–5. Tackling—start with the ball against a wall progressing to an opponent.

Figure 37–6. Control the ball with different parts of the body.

Figure 37–7. Shield the ball from an increasingly active opponent.

Table 37-2

Kicking sequence
1. Side foot a moving ball
2. Chip a moving ball
3. Side foot a dead ball (Fig. 37–2)
4. Chip a dead ball
5. Drive a moving ball
6. Drive a dead ball (Fig. 37–3)

Table 37-3

Position Sequence (Defender)
1. Backpedal: player must plant and push-off in all directions
2. Turning: (Both ways) begin with a predetermined turn and progress to on-demand
3. Shadow: passively defend an attacking player moving side to side with the ball (Fig. 37–4)
4. Jumping: jumping to head the ball
5. Tackling: begin with the ball against a wall (controlled) and progress to an opponent with a ball (Fig. 37–5)

Table 37-4

Position Sequence (Forward)
1. Dribbling: begin passively then with a passive defender
2. Control: control the ball with different body parts. Begin with balls chipped in and progress to driven balls and finally add defensive pressure (Fig. 37–6)
3. Turning: control then turn to attack (Both direction)
4. Shielding: with increasing pressure from defenders (Fig. 37–7)
5. Shooting: both feet from varying positions

Conclusion

Rehabilitation is a continuum (i.e., functional progression), culminating in a return to play decision. Athletic activities should be broken down into ordered, component skills. There should be a balance between clinical treatment and functional rehabilitation.

SUGGESTED READINGS

Kegeffeis S. The construction and implimentation of functional progressions as a component of athletic rehabilitation. J Orthop Sports Phys Ther 1983;5:14–19.

Kegeffeis S, Malone T, McCarrol J. Functional progressions: an aid to athletic rehabilitation. Phys Sports Med 1984;12:67–71.

Kegeffeis S, Weatheraid T. Utilization of functional progressions in rehabilitation of injured wrestlers. Athl Training 1987;22:32–35.

Noyes FR, Grood ES, Butter DL, et al. Clinical laxity tests and functional stability of the knee-biomechanical concepts. Clin Orthop 1980;146:84–89.

VI

• Youth in Soccer

38  Epidemiology of Youth Injuries

John Lohnes

Soccer is the fastest growing team sport among American youth. The game is promoted for school-aged children because it is relatively safe, requires little special or expensive equipment, is simple to learn, and does not require unique physical characteristics.

The Federation International de Football Association (FIFA) reported over 60 million registered players in 1984 and estimated an additional 60 million unregistered players worldwide. In the United States, soccer receives less attention as a spectator sport than it does in other countries. Nevertheless, the sport has become extremely popular among American youth. Exact statistics on participation are difficult to acquire due to municipal programs, recreational programs, and club teams not affiliated with schools or registered with the U.S. Youth Soccer Federation. However, the Soccer Industry Council of America estimated that more than 6 million children under age 12 played on a team in 1990. Over 1.6 million players under age 18 are currently registered with the U.S. Soccer Federation and another 300,000 are registered with the American Youth Soccer Organization.

Incidence of Injury

Despite the worldwide popularity of soccer, there have been few epidemiologic studies of soccer injuries, particularly in youth players. In recent years, several studies of soccer injuries have been published in the english language. The results of these series are summarized in Table 38–1.

Four studies reported on injuries sustained in large youth tournaments. Although the populations were large and the conditions well-controlled, the definition of an injury varied. The incidence of injuries reported in these four studies was higher than those observed in other studies. This may be due to the provision of on-site medical care, which made it more likely that participants would seek medical attention for an injury. Four studies examined soccer injuries using reports from emergency rooms, clinic visits, or insurance companies. Although the population sizes were fairly large, there was considerable reporting bias inherent in these studies and it was impossible to determine injury incidence. Most of the remaining studies reviewed reported injuries sustained by one or several teams during a league or club sea-

Table 38-1

Epidemiological Studies of Soccer Injuries						
Study Year	Authors	Player Age	Player Sex	Number players	Total injuries	Injury rate/ 1000 hours
Europe						
1978	Nilsson & Roaas (Norway)	adolesc.	M/F	25,000	1534	23 M 44 F
1980	Sandelin, et al. (Finland)	10–58	M F	? ?	1989 83	?
1983	Ekstrand & Gillquist (Sweden)	17–38	M	180	256	?
1985	Schmidt-Olsen, et al. (Denmark)	9–19	M/F	6600	343	19
1986	Berger-Vachon, et al. (France)	10–35	M	123,175	6153	1.7
1986	Maehlum, et al. (Norway)	12–18	M/F	14,800	411	11.7 total 8.9 M/17.6 F
1989	Nielsen & Yde (Denmark)	16+	M	123	109	14.3 game
1990	Hunt & Fulford (U.K.)	10–45	M	?	200	?
1990	Yde & Nielsen (Denmark)	10–18	M	152	62	5.6
1991	Engstrom, et al. (Sweden)	16–28	F	41	78	?
1992	Høy, et al. (Denmark)	5–54	M/F	?	715	?
U.S.						
1980	Sullivan, et al.	7–18	M/F	1272	34	0.51 M 1.1 F
1981	Pritchett	14–18	M/F	10,634	436	?
1986	DeHaven & Lintner	all ages	M/F	n/a	111	?

Table 38-1 (continued)

Study Year	Authors	Player Age	Player Sex	Number players	Total injuries	Injury rate/ 1000 hours
U.S.						
1986	Hoff & Martin	8–18	M/F	455 outdoor	46	?
				587 indoor	74	
1988	Backous, et al.	6–17	M	681	109	7.3
			F	458	107	10.6
1993	Kibler	12–19	M/F	74,900 player hours	179	2.4

son. The only ongoing study of soccer league injuries in the US is being conducted by the National Collegiate Athletic Association (NCAA), although the study only represents college-age athletes.

There is considerable variability in population size and demographics, levels of play, definitions of injuries, and injury reporting methods. This makes it impossible to directly compare or compute averages of injury statistics by pooling the various results of the studies reviewed. However, there are some consistent trends (Table 38–2).

Types of Injuries

Contusions, muscle strains, and ligament sprains account for most of the injuries resulting in time lost from games and practices for all age groups. In children, contusions and abrasions are the most common injuries and approximately 75% of these are not serious (i.e., no lost playing time). Most of these injuries involve the lower extremities. Fractures account for approximately 10% of all injuries and typically involve the upper extremity due to a fall. Fractures are apparently not more frequent in youth players, despite the decreased strength of growing epiphyseal plates. Less than one-quarter of growth plate injuries occur in team sports. Soccer ranks third behind football and basketball in terms of frequency of injuries. Serious injuries, such as head and spinal cord trauma, account for less than 0.1% of all injuries.

Head and Neck

Despite the absence of protective headgear, soccer injuries to the head, mouth, and face account for approximately 10% of all injuries in youth. This figure is greater than that for adult players. This difference may be related to less skill, greater head-to-body weight ratio, or greater ball-to-body size ratio. Although serious concussions, skull fractures, and cervical spine trauma are rare, facial lacerations and nasal fractures are not infrequent. Goalkeepers may be more susceptible to head and neck injuries since they are more likely to approach a play headfirst. Head and facial injuries may occur with improper heading or collision with the ground, goalposts, or other players.

Table 38-2

Injury Trends in Soccer

1. The incidence and severity of injuries increases with age, level of play, and frequency of competition up to tenfold in high school players.
2. Players are more likely to be injured in game conditions than they are during practice, although preseason practice has a higher injury incidence than midseason practice in scholastic teams.
3. Injuries in players under 12 are uncommon, generally occurring in less than 5% of participants.
4. When injuries do occur in this age group, they are typically minor and do not result in significant lost playing time.
5. For unknown reasons, females appear more likely to be injured than males in the younger age groups. This difference tends to disappear as players reach adulthood (with the notable exception of knee injuries, which are more common in women than in men).
6. Center midfielders and forwards are more frequently injured than defenders.
7. Youth goalkeepers are more likely to sustain upper extremity injuries than are their adult counterparts.
8. Contusions, ligament sprains (especially ankle sprains), and muscle strains account for approximately 3/4 of all injuries.
9. Injuries to the lower extremities account for between 1/2 and 2/3 of all injuries.
10. Catastrophic disabling or fatal injuries are fortunately very rare, accounting for less than 0.1% of injuries in all populations studied.

Hyperflexion-extension injuries to the neck can result when a player is kicked or struck by the ball. Maxillofacial and dental injuries account for approximately 6% of all injuries and affect the teeth, alveolar processes, and lower or middle third of the facial skeleton. The most common cause of these injuries is direct contact with another player. Players under age 20 are less likely to sustain dental and maxillofacial injuries than older players; only 4.3% of these injuries occur in children under age 15. Due to the high cost and potential for permanent impairment from dental injuries, mouthguards are recommended. The Minnesota State High School leagues instituted a rule requiring soccer participants to wear mouthguards. However, the rule was recently rescinded due to the expense and lack of evidence supporting a strong need for mouthguards.

The most common responses to soccerball-induced eye injuries are hyphema and retinal edema. Vitreous hemorrhage, retinal hemorrhage, corneal abrasion, traumatic iritis, angle recession, retinal tear, and traumatic pigmentary retinopathy also occur. Although there have not been permanent impairments in any injured players, there are recommendations supporting the use of protective goggles. Proper heading technique should also be stressed for beginning players.

Little is known about the chronic effects of repetitive heading. One study observed a higher incidence of electroencephalogram (EEG) changes in a group of soccer players compared with a control group. In this study, changes were most significant in the younger players (16–20). This is most likely due to neuronal changes caused by repeated minor head traumas. Although the value of helmets has been observed in American football, hockey, and lacrosse, no study has evaluated the effectiveness of protective headgear in soccer.

Upper Extremity

The incidence of upper extremity injuries in youth soccer participants has been reported to average 15%–20%. This compares with 10% in most adult series. Typically, these injuries involve sprains, fractures, or dislocation of the thumb or fingers. Goalkeepers are more likely to be injured due to the specific demands of the position. Frequent falls, illegal ball contact, decreased technical expertise, and greater fragility of upper extremity epiphyses could account for the higher incidence of upper extremity injuries in young players.

Hip, Pelvis, and Groin

Most studies combine injuries to the trunk, back, pelvis, and groin. Incidences have been found to range from 3%–10% for outdoor soccer and 15% for indoor soccer. The most common injuries to the hip, pelvis, and groin in soccer are the hip pointer, pelvic avulsion fractures, and groin strains. Iliac crest apophysis and slipped capital femoral epiphysis are less common.

Lower Extremity

Injuries to the lower extremities are the most frequent, accounting for 58%–81% of all injuries in the published studies for all ages. Contusions have been found to be the most frequently occurring injury in youth soccer, accounting for approximately 30%–40% of all injuries. Most of these contusions involve the anterior thigh, calf, shin, or foot. These injuries are usually minor and do not result in lost playing time. The use of shinguards, now mandatory in most leagues, has reduced the severity of lower extremity contusions. Ligamentous sprains and muscular strains around the knee, ankle, and foot are the second most common injuries sustained by youth soccer participants. Ankle sprains are the most common injuries that result in lost playing time at any age and level of competition. In the NCAA survey, ankle sprains were the most frequent injury reported in each of the six observed seasons.

The feet are susceptible to trauma in soccer due to the stresses of dribbling and kicking and because the shoes offer little support or protection. Metatarsal fractures, turf-toe, sesamoiditis, subungual hematomas, plantar fasciitis, posterior tibial tendinitis, and midfoot sprains are frequently encountered.

The chronic effects of soccer playing on the foot and ankle were seen in radiographs of the feet of United States National Team players (World Cup and Olympic teams). Radiographic abnormalities were seen in 97% of these young players (average age, 22). These abnormalities included osteophytes of the ankle, midfoot, and toe joints as well as a higher than normal incidence of accessory ossicles, os trigona, and partite sesamoids. The majority of these osseous abnormalities were clinically silent. It is not known whether these abnormalities have clinical significance with increasing age. The higher incidence of injury in accessory and bipartite bones may be the result of chronic stresses to the foot during childhood and adolescence as growth centers ossify.

Other Injury Patterns in Youth Soccer

Indoor Soccer

The incidence of injuries in indoor soccer is estimated to be 4.5 times higher than that observed in outdoor soccer. Reporting methods are variable and based on survey response rather than prospective analysis. Therefore, the numbers may be imprecise. Differences in field size and surface, game speed, officiating and player numbers are all possible causes for the increased incidence of injury observed in indoor soccer.

Playing Surface

Most authors report no significant increase in injury frequencies on artificial turf. It may be that players who alternate frequently between grass and an artificial surface may be at a higher risk for injury. A period of adaptation and the use of proper shoes may reduce the risk of injury.

The risk of injury associated with playing surfaces for youth soccer participants is unknown. It has been suggested that young players should wear uncleated shoes to reduce injury risk, although there is no research to support this concept.

SUGGESTED READINGS

Backous DD, Friedl KE, Smith NJ, et al. Soccer injuries and their relation to physical maturity. Amer J Diseases Children 1988;142:838–842.

Ekstrand J, Gillquist J. Soccer injuries and their mechanisms: a prospective study. Med Sci Sports Exerc 1983;15:267–270.

Hoff GL, Martin TA. Outdoor and indoor soccer: injuries among youth players. Amer J Sports Med 1986;14:231–233.

Keller CS, Noyes FR, Buncer CR. The medical aspects of soccer injury epidemiology. Amer J Sports Med 1987;15:230–237.

National Collegiate Athletic Association Injury Surveillance System: Men's and Women's soccer injury/exposure summaries, 1986–1987 to 1991–1992. Overland Park, Kansas: NCAA.

Nilsson S, Roaas A. Soccer injuries in adolescents. Amer J Sports Med 1986;14:218–224.

Pritchett J. Cost of high school soccer injuries. Amer J Sports Med 1981;9:64–66.

Schmidt-Olsen S, Bunemann L, Lade V, et al. Soccer injuries of youth. Br J Sports Med 1985;19:161–164.

Sullivan J, Gross R, Grana W, et al. Evaluation of injuries in youth soccer. Amer J Sports Med 1980;8:325–327.

Yde J, Nielsen AB. Sports injuries in adolescents' ball games: soccer, handball and basketball. Brit J Sports Med 1990;24:51–54.

39   Soccer Injuries in Adolescents

Peter Krumins
Bruce Reider

Introduction

Clinicians treating adolescent soccer players must be aware of how this age group differs from children and adults in physical development and potential injury patterns. Several factors contribute to this unique period of susceptibility. First, adolescents have certain vulnerabilities dictated by their stage of development. Their physes and apophyses are still open and at risk of traumatic disruption. Their ligaments and tendons are probably at their peak of tensile strength and may prove stronger than the bone to which they are attached, resulting in avulsion fractures. There appear to be other factors that put their skeleton at risk. These factors predispose adolescents to conditions such as isthmic spondylolysis and osteochondritis dissecans, which peak in this age group for reasons not understood.

The second factor that plays a role in the epidemiology of adolescent injuries are minor congenital or developmental anomalies. These anomalies can be manifested as accessory tarsal navicular, discoid meniscus, or extensor mechanism abnormalities that predispose to patellar instability.

The third major factor contributing to adolescent injury patterns is the dramatic increase in forces placed on the immature skeleton. This increase is due to the muscle hypertrophy made possible by the abundance of adolescent hormones and cultural forces, which dictate longer and more intensive training sessions. Essentially, the child's skeleton meets the adult world.

This chapter describes some of the various types of injuries encountered by the adolescent athlete when confronted with the demands of soccer.

Growth Plate Injuries

Members of the medical team must be aware of the immature skeleton and potential for fracture in and around the physes. Injury mechanisms that would produce a sprain in the skeletally mature player may cause a physeal fracture in the adolescent.

Ankle Fractures

Fractures involving the physes of the ankle are common in childhood and during adolescence. As somatic growth ends, the sequential closure of portions of the distal tibial physis can lead to peculiar injury patterns. Between the ages of 12 and 15, the distal tibial physis begins to close. This process occurs approximately 18 months before completion of tibial growth. The distal tibial physis closes asymmetrically. It begins in the central portion, proceeds medially, and finally closes along the anterolateral aspect. The posterior lateral physis closes before its anterolateral counterpart. External-rotation injury during this period can often fragment the physis. This occurs primarily along the anterior lateral portion of the distal tibial epiphysis due to the attachment of the anterior inferior tibiofibular ligament.

The Tillaux fracture follows the anterolateral distal epiphysis of the tibia (Fig. 39-1). The facture occurs through this area of the physis because the medial portion of the physis has already closed. The avulsed fragment of the epiphysis is attached to the anterior inferior tibiofibular ligament. Reduction is not necessary if the fragment is small or minimally displaced, which is the most common scenario. With displacement, however, the disruption of articular cartilage demands accurate reduction. This may be accomplished with closed methods, combining internal rotation with direct pressure over the fragment. Open reduction and internal fixation is undertaken if more than 1–2 mm of displacement or step-off remains after closed treatment. The fragment is reduced through an anterolateral incision and fixed with a lag screw. When the physis is almost closed, the screw may cross it. Otherwise, it should be placed parallel to the epiphysis.

The tri-plane fracture of the ankle also occurs between the ages of 12 and 15 (Fig. 39-2). This fracture involves three planes through the epiphysis, physis,

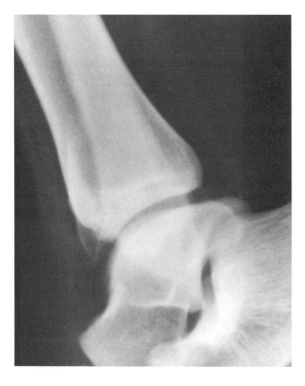

Figure 39-1. A displaced Tillaux fragment in a 14–year–old girl is seen to project anteriorly on the lateral radiograph (arrow).

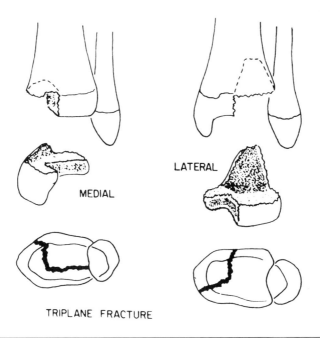

Figure 39-2. Two different patterns of tri-plane fracture.

and metaphysis. It combines features of a salter III fracture, since it crosses the epiphysis, and a salter II fracture, involving the distal tibial metaphysis.

The radiographic presentation of this unusual fracture may be confusing. On anterior-posterior (AP) radiographs, the fracture appears to be a salter type III fracture. On lateral views, the metaphyseal fragment is visible, classifying the injury as a salter IV fracture. The tri-plane fracture has been described as resulting in two or three major fragments.

Because the fracture line crosses the tibial plateau, anatomic reduction is essential. Nondisplaced fractures can be treated with closed methods. Displaced fractures can occasionally be reduced closed with internal rotation and reduction confirmed by tomogram or computerized tomography (CT). Most displaced fractures require open reduction and internal fixation to achieve and hold a satisfactory reduction. Internal fixation is accomplished with pins and/or screws, taking care to avoid crossing the open physis.

Knee Injuries

The clinician must also be aware of physeal injuries about the knee (Fig. 39-3). These must not be misdiagnosed as sprains. Fractures of the distal femoral and proximal tibial physis need attention, particularly if displaced, because of their potential for neurovascular involvement. Although the nature and severity of these injuries will usually be apparent, plain radiographs will sometimes appear benign. When a physeal fracture about the knee is suspected but unproven from plain radiographs, gentle stress views, CT, or magnetic resonance imaging (MRI) may be necessary to delineate the diagnosis (Fig. 39-4). Treatment for these injuries includes closed or open reduction with internal fixation as needed. Attaining and maintaining anatomic reduction is essential in these injury patterns.

Apophyseal Fractures

Apophyses are accessory growth plates that occur at the origins or insertions of major tendons into bone. Like the physes, they are areas of relative weakness in the adolescent skeleton and common sites for structural failure. This is truly a situation in which the child's skeleton meets the adult world as the hypertrophied muscles of the adolescent, particularly the adolescent male, avulse the apophysis through the apophyseal plate.

Most apophyseal avulsions in soccer players occur about the pelvis and proximal femur at the sites of attachment of the thigh muscles. These injuries are more common in males, especially between the ages of 14 and 16 as they approach apophyseal closure (Fig. 39-5). Common sites of avulsion are the anterior superior iliac spine (sartorius origin), anterior inferior iliac spine (rectus femoris origin), ischial apophysis (hamstring origin), iliac crest (abductor origin and abdominal insertion), and lesser trochanter (iliopsoas insertion). The majority of these injuries are mildly displaced and can be treated conservatively. Because the muscles involved are usually large and important in locomotion, crutches may be required for 1–2 weeks after the injury. Bony healing requires approximately 8 weeks, during which time the athlete may be allowed to gradually increase rehabilitation activities at a pace dictated by

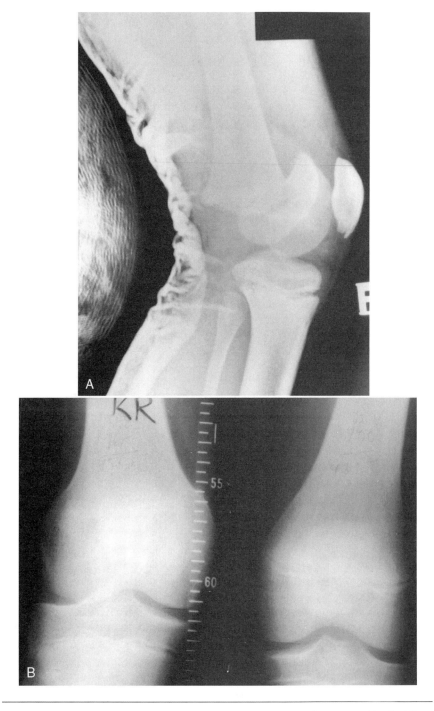

Figure 39-3. A badly displaced fracture through the distal femoral physis of a 13–year–old male. (A) Despite anatomic reduction, premature physeal arrest occurred (B).

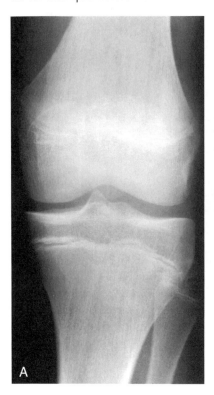
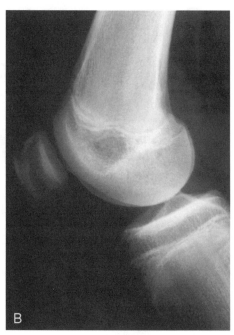

Figure 39-4. After a direct blow from another player, this 16–year–old male had a swollen knee but no obvious radiographic abnormality. (A and B) MRI showed a Salter 3 fracture of the distal femur and intrasubstance ACL rupture (C and D).

the resolution of symptoms. Full recovery of muscle strength and coordination may take several months.

These injuries rarely require reduction and internal fixation. Potential candidates are large, displaced fragments, particularly from the ischium, where they may cause discomfort with sitting.

Avulsion fractures may be missed, since they typically occur in noncontact situations in which a fracture may not be anticipated. These fractures should be considered when muscle pulls occur about the hip and pelvis in the adolescent. To ensure accurate diagnosis, radiographs should be obtained. Slipped capital femoral epiphysis, a more serious injury that can occur about the hip, should also be considered in the differential diagnosis of these cases.

Avulsion of the tibial tubercle is a serious avulsion fracture that can occur in the knees of adolescent soccer players (Fig. 39-6). The tibial tubercle is unusual in that it begins as a separate ossification center that ultimately fuses with the proximal tibial epiphysis prior to closure of the growth plate. Therefore, avulsion fractures may involve the tubercle alone or extend through the epiphysis. Ogden has classified avulsion fractures as Type 1 (fracture through the apophysis), Type 2 (fracture through the apophyseal-physeal junction), and

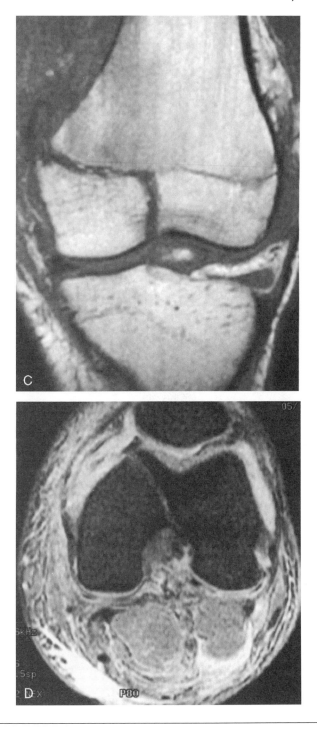

Figure 39-4. continued

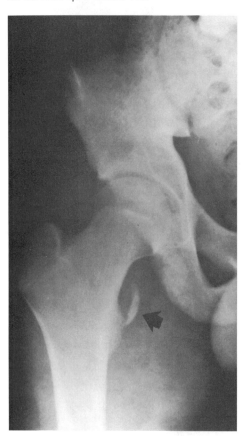

Figure 39-5. Avulsion fracture of the lesser trochanter in a 15–year–old male (arrow).

Type 3 (avulsion of a large fragment including the entire apophysis and adjacent anterior epiphysis). Since this injury constitutes an avulsion of the insertion of the quadriceps complex, displaced fractures must be reduced and rigidly fixed. Nondisplaced fragments may be treated in a cylinder cast.

Apophysitis

Apophysitis may be thought of as a stress fracture variation of the apophyseal avulsion fracture. Instead of a single violent episode of force, it is produced by the accumulation of the repetitive stresses of sports participation. The apophysitides, which is most important in the young player, involves the iliac crest and calcaneal tuberosity.

Iliac crest apophysitis usually occurs prior to the age of closure of the iliac apophysis; age 14 in females and 16 in males. It normally involves the anterior one-third to one-half of the iliac crest. The onset of pain is insidious, although the intensity may be great enough to require the use of crutches. The diagnosis relies on careful palpation of the pelvis, with the finding of tenderness localized to the anterior iliac crest. Plain radiographs may demonstrate widening of the apophyseal line in the area of involvement. This finding is usually subtle and radiographs often appear normal. Treatment is

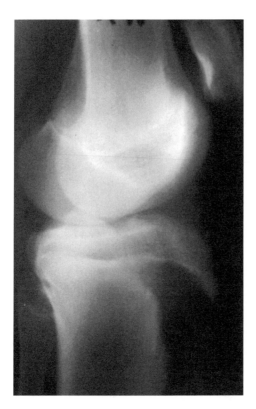

Figure 39-6. Ogden type 3 avulsion of the tibial tubercle in a 15–year–old male.

symptomatic. Because running should be avoided until the tenderness resolves, cross-training is used to maintain cardiovascular fitness. Nonsteroidal antiinflammatory drugs (NSAIDs), such as ibuprofen, may be taken as necessary for pain. Soccer training can usually be resumed within 1–2 months, although longer healing times are occasionally required.

Apophysitis of the calcaneal tuberosity is often called Sever's disease. It typically occurs in young players, manifesting itself as early as age seven or eight. The injury is characterized by low-grade pain in the posterior aspect of the calcaneus. It is thought to be caused by increased stresses across this region or indoor play on hard surfaces. Examination reveals tenderness to palpation at the posterior heel. Radiographs can be normal. However, if the condition is severe, sclerosis and fragmentation may be encountered. These changes may be difficult to distinguish from normal variations in the ossification of the calcaneal apophysis. Treatment of this problem includes stretching of the Achilles tendon and the use of a heel wedge to take stress off of the area during play. Symptoms are often mild enough to allow the player to train with this condition, although time off may be necessary in severe cases.

Osgood-Schlatter's Disease

Osgood-Schlatter's disease is a painful condition that occurs at the insertion of the patellar tendon into the tibial tubercle. Although it is often thought of as an apophysitis, Ogden has shown that the condition does not occur at the apophyseal growth plate. Rather, it occurs at the junction between the tendon and the tuberosity at approximately the time that the tuberosity is transforming from cartilage to bone. The pathology appears to substantiate the concept of localized avulsion of portions of the tendon insertion with small bits of cartilage or bone.

Osgood-Schlatter's disease typically affects males age 11–15 and females 9–13. It is more common in males. The athlete typically describes a dull aching pain at the tibial tubercle, which increases with running and kicking. Examination reveals localized swelling and tenderness at the tibial tuberosity (Fig. 39-7). The physical examination is usually so diagnostic that radiographs are not necessary. If taken, lateral radiographs usually demonstrate fragmentation of the tuberosity and soft tissue swelling. Treatment is symptomatic and includes quadriceps stretching and strengthening, activity modification, and ice after exercise. NSAIDS are used sparingly and only as necessary for pain. If the pain and disability are severe, a few weeks away from soccer may be necessary to bring the acute symptoms under control. Activity modification, such as reducing the length or intensity of practice sessions, is often sufficient. The athlete should be reassured that symptoms usually resolve as skeletal maturation progresses, although the characteristic prominence of the tibial tubercle is permanent. Occasionally, the skeletally mature player in the late teens or early twenties may complain of persistent or recurrent pain with tenderness localized to a large ossicle at the tendon insertion (Fig. 39-8). Excising the ossicle through a longitudinal split in the tendon usually relieves the symptoms in these cases.

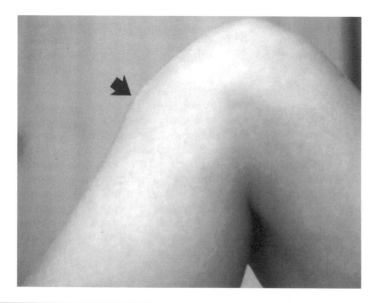

Figure 39-7. Typical area of swelling and tenderness in Osgood-Schlatter's disease (arrow).

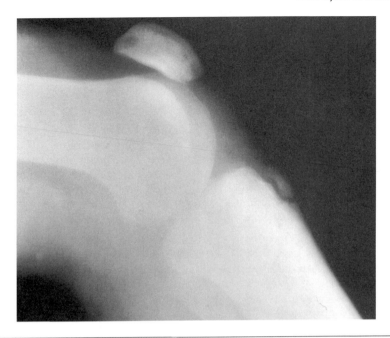

Figure 39-8. Large painful Osgood-Schlatter's ossicle in a 19–year–old male.

Sinding-Larsen-Johannson disease is a similar condition that occurs at the junction of the patellar tendon and the distal pole of the patella. It is typically found in children aged 10–13 years. Athletes complain of pain in the inferior aspect of the patella. Localized swelling, tenderness, and pain produced with quadriceps contraction can be found. Radiographs may reveal calcification at the inferior pole of the patella. Treatment for this condition is similar to that for Osgood-Schlatter's disease. Operative intervention for this condition is rarely indicated. However, excision of a calcified fragment may be performed if symptoms persist and are localized to the ossicle.

Anterior Cruciate Ligament (ACL) Avulsion

Another injury typical of the skeletally immature athlete is bony avulsion of the ACL, which is usually called tibial spine avulsion. The legitimacy of this association has been challenged since adolescents, particularly those close to skeletal maturity, frequently sustain midsubstance ACL tears and adults sometimes experience bony avulsions. Nevertheless, the large avulsion fragments, which may include significant portions of the adjacent tibial plateaux, are typically found in the skeletally immature athlete.

Meyers and McKenzie classified ACL avulsions into three types. In Type I, the fragment is nondisplaced; in Type II, the fragment is elevated from its bed on a posterior tissue hinge; and in Type III, the fragment is displaced completely out of its bed. In all types, closed reduction may be attempted by immobilizing the knee in full extension for 4–6 weeks. In Type III, arthroscopic surgical reduction or reduction through a small arthrotomy with fixation using screws or sutures will usually be necessary. If significant elastic elongation of the ligament occurred prior to avulsion, it may be necessary to excavate the bed and advance the avulsed fragment to reestablish functional length.

Osteochondritis Dissecans

Osteochondritis dissecans (OD) is a condition that occurs in the knee and is characterized by separation or collapse of a segment of subchondral bone and secondary fragmentation of the overlying articular cartilage. Since the nature or cause of this condition is not understood, it is not clear why its incidence peaks in adolescence. In fact, the declining incidence and decreased healing potential seen with age suggest that cases appearing in adulthood may have arisen at an earlier age.

Although trauma is frequently cited as an etiologic factor in OD, its high incidence in adolescence raises the question of a developmental contribution, such as an unknown skeletal risk factor. The 2:1 ratio of males to females may be related to hormonal factors or increased exposure to the cyclic trauma of athletic participation in males. The classic site for OD is at the lateral aspect of the medial femoral condyle. However, lesions may occur in the lateral femoral condyle, tibial plateau, or patellofemoral joint. There may also be subtypes of OD. In some cases, a bone fragment is present that has been dissected from the surrounding condyle. In other cases, the bone seems to evaporate, leaving an empty hole in the condyle.

The athlete describes a vague pain that may be accompanied by mechanical symptoms or effusion if the fragment has begun to separate. Physical examination findings are typically nonspecific. There may be tenderness of the affected condyle, effusion, or a positive Wilson test (pain with internal rotation of the knee in extension).

Radiographs are essential to diagnosis (Fig. 39-9A). The lesion may be localized on the lateral and tunnel or AP views, depending on the precise location on the femoral condyle. Posterior lesions are best seen on the tunnel view, while anterior lesions are best seen on the AP view. MRI may be useful to delineate the extent of the lesion or document the presence of synovial fluid deep in the fragment, which implies some degree of failure of the articular cartilage at the edges of the fragment.

The goal of treatment for this condition is to achieve bony union. This is not possible if an empty crater is seen at the time of presentation. Some lesions in young patients heal spontaneously when treated with activity reduction and restricted weight bearing. As physeal closure approaches, the potential for spontaneous healing appears to decline.

Fragments that do not show signs of healing or appear to be in danger of separating at the time of diagnosis should be treated surgically. This may include in situ drilling, internal fixation, and bone grafting, depending on the status of the overlying articular cartilage and the stability of the fragment (Fig. 39-9B).

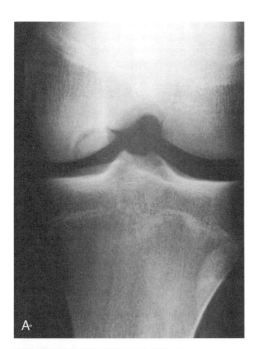

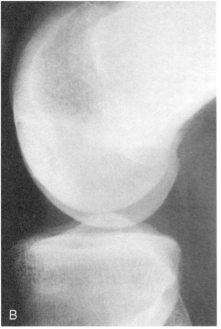

Figure 39-9. Large osteochondritis dissecans fragment in a 16–year–old male. (A and B) At arthroscopy, the fragment was found to be just starting to separate and was treated with drilling and internal fixation with Herbert screws (C and D).

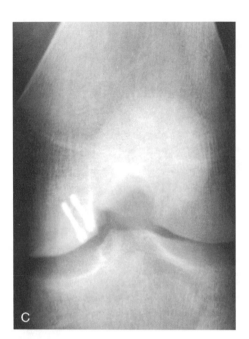

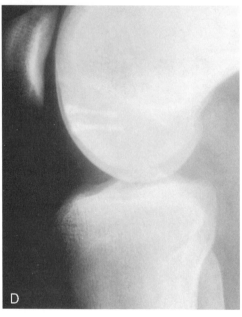

Figure 39-9. continued

Spondylolysis

Spondylolysis is a fairly common condition that is typically seen in the adolescent athlete. Although it is thought to occur in athletes who participate in sports requiring hyperextension of the lumbar spine, such as gymnasts and football linemen, we have seen cases related to soccer and less traumatic sports.

Spondylolysis is a general term for a heterogeneous group of conditions that may have congenital, developmental, degenerative, or traumatic etiologies. Wiltse et al developed a complete classification system for the broad spectrum of conditions known as spondylolysis. The type that we typically encounter in adolescent athletes is isthmic spondylolysis, a defect in the pars interarticularis of a lumbar vertebra, most commonly L5. Its incidence peaks in the 13–16 year age group, especially in males. Some adolescent spondylolysis is associated with dysplastic abnormalities at the lumbosacral junction. The type we see in athletes usually occurs in what appears to be an otherwise normal spine. The increased incidence in a narrow age range suggests that there is a factor in the adolescent anatomy or physiology that puts the skeleton at risk for this injury. Perhaps this is another instance in which the childlike skeleton is overwhelmed by adult muscular and impact forces.

The condition commonly appears as a stress fracture, with an insidious onset of pain that can become severely disabling. The athlete typically localizes the pain to the posterior beltline, midline, or unilateral (Fig. 39-10). Although pain is usually exacerbated by activities that require hyperextension, it may be produced simply by running.

Examination typically reveals localized pain exacerbated by active or passive hyperextension. Since this finding is typical, it should prompt a presumptive diagnosis of spondylolysis until disproven. Hamstring tightness may also be present. It is rare for spondylolysis in an athlete to be associated with greater than a grade I spondylolisthesis. If a grade II or greater spondylolisthesis is present, a step-off may be palpable between the spinous processes of L4 and L5.

Radiographic evaluation should include anteroposterior, lateral, and oblique views. The oblique views may allow visualization of the pars intraarticularis defect. The Scotty dog of Lachapele with a collar on its neck is a well-described radiographic finding signifying a defect in the pars intraarticularis (Fig. 39-11). In many cases, the defect is easier to see on the lateral view than the obliques. If plain radiographs are normal but clinical suspicion is high, a technetium-99 radionuclear bone scan should be obtained to evaluate the metabolic activity in the involved area. In some cases, SPECT scan imaging may be necessary to document increased uptake in the pars interarticularis.

Treatment of an athlete with a symptomatic pars defect is controversial. If the clinical picture is of an incipient stress fracture, with normal radiographs and positive bone scan, then the goal should be to obtain a solid bony union. There are two schools of thought regarding treatment for these cases. One school recommends immobilization in a lumbosacral orthosis, while the other restricts activity to the level at which the patient becomes symptomatic. We recommend the orthosis if financial conditions permit and the adolescent

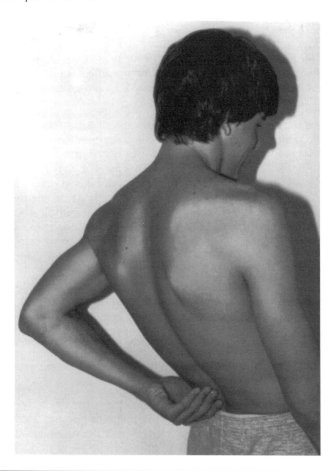

Figure 39-10. Pain of spondylolysis is typically localized to the posterior beltline and is exacerbated by hyperextension.

athlete agrees. We maintain use of the orthosis for at least 3 months. If plain radiographs remain normal during that period and the back pain resolves, we start the athlete on a rehabilitation program and progressive return to sports. Due to expense, we follow the clinical symptoms and plain radiographs rather than repeat the bone scan. If pain does not resolve after 6 months of treatment, we discontinue the orthosis, feeling that prolonged immobilization would not be successful.

For cases with a clear-cut spondylolysis on radiographs or such a finding while under observation, symptomatic relief should be the goal because bony union is unlikely. Activity modifications and analgesics are used, as necessary, to minimize symptoms. A physical therapy program is started and emphasizes flexibility, particularly of the hip flexors, with stretching of the lumbodorsal fascia, hamstrings, and strengthening of abdominal musculature. Corsets, or rigid orthoses, are occasionally used when pain relief is

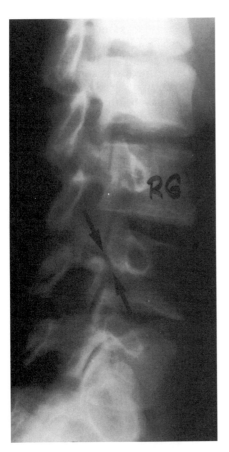

Figure 39-11. A well-established spondylolytic defect in the pars interarticularis of L4 in an 18–year–old male appears as a collar on the Scotty dog of Lachapelle on the oblique radiograph (arrow).

not experienced within the first several weeks. Sports participation is allowed, as permitted by symptoms. Surgery for intractable pain or progressive spondylolysis is rarely required.

Symptomatic Accessory Navicular

A number of minor congenital or developmental anomalies may become symptomatic in the adolescent athlete. Examples include discoid meniscus, hypermobile lateral meniscus, bipartite patella, and the spectrum of dysplastic variants that can result in patellar instability. Symptomatic accessory navicular, an example of this type of anomaly, is a condition that can be a hindrance to soccer players and other running or jumping athletes.

Sella described three types of accessory naviculars. Type I consists of a small accessory bone with a well defined, round outline. Type II is triangular and attached to the navicular by a fibrocartilaginous synchondrosis. Type III is typified by a partially fused osseous bridge between the accessory bone and the navicular body.

The young athlete typically has localized pain along the medial arch of the foot at the insertion of the posterior tibial tendon. Symptoms may begin after an acute episode of trauma or progress insidiously from overuse. Examination reveals localized swelling and tenderness over the medial aspect of the navicular. When the area is swollen and inflamed, even shoes can become problematic. The navicular and its accessory bone are often prominent to palpation. When the onset is acutely traumatic, the injury is easily misdiagnosed as an ankle or hindfoot sprain unless the foot is carefully palpated. Radiographic evaluation demonstrates the accessory navicular lesion, usually a type II lesion (Fig. 39-12).

The injury appears to be a partial disruption of the previously asymptomatic synchondrosis. If there has been acute trauma, we treat the injury as an acute fracture and immobilize the area in a short-leg cast, which is well molded under the arch. The patient is kept in a cast for 6 weeks; the first two nonweight bearing and the final four with full weight bearing. When the cast is removed, the athlete is fitted with an arch-supporting orthotic. General leg and ankle strengthening is begun with emphasis on tibialis posterior development and the athlete is allowed to progressively return to sports activities. When the symptoms are more insidious in onset or the condition is chronic or recurrent, we have forgone casting and treated the player with an orthosis and/or taping to support the arch. Brief courses of NSAIDs are used as necessary.

When conservative treatment fails to adequately control symptoms, surgery should be considered. This typically involves shelling out the fragment while maintaining the integrity of the posterior tibial tendon and its insertion. The tendon insertion is split longitudinally to excise the fragment. The longitudinal split is usually imbricated to make up for the void caused by removing

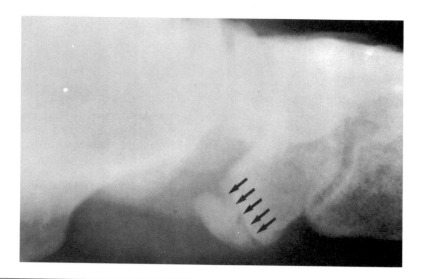

Figure 39-12. Sella type II accessory navicular in a 16–year–old female (arrows). Despite prolonged conservative treatment, this fragment remained extremely painful and required excision.

the accessory fragment. The portion of the tendon insertion that was attached to the excised fragment is firmly anchored to the remaining navicular. Casting is used postoperatively to allow adequate healing of the involved area, followed by an orthotic device and rehabilitation.

Conclusion

Medical staff members overseeing adolescent soccer players must be aware of the ways in which the adolescent skeleton differs from the adult. Although open physes contribute to skeletal growth, they represent vulnerable areas susceptible to particular patterns of injury. Similarly, ligaments and tendons in young athletes can be stronger than the bone, which may cause additional variations in the types of injuries. Minor congenital anomalies may manifest themselves during this period of growth and increased activity. Clinicians evaluating and treating these young athletes must be aware of these conditions and how they may effect the athlete's ability to play in the short-term and, more importantly, their potential to affect the athlete's performance and physical development on a long-term basis.

SUGGESTED READINGS

Cahill B. Treatment of juvenile osteochondritis dissecans and osteochondritis dissecans of the knee. Clin Sports Med 1985;4:367–384.

Clancy WG, Foltz AS. Iliac apophysitis and stress fractures in adolescent runners. Am J Sports Med 1976;4:214–218.

Gronkvist J, Hirsch G, Johansson L. Fracture of the anterior tibial spine in children. J Pediatr Orthop 1984;4:465–468.

Jackson DW, Wiltse LL, Cirincione RJ. Spondylolysis in the female gymnast. Clin Orthop 1976;11:68–73.

Mediar RC, Lyne D. Sinding-Larsen-Johansson disease. J Bone Joint Surg 1978;6OA:1113–1116.

Mital MA, Matza RA, Cohen J. The so-called unresolved Osgood-Schlatter lesion. A concept based on fifteen surgically treated lesions. J Bone Joint Surg 1980;62A:732–739.

Nilsson S, Roaas A. Soccer injuries in adolescents. Am J Sports Med 1986;14:218–224.

Ogden JA, Southwick WO. Osgood-Schlatter's disease and tibial tuberosity development. Clin Orthop 1976;116:180–189.

Ogden JA, Tross RB, Murphy MJ. Fractures of the tibial tuberosity in adolescents. J Bone Joint Surg 1980;62A:205–215.

Sella EJ, Lawson JP, Ogden JA. The accessory navicular synchondrosis. Clin Orthop 1986;209:280–285.

Spiegel PG, Cooperman DR, Larson GS. Epiphyseal fractures of the distal ends of the tibia and fibula. J Bone Joint Surg 1978;6OA:1046.

Steiner ME, Micheli LJ. Treatment of symptomatic spondylolysis and spondylolisthesis with the modified Boston brace. Spine 1985;10:937–943.

Thomson NL. Osteochondritis dissecans and osteochondral fragments managed by Herbert compression screw fixation. Clin Orthop 1987;224:71–78.

Wilson JN. A diagnostic sign in osteochondritis dissecans of the knee. J Bone Joint Surg 1967;49A:477–480.

Wiltse LL, Newman PH, Macnab L. Classification of spondylolysis and spondylolisthesis. Clin Orthop 1976;117:23.

VII

- ## Women in Soccer

40 The Female Soccer Player

Michelle Akers

As the roles of women have changed around the world, both culturally and socially, there has been an increasing popularity of and participation in women's soccer. There are national team programs and leagues for women as well as female coaches, officials, and administrators in a sport that has been traditionally known as a male only activity. Some statistics on the level of participation of women in soccer are presented in Figures 40–1 and 40–2. As the fastest growing team sport in America, in 10 years soccer has had an 83% increase among high school participants and adult (women and men) participation has increased 34% since 1987. With the increase in the number of players comes the need for qualified coaches. Table 40–1 lists the approximate number of coaches licensed by the coaching school of US Soccer and the National Soccer Coaches Association of America.

The Women's Game

This chapter expresses the views of a female athlete. I have been a US Women's National Team member since the inception of the team in 1985. The team has been very successful in its short history. In 1991, the US won the inaugural Federation International de Football (FIFA) Women's World Championship in Sweden and recently took third place in the 1995 World Cup in Sweden.

Currently, the US does not have professional or semiprofessional leagues for women. After graduating from college, elite players looking for competitive environments are forced to play overseas (i.e., Sweden, Japan, or Germany). This will be a detriment to the early success of the sport unless changes occur in the immediate future.

To rectify this problem, the United States Inter-Regional Soccer League (USISL) has begun organizing women's teams in conjunction with USISL men's teams. Also, with Major League Soccer (MLS) in place and due to begin competition in 1996, it is hopeful that US Soccer will develop a plan to coordinate a women's league with the MLS. Creating a competitive league for both men and women is essential if the US is to continue its progression toward becoming a global soccer power.

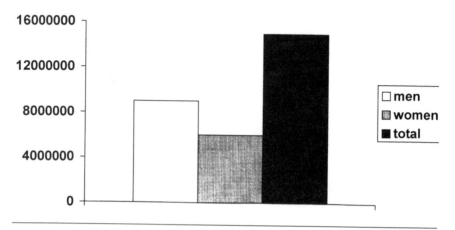

Figure 40-1. Estimated number of soccer players in the United States.

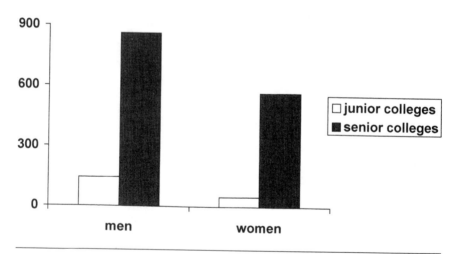

Figure 40-2. Number of collegiate soccer teams by sex and level of school.

The first FIFA Women's World Championship (WC) in 1991 marked the beginning of international acceptance of women playing soccer. This tournament was a trial to examine the skill level, athleticism, and popularity of women's soccer. The WC was a success and has set the precedent for future World Championships and further growth of women's soccer. Approximately 22% of the world population of soccer players are females and this figure is growing rapidly. More than 40% of the US soccer population are females. That is almost half of the 15 million total soccer players in the US.

Marketability

Soccer manufacturers recognize the large number of females in the game and involve women as spokespersons and endorsers to enhance promotional agendas. Several companies have aggressive campaigns with selected female players. These major athletic manufacturers include Umbro (Michelle Akers), Reebok (Julie Foudy), Nike (Mia Hamm, Tisha Venturini, Briana Scurry, and others), and Diadora (Carin Gabarra and Joy Fawcett). In addition, mainstream corporations such as Procter & Gamble, General Motors Corporation, MasterCard, Snickers, and Sprint have identified the tremendous advantage of including female endorsers in their marketing plans. Newspapers and soccer magazines are also featuring more female players, coaches, and columnists to address the rapidly growing population and demand for equal recognition and information.

The Medical Side of the Game

Many people are not directly involved in women's soccer and need to be aware of the physical demands that are part of the game, for both men and women. For example, I have had eight arthroscopic surgeries; four on each knee for various meniscus and ligament tears. In addition, I have rehabilitated at least five other knee injuries that did not require surgery. I have a history of sprained ankles, concussions, stitches, and knocked out teeth. This is the usual wear and tear an elite athlete must endure to be successful.

US Women's National Team Programs

The US Women's National Team has made impressive strides in their 10 year international history. The US Women's team was founded in 1985. Seven years later they became the first FIFA World Champions. In 1994, the team took first place in the CONCACAF World Championship Qualifying Tournament in Montreal, Canada. Also, the US placed third in the 1995 World Championships in Sweden. In the summer of 1996, the US will be among eight teams to make history when women's soccer becomes a medal sport in the Olympics. Besides the Women's National Team, US Soccer has begun to develop consistent schedules for the U–16, U–20, and Women's B Team Programs.

Female coaches in the US have also made great improvements in numbers, opportunities, and licensing programs (Table 40-1). Although the numbers still favor the men, with better education, organization, and opportunity, the coaching opportunities will improve.

The First FIFA Symposium for Women's Soccer

In October of 1992, I attended FIFA's first Women's Football Seminar. It was informative and I heard positive and encouraging information. The seminar

Table 40–1

Numbers of Licensed Coaches in the United States		
Coaching License Programs	USSF	NSCAA
Total A,B,C Licensed Coaches	9000	1729 (A,B only)
Licensed Female Coaches	450	143 (A,B only)
A License	28	41
B license	95	102
C license	325	Not available
Total C,D,F Licensed Coaches	50,000	Not available
Total Instructors	40 (A,B,C only)	22
Female Instructors	3	4

All statistics provided by USSF and NSCAA. Special thanks to Eva Ferara (Umbro USA), Paula Martin (USSF), and Steven Veal (NSCAA Program Director).

inspired renewed enthusiasm about the game and the progress that was occurring. However, several presentations were surprising and intriguing. Many of the debates and topics of these discussions had been resolved in the US. To find medical officials still concerned about some of these issues was distressing.

For example, one medical official spoke of his surprise that only one team had a gynecologist in attendance at the inaugural WC in 1991. In fact, he thought women players should wear padding to protect their uterus and chest during competition. In my 20 years of experience on the field, I have never seen a team travel with a gynecologist. I have never observed injury or complications to the female reproductive organs due to collisions with other players or the ball.

The few minor chest injuries I have observed and the reactions of the injured players were less severe than the reactions of male players when elbowed, kneed, or hit in the groin. In fact, the male reproductive organ is more likely to be injured than the female reproductive organs. Yet, men's teams do not travel with a urologist or wear protective padding.

Soccer teams (male and female) need to travel with a medical doctor (an orthopaedist or family physician), trainer, and massage therapist to cover the various medical needs. Women do not need the specialized attention of a gynecologist when traveling or competing in soccer.

The Menstrual Cycle

There are a few myths about the menstrual cycle in athletes. First, menstruation does not limit a woman's ability to participate in competition. World class performances and records have been set by women at every phase of their menstrual cycle. There is no research to suggest that performance is influenced by the menstrual cycle. Although menstruation can be uncomfortable (i.e., cramps), in most cases physical activity and fitness reduce symptoms related to the menstrual cycle.

The problems to be concerned with in female athletes are the female athlete triad; menstrual dysfunction, osteoporosis, and eating disorders. Amenorrhea (cessation) or oligomenorrhea (infrequent) are a result of the interaction of low body fat, poor diet, psychological stress, and high levels of intense exercise. Many athletes accept menstrual dysfunction as a result of training. Any change in menstrual function should be evaluated by a physician. Although there is little danger to the reproductive organs, there is cause to worry about the possibility of decreased bone density that can lead to increased stress fractures and osteoporosis at a later age. If a female player experiences these symptoms, it is important to get medical attention. It is commonly remedied with a prescription of birth control pills, vitamin and mineral supplements, and guidance in proper diet.

Eating disorders are more commonly seen in aesthetic sports (i.e., gymnastics, skating, dancing) than in women's team sports. Yet, it should not be assumed that eating disorders do not exist. Anorexia and bulimia, while rare, can be found in any sport. The most common eating problems in female soccer players are severe caloric restriction and alternative nutritional practices. Female athletes must be educated about proper nutrition, the importance of the menstrual cycle, and the potential problems associated with intense training.

Knee Injuries

There are studies concerning the differences in female anatomy that may cause an increased incidence of anterior cruciate ligament (ACL) injury and reconstructive surgery in women. However, due to my personal history of knee injuries and the histories of teammates, I have come to believe that it is not only anatomical differences that result in an increased incidence of knee injuries in women. I believe it is a combination of anatomy, lack of quality coaching, and poor technique, fitness, and decision making during competition.

In the past, female athletes have not received the best coaching available because women's soccer was not a priority. Therefore, women did not obtain the necessary information to develop proper technique, decision making skills, and fitness base that allow players to remain free of injury. Add this to increased opportunity and competition levels and the result is an increased rate of injury.

The question still remains as to why there is such a high incidence of knee injuries in particular. Doctors have many theories to explain this phenomenon. As the number of injuries increase, it seems of immediate concern to learn the explanation. The problem will continue to grow as competition becomes more intense. Therefore, I urge FIFA to initiate a study on the cause of severe knee injuries in female soccer players.

Summary

From the elite players to the young women just beginning the sport, female athletes need to be treated with the same importance and respect at all levels to prevent further injuries, provide proper training environments, and develop talented female players. Athletes, parents, coaches, and doctors must be educated in ways to protect the female athlete from injury with proper fitness, strength training, correct techniques and tactics, proper medical care, and nutritional information.

Everyone must work together to educate and prepare the young female athlete for the rigors of the sport. Doctors and trainers must provide the athletes and coaches with the information needed to remain healthy and yet compete at the highest level possible.

Finally, it is important that the medical profession and the rest of the world treat women's soccer as a serious sport with talented, ambitious athletes. The fact remains that women play soccer and the trend is growing rapidly throughout the world. It is the responsibility and to the benefit of our soccer leadership to further educate, prepare, and support these athletes in health issues, competition, coaching, and player development.

41   Female Collegiate Soccer Injuries

Elizabeth A. Arendt
Randall Dick

Soccer is the most popular sport in the world. Until the 1970s, the game was played mostly by men. The first Women's European Soccer Championship was played in 1983–1984. There has been growing interest and participation since that time. Female soccer is currently played in over 50 countries.

Soccer is a growing sport in the United States, particularly among women. At the high school level, participation has grown five-fold among males from 1972–1995. Among high school females, participation levels in 1995 were over 237 times that in 1972, the greatest growth occurring in the last decade.

The growth of intercollegiate soccer, especially among women, also shows a rapid upward trend. This growth is reflected in the increase of soccer participation by member institutions in the National Collegiate Athletic Association (NCAA). Member participation can be closely followed and compared since 1982, when women's sports were added to the NCAA purview. In 1982, there were 521 men's teams resulting in approximately 13,000 participating athletes, compared to 80 women's teams resulting in 1855 participating athletes. Currently, there are over 600 NCAA men's soccer programs and approximately 450 NCAA women's soccer programs. This reflects an increase of approximately 17% in men's programs and 458% in participating women's teams (Figs. 41-1 and 41-2). These facts indicate that collegiate women's soccer programs are enjoying a large increase in popularity and participation as reflected in the number of NCAA institutions sponsoring the programs.

Although male soccer injuries have been reported in many studies, few studies have looked at soccer injuries in females. This chapter reviews the current injury data in the college-age group in the United States for soccer as reported by the NCAA Injury Surveillance System. The NCAA developed an Injury Surveillance System (ISS) in 1982. This surveillance system was designed to collect current and reliable data on injury trends in intercollegiate athletics in the United States. The ISS has been collecting information on soccer since 1986. This chapter reviews the material and methods of the ISS, reports some interesting data from the ISS, and reflects on some of the findings.

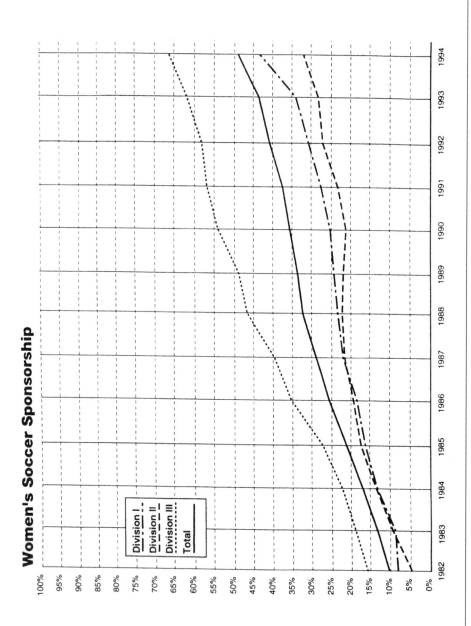

Figure 41-1. Percent of American colleges sponsoring women's soccer by NCAA division and year.

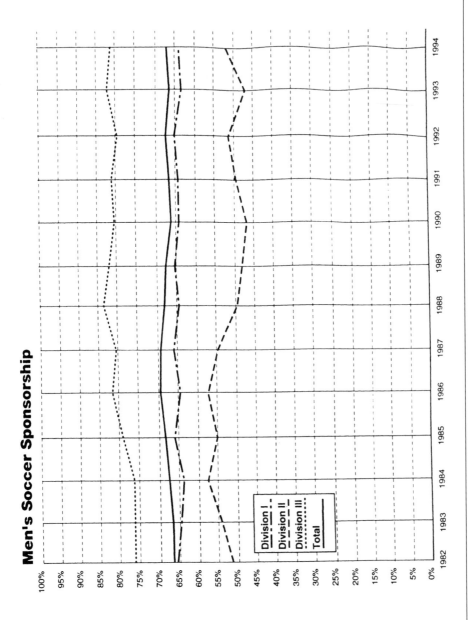

Figure 41-2. Percent of American colleges sponsoring men's soccer by NCAA division and year.

Methods

Sampling

Participation in the ISS is voluntary and limited to the 906 NCAA institutions (as of September 1994). Selections are random, within the constraints of a minimum 10% representation of each NCAA division (I, II, and III) and region (East, South, Midwest, West). This sampling scheme is used to assure a national cross-section, which expresses injury rates representative of the total population of the NCAA institutions sponsoring a particular sport.

Subjects

The student athletes monitored by the ISS are participants in varsity intercollegiate athletics programs at NCAA member institutions. The age of the participants ranges from 17–23 years.

Data Reporting

Injury and exposure data are recorded by certified and student athletic trainers from participating institutions. The system is designed to allow these individuals to give an accurate response to each of the injury or exposure questions. Injuries not attributed to the actual sport activity are not collected. Information is collated from the first official day of preseason practice to the final postseason contest.

Injuries

No common definition of injury, measure of severity, or evaluation of exposure exists in the athletic injury literature. The information discussed in this chapter must be evaluated under the definitions and methodology outlined by the ISS. In the ISS, a reportable injury is defined as one that occurs as a result of participation in an organized intercollegiate practice or game, requires medical attention by a team athletic trainer or physician, and results in restriction of participation for one or more days beyond the day of injury. Each reported injury is detailed in a variety of categories by a single response that best describes the injury. There is a category for injury mechanism, with four possible responses, including no apparent contact and contact with another player.

Exposures

An athletic exposure (A-E), the unit of risk in the ISS, is defined as one athlete participating in one practice or game in which he or she is exposed to the possibility of an athletic injury. A one-page exposure form, submitted weekly, is used to collect the number of practices and games, types of playing surfaces, and number of participants in the daily activities.

Injury Rate

An injury rate is determined by comparing the number of injuries in a specific category to the number of athletes at risk in that category. In the ISS, the value is expressed as injuries per 1000 athlete exposures.

Early ISS data reveals the knee as one of the top three body parts injured in 14 of the 16 monitored sports. To gain more insight into knee injuries, a question concerning specific knee structures was added to the ISS in 1989. This question asks which knee structures were injured and includes the categories of collateral ligament, anterior cruciate ligament (ACL), posterior cruciate ligament, cartilage (including meniscus), patella, and patella tendon.

Results of ISS Data for Soccer (1986–1994)

Reviews of men's and women's injuries show a similar pattern for injury rate in games versus practices (Figs. 41-3 and 41-4). Despite the greater exposure to injury in practices, there is a higher injury rate in games.

The type of playing surface was looked at in relation to injury. Although the data report a small number of exposures on artificial turf, the numbers are skewed. The overall data for men show a similar incident of injury on natural and artificial turf. However, the overall rate of injury was slightly lower for the women as compared to the men (Figs. 41-5 and 41-6).

When reviewing the most frequently injured body parts, there is a consistent pattern of injury in the men's data. The ankle is the most frequently injured body part for almost every year sampled (Table 41-1). For women, the primary body part injured has been variable, with a greater percentage of injuries in the knee and upper leg than seen in the men (Table 41–2).

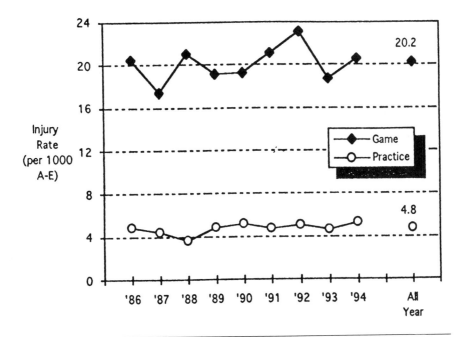

Figure 41-3. Game and practice injury rate in men's collegiate soccer by year.

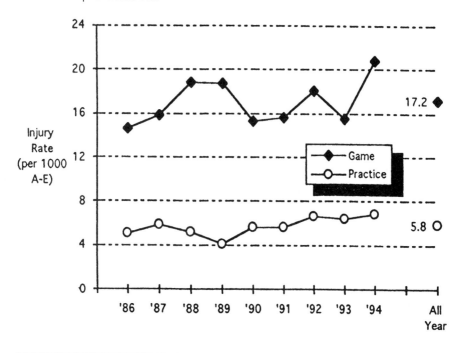

Figure 41-4. Game and practice injury rate in women's collegiate soccer by year.

Table 41–3 illustrates total injuries and total knee injuries by gender in soccer. From 1989–1993, 461 male teams (average of 92 per year) and 278 female teams (average of 56 per year) submitted data. Participation values reflect 15% of the NCAA institutions sponsoring soccer each year. The higher number of men's teams participating reflect the greater absolute number of NCAA schools sponsoring the sport and result in a higher number of athlete exposures.

Knee injuries are more prevalent in female soccer players than in male players (Table 41–4). This is true whether expressed as an injury rate (number of knee injuries/athletic exposure) or as a percentage of all injuries (number of knee injuries versus all soccer injuries).

Injured knee structures are shown according to gender in Figure 41–7. The ACL injury rate in women's soccer (0.31) is more than double that of men's soccer (0.13); a statistically significant difference. Torn cartilage, including the menisci, are also significantly higher in women's soccer (0.34 versus 0.19). Further analysis reveals that 48 of 81 reported men's ACL injuries (59%) and 66 of 97 reported women's ACL injuries (68%) resulted in surgery. The ACL injury rate difference between the genders is consistent in practices and games.

Men's Soccer
GAME Surface Injury Rate

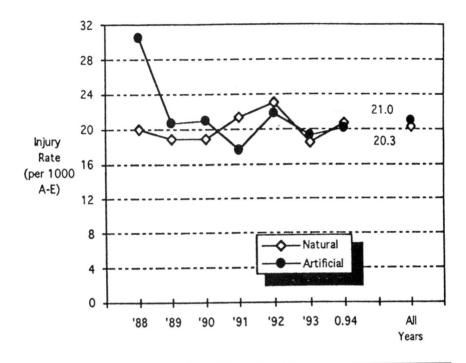

Figure 41-5. Game surface injury rate in men's collegiate soccer by year.

The soccer ACL injury rate difference between the genders over the five-year sample period is shown in Figure 41–8.

The mechanism of ACL injury in soccer is shown in Figure 41–9. In the women's game, no apparent contact is the primary injury mechanism followed by player contact. Player contact, followed closely by no apparent contact, are the primary ACL injury mechanisms in the men's game.

The etiology of the increased injury rate in females, particularly the risk of an ACL injury, is unclear. There has been much discussion concerning the increased rate of ACL injuries in women. The factors can be divided into extrinsic factors (level of skill, level of experience, muscular strength, and coordination) and intrinsic factors (ligament size, notch dimensions, limb alignment, and joint laxity). Complete discussions and reviews of this matter can be found in the literature. A few items are worthy of mention.

According to the ISS data, female basketball players have an ACL injury rate at least three times that of males in four of the five years sampled with an average of 4.1 times the number of ACL injuries as their male counterparts over the same study period (Fig. 41–10). Examination of frictional forces created at the shoe-surface interface and muscle strength at the knee joint are two fac-

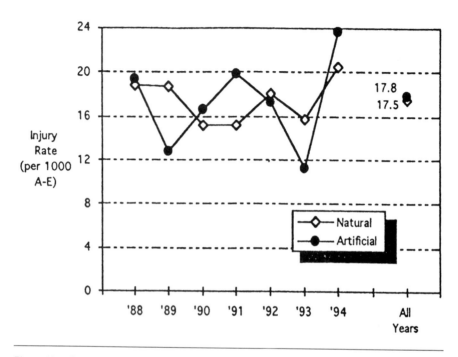

Women's Soccer
GAME Surface Injury Rate

Figure 41-6. Game surface injury rate in women's collegiate soccer by year.

Table 41-1

	No. of Teams	No. of Injuries	1		2		3	
					Top Three Body Parts Injured (Men's Soccer)			
1986–87	62	729	Knee	(19%)	Ankle	(18%)	Upper leg	(13%)
1987–88	76	823	Ankle	(21%)	Knee	(17%)	Upper leg	(15%)
1988–89	45	527	Ankle	(21%)	Upper leg	(20%)	Knee	(17%)
1989–90	75	898	Ankle	(20%)	Upper leg	(17%)	Knee	(14%)
1990–91	88	981	Ankle	(17%)	Upper leg	(17%)	Knee	(16%)
1991–92	106	1,236	Ankle	(21%)	Knee	(17%)	Upper leg	(17%)
1992–93	110	1,203	Ankle	(20%)	Upper leg	(17%)	Knee	(15%)
1993–94	83	773	Ankle	(22%)	Upper leg	(16%)	Knee	(12%)
1994–95	102	1,106	Ankle	(20%)	Upper leg	(17%)	Knee	(15%)

Table 41-2

	No. of Teams	No. of Injuries	1		2		3	
					Top Three Body Parts Injured (Women's Soccer)			
1986–87	33	288	Upper leg	(20%)	Ankle	(20%)	Knee	(15%)
1987–88	43	418	Upper leg	(22%)	Ankle	(18%)	Knee	(17%)
1988–89	39	391	Ankle	(27%)	Upper leg	(16%)	Knee	(16%)
1989–90	42	362	Ankle	(20%)	Knee	(20%)	Upper leg	(14%)
1990–91	52	476	Upper leg	(21%)	Ankle	(21%)	Knee	(17%)
1991–92	63	605	Ankle	(21%)	Upper leg	(18%)	Knee	(16%)
1992–93	62	569	Knee	(24%)	Ankle	(21%)	Upper leg	(16%)
1993–94	59	530	Upper leg	(19%)	Knee	(16%)	Ankle	(15%)
1994–95	82	910	Ankle	(21%)	Knee	(18%)	Upper leg	(15%)

Table 41-3

Men's Soccer	**Total Injury and Knee Injury Summary (1989–1993)**	Women's Soccer
461 (92)	Teams submitting data (average/year)	278 (56)
5100	All injuries	2542
788 (16%)	Knee injuries (% of all injuries)	485 (19%)
626,223	Athletic exposures (approximately 2:1)	308,748
1.3	Knee injury rate (per 1000 A-E)	1.6

Table 41-4

Knee Structures Injured (1989–1993)					
Men's Soccer			*Women's Soccer*		
Number	*Rate*[a]		*Number*	*Rate*[a]	*P*[b]
316	0.51	Collateral	192	0.62	0.02
119	0.19	Torn Cartilage (meniscus)	105	0.34	0.00
130	0.21	Patella and/or patella tendon	92	0.30	0.01
81	0.13	Anterior Cruciate	97	0.31	0.00
22	0.04	Posterior Cruciate	12	0.04	
626,223		Athletic Exposures	308,748		

[a]*Rate = Injuries per 1000 A–E*

[b]*P from table χ2 (see Materials and Methods)*

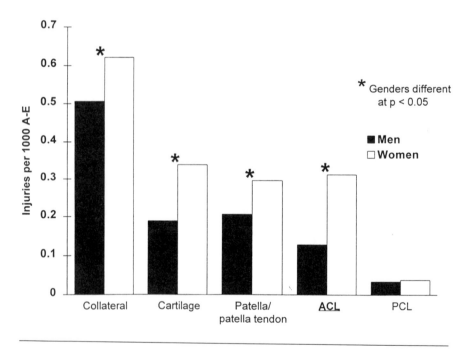

Figure 41-7. Injury rate (1989–1993) in collegiate soccer of selected knee structures by gender.

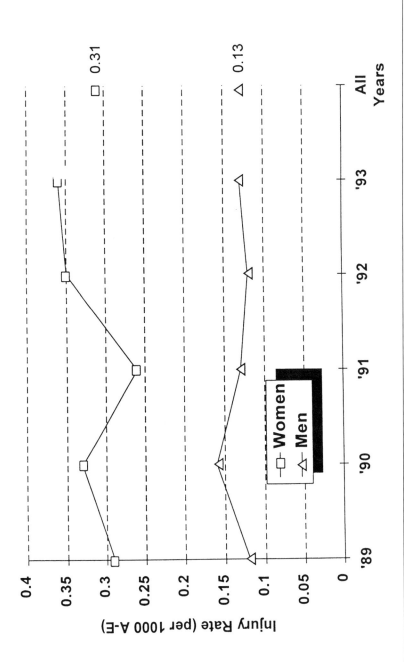

Figure 41-8. ACL injury rate (1989–1993) in collegiate soccer by year and gender.

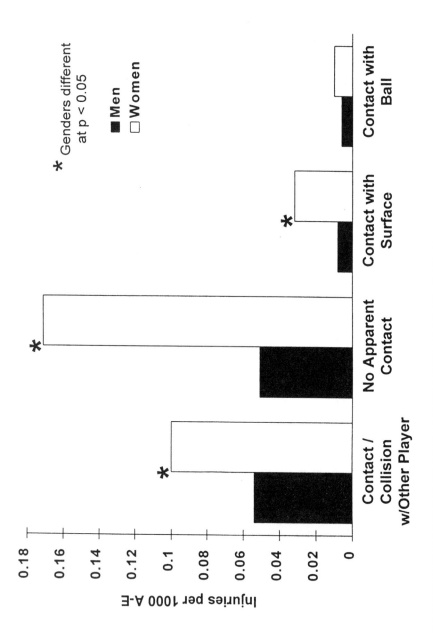

Figure 41-9. ACL injury rate (1989–1993) in collegiate soccer by mechanism and gender.

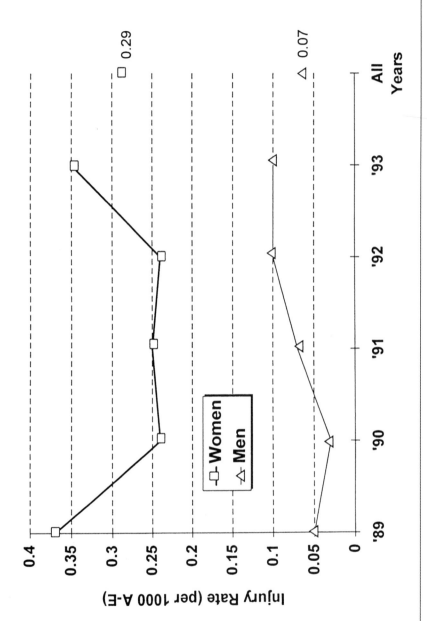

Figure 41-10. ACL injury rate (1989–1993) in collegiate basketball by year and gend

tors relevant to ACL injury and worthy of further research. The incidence of ACL injury in the NCAA ISS review is high in two sports (basketball and soccer) that share similar body mechanics (deceleration, plant, and pivot) but different shoe-surface requirements (field surface with a cleated shoe versus court surface with an uncleated shoe).

A study of team handball in Norway also implicates the shoe-surface friction rate. This study reports that certain shoes on specific surfaces, particularly green turf, show a higher friction rate and correlate with a higher incidence of ACL injuries on those surfaces.

There is little scientific investigation involving analysis and evaluation of the way soccer is played by males and females. Current research on soccer suggests that the demands of the game, including distance covered, exercise intensity, and physical and physiological characteristics, are similar for men and women. There is still considerable scope for further research in this area.

Skill level has been implicated as a contributing factor to injuries in both men and women. There is concern that the recent increase in soccer participation may decrease the average skill level of players. A recent survey from Norway, reviewing injuries sustained during the Norway Cup, show a decrease from 32 injuries per week to 17 injuries per week among the female players over 3 years. It is likely that the increasing skill level of the participants was the reason for the decrease in injuries. Concerning knee injuries in general, and ACL injuries specifically, the injury rate for females has remained relatively constant over the 5 years reviewed by the NCAA ISS data. Injury data with a more direct measurement or quantification of skill level and matched skill levels of tournament participants will help to support or dispel this belief.

Although gender differences in ACL injuries have been confirmed in this review, even in a high-risk sport such as soccer injuries to the ACL are infrequent in the college environment. Assuming 20 people participate in each practice or game, the ACL injury rate translates to one ACL injury every 385 activity sessions (practice or game) in men's soccer and one ACL injury every 161 activity sessions in women's soccer. Both genders are nine times more likely to receive ACL injuries in a game as compared to a practice.

Examination of injury mechanisms can be instructional in developing safety recommendations or possible rule changes. Contact and collision with another player contribute to ACL injuries in both genders. Therefore, future research may want to specifically examine these contact mechanisms. The role of contact and collision as injury mechanisms is consistent with the study by Engstrom reviewing injuries in elite female soccer players. This study revealed that the majority of traumatic injuries occur during contact with an opponent. The study further found that extrinsic factors, such as weather, playing surface, temperature, or the position of the player, did not influence injury rate. During the year studied, 17% of the elite female soccer players sustained major knee injuries, although ACL injuries were not specifically analyzed.

Of greater importance in this study, however, were the number of noncontact ACL injuries. Female basketball and soccer players had a significantly higher injury rate for noncontact ACL injuries than their male counterparts. The etiology of noncontact ACL injuries is speculative and can include many of the intrinsic and extrinsic factors discussed previously.

The NCAA ISS data shows that ACL injury mechanisms may differ between comparable men's and women's sports. No apparent contact is the primary injury mechanism for ACL injuries in female soccer, accounting for over one-half of the reported injuries. Player contact is the primary ACL injury mechanism in the men's game. These findings suggest that internally generated forces may be responsible for this type of injury. This may implicate an anatomical explanation for ACL injuries. Therefore, further exploration of notch and ACL dimensions may be instructional.

Conclusions

Data collected through the NCAA ISS on a national sample of collegiate soccer athletes from 1989–1993 reveals that female athletes experienced a significantly higher knee and ACL injury rate as compared to their male counterparts. No other knee structure examined (collateral, posterior cruciate, patella, patella tendon), except cartilage and meniscal injury, exhibited such a significant gender difference. A significant number of meniscal injuries occured with the ACL injuries. Noncontact was the primary ACL injury mechanism for females in soccer.

Other soccer injuries did not reveal major differences between the genders. This includes practice and game injury rate and injury to other body parts.

The increased risk of ACL injuries in females is probably multifactorial, with no single structural, anatomic, or biomechanical feature solely responsible. Contributing forces may include extrinsic factors, such as muscle strength, shoe-surface interaction, skill level, experience, and conditioning. Intrinsic factors may include ligament size, intercondylar notch variation, limb alignment, and joint laxity.

This review verifies that an increased risk of ACL injuries in female soccer players exists within the population measured. Despite a variety of studied hypotheses, there is no conclusive explanation for this increased risk. Although such an injury does not happen frequently, it can produce extended disability when it does occur. The current challenge is to explain the gender specificity associated with ACL injury and develop measures to address the problem.

SUGGESTED READINGS

Albert M. Descriptive three-year data study of outdoor and indoor professional soccer injuries. Athletic Training 1983;18:218–220.

Arendt L, Dick R. Gender specific knee injury pattern in collegiate basketball and soccer: NCAA data and review of literature. Am J Sports Med, Accepted for publication.

Backous DD, Friedl KEG, Smith NJ, et al. Soccer injuries and their elation to physical maturity. Am J Dis Child 1988;142:839–842.

Berger-Vachnon C, Gabard G, Moyen B. Soccer accidents in the French Rhone-Alps Soccer Association. Sports Med 1987;3:69–77.

Brynhildsen J, Ekstrand J, Jeppsson A, et al. Previous injuries and persisting symptoms in female soccer players. Int J Sports Med 1990;11:489–492.

Davis JA, Brewer J. Applied physiology of female soccer players. Sports Med 1993;16:180–189.

Ekstrand J, Gillquist J. Soccer injuries and their mechanisms: a prospective study. Med Sci Sports Exerc 1983;15:267–270.

Engebretsen L. Soccer injuries in Norway. J Nor Med Assoc 1985;105:1766–1769.

Engstrom B, Johannsson C, Tornkvist H. Soccer injuries among elite female players. Am J Sports Med 1991;19:372–375.

Keller CS, Noyes FR, Buncher LR. The medical aspects of soccer injury epidemiology. Am J Sports Med 1987;15:230–237.

McMaster WC, Walter M. Soccer injuries in adolescents. Am J Sports Med 1978;6: 358–361.

Myklebust G, Strand T, Engebretsen L. Registration of ACL injuries in Norwegian team handball. A prospective study. Presented at the American College of Sports Medicine Meeting, Seattle, WA, June 1993.

National Collegiate Athletic Association. Injury Surveillance System, Men's Soccer 1994–1995.

National Collegiate Athletic Association. Injury Surveillance System, Women's Soccer 1994–1995.

National Collegiate Athletic Association. Participation Statistics Report. April 10, 1995.

42  Nutritional Concerns for Women

Emily M. Haymes

Nutrition can play an important role in athletic performance. Team sports like soccer that include intermittent, high-intensity sprints require carbohydrate as the primary source of energy. Endurance sports require adequate hemoglobin in the blood to transport oxygen to the muscles for energy production. Low iron intake can lead to iron deficiency and anemia, which reduces endurance.

Little information is available on the nutritional habits of female soccer players. Most of the data on nutrient intake presented in this chapter are from studies of female athletes involved in team sports, especially field hockey and lacrosse. These two sports were selected because of their similarities to soccer in the way the games are played and the energy expended during play.

Energy Requirements

The time-motion characteristics of female soccer players show similar patterns to that of men, but at a slightly reduced distance. One study showed that during an 80 minute match, 13% of the time was spent standing, 38% walking, 23% jogging, 17% running at low intensity, 6% running at moderate intensity, 2% running at high intensity, and 1% sprinting (Fig 42–1). The percentage of time spent in each activity was similar to that of elite males competing in Danish League soccer matches. Distance covered by a female midfielder in an international match was 9500 m. The average distance covered by elite Swedish female soccer players during competition was just under 8500 m.

Energy expenditure during a soccer match can be estimated from heart rate data. The average heart rate of a Danish international player averaged 171 beats/min during the first half and 168 beats/min in the second half. For this particular athlete, the estimated oxygen consumption (VO2) was 2.79 and 2.63 L/min for the first and second half. Assuming a caloric equivalent of 5 kcal/L of O_2, the estimated energy expenditure for this female player was 1084 kcal for the match. This Danish female midfielder had a relatively high VO2max (61 ml/kg/min) compared to the VO2max of typical elite female soccer players, which ranges from 47–58 ml/kg/min. It was estimated that a

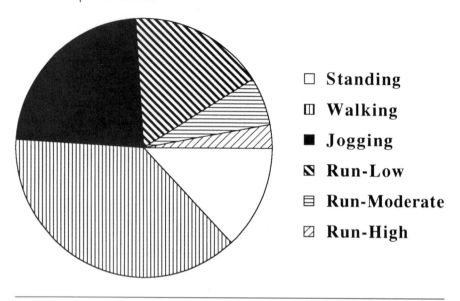

□ **Standing**

Ⅲ **Walking**

■ **Jogging**

◨ **Run-Low**

☰ **Run-Moderate**

▨ **Run-High**

Figure 42-1. Amount (%) of time spent doing different activities during a Danish League soccer match by a female midfielder. (Adapted from: Bangsbo J. The physiology of soccer—with special reference to intense intermittent exercise. Acta Physiologica Scandinavica (suppl) 1994;619:1–155).

female soccer player weighing 60 kg with a VO2max of 50 ml/kg/min would expend approximately 1100 kcal during a match. Athletes with a lower VO2max and lower weight have a slightly lower energy expenditure.

Mean heart rate during soccer matches is also used to determine exercise intensity. Average heart rates of 173–177 beats/min during soccer matches have been reported for female players. This corresponds to an average exercise intensity of approximately 70% of VO2max. The elite Danish midfield player mentioned earlier exercised at 84% VO2max during the first half and 79% VO2max during the second half of the international match.

Carbohydrate

At exercise intensities above 65% VO2max, muscle glycogen becomes the primary source of carbohydrate used for energy purposes. Studies of male soccer players show that a greater amount of muscle glycogen is used during the first half and the muscle is nearly depleted of glycogen by the end of a 90 minute soccer match. To maintain muscle glycogen, adequate carbohydrate intake (> 55% of total calories) must be included in the diet.

Studies reporting carbohydrate intake of female team sport athletes suggest that many female athletes do not consume enough carbohydrate (Table 42-1). Published data on female field hockey, lacrosse, basketball, and volleyball players report mean carbohydrate intakes as ranging from 47%–54% of total energy intake. Table 42-1 shows that carbohydrate intakes of female team sport athelets range from 204–257 g/day. Many of these female athletes appear to have relatively low energy intakes with the means

Table 42-1

Sport	Energy kcal	Carbohydrate grams	Carbohydrate %kcal	Fat grams	Fat %kcal	Protein grams	Protein g/kg	Protein %kcal
Nutrient Intake of Female Team Sport Athletes								
Field Hockey								
Wake Forest[a]	1513	204	54	45	27	56.7	0.95	15
Ohio State[b]	1956	228	47	84	39	76.0	1.26	16
Dutch National[c]	2151	253	47	81	34	62.1	1.0	12
Lacrosse[d]	2219	257	50	95	35	89.0		16
Basketball[e]	1797	227	50	52	26	69.4	1.0	15
Volleyball[e]	1608	216	54	54	30	69.7	1.05	17

Adapted from:

[a]*Nutter J. Seasonal Changes in female athletes' diets. Int J Sports Nutr 1991;1:395–407.*

[b]*Tilgner SA, Schiller MR. Dietary intakes of female collegiate athletes: the need for nutrition education. J Amer Diet Assoc 1989;89:967–969.*

[c]*van Erp-Bart AMJ, Saris WHM, Binkharst RA, et al. Nationwide survey on nutritional habits in elite athletes. Part I. Energy, carbohydrate, protein, and fat intake. Int J Sports Med 1989;10:S3–S10.*

[d]*Short SH, Short WR. Four year study of university athlete's dietary intake. J Amer Diet Assoc 1983;82:632–645.*

[e]*Risser WL, Lee EJ, LeBlanc A, et al. Bone density in eumenorrheic female college athletes. Med Sci in Sports Exer 1990;22:570–574.*

ranging from 1512–2219 kcal/day. Soccer requires approximately 1100 of these calories. Low energy and carbohydrate intakes reduce the amount of muscle glycogen stored, which could negatively effect performance. In 1982, Jacobs showed that muscle glycogen stores in male soccer players had not returned to normal levels 48 hours after a match (Fig. 42–2). In 1973, Saltin reported that players who began a soccer match with low muscle glycogen stores used most of their muscle glycogen during the first half and covered less distance and spent more time walking during the second half.

Female athletes should be encouraged to increase their carbohydrate intakes to at least 6 g of carbohydrate per kilogram of body weight per day. Many foods are rich in carbohydrate. Sugar is almost pure carbohydrate. Chocolate candy, cereals, flour, cookies, crackers, jams, and dried fruits are also very high in carbohydrate. Other good sources of carbohydrate are bread, rice, pasta, and starchy vegetables (i.e., potatoes). An adequate carbohydrate intake can be achieved by eating both simple and complex carbohydrates. Table 42-2 lists the amounts of simple and complex carbohydrates that must be consumed to equal 50 g of carbohydrate. Because most soft drinks have a higher concentration of sugar than carbohydrate-electrolyte drinks, the athlete has to drink more of the carbohydrate-electrolyte drink to receive 50 g of carbohydrate.

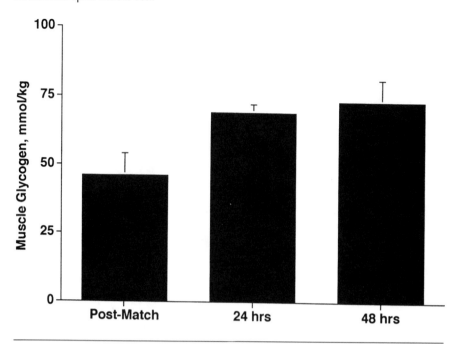

Figure 42-2. Muscle glycogen resynthesis in elite soccer players after a match. (Adapted from: Jacobs I, Westlin N, Karlsson J, et al. Europ J Appl Physiol 1982;48:297–302).

Protein

Protein is needed for growth and repair of body tissues and formation of new cells, enzymes, some hormones, and antibodies. During prolonged endurance exercise, athletes may use protein as an alternative source of energy. The recommended dietary allowance (RDA) for protein is 0.8 g/kg of body weight for adult males and females. The RDA for protein may not be optimal for some athletes, including soccer players. However, this belief is based on studies of endurance and strength athletes rather than soccer players. The protein intake of most athletes will exceed the RDA if they consume a variety of foods and adequate calories.

The protein intake of female team sport athletes varies from 0.95–1.26 g/kg of body weight (Table 42-1). Protein composes 12%–17% of the total caloric intake of these female athletes. The best sources of protein are meat, fish, poultry, and cheese, which are 19%–30% protein by weight. Other good sources of protein are cottage cheese, nuts, and eggs (13%–16% protein), cereals (7%–14% protein), and bread and legumes (7%–8% protein).

Fluid Intake and Replacement

Fluid loss during a soccer match varies depending on the environmental temperature and humidity. Male soccer players lost 3% of their body weight (> 2 kg) during soccer matches in hot dry (91°F and 40% humidity) and hot humid (79°F and 78% humidity) environments and 1.2% of their body weight

Table 42-2

Food Equivalents which Contain 50 Grams of Carbohydrate	
Simple Sugars	*Complex Carbohydrates*
3 tbsp. Honey	4 slices Bread
3 Doughnuts	50 Potato chips
16 oz. Soft drink	1.5 Baked potatoes
28 oz. Carbohydrate-electrolyte drink	1 1/3 c. Rice, cooked
3 oz. Milk Chocolate bar	1.5 c. Pasta, cooked
2 Apples (large)	2 slices Pizza (14 in.)
2 Bananas	2 Bagels
15 oz. Orange juice	2 Waffles
1/6 Lemon meringue pie (9 in.)	2.5 c. Corn flakes

during matches in a cool (55°F) environment. Fluid intake during these matches was inadequate to replace fluid loss. Dehydration and heat illness can result from inadequate fluid replacement during exercise. When fluids are consumed during exercise, body core temperature rises for the first 30–40 minutes and then plateaus. If no fluid is consumed during exercise, core temperature continues to rise due to dehydration. Rectal temperatures of male soccer players after matches in thermoneutral environments were found to average 39.5°C while the rectal temperatures of female soccer players averaged 38.7°C. The difference in rectal temperatures after the match may have been due to lower exercise intensities for the female players.

When soccer is played in warm environments, the danger of dehydration and heat illness should always be anticipated. Elias and colleagues (1991) covered the US Youth Soccer Tournament in July 1988 where the temperature approached 100°F (38°C) and the humidity exceeded 80%. Thirty-four heat exhaustion cases occurred in male and female players in approximately equal numbers. There were twice as many males as females participating in the tournament, which means the female players were twice as likely to experience heat exhaustion. After the second day of play, game times were shortened and breaks were lengthened to allow for greater fluid intake. The number of heat exhaustion cases declined after the second day, which suggests that game modifications were effective in reducing the incidence of heat illness.

Soccer players should consume 300–500 ml of fluid 15–30 minutes prior to training and competition. During training, female athletes should consume 150–250 ml (5–8 oz) of fluid every 15–20 minutes. During competition, the volume and composition of the fluids consumed at half-time should be based on the requirements and preferences of the individual. In hot weather, fluids should be available on the sides of the field and players should be allowed to drink when play is stopped. After training and competition, athletes should drink enough fluid to replace the fluid lost through sweating. After exercise, consumption of fluids and foods containing carbohydrate and electrolytes will enhance the recovery process.

Calcium

Calcium is most important during growth for the formation of bone (99% of the body's calcium is stored in bones). Low calcium intake can lead to a reduction in peak bone mass, which is achieved by the age of 30. Inadequate calcium may also increase the risk of stress fractures. In studies, young adult athletes (male and female) with stress fractures in the lower extremities had lower bone mineral densities (BMD) than matched athletes without stress fractures. The injured athletes had significantly lower calcium intakes compared to the athletes who had not experienced stress fractures.

The RDA for calcium for both females and males, ages 11–24 years, is 1200 mg/day. College-age female team sport athletes report mean calcium intakes ranging from 744–830 mg/day, which is 62%–69% of the present RDA (Fig. 42-3). One of the reasons many young women have low calcium intakes is because they restrict their caloric intake and restrict or eliminate dairy products from their diets. Dairy products are among the best sources of calcium. Other good sources include most leafy green vegetables (i.e., broccoli), tofu,

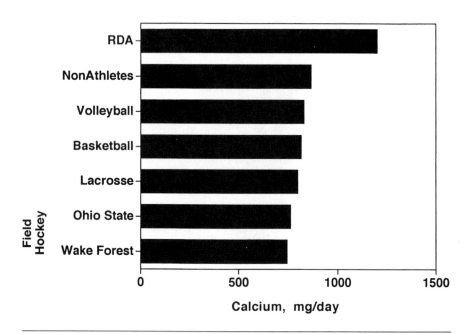

Figure 42-3. Daily calcium intake of female team sport athletes and the recommended dietary intake (RDA), ages 11–24. (Adapted from: Nutter J. Seasonal changes in female athletes diets. Int J Sports Nutr 1991;1:395–407; Risser WL, Lee EJ, LeBlanc A, et al. Bone density in eumenorrheic female college athletes. Med Sci Sports Exer 1990;22:570–574; Short SH, Short WR. Four year study of university athlete's dietary intake. J Am Diet Assoc 1983;82:632–645; Tilgner SA, Schiller MR. Dietary intake of female collegiate athletes: the need for nutrition education. J Amer Diet Assoc 1989;89:967–969).

canned sardines and salmon (with bones), waffles and pancakes made with milk, and foods that have been fortified with calcium (i.e., orange juice).

Iron

Iron is found primarily in hemoglobin, which carries most of the oxygen in the blood. Inadequate iron intake over a prolonged period of time can deplete iron stores and reduce hemoglobin levels. Females, ages 11–50 years, have an RDA of 15 mg/day of iron. The RDA for iron is higher in females between menarche and menopause because iron is lost in the menses. Many adolescent and adult females consume diets low in iron because they restrict their intake of meat. Meat, fish, and poultry are the richest sources of food iron. Studies of female team sport athletes report iron intakes from food as ranging from 9.4–14.0 mg/day (Fig. 42-4). Although, the Dutch National field hockey team had a mean food iron intake of 11.5 mg/day. Because the women took iron supplements, their total daily iron intake exceeded 50 mg/day.

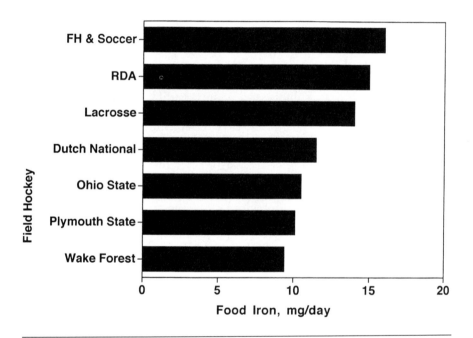

Figure 42-4. Daily iron intake of female team sport athletes and the recommended dietary intake (RDA) for women, ages 11–50. (Adapted from: Diehl DM, Lohman TG, Smith SC, et al. Effects of physical training and competition on the iron status of female field hockey players. Int J Sports Med 1986;7:264–270; Douglas PD. Effect of a season of competition and training on hematological status of women field hockey and soccer players. J Sports Med and Phys Fitness 1989;29:179–183; Nutter J. Seasonal changes in female athletes diets. Int J Sports Med 1991;1:395–407; Short SA, Short WR. Four year study of university athletes dietary intake. J Amer Diet Assoc 1983;82:632–645; Tilgner SA, Schiller MR. Dietary intake of female collegiate athletes: the need for nutrition education. J Am Diet Assoc 1989;89:967–969; van Erp-Bart AMJ, Saris WHM, Binkhorst RA, et al. Nationwide survey on nutritional habits in elite athletes. Part I. Energy, carbohydrate, protein, and fat intake. Int J Sports Med 1989;10:S3–S10).

Many female athletes have low iron stores. The best indicator of depleted iron stores is a low serum ferritin level (< 12 µg/L). Low iron stores may be due to inadequate iron intake or increased iron loss through the menses, gastrointestinal bleeding, or sweating. Depletion of iron stores may occur over a season of training and competition. In a college field hockey team observed over three seasons, there were decreases in serum ferritin levels during the second and third seasons. The mean iron intake of the field hockey players during these two seasons was 10.1 and 13.9 mg/day. In contrast, female field hockey and soccer players with iron intakes of 16 mg/day increased their hemoglobin over the course of a competitive season.

When serum ferritin levels are low in female athletes during training, iron supplements will increase iron stores. Eight weeks of iron supplementation in women can significantly increase serum ferritin levels. This can cause a significant increase in maximal oxygen uptake and reduction in blood lactate after treatment. Iron supplementation will improve performance if an athlete is anemic. The iron status of female soccer players should be evaluated as a part of the annual physical examination. Iron supplements should be recommended to athletes who are diagnosed as iron depleted or anemic.

Eating Disorders

Some female athletes develop eating disorders, such as anorexia nervosa and bulimia nervosa. Studies show that the greatest prevalence of eating disorders (anorexia nervosa, bulimia, and anorexia athletica) occur in aesthetic and weight dependent sports followed by endurance sports. The prevalence of eating disorders in ball game athletes (which includes soccer) is 11%; a figure that is not significantly different from the female nonathlete population. Types of pathogenic weight control most commonly practiced by ball game athletes are vomiting, fasting, binging, and excess exercise.

Athletes with eating disorders typically eat less than optimal amounts of some nutrients, especially carbohydrates, calcium, and iron. Athletes diagnosed with anorexia nervosa and anorexia athletica have energy intakes below that required for highly active women. Although nutrient intake appears adequate for most ball game athletes, the practice of vomiting by the bulimic athletes reduces the amount of nutrients absorbed.

Eating disorders are a part of a triad of disorders that includes amenorrhea and osteoporosis and has been called the female athlete triad. Eating disorders in female athletes may result in menstrual disorders and amenorrhea. Approximately 2/3 of female athletes with eating disorders have menstrual irregularities or amenorrhea. Both menstrual disorders and amenorrhea may lead to reductions in BMD and premature osteoporosis. Compared to eumenorrheic female athletes, the amenorrheic athlete usually has a lower BMD in the lumbar vertebrae and femur than her normally cycling counterpart. Drinkwater and colleagues (1984) note that the lumbar BMD of amenorrheic athletes (age 26) is similar to that of postmenopausal women. Low bone density in amenorrheic athletes can increase the risk of stress fractures.

Eating disorders that are left untreated may result in death due to heart problems, electrolyte imbalances, or other problems related to malnutrition. Efforts should be made to identify athletes with eating disorders. Treatment should include medical and nutritional interventions and psychological counseling.

Summary

Although little information is available on the nutrient intake of female soccer players, other female team sport athletes consume diets that are low in carbohydrate, calcium, and iron. Low carbohydrate intakes reduce muscle glycogen stores, which can impair performance in soccer. The recommended training diet for female soccer players should contain 55%–65% of the calories as carbohydrate, 25%–30% fat, and 10%–15% protein. Inclusion of dairy products, meat, fish, and poultry in the diet will ensure adequate calcium and iron intakes. One method of ensuring adequate nutrient intake is to follow the Food Guide Pyramid in selecting foods. The athlete should eat a variety of foods from the bread, cereal, rice and pasta (6–11 servings), vegetable (3–5 servings), and fruit (2–4 servings) groups, which are all excellent sources of carbohydrate. Foods in the dairy group, such as milk, yogurt, and cheese (2–3 servings) are the best sources of calcium while foods in the meat, poultry, and fish group (2–3 servings) are the best sources of iron.

SUGGESTED READINGS

Bangsbo J. The physiology of soccer—with special reference to intense intermittent exercise. Acta Physiologica Scandinavica (suppl) 1994;619:1–155.

Davis JA, Brewer J. Applied physiology of female soccer players. Sports Med 1993;16:180–189.

Drinkwater BL, Nilson K, Chesnut CH III, et al. Bone mineral content of amenorrheic and eumenorrheic athletes. New Eng J Med 1984;311:277–281.

Ekblom B. Applied physiology of soccer. Sports Med 1986;3:50–60.

Elias SR, Roberts WB, Thorson DC. Team sports in hot weather: guidelines for modifying youth soccer. Phys Sportsmed 1991;19:67–80.

Haymes EM. Dietary iron needs in exercising women: a rational plan to follow in evaluating iron status. Medicine, Exercise, Nutrition, and Health 1993;2:203–212.

Saltin B. Metabolic fundamentals in exercise. Med Sci Sports 1973;5:137–146.

Short SH, Short WR. Four-year study of university athletes' dietary intake. Journal of the American Dietetic Association 1983;82:632–645.

Sundgot-Borgen J. Nutrient intake of female elite athletes suffering from eating disorders. Int J Sport Nutrition 1993;3:431–442.

van Erp-Bart AMJ, Saris WHM, Binkhorst RA, et al. Nationwide survey on nutritional habits in elite athletes. Part I. Energy, carbohydrate, protein, and fat intake. Int J Sports Med 1989;10:S3–S10.

Yeager KK, Agostini R, Nattiv A, et al. The female athlete triad: disordered eating, amenorrhea, osteoporosis. Medicine and Science in Sports and Exercise 1993;25:775–777.

VIII

- **Sociological and Psychological Aspects**

43  Sport Psychology Issues in Youth Soccer

Robert A. Swoap

Soccer is a very popular sport for children around the world. In the United States, several million children participate in organized youth soccer programs. Children encounter a variety of experiences in youth soccer. Children's participation in soccer is not inherently beneficial or detrimental, but depends on a great number of factors, including the ways in which participation is structured and supervised.

In this chapter, the nature and quality of the youth soccer experience will be presented by reviewing three major areas in the sport psychology of youth soccer: participation motivation, competitive stress, and coaching.

Participation Motivation

Why Children Play Soccer

Participation in youth soccer, and youth sports in general, can be beneficial. Physical benefits include developing coordination, improving muscular strength and endurance, and attaining sport-specific skills. Psychosocial benefits include developing leadership skills, cooperativeness, and sportsmanship; making friends; having fun; and building self-confidence, self-discipline, and perseverance.

To assess participation motives for youth sports, researchers have asked children about their reasons for playing. The most frequently mentioned reasons include having fun, being with and making new friends, learning and developing skills, succeeding or winning, and the excitement of competition. Children usually cite more than one reason for participation. Although there are not clear gender differences in the motives for participation, females typically rate fun and affiliation as more important motives than do males.

Socialization influences are an integral aspect of youth sports participation. In sport, socialization is "the social and psychological influences that shape an individuals initial attraction to sport." The influence of peers, siblings, and parents are critical to a child's initiation into soccer. Community and societal factors are also important in participation motivation (hence, the hope that the U.S. World Cup Team's play in 1994 will amplify American's interest and participation in soccer). Therefore, sport socialization and participation motivation research must be integrated.

To examine children's motivation for participating in sports, it is necessary to understand the developmental stages and needs of children. Research in this area emphasizes the need for children to demonstrate competence, ability, and achievement in sports. Youth soccer provides a fertile testing ground for children to assess their abilities, compare themselves with peers, and establish feelings of competency. However, some children may have difficulty achieving feelings of competence and achievement on the soccer field.

To assist children in their attempts at mastery and achievement, youth soccer should focus on skill development rather than competition. Competitive sports often focus more attention on outcome than on the process necessary for skill development and mastery. For example, coaches who are concerned with reaching the playoffs may not allow all of their children to play, thus limiting skill development. Highly competitive situations make it difficult for children to improve skills and have fun. It is difficult for children to play and improve when they become so concerned about the outcome that they are afraid to make a mistake.

Children appear to be more interested in skill development and personal improvement than winning. For example, to assess the competitive orientation of over 2000 participants in the National Youth Sports Program (average age = 12), the participants were asked what is most important in playing a sports game. The following choices were provided: (A) to defeat your opponent or the other team (win); (B) to play as well as you can (skill or personal performance); (C) to play fairly, by the rules at all times (fair play); and (D) everyone on the team should get to play (total participation).

As can be seen in Table 43–1, these children clearly endorsed personal performance as the most important aspect of sports.

Children must also have the neurodevelopmental maturation to be able to understand, identify, and cope with the demands of the sport (i.e., the speed and trajectory of a soccer ball in flight) and respond in a way that will maximize opportunities for success. If a child does not have the cognitive devel-

Table 43-1

Competitive Orientation Among Youth Sport Participants		
	Males (N=1236)	Females (N=1096)
Personal Performance	51.0%	48.3%
Fair Play	24.4	37.6
Winning Orientation	13.5	4.6
Total Participation	11.0	9.4
	100.0%	100.0%

(Adapted from: McElroy & Kirkendall, 1980)

opment to understand and follow directions for a play, such as a corner kick, then the child will be less likely to experience feelings of competency and achievement. It has been demonstrated that the addition of cognitively demanding elements during a soccer-dribbling task causes significant decrements in performance, especially for soccer novices. A lack of athletic success can be associated with threats to self-esteem and confidence, excessive stress, and potential dropout. Therefore, sensible choices need to be made about the readiness of a child to participate in soccer and necessary modifications to the game (i.e., smaller field dimensions, appropriate goal size).

Why Children Drop Out

Involvement in youth sports, including soccer, typically increases up to the age of 12 or 13, and then rapidly declines. Various research estimates of children's dropout rates range from 25%–80%. In a survey of approximately 3000 soccer-playing children aged 10–18, 57% of the males and 41% of the females had stopped playing or were not planning on playing the following year (Table 43–2).

In assessing dropout from sports, researchers usually take a descriptive and retrospective approach. They ask children who are no longer participating about their reasons for ending sports involvement. For example, in 10–15–year–old male soccer dropouts, 33% attributed quitting to an overemphasis on competition combined with negative coaching (i.e., frequent criticism). Typical reasons that children give for ending participation include having other things to do (time and activity conflicts), lack of success or skill improvement ("I wasn't good enough"), lack of fun ("practices were boring"), competitive stress ("Coach yelled at me when I made a mistake"), lack of playing time, overemphasis on winning, and injury.

Conflicts with other activities are routinely cited as primary motives for discontinuing involvement. These conflicts are less likely to arise for children who are succeeding, developing skills, and having fun. Children who cite other interests as the primary reason for quitting may actually encounter negative aspects of their participation, experience a natural change in interests, and subsequently discontinue soccer involvement. An important group of dropouts to consider are those children who quit because participation was unpleasant.

Table 43-2

Reasons Children Quit Playing Competitive Sports
• An overemphasis on competition and performance
• Hard physical training
• Parental pressure to participate
• Perceived failure
• Punitive coaches
• Negative peer attitudes

Another important factor to consider when examining participation in soccer is the attributional style that children adopt. How do young soccer players explain their successes and failures? As shown in Table 43-3, children who enjoy and continue soccer participation may have a different attributional style than some of their dropout counterparts.

After achieving success, children who attribute their positive outcome to internal factors, such as high effort and high ability, experience feelings of competence and achievement and are likely to continue participation. Children who attribute their success to external and unstable factors, such as luck or an easy task, may be more likely to drop out. The opposite pattern occurs when children experience failure in soccer. The long-term participant often attributes negative outcomes to unstable factors, such as high task difficulty (i.e., a superior opponent) or low effort, rather than to low ability. On the other hand, the potential dropout may see failure as consistent and expected and will attribute negative outcomes to internal, stable factors (i.e., "I am a terrible player," "I will never get better"). Although this attributional model is supported by traditional psychological research and sport psychology research, these suspected differences in attributional styles as they relate to participation for young soccer players need to be investigated empirically.

Enhancing and Maintaining Participation

Since children experience feelings of competency and achievement when they succeed, practices should foster skill development and learning. For motivation and participation to remain high, skills must improve for all children on a team, not just the best players. Structured practices must also be fun. Since a primary reason most children give for their participation is fun, skills are best developed through drills and exercises in an atmosphere of excitement and enjoyment. Creativity in coaching is a strong attribute. Social support should also be promoted among team members. Since many children play soccer to be with friends, there should be time allotted for social interaction. Providing strategic breaks during practices, going out for pizza after a match, and encouraging team members mutual support are all strate-

Table 43-3

Attributions for Outcome: Active Participants vs. Dropouts		
Outcome	Active participant	Dropout
Success	High ability	Luck
	High effort	Easy task
	Internal	Unstable, external
Failure	Low effort	Low ability
	High task difficulty	Internal, stable
	Unstable	"I'm a terrible player"
		"I will never get better"

gies that will increase the positive aspects of participation. Also, children must play in the games. Many soccer leagues have a rule that each child plays for 50% or more of each game. Most children remain motivated when playing as opposed to sitting on the bench.

Team decisions should be allowed whenever possible. Giving players the chance to make decisions (i.e., their position, strategy) that affect their participation can improve their self-determination. Also, adults should not coerce a child to participate. Children are the best at deciding when and whether they want to play.

Competitive Stress

In addition to providing fun, skill development, and social development, youth sports can provide children with opportunities for coping with the challenges of competition. Coping with these challenges is typically not much of a problem psychologically since most children report minimal pre and postcompetitive stress. Unfortunately, a significant number of children are exposed to the high pressures of a win-oriented competitive situation before they are developmentally prepared. In these cases, children may perceive competition as stressful, threatening, anxiety provoking, and aversive rather than challenging or exciting.

The experience of competitive stress results from a combination of environmental factors (i.e., win-oriented sports model, parental pressure, punitive coaches) and individual factors (i.e., coping skills, past experiences, low self-esteem). To illustrate this interactive nature of competitive stress, it is helpful to examine the four stage process of competitive stress.

Stages of Competitive Stress

Figure 43–1 shows the model of the four stages of competitive stress that athletes experience. Stage 1 represents the context in which the child competes, that is, the situational factors (i.e., game situation, opponent, parental demands, meaningfulness of the match). Higher levels of competitive anxiety are typically found under competitive conditions as compared to practice conditions and in critical game situations as compared to noncritical game situations. For example, an intrasquad scrimmage will usually lead to less stress than a playoff match.

Table 43-4

Signs of Competitive Stress
• Consistently perform better in practice than in games
• Have trouble sleeping the night before competition
• Make negative self-statements (e.g., "I'm no good")
• Have little self-confidence
• Experience gastrointestinal discomfort ("Upset stomach")
• Have marked personality changes before a match (e.g., become shy and withdrawn)

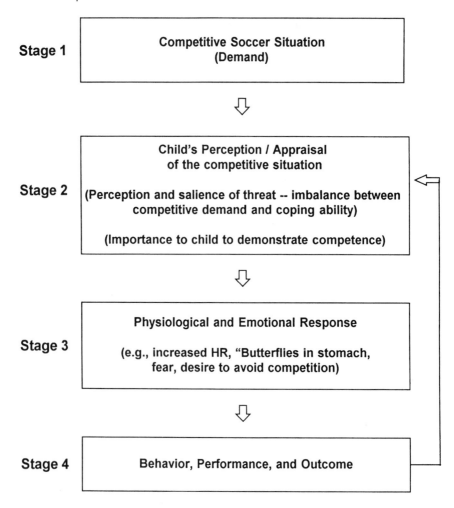

| Stage 1 | **Competitive Soccer Situation**
(Demand) |

⇩

| Stage 2 | **Child's Perception / Appraisal**
of the competitive situation

(Perception and salience of threat -- imbalance between
competitive demand and coping ability)

(Importance to child to demonstrate competence) |

⇩

| Stage 3 | **Physiological and Emotional Response**

(e.g., increased HR, "Butterflies in stomach,
fear, desire to avoid competition) |

⇩

| Stage 4 | **Behavior, Performance, and Outcome** |

Figure 43–1. A model for competitive stress in youth soccer. (Adapted from McGrath, 1970).

Stage 2 refers to the child's perception of the competitive situation. How children perceive their ability to cope with the demands of the competitive situation will largely determine their physiological, emotional, and behavioral responses. Children who assess the demands of the situation as overwhelming for their skill level may perceive the situation as threatening. If children perceive competitive situations as threatening and respond to them with elevations in anxiety, they are said to have competitive trait anxiety. In other words, when competition is seen as a threat to important goals (i.e., competence, self-esteem), then competition will likely be a negative experience. For example, when comparing male soccer players (ages 9–15) with high competitive trait anxiety to males with lower anxiety, the males with the high trait anxiety experienced greater perceived threat to mastery and competitive achievement goals.

Stage 3 refers to the child's emotional and physiological response to the cognitive appraisal or perception of the competition. If a threat has been perceived, then the body and mind react in predictable ways: increased heart rate, muscle tension, changes in skin conductance (sweaty palms), gastrointestinal symptoms (upset stomach), pupil dilation, anxiety, or fear. A child who perceives the situation as a challenge rather than a threat may also undergo physiological changes, but experience concomitant feelings of excitement rather than dread.

Stage 4 refers to the behavioral outcome in the competition. Children who are negatively affected by competitive anxiety may perform poorly for a number of reasons. Biomechanically, their motor performance may become less smooth. Under a judged, competitive condition, the ankle characteristics of children's stepping become less smooth and efficient. This is most likely due to the anxiety associated with the potential threat of being evaluated in competition.

Performance under stress may also be impaired by poor decision-making, diminished perception and attention, and reduced retention of learned material. The latter explanation may be particularly relevant for the child who has only recently learned the necessary skills to play soccer. As children experience increasing levels of stress, their retention and execution of skills suffer. Once performance begins, aspects of children's behavior are fed back for cognitive appraisal (Stage 2), which may further increase anxiety. For example, if children are not performing well during a match, they may become more anxious, feel more threatened, and continue to make errors. This may constitute a vicious cycle of spiraling stress, poor performance, and plummeting feelings of competency and enjoyment.

Antecedents of Competitive Stress

Several interdependent factors are associated with the experience of competitive stress, including child factors, parent-child interactions, and coaching styles. Coaching will be examined in the next section.

CHILD FACTORS

The extent to which children experience competitive stress may be dictated by at least four cognitive mediators.

Perceived Ability

As demonstrated in the competitive stress model (Fig. 43–1), when a child perceives his or her ability to be less than the demands of the situation, the probability of experiencing excessive stress increases. A low perceived ability level is associated with higher levels of competitive anxiety.

Success Expectancy

Children who experience excessive competitive anxiety often feel that they are as physically talented as less anxious players. The main difference is that they consistently report a lower expectancy of success.

Expectancy of Negative Evaluation

In addition to evaluating themselves, children seek approval and evaluation from external sources such as peers, siblings, parents, and coaches. Children who expect negative evaluations from significant (and nonsignificant) others tend to experience higher levels of competition anxiety. The situation becomes a threat to competency and self-esteem (i.e., "I am concerned about choking," "I am concerned about letting my parents or coaches down," "I am concerned about what my teammates will think or say"), rather than one of enjoyment and challenge. Young athletes often look to the stands (for parents) when an error is made. Expectancy of negative evaluations can usually be confirmed by verbal and nonverbal signs of disappointment or disapproval.

Expectancy of Negative Affect

Children who experience high levels of competitive anxiety expect the results of a poor performance to be more emotionally aversive than do children who experience less competitive anxiety. For example, shame and upset feelings are most common among children with high competitive anxiety who perform poorly. Children who expect to perform poorly (regardless of ability), be criticized, and feel bad after competition will likely view the competitive situation as threatening, aversive, and stressful.

PARENT FACTORS

Parents play important roles in the creation and maintenance of a positive sports environment. Parents typically enjoy their children's participation in sports and are vital in volunteering, coaching, or being supportive to the program. Unfortunately, parental involvement can also be a source of stress to youth soccer participants. Many overinvolved parents become a distraction when they argue with the referee or yell at their children. Children and coaches may have to deal with parents who are disinterested, overcritical, overprotective, scream from behind the bench, or act like sideline coaches.

To prevent excessive stress due to overinvolved parents, it may be necessary to establish guidelines for how parents conduct themselves during practices and games. Parents with little background in soccer should be encouraged to read about the sport, attend practices in which the fundamentals are taught, and have their children demonstrate what they have learned. Most important, parents must recognize that the sport is for the children and not for any vicarious motives.

Recognizing Competitive Stress in Children

When children experience competitive stress, they may exhibit decreased enjoyment, diminished skill development, excessive anxiety, somatic complaints, injury, and dropout. Children may complain about excessive competitive stress directly or, more often, exhibit various symptoms revealing that they are experiencing stress. Table 43–4 lists the signs of competitive stress. If these symptoms occur in clusters, it is likely that the child is experiencing excessive stress related to performance.

Reducing Competitive Stress in Youth Soccer

To reduce competitive stress a healthy philosophy of winning should be encouraged for the soccer league, coaches, parents and children (i.e., adopt a "Winning Philosophy" for youth sports). A winning philosophy points out that winning is not everything. Young athletes cannot derive the full benefits of sports if they think that the only objective is to beat their opponents. It also states that failure is not equivalent to losing and success is not equivalent to winning. Young athletes should not view losing as a sign of personal failure or as a threat to their personal value. Whereas winning and losing pertain to the outcome of a competition, success and failure do not. Rather, success is found in striving for victory and excellence. It is gained in giving full effort and improving skills. Given that a major source of stress for children is the fear of failure, it is important that children know that making a mistake or losing a game is acceptable to coaches, parents, and themselves.

Establishing league guidelines that promote positive aspects of competition (i.e., fun, skill development, effort) and minimize stressful situational demands (i.e., "All-Star teams," "Win at all costs" mentality) can also reduce competitive stress. For example, some youth sport leagues that emphasize fun and skill development do not keep league standings or individual performance statistics. Guidelines should also be established for parent-child-coach interactions in a meeting with parents prior to the start of the season. This meeting should focus on the objectives of children's athletics, details of the soccer program, coaching roles and relationships, parent roles and responsibilities, and coach-parent relationships. Two-way communication and respect are emphasized. Guidelines for sideline behavior are also established (i.e., demonstration of good sportsmanship, no derogatory comments, no interference with coaching).

Also, young players should not be compared. All children have individual skill levels, strengths, and weaknesses. Adults can help children learn and improve skills, but must avoid insensitive statements such as, "If Susan can do it, why can't you?" It is important to recognize that children excel at different skills and sports. Furthermore, young athletes of the same age can have a 4-year difference in biological or maturational age. Therefore, members of the same team may have vastly different abilities. It is clear that comparisons among teammates can be unfair and potentially harmful to children.

Coaching Youth Soccer

Assessment of Coaching

The coach is a central figure in the youth sport environment who provides technical instruction and evaluative feedback. The majority of coaches act on a voluntary basis. Although most of these men and women have desirable motives for coaching, some may not have the technical knowledge or communication skills needed for effective coaching.

The process of coaching has been evaluated using guidelines for coaching and communicating effectively. Several behavioral assessment techniques have been used to examine leadership behaviors in youth sports and the effects of coaching behaviors on children. One such technique is the Coaching Behavior Assessment System (CBAS) developed by researchers at the University of Washington. These researchers initially observed soccer coaches to determine the range of coaching behaviors that occur during practices and games. CBAS appears to be a reliable and valid observation system that has been used as an evaluation tool in a number of sports. In the CBAS, trained observers assess and record a wide range of coaching behaviors that can be condensed into three general categories: supportiveness, instructiveness, and punitiveness.

Supportiveness includes reinforcement for desirable behaviors (i.e., a pat on the back after a good play) and mistake-contingent encouragement (i.e., encouragement of a player after a mistake).

Instructiveness includes general technical instruction relevant to techniques or strategies of the game (i.e., how to set up for corner kicks) and mistake-contingent instruction (i.e., in a nonpunitive manner, telling or showing a child who has made a mistake how to make the play correctly).

Punitiveness includes punishment or a negative response by the coach following an undesirable performance (i.e., showing disgust or making a sarcastic remark after a child throws the ball incorrectly) and punitive technical instruction, which is instruction given in a punitive or negative manner (i.e., "How many times do I have to tell you to use both hands on a throw-in").

The Effects of Coaching Behaviors on Children

The effects of coaching behaviors on children's enjoyment, self-esteem, and participation in sport have been examined using the CBAS. It has been demonstrated that children respond more positively to coaches who are high in supportiveness and instructiveness. This is especially true for children who have low self-esteem and strong needs for self-enhancement. Children with low self-esteem want to play for supportive, instructive coaches and do not want to play for coaches without these qualities. It appears that while support and instruction are important to all children, those with low self-esteem are maximally responsive to instruction, evaluation, and feedback (positive and negative). It is also known that players on teams with supportive coaches like their teammates more. Also, how players feel about their coaches or teammates is unrelated to the win-loss record.

Although winning may not be important to young athletes, children recognize its importance to adults. For coaches, this means that it is not whether you win or lose, but how you coach the game. Children feel that their parents like the coach more when the team is winning and that coaches of winning teams like the players more than coaches of losing teams.

The effects of coaching behaviors on children have been demonstrated in a variety of sports. A study of swimmers between 10–18-years-old evaluated the perceived coaching behaviors and the athletes' self-perceptions of ability and motivation. According to self-report measures from the athletes, coaches who are perceived as giving more reinforcement and more support and technical instruction after an undesirable performance are associated with athletes who have higher levels of perceived competence and enjoyment and a preference for optimally challenging activities.

In another set of studies, coaches participated in a coaching effectiveness training program (CET). Among other things, the CET trains coaches to raise awareness of their behaviors through self-monitoring, reinforce good performance and effort, respond to mistakes in a nonpunitive manner with encouragement and technical instruction, and use clear, concise, technical instruction. One year after the CET intervention, the dropout rate for players of nontrained coaches was five times higher (26%) than the dropout rate for players of trained coaches (5%). Furthermore, children with low self-esteem who were instructed by CET trained coaches showed significant improvement in self-esteem.

The results of these studies indicate that coaches can be taught to relate more effectively to young athletes and that training coaches has a positive effect on children's sports experience. A coach who gives positive feedback, is encouraging, and provides high-quality technical instruction helps children acquire athletic and general competencies. Coaches can also assist children with poor self-concepts to emerge from the sport experience feeling more self-assured and convinced of their self-worth.

Research in coaching behaviors has been conducted primarily on male coaches of male children in Little League Baseball. More comprehensive research is needed to examine the impact of coaching behaviors on children across sports and genders. For example, it is not known whether female soccer players value support and reinforcement more than males. Anson Dorrance, past coach of the US Women's National Soccer team, stated that "with women, it's a constant process of building egos up. I am constantly amazed by how little confidence even my most talented players have." Another issue that needs to be evaluated is how the needs for supportiveness and instructiveness change at different stages in children's development. The need for more research to answer these and other questions regarding coaching youth sports is apparent.

Implications for Coaching Youth Soccer

Consistent with the recommendations for reducing competitive stress, coaches should promote a healthy philosophy of winning related to effort and skill improvement. Coaches should give praise and encouragement freely, but sincerely. Although encouragement is important, it means little to the young soccer player to hear "good job" if the player knows that he or she has not done a good job. Also, all players should be rewarded. Although not every child can be the star player, each child can show improvement in skills and effort and should be rewarded. When children make errors, coaches should help them to realize that they can improve. Both supportiveness (i.e., mistake-contingent encouragement) and technical instruction are necessary. Coaches can help children to see mistakes and errors as opportunities and challenges, rather than threats to their personal well-being or self-esteem. Finally, the sport should be fun for everyone involved.

Conclusions

In this chapter, research on participation motivation, competitive stress, and coaching has been summarized. From this brief review, it is clear that children play sports for many reasons, but mostly for enjoyment. Soccer is a wonderful, fun game when played under the right circumstances. Unfortunately, some children have stressful athletic experiences when they expect (and receive) negative evaluations, feel overwhelmed, or are simply not having fun. Occasionally, external pressures from spectators, parents, and coaches can create a less than optimal environment in which to develop soccer skills and personal attributes. Sometimes children have less fun and do not get the opportunity to develop their skills due to an overemphasis on winning. When winning becomes the most important element of participation, the needs of the children become secondary. If children's feelings of self-esteem are dependent on performance or praise from parents and coaches, then something is awry.

If children have fun, develop soccer skills, improve social skills, and gain feelings of competency and self-esteem, the program can be considered a success. More children will enjoy and remain in those sports that provide these types of experiences and opportunities. Despite the large amount of research conducted on children in sports, more investigations of youth sports participation are warranted. This is especially true for research that integrates related fields such as sociology, psychology, child development, and medicine. Further research that examines female participation in sport is also strongly needed. Lastly, collaboration between sport psychology researchers, sports medicine practitioners, and youth soccer organizations would provide excellent opportunities for both theoretical and applied studies, ultimately enriching the experiences for children playing soccer.

SUGGESTED READINGS

Anshel M. Sport psychology: from theory to practice, 2nd ed. Scottsdale, AZ: Gorsuch Scarisbrick, 1994.

Duda JL. Toward a developmental theory of children's motivation in sport. J Sport Psych 1987;9:130–145.

Gould D. Promoting positive sport experiences for children. In: May J, Asken M, eds. Sport psychology: the psychological health of the athlete. New York: PMA Publishing, 1987;77–98.

Gould D, Petlichkoff L. Participation motivation and attrition in young athletes. In: Smoll F, Magill R, Ash M, eds. Children in sport, 3rd ed. Champaign, IL: Human Kinetics, 1988;161–178.

Hopper C, Guthrie GD, Kelly T. Self concept and skill development in youth soccer players. Perceptual and Motor Skills 1991;72:275–285.

Ommundsen Y, Vaglum P. Soccer competition anxiety and enjoyment in young boy players. The influence of perceived competence and significant others' emotional involvement. International Journal of Sport Psychology 1991;22:35–49.

Passer MW. Fear of failure, fear of evaluation, perceived competence, and self-esteem in competitive-trait-anxious children. J Sport Psych 1983;5:172–188.

Passer MW. Determinants and consequences of children's competitive stress. In: Smoll FL, Magill RA, Ash M, eds. Children in sport, 3rd ed. Champaign, IL: Human Kinetics, 1988;153–177.

Smith RE, Smoll FL. Self-esteem and children's reactions to youth sport coaching behaviors: a field study of self-enhancement processes. Developmental Psychology 1990;26:987–993.

Smith RE, Smoll FL. Behavioral research and intervention in youth sports. Behav Ther 1991;22:329–344.

Smoll FL. Enhancing coach-parent relationships in youth sports. In: Williams J, ed. Applied sport psychology: personal growth to peak performance. Mountain View, CA: Mayfield, 1993;58–67.

Smoll FL, Smith RE. Developing a healthy philosophy of winning in youth sports. In: Seefeldt V, Smoll F, Smith R, et al, eds. A winning philosophy for youth sport programs. East Lansing, Michigan: Michigan Institute for the Study of Youth Sports, 1981;17–24.

Smoll FL, Smith RE, Barnett NP, et al. Enhancement of children's self-esteem through social support training for youth sport coaches. Journal of Applied Psychology 1993;78:602–610.

Wandzilak T, Ansorge CJ, Potter G. Comparison between selected practice and game behaviors of youth soccer coaches. J Sport Behav 1988;11:78–88.

Weiss MR. Children in sport. In: Murphy S, ed. Sport psychology interventions. Champaign, IL: Human Kinetics, 1995.

44   **Drug Abuse In Soccer**

Eduardo Henrique de Rose

Historical Aspects

According to Philostratus, the athletes in the ancient Olympic Games believed that drinking herbal teas and eating mushrooms could increase their levels of performance. Another interesting form of ancient doping was to prepare a powder with the oil, dust, and sweat taken from the skin of the athlete after the competition. This mix was removed in the dressing room with a strigilo, a metallic instrument in the shape of an "L." The athlete sold it to other participants who believed that by drinking the mix they could have the same physical capabilities as the champion.

The modern Olympic Games were inaugurated by Pierre de Coubertin at the city of Athens in 1896. From 1896–1932, nine Olympic Games were held, excluding the years of the first World War. At that time, doping was not common except for some drug use among cyclists. The most common mix used to increase performance was a cocktail with cocaine, caffeine, and strychnine.

From 1936–1964, six Olympic Games were held, excluding the period of the second World War. At this point in history, the games were used as a marketing instrument to promote political systems. This changed the original ideal of Coubertin and winning started to become more important than the competition. The most commonly used substances at this time were amphetamines and, after 1954, anabolic steroids. To control the use of doping agents, the International Olympic Committee (IOC) appointed a Medical Commission. Under the chairmanship of Prince Alexandre de Merode, the Medical Commission started medical controls during the 1968 Olympic games.

From 1968–1980, four Olympic Games were held. The first list of banned pharmacologic classes was introduced and included psychomotor stimulants, sympathomimetic amines, stimulants of the central nervous system, and narcotic analgesics. After 1975, just before the Olympic Games of Montreal, anabolic steroids were added to the list. During this period, positive cases were found in a small number of athletes in every Olympic Game, except in Moscow in 1980.

The Olympic Games from 1984–1992 should be considered separately considering the high number of positive cases and important changes made in the list of banned pharmacologic classes and methods implemented by the IOC Medical Commission.

In Los Angeles the cases of doping increased, probably due to the professionalism and marketing of the games. Athletes were obliged to win at any cost. Consequently, there were a great number of positive cases (11) and false medical certifications of hypertension to justify use of beta-blockers in shooting, blood transfusions in cycling, and manipulation of the urine by physical, chemical, and pharmacologic methods. For this reason, in 1987, the IOC Medical Commission modified the list of banned pharmacologic classes to include beta-blockers and diuretics. Restricted substances and forbidden methods were also included to prevent the use of local anesthetics, corticosteroids, blood transfusions, and manipulation of the urine.

In Seoul, a total of nine cases of doping were detected and the exclusion of Ben Johnson had a great impact in the media all over the world. After these games, there was evidence of the use of erythropoietin (EPO) and growth hormone. Therefore, the IOC Medical Commission included peptidic hormones in the list of banned pharmacologic classes. Marijuana was also included in the list of restricted substances.

In Barcelona, the cases of clenbuterol caused a new change in the list of banned pharmacologic classes and methods. The concept of related substances was changed to include chemical structures and pharmacologic action. For this reason, a new class of anabolic agents was established, including the anabolic-androgenic steroids and beta-2-agonists. The pharmacologic class of beta-blockers was removed from the banned area and moved to the restricted area. The most important decision after this competition was to include the possibility of blood sampling, in conjunction with urine sampling, to permit a better determination of the use of hormones.

Doping Control in Soccer

Doping control in the Federation International de Football (FIFA) World Cups started in Mexico, in 1970. So far, just two athletes have been disqualified. The first case involved the use of stimulants by an athlete from Scotland who was playing in Cordoba, Argentina in 1978. The second case involved an Argentinean player who was disqualified for using stimulants during the 1994 World Cup in the United States.

In the United States, 24 teams will perform during the World Cup and 240 samples will be collected. Today, FIFA uses the same list of banned classes of substances proposed by the IOC Medical Commission. The methods for the collection of samples and chemical analysis are standard for all sports.

Only in Western Europe, the United States, Canada, Japan, and Australia is regular doping control performed in soccer championships. In the other areas of the world, mostly due to the absence of national regulation or IOC accredited laboratories, doping control is only performed in international competitions under the supervision of FIFA.

According to the data presented in the report of the IOC Medical Commission, issued annually by Professor Manfred Donike, doping does exist in soccer, although the incidence is lower than in other sports modalities. Table 44–1 shows the number of controls done during the 1992 games and the incidence of positive cases detected in six Olympic sports.

Approximately 5% of the total number of controls done in soccer were from out-of-competition doping tests. The 0.39% of positive cases is a weighted average for the total number of tests. For in-competition tests, there is a 0.24% of positive cases and for announced out-of-competition tests the positive cases rise to 0.50%.

Table 44–2 shows the breakdown of doping agents found in the positive cases, according to the report of the IOC Medical Commission. Only stimulants and anabolic steroids are considered.

The doping classes used are stimulants and anabolic steroids. The primary stimulant used is pseudoephedrine and the primary anabolic agent is testosterone. Anabolic agents were mainly found in announced out-of-competition doping controls, while stimulants were detected during in-competition testing.

Conclusions and Recommendations

Although doping is used in soccer, the incidence is lower than in other sports modalities. The doping classes used are stimulants and anabolic steroids, in similar proportions. The primary stimulant used is pseudoephedrine and the primary anabolic agent is testosterone.

The fact that announced out-of-competition tests in soccer show more than twice as many positive cases as in-competition controls indicates that it is vital to shift the focus of the medical commissions on out-of-competition testing, either announced or short notice.

The positive cases hereby reported are the ones detected by the IOC accredited laboratories in 12 of the 28 participating countries. Doping control is not a major problem in the FIFA World Cup. It is important to perform drug tests at the national and international levels. In addition, to expand the breadth of testing, it is also necessary to perform controls in independent and accredited laboratories.

Table 44-1

Incidence of Doping Cases in Different Sports in 1992 Olympic Games			
Sports	Controls	Positives	Percent
Weightlifting	4164	86	2.07
Athletics	11,266	108	0.96
Cycling	11,606	87	0.75
Swimming	2262	9	0.40
Soccer	9936	39	0.39

Table 44-2

Classes of Doping Agents Used in Soccer	
Stimulants (n=15)	*Anabolic agents (n=12)*
6 pseudoephedrine	11 testosterone
3 ephedrine	1 methandienone
3 PPA	
4 amineptine	

Based on the history of doping control, it is possible to conclude that peptic hormones will soon be detected in the urine and blood of Olympic athletes. But, at this time, other methods will probably be developed to beat drug testing methods and to help athletes increase performance in unethical ways.

SUGGESTED READINGS

Coombs R, West JW. Drug testing: issues and options. New York: Oxford University Press, 1991.

Dirix A, Knuttgen H, Tittel K. The olympic book of sports medicine. Champaign, IL: Human Kinetics, 1988.

Donike M. Statistics of the IOC accredited laboratories. Cologne: DSHS, 1992.

Drug Use and Sports: Current Issues and Implications for Public Health. Geneve: World Health Organization, 1993.

Strauss R. Drugs and performance in sports. Philadelphia: WB Saunders, 1987.

The Fourth Permanent World Conference on Anti-Doping in Sports. Conference Proceedings. Sports Council, London, 1993.

XV FIFA World Cup, USA 1994. Doping Control Regulations. Zurich: FIFA, 1994.

Index

Italic pages indicate figures; pages with *t* indicate tables.